Celtic Cubs

Inside the Mind of the Irish Teenager

Orla McHugh

LIB
ERT
IES

Contents

Introduction

As I write this foreword I have just finished reading an interview in an English newspaper with Matt O'Connor, the founder of Fathers 4 Justice, the British organisation that attracted huge publicity for its superhero protests in support of parenting rights for fathers. The interviewer was a woman, undoubtedly a feminist. The tone was instantly familiar: sneering, hostile, dismissive. What had fathers done to deserve equality? Weren't mothers more important than fathers anyway?

Why was he so angry? the journalist asked. Why was he trying to help other angry men to exert control over women? Matt O'Connor alone knows why he feels a need to talk to journalists like this. In the course of the interview he described journalists as 'c—s', leaving his willingness to place his head on the block all the more perplexing. Perhaps he is not so much angry as mad: a working definition of madness I've occasionally heard is, 'doing the same thing over and over, each time expecting a different result'. The interview comprised the same ignorant stuff I've read a thousand times over the past decade, usually written in an Irish newspaper about myself and my own modest efforts to draw society's attention to the dangers of its prejudices about men. O'Connor rose to the bait and allowed himself to be portrayed in exactly the way the interviewer had set out to betray him. Sometimes, bad publicity is merely bad publicity. In this case, however, the bad publicity afflicted not just the subject of the interview but the gamut of issues he is seen to stand for. In the end it achieves its true purpose: the strengthening of public prejudice towards an unpalatable set of truths.

The strange thing is that it never seemed to occur to either Matt O'Connor or his interviewer that it doesn't matter whether fathers are angry or not. I would certainly be suspicious of a father who was not angry about being 'disappeared' from his children's lives, but otherwise wouldn't regard the issue as relevant. It often strikes me as odd that, in societies that ritualistically invoke the 'rights of children' and the 'best interests of the child', we can continue to have these discussions, year after year, without mentioning that the rights of father are conterminous with the rights of children. It isn't possible to deny the rights of fathers without also denying the rights of children. It isn't a question of what fathers have done to 'deserve' equality but what children have done to deserve losing their fathers. As for the question as to whether fathers or mothers are 'more important' – I put this in the same category as the question about whether my right leg is more important than my left.

Our children are not as happy as we would like them to be – that much is becoming clearer as we move forward with what we otherwise describe as progress. They are drinking too much, taking drugs to reach the pains that alcohol can't get to, and, in extreme cases, seeking final solutions to something that remains unnamed. But every attempt to name the problem runs into a bigger one. Certain things cannot be said because they make some of us feel uncomfortable, or guilty, or stigmatised. It takes courage to state the obvious – that, for example, we are only now beginning to experience the initial fallout from the divorce culture we ushered in just over a decade ago. Or that our non-judgemental attitude towards single parenthood may yet deliver us a serious tab.

Nothing speaks as eloquently of our errors as the state of our adolescents. The teenage phase can be a difficult one for individuals and those who love them. This has always been true. But what may be true now for perhaps the first time in Irish society is that the teenage phase – in the sense of the overall condition of Irish adolescent – may be about to speak to us about our overall health as a people and as a society. The children of that first generation of divorced parents, together with the children of the fatherless households created by our manufactured hostility towards men and maleness, are entering into the phase of life that tells us more clearly what our society is like than almost anything else.

A couple of years back, just prior to his retirement from the bench, the then Chief Justice, Mr Ronan Keane, spoke in a newspaper interview about the connection between juvenile delinquency and absent fathers. What he said was wholly unexceptionable because it was entirely true. The only regret about his saying it was that he had not done so at a time when he might have been in a position to do something practical about the problem. But then we observed the probable reason he had kept his counsel until this last minute of his public career: he was immediately set upon and savaged by journalists and self-styled 'experts' seeking to dismiss what he said because of the 'offence' it might cause to certain interested parties.

One of the symptoms of the sickness that afflicts post–Celtic Tiger Ireland is an inability to hear unpalatable truths, or even theories, about what is wrong with our society. The bearer of such messages is invariably set upon like a crow that has stolen twigs from his neighbour's nest. The trouble is that, although the attack on the errant crow actually assists in the maintenance of societal cohesion among the crows, the habit of attacking those who offer uncomfortable truths to the human society of modern Ireland has the opposite effect: those who attack the messengers are destroying themselves and the rest of us, perhaps our children most of all.

I regard this as an important and timely book, and not only because it is written by a woman who values men and regards fatherhood as a vital force in the lives of children and in the life of society. It is valuable because it seeks to put pieces of the picture in the correct place and sketch in the missing bits. It is welcome because it does not flinch from delivering unpalatable messages. Orla McHugh comes to her subject as a parent, a citizen, a woman and a psychologist, in more or less that order. Her book is all the more timely because it address a theme that has been overlooked by virtually every other instrument of discussion and transformation, including politics and journalism. I am glad, finally, that Orla McHugh is a woman – for her own sake, in the matter of making the argument, and for all our sakes in the matter of getting to hear it. I welcome her book and its uncomfortable messages and wish its author well in her efforts to get her unpalatable truths to the ears of those who need to hear them, over the hurdles of ignorance and through the gauntlets of hostility that lie waiting for anyone who dares to question the invisible establishment seeking to tell us all how to think.

John Waters, July 2006

Acknowledgements

First and foremost I would like to acknowledge my thanks to my publishers Seán O'Keeffe and Peter O'Connell for their enthusiasm and belief in this endeavour from the very outset.

I would like to thank my colleagues and peers for their encouragement and support, with especial thanks to Ann Cahill and Jack Milton for their patient guidance and deep compassion.

Lastly I would like to thank all the young teenagers who have come into my life, and shared with me their deepest fears with courage and honesty: they hold a special place in my heart.

*

The quotation on pages 13 and 14 is reproduced by permission of the *Irish Independent*. The quotation from Anna Freud on page 25 originally appeared in *Young People, Health and Family Life* (Open University Press, 1994). The quotation from Eric Ericson on page 27 originally appeared in *Identity and the Life Cycle* (Norton, 1980). The quotation from Laurence Steinberg on page 48 originally appeared in *Time* magazine, 7 June 2004. The quotation from Alice Miller on pages 56–7 originally appeared in *The Drama of Being a Child* (Virago, 1997). The quotation from Alexander Lowen on page 159 originally appeared in *Narcissism* (Simon & Schuster, 1997). The author and publishers have made every effort to trace holders of copyright material and will be happy to make good any omissions in this regard in future printings of the book.

Foreword

On Saturday the 16th of October 2004, the editorial in the *Irish Independent* ran:

TEENAGE MURDERS

Many people will be asking themselves today what it is that drives two teenage boys to murder two other adolescent boys in as brutal a manner as found in the cases of Darren Goodwin and Christopher Dunne.

Yesterday Goodwin (16) received a life sentence for hammering to death Darragh Conroy. Dunne (17) was found guilty of stabbing to death Alan Higgins.

It is hard to know which case is more disturbing. Goodwin seems to have been driven by a generalised feeling of rage and anger which he vented on the hapless Darragh Conroy, someone he thought would not be missed.

Dunne murdered Alan Higgins over a mobile phone, although in truth this motive seemed to take second place to a desire to wreak havoc.

The adolescent and early adult years have long been associated with crime. It is at this stage, between childhood and the responsibilities of adult life, that young males — and it is usually males — are most likely to be drawn into crime.

Factors other than the age and sex must exist of course. Often these factors work in combination with each other. Frequently there are conditions of social deprivation. Often there is no father present and hence no male role model. If there is a non-paternal role model, it often is a negative one, perhaps to be found in a street gang.

The psychological make-up of the criminal himself cannot be overlooked. Is there a predisposition towards violence, for example? Also we must be careful not to forget that at the end of the day, a large element of responsibility remains.

Almost certainly the young person will lack a clear moral compass to guide them through life. This may not be the fault of the parents because the parent, or parents, often find themselves competing against a frequently toxic youth culture.

This culture is fed on a cascade of violent images that come from films, television programs and computer games. It is fuelled by drugs and alcohol. It is formed by a particularly brutal and primitive idea of what it is to be a man. Peer pressure comes into play. So does the absence of religion or some other competing source of morality.

It is clear that Irish society is becoming more violent. If the above elements are indeed leading to this situation, and there can be little doubt that they are, we must ask ourselves what we intend to do about it?

I was profoundly disturbed by this particular case, and similar cases that occurred around the same time – including the beating to death of Brian Murphy outside Anabel's nightclub at the Burlington Hotel, Dublin – and was led down a path of questioning that eventually prompted me to put pen to paper. I was disturbed not only by the events but also by the public's reaction to them, especially in the case of the Annabel's boys. As the tabloid press became increasingly vindictive in their portrayal of the lives of the perpetrators of these crimes post-sentencing, laughing at their tears and in general ridiculing them, I became increasingly incensed. It is not that I believed that these boys had not committed a crime for which they were responsible and accountable – they had and they were – but a strong feeling arose within me that they were in some way being scapegoated by society at large. I asked myself the question whether, if my fifteen-year-old son was faced with the same situation, with the myriad elements of that tragic evening, I could guarantee that he would not have behaved in the same way. In all honesty, I could not.

I was left with the question of why these events happened,

and was forced to look at the wider issue of responsibility. I did not doubt that each of these boys, as individuals, were responsible for their actions, but what of the larger community? How are we all, collectively, responsible? My partner recently commented to me that with money comes responsibility. As a society which has gained sudden, great, and ever-accruing wealth, are we taking seriously the responsibilities that accompany that wealth? As material gain and self-obsession increasingly become the driving forces in our lives, what other areas of life are we neglecting? Are we encouraging competition at the expense of others? Was competition not a contributing element on the night of the Annabel's episode? Was the societal estrangement and marginalisation of Darragh Conroy and Christopher Dunne not an element in this case – that, in the competitive society in which we live, they felt like failures and losers (an all-too-common word in teenage parlance) and were raging? And what of us as parents? Do we place untold pressure on our children to perform and compete, to shine bigger and brighter, so that we look good in the company of our friends and work colleagues? So that people will look at us and comment about what a great job we are doing with our children? Have we failed to teach the necessity of tolerance, sympathy, inclusion and care? Do we take adequate responsibility for how we serve as role models to our children? And what of our schools? Are they not in some way responsible too? Have they not embraced the notion of competition, of winners and losers? Has academic performance and athletic achievement been fostered and prioritised, at the expense of individual growth? Is a school's place in the league table seen to be more important than the balance and well-being of the students?

All these questions seem to me to be of fundamental importance when looking at the issue of teenage distress in Ireland. These questions must be explored if we, as parents and as people involved with the care of adolescents, intend in any way to address the malaise that underlies this distress. With this in mind, I intend in this book, firstly, to give a broad outline of the nature of adolescence and the developmental tasks involved. Secondly,

I will examine the relevance of various psychological theories that have been propounded in relation to adolescence, focusing on those which, I believe, most adequately explain the negative experiences within a child's life – experiences which drive him or her to adopt aberrant behaviours by the time of adolescence.

I will examine the prevailing theories which emphasise the primacy of the maternal relationship, and the necessity of a secure loving environment, as the precursor for the development of a healthy and balanced teenager. Having looked at the relevant studies in relation to the development of adjusted and maladjusted adolescents, and the factors that are classically seen to determine this, I will examine classical and modern-day stressors that intervene to disrupt the ongoing healthy development of the teenage psyche, and the various contemporary issues that are contributing to adolescents' social estrangement. The effects of family breakdown, the increase in the number of single-parent families, youth culture, growing wealth and materialism, with a commensurate striving for all-round perfection. The lack of a spiritual dimension or any cultural ideology to counteract the narcissism and self-obsession that characterise the teenage years will also be examined, and the way in which teenagers are communicating their distress will then be explored.

I will examine parenting roles, and the need for these roles to be adapted to modern-day circumstances. The important part schools can play as a first line of defence in this area will be outlined. The place of counselling, mentoring and guidance during the crucial adolescent years will be investigated. Lastly, I will put forward suggestions that would, if enacted, ease the pain that some of our teenagers are experiencing.

Perhaps most importantly, I must stress that I do not want to sensationalise and misrepresent the world of our teenagers. (A 2004 World Health Organisation report estimated that 80 percent of teenagers negotiate the vagaries of adolescence successfully, and emerge from these turbulent years as responsible, well-adjusted, 'normal' young adults.) Rather, I am speaking about the small but growing minority that needs help, and attempting to draw from the experiences of these youngsters lessons which we must learn in order to stem the tide of mental illness and improve the quality of life for our teenagers and future generations.

Part One

The Adolescent Experience

1

The Period of Adolescence

The word 'adolescence' is derived from the Latin words *'ad'*, meaning 'towards', and *'essence'*, meaning 'maturity'. It is in effect the period of time between childhood and full maturation as an adult, which, classically, was seen to extend from twelve to eighteen, but in modern times often extends into the mid-twenties. The period of adolescence as we know it is a relatively modern creation, born out of history and social change. Economic conditions created by the industrial revolution of the 1850s onwards dictated that children attended school up to the age of puberty, after which time they entered adult society within the workforce as apprentices, factory workers, farmer's hands and so on. In Ireland, it was most often the case, that these young people helped out on the farm until they were old enough to emigrate. By the age of eighteen, they were expected to be economically independent and ready to take on the responsibilities of work, marriage and childrearing.

In the wake of the Second World War, this situation changed in most of the developed world, with the introduction of compulsory education; in Ireland, however, compulsory full-time education until the age of sixteen was not introduced until 1965. Young teens often now remain at home, economically dependent on their parents until their late teens at least, discovering the ways of the world not from their employer – who often also acted as their mentor in days gone by – but from their peer group. This is now particularly the case in Irish society, where the attainment of at least a primary degree is the norm. The notion of a separate youth culture, with its own musical tastes and dress code, mirroring the rebelliousness associated with this period of life, was quick to be capitalised on by the market system almost as soon as this youth culture emerged. Now, catering to teenagers has become a multi-billion-dollar business.

Some believe that the creation of the period of adolescence, during which little economic responsibility was required of the adolescent, was in some way connected to the great loss of youth sustained during the wars, when many thousands of young people were cut down in their prime. The young people who grew up in the post-war period believed that they were owed something in return, and there was a greater readiness to put off the age at which the full responsibility of adulthood was taken on. As a result, from the early 1950s the period immediately after puberty became generally recognised as a distinct space between childhood and adulthood when the young person could delay major identity choices, and experiment with roles, in order to discover the sort of person he or she wished to be. This period of respite was embraced quickly by the youth of the day, and they reacted by establishing the peace movement, and espousing the principles of love and peace that became associated with the hippie movement of the 1960s. Teenagers first found their voice in America and sought to influence political policies. The great loss of youth that was being sustained as a result of the Vietnam war soon became a rallying point for young people, who protested against what they viewed as a senseless loss of young lives. Then-emerging popular artists, notably Bob Dylan and Joan Baez, became the focus for this protest. The Vietnam war and the music associated with this era more than anything else to date solidified the concept of youth culture and identity.

In more recent times, a number of factors, most significantly changes in the labour market, have combined to prolong the period of adolescence. The advent of the Celtic Tiger in Ireland has done much to alter labour trends amongst young adults. The economic stagnation of the 1970s and 1980s, with its commensurate high levels of unemployment, meant that many teenagers had to emigrate to seek employment immediately after finishing secondary education. This in effect dictated that they sever their economic dependence on parents, leave home and enter into adulthood. The exception to this were the teenagers of the upper and upper-middle classes, who were able to postpone this move by attending fee-paying third-level educational institutions.

The economic boom of the 1990s has markedly changed this pattern, however. The recognition of the need for an educated and skilled workforce prompted the government to introduce a large number of job-training and job-preparation schemes to accommodate this demand. Access to third-level education was made available to all through the abolition of fees. Entrepreneurs were also quick to see an opportunity, and established private fee-paying courses and colleges. All of these initiatives had the effect of delaying entry into the labour market, with young adults remaining at home until their twenties. (This is particularly the case in Ireland due to the concentration of population around the country's major cities, each of which has at least one university. As a result, unlike in England, most Irish students are able to remain living at home through their student years.) The most far-reaching implication of this changing labour market is that, among teenagers, economic independence, the most tangible sign of maturity, is by and large being delayed.

Another noticeable result of this delay in establishing independence among teenagers is the fact that young adults are delaying getting married. Rising property prices, and more prolonged periods spent in education, means that many are not in a position to marry until their late twenties or thirties. Instead, young people often continue to reside in the parental home until they have saved enough to afford a deposit on a place of their own. This phenomenum is becoming so commonplace that it has been assigned its own acronym: these young adolescents are now known as 'Kippers' – which stands for 'Kids Invading Parents' Pockets, Eroding Retirement Savings'! The rise in separation and divorce in modern-day society has also contributed to people tending to live at home: young people in general appear more reluctant to commit to long-term relationships and marriage. The emotional and financial loss being sustained as a result of separation and divorce is making the institution of marriage less attractive for the young, especially for men.

Another factor that has prolonged the period of adolescence is that puberty appears to be starting earlier: a better diet and all-round improvement in health means that children are reaching puberty at an earlier age than before. This is accompanied by an earlier maturing on the social front. There is an earlier awareness of sexuality, and dating and other adolescent behaviours – including a particular interest in clothes and music – commence at a younger age. As a result, the adolescent stage now begins for some as early as nine or ten and continues for many until well after their twenty-first birthday – which was traditionally seen as the age at which young people reached maturity.

This prolonged state of adolescence has presented many modern-day families with increased challenges. Finding the balance between parental authority and the increased emotional and psychological independence of the young adult, together with their growing need for autonomy, requires strong negotiation on the part of both teenagers and their parents and guardians. The long-term psychological impact on the young adult of this continued dependent state often depends on how well this balance is achieved.

To understand the condition of adolescence fully, a knowledge of the various psychological, physiological and neurological changes that occur during this period of development is necessary as a foundation from which to build an insight into changes that can be effected to help teenagers in general, and those undergoing crises in particular.

2

Psychological Changes

Adolescents are excessively egoistic, regarding themselves as the centre of the universe and the sole object of interest, and yet at no time in later life are they capable of so much self sacrifice and devotion. They form the most passionate love relations, only to break them off as abruptly as they began them. On the one hand they throw themselves enthusiastically into the life of the community, and on the other hand they have an overpowering need for solitude. They oscillate between blind submission to some self-chosen leader and defiant rebellion against any and every authority. They are selfish and materially minded and at the same time full of lofty idealism.

ANNA FREUD
IN *YOUNG PEOPLE, HEALTH AND FAMILY LIFE*

Traditionally the word 'hormones' has been used as a blanket explanation for the peculiarities that characterise the teen years, reducing complex and massive change to an aside and trivialising the sometimes monumental challenges that the adolescent has to negotiate. Normal adolescence is characterised by a range of distressing, turbulent and unpredictable thoughts, feelings and actions and, as a consequence, adolescents will often display symptoms and behaviours that in an adult would suggest a definite psychological disturbance.

Adolescence therefore has the propensity to create great

insecurity, which needs to be alleviated by the surrounding environment in general, and parental guidance in particular. Numerous tasks need to be negotiated and completed by each adolescent during this stage, in order to ensure the development of a balanced and well-adjusted adult. These tasks are as follows:

1 Accepting one's physique and sexual role:
   the development of sexuality

2 Establishing new peer relationships with both sexes:
   individuation

3 Achieving emotional independence from parents:
   individuation

4 Achieving assurance of economic independence:
   individuation

5 Selecting and preparing for an occupation:
   social self-development

6 Developing intellectual skills and concepts necessary for civic competence: *social self-development*

7 Acquiring socially responsible behaviour patterns:
   social self-development

8 Preparing for marriage and family life: *individuation*

9 Building conscious values that are harmonious with one's environment: *social self-development*

On reading this list, it is little wonder why emotions during this period may be exceptionally varied, extreme and conflicting. Furthermore, everything is felt more intensely as a teenager, and reactions are in many cases extreme, prompting behaviours that are often seen to be out of character. From this list, it is possible to separate these tasks into three distinct categories and examine them in this way:

Individuation

Eric Ericson, a leading developmental psychologist, believed that the real task of adolescence was the formation of the ego identity:

> The need for an ego identity, which expresses their individuation, is filled with energy, and requires a strong supportive environment, in which their achievements within their own real culture are recognised. The absence of such an environment leads to many a revolt as the young teen, driven by his developmental need to form his own identity, reacts against attempts to negate it. Should a child feel that the environment tries to deprive him too radically of all forms of expression which permit him to develop and integrate the next step in his ego identity, he will resist with the astonishing strength encountered in animals who are suddenly forced to defend their lives.

> ERIC ERICSON
> IN *IDENTITY AND THE LIFE CYCLE*

Psychologically, this is a time when emerging adults must leave behind the security of identifying with parents and families, and 'individuate', taking on and owning their own identity and personalities. Individuation is in fact the primary aim of the teenage years, and its successful negotiation is essential to the healthy development of a young person. A healthy individuation is necessary for a young adult to be able to leave home and make his or her own way in the world. Ericson believed that 'societies offer, as individuals require, more or less sanctioned periods between childhood and adulthood, institutionalised psychosocial moratoria, during which a lasting pattern of "inner identity" is scheduled for relative completion'. Adolescence can therefore be seen as a period in which feelings of loss and grief can be strongly felt, as the safety and security of childhood is left behind and the individual is forced to take on the growing responsibilities and personal challenges that accompany adulthood. That said, the youngster also generally feels excited and energised at the prospect of becoming a separate, independent individual, and this fuels their quest for individuation.

Identity, for the teenager, is created through a series of individual struggles to determine the exact nature of self, and through a succession of choices that establish this identity as being separate from that of parents and others. This often involves, on the part of the teeanger, a clash with parental values and expectations, as in this way young teens demonstrate that they have an individual will that is not dependent on that of others and that they are responsible and accountable for their own choices and decisions, even if it transpires that they are ill-conceived. Parents often take this determination by teenagers to make their own choices as a threat, and try to exert increasing control and authority over them, especially during mid-adolescence, from fourteen to seventeen, but they often fail to realise that their teenage children, while seeking to establish their autonomy, also need their love and approval as much as ever. The teenager is often in a quandary: torn between rival loyalties, they wish to assert their independence while at the same time receiving strong parental guidance and love in order to make them feel secure. It is imperative that they know that they will not be rejected or abandoned as a result of their drive for autonomy, and that they are valued as individuals.

Parents and adolescents must therefore work together to redefine their relationship: close ties must be maintained, without the young person's individuality being threatened. Research shows that, on the whole, this work does occur harmoniously, and that the popular view of conflict between parents and teens during these years is exaggerated. Basic attitudes towards education, careers and morality appear to be convergent within families. Young adolescents endorse the values and attitudes of their family, and in general they respect their parents' views and seek their opinions on major issues. Conflict occurs by and large around day-to-day behaviour, such as bedroom tidiness, household chores, finances, eating habits, bedtimes and the time they return home after evenings out. In fact, research in the UK shows that teenagers view their parents as being more conservative than they actually are, and parents, conversely, see their adolescents as being more radical than is the case. It therefore appears that the generation gap is more about perception than reality. Conflict at this time, of which we hear so much, is generally limited to a small percentage of families, in which relationship difficulties were prevalent during childhood and poor family communication and negotiation exist.

During the process of individuation, attention is diverted away from parents and family to the peer group, which plays an increasingly important role in the life of teens, giving them a sense of belonging outside of the family, and solidifying their feeling of autonomy. This sense of belonging is crucial to the developing teen identity, and often its absence is a major driving force behind teen depression and suicide, which will be examined in greater detail in Chapters 15 and 16. Personal needs and social pressure direct teenagers towards at least one friendship group, because the alternative is loneliness and isolation. The intense relations with same-sex friends that characterise the childhood years gradually wane as the period of adolescence progresses, and a wider network of friendships evolves. In this wider circle, the role of opposite-sex friends becomes more pronounced. Friendships are vital to the developing identity of the teen, providing them with the necessary affirmation, security and support that were previously afforded them by parents, and offering them understanding, partnership, and companionship. It is with their close friends that they explore the realities of adulthood and share their fears, worries and times of sorrow. It is with them, too, that they begin the process of seeing their parents as fallible individuals as opposed to demi-gods, and by so doing initiating the process of individuation.

The growing social network of the developing teen is often complex and variegated, but, like adult relations, it can be seen to have distinct forms. At the centre is the 'close friends' group – or clique – referred to above. There is then the wider peer group, which contains same-age and same-gender peers. Within this exists a plethora of sub-groups who adopt their own identity, such as skateboarders, rugby 'heads', 'druggies', goths and so on. These groups set the norm of behaviour for their members, and adherence to this norm is a prerequisite for membership of the group. They operate their own specific value system – relating to attitudes to drugs and alcohol, for instance – and demand the wearing of specific signs and symbols, including particular clothes and hairstyles, that identify their members. Generally, teens choose the groups which most closely embrace their own value systems and thereby provide them with a sense of ease surrounding their identity. At times, they may experiment with other groups, but they will generally return to that which is most supportive of their own family environment and value system.

Like the perceived existence of a conflict-ridden generation gap, the notion that the teen peer group exerts negative pressure on its members appears to be ill-conceived. Studies in this field indicate that adolescents are, in general, attracted to groups that support their family's value systems, and reflect their sense of themselves in the world. They will be drawn to groups made up of people who have similar hobbies and leisure interests, who dress like themselves, and who have similar attitudes to school, music and other things. Instead of exercising negative pressure, such as promoting drug use and advanced sexual behaviour, peer groups more often than not operate a positive pressure, dictating that their members stay within the group's collective, family-value system. For instance, the group may demand that drugs are not used, and that sexual promiscuity is unacceptable. The group thus often operates a policing of behaviours: the giving and receiving of support, and the space to resist group pressures – all of which are necessary in order to enhance a sense of self. While individual groups may go through a stage of experimentation during the middle adolescent years, this tends to be contained by the group and is generally a passing phase. As individual members mature and become more confident in their independence, the level of conformity among members gradually decreases. The development of romantic relationships is seen to encourage this independence from the group. While groups that support and sustain delinquent behaviour do exist, these are not the norm – and are generally a reflection of familial difficulty and the wider social environment of the adolescent.

As adolescence progresses, especially from mid-adolescence, these smaller groupings or cliques usually enter larger groupings – generally known as crowds – which typically consist of between two and four cliques. There are two basic reasons for this. Firstly, it facilitates association with opposite-sex cliques, so that heterosexual behaviours can be learned and practised, which is a necessary stage in sexual development. Secondly, it facilitates the process of identity creation, where the tight security provided by the clique, as an alternate to the family environment, is no longer as necessary as it was before. These crowds give the adolescent greater opportunity to experiment with and reinforce their developing identity, while maintaining a sense of belonging. Adolescents leave their close-knit cliques to become members of larger crowds of boys and girls. In so doing, they consolidate their individual identity and learn to function in a wider social context, which is necessary for entry into the adult world, where tolerance of difference is essential for the effective functioning of any society. Studies in the UK show that the dominant crowds in most schools are perceived as socially and academically competent, and engage in school activities more readily than more marginalised crowds. Groups with the lowest levels of involvement in school activities, such as the 'druggies', are generally viewed fairly negatively by other groups.

Navigating a positive path through the often intensely political nature of the teen peer group is a huge learning experience in interpersonal relationships for young people, and one which often has a big impact on their future ability to relate effectively as individuals. In this transient world, where loyalties change to facilitate the ongoing creation of identity, teens often experience loss for the first time in their lives. Through the negotiation of these losses, they learn invaluable lessons that will stay with them throughout their life. The teen who relates effectively within the peer group, maintaining an individual sense of self, and learns to accept loss as a necessary part of the human experience will, by and large, display greater mental health in later life than one who does not. Parental empathy, support and guidance can also have a major life-enhancing affect at this stage of their development. The ability to enter the emotional world of the young adult and give guidance, rather than seeking to control his or her life, should be the primary aim of parents.

Social Self-development

The tasks in this category are generally concerned with the development of the teenager's abilities to function effectively within the world at large, and by so doing adopting a positive and contributory place within their social system. Their propensity to do this will be directly linked to their sense of worth, and hopes for their future.

During the mid and later teenage years, the executive functions of the brain develop, allowing the young adult gradually to turn away from the narcissistic, egocentric world that characterises early adolescence. Cognitive functions develop, and these enable the young teen to judge the consequences of their actions – on both themselves and others – more readily. Organisational abilities develop, and teenagers begin to be able to plan tasks and to examine alternative strategies and perspectives. Furthermore, they develop the ability to examine their own thinking, and are more capable of identifying distortions in their thinking and in that of other people. Their view of other people moves from an egocentric to a more empathic foundation. In other words, the notion of personal responsibility in a wider social context develops, as does the youngster's perception of their future and their place in the world in general.

A teenager often develops a social and political conscience at this stage, and young adolescents are frequently attracted to 'causes' and display an interest in both national and international politics. This marks the beginning of their ability to experience themselves as part of a wider social system, and their attempts to create an identity for themselves within that system. It again fosters a sense of belongingness, rather than social isolation. A sense of justice and injustice are passionately adopted by the teenager, whose thinking is dominated by black-and-white thinking, and idealised aims appear tangible and attainable.

It is no coincidence that many of the suicide bombers in the Middle East are teenagers, and that it is young youths that pelt Israeli tanks with stones in defiance of authority. Believing that they can take on such might, they are unable to judge the full consequences of their actions, and too often pay the price. Indeed, they often prepared to die, hoping that their deaths will in some way contribute towards the realisation of justice. Closer to home, in Northern Ireland, the IRA enlisted their staunchest and bravest supporters from the ranks of youth, who were driven by a determination that justice and equality would prevail. In this context, it should be noted that the hunger strikers of the 1980s were all between the ages of twenty-three and twenty-nine. In the rioting in Dublin in March 2006, as a result of the proposed 'Love Ulster' parade, it was the disaffected youth of the inner city who were drawn on by larger organised groups to fuel the violence. While more mature adults may see these notions as hopelessly unattainable, or at least foolhardy, or have the capacity to view the situation from more than one perspective, idealistic – or disaffected – youths frequently fail to look at the consequences of their own and others' actions, and either push change forward or, in some cases, create mayhem.

This sense of fairness and justice, and the questioning of authority and beliefs often associated with it, is also frequently introduced into the home by the teenager, often creating friction with parents. The justness of parental authority is questioned – and often found wanting. The teenagers begin to notice the sometimes arbitrary nature of rules, and how they are bent. With parental judgement no longer seen to be infallible, teenagers either grudgingly acquiesce to rules or rebel against them.

The idea that one has a part to play in the wider community

should be encouraged by parents and schools at this stage in the teenager's development. The President's Award – in which involvement in charity or voluntary work is an integral part – during transition year has done much to instil this notion amongst young teens. So too has schools' Civics, Social and Personal Education programme, which aims to promote the ideas of social and civic responsibility. A growing consciousness of the environment is also noticeable amongst young people, with recycling, animal rights, vegetarianism, and other issues often being championed by them. In school and on playing fields, young teens learn the need to adhere to rules for the common good, the need to negotiate and compromise, respect for difference, personal responsibility, the need to deal with disappointment, and so on. These are all necessary experiences that promote a sense of responsibility. The school environment should therefore seek to prepare teenagers for the wider social and civic environment, in which they will have to take their place.

It is during this period, especially from the age of fifteen, that teens need to start thinking of their future careers, which will furnish them with economic independence. This is often a daunting prospect to the many teenagers who have no clear idea of what they would like to do. Guidance from parents on these issues is generally sought, and in most cases respected. It is parents, more than anyone else, who are responsible for giving young teens a vision of their future. Transition-year work experience gives many the opportunity to experience various industries at first hand. Part-time work at this stage helps to imbue teenagers with an understanding of the importance of hard work, of self-worth, value and achievement, an appreciation of money, and the confidence of being involved in the wider working environment.

Development of Sexuality

Sexual development is one of the most significant aspects of adolescence, and one which, in many ways, creates the most challenges to developing teenage identity. It involves not only the obvious physiological changes that occur during puberty but also a change in social definition. Teenagers need to adjust to their identity as sexual beings, and for many, this task can be daunting, both emotionally and socially. How they view their budding sexuality is influenced strongly by the society in which they live, and by their family, peers and religious and other beliefs.

Modern-day openness to sexuality has no doubt helped adolescents to feel less self-conscious and fearful about their sexual development, and in general they no longer view it as a taboo subject. This new openness, however, by its very nature means that teenagers are exposed to sexual encounters at a much earlier age than in previous eras, and have less time to develop their own values and beliefs around the issues involved in relationships. While no comprehensive surveys have been conducted on the sexual behaviour of Irish teenagers, it is reasonable to assume that trends here similar to those in England. These surveys indicate that the number of teens who engage in sexual intercourse before the age of sixteen has been steadily rising until quite recently, although the change for females is slower than that for males. There is also evidence that young people today are likely to engage in a wider range of sexual behaviours, particularly oral sex, than previously. The rising popularity of oral sex can be accounted for by the fact that it will not lead to pregnancy, or, in general, the spread of sexually transmitted diseases. It is often engaged in with casual partners, while full intercourse is reserved for more steady liaisons.

In the past decade, the issue of teen pregnancy has been creating growing concern. In 2005, the Rotunda Hospital opened a separate wing for teenage mothers in an attempt to make the experience of childbirth more positive for them, and to provide support for their particular needs, and some secondary schools have recently felt the need to introduce maternity uniforms in order to facilitate the growing number of pregnancies amongst their students. However, results from the 2006 Census are both welcome and positive in relation to this issue. There has been a sharp fall in the number of teen births: last year, 2,427 Irish women under the age of twenty gave birth, compared to 3,116 in 2000. Likewise, the number of births to teenagers under the age of seventeen fell from 273 in 2000 to 224 in 2005 There were only seven births last year to girls under the age of fifteen, compared to ten in 2000 and thirteen in 1980. Among fifteen-year-olds, there were thirty-five births in 2005, compared to fifty-seven in 2000, and among sixteen-year-olds, births fell from sixty-seven in 2000 to forty-two in 2005. These decreases are both significant and heartening, and indicate that the increased awareness and availability of contraceptives to teenagers is having a significant impact. The introduction of compulsory sex education in schools in 2003, through the Social, Presonal and Health Education (SPHE) curriculum, can also be seen to be exerting a positive influence in the area of teen sexuality. When taking account of these figures, however, it must be noted that the number of births to teenagers does not necessarily equate with the number of teenage pregnancies: it must be acknowledged that a growing tolerance of abortion, together with a decrease in the cost of having an abortion due to cheap air travel, may well have an impact on these figures as well.

Findings from two in-depth studies on sexuality, contraception and unplanned pregnacy carried out in 2004 by the Crisis Pregnancy Agency support these views. The studies confirmed that sexually active young adults have a strong tendency for sexual risk-taking and have poor levels of knowledge about fertility. The chairperson of the agency, Olive Braiden, believes that these factors are making a significant contribution to the scale and seriousness of crisis pregnancy in Ireland. Furthermore, it was reported that the age of first sexual intercourse in Ireland is dropping, with the majority of young people now having their first sexual experience by the age of eighteen, with the average age for first sexual experience being fifteen and a half years.

Eighteen- to twenty-five-year olds were less likely to use contraception consistently when compared to the adult population, with 58 percent citing the fact that they had not planned to have sex as the reason why they had engaged in unprotected sex. Twenty-one percent stated that drinking alcohol and using drugs had inhibited their judgement in making the decision not to protect themselves. Other reasons given were that they were afraid that their parents would find their contraceptives and know that they were sexually active, and that they found it difficult or were embarassed to get contraceptives. The abortion rate for twenty- to twenty-four-year-olds was also higher than for any other age group. The authors of the study concluded that sex education in Irish schools and by parents is 'inadequate, and too biological, too narrow, and too late.'

Teenage sexual behaviour must be looked at in the wider context of society as a whole. Modern society has become more sexual in all respects, with sex increasingly being viewed as a commodity. Young people see sexual material on television, on film and video, on advertising hoardings and in teenage magazines, and the fact that adults are engaging in sex outside of marriage, and at times pursue sexual gratification regardless of the consequences, may also be removing traditional barriers to early sexual activity. The weakening of religious values in relation to sex, especially in the wake of the recent sexual-abuse scandals within the Catholic Church, has also weakened inhibitions. In the teenager's view, everyone is at it, so why not them? Parental guidance on, and monitoring of, sexual behaviour has a major influence on teenagers' developing sexuality, as does their behaviour as role models. As in other areas, open discussion and negotiation around sexual behaviour is necessary, and appears to produce the best results. Refusal to discuss sexual issues, or to acknowledge teenagers as sexual beings, does not prevent teens from becoming sexually active, and does not allow space for discussion of other important issues, such as sexual health and contraception. Allowing an open forum for discussion of such issues gives the young adolescent the security of being able to discuss any difficulties they may experience in this area.

Irish society has to date paid a very high price for sexual repression, as sexual energy does not simply dissipate but finds expression in more dysfunctional forms. This can be seen to account for the extent of sexual abuse in our society – not restricted to incidences of clerical sexual abuse. Indeed, it could be argued that the clergy has been scapegoated and used to deflect attention away from the fact that deviant sexual practices have in the past been far more common within our society than we care to admit. Moreover, it has been far easier for abuse victims to come forward and testify to abuse at the hands of the clergy than within their own social networks and immediate families.

It is also important to remember that sexual behaviour is only one aspect of sexual development, and that the importance of the emotional experience involved in teenage relationships should not be overlooked. Falling in love – as written about in so many songs and poems – is a major part of the adolescent experience, and of the teenager's search for self-definition and a sense of identity. An experience of intimacy involves levels of openness, sharing, trust and commitment that have hitherto not been experienced by the teenager. Teen love relationships tend to be intense but short-term, and the way in which the young teen manages the loss or break-up of a relationship is integral to their development, as it affects their future choices in relationships, and their perception of themselves within these relationships.

Adolescents who either know that they are homosexual or are unsure of their sexual orientation experience the most difficulty when negotiating their sexual development. Some may know from an early age that they are either gay or lesbian, while others will remain confused and uncertain throughout their teenage years. Stereotyping and prejudice towards gays and lesbians, which are pervasive in our society, make it increasingly difficult for young gay people to own their own sexual identity, and are major contributing factors in the mental ill health that is commonly found among members of this group. A lack of acceptance by society in general stigmatises them, making them feel it is necessary to conceal their doubts about their sexual identity. Very few have access to an outlet for help or support, and they are usually not in a position to share their anxieties with their families, fearing the response of other family members.

In the initial stages of sexual identification, the young person generally experiences great anxiety as it becomes increasingly clear to them that they are different from most of their peers. It may take some time for them even to admit this difference to themselves. If and when they eventually accept that they are either gay or lesbian, they then have to develop coping strategies to defend themselves against the stigma they believe may exist towards gays and lesbians. Most do this by keeping their sexual preferences a secret initially. While some then move on to disclose their sexual identity to close friends, some never manage this step, and these people then have to decide whether they can disclose their sexual orientation to their parents or not: for most, the thought of doing so is terrifying, as they fear the reaction that they may receive. The feeling of isolation that ensues creates great stress. A survey conducted in the US in 1993 found that 42 percent of the gay and lesbian young people that were studied had attempted suicide in the previous year, and similar findings have been reported in various European countries. As yet, no such studies have been conducted in Ireland – which can itself be seen as a reflection of our own reluctance to consider the impact of sexual-identity confusion.

There is an urgent need for an adult who suspects that a teenager may be experiencing difficulties around sexual-identification issues to convey to these distressed teenagers that support is accessible through such agencies as Outhouse, where they can seek advice and meet others who are experiencing the same difficulties. This eases their sense of isolation and creates a sense of belonging, which is crucial during these years.

In 2003, the Department of Education, acknowledging the special difficulties faced by gay, lesbian and transgender teenagers, made a decision to fund a special youth project, BelongTo, that had been set up by Outhouse on a voluntary basis. This project, which caters for fourteen- to twenty-three-year-olds, has a subsidiary group called BelongTeen, which addresses the needs of the under-eighteens. Individual counselling and group support is offered by trained facilitators to its members. Social meetings, which take place every second week, aim to make it easier for under-eighteens to meet and make friends of their own age in a safe enviroment. Group activities such as drama, photography and alcohol-free youth-club nights are also organised.

3

Physiological Changes

As well as these psychological challenges, teeangers have to deal with the fact that their bodies are changing drastically during this time – and indeed appear to take on a life of their own. As well as coming to terms with their new shape, young teens must step into their sexuality, adopting the adornments of femininity or masculinity, adjusting to the new rhythms of their bodies, and becoming comfortable with the biological changes in their sexual organs.

Puberty in fact begins at the age of about eight, when the pituitary gland begins to pump increasing amounts of sexual hormones to the sexual organs of both boys and girls. In the second stage, the breasts begin to bud in girls, and a few wisps of pubic hair may become noticeable; in boys, the testicles begin to enlarge and the scrotal sac starts to hang lower. In stages three and four, the genitals in both sexes enlarge and grow darker in colour. In stage three, the penis begins to get bigger, and one testicle may hang lower than the other to avoid discomfort while walking. Sperm production is possible from the age of twelve. Pubic hair grows thicker and curlier in girls, and begins to appear in boys from stage four. Menstruation occurs in stage four, generally two years after breasts begin to bud, and vaginal discharge is noticeable. In girls, a little extra fat around the thighs and bum appears, as body fat is essential for menstruation.

Physiological change during this period is not confined to sexual organs. The heart doubles in size, and the lungs expand to fill the widening ribcage. The body does not grow uniformly: head, hands and feet reach adult size first. After the limbs have stretched, shoulders widen in boys and hips in girls, and the final part in the body to lengthen is the trunk. It is this rapid growth that accounts for the clumsiness that accompanies adolescence, as these new physical attributes are only slowly assimilated mentally by the teenager themselves. Bones become denser and harder, and the skin becomes rougher, particularly around the upper arms and thighs. There are subtle changes to the face as it becomes more angular, the forehead becomes higher, and the lower part of the face gets longer as the chin juts forward more. The mouth widens and the lips become fuller. Muscles grow too, and both sexes discover a marked increase in their physical strength and endurance. The average teen puts on about ten pounds a year between the ages of ten and eighteen. There is a marked increase in body hair in both sexes. Hair darkens and grows thicker on limbs, and begins to appear under arms, and on the face in boys. Some girls also grow fine down on their top lips, and may find the odd hair on their breasts. Glandular activity increases too, with oilier skin and increased perspiration under the arms and in the groin area.

The young teen, powerless over the physiological changes happening to their bodies, waits apprehensively to see the final product. They fear that what might emerge is a shape that would be scorned by their peers and will be a lifelong source of embarrassment to them. Inevitably, in a world where the idea of a perfect body is clearly defined and perceived to be increasingly necessary, they find many thing wrongs with theirs, and fret. Their calves are too thick, their thighs too round, their ears too big, their legs too long, their torso too skinny, and so on. Self-consciousness and self-obsession take over.

Given the extent of such change, it is not surprising that so many adolescents feel awkward about their developing bodies. Indeed, most adults have little difficulty in recalling the insecurity they felt around their physiological development during their teenage years. Nowhere was self-consciousness on this issue as marked as in the school changing rooms. Instead, it could be argued that modern society's increased tolerance of nudity, or at least a more liberal dress code, has eased the level of self-consciousness for many. However, for those suffering from obesity, for instance, this increased level of exposure merely accentuates their plight.

Adolescents' concerns surrounding their bodies should not be dismissed as immaterial. It is OK to discuss with them the difficulties they are experiencing and to reassure them about their development. Above all else, uninvited negative comments about their bodies should be avoided at all costs, as these are often perceived to be shaming.

4

Neurological Changes

As in other areas, neurological development and change during the teen years is profound. Until the early 1990s, most scientists believed that the brain was a finished product by the age of twelve. But, as reported in *Time* magazine on 7 June 2004, a giant study led by Dr Jay Giedd of the National Institute of Mental Health in Bethesda, Washington, was initiated in 1991, with the stated goal 'to determine how the brain develops from childhood into adolescence, and on into early adulthood.' His findings were groundbreaking in that he concluded that, far from the teenage brain being fully formed from childhood, as had been believed, the brain of the adolescent 'is far from mature; both grey and white matter undergo extensive structural changes well past puberty, up until the age of twenty-five in most cases.'

Given this premise, researchers are now investigating how the absence of adequate cognitive controls due to a lack of neurological development may account for disturbed behaviour during the teenage years. A link between the onset at this time of major mental illnesses such as schizophrenia and bipolar disorder, and neurological development, is being studied. Dr Jay Giedd has identified that subtler changes in grey matter within the brain reflect experience and environment and that, by examining these more subtle changes, it may be possible to tease apart the influences of nature and nurture. As he puts it, 'the brain more than any other organ is where experience becomes flesh.'

When studying twins, he was able to identify that, while one part of the brain, the corpus callosum, which deals with instinct and emotion, is identical in identical twins, and thus it can be inferred that it is largely controlled by genes, the cerebellum, which contains the executive functions, is different in each twin. He thus believes that it is this part of the brain that develops according to experience and environment, and which holds the key to the future development of the adolescent.

The delay in the area of neurological research in adolescents may in part be accounted for by the fact that, by the time a child reaches six years of age, the brain is 90 to 95 percent of its adult size. Morevoer, subtler changes in structure that occur during adolescence were undetectable until the recent development of MRI facilities. In fact, humans achieve their maximum brain-cell density between the third and sixth month of gestation, after which a dramatic pruning occurs, in which unnecessary brain cells are eliminated. It is believed that some conditions, including Asperger's, may be caused by the pruning that occurs at this time. Through the use of MRI scans, Giedd has discovered that a second period of 'proliferation and pruning' occurs later in childhood, with the final and critical part of this process affecting some of humans' highest mental functions, occurring in the late teens. Unlike the initial growth spurt within the womb, however, this phase does not involve brain cells as such, but the number of connections between them, known as synapses. Between the ages of six and twelve, the neurons become bushier, with each making dozens of connections to other neurons, and creating new pathways for nerve signals, thus enlarging the grey matter in the brain. This enlargement can be seen as the foundation of opportunity, laying the groundwork for the individual to become whatsoever he or she may wish to be. By the age of twelve, the second wave of pruning commences. During this period synapses that are not being used are thinned out, and those that are being used are strengthened by being wrapped in white matter, known as myelin, which protects and thickens the synapses, making nerve signal transmissions faster and more effective.

Direct experience at this stage of development is believed to determine the future capabilities of the emerging adult. As *Time* magazine reported on 7 June 2004: 'The brain becomes a more efficient machine, but there is a trade-off: it is probably losing some of its raw potential for learning and its ability to recover from trauma.' The pruning process is believed to be driven by the use-it-or-lose-it principle: synapses that are directly connected to activities that are being engaged in are thickened. (For instance, playing the piano thickens neurons in the brain region that controls the fingers.)

The development of the brain can be compared to the development of a national road network. Originally, a large number of lanes and small roads would be developed. As time goes on, and the country develops, the roads that experience the most usage are widened and reinforced, while those that are barely used fade away. A similar process occurs within the teenage brain. Thus, the activities of developing teenagers may have a profound effect on the way in which their brains develop, and thus on their future capabilities. In the case of the twins being researched, Giedd believes that he will be able to predetermine the future career paths of each of the twins. Thus genetic inheritance does not of itself determine future ability, and Giedd's findings reinforce the adage that 'Genius is 99 percent practice and 1 percent ability.'

As a result of these findings, one cannot underestimate the significance of the nature of the activities in which teenagers engage during these vital years on their future development. Teenagers who are understimulated will fail to strengthen many of their synapses sufficiently, while teenagers who concentrate all their energies on a few activities will have some synapses that are over-developed, while others will not be developed at all. By concentrating all their attention on one activity, such as studying, sport or music, such teens will have little to fall back on if they experience difficulty in their chosen activity. Balancing activities is therefore of great importance at this stage.

Brain development goes through certain stages. The back of

the brain, called the amygdala, develops first. This part of the brain mediates direct contact with the environment; it controls sensory functions such as vision, hearing, touch and spatial processing. It is involved in the production of a fear response, and other negative emotions.

Next to develop is the area that coordinates these functions: the anterior cingulated cortex. This part of the brain helps you know where the light switch is in your bathroom, even if you cannot see it; it is associated with emotion and gut responses, and is more dominant in the teenage years. The adolescent therefore has a more emotional response than an adult: the prefrontal part of the brain, which restrains emotion through advanced discerning powers, is not yet fully developed. The ability to check emotions through rational thought is not properly developed, and the ability to differentiate between different emotions is more developed in this part of the brain in teenagers compared to adults. Research has found that teenagers are far less able to identify an expression of fear, confusing it with other emotions, such as anger. This is seen to account for the propensity in teenagers to respond to situations with irrational levels of emotion.

The last area of the brain to develop is the part that contains the executive functions; it is here that the pruning process occurs. It is only now that the brain's decision-making faculties are fully developed – the ability to plan, set priorities, organise thought, suppress impulses, weigh up the consequences of actions, and so on. These facilities allow people to respond rather than merely react: they help distinguish an adult from a child.

The idea that hormones are alone accountable for bad and seemingly irrational decisions made by teenagers is being challenged by recent research, which suggests that a lack of full neurological development plays a large role in this phenomenon. This lack of development, coupled with the effects of the hormonal onslaught in puberty, combine to make adolescence a volatile and risky time.

Adrenal sex hormones are extremely active in the brain at this time, attaching to receptors everywhere and directly influencing levels of serotonin and other brain chemicals, which regulate mood and excitability. These hormones are especially active in the brain's emotional centre; as a result, not only do feelings reach a flashpoint more easily, but adolescents tend to seek out situations where they can allow their emotions and passions to run wild. The dangers inherent in this situation are aptly described by psychologist Laurence Steinberg:

> The parts of the brain responsible for things like sensation-seeking are getting turned on in big ways around the time of puberty, but the parts for exercising judgement are still maturing throughout the course of adolescence. So you've got this time gap between when things impel kids toward taking risks early in adolescence, and when things that allow people to think before they act come on-line. It's like turning on the engine of a car without having a skilled driver at the wheel.

Part Two

The Psychological Background

5

Psychological Theories of Adolescence

Most theorists agree that nothing has a greater impact on the developing teen than his or her childhood experiences within the family of origin. Eric Ericson, when propounding his theory of human psychological development, asserted that continued mental health rests on the individual's propensity to successfully negotiate the development tasks of each preceding stage of life. Failure to do so resulted in the development of a split within the personality of the individual. For a teenager to successfully complete the tasks of adolescence, he or she must be adequately equipped with a strong sense of self. This is achieved by successfully completing the previous stages of development, through the provision of a secure and mirroring primary-caregiver relationship, the existence of a healthy family dynamic based on unconditional love and self-expression, and the absence of major childhood trauma. We can therefore assume that, in most cases, the answers to crises in adolescence can be found in childhood experience. Negative events or experiences in adolescence including bereavement and parental separation – may, however, intervene and disrupt development; in general the more secure their childhood has been, the better able the adolescent will be to cope with these experiences.

Trauma and loss are seen to be central to the genesis of neurosis. Freud based his theory of neurotic development and sexual identity on the Oedipal and Electra complexes, believing that, between the ages of three and six, each child develops a romantic love for the opposite-sex parent. The successful negotiation of feelings that are aroused by this situation, by both parents and child, determine the future ability of the child to remain true to themselves, and integrate the feelings of loss that ensue. He noted that: 'What happens in the Oedipal conflict is critical to determining and qualifying a boy's sexual identity, as well as establishing the foundation of his later psychological development.' In the Oedipal situation, the son feels an antipathy towards his father, and his attachment to his mother arouses an emotional reaction in the father, whose primal instinct is to feel threatened by the strength of the bond between mother and son:

> The boy becomes a competitor with his father for his mother's interest and admiration, for her desire. He wants to be the love preference of his mother, his mother's boy, first in her attention and affection.

The son senses a threat of punishment from his father for his 'designs' on his mother. He may experience deep feelings of hatred towards his father, sometimes fantasising about his father's death. The role of the father during this period is pivotal to the future development of his son's masculinity. The father's role at this stage is to gently but emphatically break the intensity of the bond between the son and mother, and bring the boy into the male world. The boy must temporarily experience defeat at the hands of his father. This defeat instigates the child's first experience of real loss, as he is forced to give up his 'love' for his mother. He now enters the latency period, where his sexual interests go under ground and he seeks out the company of other boys. During this period, the father becomes an active role model, and in so doing eases the feeling of loss being experienced by the boy. The boy's new identification with his father, and his father's rules, introduces the boy into the world of maleness, and compensates for the loss of the mother, who becomes increasingly less important in his psychological make-up. This experience will be further explored later in the section on fatherhood in Part Six.

Thus, if the boy child's original feelings of fear and rage are accepted and understood by his parents, and the tasks laid down in the Oedipal conflict are properly negotiated by all three parties, the child will avoid the development of neurosis, and develop a strong sexual identity. When this is not the case, repression is adopted as a defence, creating internal conflict and anxiety for the child. In cases where there is no father to break the bond, similar problems develop, especially with regard to the developing masculinity of the child..

The idea that experiences prior to the Oedipal stage were important in regard to psychological development were developed substantively by the renowned theorist Melanie Klein. Klein founded the object-relations school, which stressed the importance of early childhood relations, especially with the mother. The first few months of life were seen to be crucial to the development of the child's future mental health. Klein, however, moved away from Freud's view that the bond between mother and child was purely libido-driven and centred on infantile sexuality. Attachment and detachment to objects, including the mothers' breasts, and the infant's reaction to these losses, through detachment, were seen to be of greater importance. Klein believed that the infant is linked psychologically as well as physiologically to the mother and her breast from birth. The self developed in relation to these objects, and ideas and feelings towards them were internalised. The satisfying, nourishing and comforting breast symbolised the 'good object', and thus the attentive mother, while the absent, withholding empty breast was the 'bad object', the product of the failures and unresponsiveness of the mother. The way in which debilitating feelings of loss are facilitated by the mother during the process of weaning is all-important, as is the way in which individuation from the mother was facilitated. Future neurosis was determined by the emotional reactions of the infant to the loss of such objects, and his or her own individuation. The way these losses were managed, or not managed, through maternal support accounted for such conditions as narcissistic disorder and borderline personality disorder.

Alfred Adler, one of Freud's initial circle, was the most significant theorist to break away from the classic psychoanalytic view of childhood, based on biological and instinctual drives. Adler asserted that it was necessary to view each individual in his or her social context, paying special attention to family constellations. He believed that the self developed in relation to other people and therefore that, while early relationships were important in setting up a person's view of themselves, relationships continued to influence self-perception throughout life. This led to a split with Freud.

David Winnicott and John Bowlby, two of the most significant theorists to emerge in the wake of World War II, supported Adler's views. While supporting the primacy of the early maternal relationship, they integrated the idea of the importance of a supportive environment into their theories. They in effect held that a child who experienced the trauma of maternal deprivation could be saved from mental ill health through the provision of a warm and affirming substitute environment.

Winnicott believed that the psyches of the newborn and the mother were inseparable, as a result of the mother's natural instinct to provide for the child's every need – which ensured the development of an emotionally and mentally healthy child. The child did not in fact view itself as being separate from the mother. By mirroring back feelings of love and safety to the baby, and by instinctually providing for all its needs, the mother developed a view, in the baby, that the environment in which it existed was secure. As the infant gradually began to view itself as separate, it had no reason to be afraid: the child was free to communicate its needs, and to expect them to be fulfilled. In such babies, the 'true self' is free to develop, resulting in a mentally healthy child.

In cases where these needs are not fulfilled, however, and neglect, either emotional or physical, exists, the seeds of neurosis are sown. The baby, uncertain about whether its basic needs will be met, begins to view its environment as threatening, and develops a deeper sense of separateness. The threat of these feelings to the baby's psyche are so overwhelming that it is driven to develop defences against reality. A split occurs and the child abandons its true self, its true feelings, and develops a false self, which represses its own needs and instead plays to the needs of the mother. The baby stops crying to have its needs met, withdraws into itself, and ceases to make demands on the unavailable mother. In other words, it develops tactics through which it hopes to satisfy the mother and win her love, while suppressing its own needs. A false self that engages in people-pleasing behaviours at its own expense develops. Once this process occurs, the practice of seeking approval is initiated, and the child continues to move further away from its true self, in the pursuit of having its unmet need for love satiated. The child goes out into the world seeking affirmation of others that it failed to secure from the maternal bond. This results in the development of neurosis, as the conflict between the true self and the false self intensifies as time goes by. This conflict can in some cases be so severe that psychosis can eventually develop.

Like Winnicott, John Bowlby, inspired by Klein, further extended and validated her ideas through his work with children during the Second World War and in its aftermath. While Bowlby firmly believed that negligent maternal care of infants led to neurosis, he also put forward the idea that neurosis, and character disturbance, could occur as a result of environmental trauma such as separation. He developed his theories of attachment, separation and loss while studying the effects of maternal deprivation and institutionalisation on young children. The basis of his theory centres on the notion that a child's ability to cope with the vicissitudes of separation and loss are directly linked to the degree of security attached to its maternal bond. A child who was securely attached to its mother as a result of a nurturing maternal relationship, while disturbed by separation, was able to cope. By contrast, children who were insecurely attached to their mother as a result of inconsistent maternal care were less able to cope with separation. These children had a mixture of feelings towards their attachment figure: intense love combined with dependency, fear of rejection, irritability and vigilance. The effects of separation on these children was found to have lasting effects on their future mental health.

Bowlby drew criticism from some quarters, especially the developing feminist movement, for the great levels of responsibility he placed on the mother in his attachment theory, which in effect dictated that to be a good mother one must, by necessity, be omnipresent. He later modified his theory to include a pyramidal system of attachment bonds and care, which were of equal importance. He embraced the idea that a supporting and loving environment could ameliorate the negative effects of maternal neglect or separation.

Later theorists brought this thinking forward, looking at the effects of maternal deprivation and neglect in a generational context. They investigated how a maternally deprived and needs-neglected mother was unable to provide adequately for the emotional well-being of her child. Given no clear map as a child, and dominated by unconscious unmet needs, the mother uses the child in an attempt to fulfil her own needs. Mothers who suffer from neurosis are therefore likely to have children who also develop neurosis. This process is succinctly described by one of these theorists, Alice Miller, in her book *The Drama of Being a Child*:

> I think that the cause of an emotional disturbance is to be found in the infant's early adaption. The child's needs for respect, understanding, sympathy and mirroring have had to be repressed, with several serious consequences. . . . If that person is missing, if the child must risk losing the mother's love or the love of her substitute in order to feel, then she will repress her emotion. But they will nevertheless stay in her body, in her cells, stored up as information that can be triggered by a later event. . . . When a woman has had to repress all these needs in relation to her own mother, they will arise

from the depth of her unconscious and seek gratification through her own child, however well educated she may be. The child feels this clearly, and very soon forgoes the expression of his own distress.

This thinking gave rise to the family-system theorists, who developed Adler's original family-constellation theories. They believed that no individual could be thoroughly understood unless they were viewed in their wider social context, i.e. with regard to how they function in relation to others. These theorists placed primary importance on the individual's interactions within the family system, seeing it as a blueprint for the individual's wider network of relationships. They also believe that the behaviour and action of any one individual within a family system affects all the others family members, and that the reciprocal reactions from other family members affect the individual. An individual's problematic behaviour may be seen to have a function within the family, be a reflection of the family's inability to operate productively, or be a symptom of dysfunctional patterns handed down across generations. These theorists believed that not only do needs-neglected mothers produce children that are likewise needs-neglected, but that in most cases their chosen partner is also the product of a need-neglected maternal relationship. This gives rise to the theory of dysfunctional families, in which both parents and children adopt various roles to keep the family system functioning. Within such families, no member is free to express their true selves, as, by so doing, the system would be threatened with collapse. These theories gained increased credence from the 1950s, and they tend to be used, in some form or another, in most psychological assessments today.

For us, in our examination of adolescents, these combined theories leave little doubt that the roots of adolescent distress are generally embedded in childhood and the family system in which they operate, and that childhood experience in most cases dictates the future mental health of the adolescent. The exception to this rule are those adolescents that suffer a stressor such as bereavement, parental sickness or separation.

In her documentary on juvenile criminals on RTÉ's *Prime Time* series, Keelin Shanley interviewed a priest from the disadvantaged area of Neilstown in west Dublin. What was remarkable about this interview was the fact that the priest emphatically stated that, when christening the children of his diocese, he was able to predict which ones would end up as joyriders, drug addicts, alcoholics, and so on. He was in fact endorsing family-system theory. If a pre-emptive mental-health policy were to be developed in schools, it would be possible to apply these theories, with a view to identifying teenagers who were potentially at risk.

In recent decades, a number of theorists have claimed that too much emphasis is placed on childhood experiences and that mental health or ill health during the teenage years is determined by the number of stressors that teenagers are faced with, and, more importantly, by when these stressors occur: the focal-point theory. The proponents of this theory point to the fact that many young adults face a wide range of transitions and stressors during adolescence and yet appear to cope without undue trauma or stress. It is believed that, in these cases, issues that arise are dealt with one at a time, and the process of adaption is spread over a number of years. As a result, the stresses that stem from the need to adapt to new modes of behaviour are not concentrated in any one point in time. Nonetheless, the more issues any adolescent is faced with at any given time, or the more issues they *choose* to face at any given time, the more likely they are to exhibit signs of stress. While this theory has a certain validity, it cannot be viewed as an alternative to the basic psychoanalytic theory. It can be argued that the adolescent who has been provided with adequate childhood security and operates within a functional family system will be able to tackle and adapt to these issues when they arise – even if some do occur simultaneously – as they have a strong sense of self.

6

Psychological Disturbance

In this chapter I am going to introduce and examine teenage distress in relation to Adlerian theory, as it is Adler who presents the most comprehensive and dynamic approach to treating the emotional and behavioural problems of adolescence. His belief in the 'value, worth and dignity of each human being' are closely aligned with belief systems within the developing psyche of the adolescent, and as a result increases the probability of a positive connection with young adults. His theoretical framework complements the emerging social conscience which, as we have seen, characterises adolescence, as does his emphasis on the 'unique and idiosyncratic manner in which individuals perceive and make use of their aptitudes, abilities and experiences.' Choice and individual responsibility therefore come into play, and they provide the disturbed teenager with the opportunity to move from destructive patterns of behaviour to constructive ones. Adler promotes the idea that young adolescents have some level of control over their development, and the way in which they negotiate crises. While maternal deprivation and childhood trauma are seen to be significant, they are not irreversible facts. The central place of self-actualisation and self-realisation in Adlerian theory provides the necessary framework for progressive healing. A view that all is not lost pervades his work: he believes that adolescents may 'overcome early feelings of inadequacy by developing successful relationships, making solid and lasting friendships, or becoming competent workers and providers.'

Social interest is, he believes, 'innate within every individual, and this natural disposition to seek out connectedness with others and contribute to the common good of society lie within every human. In some it may, as a result of experience, lie deeply hidden but it is always there ready to emerge, given the correct conditions.' In other words, different factors may come in to play to counteract the original stressor, and each individual with behaviour problems must be examined in relation to his or her wider social world, and not just in relation to their family. Respect for the individual is crucial, leading Adler to describe psychopathology not as a 'sickness' but as a 'discouragement'. He believed that 'When individuals cannot cope effectively and constructively with feelings of inferiority, they become discouraged and, as a consequence, develop disordered beliefs, emotions and behaviours in their efforts to manage the difficulties of life.'

Adler's approach to child and adolescent therapy was founded on his belief that all misbehaviour was goal-orientated and sought to redress an imbalance. His work was later taken up and developed by his protégé, Rudolf Dreikurs, who outlined the specific purposes of these behaviours as being attention-seeking, the desire for power, revenge and assumed disability. It is from this goal-orientated perspective that I intend to examine the misbehaviours in which teenagers are currently indulging.

As a general rule, attention-seeking behaviours are adopted by adolescents who believe that they are insignificant unless they are at the centre of adult attention. These behaviours can be seen to be admirable. They strive to be successful, charming, cute, precocious or destructive, playing the class clown, showing off, and being bashful or fearful. The more uncertain the individual is about his or her importance within their social environment, the more pronounced these behaviours will be. As Prout and Brown point out in *Counselling and Psychotherapy with Children and Adolescents*: 'Too much or too little attention by parents may leave a child overemphasising or questioning his or her value as an individual, or place of importance within the family.' The danger in these behaviours is that the young adult is adopting them not for themselves but to provoke a reaction in others.

Power-seeking behaviours are adopted by adolescents to help them gain a sense of significance and self-importance, and to demonstrate to adults that they will not submit to their rules or to their threats of punishment. They deliberately tempt adults into power plays in order to make themselves feel powerful. They may display openly rebellious behaviour, such as arguing or throwing temper tantrums, or be more passive-aggressive, indulging in laziness, forgetfulness or stubbornness. Adler believed that this type of behaviour was a direct result of poor role modelling and of media influences, which 'often model the use of power, control, threats and domination as a method of dealing with interpersonal problems.' Such approaches typically lead to an escalation of conflict, which invariably leaves the child feeling unimportant and hurt. A child who is made to feel like this too often inevitably develops a desire to seek vengeance, and this leads to the third form of misbehaviour, revenge.

An adolescent who is involved in revenge-seeking behaviour seeks to hurt his or her parents by exploiting their vulnerabilities. The adolescent chooses the problem area that will have maximum retaliatory impact on the parents who, as they see it, have hurt them. Some of the more damaging forms of behaviour, such as drug addiction, eating disorders and self-harming, happen in this phase.

Lastly, if this behaviour fails to attain its goal, the adolescent resorts to the fourth and final form, which is assumed disability. Of all the behaviours, this one is the most dangerous. The adolescent has in effect given up hope of being able to have his or her needs met, has ceased to act out, and withdraws and isolates him- or herself. Depression often enters the arena at this stage. The adolescent loses interest in academic and sporting achievement, and withdraws socially. The goal of this behaviour is to get people to give up on them, so they can 'escape the countless day-to-day occasions where their insignificance, incompetence and helplessness are exposed and reaffirmed.' This is the most dangerous type of misbehaviour, and parents of an adolescent displaying these symptoms should seek professional help.

Of great importance to Adler's theory of discouragement is the adolescent's position within the family constellation. The firstborn is generally seen to bear the most pressure in relation to parental expectation, and enjoys the position of being the most mature. Historically, firstborns have been less likely to die in infancy, less susceptible to disease, and, as adults, more likely to reproduce. They enjoy the unique position within the family of having received a good deal of attention as the only child for a certain period of time. Parents experience the 'first' everything with them, and they therefore tend to be approval-seeking, identifying strongly with success. They are dependable, hard-working and achievement-oriented. Firstborn adolescents tend to achieve more than any of their siblings academically, and failure to achieve will have a more negative impact on firstborns. On the negative side, firstborns have to experience 'dethronement' when their valued position as the only child is taken from them by the birth of a sibling. This is said to account for the fact that firstborns tend to be more anxious and emotionally intense than their other siblings, and are defensive and prone to jealous rages. How this dethronement is accommodated by the parents is crucial for firstborns' future development.

On the birth of a second sibling, they experience what Adler described as 'dethronement': the loss of their unique position. How this dethronement is accommodated by the parents is important for the child's future development. Generally, eldest children are dependable and hard-working, and failure to achieve will have a more negative impact on the firstborn than on those siblings that are born subsequently.

The second child is different in that from the time he or she is born, he or she will have to share the attention of the parents. This generally results in the presence of a highly competitive streak in the second child, as they compete for their parents' attention. They will deliberately seek out and expose the eldest child's vulnerabilities, in order to win praise from the parents. They will seek to achieve in areas where the eldest child has either failed or displays no interest.

The middle child is often the lost child. Faced with the established position of the firstborn, and in some cases the highly competitive nature of the second, they find it difficult to find their place within the family. They often develop the knack of attracting negative attention, setting themselves up with a counter-identity to the other two. They are approval seekers and frequently indulge in people-pleasing behaviours. Within families that are prone to conflict, they are the peacemakers, attempting to negotiate between various siblings, or between siblings and parents. This may be accounted for by the fact that they have a weaker sense of self than eldest or youngest children and are therefore less resilient in the face of anxiety and conflict. In families where there are four children, the third child is generally more easygoing and has a closer affiliation to the eldest sibling.

The youngest child remains the baby, and tends to be pampered by their siblings throughout their life. They tend not to get involved in the competitive environment that the older siblings inhabit, are more independent, and often develop in ways that are more individualistic in nature. They are also more likely to developing their creative capacities than their older siblings.

The only child holds a place of their own in the world. They often share many of the characteristics of the firstborn in that they are high achievers and responsible individuals. However, they do experience drawbacks in their development. They are often pampered by their parents, and are imbued with their own sense of specialness, and therefore have difficulty with sharing centre stage or being upstaged. As only children, they do not experience the need to share, negotiate or compromise, neither are they challenged to assert themselves or fight their corner.

Adler firmly believed that 'discouragement' was the direct result of childhood conditions and experiences. He clearly defined these conditions. Firstly, children born with disabilities or illnesses find it more difficult to develop a healthy, autonomous sense of self. Secondly, a child that is neglected, ridiculed or directly abused perceives himself to be 'bad', or a burden. Such children do not feel worthy of love and affection, and therefore hate themselves. They find it difficult to experience empathy, compassion or love. The third condition that interferes with healthy development is spoiling, which leads the child to expect immediate success with minimum effort. They become overly dependent on others and develop an unhealthy sense of self-importance, which interferes with their social relations. Fourthly, the fact that competition and achievement are openly fostered in modern society means that adolescents are goaded on in the pursuit of self-serving goals, with little thought being given to the effects of this on others. Problematic behaviours such as stealing, cheating, lying, criticising and bragging are stimulated by highly competitive environments.

Adler's theories are, I believe, of most significance when it comes to dealing with adolescents' behaviour, and the conditions they present with are easily identifiable within his theory of the four conditions of misbehaviour. Most professionals now accept his premise, that children need to be encouraged through positive discipline, empathy and a deeper understanding of behaviours, rather than being subjected to traditional punitive discipline, which discourages children and damages their self-esteem and sense of worth. We will see in later chapters how his views are embodied in authoritative-style parenting, which is seen to be the most conducive to good mental health among adolescents.

Part Three

Stressors for Adolescents

While childhood experience for the most part determines the psychological world of the adolescent, and how well they accomplish the individual developmental tasks that they are faced with at this stage of their life, other life stressors may intervene during the teenage period to rupture this development. While the past experience of each adolescent who faces such a stressor will influence how well they cope and adjust to it, the stressor will nevertheless have a significant impact on the emotional world of the young teen, and in some cases may be the trigger for them to indulge in self-destructive behaviours. Although some teeangers will cope with a number of stressors simultaneously and remain stable, others may not. Communication, support and tender loving care will often save them from such a fate. It is therefore necessary for any adult who is in contact with a young adolescent who is experiencing a stressor to be well-equipped with knowledge as to how each particular stressor affects a teenager, and what the teenager needs to help them through the crises. The resilient nature of teenagers is nowhere more evident than in their ability to face and negotiate these stressful times, and to move on with their lives – if they are given adequate support.

Various factors are seen to combine to help adolescents cope with these stressors, and it is believed that the absence of these conditions adversely affects the adolescent's copying skills. Thus, strong parental and peer support, combined with a settled, economically stable environment, will inevitably help a teenager cope more successfully than a contemporary, who is growing up in a disadvantaged area or in a dysfunctional family, or who is experiencing some form of abuse or neglect.

Stressors can be divided into three main categories: normal stressors, individual stressors and daily stressors. Normal stressors are those that are experienced by all individuals during adolescent development, such as puberty, the transition from primary to secondary school, peer pressure, exam stress, and so on. Individual stressors are those that are unique to the particular adolescent, such as parental illness, parental separation, divorce, friendship break-up, bereavement, and so on. Lastly, daily stress may appear to be relatively minor in scale but can have a powerful impact when experienced in combination with other stressors. The number of stressors, the timing of such stressors and the synchronicity of the stressors all determine how well a teenager copes.

Below is an outline of the more significant stressors that they may have to face, how the teenager experiences these stressors, and how they can best be helped through the stressful ones.

7

Bereavement

Adolescents may be more prone to negative consequences of
bereavement because unlike children they are no longer protected psychologically by immature cognitive skills and concrete thinking that could buffer them from the full impact of
bereavement.

HELEN FITZGERALD
IN *THE GRIEVING TEEN*

Of all the stressors that can intervene and disrupt the life and
development of an adolescent, bereavement is the most devastating. Like most things in life, there are degrees of bereavement.
The death of a parent is by far the most extreme form of
bereavement a teenager can experience, especially if that death is
sudden or, worse still, by suicide. The death of a sibling is nearly as devastating, followed by the death of a close friend or
grandparent. However, bereavement has a shocking impact, no
matter what the nature of the relationship of those involved
might be, and is the most powerful stressor an adolescent can
face. At a time when teenagers are already facing the developmental tasks of adolescence, which in themselves can be arduous and create great uncertainty, the death of a parent or sibling
can rob a teenager of the security of a warm and supportive
family environment at a time when it is most needed.

Death of a parent

The death of a parent is the most traumatic event that an adolescent can face. Such a loss is so profound and shocking, and the commensurate pain so deep, that the whole period of adolescence can be tainted by it. For a young teenager who is finding adolescence difficult, the sudden loss of the security of family that the death of a parent brings often seems unbearable. It also comes at a time when conflict with parents is par for the course: in the aftermath of the death, feelings of guilt surrounding this conflict can be overwhelming. The deep emotional pain into which the teenager is thrown as a result of a death calls on all their available coping resources and also brings them face to face with their own mortality, often for the first time.

The teenager suddenly feels that there is no certainty in life and that nothing can be relied on as permanent. They are faced with a shocking and painful loss, and often left feeling confused and overwhelmed by the extent and range of emotions they are experiencing. Often they feel that all their dreams and aspirations have been shattered, and are no longer worth pursuing. Saddest of all, those closest to them, who would normally be available to help them through such difficult times – namely the surviving parent and other siblings – are often so caught up in their own grief process that effective communication and reassurance is impossible. The teenager is left feeling isolated, sometimes bitter and resentful that no one is available to them to listen to and understand their pain. They long for a return to the way things were, while at the same time having to come to terms with the fact that such a return is impossible. In such situations, the importance of having someone outside the family to help them through these times cannot be underestimated. In some cases this does happen: close friends of the parents, aunts or uncles, or teachers and counsellors come forward and provide them with a safe haven to express their pain and fears, and ease the dreadful isolation they are feeling. Friends can, at this time, provide invaluable support just by being there to listen.

Having had no previous experience of death, the young adolescent is often overwhelmed by the extent of their mental and emotional anguish. To be able to speak to someone who understands, and can explain the grief process to them, is vital. While feeling that someone understands the range of emotions they are experiencing cannot prevent them from feeling the pain with which they are gripped, it provides them with security and with the assurance that they will pass through this painful period and return to a different, but normal, life.

Death of a sibling

The death of a sibling presents a young adolescent with a very different set of challenges than that of a parent. While the level of dependence on a sibling is far less defined than in relation to a parent, the impact of the loss of a sibling should not be underestimated, especially if a special bond with the dead sibling existed within the family dynamic. If many activities were shared, the sense of loss will feel excruciatingly painful, especially in cases where bedrooms were shared. The early loss of life also exacerbates the grieving process, and often the teen is left with a sense of survivor's guilt. If sibling rivalry existed, the situation is complicated further. Clear, direct communication, where the expression of guilt and fear is allowed, can be invaluable at such a time. Furthermore, the sense of the teenager's own mortality is more pronounced in this grief, as the sibling would in most cases be close to them in age.

Death of a grandparent

The severity of the grief associated with the death of a grandparent will be directly linked to the quality of the relationship that existed. For some, the grandparent may have been a remote figure with whom the teen had little contact, but for others the bond may have been very strong, especially if circumstances had dictated that the grandparent assumed parental roles. Often the relationship between grandparent and grandchild is a very special one. The lessened responsibility and expectation that a grandparent has towards grandchildren often creates the space for a very loving and warm relationship, and the grandparent has after all gone through the parenting experience themselves. Often teenagers feel that they have lost an important arbiter, to whom they turned when they were experiencing conflict with their parents.

The Grief Process

A clear understanding of the grief process is invaluable to any adult who is in contact with a bereaved teen, as it gives them insight into what stage of grief the teen is experiencing and alerts them to any signs of complicated grief (where an individual has got stuck in a particular stage). The single most important part of the grief process is to be able to identify and express feelings. The adolescent who is not given this opportunity will bottle up their emotions, and these emotions will continue to exist, waiting for relief in the form of emotional flare-ups or physical ailments.

One aspect of grief that often affects young teenagers is the fear that their reaction to the death is not normal. This is especially so in cases where the bereaved feels unable to cry. They look around them and see people weeping their hearts out, and are frightened that they only feel numb and cannot shed a tear. They are left in the frightening position of questioning their connection with, and love for, the deceased. The teenager may not realise that, for many people, this is a common reaction, and part of the shock/denial stage of the grief process.

Grief is unique for each individual and is often dependent on the relationship each member had with the deceased: some might feel angry, others guilty, others sad. This uniqueness is reinforced by the fact that each individual develops different coping skills during life – some positive, some negative. Individual coping skills affect the grief process. However, while grief is unique, there are clusters of feelings that are commonly identifiable in the process. The acknowledgement and negotiation of these feelings, together with the different stages of grief, aids the grieving process and gives the bereaved a structure through which to understand what they are experiencing.

Shock and disbelief

One of the first experiences on hearing about the death of a loved one is a feeling of shock and disbelief, which will last differing lengths of time for different people, and in different circumstances. Shock is the psyche's way of defending the individual from the effects of the reality of the loss, until it is able to fully accept the situation. Little by little, the truth is allowed to sink in. During this stage, the young adolescent oscillates between intellectually knowing that a loved one has died, and emotionally feeling it. The truth feels very unreal, and they find it very difficult to understand what is happening. Only by talking things through are they able to experience the reality, and by so doing initiate the grieving process. Often a need to know the exact circumstances surrounding the death is necessary, even if the family believes that such details would cause additional pain. Revisiting the place of death, such as the hospital room, often provides some opportunity for healing.

Denial

The next stage of the grief process that the adolescent moves into is denial. For many, the pain of the fact of death can be unbearable, and the feelings surrounding this realisation can be too great to bear. The adolescent may feel that they will not be able to survive the pain of the bereavement. Often in such cases the young teenager shuts down from the reality of the situation and refuses to engage with it. They may refuse to talk about the deceased, leaving the room if that person is brought up in conversation. They may also bury themselves in school work to avoid thinking about the reality of their situation, they may use drugs or alcohol to numb themselves, or they may simply avoid coming home. Some initially come to terms with the news of the death by pretending that the deceased has simply gone away for a period of time.

This is all quite normal. However, if an adolescent does not come out of this stage of grief, and continues to live in denial, they will need help, as the necessary grief process is being blocked. Grief cannot be prevented, and a failure to engage with the process will end up affecting the teenager eventually. They may become depressed, develop addiction problems, experience unstable personal relationships and have difficulty at school.

Anger

As the young adult leaves behind the defence of denial, they enter the most painful part of the grieving process. For many, their anger feels overwhelming. They cannot believe that this has happened to them, and feel angry at the world. Why me? they ask. Their anger may be expressed in various ways. At its essence, the anger is directed towards the deceased for abandoning them. They blame the deceased – for not looking after their health properly, for not exercising, for drinking too much alcohol, and so on. Doctors also often become the focus of their anger because, as strangers, they are easy to blame. The teenager may live with the idea that there was something the doctor could have done to save the patient and that they did not, and that therefore the death is their fault. Often the young teen feels angry about the changes in the family that have come about as a result of the death. They often have less freedom, as they are expected to take on more responsibility in the home. Also, in the case of the death of a parent, they may feel angry because the surviving parent is overwhelmed by the death of their loved one and is not as available to them as they used to be. That parent may become the focus for their pent-up rage. In school, they will be angry because they feel that no one understands their pain. Often they feel resentment towards their friends because *their* parents are alive, and this sets feelings of guilt in motion. A teen experiencing this stage of grief needs to be related to and given the space to talk about their anger. Otherwise, in their confusion they will lash out and become destructive, hurting either themselves or others. Feelings of anger keep the bereaved from feeling the sadness of their loss and should therefore be watched out for.

Sadness and depression

The period of sadness and depression can run alongside the previous stages, but when all these defences are fully dropped, the sense of sadness is profound. Feeling the extent of this sadness is a necessary step in coming to terms with the death and accepting it. The bereaved teen should be given the time to talk about, and cry for, the deceased. Reminiscing and telling stories is essential to this process. It keeps the memory of the loved one alive, as the biggest fear of the grieving teen is that their loved one will be forgotten. Looking at old photographs or writing a poem can help. Being able to talk about how special the deceased was, what their quirks were, and so on, can bring relief. The bereaved should never feel that people are tired of listening to them, or that others are getting on with their own lives and want them to move on too. Although it is necessary to move on, this should be done only when the individual is ready. However, it is necessary to look out for the adolescent and ensure that they do not sink into an interminable depression where nothing related to the grief process is being negotiated. This is counterproductive. The young teen may feel that they, too, want to die, but it is not so much that they want to die as that they do not know how to live with their unbearable loss. The future looks too daunting for them without the love and security that the deceased gave them.

Acceptance

This is the last stage of grief and comes with time. It involves the young adolescent getting on their life again, and coming to terms with the change that has occurred. Returning to school may be a daunting prospect, and the teen will probably experience difficulties, but often, despite this, getting back to normal life is viewed with a sense of relief. There is less time to think, and involvement with others is necessary. This allows the adolescent momentary periods of relief from their plight. Also, the immersion in an environment that is not dominated by sadness helps to bring them on. While nothing will ever be the same, the young teen realises that life can, and does, go on, and that they have a place in it.

The single most important way of helping a teenager through the process of grief is to provide them with a space where they can come and talk without being judged or made to feel a burden. In this space, they need to be allowed to express the wide range of feelings they are experiencing, including their fears about the future. Studies have consistently confirmed that the single most important factor cited by bereaved teenagers that helped them in their grieving process was the ability to discuss their plight with people close to them. They may not be able, at times, to discuss the death itself, but they can vent their frustrations about their changed circumstances. Most importantly, they can be given a sense of hope that things will get better for them – that they will adjust to their new reality and be able to engage in day-to-day life without feeling overwhelmed by the emotion associated with their loss. In these circumstances, adolescents need very special care for a prolonged period of time. Having this space and care will ensure that they do not become involved in destructive behaviours as a result of their loss.

Signs of Complicated Grief

While the majority of teenagers will pass through the bereavement process naturally, the presence of certain signs indicate that the adolescent is stuck in a particular stage of grief and may need outside intervention to help them through the difficult time they are experiencing. Signs to look out for are as follows:

1   An extended period of depression where the young person withdraws from society

2   Insomnia, loss of appetite and a prolonged fear of being alone

3   Acting much younger than their actual age

4   Excessively imitating the deceased person

5 Repeated statements that they would like to join the dead person

6 A sharp drop in school performance or a complete refusal to attend school

7 A noticeable lack of concentration

8 Being over-active and consistently busy

9 Over-consumption of alcohol, taking drugs or indulging in other risky behaviourss

10 Becoming increasingly sexually promiscuous

11 Indulging in criminal behaviour

12 Suicidal thoughts

13 Fits of unprovoked rage

If a bereaved teenager is exhibiting a number of these indicators for a prolonged period of time, professional help should be enlisted.

8

Parental Separation and Divorce

> A divorce undertaken thoughtfully and realistically can teach children how to confront serious life problems with compassion, wisdom and appropriate action.
>
> JUDITH WALLERSTEIN
> IN *THE UNEXPECTED LEGACY OF DIVORCE*

As separation and divorce become more commonplace in Ireland, thousands of children and teenagers are left reeling from the impact. While one often hears of the adverse effects that separation and divorce have on younger children, the emotional impact of these things on teenagers – which can be worse than for younger children – is often overlooked. Teens, being older, have developed longer and stronger relationships with both parents in most cases. As a result, they have a stronger investment in the security of the family home. They are often very self-conscious and find the break-up of the family home embarrassing: they may feel a sense of familial failure and try to conceal the break-up from their peers. They have often been living in tense situations for quite some time, hoping that the situation will rectify itself, but fearing the worst. They feel great disappointment and hurt when faced with the reality of the situation. It is important to remember, however, that divorce is a process and that, while initially it may have a severe emotional impact on children, they do adjust, and can move on from the experience to live happy, balanced lives.

In the immediate aftermath of separation, adolescents have to face the day-to-day absence of a parent, and the great feeling of loss and abandonment that this often triggers. They may experience feelings of guilt and sympathy for the parent who may have been forced, through circumstances or the courts, to leave the parental home. On a practical level, at weekends they often have to leave their family home and friends to go and stay with the departed parent. That parent is sometimes living in accommodation that is much smaller than the family home. In some cases, the parent may, at least temporarily, be living in single-room accommodation, and children as a result may only get to spend short periods of time with that parent. Worse still, the legal system in Ireland, in order to avoid the accusation of abandonment, now dictates that neither parent leave the family home until a proper financial settlement has been established. This results in children and teenagers being left to live in highly acrimonious and volatile circumstances that merely prolong the agony for them; they are stuck in the middle of opposing forces, and often come under undue pressure to take sides.

Financial insecurity often dominates the family atmosphere as each parent awaits the settlement agreement. In most cases, after a settlement has been reached, the teens find themselves in far more stringent financial circumstances, with family budgets having to be stretched to cover two households. They are often left feeling deprived of items and outings that they would previously have enjoyed, and which they see their peers enjoying. In some cases, severe financial deprivation may occur following a divorce.

The teenage child then has to adjust to life in a one-parent family. From the outset, teenagers living in these families are faced with the perception that their family is not complete. They live with the sense that they are somehow missing out, even if the home they live in is perceived to be secure. Although separation and divorce is becoming increasingly common, teenagers may feel that they are different when they spend time in friends' houses where both parents are living together happily. Nothing can be done to eliminate these feelings, but being able to talk about them helps.

Sexual development is often affected in a number of ways. Firstly, as young adults, they suffer from the lack of a loving parental relationship as a role model. They are less optimistic about the possibility of finding enduring love, and may in some way hold that relationships are temporary. The flip side of this is that they may become involved in a serious long-term relationship at too young an age. By doing this, they avoid the ups and downs of the teenage love life, where many lessons are learned and emotional maturity and resilience can be built up.

Studies have found that young females who have little or no relationship with their father as a result of divorce or absenteeism tend to become involved in sexual activity earlier than girls who have a father who is present, and available to them. Young female adolescents develop strong feelings of admiration for their fathers from the ages of twelve to sixteen. They tend to view their father as the perfect man, the epitomy of maleness. In cases where a father is mainly absent, those feelings are transferred elsewhere. Their developing sexuality dictates that they seek male connection. They often become sexually promiscuous as they attempt to replace the male love of a father. Often the absent father becomes idealised, with the result that they meet continuous disappointment in their own relationships, as their boyfriends fall short of the ideal and fail to fill the void that has been created.

Evidence tends to support the belief that young boys are more adversely affected developmentally by the absence of a father than girls. Adolescence is a time when young people seek identification with the same-sex parent as part of the process of moving into adult roles. They look to emulate their fathers in adulthood, and need strong role models. The absence of a strong paternal relationship leaves them without a role model. Often this situation is exacerbated when the character of the father is called into question by their mother: not only are they lacking a positive male role model, but they also feel a pressure to disassociate from, or even denounce, their father. This results in the repression of natural feelings of identification that are necessary to their development. Too often – especially in the case of the eldest son – they are wrongly forced to fill the emotional void created for the mother by the absence of a partner. The new role of being the new man of the house is foisted on them. In cases where this occurs, the maternal relationship becomes enmeshed and can feel stifling to them. Furthermore, negative attitudes towards males within the home lead to a sense of inadequacy and defensiveness, and, too often, to an internalised rage. It is imperative that the resident parent takes responsibility for themselves, and their lives, in the wake of separation in order to ensure that their children are not overburdened or given too much power.

Young teens are too often faced with the, at times, overwhelming emotional world of the divided family. Parents abandon the best interests of their children in the eye of the storm. Primarily they become self-obsessed, caught up in their strong feelings of anger and hurt. Their young-adult children are used as allies as they dump their feelings on to them, often trying to arouse feelings of resentment towards the other parent, and disclosing information about that parent which is either distorted or inappropriate. Faced with this situation, the life of the young teen is turned upside down. They are increasingly dragged into a battle of loyalties, hurt and angry about what they are hearing and witnessing, and often feeling unable to express themselves or their views, or afraid to defend a parent. Feelings of trust are annihilated. At a time in their development when emotional cognisance is only in its infancy, they are not only not being given guidance on how to manage their new emotional worlds, but instead are being brought into an intensely emotional experience which appears to lack any security. Their role models too often display how *not* to behave or react in cases of conflict.

In painting this picture, however, I must stress that such outcomes are not predetermined but are rather the worst-case scenarios. Teenagers whose welfare continues to remain the primary concern of their parents do not suffer in such a way. Open, honest and loving communication can assuage their fears, once these fears are properly addressed. A semblance of respect for the other parent, as well as the children involved, can go a long way towards alleviating distress. Ego, and a feeling of victimhood, needs to be left out of the equation. As the negative effects of conflictual divorce continue to be researched and publicised, parents are becoming more aware of the need to temper their feelings and behaviour, and to focus on a just and damage-limiting resolution of their affairs. Family mediation services that include counselling facilities are becoming increasingly popular with divorcing couples, helping them negotiate their separation outside of the legal sphere.

While little can probably be done to stem the tide of divorce, the way in which the situation is handled by the parents is the single most important factor in helping adolescents come to terms with the new situation. Indeed, divorce is viewed by many children as being preferable and less damaging than living in an atmosphere of continuous conflict and estrangement. In such instances, they are never free to get on with their lives and are instead dominated by the emotionally turbulent atmosphere of the home. There is a right way and a wrong way to separate and divorce, however, and this message needs to be brought home to parents. Often it is not the divorce itself that damages the children and adolescents involved, but the level of inter-parental conflict and acrimony that accompanies it. Parents that indulge in such behaviour are being selfish and self-indulgent and are shirking their responsibility to look after the emotional welfare of their children.

While divorce is painful, outright animosity helps nobody. It is of crucial importance that children have access to, and are free to spend time with, both parents. Custody battles and restricted access cause untold damage: children have both the need and the right to see both their parents, no matter what the circumstances. Thankfully, as we grow more accustomed to divorce in Ireland, parents are becoming more aware of the impact of their behaviour on their children.

It would be wrong, though, to suggest that in all cases of divorce parents abandon the interests of their children and seek only to further their own. Many succeed in cushioning their children from the pain and animosity they may feel – difficult as this may be for them. Their courage is admirable. By refusing to allow themselves to become overwhelmed by negative emotions, maintaining a reasonable and just outlook, and keeping the best interests of all involved in mind, they make their children feel secure and provide them with strong role models when it comes to dealing with conflict.

Lastly, it is important to debunk the myth that teenagers of one-parent families are irretrievably damaged and suffer from greater psychological disturbance than the average teenager. While the initial impact of a parental separation may present them with a severe stressor that others do not have to face, most teenagers, particularly if the parents involved behave in a responsible fashion, adjust well to their changed circumstances. In contrast, teenagers who are forced to continue living in environments where inter-parental conflict exists have to deal with tension and insecurity on an ongoing basis. Instead of a short sharp pain, they are left with a continuous ache to deal with. In fact, some professionals believe that young adolescents who go through parental separation benefit, as the experience increases their emotional depth. They learn that loss, though hugely painful, can be managed and processed without resulting in personal annihilation.

Moreover, recent research in the UK suggests that changed circumstances due to divorce provide young adolescents with increased autonomy and responsibility within the family, leading to the development of more mature and developed individuals. Resilience is enhanced. More long-term and thorough research in this area needs to be conducted, as most research results at present focus on the adolescent's wellbeing immediately after divorce, and no account is taken of other stressors, such as alcoholism and depression on the part of one or both of the parents, that may have been the driving force behind the divorce.

9

Parental Illness

Parental illness, either physical or mental, can land like a cruise missile into the life of a teenager, irretrievably changing their world. The sense of loss they feel is often complicated by the fact that the parent is still alive but may appear like a different person and require special care. All of a sudden, the whole family dynamic is disrupted, and the teenager's secure position within that family disappears. In such circumstances, children often have to take on new roles and responsibilities, as the family adjusts to the stressor. Eldest children often find themselves in a position where they have to assume parental responsibilities towards other siblings. Any distress caused by changed circumstances often goes unaired, as the young teenager may feel that they are in some way being selfish by communicating their distress openly. They ruefully wish for a return to life as it was before. When parental illness hits a family, no matter how well that family has been functioning to date, it becomes dysfunctional. How the healthy parent reacts to the new stress is all-important. When it comes to the healthy development of offspring, it is more important that a family is headed by a mature, well-balanced and emotionally stable parent than by two parents who are dysfunctional. To be a good parent, in the face of personal illness, is difficult for the partner who is in full health, but an awareness of how essential it is to the well-being of their offspring that they do not become emotionally overwhelmed by the situation they are facing goes a long way towards minimising the effects of illness.

In cases of physical illness such as cancer, the whole routine of the family is disrupted. Long hospitalisations dictate that both parents are often absent, with parenting being left in the hands of siblings or close relatives. Then, when the ill parent returns to the home, there is a complete change in atmosphere. Full-time care is often needed, and in many cases the house needs to be quiet. As a result, teenage children are no longer free to spend time with friends and engage in normal activities, and friends may not be free to drop in and hang out. When they have to leave the home to go to school or elsewhere, they fear for the welfare of the sick parent.

Such children are caught in a bind: they are burdened by the overwhelming sadness they feel for their parent but also feel guilty about their own feelings of anger. Teenagers in such situations will feel angry and resentful that their world has been turned upside down, and that they can no longer live life as they had done before, or as they see other teenagers doing. They will ask 'Why me?', 'Why us?' Often they will be unable to express this anger, deeming it to be unacceptable, and try to bury it, for the common good, as they see it. Inwardly, they have great difficulty in adjusting to the reality of their new situation. Finding someone with whom they can share their 'poor me's, as well as their anger and fears, is an invaluable experience for them, and goes a long way in helping them adjust. Failing to do so leaves them with ill-defined doubts and fears.

Mental illness in a parent is, in most cases, more devastating for a teenager than physical illness. It is less tangible and less predictable, and thereby creates heightened feelings of fear. While physical illness is visible and measurable, mental illness often seems confusing to teenagers, as a strong sense of self is necessary around mental ill health. One needs to be able to judge what is normal or not, and what is real or not. For teenagers who are only developing a self-identity, this is particularly challenging.

They also have to deal with the stigma that is still associated with mental illness in Irish society. Teenagers often question whether a depressed parent is merely choosing to be down and in a bad mood. In cases of anxiety disorders, the teenager has the feeling transferred on to them that their environment is threatening and ominous, while at the same time doubting that this is the reality. They find the parent's anxiety confusing, as it continuously prompts them to question their own reality.

Case Study: The Alcoholic Parent

> When is a child not a child? When the child lives with alcoholism. . . . You looked like a child, you dressed like a child, but you sure as hell didn't feel like a child.
>
> JANET WOITITZ
> IN *ADULT CHILDREN OF ALCOHOLICS*

One of the most damaging mental illness to strike a home is alcoholism. An examination of the effects of being brought up in such an environment will be presented here, to give a worst-case scenario. All children who experience parental illness will be affected in similar ways as those brought up in alcoholic homes, but the degree to which they are affected will vary according to the type and severity of the illness, as well as the way in which the other parent deals with the illness.

For many teenagers, living in an alcoholic home is a psychologically and emotionally abusive experience. In some cases, it is also physically and sexually abusive. It is also the one clear case of mental illness where the question of choice and responsibility can be stringently challenged. The untold damage created by an alcoholic parent is well documented and, I believe, deserves special attention, as countless thousands of children in this country grow up in such homes.

In the home of an alcoholic, nothing is predictable. The uncertainty created by this leads to children being consumed by fear about what will happen next. They fear leaving the home in case something happens that they could have prevented, and dread returning for fear of what they might be met with. Will it be Jekyll or Hyde? Their loving, conciliatory parent, or that other one, to whom it is impossible to relate? How will their other parent be? Angry, irritable, depressed, morose, anxious, blaming, cut off? Worst of all, children living in these environments find it very difficult to confide in anyone about what is going on, and how they feel about the situation. To do so feels disloyal, and involves admitting a reality that they do not want to face. Instead, they live in hope that the problem will simply go away and things will return to normal. This is the unrealisable fantasy of anyone who lives with an alcoholic.

Teenagers from alcoholic homes display common traits in school. They either super-achieve or underachieve. The super-achiever is driven by a desperate need to prove their worth, and to be acceptable and admired. While they may be unable to control their life in the home, at least in school they can do so, by performing and achieving. This achievement masks the reality of their life, however. The underachiever acts out the problems they are experiencing at home in a different way. The overriding behaviour they learn and adopt from their alcoholic parent is not to take responsibility for themselves or their lives. Avoiding responsibility, and rebelling, allows them to get away from their feelings and provides them with some type of identity. While that identity might be frowned upon by the adults that surround them, it often gives them a feeling of kudos amongst their peers, and in some way gains them affirmation. However, this behaviour has a propensity to become more and more delinquent, and often such children will end up finding themselves in difficulty with authority, or even the law. One must realise that these behaviours are a defence, and in many cases serve their purpose well, as they save the teenager from becoming submerged in their emotional world. Only in the case of juvenile crime can such behaviours be dismissed completely as inappropriate.

Teenagers from alcoholic homes have trouble concentrating in school and can be prone to daydreaming. They often live a fantasy life in their heads, where everyone, including themselves, is happy. In these fantasy lifes, they are in control of their situation and are not faced with negative experiences. These lives are far removed from the reality they live in but perform the function of allowing them to escape that reality, albeit briefly.

The most damning effect of growing up in an alcoholic home is that the adolescent inherits and develops a distorted sense of self. A child or adolescent develops a sense of worth from the messages he or she receives about himself or herself from his parents, and internalises these messages. But in an 'alcoholic home', two very different realities are running parallel to each other, and double messages and double standards are the norm. This creates the distortion. The youngster is told that they are loved, but generally the reality is that their absence would be preferred. The pressure on them to be perfect ensures that they are constantly criticised and berated for not being good enough, even if their performance is admired outside the family. While at times they are berated, at other times they are told that they are wonderful and indispensable. This creates great confusion. They are also exhorted, like all children, to tell the truth, even though they see their parents being dishonest frequently. Promises are rarely kept. They are to tell the truth – but not about what is going on in the family home. Loyalty is the single most important prerequisite for membership of and acceptance within the family. Lastly, adolescents in these homes witness bad behaviour being accounted for by alcoholism: bad behaviour is justified on the grounds that the parent was drunk at the time, and therefore not accountable for their actions. This get-out clause creates a deep malaise because it teaches the children involved that they too do not have to be accountable for their behaviour.

Two support groups that run twelve-step programs exist to help the children of alcoholics recover from the effects of living with an alcoholic parent. They are Alateen and ACOA (Adult Children of Alcoholics). There are thirteen main traits and issues that these groups deal with, which would be helpful to outline here:

1   Children of alcoholics guess at what 'normal' is

This is an overriding characteristic of teenagers from alcoholic homes. Because they have grown up in a home that is not normal, and at times bizarre, they view this as normal. Behaviours that are demonstrated every day by both parents are seen as normal. The teenage children lack any frame of reference. When faced with situations where their view of normality is challenged, they have to guess at what would be considered normal. This confuses them. They do not know what is OK to say or not, or what is OK to express or not. They fear conflict but at times fly into rages. They engage in people-pleasing behaviours, or withdraw, in order to avoid being exposed. They are in general highly 'defended'. That is, they hide their true thoughts and feelings and are hyper-sensitive when their perception of reality is challenged, often seeing that challenge as an attack. In such situations, they will react strongly, as the reality of their situation and their home life is too much for them to bear psychologically. In most situations where the acknowledgement of reality will be overwhelming, the psyche defends itself by removing the individual from the facts of the true situation and will defend itself strongly against any attempt to force these facts onto the individual.

2   Children of alcoholics have difficulty seeing projects through to the end

Children and teenagers learn from their role models, generally their parents. In functional families, they see a project developing from beginning to end, from the idea to the actuality. In developing their own projects, they are given support and guidance from beginning to end. This is rarely the case in alcoholic homes. Projects may be initiated but never completed; they may indeed never get past the idea stage. Therefore, these children have no one to model how things are done. Often when they initiate projects themselves, they are either belittled for it and told that they will fail, or they are greeted initially with enthusiasm, which peters out, leaving them with no support or guidance.

3 Children of alcoholics lie when it would be easier to tell the truth

More often than not, the children of alcoholics are living a lie. The gap between what the family projects itself as being, and what it actually is, is generally huge. Denial means that the family is permeated with a basic dishonesty. Furthermore, lie after lie is told to cover up the reality. It becomes the natural impulse to lie and not to admit to anything, because to be honest may result in dreadful consequences. Lying is therefore seen as normal within the household and becomes habitual.

4 Children of alcoholics judge themselves mercilessly

As constant criticism and blame is the norm in 'alcoholic' households, negative self-feelings are internalised by children. Perfection is the only standard that is acceptable, and by its very nature this is unrealisable. It is difficult for such children to accept praise and acknowledge their successes. To do so would involve changing their image of themselves. To see themselves in any way differently requires huge change and blind trust, the resources for which they often cannot muster. Instead, their successes are put down to luck or coincidence, or the child says that the success was bound to happen, whether they were involved or not.

5 Children of alcoholics have difficulty having fun

6 Children of alcoholics take themselves very seriously

These two traits are interrelated and can be treated together. Growing up in a house that is shot through with an undercurrent of tension and anxiety inhibits spontaneity. While there may be periods of time when the atmosphere lightens, these periods cannot be trusted as they will inevitably end in hurt and disappointment. As a result, children from these homes are reluctant to have fun. They do not trust it: what may be considered amusing one day may induce rage the next. Therefore, these children tend to keep things serious, for safety's sake. Because they live in serious circumstances, they grow up serious. They have never learned how to have fun and, because they feel threatened by it, often dismiss it as silly. Ironically, often the only times they feel free to have fun is when they consume or take drugs themselves. Their defences drop and they become less inhibited. However, the following day they have to face themselves, and with great seriousness they castigate and criticise themselves for their behaviour the night before.

7　Children of alcoholics have difficulty forming intimate relationships

This characteristic is prevalent amongst children of alcoholics for a number of reasons. Firstly, they have not had an intimate relationship role modelled to them, so they lack a frame of reference. Due to the inconsistency of the love that was made available to them as children, they suffer from dreadful fears of abandonment. They feel loved one day and rejected the next. They exaggerate the importance of their parents' feelings for them, and they transfer this importance into adult relationships. They believe that eventual abandonment is inevitable and are primed and ready for the first hint of rejection. Minor disagreements therefore get blown out of all proportion. Their experience of mature conflict resolution is minimal; instead, they witnessed huge blow-outs, which were subsequently completely ignored, with no negotiation. Furthermore, a basic feeling of worthlessness and unlovability permeates their being. This dictates that they gain their sense of worth not from their own self-belief but from what other people believe about them. The end result is that they do not feel free to express themselves – a necessary ingredient of a healthy relationship. To do so means to risk abandonment, as they see it. Lastly, such children, knowing that they do not have the internal resources required to form intimate relationships, are generally attracted to partners who suffer from the same problem. In this way, they remain unchallenged in their behaviours and thought processes. Furthermore, they view dysfunctional behaviours in their partners as normal, and display a higher tolerance of them.

8   Children of alcoholics overreact to situations over which they have no control

Adolescents from such homes often try very hard to control their environment outside of the home. This is natural, as they had no control when they were in the home. The alcohol consumption of the alcoholic parent is the real controller, even though it leads to many situations that are clearly out of control. Such adolescents feel secure when they are in control but, if any change is made in which they have no say, or are not part of, they react with fear. This reaction often confuses others and is misunderstood. Change, no matter how small, brings them back to the insecurity and powerlessness they felt around their alcoholic parent. The fear of abandonment again lurks for them.

9   Children of alcoholics constantly seek approval and affirmation

Because love is conditional in the homes of these teens, they constantly need to see that they are loved and approved of. The volatile nature of this love, being given and withdrawn for no reason, means that these children need constant attention and approval in order to feel secure. However, because of their own lack of self-worth, they can never take on for any length of time the affirmations they are given. Their insecurity leads them to believe that love will be withdrawn at any stage without warning and that they must therefore constantly work at being loved and must feel that they are the centre of attention.

10   Children of alcoholics feel they are different from others

Because they are raised in homes that they view as different from 'non-alcoholic' homes, these teenagers feel different – marginalised in some way. Because they do not feel free to say what is going on in their home, or to divulge the extent of the troubles therein, they are left feeling isolated and not part of normal day-to-day life. Moreover, they have not had the experience of feeling comfortable and at ease in a group, and therefore find socialising on a genuine level difficult. The image they project to others is more important than exposing who they really are, and this leads to a sense of being removed from others. As in relationships, these teenagers tend to identify with other teenagers who feel marginalised, as they feel more secure and less threatened in their company. Unfortunately, they also remain unchallenged.

11 Children of alcoholics are either super-responsible or super-irresponsible

Teenagers living in alcoholic homes generally do either too much or too little. Those who do too much are driven by a need to be noticed and approved of. They do not know their limitations and have a fear of saying no, in case this is taken as an indication that they are incompetent. They drive themselves on in the hope that, by proving they are perfect, they will gain approval. The flip side is the teenager who refuses to engage in this dynamic and simply gives up. They believe that they will never succeed in winning this approval and therefore do not even seek it. They tend to cease trying and rebel. Believing that they are no good, they seek to prove that this is the case. Many of the teens who display this behaviour pattern end up becoming addicts of one kind or another themselves. While others try to prove their worth, they attempt to prove their lack of worth.

12 Children of alcoholics are extremely loyal, even when that loyalty appears to be undeserved

Teenagers from such homes demonstrate huge loyalty – out of fear and insecurity rather than choice. They witness one parent standing by another long after they should do, and model this. They learn that you should never walk away from a situation, no matter how bad it may appear. Because they find the establishment of friendships and relationships difficult, they hang on to them. They believe that, if someone demonstrates that they are their friend and does not abandon and reject them, they have an obligation to stay in that friendship no matter how the other person behaves. Moreover, they prefer what is known to what is unknown, even if it is destructive, and the thought of change, or their fear of what life would be like without that person, holds them paralysed. Their own negative self-image allows them to hold themselves to blame, in some way, for the bad behaviour, and thereby enables them to stay within the dynamic of a bad relationship long after they should.

13   Children of alcoholics are very impulsive

This is very much modelled or learned behaviour. Adolescent children of alcoholics witness their alcoholic parent continuously acting on impulse, without seriously considering alternatives or other prior responsibilities. When they see their parent doing what they want, when they want, they believe that they can behave in the same way. The teenager does not reflect on the consequences of their actions. Even if their parents do try to relate to the way in which they are behaving, their credibility is tainted by hypocrisy. These children are also used to functioning in crises; they often feel uncomfortable when there is not a crises, and so they create one for themselves by behaving impulsively. They lack patience and seek immediate gratification. This is directly linked to the fact that, more often than not as children, whenever they asked for something from their parents, it was promised at some time in the future but never subsequently materialised. They therefore learnt that, unless they nailed something down in the present, it would never happen.

*

From the above list of traits, it is easier to understand the profound effect that parental illness may have on a family. Adolescents who live under such a stressor are at higher risk than most teenagers, as they are under constant and ongoing pressure. Their coping skills are severely tested when faced with additional stressors. They need special attention and their well-being at times of extra stress, such as exams, shoud be monitored. Counselling benefits such teenagers as it provides them with a neutral space where they are allowed to be completely honest, without guilt or fear of reproach.

10

Social Deprivation

There is no doubt that social deprivation has an adverse effect on the development of adolescents. If a strong sense of self-worth, in both parents and children, is a necessary prerequisite for healthy development, and social deprivation annihilates feelings of self-worth, it is no surprise that many adolescents who live in deprived areas in this country experience difficulties. While it is true to say – and it has been my experience working with adolescents from such areas – that there are some families from socially deprived areas that value themselves strongly and produce mentally healthy offspring, this is not always the case. So what is the relationship between deprivation and psychological distress?

One of the main contributing factors to a lack of self-worth is unemployment. Employment gives an individual a sense of worth and purpose. It makes them feel that they are contributing to society and providing for either themselves or their loved ones. It gives them a function in life and the opportunity to be able to enjoy their leisure time. This is possibly especially true for men, whose traditional role has been that of the hunter-gatherer. In areas of social deprivation, unemployment is high. Men who are unable to secure employment begin to feel useless. They find it difficult to sit at home and do nothing and may either get depressed, turn to alcohol or become involved in crime. Their young teenage children are therefore provided with poor role models, and the parent's lack of self-worth pervades the family atmosphere. Teenagers who grow up in such an environment take on the parent's hopelessness and lack of self-worth. Their lack of confidence in themselves and their prospects inhibits them from going out and securing employment – if suitable employment is available. They become trapped into the same mental ill health as their parents.

Many of the children of those who experienced unemployment in the 1960s and 1970s are now in their teenage years. They would have been brought up in the insidious atmosphere of unemployment, and their mental health been affected by it. It is therefore no surprise that so many of these children are experiencing serious difficulties. While the opportunity for employment is available to them, as is a better standard of education and government-sponsored training programmes, their psychological make-up is such that they sometimes cannot avail of these opportunities. Addiction and alcoholism is rife in their homes. Many are depressed without even realising it. For others, the anger that they and their parents feel is acted out in violence. For many males, living in these circumstances, criminal activity is a viable option to ensure that they get their piece of the Celtic Tiger.

Successive governments have abjectly failed to deal with the issue of mental health in these areas. No amount of new training programs, increased Garda funding to deal with crime, or cash handouts will serve any purpose until this issue is addressed. While working as a volunteer school counsellor in the disadvantaged area of Clondalkin in west Dublin, I at times felt overwhelmed by the extent of the problem. Teenager after teenager spoke to me of the difficulties they were experiencing at home, and in life in general, and few held out any prospects for their future. Depression, eating disorders, anti-social behaviour and other problems were the norm. Racial tension and abuse were raising their ugly heads, as the number of immigrant students within the school swelled. However, not one government-salaried counsellor was on the school's payroll, when in fact a team was needed. Within the wider community, government-sponsored help and initiatives were practically non-existent. For a community that lacked a feeling of self-worth, that feeling was being validated by the government: they appeared to be deemed unworthy of help.

While certain initiatives undertaken by the government, such as the Drugs Task Forces and inner-city rejuvenation schemes, are alleviating the disadvantage felt in these areas, more needs to be done. It is in these areas that the government needs to address the issue of mental health, providing help where it is needed, in the form of government-salaried counsellors, and helping local community initiatives to tackle these issues. A comprehensive policy needs to be drawn up by professionals in the field, if the government wants seriously to tackle the issues of drugs, crime and so on in these areas and beyond. Young disadvantaged adolescents are facing too many stressors simultaneously to be able to cope using only their own resources. Relevant help provided at a young enough age would alter these teenagers' future and would have a huge impact on levels of dysfunction, both social and individual, in this country. Unfortunately, government policy to date has focused on trying to mend problems after they have come into existence rather than taking preemptive measures to prevent them from happening. If young adults were helped to cope with dysfunctional families and communities, the likelihood of them falling victim to the same destructive behaviours would be strongly challenged.

11

Bullying

Bullying is a conscious, wilful and deliberate hostile activity, intended to harm, induce fear through the threat of further aggression, and create fear.

BARBARA COLOROSO
IN *THE BULLY, THE BULLIED AND THE BYSTANDER*

Of all the stressors that may intervene to disrupt the healthy development of a teenager, bullying is the most pernicious. Unfortunately, bullying is becoming an increasingly prevalent feature of modern societies, with competition going beyond the individual self and involving the devaluation of others in the pursuit of achievement, or a feeling of self-worth. Bullying is the natural by-product of the 'loser' mentality that is becoming more pervasive within our society.

But children and teenagers are not born bullies. Bullying is a learned behaviour: children learn how to behave and think by absorbing the attitudes and values of the environment around them, particularly their immediate environment. In particular, they mimic the adults around them. If stereotyping and prejudice exists within the home, the school, the community and the society, then it is fostered within our children. As Irish society becomes more affluent and heterogeneous, these features are creeping into our psyches and becoming more evident in everyday life.

It is not that prejudice never existed in Ireland: in fact, it has always been a strong element in our cultural make-up. Traditionally, we looked down on Travellers and those 'without land' and demonised those who did not share our religious affiliation. The regulations put on our behaviours by the Catholic Church called for the ostracisation of those who did not conform. Individuality and difference were viewed with scepticism and perceived as threatening. Now, however, we are faced with bigger challenges as a society. Our economic success has dictated that, with the lack of available labour resources, we open up our borders and our society to 'foreign nationals'. The attitudes we adopt, and the tolerance we demonstrate with regard to difference, will dictate our future harmony as a society, if we are to avoid the kind of scenes and politics that we are now witnessing in France and other European countries. If racism is not to take root, it is now up to us to model these values to our young teenagers and children.

My son Carl recently engaged two African ladies in conversation at a bus stop in Rathmines, asking them about the countries they came from, and telling them about how his grandfather had worked in Africa. A bus pulled in and everyone piled on. The African ladies were the last to embark. They were immediately told by the bus driver that there was no more room left on the bus, even though a number of seats were unoccupied. Carl, deciding to confirm his suspicions, went to board the bus. His fare was about to be accepted when he turned around and said 'Ladies first', beckoning the two African ladies to re-board the bus. Immediately, the driver retorted that the bus was full. Carl challenged the driver, saying that the reason the ladies were not being allowed on to the bus was due to their racial origin. Again the driver objected, but fearing an even bigger scene, he eventually acquiesced. He did not do so graciously, however, but proceeded to blurt out a spate of racial slurs. I was left asking myself where were the voices of all the other adults present, who witnessed this scene, and why it was left to a fifteen-year-old boy to challenge such a blatant piece of racism.

It is therefore the responsibility of us as adults to examine our thoughts, words and actions in order to identify if and where our prejudices exist, and to root them out. In any situation where demeaning the value and worth of another individual or group is necessary in order for a person to boost their feeling of self-worth, prejudice exists. Racial prejudice, bigotry, snobbery, scapegoating, demeaning of a partner, and child neglect or abuse all play a part in the psychological development of a bully. In most cases, the bully was himself bullied.

But what exactly is bullying and what is its effect? Three distinct types of bullying have been identified, which sometimes exist independently or, in more extreme cases, in combination. These are verbal, relational and physical bullying.

Verbal bullying

Verbal abuse, which constitutes bullying, accounts for 70 percent of reported incidents of bullying, and is used equally by boys and girls. It is the least detectable and most easily deflected or denied form of bullying and is often the precursor to the other two forms. It takes the form of taunting, belittling, name-calling, slander, gossip, threats, abusive phone calls, voice mails and texts, and so on. It leads to rapid marginalisation for the target, as others are often quick to join in. For any child who does not have a strong sense of self, it can be debilitating, and prolonged exposure to verbal abuse can greatly reduce any teenager's sense of self-worth and self-identity.

Relational bullying

This form of bullying is the hardest to detect and is used to alienate and reject an individual and ruin a friendship. Due to the nature of female friendships, it is most commonly used by girls. Its primary aim is to ostracise and reject the target, and it has the maximum impact at the onset of adolescence, when strong peer relationships and a feeling of belonging are necessary to bolster a young teenager's burgeoning identity. Any action that seeks to exclude an individual from a group, community or society constitutes relational bullying. It is generally reinforced by the persistent use of intimidating body language, such as sneers, aggressive stares, sniggers and so on. It is subtle and innocuous, with the target sometimes being unaware that it is even going on, but feeling the impact of it nonetheless.

Physical bullying

This type of bullying accounts for less than 33 percent of reported incidents of bullying. It is the most evident form of bullying as it is very difficult to deny. If a young boy is wandering around with a black eye, the chances are he did not do it to himself. It is most commonly used by boys, but is increasingly being used by girls as well.

*

Most bullies have certain characteristics in common. Bullying is driven by contempt – a deep-seated dislike for a person who is viewed as being inferior and unworthy of respect. The bully maintains a position of superiority in order to mask their own lack of self-worth and their feelings of inadequacy, and has often been bullied themselves. Bullies like to dominate other people, and use them to get what they want. They are self-centred and unable to view situations from other people's perspective. In the absence of any figure that would challenge their actions, they prey on the vulnerable. They use blame, criticism and false allegations to project their own inadequacies onto others, and refuse to accept responsibility for their actions. Above all, they are attention-seekers.

In any given bullying situation, there is an imbalance of power, an intent to inflict pain on another person, a threat of aggression and, in the final stages, an intention to strike terror into the heart of the bullied. When this sense of terror has been established, the victim has been rendered sufficiently powerless to ensure that the bully can act without fear of recrimination or retaliation. Witnesses are intimidated into being drawn into the situation through fear of the bully, and either participate themselves or fail to intervene on the victim's behalf.

When a bully is challenged for his (or her) bullying behaviours, he tends immediately to deny any wrongdoing, trivialises the event, adopts the role of victim – claiming that he was simply acting in defence – and relies on bystanders to collude with him. Bullies do not act in isolation. One must remember that, deep down, they are insecure, and are therefore seeking attention and recognition from others. They seek out allies, and intimidate others enough to ensure that they are at least colluded with, through silence. In this way, they contribute to desensitising witnesses and often gain support for their activities.

These 'bystanders' hold the key to breaking the cycle of bullying. They are immediately drawn into the bully's toxic world. Their self-confidence and sense of self-respect plummet, as they too are gripped with a fear of the bully, and react by either getting involved themselves, or turning a blind eye to what is going on. Guilt assails them as they increasingly realise that they are morally blighted by not defending the bullied and are no longer innocent of wrongdoing. Often they become increasingly involved, in order to blot out the feeling of wrongdoing, and seek to rationalise the situation. But thankfully, some do muster up the moral courage to intervene, and bring the situation out into the open. If bullying is to be adequately dealt with, an environment that makes it safer for witnesses to intervene is vital.

The one factor that children who are bullied have in common is that they are targeted by a bully; in all other aspects they may differ, and the reasons why they were bullied vary greatly. They may be targeted for being beautiful, for being intelligent, or for being new to the class; they may have a submissive demeanour, be shy, be poor – or rich – and so on. Once a child has been targeted, how they respond to the first slight determines whether they will be left alone or will become a victim of bullying. Any show of fear or intimidation, or a failure to assert themselves, encourages the protagonist. The victim is immediately affected, and embarks on a downward cycle of emotional change. Their failure to stand up for themselves, and the sense of shame, unworthiness and powerlessness they feel, escalates with each incident, making them increasingly easy pickings for the bully. Their growing fear of the bully, along with their diminishing sense of self, ensures that they do not alert their parents to the problem. They feel that no one can or will help them, and that the adult world is colluding with the bully: they may be told to 'ignore' him, to stand up for themselves, that it is 'all part of growing up' and that things are not that bad. Sometimes the victim of bullying is simply not believed.

Warning signs begin to surface but often go unnoticed, or unexplained. The teenager may lose interest in going to school or flatly refuse to go, their grades plummet, and they withdraw from family life. They may bad-mouth their peers at home, or stop talking about them completely; adopt avoidant behaviours, such as taking different routes to school or deferring using the bathroom at school; and look and behave put out after receiving phone calls or text messages. They may come home from school hungry, claiming to have lost their lunch money, or steal money, look dishevelled or lose expensive clothes. They do things that are out of character for them. Eventually, the trauma they are suffering begins to manifest itself physically: they get headaches and stomach aches, suffer from panic attacks, are restless and cannot sleep – despite spending hours in bed – and may experience kidney problems. Their life is not their own, and is out of control. Eventually, they will either 'implode' or 'explode'. This usually involves an act against the self, which at its extreme is 'bullycide' (suicide as a result of the pain experienced by bullying), or they will lash out violently, and commit a crime or, worse still, an atrocity. A study conducted by the US Secret Service found that, in more than two-thirds of the school shootings that had occurred in the US, the perpetrators of the violence had been bullied.

Though bullying has always existed within our schools to a

certain extent, it now seems to be taking a new and more sinister turn. The increasing value that is placed on wealth in our society is making social bullying more pervasive within our schools. As we adults place more and more worth on our external image, our young teens are picking up on our cues. How wealthy their parents are, how much their houses are worth, what car their parents own, and whether it is the latest model are all used to compete with others and establish a position of superiority. In 2005, an incident was comically reported in the press, where a young boy was removed from school in an ambulance after a violent altercation with another student: at issue was whose father had the capacity to 'buy' the other's father out. We are to some extent teaching our children that a person's worth is dictated by his financial capacity. Although we have not yet reached the extremes that are evident in the US and England, we should be taking note what is happening there, and put in place counter-measures, if we are to avoid problems similar to the ones experienced there. The place to start is in the home.

Part Four

Manifestations of Distress Among Adolescents

Adolescence is a time when it is natural for a young person to flirt with danger, to push the boundaries out, and to experience new and powerful emotions, and by so doing learning to master them. It would appear by and large to be the case that young adolescents who have a stable and supportive home life, with adequate parental communication and a healthy peer group, are managing to emerge into adulthood well-balanced, and with a sufficiently strong sense of self to take on the responsibilities with which life presents. However, the evidence indicates that an increasing number of young teens are losing themselves in the process, resorting to aberrant behaviours to communicate this loss. The World Health Organisation estimates that up to 20 percent of teenagers in Western developed countries are failing adequately to pass through this period of development. In other words, they are experiencing developmental, emotional or behavioural problems and are turning to self-destructive behaviours to relieve and bring attention to their distress. Eight percent of these people are said to meet the criteria for a mental disorder.

One of the largest studies to date on adolescence mental health carried out in Ireland, by the National Suicide Research Foundation, confirmed this. It concluded that 80 percent of Irish adolescents appeared to have positive emotional health and well-being but that 20 percent showed signs of depression and were at risk of experiencing mental-health problems. These young adults have either entered adolescence without a sufficiently strong sense of self to negotiate adequately the developmental tasks they face, or experience a stressor, such as parental separation or bereavement, with which they are unable to cope. Adolescence, with its underlying susceptibility to depression, has now overtaken infancy as the most dangerous stage of life. While there are no hard-and-fast rules, it is possible to notice a pattern whereby girls turn this distress in on themselves, developing food disorders, depression and self-harming, whereas boys are more likely to act out, indulging in aggressive behaviour and crime, joyriding and, most alarmingly, attempting suicide. Both sexes are increasingly using alcohol and drugs to help them cope with the difficulties they face and to dull the pain they are experiencing.

When looking at the various ways in which teenagers are communicating their distress, we must take into account recent neurological research which indicates that the facilities people need to assess the consequences of their actions properly are not adequately developed until the age of twenty-five. Adolescents are therefore often unable to recognise the implications of their self-destructive behaviours and actions. I will next examine the various ways in which teenagers are manifesting their distress in today's Ireland.

12

Eating Disorders

Anorexia nervosa and bulimia are the two most common – and most destructive – eating disorders, and are considered to be an extreme cry for attention and help. It is believed that one in five women in Ireland will develop an eating disorder of some kind between the ages of fifteen and thirty. Bodywhys, the voluntary agency that supports those affected by eating disorders, estimates that ten thousand people aged between fourteen and twenty are thought to suffer from eating disorders in Ireland, with females accounting for nine out of ten of these cases. Recent figures show that young males are increasingly turning to anorexia.

Anorexia

Anorexia is most common among women aged twelve to twenty-five years, and is clearly associated with the preoccupation with body image that accompanies puberty. Anorexics experience difficulties coping with the physical changes that occur at this time, and lack the emotional capabilities that would allow them to accept these changes. They look on with alarm, and sometimes horror, as their bodies take on their new form, and become obsessed with body weight, stringently monitoring food intake and exercise. This is coupled with an inability to gauge normal body weight: the anorexic has a highly distorted view of thinness. Extreme weight loss is achieved through excessive dieting, avoiding fatty foods, use of laxatives and diuretics, self-induced vomiting, and exercise. Body weight is maintained at least 15 percent below that expected for the person's height. Controlling food intake gives the anorexic a sense of power, while feelings of self-hatred and guilt are aroused by eating. However, food itself is rarely the problem but is rather a means of avoiding other problems. The growing reality of the experience of childhood neglect or trauma becomes more accentuated during the process of individuation that takes place during adolescence. Food may become a way of diverting attention away from that reality, and a feeling of lack of self-worth is often overwhelming. Feeling ill-equipped to 'grow towards' adulthood, teenage girls sometimes resort to anorexia in an attempt to maintain their childish physique and forestall menstruation. By becoming ill, they perpetuate their dependency on parents, and thus avoid individuating. Other teens may use food as a way of expressing their individuality and their need to make choices for themselves; this is particularly the case in families where heavy emphasis is placed on eating. It is seen as a means of rebelling against parental control.

Still others may use anorexia in a more calculatedly manipulative way. This is the case in situations where the condition is used to divert attention away from a more threatening problem, such as parental conflict, alcoholism in the home or another form of dysfunction. Sensing impending parental separation, a young teen may resort to anorexia, making the fear of divorce the central motivating factor. In such cases, it is extremely difficult for parents to choose separation over the health of their child. The teenager is thus using anorexia as a way of demanding attention and controlling outcomes. Lastly, adolescents who come from success-driven and focused homes are susceptible to anorexia. They wish to be viewed as successful by their parents, and to many teenage girls success is judged by maximal good looks, minimal weight and high academic achievement. It is therefore common to find that those who are suffering from examination stress have a food disorder as well. Anorexics are loath to have their condition exposed and go to great lengths to hide their weight loss. Like many addictions, any form of confrontation is met with vociferous denial, as the victim battles to defend his or her delusion and feeling of power.

It is often argued that media images of thinness, and the deliberate use of apparently anorexic models by the fashion industry, are to blame for the prevalence of anorexia. However, while such images without doubt influence anorexics, they do not account for the condition. Teenagers with a strong sense of self-worth have no need to imitate the thinness of models, and while they may wish that their figure more closely resembled that of Naomi Campbell, they are not driven into the arms of a food disorder with the aim of achieving this.

Serious long-term risks associated with anorexia include osteoporosis, and heart, liver, kidney and brain damage. It can also impede growth in the young and cause difficulties with concentration. Tooth decay and damage, due to prolonged self-induced vomiting, is also common. People who do not receive psychological treatment for this disorder may become chronically ill or even die. The earlier a food disorder is detected and confronted, the less severe the overall damage, both physically and psychologically.

Warning signs

Like most conditions, there are specific warning signs that a teenager has developed an eating disorder, as well as more broad-based indications.

1   As anorexics do not like exposure of their condition, they engage in specific behaviours to hide their weight loss. These include wearing baggy clothes that conceal their figures, pretending to eat by putting tiny morsels of food into their mouths, and giving the appearance that they are eating. They may play with their food and

eat very slowly, chewing everything carefully, or compress the remaining food on their plates to make it seem like more has been eaten. They blatantly lie about when and where they have eaten. Packed lunches are thrown away en route to school and family pets are fed under the table. In all situations, they endeavour to consume as little food as possible.

2   Anorexics try to reduce the impact that ingested food has on their weight. They exercise with the sole intention of losing weight, often becoming obsessed with exercising. Laxatives and enemas are taken to remove food from their systems.

3   They become increasingly obsessed with their weight, and have an exaggerated and distorted view of their weight and size. They refuse to accept assurances from others that they are not fat. They become preoccupied with the perfect body, and increasingly strive for perfection in general. They equate slimness with success, and fatness with failure.

4   Psychologically, their thinking around food becomes increasingly obsessive and self-punitive. They experience poor self-esteem, and feel as though they are no longer in control. They experience intense shame and guilt when eating, or after having eaten. They experience excessive mood swings and are afraid to express their emotions, and they withdraw from others, becoming anxious, lonely and uncertain. They often experience their bodies as being separate from themselves.

5   In girls, weight loss often leads to the cessation of menstruation, as the fats that are necessary for the process are simply not present.

Bulimia

Bulimia, which literally means 'ox hunger', is far more widespread – and far more insidious – than anorexia. Bulimia is defined as the ingestion of a huge amount of food – up to eight thousand calories – followed by self-induced vomiting or diarrhoea. The bulimic will often use drugs that induce vomiting, or abuse over-the-counter laxatives or diuretics.

For centuries, it was believed that bulimia was caused by a stomach malfunction in which food that had been consumed was indigestible and therefore had to be vomited up out of the system. Only in recent times has it emerged that bulimia is driven by emotional distress. Bulimia is not as common in the early teenage years as anorexia is, but it is more prevalent in older adolescents and young females. Only those who binge and purge twice a week are considered to be bulimic. Each binge is usually triggered by some form of stress or anxiety, and generally involves the consumption of high-calorie foods. A feeling of calm immediately descends on the bulimic, but this is generally short-lived, as feelings of guilt and shame, accompanied by physical discomfort, quickly arise.

Bulimia has a propensity to cause huge physical damage to the sufferer. Drugs used to enhance the process of purging dehydrate the body and deplete it of important minerals such as potassium, which is essential for normal heart and kidney function. The body's potassium balance may become sufficiently disrupted that a heart attack ensues, or the kidneys may fail. The excessive vomiting can cause the stomach to rupture, and hydrochloric acid from the stomach is pushed into the mouth, which can destroy tooth enamel and cause severe dental and gum problems. Vomiting also causes a rise in blood pressure in the head, leading to broken blood vessels in the eyes, which impairs vision. Bowel damage can also occur from the overuse of laxatives.

Warning signs

Bulimia is far more difficult to detect than anorexia because the bulimic typically remains within ten pounds of his or her normal weight. However, there are a number of tell-tale signs that should be watched for:

1 Bulimics become increasingly anxious to get to the bathroom immediately after a meal is consumed, as they fear that the food will be absorbed by the system before they get the chance to vomit it up.

2 Forbidden foods are often hidden in their bedrooms.

3 The habit of overeating can be very expensive due to the large quantity of food being consumed, and the young teen may therefore resort to stealing.

4 Other compulsive behaviours often go hand in hand with bulimia, and these are often more visible.

5 Physical symptoms emerge, such as calluses on the knuckles, a sore throat and swollen glands.

If you believe that your teenage child or a teenager you are in contact with is suffering from bulimia, you should seek professional help immediately. While bulimics can survive for a much longer period of time than anorexics, untold damage is being done to their bodies, and they are equally at risk. Like anorexia, some form of psychotherapeutic intervention is necessary. Bodywhys is again the first place to contact. (Details of this organisation can be found at the back of the book.)

Obesity

Obesity, which can lead to heart disease, kidney failure and a number of orthopaedic and respiratory problems, is becoming endemic in today's Ireland, posing a serious health risk to Irish teenagers. Up to 18 percent of the population is obese, and a report published by the National Taskforce on Obesity in April

2005 stated that three hundred thousand Irish children are over-weight, and that this figure is set to increase by 10,000 a year unless drastic action is taken.

There has been a huge increase in the consumption of energy-dense foods in this country, and in the Developed World in general. Sugar-sweetened carbonated drinks, high-sugar and high-fat snacks, and fast foods are major contributors to obesity. Added to this is the increasingly sedentary lifestyles we are leading, with a sharp drop in leisure time due to longer hours spent at work. Trends in our national diet indicate that we have a high propensity to eat high-fat foods.

Obesity is driven by emotional disorders as well, however. Teenagers who are experiencing difficulties in life are turning to comfort eating; the weight gained as a result merely adds to their feelings of low self-worth and hopelessness, however. Adolescents who feel that they are not appreciated, have lost their self-esteem or are consistently dependent on others and engage in people-pleasing behaviours binge-eat to overcome these negative feelings. If this behaviour continues over a long enough period of time, they become obese.

Obesity is a social stigma: fat adolescents are seen as being stupid, dirty, lazy and smelly. They are discriminated against by other students at school, romantically, or when seeking employment. These attitudes naturally affect the emotional well-being of many fat adolescents and drives them to lose weight by adopting fad diets. The relief they feel as a result of this is often momentary, however. Initial weight loss improves their moods, depressive episodes become less frequent and self-esteem rises. But without proper emotional support, they invariably return to their old eating habits, and their psychological symptoms return, often with greater severity.

While the National Obesity Taskforce recommends that Irish teenagers who are obese be treated with Xenical, a fat-busting drug, to stave off medical complications, it also stresses the need for the government and the private sector to address the issue of obesity. The promotion of healthy eating and active living is vital, and emotional support is necessary to help teenagers who are obese face their personal problems and change their lifestyles. A new obesity clinic has been established at Loughlinstown Hospital in County Dublin to deal with the medical implications of obesity.

Recovery from food disorders

It is important to realise from the outset that food disorders do not simply go away of their own accord; neither can a young adolescent be forced to eat healthily. People who suffer from food disorders are highly deceptive and, as with other individuals with addiction problems, need outside and professional help to help them overcome their pathology. Even with adequate professional support, recovery can be very slow, the underlying problem being such that it can be years before the anorexic teenager gains the insight required to understand and control his or her behaviour.

Hospitalisation may be necessary initially if the condition is very severe, and life-threatening. Often it will be necessary to feed through a tube or intravenously until a critical weight has been reached. When the adolescent's health is no longer in question, rehabilitation begins. Nutritional counselling helps to reprogramme eating habits. Individual, and often family, therapy can be used to deal with the unhappiness and despair that the adolescent is experiencing, and to examine and correct dynamics within the family that may be driving the disorder. Support groups such as Overeaters Anonymous and Bodywhys help teenagers to become more expressive about their difficulties, and provide invaluable help.

13

Alcohol and Drug Abuse

Teenage abuse of alcohol and drugs in Ireland is a cause for concern: reference is made to it in the press on an almost daily basis. Teenagers have always indulged in the consumption of alcohol; what has changed recently is that the average age of the consumer has dropped, and the number of units being consumed on an average 'binge' has increased, especially amongst young teenage girls.

In 2005, 83 percent of fourteen- to seventeen-year-olds surveyed drank alcohol, and the average age at which they took their first drink was twelve years. Ireland's teen alcoholism rate is 6 percent – double that of the USA. An alcoholic in this survey was defined as someone who has 'a high tolerance to alcohol, has experiences of being harmed or causing harm (when under the influence), and has experienced problems as a result of drinking (e.g. conflict in relationships, financial difficulties or a decline in school performance).' Since 1996, there has been a 390 percent increase in intoxication in public places by underage drinkers. The survey also revealed that 37 percent of Irish teenagers smoked cannabis, compared to a 12 percent average in the remaining 25 European countries.

In the European School Survey Project on Alcohol and Other Drugs (ESPAD), carried out in 2003, Irish teenagers topped the league as the worst binge drinkers in Europe. Binge drinking is defined as the consumption of more than five alcoholic drinks in a row, at least three times, in the previous thirty days. Thirty-two percent of Irish sixteen-year-olds fitted this criteria, and one can assume that these are the baseline figures. The figure for girls was 33 percent, and 31 percent for boys. Ireland came second in terms of consumption of beer for boys, and alcopops and spirits for girls. Our teens had the highest consumption of cider for both sexes. In an article in the *Irish Independent* on 1 December 2004, it was claimed that young teenagers are now drinking a week's recommended intake of alcohol in the space of only a few hours. The huge increase in alcohol consumption, especially amongst young females, has been blamed on the new sugar-based alcoholic drinks, which contain high levels of alcohol and are easy to drink. The high sugar content facilitates quick absorption of the alcohol into the bloodstream and makes the drinks easy to consume for young people, who may not like the taste of traditional alcoholic drinks. These drinks contain up to four and a half units of alcohol. They are branded, and marketed, directly at young teens. A barman with relevant experience on the issue was quoted as saying: 'Young drinkers in the past stuck to pints, but it would be much harder for a girl to drink seven pints or a lad to drink ten before they had reached their weekly limit. But it's easy enough to drink bottles and bottles of alcopops in one sitting, and find yourself drinking your weekly quota of units quite quickly.'

In its 1996 report, the Department of Health confirmed that the use of alcohol and drugs by Irish adolescents was widespread: 'Today adolescent drug users do not identify with any particular subculture, but rather it seems to be a normal part of youth culture, straddling all classes and all geographical boundaries.' What was most noticeable in the ESPAD survey was the fact that, compared to other European teenagers, Irish teens had little appreciation of the risks involved in alcohol and drug use.

In a qualitative study of young teens from Dublin's inner city, it was found that the motives for drug use were deemed, by the teens, to be positive. In other words, they focused on what they believed were the positive effects of drug-taking rather than the negative ones. The report pointed to certain trends that were identifiable from various surveys that had been conducted into this issue. These were:

1   Ninety percent of Irish teenagers believe that drinking alcohol is for life.

2   Illicit drug use is relatively high, but there are indications that it has stabilised or decreased in recent years.

3   Lifetime use of solvents among fifteen- to sixteen-year-olds is relatively high, at 22 percent.

4   Drug use is most prevalent amongst young Dublin males.

5   The typical problematic drug user in Ireland is a young, unemployed male, leaving school at an early age and living in a socially and economically deprived area.

6   One-fifth of all new clients in treatment for drugs in Dublin between 1990 and 1999 were under eighteen years of age. The main drug of misuse was heroin in almost half of these cases. These young people were more likely than their adult counterparts to be female and to be homeless.

7   The number of drug-related deaths under the age of twenty is low, but it is higher for some other age groups.

8   Of the juvenile offences committed in 2003, 1,050 were for the possession of illegal drugs.

The greatest concern voiced by the Irish public in submissions to the Department of Health in 1996 concerned the access teenagers have to alcohol. The government has reacted to this situation by introducing severe penalties for anyone selling alcohol to teenagers, and by banning children under the age of sixteen from being present on any licensed premises, whether alcohol is being served at the time or not. While many regard these attempts to tackle the problem of teenage drinking as admirable, I believe them to be misguided and naive. In adopting these measures, we, as adults, are taking responsibility for teenage drinking into our own hands, and are suggesting that young people cannot, or should not, be held responsible for their own actions in relation to alcohol and drugs. Teenagers need to feel responsible for their actions, however. We need to promote the idea that, when provided with the facts needed to make informed choices, and when treated with respect, teenagers are capable of acting in a responsible manner.

Until we accept that there is a problem with regard to teenage drug use, and relate to it in a real way, our attempts will be futile. Adopting a zero-tolerance policy drives the issue underground, making the detection of the problem more difficult. Understanding the reasons why our teenagers are drinking or taking drugs should be the first step. It is only when these reasons are clearly understood that we can discuss the issue in a real and undefended way with young teenagers. We must also accept that the very nature of adolescence invites young teens to experiment, and most do! As these young adults mature, the initial thrill and excitement that alcohol and drugs provided generally wanes, and they go on to drink in a more normal and controlled fashion. While many of our teens drink to excess, it is wrong to sensationalise the problem and infer that, as they mature, a large majority of them will develop serious issues in relation to drink. That said, a small but growing number of them will.

In the survey conducted in Dublin's inner city, it was found that the young adolescents had tolerant views on the use, and benefits, of drugs. Motives for use included curiosity, pleasure, enhancement of self-esteem, alleviation of boredom, management of negative self-thought and, of course, the fact that drugs were available. We can take it that these motives underlie all teenage drinking as well, to a greater or lesser extent. Any substance that provides pleasure and alleviates self-consciousness will be seen as irresistibly attractive to a developing teenager. Drinking is seen as 'adult', and a testimony to the young person's individuation. It overcomes shyness and masks inhibitions, and it breaks down barriers between the sexes in social situations, at a time when issues around sexuality are a torment to many. However, a relatively secure, well-guided and well-adapted teen who is valued as an individual and looks forward to a bright future, and who is taught self-responsibility and self-respect, will by and large not go on to develop an addiction to either alcohol or drugs.

However, the teen who does not have this security, who has suffered neglect and deprivation, both personal and social, and who sees little to look forward to in life, will be vulnerable. The investment these vulnerable people place in alcohol and drugs, to assuage their feelings of low self-esteem, to relieve boredom and a sense of uselessness, and to manage their negative self-thought, may become so great that they eventually use alcohol and drugs compulsively. They will use it to mask depression, and escape the reality of their daily lives – lives in which they may experience parental conflict or neglect, extreme exam pressure or unbearable loss.

The real solution to the problem of underage drinking lies not in prohibition but in helping teenagers become secure, independent and responsible young adults. It lies in building their self-esteem and ego strength through adequate communication and care, in instilling in them self-worth and a vision of their future that holds out promise to them. It lies in reaching out to young people who are experiencing difficulty and helping them to develop a positive self-identity that will allow them to trust both themselves and life in general. They must, above all, be given hope.

Relating to Teenagers about Alcohol

Many of us as adults, driven by fear, feel at a loss as to where to begin relating to teenagers about alcohol. Often this fear is so great that discussions about alcohol are dictatorial rather than open, and censorious rather than negotiated. This fear is understandable: very few of us have not been closely touched by the devastating effects of drug and alcohol abuse, and a plethora of media reports is identifying teenage alcohol abuse as an ever-increasing problem. Often we simply do not know what to do, other than prohibit usage, or we ignore the problem, hoping that it is other people's children, and not our own, that are at risk. In many cases, by the time we see a potential problem in our children, it has already deeply taken root.

Before any parent sits down to discuss the issue of alcohol use with their children, they would be well served to examine their own attitude towards, and behaviour around, alcohol. We as a society have a permissive attitude to alcohol usage; in fact, in many cases we attach a degree of notoriety, even admiration, to drunken escapades. Teenagers are often party to adult conversations in which the drunken escapades of family or friends are recounted with great hilarity, and the lack of responsibility, and often inappropriate nature, of their behaviour is completely overlooked. The impressionable young teen hears these stories and deduces that one can gain great notoriety from such behaviour. If lack of moderation is acceptable to adults within the family unit, then teenagers will likewise surmise that over-indulgence is acceptable. If adults object to this, their arguments will bear little credence and will be dismissed as inherently flawed.

Indeed, alcohol consumption is in some ways perceived to be an acceptable reason for abrogating responsibility. I recently heard a judge protest in court about how the general public appears to believe that the consumption of alcohol is a reasonable excuse for being abusive to members of the Garda Síochána. We appear in some way to believe that we are not accountable for our actions if we are 'under the influence'. The 'Ah sure, he had drink taken' philosophy is alive and well as a defence in our judicial system!

Having clarified our own position on consumption, we are better equipped to discuss the issue with our teenagers. In any initial discussion, one would do well to focus on the teenager's perceived expectations about the effects of drinking. By so doing, the teenager's distorted thinking and beliefs around the issue, which are often contradictory, can be discussed. Various studies on this question report the same expectations. Teenagers' positive expectations of alcohol are as follows:

1 Alcohol generally alters experiences in a positive way.

2 Alcohol adds to social and physical pleasure.

3 Alcohol contributes to sexual experiences and performances.

4 Alcohol increases aggression and dominance.

5 Alcohol improves sociability and social assertiveness.

6 Alcohol reduces tension.

Some of the negative expectations cited are:

1 Alcohol increases clumsiness.

2 Alcohol delays responsiveness.

3 Alcohol affects memory and concentration.

4 Alcohol can bring on bouts of nausea and dizziness.

Research also found that adolescents with drinking problems believed that alcohol improves their intellectual and physical performance. Non-drinkers and non-problem-drinkers did not share this expectation.

The Facts about Alcohol that Should Be Communicated

The amount of alcohol in the blood, which determines an individual's level of intoxication, is typically referred to as the blood alcohol concentration, or BAC. The rate at which alcohol is absorbed into the bloodstream affects the BAC. Therefore, consuming very diluted alcoholic beverages, and drinking on a full stomach, tends to slow down absorption, since it takes longer for the alcohol to reach the intestine. Carbonation in drinks relaxes the stomach valve, allowing material to move into the intestine and speeding up rates of absorption.

As soon as alcohol enters the bloodstream, the liver starts working to eliminate this poison from the blood system by producing enzymes. In general, it will take up to two hours to eliminate the amount of alcohol that is contained in a glass of wine, a single measure of spirits or a 300 ml glass of 4 percent-strength beer. In general, there is an equal amount of ethanol in every drink, therefore the type of alcoholic beverage drunk is not nearly as critical to the BAC as the number of drinks consumed. This is not the case with alcopops, however.

The speed with which the alcohol is consumed also affects the BAC. Consuming drinks quickly and in rapid succession results in a sudden elevation of the BAC; on the other hand, because the body is constantly metabolising any alcohol that is present, lower-volume or spaced drinking gives the body a chance to 'burn up' the alcohol that is already in the system before more is introduced. Thus, the amount of time spent drinking, as well as the total amount of alcohol consumed, is critical to the BAC.

The final major factor that influences the BAC is the drinker's body weight. The larger the individual, the more fluid there is to absorb and dilute the alcohol. This is why larger people do not seem to get as intoxicated as smaller ones who drink the same amount. Another important factor is gender-based. A greater proportion of the male body weight is made up of fluids, whereas females, by nature, generally have more low-fluid fat and less high-fluid muscle.

What alcohol does when introduced into the system

Alcohol acts as a general depressant on the central nervous system, which includes the brain and spinal cord. The ability of nerves to produce and transmit electrical impulses essential for the proper processing of information that comes to the brain from the skin, senses and muscles, is reduced.

It is thought that, at a low BAC, alcohol acts as a stimulant, but as the BAC increases, it becomes a depressant. Therefore, those who drink only small amounts of alcohol are stimulated, while those who consume a large amount in any given session are initially stimulated, but then the depressant effect kicks in. Heavy drinkers are continuously lured back into the 'alcohol trap': they want to experience the initial high but then fail to stop as the depressive effects kick in.

Debunking the Myths

It is generally believed that alcohol alleviates anxiety and reduces tension. However, when the direct effect of alcohol on the body is examined, it appears not to reduce muscle tension or increase the heart rate. It has even been shown to increase muscle tension and reduce heart rate. It is therefore reasonable to assume that the perceived reduction in tension and anxiety from alcohol consumption is based more on expectation and the fact that drinking is generally done during leisure times, when an individual would naturally feel more relaxed anyway. There is also a commonly held belief that alcohol enhances sexual encounters. Again, evidence does not support this theory: in many cases, alcohol actually negatively affects sexual performance, especially in males.

There can be little doubt that alcohol, as the most widely used drug, is also the most abused. Teenage drinking problems seem to be worse among older adolescents, especially boys, and have been associated with approval and modelling of drinking by both parents and peers, with an atmosphere of poor parenting contributing to early and excessive dependence on peer relationships.

We certainly have a growing problem to address in relation to this issue. As well as many juvenile offences being alcohol-related, overconsumption of alcohol is also seen to be behind a significant number of teenage pregnancies and sexual assaults. Mary Holohan, director of the Rotunda Hospital's sexual-assault unit, has stated that more than one hundred alcohol-induced memory-loss cases occurred in 2003. Alison Begas, chief executive of the Well Woman Clinic, confirmed that a large number of women were seeking the morning-after pill after having unprotected sex the previous night, while under the influence of alcohol. This also has a bearing on the rise of sexually transmitted diseases among teenagers.

Relating to Teenagers about Drug Abuse

Naturally, when we are faced with the evidence that our young teenagers are increasingly using drugs for recreational purposes, we are filled with alarm. However, it is again necessary that we do not go into panic mode and exaggerate the problem. Adolescents who use drugs in Ireland are generally taking cannabis, which is less addictive than chemical drugs and which does not result in fatalities. While teenagers may experiment with drugs, this tends to be a passing phase and rarely develops into full-blown addiction.

Tell-tale Signs

It is important to be familiar with, and keep an eye out for, the tell-tale signs of drug use, as any teenager who is using drugs needs to discuss this issue with an adult and believe that they will receive positive guidance from them. Sudden mood swings or personality changes are often discernible, and behaviour may become aggressive and challenging. The adolescent may appear euphoric or 'giddy' and be excessively active when they return after a night out. In general, however, they will be more lethargic and less interested in activity than others. Often, they will have recently changed their friendship group, and new friends may appear to be quieter, or may be reluctant to enter your home. The individual's school work may become less focused, or they may not even go to school. Those who are using hard drugs may have difficulty getting up in the morning, lose their appetite and experience subsequent weight loss, and leave drug paraphernalia, such as syringes and burnt silver paper, in their room.

Again, like alcohol, it is important that parents do not over-react and become panicked, as this inhibits meaningful communication and drives the problem underground. An honest discussion on the effects of drugs, especially on the teenager's future prospects, should be initiated. Increased supervision is necessary to monitor the whereabouts of the young teen. Efforts should be made to secure the teenager emotionally, and this should in general be accompanied by a level of self-examination by the parents and teenager involved. In the case of hard drugs, the extent of usage needs to be identified immediately, and advice should be sought immediately from an addiction centre. It is imperative to establish whether the teenager is indulging in once-off experimentation or is actually in the grip of an addiction.

14

Juvenile Criminal
and Anti-social Behaviour

Anyone who feels himself cheated by life, will rob.

ALFRED ADLER

In recent times in Ireland, we have experienced huge increases in juvenile criminal behaviour. Sensational cases such as the manslaughter of Brian Murphy outside Anabels nightclub in Dublin meant that the government and the public at large could no longer dismiss juvenile criminal activity as the work of deranged teens from disadvantaged areas.

Young teens that are indulging in criminal behaviour are acting out their anger at a world that appears oblivious to their plight. The messages they receive from adults are contradictory: they are told that they should not drink alcohol, while the adult population has gone on an almighty bender; they are told not to be aggressive, while they are actively encouraged to increase their physical strength to the point of taking steroids, so that their performance on the rugby or GAA pitch will bring credit to their school and personal prowess amongst their peers. (In a recent schoolboys rugby match, I witnessed a father praising his son from the sidelines for his 'Great show of aggression'!) And what of the young teens from disadvantaged communities who feel like failures before they start, who often come from a background of physical, emotional or sexual abuse, and who are educated in schools the inner workings of which bear a greater resemblance to a prison than an educational institution, with attendance and behaviour maintenance and control, rather than academic growth, seeming to be the primary aim. They are filled with teens who are dying of boredom through the lack of any facilities that would motivate them to become more active and participatory in life, and angry that access to wealth seems to be attainable only through criminal activity. We should not be surprised that they are venting their anger against society at large.

According to the 2003 Garda Annual Report, 19,915 individuals were referred to the National Juvenile Office in 2003. Drink-related offences topped the table, with 4,117 offences; 3,539 were related to theft; and 2,125 involved criminal damage. A further 1,394 were referred for traffic offences, fifty-three for sexual assault, thirty for rape or unlawful carnal knowledge, including attempted rape, and three were charged with murder. The vast majority were male, with dramatic increases in criminality from the age of seventeen. The good news is that the majority of these categories have shown a marked decrease since 1999, except in the case of drinking offences, which are rising steadily every year.

Many of those who are referred reoffend: in fact, a majority of the offences are being committed by a fraction of the teen population. In a recent case, a seventeen-year-old was convicted of having committed his eighty-fifth offence. There is thus room for optimism in that there would appear to be a coherent and identifiable group of offenders who may benefit from active intervention. Speaking at the end of Keelin Shanley's acclaimed *Prime Time* investigation into juvenile offenders, a young Limerick man who experienced a successful therapeutic intervention spoke about how, looking back, he realises that all that he had needed was an adult to listen to him and guide him, and that, having been provided with that, he was able to function positively in life.

In response to increased criminality amongst youth, the Garda Juvenile Division program was established in 1963 to 'provide an opportunity to divert juvenile offenders from criminal activity. . . . Every child who is admitted to the programme receives a caution. The caution can either be formal or informal, depending on the nature of the offence. A child who is given a formal caution is placed under Garda supervision for twelve months.'

The Gardaí and the courts are now attempting to intervene in the case of multiple offenders, with many being sent on rehabilitation programs and given therapy. While such interventions do not necessarily produce results, they at least provide the young adults concerned with an alternative.

There has been no comprehensive research done in Ireland into the nature of juvenile anti-social behaviour, but it would be fair to assume that trends here are not dissimilar from those in the UK and America. I will use research from these countries to outline results that have come to light.

All research into this field indicates that there has been a continuous and significant growth in anti-social behaviour in recent decades. Furthermore, it is general believed that official statistics give only a partial picture and that, when they are correlated with the results of self-reporting research, there is a huge discrepancy between the number of offences that are committed and those that result in convictions. The number of offences admitted to was far in excess of the number of actual convictions. While 55 percent of males and 31 percent of females between the ages of fourteen and twenty-five who participated in the self-reporting research admitted to having committed at least one offence in their lives, only 28 percent of males and 12 percent of females had actually been charged with committing an offence. The more serious the crime, the more the figures correlated. We can thus deduce that the actual incidence of crime in this age group is far greater than we would expect based on statistics, and that less serious offences are either going unnoticed or do not result in a change.

Also of note is the conclusion that, while the level and number of self-reported offences did not vary to any great extent across the class and social divide, convictions indicated that anti-social behaviour is mainly the preserve of those from disadvantaged areas who are socially marginalised. Adolescents from these groupings felt that the police were less tolerant of them and harsher in their treatment of them, and that they were far more likely to be targeted and arrested by the police than young people from more affluent and influential communities.

It would also appear that the incidence of offences is age-related. Starting from the age of ten, it peaks for males at eighteen and females at fifteen. Therefore, mid-adolescence can be seen as the most vulnerable time. This correlates with the views of both developmental theorists, who believe that youngsters test boundaries most frequently between the ages of fifteen and eighteen, and neurologists, who believe that the executive functions of the brain – which enable teenagers to judge the consequences of their actions – develop in late adolescence.

From various studies of anti-social behaviours, certain risk factors are clearly identifiable. Firstly, gender would appear to be a key variable. The vast majority of reported offences are committed by males. A number of reasons are put forward for this. Firstly, the more aggressive, competitive and macho nature of male peer groups are seen to be an influence. Secondly, young males are afforded greater freedom by their parents, and therefore have greater opportunity to commit crime than females, especially at night. Thirdly, hyperactivity and other conduct disorders linked to criminality are more prevalent in males.

Fourthly, it is claimed that young females are treated more lightly by policing authorities and the courts. This view is backed up by self-reporting research, which indicates that far fewer offences committed by females end in criminal charges. Lastly, it is believed that, as young women leave home at an earlier age, have families earlier and make the transition to adult roles at a younger age, this goes some way towards accounting for the differences. This is backed up by the fact that female adolescents' level of criminality peaks at fifteen.

Family factors are also of great significance when assessing risk factors. Research shows that teenagers whose parents spend little time with them and are unaware of where they are and what they are doing, are more likely to offend. Family conflict is also a major contributing factor, either through direct aggression, or through harsh and erratic disciplining. Deviant values or behaviours on the part of parents also plays a key role. Inadequate parenting as a result of the presence of a stressor is also believed to be significant.

Of all the social and environmental factors that are seen to influence criminality, poverty is seen to be the most relevant, because parents who experience poverty are generally less effective in providing support and supervising behaviour. As poverty undermines the social fabric of the neighbourhood – as discussed previously – it is more difficult for the parents in such neighbourhoods to provide role models, leisure activities and avenues to help young people move into adulthood. In areas of unemployment, young males find it more difficult to carve out a place for themselves in life and tend towards aggressive behaviour as an alternative mark of status and power within the community. Lastly, the increased incidence of violence in these areas makes it more acceptable than elsewhere.

15

Depression

Depression is the most common manifestation of teenage distress and mental illness and is the underlying factor in many aberrant behaviours. Until the last two decades, however, it was widely believed that depression did not exist in childhood and adolescence, as young people were seen to be lacking in the necessary cognitive and emotional maturity necessary for such a condition. 'Bad moods' were seen as not only normal but as something to be expected during the adolescent period. However, while such moods are normal, prolonged sadness, irritability and so on are not, and need immediate treatment. Harold Koplewicz, a leading authority in the field of teenage depression, points to this in his book *More Than Moody,* stating that 'Anna Freud said that affective fluctuations or moodiness in adolescence merely resembled illness or psychopathology. She believed, as did the field, that adolescents who didn't exhibit depressive or sad periods were actually abnormal – that they had an inability to cope with internal struggles.' Koplewicz warns, however, that 'Depression in adolescence is real, and it is not trivial: left untreated it can lead to school failure, social isolation, family breakdown and even sometimes psychosis or suicide.' He also points to emerging neurological research which is confirming that much more structural change is taking place in the brain during this period than has previously been recognised. He links the groundbreaking research being conducted by Jay Giedd to teenage mental health. Koplewicz points out: 'This burst of brain maturation occurs at a time when rates of major psychiatric disorders, including depression, increase markedly.' In research into teenagers who had attempted suicide, very low levels of serotonin were identified when spinal taps were conducted.

Recognising that depression exists not only in teenagers but also, in some cases, in children as well has been a major breakthrough in mental health, as it is believed that early diagnosis and treatment at this stage often prevents recurring depressive episodes in adulthood. It is estimated that 33 to 40 percent of adolescents in the US are affected by depression – indeed, depression now affects more teenagers than adults. According to the Journal of the American Medical Association (1989), it seems to be occurring earlier in life than ever before. A brief examination of the age groups of completed suicides confirms this theory, as it was the huge rise in the number of suicides amongst teens over the past four decades that made it impossible to deny that depression existed during adolescence. Diagnosis of this condition is, however, still wanting, and often it is only when the depression has a powerful and debilitating hold on the young adult that intervention is sought. Increased awareness of the incidence of teenage depression amongst parents, teachers and GPs would go a long way towards reducing its impact and strength – and reducing Ireland's suicide figures.

Diagnosis

Before examining the symptoms and tell-tale signs that herald the onset of a depressive episode, it would first be helpful to examine the various forms of depression that exist, their severity, and their incidence amongst teens. A clear understanding of the different types of depression makes it easier to predict what to expect.

Major depressive disorder (MDD)

This is a serious depression in adolescence and lasts on average between seven and nine months. Many of its features are similar to those found in adult depression – sadness, pessimism, sleep and appetite disturbance, and a decrease in concentration and sex drive – but in other ways it is distinct. For instance, anxiety symptoms and irritability are more common in depressed teenagers than in adults. This is believed to be the case because young teens are still by and large novices when it comes to knowing what is going on for them emotionally. They experience difficulty expressing feelings, and this difficulty manifests itself in irritation. 'Atypical' depression, which is most common among teens, is characterised by oversensitivity to the enviroment and responding to perceived negative interactions, with symptoms opposite to those in the classic picture. These include eating and sleeping too much rather than not enough.

Dysthymic disorder

This is a milder but more chronic depression. Also called 'dysthymia', it is a low-level depression that is felt for most of the day, on most days, and continues for years. In adolescents, the average duration is four years – which means that they spend virtually their entire adolescence depressed. A low mood for such a long time during such a crucial developmental stage is likely to affect a person's mental state as an adult. Teenagers often find that prolonged bouts of depression leave them so far behind in terms of social development and school work that they feel isolated, and daunted by the amount of ground they have to regain. These feelings perpetuate the depression, feeding lack of self-esteem and inadequacies.

Double depression

A combination of major depression and dysthmis: a depression that is both serious and chronic.

Bipolar disorder

Also known as manic depression, this is characterised by unusual shifts in mood and energy. Although there is debate about how prevalent it is in young people, the condition frequently begins with a depressive episode during adolescence. Research has shown that anything from 20 to 40 percent of adolescents with major depression develop bipolar disorder within five years.

Reactive depression

The most common form of mood problem in children and adolescents, but the least serious. This is a depressed state brought on by difficulty adjusting to a disturbing experience – from something as serious as the loss of a parent to something as relatively inconsequential as a rejection or slight. It usually lasts anything from a few hours to a couple of weeks and is not considered to be a mental disorder.

Warning Signs

Differentiating between ordinary teenage moodiness and the actual presence of a depression is often difficult for anyone undertaking the task. Nonetheless, a fairly straightforward list of symptoms exists that goes a long way towards determining a diagnosis. While some of these symptoms are a carbon copy of adult ones, important differences do exist and must be noted in order to avoid discounting some of the symptoms.

Firstly, a change in mood over a prolonged period of time (three weeks or more) is indicative that something more than 'hormones' is at work. Feelings of sadness and irritability, and a withdrawal from pleasurable activities, including meeting friends, should be noticeable. However, depressed teens, unlike depressed adults, are able to snap out of their gloominess for brief periods, and by all accounts appear fine. They can feel good if something good happens, and thereby confuse their parents, who deduce that they do indeed have control over their situation.

This is not the case, however: depressed teenagers are simply capable at times of experiencing pleasure.

Concentration levels are seriously affected by depression and, as a result, a marked decrease in academic performance is a primary indicator that something is afoot. A drop in school performance should be taken seriously if it is seen to be unusual.

Unlike depressed adults, who often experience a loss in appetite and hence in weight, teenagers frequently respond to depression by over-eating and putting on weight. They comfort-eat, and the commensurate weight gain may then add to their depression.

Depressed adults generally find it difficult to sleep and suffer from insomnia; teenagers, however, frequently want to sleep around the clock when they are depressed. They are increasingly lethargic and often find it difficult to stay awake. It is their way of cutting off from the pain they are experiencing: they believe that they can in some way sleep their way through the depression. One must also remember, however, that, as a result of chemical changes that are taking place in their brains, teenagers require more sleep than adults.

While depressed adults tend to see their libido diminish, this is not the case in teenagers, who continue to feel sexual. The only noticeable difference in their sexual activities is that they generally do not actively go out and pursue sex. They either masturbate or are responsive to other people's sexual advances.

As mentioned earlier, there is a closer relationship between irritability and depression in younger people than in adults. This is due to the fact that teenagers are less able to verbalise their emotions, and react angrily, due to an inability to express their emotions properly. In other words, where adults tend to be sad and their depression is nearly 'feelable', teenagers are more likely to be angry and irritable, or to act out and misbehave. This behaviour often masks the depression and throws adults off the scent.

Below is a list of symptoms released by the US National institute of Mental Health that are associated with teen depression, the persistent occurrence of which indicates the need for intervention:

1 Persistently sad or irritable

2 Loss of interest in activities once enjoyed

3 Significant change in sleeping and eating patterns

4 Loss of energy

5 Feelings of worthlessness or inappropriate guilt

6 Difficulty concentrating

7 Recurrent thoughts of suicide

8 Frequent vague, unspecific physical complaints – headaches, muscle aches, fatigue

9 Frequent absences from school, mitching, or a drop in academic performance

10 Outbursts of shouting, complaining, unexplained irritability and crying

11 Excessive boredom

12 Social isolation: lack of interest in friends and poor communication

13 Alcohol and drug abuse

14 Fear of death

15 Extreme sensitivity to rejection or failure

16 Reckless behaviour

Inherent Susceptibility in Teenagers

While all teenagers are susceptible to developing depression during adolescence – it is possible, on perusing the statistics, to notice certain fundamentals that may lead to depression or which make a teenager more at risk of it.

First and foremost amongst these factors is a history of depression within the family. 'Statistically, children of depressed parents are three times more likely to become depressed themselves than children whose parents do not have depression,' Koplewicz notes. These findings have fuelled the debate as to whether depression is the result of nature or nurture: no definitive answer to this question has been arrived at yet, and it is probable that a combination of both play a part. A depressed parent will psychologically have an adverse effect on the mental health of both their partner and children. If either or both parents are depressed, the family will no longer be operating as a functional unit but will become dysfunctional. The stress placed on the family system will force a change in roles and promote enmeshment. It is also proposed that a whole family can become depressed as the result of a common family situation. Studies also reveal, however, that genetic make-up leaves adolescents more vulnerable to depression.

The second most noticeable factor in susceptibility to depression is gender. As in adulthood, teenage girls are far more likely to be diagnosed with depression than boys. But why is this the case? A popular belief is that, during adolescence, girls adopt personality characteristics that make them prone to depression. Girls place more importance on affirming relationships and friendships and as a result are more affected when problems arise within these relationships. Their levels of investment in and expectation of friendship are generally far greater than with boys. Girls also tend to be more self-critical and self-blaming: they turn failure in on themselves. In general, young girls are seen to find adapting to their new sexual roles and physiological changes more difficult than boys. The modern preoccupation with the perfect female body fuels this difficulty. They are in general more self-conscious. It has also been suggested that the fact that more girls are sexually abused during childhood must have an effect on figures for depression among adolescents. While it would be wrong to say that teenage boys do not get depressed, they in general adopt different defences to cope with their negative feelings. Wallowing in depressed feelings goes against their developing male sexuality, which identifies with power, strength and action. The overall effect of these alternative defences on teenage boys' personal well-being are not, however, any less painful for them: their objective is to bury or hide their pain. They often act out, becoming aggressive and at times turning to crime. Others put all their energies into pushing themselves forward and seeking to achieve, neglecting other areas of their lives. These alternatives are often dangerous, as their success is not based on any great feelings of self-worth, or a strong sense of self. A sudden breach in their armoury can allow feelings of inadequacy to flood in and overwhelm them, and this may lead them to turn to suicide.

The third key factor in an individual's susceptibility to depression is the prior existence of an anxiety disorder: social phobia (pathological self-consciousness), separation-anxiety disorder (marked by fears about the well-being of the family), or generalised anxiety disorder (a fear of the future and constant worries about one's performance). Research shows that, among those who have an anxiety disorder coupled with depression, in 85 percent of the cases the anxiety disorder existed first. Thirty percent of those preadolescents who were diagnosed with an anxiety disorder went on to develop depression. Therefore a pre-emptive strike against depression – in the form of developing social skills in children who suffer from an anxiety disorder – is possible in these cases.

Anxiety disorders centre around poor self-esteem and lack of self-worth. Performance levels are seen to be wanting, and those affected view themselves as social failures. They see themselves as defective and inadequate, and have an exaggerated view of their own flaws. They fail to connect with their peers, as they are so caught up in themselves that they neither listen to others nor have the capacity to empathise with them. Peers pick up on this and move on to greener pastures, seeking out people who are more emotionally available. The oversensitivity of anxiety-disordered children unnerves these peers and presents a challenge to their developing ego identities that they feel they can do without. The socially phobic child is left isolated, in a self-perpetuating belief system that supports rather than negates his or her disorder. Active intervention is required to help the individual develop new social skills, which they should try out at first in support groups for children with similar disorders.

Stressors

Stressors are situations or experiences that occur in an adolescent's life that set off a depressive episode. While they do not necessarily cause depression, they may trigger it, especially if a susceptibility to depression already exists. These stressors are either 'loss events' or events that affect self-esteem. Loss events include bereavement, parental separation, leaving home to go to college, and so on. In such events, the teen has no control over situations and feels powerless. Events that affect self-esteem are more prevalent; these include rejection (including physical and emotional abuse), by parents, friends or a love mate, and a perceived difference, such as a learning disability, sexual alignment, racial origin, or being gifted and talented. In the last case, the child's identity has been formed around the approval they have always received from adults as a result of their ability. They increasingly put pressure on themselves to perform brilliantly. The importance they place on their performance becomes distorted, and if or when they do not perform as well as they had hoped, they go into a depression.

A teenager's emotional make-up – how he or she responds to loss – is a critical factor in distinguishing a person who is vulnerable to becoming depressed from someone who is resistant to it. In other words, an adolescent with a strong sense of self, who has had a secure and nurturing upbringing, and has no predisposition to depression, will demonstrate great resilience to any stressor that they may have to face in life. For those who do not have this sense of security, who have a family history of depression, who have a previous or present anxiety disorder, or who have a prior episode of depression, vulnerability to depression following a stressful life event is significantly increased.

Also of note is the fact that one significant stressor can trigger a series of smaller ones, which accumulate to make the experience more pronounced. For example, the loss of a boyfriend may also lead to the loss of his circle of friends, which merely serves to make the sense of loss more acute and the displacement more severe. In the case of parental separation, other factors that may be the result of the separation, such as strained finances or the loss of the family home, all add to the original stressor.

Action Plan

The recent huge increase in the incidence of depression amongst Irish teenagers, coupled with the fact that early intervention for depression can not only lessen the impact of future episodes but may also, in some cases, ensure that no future episodes occur, points to the need to increase awareness surrounding the issue amongst both parents and schoolteachers. Indeed, teachers are often more likely to notice the symptoms of depression before parents due to the objective nature of their relationship with the child. In America, where depression amongst teenagers is both recognised and responded to, a clear mental health programme centred on schools exists. To date, no comprehensive policy has been adopted by the Irish government to tackle these issues, however. Talks for parents that increase the awareness of the various aspects of mental health are crucial. Often parents only learn about mental health issues when they are faced with them, and go on to feel guilty and blame themselves for not having identified the problem sooner.

If you believe that your child, or a child that you are in contact with, is suffering from depression, take action. While you may have your doubts, the sin of omission is worse than the sin of commission. If the adolescent in question is not your child, it is necessary to talk to the parents, despite your misgivings. The first port of call for a parent of a child with suspected depression should be their GP. If the GP deems the depression to be mild, he or she may refer the child to a counsellor or therapist, who will explore the difficulties the teen is experiencing and attempt to develop their coping skills. Often, cognitive behavioural therapy is used to challenge negative thought patterns and improve the teenager's outlook. In cases where the depression is seen to be more severe, the physician may prescribe a course of antidepressants to give more immediate relief to the troubled adolescent, while also recommending therapy as a more comprehensive treatment. In some cases, both physicians and parents can be reluctant to use medication as a treatment for adolescents. Medication is the lesser of two evils in many cases, however, and need not be seen as a long-term solution – and in most cases indeed *should* not be a long-term solution. In some cases, however, the physician may deem it safer to refer the teenager to a psychiatrist, who will prescribe medication on a more long-term basis if he or she diagnoses a more severe syndrome.

Parents would be advised to increase their knowledge of depression and to seek advice on how best to help their child through their difficulty. Although our attempts to help can often be misguided, early intervention can have a profoundly positive effect when it comes to treating depression. The voluntary organisation Aware deals specifically with depression and provides information and support to those experiencing depression and those who are affected by depression in a loved one.

16

Suicide

Although reports in the media would have us believe that the suicide rate amongst teenagers is inexorably rising, figures from the Central Statistics Office prove that this is not the case. The rate of suicide has in fact dropped sharply, particularly amongst teenage boys. The incidence of suicide in the fifteen-to-twenty-four-year-old age group of boys rose steadily in the 1990s, peaking at 120 in 1998 (36 per 100,000), and has fallen consistently since, with eighty-three suicides (24 per 100,000) for this age group recorded in 2004. For females in this age group, the figure peaked at eighteen in 1997 and fell to ten in 2004. In the case of males up to the age of fourteen, eight boys took their lives by suicide in 1993, while in 2004 there was a single suicide in this group. The incidence of suicide in this age group for girls is practically nil. This decline can be accounted for in part by the work of Aware, the Suicide Awareness Group, Barnardos and various government-sponsored campaigns. It also demonstrates, as in the case of teen pregnancy, the effect that coordinated awareness campaigns can have.

The results of a study carried out to determine the frequency of reported suicidal thoughts and acts in a school-based sample of Irish adolescents, and also in adolescents attending a community child and family mental health service are cause for great concern. Within the school sample, while 3 percent of parents reported that their child had talked of harming him- or herself, 15 percent of the teenagers reported that they had had thoughts of harming or killing themselves, while 7 percent claimed that they had tried to harm or kill themselves. In other words, many parents were unaware of any suicidal ideation in their teenage children, and some were unaware that their children had actually attempted to harm themselves. Among the mental health clinic attendees, 37 percent of parents reported that their child had spoken of harming him- or herself, and 32 percent reported that their child had thought of self-harming; 21 percent of the attendees reported that they had tried to harm themselves. These figures give an idea of the mental anguish teenagers may be suffering, unbeknownst to their parents.

What Is Driving Suicidal Thoughts in Teenagers?

The single most identifiable factor underlying the majority of suicides is a sense of social isolation. The greater the ability of an individual to integrate socially, the lower the risk of suicide. Teens who identify strongly with their society and their place within it feel less isolated than those who do not. The belief that they have an active part to play within a group, and that their future within that group is promising, fuels their zest for life. By contrast, those who feel 'different', or disadvantaged or disabled for some reason, are more susceptible to suicide.

Factors of modern-day living that promote isolation also come into play. The degree to which Irish people have turned away from the Church and religious organisations in general fuels a sense of isolation on an existential level. The more secular and individualistic a society becomes, the more insignificant its members tend to feel. Members of religious affiliations are less prone to suicide due to the fact that religions are fairly tightly socially organised and controlling of individuals; it appears that the more socially controlling an organised religion is, the less likely its adherents will be to attempt suicide. Religious affiliation also fosters a sense of community and belonging, as well as providing teachings that encourage individuals to see the bigger picture. In times of mental anguish, this can provide hope as an antidote to despair.

As previously mentioned, the period of adolescence is a relatively modern creation. Although this period of dependency, with little responsibility, can provide young adults with the space to develop themselves and their abilities, for those who are less motivated or are lacking in self-worth, and who do not receive adequate guidance, it may become a yawning abyss of isolation. The period of adolescence may be likened to the transition year in school, which for some is used as a period of character-building and self-development, but which for others lacks meaning, structure and guidance. The large amount of leisure time afforded to young adolescents can leave them with a sense of boredom and purposelessness, if it is not constructively used. In such cases, it can become a breeding ground for high-risk behaviours and mental distress. This is especially the case in families where most members are active and leading full lives. The teen can in some ways feel left behind.

A growing body of opinion holds that the increasing freedom of choice within modern society has a down side. The freedom teens have to make their own choices, and the lack of control over them on the part of adults, allows for the possibility of the choice of suicide. Greater choice inherently requires greater responsibility, and the modern teenager living in a democracy is now responsible for making a wide array of choices, about their careers and how they live their lives, that did not exist in traditional society. For some, the sheer responsibility of making these choices appears too much: they often feel disempowered by the lack of self-esteem that is prevalent during adolescence, and feel unable to make the right choices for themselves. They seek to escape or shirk their responsibilities, and, lacking the neurological facilities to judge the consequences of their actions, the choice of ending their life becomes more tangible and real to them. Tunnel vision, 'either or' thinking, and a lack of problem-solving abilities contribute to their consideration of suicide as an answer to stress.

The nature of adolescence itself is isolating. Young teens need to rebel against their parents and adult society in general to complete the task of individuation adequately. A close identity with contemporary teen culture enables this. However, while teen culture is in essence rebellious, and teens identify with that culture in their individuation process, they rarely get a real sense of belonging in this culture as they know that, by its very nature, it is transitory. Therefore, they maintain a strong need to belong to an adult culture and be accepted by it. This is the anomaly presented to the parents of teenagers. The teenager's need to rebel has to be respected as a necessary process, and while they need strong boundaries with regard to what is seen to be acceptable or unacceptable, the parent who goes too far down the authoritarian path may leave their young adult child feeling rejected and ostracised. In such cases, severe feelings of isolation can be fostered. In other cases, more vulnerable teenagers may have an exaggerated reaction to the conflict with which they are presented, between teen culture and parental authority. This reaction feeds isolation.

With suicide rates increasing at an alarming pace in Ireland in the past decade (by 36 percent in Ireland, compared to 12 percent in the UK), the issue is becoming less taboo. The greater its prevalence, the more it is perceived as a viable option by the teenager. This is particularly noticeable within families that have a history or recent experience of suicide. The very fact that a member of the family viewed the choice to take his or her own life as acceptable breaks a barrier and presents other family members with the fact that such a choice exists. This problem is aggravated by the fact that mental illness, such as depression, generally 'travels' within families.

Young teenagers are also very impressionable, and our increasing fascination with celebrity culture must be noted when looking at suicide rates. Celebrities that commit suicide profoundly affect some teens and play a part in creating the idea that suicide can be acceptable. This is evident in the phenomenum of so-called cluster suicides, where several teenagers die in a concentrated period of time in a way imitative of the celebrity suicide. This appears more frequently when teens glorify the celebrity death and the media romanticises or dramatises it.

Risk Factors for Suicide

Given that our suicide rates are so high, and parents are by and large unaware of the extent of suicidal-thought ideation, a greater understanding and awareness of the mental conditions that precede suicidal intent must be attained in order to try to reverse this trend within Irish teen culture.

Multiple studies have shown that, in 90 percent of suicide cases, there is an underlying psychiatric disorder – a foundation risk factor. This is consoling in that, in the majority of cases, it is possible to identify those who are susceptible to suicide; however, within this group it becomes increasingly difficult to identify who is at greater risk.

Teenagers who are suffering from depression are by far the most endangered group. It is estimated that between 50 and 70 percent of teenagers who commit suicide suffer from depression. Anti-social behaviour is the second-most-important condition accompanying suicide: many of those who commit suicide have had problems with their behaviour either in school or with the law. It is thought that these teens are impulsive, and the impulse that leads them to get into trouble can also lead them to make an attempt on their lives, especially if they are under the influence of drink or drugs.

Thus substance abuse is also prevalent amongst suicides, and is associated with more lethal means, more frequent attempts and more serious suicidal intent. It is both a foundation and a risk factor, in that not only are teenagers who have a problem with substance abuse more likely to commit suicide, but also a large number are under the influence of drugs when they commit suicide. This is not surprising, as the use of substances breaks down defences and inhibitions and distorts one's capacity to make judgements.

Anxiety disorders are also a foundation risk factor, as is family violence or abuse, and the suicide of a family member or friend – as discussed above – also greatly increases the risk of suicide. Sexual orientation is also seen to be a factor in teen suicides, as suicide attempts among gay people are at their peak during the adolescent years due to their struggles with issues of sexuality, isolation and identity. The exact extent of the influence of sexuality as a contributing factor in an individual's decision to commit suicide is hard to determine. This is due to the fact that sexual identity is often hidden.

The experience of physical and verbal abuse, as well as sexual abuse, can set up negative thought patterns about self, which may eventually lead to suicidal ideation. For most teens who are abused in such a way, they believe that the abuse is not only acceptable but also that it was their fault and that they deserved it. They feel isolated from other family members and believe that they do not belong. Feelings of self-hatred can become overwhelming, and there is no greater expression of self-hatred than the taking of one's own life.

Warning signs

Various studies of teens who have committed suicide point to a number of warning behaviours or signs that can help to identify those who may be having suicidal thoughts and serve as a forewarning. A thorough awareness of these signs is the first step in helping to stem the tide. Listed below are a number of the more obvious tell-tale signs:

1 *They become preoccupied with death:* they joke about it, write about it and discuss the notion of death in broad philosophical terms. They ask probing questions about how the parent would feel if they died. No expression of a wish to die or an allusion to suicide should be dismissed, even if it is said in a humorous context. Many

parents believe that, if their child talks about suicide, he or she will not actually try it, because if they were serious about it, they would keep it secret. Experience shows that this is not the case. Many young people who are thinking about suicide would like to be stopped, and talking about it is often a cry for help.

2 *Increased isolation and apathy* increase the risk of suicide. Teenagers who are withdrawn, and have few friends – at a stage in their development when peers play such an important role – feel acutely lonely. They lack a sense of connectedness in school, at home and in life in general, and thus also lack a sense of purpose. They may watch television continuously, listen to music for hours, or appear to be daydreaming all the time. These are classic ways of taking their attention away from the reality of their pain. They may refuse to talk in anything but monosyllabic language, and often ridicule others, or make sarcastic and vicious comments.

3 In cases where the above symptoms are acute, *depression is likely to be present*. These symptoms may be accompanied by eating and sleeping disturbances, and declining school progress.

4 *Other noticeable changes* include developing addiction, becoming more introverted – or, conversely, extroverted – or becoming either more passive or more aggressive. They may change friendships or involvement with peers.

5 *Tidying up their room and sorting out their possessions,* especially giving away things which they had previously treasured. Ascertaining that a pet would be properly cared for if anything were to 'happen' to them.

6 *Contacting old friends and relations,* visiting grandparents, or having any unexpected resurgence of interest in others. Unexpected hugs, or being especially attentive

to younger siblings, particularly when this is out of character.

Usually a loss of some form provides the trigger, and the feelings of despair that this loss arouses lead to the decision to end their life. Parents who fail to support their teenagers at times of loss, no matter how trivial that loss may appear, underestimate the power of that support.

Professor Alan Apter of Tel Aviv University, while addressing the Fifth Annual Conference of the Irish Association of Suicidology, pointed to several personality characteristics that stand out as being important for both fatal and non-fatal suicides.

In the first group of traits, he identifies individuals who appear to be highly sensitive to minor life events, which cause them to become anxious, angry and then depressed. They display an emotional frailty. Many have histories of abuse as children, are extremely unstable emotionally, and abuse drugs and alcohol. They are usually young, with multiple attempts at suicide and self-mutilating behaviour. They use psychological defences such as regression, displacement and splitting.

In the second group, a cluster of traits seems to revolve around narcissism and perfectionism. Individuals in this group appear to have depression related to self-criticism, and are unable to tolerate failure or imperfection. Many of these subjects seem to be quite successful in their lives, and their suicides often come as a complete surprise. Their suicide attempts are usually well planned, not impulsive, and quite lethal. These individuals are often described as private people, and on empirical measures they seem to be low on self-disclosure and intimacy, and high on loneliness – though this is often well disguised.

The third and final group are individuals who have an obvious psychopathology, such as schizophrenia, eating disorders and anxiety syndromes. They feel hopeless and helpless, and are overwhelmed by their psychiatric illness.

Although all of the above information is sobering, it is possible to alleviate the problem. In the US, where teenage depression and suicide have been recognised as a problem that requires active attention, suicide rates have been declining since the early 1990s. This can be seen to be mainly due to the launch of nationwide suicide-prevention programmes in schools, an increase in the numbers of properly trained student counsellors working in schools, and the increased prescribing of SSRIs (Selective Serotonin Reuptake Inhibitors). One must also, however, question whether the increased conservatism in US culture in general, and an increased participation in religious groupings, have also contributed to this trend.

What To Do if You Suspect that a Teenager May Be Contemplating Suicide

1 *The first step is risk evaluation.* An adult who is very close to the teen should be contacted, and any fears surrounding the teen expressed. The adult in question should be made to understand the risk clearly.

2 *The teen should be approached and asked directly if they are considering suicide.* Those who talk about suicide to a compassionate listener are far less likely to go through with it. While it may take a few attempts to 'reach' them – they need to feel sufficiently secure to trust their confidant – most teens are relieved to be able to talk about suicide, and feel emotionally relieved when they do. Such conversations require those close to the teen to put their own reactions – such as hurt, anger, withdrawal and denial – on hold in order to listen.

3 *Do not allow any opportunity for suicide.* If parents think that suicide is impending, they must not leave the teen alone and, as much as is practical, all means by which they may kill themselves must be removed.

4   *Get help.* Contact your physician and begin a course of therapy. In cases where danger is acute, hospitalisation may be the only safe alternative. A suicidal crisis is no time to allow teens to make their own choices: they need to have protection until they are able to function normally again.

5   *Stay involved after the crisis has passed.* Suicide takes energy, planning and organisation. Often teens wait some time after the first crisis before trying again, when they are feeling more energetic. Parents and others need to continue to listen, and to be available to the teens for a long time, even if the crisis appears to be over. They should not seek to downplay the significance of the suicide attempt. By categorising a suicide attempt as not serious, parents can excuse themselves from having to do anything to help. It means that they do not have to face the problem, and the self-questioning and accountability that such a process would involve. Such an attitude exacerbates the teen's isolation and despair, and increases the possibility of a second suicide attempt.

6   *Family therapy is recommended.* The suicidal teen is often acting out the family distress and dysfunction, and their condition may sometimes be used by the family to scapegoat them. In a family where suicidal ideation has a place, the whole system is corrupt in some way and needs to be attended to.

Part Five

Adolescence in the Age of
the Celtic Tiger

On the cultural level narcissism can be seen in a loss of human values – in a lack of concern for the environment, for the quality of life, for one's fellow human beings. A society that sacrifices the natural environment for profit and power betrays its insensitivity to human needs. The proliferation of material things becomes the measure of progress in living, and man is pitted against woman, worker against employer, individual against community. When wealth occupies a higher position than wisdom, when notoriety is admired more than dignity, when success is more important than self-respect, the culture itself overvalues 'image' and must be regarded as narcissistic.

ALEXANDER LOWEN
IN *NARCISSISM*

Never before in the history of this country has a generation of teenagers stood at the threshold of such opportunity. The increased secularisation of Irish society, together with the unprecedented levels of economic growth and modernisation, that has been our recent experience, has produced a generation which, like their parents, believe that the world is their oyster, and we are deservedly revelling in it. Walking down Grafton Street on a Saturday afternoon, I am often in awe of these bright, happy children, who appear so at one with themselves, their friends, and life in general. Most of all, I am struck by their sense of confidence – a far cry from the teenagers who hung out in the Gaiety market in the early 1980s. Their inherent belief and trust in the fact that life will provide well for them has imbued in today's young people a freedom of self-expression that will in most cases ensure that this comes to pass. They have come of age in a country that has come of age.

To fully understand the significance of what is coming to pass, it is necessary to cast an eye backwards into our most recent past, and identify the changes that have occurred within our society that have facilitated this spirit of opportunity. But of equal note are the changes that have not occurred, and these can often be overlooked. While we often hear about how we have turned away from Catholicism, and how it is playing an increasingly diminished role in our national culture, it would be wrong to conclude that, because we are not flocking to church on Sunday mornings, we are bereft of any form of value system. Indeed, it is because we have inherited this strong value system through our cultural history that such success has been possible. Ireland was strongly spiritualistic from Celtic times on, with a robust tradition of monastic piety that predated the rise to power of the Catholic Church in Ireland. Even if we no longer attend church or engage in any formal religious practice, our parents' words still ring in our ears. In order to avoid becoming a narcissistic society – as so brilliantly described by Alexander Lowen above – it is imperative that this value system is fostered and maintained. If it is not, we are more likely to be standing at the threshold of our own self-destruction than at one of great opportunity. To avoid the latter fate, we must ensure that our words ring in the ears of our teenagers – that we give them adequate guidance and values to ensure that they can seize, and fully enjoy, the opportunity with which they are being presented. When it comes to values, it is imperative that we do not throw the baby out with the bathwater.

Secularisation, modernisation and newfound wealth are presenting our teenagers with challenges that we, as parents, have rarely had to face. While the authoritarian nature of traditional society stifled our individuality and inhibited our self-confidence, it did provide a sense of security. In modern-day Ireland, we have taken a leap into individualism and are faced with massive individual choice, without the traditional structures that previously existed to hold us in check. Our teenagers have far more choice, and far more decisions to make for themselves, than we ever had, making the existence of a strong value system a necessity. As a result, they are under enormous pressure. In a society where the number of people in third-level education increased by almost 40 percent between 1996 and 2002, academic performance is becoming increasingly important. On our athletic fields and playing pitches, increased competition and the rise of the celebrity sportsman is leaving less and less room for mistakes or poor performance. Increased exposure to drugs and alcohol means that young people also need to strike the right balance on these issues for themselves.

Aspects of modern-day society are also presenting them with increased challenges. Parental separation, the cult of celebrity – particularly around musicians and reality-show stars – violent media games, a waning of spiritual guidance, an inexorable desire for the acquisition of wealth to bolster self-esteem are all playing their role in destabilising adolescents. This drive for perfection is putting intolerable pressure on teenagers to succeed, spurring a sense of failure and lack of self-worth in those that view themselves as less than perfect. Our young people are being asked to succeed academically, athletically and creatively, as well as to wear the right clothes and own the increasingly expensive paraphenalia of modern-day youth. By and large, they are facing these challenges head on and proving how resilient they are.

It is only by understanding these pressures, and the monumental challenges that our teenagers are often negotiating successfully, that we, as parents, will be able to provide them with what they need from us. These are therefore challenging times for parents too. Traditional parenting methods, backed up by an authoritarian society, are losing both their relevance and their effectiveness. Our challenge is to recognise the changes that have occurred and the effect they are having on our young people, and to adapt our parenting skills accordingly.

Secularisation

I remember vividly arriving in Ring College, County Waterford, at the ripe age of ten years, having lived abroad for all of my life at that stage, and the trepidation I felt being immersed in an Irish-speaking school without a single *focal Gaeilge*. Learning history and geography by rote, in a language I neither understood nor spoke, was a bizarre experience for me. It is no doubt as a result of this that a sentence I learnt from an ageing, crumbling history book is indelibly printed in my memory. It ran:

Is iad cuspoiri na bpein dLithe, muintir na hEireann a coimead bocht agus enoleach.

(It was the aim of the penal laws to keep the Irish people poor and ignorant.)

With the naivety of a ten-year-old, I was roused into a nationalistic fervour. Now, thirty years later, I look back, with the help of more enlightened history books, and realise that it was the aim of the *Catholic Church,* as well as the Penal Laws, to keep the people of Ireland 'poor and ignorant'. For decade after decade, the Church used its power and influence over the political leaders of this country to scupper any attempts at secularisation, such as Noel Browne's Mother and Child Scheme, rightly believing that this would lead to the erosion of its power base. It cloaked its anti-modernist bias in terms of greed, describing secularisation and the quest for material gain as a sin, and therefore not something which Irish citizens should engage. Instead, we were to suffer in this world, to secure for ourselves a more exalted position in the afterlife. Only by acquiescing to the clergy's authority in this life could peace in the afterlife be guaranteed. The monumental power the church had been allowed to amass, which dominated nearly every aspect of the country's social and cultural environment, enabled it to head off any attempts at modernisation until the 1950s. Its control over educational policy can be seen to have been the single most stultifying factor in preventing Irish society from going forward. It is only by recognising the negative effect of this power that we can truly understand the nature of the sudden changes that have occurred within our society of late. Like a couple who have existed within the confines of a bad marriage long after they should have called it a day, and then suddenly separate, we as a society stayed within a relationship with the Catholic Church that was clearly inhibiting if not at times abusive, and are now rapidly recoiling from it. The fact that many citizens of this country have no idea of how that power was amassed and utilised is a poignant indication of the insidious nature of its control. In short, we accepted without questioning.

It is remarkable how many Irish people believe that it was the post-revolutionary nationalist leaders of the Irish Free State that handed over control of many of Ireland's social affairs to the Catholic Church, seeing Catholicism as a form of nationalist protest against Protestant England. This is simply not the case: the nationalist leaders in fact inherited the power of the Catholic Church and were in effect only allowed to operate at its behest. It was the British government, during its long period of rule over Ireland, that forged a partnership with the Catholic Church. It regularly made substantial financial donations to Maynooth, believing that the priests in Ireland would root out any anti-clerical insurrectionist politics after the French Revolution of 1789. The British were solely interested in their political authority in Ireland and had little time or inclination to be involved in the day-to-day functioning of Irish society in general. Rather, they sought control, and the Catholic Church was seen as the perfect instrument by which to control the masses – given the inherently doctrinaire and authoritarian way in which it governed. This partnership was to have far-reaching effects on our society, extending far into the next century. While the Catholic Church was given control over the health, social and psychological lives of Irish citizens, it was its control over education that was its real trump card. It had a vested interest in keeping the masses uneducated, lest an intelligentsia came into being that questioned its power. During this period of its history, the clergy were mainly made up of Anglophiles who were drawn from the ranks of the 'Old English' (descendants of the Cromwellian settlers), were middle-class and urbane, and remained removed from the general citizenry.

By the end of the twentieth century, the church had become more popularised. The clergy was increasingly Gaelic in descent, and largely drawn from the rural masses, thus closing the gap between their identity and that of the population in general. The population had given itself over to Catholicism and the Church, as an expression of its anti-British identity. Piety and devotion were the order of the day. With the lack of any popular lay political leadership with which to align, the Church stepped into the breach. At this time, the Church was quick to discern that a shift in the political atmosphere was afoot that could pose a threat to its position. Nationalist thought was on the rise and gaining momentum, at a time when England was becoming colony-weary. Opportunism, coupled with the change in the nature of the make-up of the clergy, motivated the Church to make a sudden about-turn politically: having previously adopted a policy that castigated the nationalists, by the turn of the century it was taking up the nationalist cause. By promoting the Catholic face of Irish nationalism, it ensured that its power base remained intact.

The great revolutionary leaders of this era were men of their time. They had grown up in a rural, agrarian country, where education was limited and communities were controlled by the local parish priest. They were Catholic through and through. Thus, for them, on entering government, deference to the Church came naturally to them: it is little wonder that they have been referred to as the most conservative revolutionaries of modern times. Their ideological base was not rooted in any great revolutionary ideas but simply propounded the aim of usurping political authority over a country that was already functioning as a well-developed democracy with an effective bureaucracy.

It is therefore not surprising that the thinking of the new political elite was closely aligned with that of the Church. By promoting the power of the Catholic Church, the country's new leaders ensured that there would be no counter-revolution by the Protestant Ascendancy, whose power base they were bent on destroying. Indeed, by the late 1920s Protestantism was seen to have no place within the new Irish state. The Protestant Ascendancy's naive adherence to an idealistic view of Ireland being 'separate' and different, with a culture and language that needed to be protected and fostered, played into the hands of the clergy. Unable for years to properly establish an Irish identity, they adopted an anti-modernist stance. As they saw it, only by insulating Ireland from the world in general could this identity be preserved. Many of these leaders, taking their model from the Catholic Church, also believed that the best form of rule was authoritarian in nature.

Educational control was seen to be the best way of preserving the new identity that these leaders envisioned for the state, and it therefore made sense for them to leave control of education in the hands of the clergy, with the school system being church-owned but state-funded. Clerical control over the educational curriculum can be seen to be the single most important factor in forestalling modernisation and economic growth. The Church believed that only a very basic education in the three 'R's was necessary for the population in general, higher education and intellectualism being left as the preserve of the political and religious elite. It was telling that, in the underground Dáil government of 1919, there was no ministerial portfolio for education: mass education at secondary and tertiary level was certainly not part of the thinking of the fledgling government.

The emphasis on the primary importance of teaching Irish was, in many ways, not a primary concern of the clergy. Religion, Latin and Greek were seen to be of far greater importance than the teaching of the sciences, modern languages, history, geography and the social sciences. The Church clearly grasped that the learning of such subjects might produce a population with the intellectual capacity to challenge the power of the Church or the ruling classes. It was argued that Ireland was, and was destined to remain, agrarian in nature, and therefore that its population had no need for a scientific education. In 1936, an interdepartmental committee concluded that there was no need to raise the school leaving age from fourteen to sixteen, as this would put untold financial pressure on families, many of would lose a wage earner. It was not pointed out that a large proportion of fourteen- to sixteen-year-olds were unemployed, and that the legal age of employment was sixteen. In reality, these fourteen-year-olds were needed by the agrarian middle classes to work the farms, and it suited the Church to keep education at a basic level.

The Church's objections to any form of education that might facilitate a move towards industrialisation and modernisation was particularly evident in the stance it took in the 1940s on the issue of the Vocational Educational Colleges. The Cumann na nGael government had, in 1930, established a secular vocational educational system which the Church begrudgingly accepted, believing that it would be of no great importance. The new system proved to be popular with the population in general, however, and enjoyed considerable growth. By 1940, the Church was becoming increasingly concerned by this growth and began lobbying the government on the issue. Archbishop John Charles McQuaid complained that no religious instruction was included on the syllabus of these colleges, even though such instruction had, by law, to be given. Furthermore, and more insidiously, he objected that there was no Church control over the teachers who taught in these colleges. In 1942, the departmental committee recommended that the VECs be involved in the language revival, and include religious instruction in its program. Henceforth, the system was starved of financing, preventing it from developing into a real alternative to the mainstream education system, and depriving its graduates of access to third-level education. While Éamon de Valera had his own prejudices against the system, which dictated his policy towards the expansion of the VECs, Church influence was integral to the adoption of this policy. In 1954, the Council of Education recommended the formal recognition of the denominational nature of the primary-school system; this was legally implemented in 1965. The Council again vetoed the raising of the school leaving age from fourteen to sixteen, citing unnecessary expense. Within the population at large, however, discontent with the system was growing: the middle classes increasingly turned to private fee-paying institutions to educate their offspring.

It was not until Sean Lemass entered government in 1959 that any really change in the system occurred, but when it happened it was definitive. Lemass and his consorts readily accepted that the goal of the education system should be the facilitation of economic growth rather than the production of 'pious patriots'. In 1962, an independent 'survey team' was established to report on the general state of the educational system in Ireland. Its findings were published in the Investment in Education Report in 1965. Tom Garvin, in his acclaimed book *Preventing the Future,* concludes that: 'The concept of education as a means by which society invested in the next generation informed the entire report, and its assessment of Irish education was devastating. It found that the Irish system was grossly neglectful of the children of the poorer classes in society, and that over half (53 percent) of children left school at, or before, the age of thirteen.' The lack of any instruction in modern European languages was pilloried. In January 1963, Patrick Hillery, as Minister of Education, sent a memorandum directly to the Taoiseach proposing a new nationwide system of post-primary education. Then, out of the blue, on 10 September 1966, Donough O'Malley announced to the press that free education to Leaving Certificate level at age eighteen was to be provided by the government immediately. He intended to increase the status of the VEC system so that it had a position equal to that of the secondary-school system, and would offer a range of non-technical educational subjects as well. He challenged the vested interests that might oppose him, asserting that they would fail in their opposition policies. The Catholic Church was suddenly sidelined.

This unauthorised announcement caused widespread surprise, and even dismay, in official circles – including on the part of Lemass – but succeeded in that it set the goal: the notion of free secondary education was now in the public mind. There were drawbacks, however, as the scheme had to be implemented with great speed and without adequate planning, and this resulted in the squandering of financing. It can, however, be argued that this was a small price to pay for what was to come in the future as a direct result of the implementation of these recommendations. Free primary and secondary education was followed by the establishment of Regional Technical Colleges, which were gradually elevated to the same status as second-level and third-level institutions. Two new technically oriented third-level colleges, known as National Institutes of Higher Education, were established. These later became the University of Limerick and Dublin City University. University attendance figures jumped from 9,000 in 1961 to 20,000 in 1971. Between 1964 and 1993, the total numbers in third-level institutions increased from 18,000 to 93,000, and this increase has continued to the present day. Today, the once-coveted primary degree does not have the value it once held. Masters degrees are increasingly becoming the norm, with growing numbers are pursuing PhDs. Irish policymakers, and the population in general, belatedly came to realise that our real industry was intellectual in nature and human-resource-centred, and they have pursued educational prowess with a vengeance. No longer were the objections of the Catholic Church to be taken into account

In the new independent Ireland, the clergy exerted its power through largely invisible channels, influencing public policy in a broad range of social, cultural and economic areas. Although it maintained this stranglehold until very recent times, government policies adopted in the 1950s signalled the beginning of the end. The Irish population slowly began to see that it was being left behind in a modern world and that to catch up and keep pace with other countries would necessitate a challenge to clerical power. Loyalty to the Catholic faith was never in question, however, and the essentially Catholic nature of the Irish population remained strong until at least the 1970s. The huge attendances at the papal visit in 1979 were testimony to this loyalty, but they can now be seen as symbolic of the ending of an era. In its wake, over the course of two decades, scandals surrounding the actions and behaviours of members of the clergy shocked the Irish nation. The ramifications of these scandals slowly began to reverberate through Irish society. While the older generations in general lived in a state of quasi-denial – excusing, rationalising and at times justifying the actions of the clergy – the younger generation was outraged and horrified by them. The long-standing relationship between the Catholic clergy and the Irish citizenry came into jeopardy, and this is still the case today. Whether a new, more healthy relationship, which respects the individual, comes into being remains to be seen. It is certainly the case that our teenagers need some form of spiritual guidance that imbues in them a strong value system. Faced with the quest for material gain that is becoming a driving force in our society, they desperately need a counterbalancing force to save them from the negative aspects of excess. Whether the Catholic clergy is able to make amends for its past actions and reinvent itself remains to be seen.

Industrialisation and Economic Development

Ireland's embracing of the concept of economic modernisation was delayed by two interlinked and equally powerful forces: the Catholic Church and the 'Independent Ireland' ideologues. The idea of a self-sufficient, agrarian and Catholic nation insulated from the rest of the world was heralded by the generation of political leaders that came to power in the wake of independence. Outside influences that might corrupt the minds of the Irish were to be abhorred. Industrialisation and modernisation were seen to be the greatest threat to this ideal, and active measures were to be taken to protect against them. Economic and social policies were adopted to protect this mistaken ideal, and these succeeded in keeping the Irish population in general poverty-stricken and uneducated. The accusations levelled at the Penal Laws had in effect become state policy.

It was not until the next generation of politicians gained power, under the leadership of Sean Lemass, that the folly of these policies began to be recognised and questioned. This new generation of leaders were no longer in thrall to the idea of a rural, pious society, and clearly perceived that industrialisation, modernisation and stronger trade relations with the outside world were imperative if the situation of the population was to be improved. Moves to modernise were taken on only slowly, however. In 1949, the IDA was established, to research what areas of industry could be developed. There was from the outset controversy over the research nature of the IDA, with some, including Lemass, arguing that decisions had to be made, and strategies formulated, immediately. It became increasingly clear was that, whatever policies were adopted, Ireland lacked a sufficiently well-trained and well-educated workforce to make any real advances. Meanwhile, mass emigration was draining the country of manpower. It fell back on the newly established semi-state enterprises to provide on-the-job training as an alternative to secondary and tertiary education. This was the inevitable consequence of the government's continued reluctance to challenge the Church's power within the educational domain. State services were also seen as an alternative way for young people to advance economically, and as a result jobs within the army, police and civil service were greatly sought after.

The idea of state investment in industry was slow to take root, even though the introduction of Marshall Aid to Ireland in the late 1940s exposed the ruling elites to the idea of the value of competitiveness and investment, and to the American business ethos in general. The economy was still foundering throughout the 1950s, even experiencing a decline in industrial output. By the 1960s, the combination of economic crises and increased overseas opportunities combined to force change, giving the policymakers enough latitude to abandon protectionist, isolationist policies and look outward towards Europe and America – and the idea of free trade. Ireland joined the United Nations in 1955 and increasingly sought to take its place within the new European order. Investment was made in industry, technical education – and education in general – and infrastructure. The IDA played a key role in attracting European and American investors, who were attracted by the low-wage economy, and Ireland's English-speaking, relatively well-educated population. These new policies paid off: economic production began to rise and eventually reached the same growth rate as other OECD countries. By the 1970s, industrial output outstripped agricultural output for the first time, and the urban population was greater than the rural population.

Industrialisation and economic growth inevitably brought about the modernisation of Irish society. The population was increasingly exposed to the popular culture that was developing in America and Europe, and it was quick to devour it. Ireland's teenagers of the 1960s markedly abandoned the concept of 'Irishness'. Instead, they coveted the music and dress styles that were in vogue in the international arena, and by so doing forced change. The Irish teenager was eventually born.

Modern Popular Culture and the Irish Teenager

One can only marvel at the extent of the changes that have occurred in our society in just two generations. Placing this change within my own family experience, if my father as a young teenager in the 1940s had been given a preview of the life his grandchildren would be living in 2006, he would have dismissed it as an Aldous Huxley–style fantasy. He well remembers the considerable outlay his parents made back in 1946 to purchase their first radio, the invention of which was considered miraculous. It was through the radio that the most of the Irish population was introduced to the concept of life beyond their immediate geographical boundaries, and the existence of Europe and America became a reality for them, rather than a concept spoken of by distant politicians.. For most people, at this time, Europe and America were foreign and alien lands to which family members disappeared, in search of a means of existence, often never to be seen again.

Recent changes in educational policy ensured that Irish teenagers, like their counterparts in the industrialised world, were being given a resting period before they took on the full responsibilities of adulthood. This generation eagerly absorbed the ideology, music and cinema of international teenage culture, which encouraged the formation of individual identity and the right to personal views and opinions. Catholic doctrine was losing its stranglehold on the Irish psychological make-up.

171

In the 1970s, the computer was to make its debut, and modern cyberspace technology was born. The computer, more than any other technological advance, has revolutionised the lives of our young teenagers. They were born into the age of the computer: they have at their fingertips instant communication, endless access to contemporary music, entertainment in the form of every kind of computer game imaginable, and unlimited access to any form of information they seek. But not every aspect of this new cyberspace is to be applauded. Young teenagers are posting up personal information and photographs on websites, leaving themselves open to indiscriminate comment, and privacy is increasingly a thing of the past. In recent times, a group of girls from a well-known Dublin Ladies school set up a 'Hateboard' website, where every inconceivable slander and slight directed at other contemporaries could be posted for all to see. Desensitisation is increasingly the order of the day.

The mobile phone is the other significant technological advancement that influences the lives of teenagers, and it too has both positive and negative effects. It is reassuring for us as parents to be able to contact our young teenagers at any time, and to establish their whereabouts. It is also reassuring that they too can contact us if they are in any immediate difficulty. On the other hand, young teenagers use the medium of text messaging to say things that they would not be able to say face to face. The more they use this form of communication to disparage and bully others, the easier it will become for them to speak them face to face. Moreover, text messaging, and the use of the internet, allows them to bypass experiences that require courage, and they miss out on an important learning lesson in communicating and relating face to face. We as parents are only waking up to these aspects of modern communication, and clearly need to guide our offspring in what is acceptable and unacceptable behaviour in cyberspace.

This rapid modernisation of our culture is presenting us with challenges other than in the field of technological communication. Aspects of contemporary youth culture can also be seen to exert a negative influence, if proper guidance is not given. For instance, while music can be life-enhancing and can open our teenagers up to new ideas and new forms of emotional expression, it can also at times exert a negative influence. On listening to the lyrics of some contemporary pop stars, I am struck by the level of emotional turmoil, angst and pain they reflect. Today's lyrics speak of discrimination and alienation, and of the pain of family breakdown, depression and suicide. They speak of maternal rejection, of abandonment, and of relationship breakdown. They portray a generation in crisis, grappling to make some sense of life. Underlying many songs is a deep anger, and these songs are popular because so many people identify with the pain and anger they express.

But if these songs are merely describing how so many teenagers feel, one may ask what is the harm in them. For the balanced, healthy teenager there is indeed little harm, and the emotions expressed probably have little impact on them or their lives. But for a young adult who is desperately trying to cope with and manage negative emotional experiences, there is no better means of evoking emotion than music. If these songs are putting forward the notion of suicide as a form of heroic protest, or as an escape from pain, they are putting lives in danger. If they are speaking of feelings of hatred and anger, they are bringing our youth further into these emotional experiences. While they may be expressing the malaise felt by many, the negative emotional impact that they are having cannot be underestimated.

We often hear of the content of video games, and the violence they promote, without actually acknowledging just how they promote it. Three-dimensional, full-motion video games that involve aggressive and criminal acts bring the game player into the reality of the game. They are not experiencing the game objectively, but subjectively. They are in fact part of the action.

The line between reality and fantasy is nowhere more smudged than in today's films and television series. As violence, abuse and depression invade our screens at an ever-increasing pace, and in ever-more-vivid graphics, it becomes increasingly difficult for our teenagers to discern what is normal or not in the real world. In the developing adolescent brain, where the powers of discernment are not fully developed until the age of twenty-five, this can be potentially fatal. Unable to judge accurately the consequences of their actions, they impulsively react in ways they have all too clearly seen on screens.

Striving for Perfection

If a person has learned never to regard his affairs as purely personal matters . . . but to consider all problems as part of a con munal life . . . he will not try to conceal defeat. . . . He will not feel himself shaken by failure, nor topple from a position of superiority, but in his humanity he will renew his courage and make a fresh start, either in a different field of activity or in a different manner of approach within his old field. And that is what we call daring to be less than perfect.

ALFRED ADLER

Striving for perfection is a very identifiable outcome of the Celtic Tiger economy, and our commensurate affluence. However, few reflect on the fact that perfection is not a realisable goal but is rather something to aim for. But many of us have failed to grasp this fact and therefore live in a world where we feel like failures – that we never measure up, and that there is always someone better, more perfect than us, against whom we must compete. Instead of accepting our inadequacies as merely human, we prefer to deny and hide them, always living in fear that we will be exposed. Our feelings of self-worth are founded on what we are seen to have achieved. A flimsy foundation indeed!

So how does this affect our society, and more importantly our teenagers? We increasingly live in an age where material wealth is held out as our main objective in life – the sign of true success and indeed perfection. It is therefore very important to be seen to have the ideal partner – the hero or heroine of the fairy tale – and we want our children to be seen as heroes too, they must perform in the classroom and on the playing field, looking good and wearing the right clothes, and being intelligent, happy, confident and, most of all, impressive. That they may have different feelings on the issue – that they may attach more importance to other things – is unacceptable to many parents.

So what is the effect of this quest for perfection on our teenagers: what does it say to them about us, and about themselves? Firstly, it teaches them that the acquisition of material wealth is their primary purpose, and that, in order to succeed, they must compete and be better than others. The principles of spirituality – of helping, caring, and serving others' needs – are to be allowed only if they do not threaten this primary goal. It is imperative in the age of the Celtic Tiger to think of ourselves rather than others. Our young adults naturally come under huge pressure as they attempt to live up to these expectations.

As our third-level educational system is increasingly seen as the bedrock of our economic growth, and our greatest national asset, competition within this sphere is becoming ever more cut-throat. While academic success is commendable, and an invaluable asset for any young teenager entering the world of adult-hood, in cases where it is used to judge the worth of an individual it can be counter-productive. Academic pressure drives some to stop engaging in the normal activities of youth, as study becomes a priority. The evaluation of the teenager's self-worth will be made by a faceless examiner based on a few days' performance in exams. Often this pressure becomes too much for some young adults, and they turn it on themselves, 'acting out' – in anger, alcohol or drug abuse, or suicide – or 'acting in' – becoming depressed, developing food disorders, and so on. This increased pressure to perform academically is fostered not only by parents but also by schools. More and more, schools have entered the arena of competition. This is increasingly the case in some private fee-paying schools, which equate their image with academic and athletic performance. Pressure can be intense, as a teenager's worth is judged on the basis of performance; individual worth and difference do not fit the picture.

More and more, the teenager's performance on the athletic field is becoming equally important. Encouraged by parents, peers, and the schools themselves, they are taught to go out on the pitch and be aggressive, and to do what is required to win. This is nowhere more evident than at schools rugby matches, where schools that value performance and image rather than participation are easily recognised. The growing aggressiveness, and even violence, on playing pitches is cause for concern. The active encouragement on teenagers from some schools to take performance-enhancing substances is no less than physical abuse of our youth. A sixteen-year-old client recently related to me that, when he refused to take these substances, he was dropped from the team and ostracised. He also spoke of the Masonic-type secrecy the team was forced to hold on this issue. To 'squeal' was seen to be contrary to team spirit, and an unacceptable disloyalty. We teach our young boys this, and then react with outrage when, under the influence of alcohol, the pressure cooker explodes, and their learned aggression is activated to the extent that the end result is a death. We then disassociate ourselves and our children, and demand justice – or a scapegoat? As parents and as a society, we need to engage in a process of self-examination, and face the fact that our actions and expectations are producing an environment that creates the space for tragedy.

Part Six

Parenting in the Millennium

Without doubt, the method of parenting used with teenagers in modern society plays a pivotal role in maintaining the mental health of our young people. If teenagers have had to adapt to an array of challenges and pressures in the twenty-first century, then so too have parents. No longer do traditional methods of parenting appear to be working in societies where choice, freedom and ample leisure time are the norm for adolescents, and where the old factors of control – employment, religion and community – are increasingly irrelevant. In the face of such loosening of control, parents often find themselves at a loss, fumbling along in their parenting roles, without any clear vision or understanding of the psyche of the modern-day teenager, hoping for the best, but often left smarting from the results of this happy-go-lucky approach. Today's hectic and over-stimulating environment puts untold demands on parents' time, leaving little space for self-reflection or observation of family dynamics. The energy required to ensure that the family unit is functioning in a reasonably satisfying manner, and that the needs of all members are being met, is often hard to muster. This burden of responsibility on parents is accentuated by the modern trend towards individualism, which often leaves parents without the support of either the extended family or the wider community. In some cases, a lone parent is left with the full responsibility of parenting their children.

Given these circumstances, it is not surprising that parents either find themselves at a loss, or simply do not notice possible flashpoints until a serious problem has developed. In a country that prides education and knowledge so much, the level of awareness on familial issues is sadly lacking. Parenting courses within communities, designed to impart knowledge and actively promote the effective functioning of families, are virtually non-existent. Some schools have attempted to step into the breach by providing talks for parents, but they are fighting an uphill battle. While there are plenty of books on how to parent infants and toddlers, few exist that provide information on the realities faced by families as children grow up. Given the pressures that are exerted on today's teenagers and parents, and the increased possibility of more serious mental health difficulties arising, parents need a helping hand to impart them with sufficient knowledge to be able to negotiate the challenges they are facing in more established families.

Family Dynamics

The family is the single most important factor in the development of the individual. It is our experience within the family unit that establishes our view of the world and provides the blueprint for the way in which we relate to each individual we encounter in life, no matter how significant – or insignificant – that encounter may be. It is through our inter-familial relationships that we acquire a view of ourselves and establish our identity in relation to the world. It is the primary function and responsibility of the family unit to ensure that each of its individual members is provided with sufficient nurturing and affirmation to enable them to leave that unit and go out into the wider world with a sense of real worth, self-value and independence. It is the responsibility of parents, as 'leaders' of the family, to provide such an environment.

Increasingly, we hear the terms 'functional' and 'dysfunctional' bandied about in relation to families, without any real understanding of the theory behind these terms. As a result, the terms are often inappropriately used, with families being categorised as either 'functional' or 'dysfunctional' – which assumes stasis and rigidity. This negates the reality that families are in fact dynamic units that are continuously changing, and are therefore better viewed on a broad spectrum. In other words, the notion of a fully functioning family is a goal to be aimed for but does not exist per se. We might be better advised to aim for the 'good enough' father, the 'good enough' mother and the 'good enough' family.

The quality of the relationship between parents is the single most important factor in determining the functioning of such a family system. In single-parent families, the quality of the relationship of that parent with both themselves and the world in general is of primary importance. In families where a new partner for the parent has been brought into the household, the quality of the relationship between the parent and the third party, together with that with the other parent, is significant. The concept of modelling is all-important: it is imperative that we as parents act as role models in relationships and display behaviours that are seen to respect and value the worth of all individuals involved. The security of children and adolescents is determined by the amount of security they evidence within these adult relationships.

In a properly functioning relationship between parents, it is vital that the value and worth of both spouses is respected and nurtured. The prerequisite for this is that each parent has a strong sense of self-worth and engages in self-reflection – in other words, that they take personal responsibility for themselves. They are therefore able to express themselves freely without feeling threatened, and at the same time to be open to the premise that, while their feelings are valid, their view of any given situation may be distorted, to some degree. In such scenarios, there is neither right nor wrong, and a secure space is created for negotiation.

Most conflict arises within couple relationships when either one or both parties feels that their needs are not being met within the relationship. It is the responsibility of both parties involved to attempt to negotiate for the provision of these needs within reason, in a reasonable and empathic manner. To do this, a basic level of love and security is necessary: each spouse needs to be able to feel that they can ask for their needs to be met without fear of being punished, ridiculed or dismissed, and that their request will be given due consideration. They likewise must respect their partner's right to reject their request, in a non-defensive manner. A strong sense of self is therefore necessary on the part of both people. In such an environment, it is possible to negotiate and determine whether the fulfilment of those needs is possible.

The basic needs that seek to be met within a couple relationship are the need to be loved and feel secure, to feel supported, to be sexually gratified, to share responsibilities, to feel autonomous and free to pursue their own individual potential, and to be financially equal. In a family where the individual needs of the parents are expressed and negotiated within a loving and secure environment, freedom of expression and positive communication exists, and the value and worth of each parent is supported and validated. In such a situation, the parents are acting as positive role models, and by resolving their conflicts in an accommodating atmosphere they provide their children with the security to be able to express their feelings and communicate openly. The children within these families intuit that it is all right for them to be themselves, and that difference is acceptable. They are able to differentiate between their behaviour and their person. Such children feel a great sense of self-worth and do not feel that they have to adapt their basic self to accommodate others and, by so doing, to avoid conflict.

In dysfunctional families, inter-parental conflict is not negotiated, and defensive forms of behaviours and communication are adopted. The core difficulty in such situations is that the parents have a poor sense of self and are plagued by insecurity, particularly the fear of being rejected or abandoned. These difficulties arise from their experience in their family of origin, and can generally only be surmounted if they take responsibility for, and deal with, the core issues that have created such insecurities. Such a task involves great courage, and is therefore avoided by many people. In such cases, defensive behaviours are to some extent adopted; these behaviours impede free expression within the family and dictate that all members adapt, and in some way deny their basic selves. This can in extreme cases have devastating effects, and lead to the declining mental health of the family.

A family that ceases to function freely becomes 'defended'. Defensive relating strategies are adopted, generally through either a domineering or an over-protective stance being adopted by one or more family members. Domineering parents typically control, blame, criticise, ridicule, over-punish, and dismiss others' declared needs. Over-protective parents use timidity, manipulation, possessiveness, non-assertiveness, neglect of self, people-pleasing behaviours, and constant seeking of reassurance. Children will often adopt the behaviours of one parent, especially when dealing with siblings. Within such a family, nobody feels free to be themselves, and high levels of insecurity predominate; this results in the adoption of behaviours and roles which, it is hoped, will stave off rejection and abandonment. Such behaviours include alcohol and drug dependence, possessiveness, control through aggression, emotional or physical withdrawal, silence, over-involvement with each other, dependence and over-neediness, suicide threats or attempts, rageful outbursts, and so on. The failure of the parents in such families to resolve the difficulties within their relationship constructively generally has a negative impact on their offspring.

Feeling that their needs are not adequately being met by their spouses, parents in defended families may turn to their children in an attempt to have these needs met. They often over-bond with particular children, and alliances are forged in a childish attempt to become the favoured parent. The child is thus being used to affirm the parent, instead of vice versa. This sets the stage for inter-sibling rivalry, as each child seeks to 'secure' themselves with one or both parents.

Parents in turn use power, control, perfectionism, criticism, contempt, blame and rage to secure themselves. The children no longer feel free to be themselves, or that they are acceptable as themselves. Instead, roles are adopted whereby personal feelings are suppressed, in an attempt to impress, and indeed control, the parent. Such roles include being the helper, the hero, the perfect child, the rebel, or the scapegoat. In the case of the 'rebel' role, the child reacts against control and not only attempts to establish their own power but also deflects attention away from the troubled parental relationship. These roles are adopted to compensate and restore balance to the whole family system: for instance, if the father is a workaholic or an alcoholic, and rarely at home, one child will generally compensate for this deficiency and step into the role of the emotional spouse to the mother. In such scenarios, children are forced to deny aspects of themselves and cut off their feelings: the hero must be courageous and strong, and will therefore not allow any fear, or feelings of vulnerability, to surface.

Love is therefore conditional, and is given on the premise that each child measures up to the rules demanded by the roles that they are playing. They are driven by their desire to please and, in so doing, they give up their independence, their self-value, and their spontaneity. This loss of self generally leads to personal difficulties later in life, especially when such children form long-term relationships and establish families themselves.

In any assessment of whether a family is functioning or not, levels of conflict are a key issue. Conflict signals a malaise or possible dysfunction within a family. However, the conflict is not in itself the marker of health; rather, the way in which that conflict is resolved determines how well a family is functioning. The first step in such resolution is the acknowledgement, primarily by the parents, that a problem does actually exist. Many highly dysfunctional families do not get even this far, as the acknowledgement of the problem is seen to be too threatening to the unit as a whole, and is therefore denied. In families that are functioning more effectively, greater self-responsibility is recognisable, and while difficulty in facing the issue may be experienced, the individuals involved acknowledge the difficulty, and each takes responsibility for their part in it. Thus step two involves a commitment to take measures to resolve the problem, seeking outside help if necessary. Next, family members need to confer about the best possible way to reach a resolution, and then attempt to execute that solution. The execution of the solution may be difficult, and it needs a commitment from all relevant members to see it through, with continued monitoring of the situation.

Success in conflict resolution brings great security to each member of a family and provides invaluable role modelling.

Through it, family members realise that they can bring difficulties to the family table and will not be rejected for doing so. They likewise realise that help and support is at hand, and that adequate action will be taken to resolve any difficulty without resorting to denial, blaming, criticising, punishing and so on. Freedom to be themselves is the resultant effect. Families who fail to resolve conflict increase their dysfunction, make love conditional, and exacerbate their difficulties in the long run.

Parenting Teenagers

One of the most poignant social effects of the embracing of secularisation and modernisation within this country has been the diminished roles of patriarchal and authoritarian forms of control within our society. Nowhere is this more evident than in the way in which we approach parenting, especially the parenting of adolescents. It is often with shock that parents realise that authoritarian-style parenting no longer holds sway, and in fact has a detrimental effect on the well-being of our children. The whole notion of alternative, non-authoritarian parenting practices is therefore receiving greater attention in Western, modernised societies, including Ireland.

Nowhere is the parenting role more uncertain than in relation to parenting teenagers; given the nature of adolescence, this is not surprising. As young children have under-developed psyches and low cognitive capabilities, they are wholly dependent on their parents and blindly trust them. However, as they progress into adolescence and seek to develop their own individual identities, the process of full separation from their parents is initiated. In most cases, this involves the assertion of their own will, opinions and judgements. Parental supremacy and infallibility is at times heatedly disputed. This is a natural course of events. In traditional societies, however, life was more structured and predetermined, and, with little choice available to them, the incidence of a conflict of will and opinion was limited. The community, particularly the religious community, played its part in determining the outlook on life of adolescents. Political rule was authoritarian in nature, and simply involved obeying. The arrival of democracy in this country, as in others, heralded a new way of thinking. People began to embrace the idea that they had the right to have a say in their lives and their futures. Freedom and choice became the new ethos. By the 1960s in Ireland, this new ethos was taking root, and began to operate in all aspects of our society, including the family. It is only in the past decade, however, that this approach has begun to have a serious impact on the way in which we parent teenagers. Our parents by and large relied on authoritarian-style parenting skills, often adapting their views only out of necessity. When the economic boom hit this country, however, bringing with it unlimited choices and possibilities, we have had to give up the last vestiges of authoritarianism, or suffer the consequences. What is clearly evident now is that, as a style of parenting, it no longer works, and indeed has a negative impact on our young teens' self-esteem, leading them to adopt aberrant behaviours in an attempt to cope with the challenges they faced in today's society.

To date, little information or support has been offered to parents to help them adopt new, more creative and more relevant ways of parenting. No clear guidelines about what is expected of them in relation to monitoring and supervision, or in setting limits or boundaries for their teenage children, have been outlined. So far, logic and reason, together with a strong value system, appear to have guided us broadly along the right path, but we need to increase our awareness on parenting in general.

Four distinct styles of parenting have been identified; these appear to be related to the level of control parents perceive themselves to have. Parents who feel in control tend to adopt healthier parenting technique than those who perceive that they have lost control over their adolescent children. Parents can be classified as 'authoritative', 'authoritarian', 'indulgent' or 'indifferent'.

Authoritative parents

Authoritative-style parenting is deemed to be the most successful style in producing healthy, balanced adolescents, who have high self-esteem, are able to look at situations from various perspectives, and do not become involved in risk-taking behaviours. Such parents are warm, supportive and understanding but also firm, providing structure to their lives of their teenage children. Their teens realise that certain reasonable expectations are placed upon them, and rules exist that encourage them to be responsible for their own behaviours. The reasons for certain rules are explained, and these reasons help teenagers to see things from a different perspective.

Authoritative parents behave as positive role models. They set standards and hold boundaries but are also more likely to give explanations, and to reason and negotiate with their young teens, than to be dictatorial and punitive. They monitor and supervise their young adults, and above all provide adequate guidance to them. They value the right of the adolescent to have different views and opinions from them, and seek to resolve conflict without resorting to controlling and shaming behaviours. The young person's autonomy is supported, in that individuality is respected and encouraged. Often, they are involved in the decision-making processes within the family, rather than being presented with the outcome of decisions made by the parents. This is seen to encourage more pro-social behaviour, and higher levels of moral reasoning. In such families, young people are allowed to move towards individuation, while remaining connected to the family, and parents in particular.

Authoritarian parents

Authoritarian parents do not feel that they are in control of their children, and therefore resort to rigid rules and punishment in order to allow themselves to feel that they are in control. They place a high value on obedience and conformity. They punish misbehaviour and do not encourage autonomy or individual thinking. Such parents are more likely to resort to anger as a tool of control, and by so doing instil fear in their teenagers. Parental expectation and the need to succeed are high in the families of such parents.

Indulgent parents

Indulgent or permissive parents behave passively in relation to their children and do not provide leadership, either due to a poor sense of self or as a result of time pressure. They fail to set boundaries and standards, and instead 'befriend' their teenagers and treat them as adults. Real guidance is lacking, and a laissez-faire attitude prevails. These parents have little expectation of their children and do not believe in any form of punishment. The resultant effect on children is that they generally feel inse-cure and unsafe, as they do not feel that they are offered any real protection by their parents, neither do they feel that any prob-lems that arise for them will be treated seriously. They are less mature and more irresponsible, and place too high a value in their peers. They also tend to be more influenced by peer pres-sure.

Indifferent parents

Indifferent parents fall by and large into the 'neglectful' catego-ry. They display little interest in the lives of their children, and spend as little time with them as possible. They are over-involved in their own lives and are emotionally unavailable to their chil-dren. They fail to either monitor or supervise the whereabouts of their adolescents. This lack of care often leads to their teenage children being more impulsive, as they receive no guid-ance on boundaries, and becoming involved in high-risk behav-iours such as juvenile crime and drug and alcohol addiction.

Guidelines for the Effective Parenting of Teenage Children

The real key to effective parenting lies in the ability to respond, rather than react to or ignore, various situations and issues that arise in relation to adolescents. This skill distinguishes authoritative-style parenting from the other three types. In authoritarian-style parenting, parents try to establish control by adopting various types of behaviour, and in indulgent or neglectful parenting they neither react nor respond. Adolescents need their parents to respond to them as a means of giving guidance and valuing them as individuals. Authoritative parents tend to use the following skills that ensure that they respond to their adolescents' needs:

1 Effective Communication

Effective communication involves certain key elements that ensure that all parties to the communication believe that their view has been listened to, taken on board, and reasoned with, whatever the outcome. In such a communication, the basic dignity and value of each individual is respected, and self-esteem is promoted.

Listening is the first key element in any communication, but it is surprising how many parents falter even at this early stage. By listening actively, one person communicates to another that they believe that what the other has to say is of value and deserves attention. Indeed, they give their full attention – which is picked up on in non-verbal communication such as eye contact, posture and so on. Encouragement is therefore given to the person to continue talking until they feel they have fully expressed what they are feeling or thinking. This is not the case in communications where reaction is the immediate consequence and where advice, blame or criticism is immediately seized upon. In such a communication, the person concludes that they are not being either listened to or understood, and seek to stop the conversation, feeling that their needs have gone unmet. By actively listening, one person communicates their unconditional acceptance of the other by not reacting. Often, in such cases, we have personalised what is being said, rather than standing back and looking at the deeper issues that are driving the communication. Clarification is often necessary to avoid misinterpretation. This does not mean that we necessarily agree with what is being said, but that we are open to another person's view and will put forward our own view in a non-aggressive or nondefensive way.

Non-judgemental language

Non-judgemental language enhances communication by focusing on the behaviour in question, rather than the individual. The person is, as such, seen as separate from the behaviour, and this leaves space for a frank discussion of the behaviour itself, thus ruling out the necessity for a defensive reaction. The communication is further enhanced by keeping the language self-focused and explaining how the behaviour impacts on you, rather than taking an accusatory and blaming stance. Therefore, one should avoid communications such as 'You are totally selfish and never think of anyone else' and instead 'own' your feelings by saying 'I feel upset when you do things like that as it makes me feel like you do not care for me.'

Non-controlling communication

In such communication, others are allowed to fully express their feelings, beliefs and opinions, without consequences. Unsolicited advice and blame are avoided. Manipulation, dominance and control do not feature. Time and space is given for full expression of each individual's concerns, and messages are not personalised but are viewed as being about the other person.

Empathic communication

This involves being able to enter the emotional world of the other person and view things from their perspective. It communicates warmth, care and safety, and the person feels that they are in some way being listened to and understood. In empathic communication, the people involved feel free to express their feelings without them being devalued, and a feeling of equal worth prevails.

Provisional communication

Provisional communication is an antidote to self-righteousness, and starts with the premise that either party may be right or wrong. Therefore, a battle of wills, that involves the assertion of one individual's views and opinions on the other, does not ensue. The space for negotiation therefore exists, and the result may be compromise rather than one person being right and another being wrong. Furthermore, in such a non-threatening environment, one party may come to the conclusion that they were indeed mistaken and reassess their view.

Direct and clear communication

In such communication, it is clear who is sending the message, to whom it is being sent, and what exactly it is saying. The speaker 'owns' the message that is being communicated.

2   Communicating the Certitude of Love

Of all the parenting skills, the ability to communicate strongly your love for your adolescent children is by far the most important. Any adolescent is more capable of taking on the challenges presented to them by the world if they know that they have a space at home where they are truly loved and supported, no matter what. Too often in modern times, however, we can be careless about our demonstration of love. It should not be assumed that, simply because we provide shelter and food, and all the material needs of our adolescent children, it is a foregone conclusion that they know that we love them. Communicating love requires more than that.

Most important is the time we give to our teens. We often assume that, as they are now young adults with their own friends and social lives, they do not need to spend time with us. While time spent with friends is important to teenagers, time spent with parents is often of more real value to them. With their growing levels of discernment, teenagers are quick to question the love of a parent who professes to love them but is in fact too busy with their own lives to spend any time with them. As the pace of our society continues to quicken, with ever-more-gruelling work schedules and increasing numbers of social engagements, it is imperative that we make room for spending normal time with our children, watching DVDs with them, discussing everyday issues, and so on. It is in these interactions that they feel valued and get a sense of their own worth as autonomous individuals. Parents who go to their adolescent children's sports activities and show an interest in their extra-curricular activities communicate to their teenagers that they value them. Teenagers need to see that at all times their needs for attention are given priority over our hectic schedules.

There are other invaluable ways of communicating love to young adults. They too, like young children, need to have it verbally communicated to them that they are loved. They also need demonstrations of physical affection, such as hugs and kisses. Do not assume that a teenage girl does not enjoy snuggling up on the sofa like a little child with her mother: teenagers often love the moments when they are allowed to be loved like little children. Likewise, teenage boys, just because they are young men, should not have the demonstration of physical affection withdrawn from them, especially by their fathers. Too often in modern society, the value of inter-family touch is dismissed.

Respecting individuality

The parent, or parents, who sets out with a rigid idea of who and what all their children are going to be will soon run into difficulty. With such set expectations, they fail to recognise the individual talents and aptitudes of each of their children, and put pressure on them to conform and perform as they see fit. The individual psychological make-up of each child is ignored, and an untold injustice is done. In the academic field, too often parents expect or demand that a child performs well in academic subjects, and fails to recognise that the child's real talent lies in the creative or musical field, or elsewhere. By putting pressurise on a creative child to do well in maths or sciences, they undervalue the child's real strengths and hit at their self-esteem as the youngster is unable to satisfy the expectations placed on them, and equates this with failure. Likewise, in the emotional field, some children are more sensitive and introverted than others: while one sibling may not blink an eye at interpersonal relations, or may not be overwhelmed by an emotional difficulty, his or her sibling may find such challenges arduous. Therefore statements like 'Look at how Laura does not let that bother her' are unhelpful and self-defeating. This is not to say that a parent should pander to a child's sensitivity by protecting them from situations they find difficult; they should instead step in with extra support, assurances and encouragement to help the youngster through their particular crises. Shielding children from difficult challenges ultimately works against the child, as important lessons go unlearnt.

In other areas, too, individual differences between teenagers exist and need to be respected. Some children like space alone, while others need the constant company of friends; some have no problem with others using their property, while others do. It is therefore necessary for parents to regularly sit down and reflect on the individual needs and strengths of each child separately, and determine how they can be facilitated on an individual basis.

3   The Teaching of Responsibility

The fulfilment of individual responsibilities is a key factor in the effective functioning of any system and is therefore essential to the development of every individual. Within the family system, it is the parents who must teach their adolescents to be responsible. Central to the learning of this lesson is the necessity for parents to demonstrate that they themselves are responsible people. The adolescent who learns to be responsible within the family system will take this sense of responsibility out into the world with them.

What exactly is it that defines a responsible individual? First and foremost, responsible individuals have a healthy regard for all other individuals, irrespective of circumstances, and therefore demonstrate an unconditional positive regard in all their interactions with others. Bullying, victimising, racism and other forms of prejudice are not part of their make-up. They therefore take responsibility for themselves in relation to other individuals and behave in socially acceptable ways, always checking the tendency to be self-absorbed. They have developed the ability to view realistically the way in which their actions affect others. They respond to others' expressions of feelings with due regard, without slighting or diminishing them, but with a level of understanding that allows them to view situations from more than one perspective. They seek to meet their own and others' needs, thereby demonstrating self- and other-care. They therefore give due attention to physical, emotional, intellectual and spiritual well-being. They communicate clearly and directly, and therefore take full responsibility for their thoughts and feelings. They treat problems seriously and endeavour to resolve conflicts through negotiation.

People who behave responsibly are primarily in control of their behaviour and believe that they are accountable for it. Within the family, it is essential that parents stay in control of their behaviour if they are to teach responsibility. No member of a family should seek to control the behaviour of another family member, but instead they should seek to make that family member responsible for that behaviour. If one spouse fails to remain in control of themselves, it is essential for their offspring to see that this behaviour is confronted by the other spouse, in a loving and constructive way. This is by far the most important learning lesson for adolescents. When parents do this with each other, it gives them more credence when confronting aberrant behaviour in their children. This is especially the case with adolescents, who are quick to pick up on double standards.

It is the responsibility of all family members to see that harmony is maintained within the family. It is here that sanctions come into play. Sanctions should, by and large, be predetermined, and applicable to all, so that fairness is guaranteed. They should by no means be accompanied by the threat of the withdrawal of love, or a demeaning of the personal worth of the individual concerned. They must be behaviour-specific, and not personalised. It is therefore necessary to sit down with young adolescents, discuss the spectrum of possible misdemeanours, and decide on appropriate sanctions with them. What is acceptable and unacceptable behaviour is thus clearly defined, and there is no room for courts of appeal and plea bargaining! Sanctions must be applied consistently to all members, so that favouritism does not become an issue. Each family member is fully aware of the sanction they will receive for specific misbehaviours, and is therefore more open to being accountable for their actions. A word of caution is necessary here, however: misbehaviours are often an indication of an underlying dissatisfaction, and parents should seek wherever possible to identify what that dissatisfaction is and to relate to it in a positive and affirming manner.

4　Guidance

Adolescence is often a very turbulent period in the life of a child, one in which they no longer have decisions made for them but instead have to make their own path in the world. Never before have teenagers in Ireland been faced with so many choices regarding themselves and their future lives as they are now, and never before have they been faced with such challenges to negotiate. As our society becomes less structured and more individualistic, the implications of individual choice and self-responsibility become increasingly significant. Career choice, which affects a teenager's ability to provide for themselves in the future, is becoming a more pressing issue in a country that is experiencing huge economic growth, and in a society that increasingly values material wealth. Socially, human behaviour in general is less bound by rules and regulations, and young adolescents are therefore left to determine their own boundaries in relation to sex, drugs, inter-personal relationships, and so on.

While they seek to establish their own identity by developing self-autonomy, it should not be underestimated how much they actually rely on parental guidance. With so much uncertainty to be navigated, the knowledge that they have wise and affirming guides to fall back on for advice and help is paramount. But in order to ensure that teenage children feel that they have this safe place to come back to, parents need to realise that it is guidance, not diktats, that is needed. Therefore, when teenagers go to their parents looking for advice, it is imperative that parents explore the issues they are facing, and the implications of various courses of actions, rather than immediately supplying a solution. They need to see things from the teenager's perspective, to ensure that the adolescent feels that the parent has a full understanding of the situation. If the parent immediately jumps to a solution, the teenager feels unheard and often misunderstood, and may therefore view their parent as being out of touch with the realities of their life.

5   A Strong Value System

Family values, or the lack thereof, can be seen as the single most important factor in the future lives of our offspring. How the family unit sees itself in relation to the rest of the world shapes the view of the world that each individual within the family adopts. A family that values all its members, shows due concern for all individuals, stresses the worth of hard work, places a value on finances that is not deemed to be over-indulgent, encourages physical exercise and sport, and values creativity, by and large produces offspring who have a strong value system, who have a robust sense of themselves and their own worth, and become responsible members of society.

It is here that the issue of the 'generation gap' comes into play! It is widely perceived that young adults hold widely divergent views on issues such as sex, drugs and morality compared with their parents, and that this creates widespread conflict and disagreement. In fact, the conflict associated with the generation gap in the adolescent years may be a misnomer. Research consistently shows that the values and attitudes of teenage children and their parents tend to be more convergent than divergent, and that greater differences exist in the values held by people from different backgrounds, than from one generation to the next. As has already been noted, teenagers tend to socialise in peer groups that foster the value system of their family of origin, and participate in negative peer groups only when there is a more serious dysfunction within the family. Research showed that beliefs relating to work, religious and moral values, and personal attributes are by and large consistent within families. Adolescents by and large report that they respect their parents' opinions, and seek their advice on the major issues they face.

Conflict with parents tends not to centre around the big issues but is more to do with daily responsibilities, and the breaking of minor rules of behaviour that affect the functioning of the family system. Conflict tends to arise around household chores, time-keeping, and the degree of autonomy that is to be granted to the teenager during the various stages of adolescence.

In relation to parenting styles, it can be argued that authoritarian-style parenting adheres too strongly to a prescribed value system, which does not have an underlying sense of the value of the individual and is enforced, rather than encouraged. In the cases of indulgent or neglectful parenting styles, the parameters provided by a strong value system do not exist, and boundaries tend to be haphazard and inconsistent. In authoritative-style parenting, a strong, clearly defined value system underlies the family ethos.

6   Supervision and Monitoring

Most studies that have been conducted into the positive and negative behaviour of teenagers agree on the issue of monitoring and supervision. It has consistently been found that parents who supervise and monitor where their teenage children are, who they are with and what they are doing, find that their children are less likely to be engaged in self-destructive or, in particular, anti-social activities. These parents allow their children to engage in activities outside the household, especially social activities, but keep a vigilant eye on what they are doing. Again, this aspect of parenting is a feature of authoritative parenting. In authoritarian-style households, adolescent children are given little freedom to engage in activities outside the home, and when they are, they are so laden down with rules that a breach of these rules in virtually inevitable. This then gives the parents the perceived right to tighten the freedoms and rules even more. They thereby fail to give their adolescents the space to develop their own autonomy. Sustained use of these principles often leads to outright rebellion on the part of the teenager, as the rage the young adolescent vents the frustration they feel about being restricted to such an extent. In indulgent and neglectful homes, little or no monitoring exists, and adolescents as a result have too much freedom and too few boundaries. In such cases, the safety of the child may be put at risk, as the innately instinctive nature of adolescence is not reined in. The lack of accountability and responsibility for their actions and whereabouts results in them failing to develop their cognitive skills and judge the consequences of their actions. Risk-taking behaviours become the norm in such cases.

Fathering and Mothering

For adolescents, the parental home still remains an important anchor point, and the attachment system will become reactivated at times of threat, illness or fatigue.

JEREMY HOLMES
IN *JOHN BOWLBY AND ATTACHMENT THEORY*

The reality of the changing and diverse nature of modern-day families, has necessitated a shift in the rather rigid understanding we have traditionally held with regard to the roles of motherhood and fatherhood. As the proliferation of families where both parents work, of single-parent families, and of families where one parent is not properly functioning in their role as a parent, abound, we as a society need to look at the masculine and feminine qualities that each sex brings to parenting, and view these qualities in a more holistic manner. In other words, it has become increasingly necessary for each parent not only to display the qualities in parenting that fit their gender, but also to reflect on and embrace the qualities which have traditionally been associated with the opposite sex as well. By developing both their masculine and feminine sides, parents are more adequately furnished with the capability to provide for all of their children's needs, encouraging them to nurture both their male and female sides. This is especially the case in single-parent families, where the presence of one mature, well-balanced adult is often better for teenage children than the presence of two immature adults. Having said that, the active involvement in their lives of two mature, well balanced parents is the preferred option to ensure optimum results.

But what exactly are 'male' and 'female' qualities?

Traditionally, feminine qualities include warmth, nurturing and affection. They encourage emotional sensitivity and expression, and movement inwards – in other words, self-reflection. They are intuitive. They focus on 'being'.

Masculine qualities traditionally seek progression: they encompass physical strength, energy and assertiveness, and favour logic over emotion. Male qualities are dynamic, and encourage drive and initiative. They value completion and achievement. They are solution-orientated, and forward- and outward-looking.

The Role of Fatherhood

The silence from my father throughout my growing-up years was deafening. My life has been full of sadness at being cheated of what is the rightful inheritance of every child – the unconditional love of both parents. The problem with never seeing my Dad is that I idealised – and idolised – him. . . . He became, in my childish imagination, a glamorised amalgam of movie star looks and Santa Claus kindliness, with the uncanny ability to know me even better than I knew myself.

AYESHA HUDSON
IN THE *SUNDAY TIMES*, 18 JUNE 2006

Too often, the role of fatherhood is seen as being of secondary importance to that of motherhood: the view that 'the right place for a child is with its mother' prevails. Little recognition is given to this function in modern Irish society, especially by our courts. Time and again, in cases of separation and divorce, the mother is favoured over the father in relation to child care, and the role of the father is diminished. Fathers are given 'access', and often their right to see their children is restricted: the only real right in relation to access is that a child or adolescent has at any given time the right to have free access to both their parents.

Any real debate on the issue of joint parenting and the important role of fatherhood is given little airing space in the public domain. John Waters stands out in my mind as the lone intelligent voice in the wilderness: he consistently attempts to bring the issue of fatherhood into the public domain, often against the odds. Prior to an edition of RTÉ's *Prime Time* at Christmas in 2005, a programme was screened that attempted to highlight the disaffection and marginalisation of a growing number of separated fathers. The programme failed properly to deal with the complexity of the issues involved, and an opportunity was, I believe, missed. By failing to place adequate emphasis on the importance of fathering, we do a disservice to our children; a more thorough knowledge of the function of fathers is necessary in our society if the rights of children and adolescents are to be upheld and protected.

The role of a father is often pivotal throughout the life of a child and adolescent. As well as the fact that fathers pass on their genetic information to their children, we are all born with an innate expectation of being mothered and fathered. Through the early months of a child's life, the father gives love and protection to the mother of a kind that she cannot get elsewhere. Through the love relationship, he protects and provides, and by so doing allows the mother to give her full attention to the newborn infant.

Then, as the child slowly develops, the father's primary function as a guide comes into play. The father comes to represent a sense of 'otherness' to the child. It is through his or her contact with the father that a child begins to grasp that a world exists outside its relationship with the mother. At this early stage in his development, the child still sees himself as 'part of' the mother. The father therefore helps the child to develop a view of himself separate from the mother, and, through his guidance, the child takes his first steps away from the mother into the world. The father facilitates this by drawing the mother out from the exclusive relationship she has with the child and back into the outside world, and the child is thus also drawn into the outside world. Intervening in this way in order to prevent the development of a dependency between the mother and the child can be difficult for the father, and requires courage and strength on his part. In cases where the parental relationship is fraught with difficulty, the mother is not effectively drawn away from the child, and the mother invests the emotion she should have for the father into the child, thus making that child 'mother-bound'.

As the child moves away from the mother he turns to the father, who helps him to develop a path of consciousness, and by so doing brings order to chaos. During this process, the father ultimately provides protection to the child while he or she makes these steps. The child begins to establish boundaries between himself and the outer world, taking on the concept of the individual will. He also develops the ability to say 'yes' or 'no to his innate drives and instincts; the building of such boundaries is a necessary part in the development of the child's personality.

As the child begins to step out into the outside world and establish his boundaries, he gradually begins to build up his 'persona', which incorporates the social skills he develops in adapting and relating effectively to the outside world. As a child by his very nature seeks to win the approval of his parents, he will by and large develop a persona that is consistent with the expectations of his parents, including their moral, social and cultural values. It is necessary, however, that the child gains some sense of his own will, in order, at times, to challenge parental expectations so that he does not lose his own individual identity.

In aiding this process, the father brings structure to the child's identity and life, giving them inner strength. If the father is either not present or represents a negative influence, the child will not develop a strong sense of self, will have a problem with boundaries, and will live out a fear of being overwhelmed by chaos and disorder. This is especially the case for boys. In future years, this sense of inner chaos will lead to the adoption of compulsive behaviours or an exaggerated need for structure and order when it comes to the outside environment. The sons of such men may have difficulty forming intimate relationships and, more importantly, committing to them, as they may fear being overwhelmed by the feminine, as they were in childhood. At this vital stage, fathers therefore help their children to develop self-confidence and the ability to fight for their needs and rights.

By investing masculine energy into the development of the

child, the father also develops the child's ability to focus and think logically. This creates a counterpoint to the emotional world of femininity and allows the child to think about their feelings, thus helping them to develop insight and preventing them from getting lost in emotion. A balance is necessary here, however: too much logic at the expense of emotion is counterproductive and causes the child to split off from feeling. The aim should be for a child to experience emotions and then to be able to apply logic to these feelings, in order to make sense of them.

Lastly, it is more often than not the father that brings the notion of discipline to the child. Discipline is bound by authority, and by the very nature of male qualities (the moving outward into the world, logic, aggression and physical strength), authority tends to lie more strongly with the father. A sense of responsibility on the part of the child comes through discipline. It is necessary, however, for the father to be authoritative rather than authoritarian.

All these aspects of fathering continue to play an important part in the life of the developing adolescent. The continued fostering of structure and boundaries is crucial to the developing adolescent identity and his or her drive towards autonomy. The father continues to encourage the adolescent's drive into the outside world by focusing on their future careers and on the need for them to achieve their potential. By helping to activate their offspring's thinking capacities, they provide a counter-balance to the instinctual drives that are characteristic of the adolescent years. It is therefore not surprising that in many cases of male juvenile crime, a strong father presence is noticeably absent. In these cases, there is no moderating influence on the instinctual aggression that exists for males in these years.

Fathering Teenage Boys

As already noted, it is one of the primary functions of the father–child relationship to break the intensity of the bond between mother and child, and to develop 'male' qualities within the child. This is especially necessary in the case of boys, who have a greater need to be drawn into the world of the masculine and gain access to their maleness. Boys look to their father as an incarnation of masculinity, and from them develop their view of how to be a man in the world. Therefore, fathers are important and necessary role models to their sons, who tend to grow up like them – sometimes in spite of themselves. A loving and strong father presence is therefore essential to the development of a mature and well-balanced son, especially during important transitional stages such as going to college, leaving home, starting their first job, getting married, and becoming a father themselves. Elements of mental turmoil tend to intrude at times of significant change, and a son needs to be able to rely on his father to provide structure and order for him at these times.

While the process of separating from his mother is initiated in the early stages of a boy's life, it gains in energy and importance from seven years of age. At this stage, it is necessary for the father to actively engage with his son and to introduce him into the world of maleness. Playing sport, going fishing, going camping and taking part in other such activities fosters this process. In going out into the world with his father, the son grasps how the father engages with the outside world and other people, and he takes his cues from him. The boy also learns from the father the need to be proactive and to go out and achieve, and it is he that generally encourages goal-setting and achievement.

It is therefore crucial for teenage boys to spend real time with their fathers, and to develop warm, loving and respect-based relationship with them. Boys need to connect with the physicality of their fathers and experience them as role models, and those who experience this have much higher levels of self-esteem and confidence, and feel more driven to achieve, than those who do not. It has been suggested by psychologists and sociologists that fathers place the condition of achievement on the relationship and that this pushes the boy forward and encourages a sense of responsibility in them.

Through their fathers, boys also learn the ability to connect with and articulate their feelings. They observe their father's interactions with the opposite sex and take note. Therefore, the father's view of women and love influence the son's sexuality, and his future relationships with women. If a boy sees his father in a genuine, responsive love relationship, it serves as a role model for him in the future, and he will seek out such a relationship himself. If his father holds women in disdain, so too in many cases will the son. If his father avoids female relationships, in many cases the son is likely to as well. Often the messages that teenage boys pick up from their fathers hinge on the unspoken rather than the spoken, as they are often reluctant to discuss the nitty-gritty with their father.

The adolescent years are marked by emotional turbulence, and a strong father presence is therefore necessary to hold the teenage boy's more aggressive and volatile male emotions in check. The father's ability to discipline, and to promote logical thinking, acts as a counter-influence to these emotions; so too does the structure and order he provides. Given all this, there is a strong argument that the increased difficulties young boys are experiencing in modern-day Ireland are to some extent explicable by the phenomenon of absent fathers, fathers being given limited access, and fathers spending too little time at home due to pressures of work or other reasons.

Fathering Teenage Girls

While a father's role and impact on the life of his son is crucial, the father–daughter relationship during the teen years is also extremely important. A loving father can make a girl feel cared for and protected, and therefore valued. The extent to which the father is present and involved in his daughter's life has a strong impact on her developing sense of self-worth, especially in regard to her sexuality. The way in which a father affirms a girl's sexuality often determines the nature of her future relationships with men. A father should therefore attempt to encourage and support his daughter's growing maturity, and embrace it, neither clinging too strongly to the idea of her still being a child, nor absenting himself, in the belief that she is now a grown woman who no longer needs the guidance of her father and whose needs will be met exclusively by her mother.

It is in the Oedipal years – roughly between the ages of seven and nine – that girls form strong romantic attachments to their fathers, viewing them as heroes, and as the incarnation of what a man should be. They idealise their fathers to such an extent that they often fantasise about ousting their mother in some way and winning the coveted prize of being their father's wife! These early fantasies are the first stirrings of a girl's sexuality and her notion of what a love relationship is and should be. Through her relationship with her father, she will learn about other heterosexual relationships, and later in life she will often seek out a man who is similar to her father. The exception to this is when a girl's father is a negative role model for her; in such cases, she will either seek the opposite in a man, or avoid intimate relationships with men completely. In other words, the way in which a father relates to his daughter is crucial to her future happiness in relationships.

Daughters will often go out of their way to gain the approval of their father. They differ from sons here in that the approval of the girl's father is bound up with the way they see themselves as a young woman. They are therefore far more sensitive to any remarks their father may make about them, especially if these remarks relate to their femininity. It is important for fathers to affirm their daughters not only when it comes to their feminine attributes but also in regard to them as individuals. Praising them for their achievements is extremely important, and therefore a balance needs to be struck.

During the pubertal years, as their sexuality develops, girls' relationships with their mothers may go through a tumultuous phase. In such cases, they often turn to their fathers for affirmation as a counter-balance to what they are experiencing in their maternal relationships. It is important that fathers do not become embroiled in this conflict but instead affirm their daughters and lend them a sympathetic ear. In cases where this does not happen – often in cases where there is a strain in the marital relationship – a father may side with his daughter against her mother and use her for his own ends – as a way of 'getting at' his partner. Such a stance can cause untold damage to a girl's developing ideas of romantic relationships. Firstly, they may over-invest in their father's energy which should instead be going out into teenage heterosexual relationships, and maintain an idealised view of their father. This results in any future man being unable to measure up to the young woman's idealised notions of what a man should be. It also sets her up in competition against her mother and at some level encourages her to dismiss her mother's worth as a woman, thus doing untold damage to an essential relationship. Her experience of being involved in a three-way relationship often establishes a pattern for her future relationships, where she will often feel herself to be in competition with another woman. Such relationships preclude intimacy. It may also result in her devaluing female company, of which she may be distrustful.

The navigation of sexual tension between adolescent daughters and their fathers can be very challenging for the men involved. Fathers at times find great difficulty with the fact that their little girls are developing into young women who may have sexual feelings for men, and the primal instinct to protect them may come in to play forcefully. Their awkwardness about their daughter's developing sexuality may lead them to avoid any physical contact with them, for fear that such contact will be viewed as incestuous. Girls often feel this physical withdrawal as a form of rejection of their womanhood.

The most constructive thing a father can do in such a position is to relate to his daughter in a non-judgemental, undefended way. He can play a vital role in discussing with his daughter how men think and behave, thereby giving them a realistic perspective on the other sex. In so doing, he will bolster her confidence to develop friendships with boys as equals. Most of all, by modelling a loving and empathic relationship with his wife, a father can model to his daughter what to expect of a relationship.

Too often, however, a father can get lost in the nuances of the father–daughter relationship and withdraw emotionally or physically, or both. At this vulnerable stage of a girl's life, this approach can have a powerful impact on her feelings of self-worth. She may grieve for the special relationship she once had with him, and start to believe that her becoming a woman is in some way unacceptable to him. Fathers who withdraw tend to criticise their daughters as a way of coping with the changed circumstances of their relationship. These girls tend to have difficulty trusting men in future relationships and may become involved with men who are domineering, adopting passive roles so as not to be rejected.

Other fathers become over-protective of their daughters at this stage. They become too emotionally involved with their daughters and try to protect them from any possible source of pain, believing that they should only experience happiness. This may result in the daughter feeling bound to accede to her father's will at all times and failing to assert herself and fight the battles for autonomy that are so necessary in this stage of her development. She does not want to hurt her father, so she engages in what is known as a relationship of reciprocity, seeking to protect him from any pain too.

A father may also become over-protective by becoming too controlling, and allow his daughter no sense of being independent. In such cases, the daughter may fail to develop either any real experience of the outside world or the coping skills they will need to overcome future crises in their lives. Such fathers adopt this style of parenting because they have an exaggerated perception of danger, from which he feels bound to protect his daughter. It results in his daughter feeling that she always needs a man to protect her, and, in her relationships, becoming reliant on men who dominate and over-protect her. In extreme cases, such a need to control can lead to outright tyranny, where all the members of the family are made subservient. In this situation, however, the father is not seeking to protect his family as such but is demanding that his own needs be met, regardless of what is best for others within the family. Daughters who grow up in such homes get a distorted view of male and female roles in relationship and grow up believing that men have to be obeyed. They are thereby left open to being abused by men as they do not know how to make a stand when they feel their boundaries are being invaded.

The Role of Motherhood

The young child's hunger for his mother's love and presence is as great as his hunger for food.

JOHN BOWLBY
IN *THE SECURE BASE*

If one of the main masculine qualities, and one that is essential to fathering, is an outward-bound movement into the world, it is the inward-bound feminine quality that contains many of the essential elements of mothering. To many, home is symbolised by the maternal presence, whether a mother is out working and is active in her own life or not. The feminine qualities of nurturing, warmth and affection, emotional understanding and expression create what is known as a 'secure base' for the child. In fact, the mother–child bond has captivated man for centuries as the most primal expression of unconditional love, as evidenced in the art and literature of all the world's cultures.

In the early months of a child's life, this bond is in fact so intense that the infant is unable to differentiate between himself and his mother. The mother is the main provider for the child's needs and soothes the infant when he is in distress. While fathers also contribute to the provision of these needs, they are still viewed from a distance – unless the father is the primary caregiver which may sometimes be the case. The quality of this initial bonding with the mother can have long-term implications for the future development of a child. A mother who is present and attuned to every need of the newborn infant ensures that a secure attachment develops between the child and his mother. A child who attaches to the mother securely is imbued with a basic trust that the world is a safe place and that their basic needs will be fulfilled. As a young child who is securely attached begins the process of separating from the mother, he confidently moves out into the world and away from his mother, knowing that his mother will be there for him when he experiences danger.

Not all children experience secure attachment, however. In cases where the mother's care is unpredictable or rejecting in the early months of life, a child develops what is known as an 'anxious' attachment bond. In such cases, a child who is uncertain that his needs will be met at any given time develops both a need to be in close physical proximity to his mother and an intolerance to separation. While a securely attached child will initially cry and object to separation, he will then be able to accept the reality of the separation and get on with what he is doing. By contrast, insecurely attached children will either pine for their mother's presence and become clingy, fearing abandonment, or, conversely, may remain detached from the mother, cutting off from warm feelings towards her, and by so doing protect themselves from emotional pain.

In cases where the mother is needy and uses the child to secure herself, the child is likely to be anxiously attached, as it takes on the role of care-giver rather than care-receiver. In such cases, the father is often unable to break the bond between the mother and child that is necessary during the Oedipal years, and the child becomes mother-bound.

Research has shown that the original type of attachment bond with the mother provides a blueprint for how an individual will attach in future relationships, especially romantic ones. Nonetheless, anxiously attached children can go on to experience secure attachments if at some stage they come into close contact with someone who is able to alleviate their insecurity and provide them with a secure attachment.

A securely attached mother is able to give her children the love, care and nurturing they need without having to 'own' the child. She thus provides the child with enough containment that they can separate and develop as an individual, knowing that she will be there for them when they need her. Such a mother needs to be active in her own life, with sufficient interests outside of her children that she does not depend on their company to feel fulfilled.

This sense of self is critical in the Oedipal years and during adolescence. As one of the primary tasks of adolescence is to develop autonomy in the teenager, a secure attachment bond with the mother is necessary. While teenagers may spend increasingly less time in the presence of their parents as they progress through adolescence, it does not necessarily follow that their need for a warm and understanding mother in whom they can confide lessens. Indeed, it could be said that, while they may not need their mother's input in so many instances, when they do turn to her, their need to feel secure is more intense. Also, given the fact that adolescence is an emotionally turbulent period, where feelings are intensely experienced, the need on the part of a teenager to have someone who will help them to negotiate their feelings may be greater. During this phase of development, the mother moves into a more equal relationship with her children and plays a different and more intimate role in their lives. While it would be wrong to say that they become friends, an element of friendship comes into play. Mothers tend to be more actively involved in their teenagers' lives, acting as confidants and being more attuned to the social interests and inter-personal skills of their offspring. Although men give their teenage children emotional support, surveys suggest that teenagers turn to their mothers more often on issues such as friendship, relationships and sex.

A mother who is able to be available to her children and listen to the difficulties they may be experiencing during their teenage years without becoming too emotionally involved in the situation plays an extremly positive role in her children's psychological development. Too often, parents believe that, once a child reaches adolescence, they are mature enough not to need maternal emotional support and advice, and that such needs will be provided by the teenager's peers. This is simply not the case: while peers do provide support, especially in the case of girls, on important issues the mother is still the primary port of call for a teenager when it comes to issues around emotional expression, with the father also helping to make sense of things for him or her.

Mothering Boys

The mother–son relationship has traditionally prompted a great deal of interest – as well as much ridicule. Maybe this is because the influence of this relationship is so readily recognisable in adulthood. There are clearly certain elements within this relationship that can be seen to influence a man's presence in the world, especially when it comes to relationships.

The nature of the mother–son relationship is more easily understood when one looks at these elements. If feminine qualities embrace the world of emotion, and place a greater importance on relationship, then the gender relationship is more acutely felt within the mother–son bond. It follows that, if a mother is not having the importance she attaches to relationship met by the outside world, she will turn to her son or sons to affirm her femininity. Similarly, if she fails to be affirmed in her womanhood, she will naturally look for affirmation in motherhood. Moreover, society appears to deem it more acceptable for women to be proud of and admire their son's sexuality than for men to do so with their daughters. This therefore, unconsciously, allows for a more psychologically incestuous bond between mother and son.

It is generally held at some level that women admire men, while men lust after women. However, another factor in the equation is that fathers tend to expect their sons to connect strongly with the masculine, demanding that they place more importance on achievement and on going out into the world, whereas mothers often feel that their partners are 'too hard' on their sons. This naturally stirs in the mother the need to provide a more protective and nurturing bond with her sons than with her daughters, who are closer to hand and more 'in touch' emotionally. Lastly, if the feminine quality is more inward-bound than outward-bound, mothers are faced with an increased challenge when faced with the needs of her son. The son will naturally go out into the world, while the mother is forced to negotiate her instinct to keep him inward-bound.

It is, I believe, because of these elements that the relationship between sons and mothers is probably the most difficult to navigate, and the one most prone to enmeshment. In the Oedipal years, the mother has to experience her first letting go of her son, and facilitate the father's need to guide the boy away from the mother and into the outside world and the world of masculinity. The more secure a mother is in her sense of self, and in her marital relationship, the easier she will find it to facilitate this process, and even be proud of the steps her son is taking. The son will not feel overwhelmed by the mother's emotions and will therefore not feel guilty for abandoning her to some degree. Instead, he will go out into the world secure in his attachment to his mother. Mothers who fail to have their needs met by the outside world or through the marital relationship will find this task more arduous, and in some cases will resist it outright. In such cases, the son will be insecurely attached, feeling that he will in some way suffer a reprisal for his abandonment of his mother. He will either cut off from his mother and emotionally detach, as a means of coping with the situation, or else, overwhelmed by the level of her emotion, will become clingy and frightened, and fail to detach at all. In the latter case, a pattern will be established which he is likely to repeat in his future relationships with women – either regarding them with suspicion and remaining aloof, of else over-attaching and becoming co-dependent, while still primarily seeking out the mother love. In this way, his relationships will, to a certain degree, tend to remain unfulfilling.

Again, it is in their offspring's adolescent years that mothers have to let go of their sons. This phase is made all the more difficult by the developing sexuality of the son, and by the fact that the eventual 'leaving' of the son is becoming more of an inevitability. Moreover, it is often the case that difficulties within the marital relationship are more pronounced at this stage; this often forges an increased reliance by the mother on the mother–son relationship and fuels a reluctance in the mother to let her son go. I believe that, deep within the heart of many women lies the – sometimes unarticulated – belief that, although their partners may abandon them, their sons never will. Some mothers may therefore seek to control and manipulate their sons, in an attempt to secure their future. Such mothers have difficulty accepting their son's girlfriends and are always looking to find fault in them. No girl will ever be 'good enough' for him, in her eyes. Their sons therefore experience great internal conflict in attempting to develop their own autonomy and to individuate fully. Some never succeed – to the detriment of their future relationships.

For some sons, the experience may be the opposite to this. Their mother may never form a strong bond with them, and may remain ambivalent towards them for an extended period – possibly for their whole life. They do not face any of the challenges of letting go, because a strong bond was never established in the first place. If there are female siblings, they may be much favoured by the mother, thus increasing the extent of rejection felt by the males in such a family. As their sons reach adolescence and start taking on their sexual identity, the relationship between the mother and son often deteriorates even more. The mother, who may in many cases have deep-seated issues with men, feels threatened by their developing masculinity, and rejects them even more. Often there is a real strain within the marital relationship at this stage – if indeed there has not already been a complete breakdown in this relationship. In such cases, mothers often justify their actions by claiming that boys are primarily the responsibility of their fathers, and in cases of separation may want the father to takes on their parenting fully and have the boys live with him. Fathers within these units are often deeply hurt themselves as a result of the breakdown of their relationship with their wife, and either rage or become prone to depression. The overriding consequence for the sons is that they are imbued with a deep sense of distrust for women, which significantly affects their future relationships.

Thankfully, such cases are not the norm, and most mothers navigate the process of letting go of their sons successfully, even thought they may find it very difficult. They value their sons as young men in the world, and support their moves towards individuation, being neither over- nor under-involved in their lives and their relationships. While such a mother may have a natural curiosity about her son's romantic relationships, she does not attempt to influence him but instead allows him to navigate this area without prejudice. Expressions such as 'I told you that that girl . . . ' do not feature in their vocabulary. In relation to their son's career, while they may guide and advise, they ultimately accept their son's chosen career path. This may also be difficult for them.

Mothering Girls

The mother–daughter relationship, while prone to dips, is enduring in nature, and becomes richer and deeper from the late teenage years on. From this relationship, a young girl learns what it is like to be female in the world, being tuned in to her mother's dreams and aspirations as a woman in the world, whether these dreams are fulfilled or not. With her mother as a role model, a girl entering the adult world learns how to love and nurture, and how to develop close and meaningful relationships and friendships. Like the 'good enough' father, the 'good enough' mother is able to provide her daughter with enough love and guidance to ensure that she grows into a self-assured woman who is able to face and negotiate the various difficulties that life may throw at her. While the 'good enough' mother will make mistakes – she may at times try to control, or dictate, and at other times be too lax – she will be able to recognise the error of her ways and learn from her mistakes. She will stay in close emotional connection with her daughter until the latter is equipped with sufficient skills to be able to make her own way in the world and fend for herself.

It is in the Oedipal years that a mother may first experience rejection at the hands of her daughter. As the young girl fantasy-bonds with her father, she may begin to view her mother as a nuisance – as someone who demands too much time from the man of whom she herself is seeking the attention. If the father fails to temper his daughter's infatuation, tension between mother and daughter will develop. If the mother suffers from insecurity herself, she will anxiously vie for her husband's attention and will also feel conflicted: the idea of vying with her daughter for the attention of her husband will seem inappropriate and hard to take on. Further feelings of hurt may enter the frame, as the young girl dismisses the mother, putting her down and viewing her as being 'cranky'. The mother may be viewed as a dictator and the father as all sweetness and light. This view is, of course, distorted, like most fantasy bonds. If both parents mediate this crucial stage of development in the girl's life, an air of realism will return: the mother–daughter bond will deepen, the young girl will return to the world of the female, investing time and energy in her female friendships, and will, with them, view the world of boyhood from a distance. Romantic notions about the father may now be turned on some hapless eight-year-old boy, who becomes the object of the girl's fantasies, and her prime target in games of kiss-chase and spin-the-bottle.

As the young girl approaches puberty, tensions between mother and daughter come to the fore again. Faced with her daughter's budding sexuality, the mother is inevitably faced with her own aging process. How at ease she is with this process often influences the level of tension between her and her daughter. The mother who feels that her worth as a woman is being shown up in some way by her youthful daughter may resort to demeaning her daughter in countless ways: making harsh comments about her weight or looks, criticising her behaviour, and questioning her competence. In a worst-case scenario, the mother will attack the girl at any opportunity, mocking her ideas and accusing her of inappropriate sexual behaviour. She will instil in her daughter a deep sense of unworthiness, often provoking a backlash, through the adoption of self-destructive behaviours by the girl. This tension is fuelled not only by female competition but also by parental fears for the girl's developing sexuality. As the same-sex parent, the mother will generally have to carry more than her fair share of responsibility for the daughter's sexual behaviour. It is she who is left to instruct, and even to police her daughter's sexual mores, especially in cases where a father is having difficulty accepting his daughter's sexuality, and simply avoids the issue. How at ease the mother is with her own sexuality often determines the level of tension between them. Too often, the mother carries both her own, and her partner's, fears for the girl's sexual well-being.

The fear of rape, STDs and pregnancy are major players in the female adolescent years, and parents would do well to reflect on these fears so that they do not drive the relationship between them and their daughters. While it is natural for parents to have these fears, seeking to control the girl's social and sexual life is often counter-productive. Girls who are overprotected in general lack the skills to be able to handle themselves when they are faced with difficult situations. Repressed sexuality, as we well know in this country, is a dangerous energy that will seek expression in some way. The most a parent can really do in this situation is to relate to their daughter, giving her adequate information on sexual behaviour and its pitfalls, and on the various consequences of these behaviours, and seek above all to instil in her a sense of responsibility about her own sexual mores. Responsibility, and the ability to set and adhere to her own sexual boundaries, are crucial, and need support. A failure on the part of parents to engage with their daughters in these matters makes the likelihood of difficulties arising in the girl's life greater.

Life is not perfect, however, and teenage pregnancies not only occur but are becoming more prevalent in Ireland. In the case of teenage pregnancy, the support of a mother for the young woman, who is likely to be confused and often frightened, is immeasurable. The mother is perceived to hold the secrets of womankind, and she is the person to whom a girl will naturally turn for help. Shaming a young girl at this stage can have extremely negative consequences, and telling a young girl that her life is ruined can cause untold damage. The pregnancy is a reality, so everyone needs to get on with it! Mothers who are able to support their daughters at such traumatic times deepen not only their daughter's but also their own sense of womanhood, and by so doing solidify the mother–daughter bond.

Mothers should not, however, seek to befriend their daughters but should instead see themselves as role models and as supportive guides. In situations where a mother becomes her daughter's best friend, an inequality always exists within the relationship, and the mother will inevitably become too powerful a force in her daughter's life. The mother may seek to relive her youth through her daughter, determining how she should look, whom she should date, what career she should choose, and so on. Often she will seek to have her unfulfilled dreams lived out by her daughter; unfortunately, however, these are her dreams and not her daughter's. The young girl may be passive and have difficulty asserting herself, demurring to her mother's wishes, opinions and beliefs. She will above all else seek to please her mother and will therefore suffer from a deep insecurity. She will emerge out of adolescence unable to differentiate from her mother, as she will have failed to fight the necessary identity battles. She will have no real sense of who she is or what she really wants. A variation of the mother who wants to stand in the limelight with her daughter is the one pushes her daughter forward to attain her unlived dreams, while she herself stays in the background in the role of semi-martyrdom.

Dual Parenting

Throughout this chapter, I have referred to the role of mother-hood, and the role of fatherhood – and the masculine and fem-inine qualities assocaited with them – as separate and distinct entities. I will now seek to qualify this, in an attempt to make sense of parenting in Celtic Tiger times.

There is increasing debate among psychologists, psychia-trists, therapists and others on the issue of the 'maternal' instinct, and the traditional roles of motherhood and father-hood. The burning question is whether these instincts are innate human traits, or whether they were seized upon and developed in earlier times, in order to put structure on, and give a sense of order to, traditional economies and societies. If the latter is true, we must ask ourselves whether this view is relevant in the con-text of modern-day parenting. In an age when both parents are often in full-time employment, or indeed where only one parent is resident in the family home, it no longer serves us to stick to the traditional view of 'mother' and 'father' roles, and 'mother' and 'father' characteristics and qualities. It is becoming increas-ingly clear through experience that a parent of either sex is able to fulfil both roles if they so choose. Increasingly, as women establish a role for themselves in the world outside the home, they are guiding their children outwards, while men, who are becoming more aware of the need for emotional expression, are nurturing the emotional world of their children.

Whether feminine and masculine qualities are innate, or were merely developed to suit the structure of traditional societies, is a moot point: of more significance is the fact that any individual can develop those qualities in which they have a deficiency. The pace and structure of modern-day life in most cases dictates that parents need to embrace and develop both their masculine and feminine qualities. As equally-shared parenting, or single parent-ing, become more common, this needs to be done to ensure that the next generation has its full range of needs adequately met. For many of us, this is a daunting task. As a single mother of two children, I can see areas where there is a shortfall in order, structure and discipline in my own household, and where I need to expand my parenting skills. It is my responsibility to seek to develop these skills; claiming that they are a father's and not a mother's responsibility does my children a disservice. But I also need to accept my fallibility. That I seek to become a 'good enough' mother or father is what counts.

Conclusion

My main aim in writing this book has been to help parents, and all those involved with teenagers, to understand the nature of adolescence better, so that the particular needs of children at this stage in their development may be more adequately met. Too often in the course of my work with adults whose lives have been negatively affected by poor parenting and a general lack of love and guidance, we say 'Ah sure, they didn't know any better, and did the best they could.' This of course holds true: no parent wilfully goes out to destroy the lives of their children, and access to relevant information was often not available. Will we be able to excuse ourselves on such grounds, however, given the abundance of information on the subject, together with the fingertip access to information that modern technology gives us?

Nonetheless, I believe that such information should be more readily available to us. Our government has to date abjectly failed us through not having adopted a comprehensive programme to increase emotional intelligence amongst adolescents and thereby stem the rising tide of mental distress and ill health in this country. Too often, they have thrown good money after bad. and have sought to treat the symptoms rather than the cause of the problem. Nowhere is this more in evidence than in the government's policy of treating heroin addiction with methadone.

Increasing the number of Gardaí on the streets will not solve the problem of juvenile crime. Expanding the drugs force to hit at the supply, instead of dealing with the issues driving the demand, is doomed to failure. Increasing social-welfare benefits and providing training to the unemployed will not on their own give them the incentive to go out into the workforce. Increasing the legal age limit for drinking, and keeping control over licensing hours, will not stop people from over-drinking. (Some under-sixteens go 'fishing' – getting those over sixteen to buy alcohol for them – or 'piking,' where they just steal alcohol.) There is a saying that 'addiction travels', and I believe it does. The drug addict gives up heroin and takes up cocaine or alcohol, the alcoholic gives up alcohol and becomes a sex addict, the sex addict gives up surfing and cruising and turns to crime or self-abuse, and the underlying malaise is never treated.

That is not to say that our government has done nothing about these issues. A drugs campaign has been initiated and treatment facilities have been expanded. The recent suicide-awareness campaign has at least brought the issue to the fore and acknowledging that our male population is particularly at threat. Schools' CPSE program endeavours to provide some level of emotional cognisance to students. It would probably be fair to say: 'Some done, but loads left to do.' As our public-health crisis deepens, and our physical-welfare needs remain unmet, the issue of mental health sleeps like a dormant dinosaur. As the number of citizens on long-term waiting lists for surgical operations increases, and our hospital corridors become nearly impassable with patients lying on trolleys, the issue of the hundreds of thousands of citizens who are unable to get on with their lives as a result of depression, addiction, extreme anxiety and other problems does not get a look-in.

Change is possible, and is necessary to ensure that the sleeping dinosaur does not awaken and gobble the much-loved Celtic Tiger. Our policies need to centre primarily around the younger generations, to ensure that the dinosaur dies off. It is our current generation of teenagers that will lead Ireland into the future: they are our wealth. The land of opportunity awaits them, but only if we keep our eye on the ball. Government, society and parents need to combine to ensure that they fulfil their potential.

So Where Do We Start?

In the home. The idea that parenting is skills-based has not yet taken hold in this country. Most of us would believe that parenting comes naturally, and when we experience difficulties, we are quick to revert to the parenting we experienced ourselves as children. All those phrases and anecdotes we despised as children come rolling off our tongues with ease. We resort to tactics rather than skills, and are quick to dismiss or rationalise the detrimental effects these tactics had on the building of our own self-esteem. The idea that parenting is in fact a skill needs to be promulgated. In order to ensure maximum success in rearing our children, we would do well to access information on these skills through public talks, courses, books and so on. We need to be proactive on this issue. While parenting courses do exist, they are few and far between, and inadequately publicised. If demand dictates supply, we need to increase our demand, in order to increase our supply.

Secondly, all parents need to take a realistic view of their family units, and the dynamics and behaviours that operate within them. This takes courage. Often, we do not like what we see, and either deny, rationalise, or justify the existence of, the problems we experience. By admitting that problems exist, we are faced with the responsibility of changing, and we as humans are afraid of change – we generally do not rush out with open arms to embrace it. We need to revert to our sense of responsibility; a commitment to responsibility will bring a commitment to change.

Outside of our families, more can be done. There is no better place to access our youth than in schools. Nowhere else provides us with an opportunity to observe young teenagers and recognise difficulty and distress. We rightly prize our education system and value our schools. We trust that our children will arrive at the other end of the school system ready to launch themselves into their respective careers. We can in most cases expect that, academically, they will emerge as capable individuals.

But will they emerge as well-rounded, balanced individuals? Most will. However, given the emphasis that is placed on academic capabilities, it is a spectacular oversight how little teenagers' emotional well-being and intelligence are addressed. One only needs to look at the ratio of teachers to mental-health specialists within our educational system to see the gross imbalance that exists here. Given that the early detection of emotional distress increases the likelihood of a full recovery, and that in no other setting are we likely to have sufficient access to children and young adults to be able to identify distress, it is remarkable that a government-employed mental-health employee is not available to every school in the country. In a survey conducted by the National Suicide Research Foundation on young people's mental health, teenagers said that they believed that a support system within schools that included counsellors would help in the prevention of self-harm by helping them to manage issues like loneliness, abuse and bereavement.

Moreover, our young people are not sufficiently educated in the area of mental-health issues. Whilst the CPSE programme does address these issues to a certain extent, the symptoms, causes and effects of various conditions are not explored. The need to get professional help to deal with various manifestations of distress is not adequately stressed. A much deeper treatment of this subject matter is necessary so that teenagers are aware of what these conditions are, how they manifest themselves, and how help can be sought accordingly.

The provision of a basic knowledge of psychology should also be made a necessary element in teacher training, so that when a student states 'I don't know what's wrong with me', somebody close by may have an answer for them. They will also be in a better position to identify students who are in difficulty. This is especially important when one considers that the more dysfunctional a family is, the higher the levels of denial, and the higher the demand for secrecy. Teachers are therefore in a better position to recognise a difficulty and intervene. In short, we need to be proactive and pre-emptive.

Lastly, there is the issue of government policy. Our government needs to take the issue of mental health more seriously and start taking a more pre-emptive approach. Awareness of issues needs to be raised at a communal level in order to end the current stigmatisation that is attached to mental ill health. Programmes need to be run that offer information, advice and support, especially in areas that are socially disadvantaged. The issue of access to counsellors and psychotherapists needs to be addressed. Until now, this work has been left to charitable support groups, who do not have the resources to access the population in general. Each and every one of these groups, including Aware, Bodywhys, the Samaritans, Women's Aid, acknowledges that it cannot keep up with the demand for their services. Is our government suffering from denial? Or is it a case that, so long as the money keeps rolling in, who on earth – or at least on this island – could be unhappy?

Further Reading

John C. Coleman and Leo B. Hendry: *The Nature of Adolescence* (London and New York: Routledge, 2004)

M. Murray and Colm Keane: *The Teenage Years* (Dublin: Mercier, 2004)

Kate Figes: *The Terrible Teens* (London: Penguin, 2004)

Eric Ericson: *Identity and The Life Cycle* (New York: Norton, 1980)

Benig Maugher: *Reclaiming Father* (Dublin: Soul Connections, 2004)

Peter Gay: *The Freud Reader* (London: Vintage, 1989)

David Winnicott: *The Child, The Family, and the Outside World* (London: Penguin, 1964)

John Bowlby: *The Secure Base* (England: Routledge, 1988)

J. Holmes: *John Bowlby and Attachment Theory* (London and New York: Brunner and Routledge, 1993)

Bernie Purcell: *For Our Own Good* (Cork: Collins Press, 2001)

Alice Miller: *The Drama of Being a Child* (London: Virago, 1997)

Helen Fitzgerald: *The Grieving Teen* (New York: Tyneside, 2000)

Elisabeth Kubler Ross: *On Death and Dying* (London: Tavistock/Routledge, 1970)

Janet Woititz: *Adult Children of Alcoholics* (Florida, USA: Health Communications, 1983)

Barbara Coloroso: *The Bully, The Bullied and The Bystander* (London: Piccadilly Press, 2005)

Harold S Koplewicz: *More Than Moody* (New York: Berkeley, 2003)

Bev Cobain: *When Nothing Matters Anymore* (Minneapolis: Free Spirit Publishing, 1998)

Dr M Kaufmann: *Overcoming Teen Depression* (New York: Firefly, 2001)

Marion Crook: *Teens Talk About Suicide* (Vancouver, Canada: Arsenal Pulp Press, 2003)

Kay Redfield Jamison: *Night Falls Fast: Understanding Suicide* (London: Picador, 2002)

Nancy Friday: *My Mother, Myself* (London: Fontana, 1979)

Dr C. Eagle and Carol Coleman: *Your Adolescent Daughter* (London: Piatkus, 1995)

Tony Humphreys: *Family: Love It and Leave It* (Cork: Carraig Print, 1994) and *Leaving the Nest* (Dublin: Gill and MacMillan, 2004)

John Bradshaw: *Bradshaw On: The Family* (Florida, USA: Health Communications, 1996)

Tom Garvin: *Preventing the Future* (Dublin: Gill and Macmillan, 2004)

H. T. Prout and D. T. Brown: *Counseling and Psychotherapy with Children and Adolescents* (New York: John Wiley and Sons, 1999)

Resources

THE DRUGS TREATMENT CENTRE BOARD
Trinity Court, 30–31 Pearse Street, Dublin 2
(01) 648 8600

ALCOHOLICS ANONYMOUS
109 South Circular Road, Dublin 8
(01) 453 8998

THE RUTLAND CENTRE (addiction centre)
Knocklyon Road, Templeogue, Dublin 16
(01) 494 6358

THE AISLING CENTRE (teen addiction centre)
Ballyragget, County Kilkenny
(056) 883 3777

BODYWHYS (support around eating disorders)
The Knocklyon Road, Templeogue, Dublin 16
(01) 494 6358; LoCall 1890 200 444; www.bodywhys.ie

BELONGTO (gay, lesbian and transgender support group)
Outhouse, 105 Capel Street, Dublin 1
(01) 873 4932; www.BelongTo.ie

GAY SWITCHBOARD (parent support)
Carmichael House, North Brunswick Street, Dublin 7
(01) 872 1055

AWARE (helping to defeat depression)
72 Lower Leeson Street, Dublin 2
(01) 661 7211; LoCall Helpline 1890 303 302; www.aware.ie

CONSOLE (foundation for those bereaved by suicide)
All Hallows College, Drumcondra, Dublin 9
FreeFone 1800 201 890

THE HAZELBROOK COUNSELLING AND ADOLESCENT CENTRE
30 Sundrive Road, Kimmage, Dublin 6W
086 898 5666

Rebecca

Solnit

L U S T

VERSO
London · New York

Grateful acknowledgement is made for permission to reprint the following copyrighted works: Selection from *Cold Mountain: 100 Poems* by Han-Shan, translated by Burton Watson. Copyright 1970 by Columbia University Press. Reprinted with the permission of the publisher.

"On Climbing the Sierra Matterhorn Again After Thirty-One Years" from *No Nature* by Gary Snyder. Copyright 1992 by Gary Snyder. Reprinted by permission of Pantheon Books, a division of Random House, Inc.

Selection from *The Collected Poems of Frank O'Hara*, edited by Donald Allen. Copyright 1971 by Maureen Granville-Smith, Administratrix of the Estate of Frank O'Hara. Reprinted by permission of Alfred A. Knopf, Inc.

ILLUSTRATION CREDITS

Page iii: Detail of postcard, ca. 1900, showing passersby in front of Notre Dame de Paris.
1: Linda Conner, *Maze, Chartres Cathedral, France*, 1983. Courtesy of the artist.

79: Cedric Wright, *Sierra Club Mountaineers on Mount Resplendent in the Canadian Rockies*, 1928. Courtesy William Colby Library, Sierra Club.

169: *March of the Mothers in the Plaza de Mayo*, April 1978. Courtesy of the Associación Madres de Plaza de Mayo, Buenos Aires.

247: Marina Abramović, from *The Lovers*, 1988, black and white photograph. Courtesy Sean Kelly Gallery, New York.

First published in the UK by Verso 2001
© Rebecca Solnit 2001
First paperback edition published in the UK by Verso 2002
© Rebecca Solnit 2002
All rights reserved

7 9 10 8 6

Verso
6 Meard Street, London W1F 0EG
www.versobooks.com

Verso is the imprint of New Left Books

ISBN-10: 1-84467-558-0
ISBN-13: 978-1-84467-558-6

British Library Cataloguing in Publication Data
A catalogue for this book is available from the British Library

Designed by Kathryn Parise
Printed and bound in the United Kingdom by CPI Group (UK) Ltd, Croydon, CR0 4YY

Contents

Acknowledgments

I owe the origins of this book to friends who pointed out to me that I was writ-ing about walking in the course of writing about other things and should do so more expansively—notably Bruce Ferguson, who commissioned me to write about walking for the catalog accompanying his 1996 show *Walking and Thinking and Walking* at the Louisiana Museum in Denmark; editor William Murphy, who read the results and told me I should think about a book on walking; and Lucy Lippard, who, while we were on a trespassing stroll near her home, clinched the idea for the book for me by exclaiming, "I wish I had time to write it but I don't, so you should" (though I have written a very different book than Lucy would). One of the great pleasures of writing about this subject was that, instead of a few great experts, walking has a multitude of amateurs—everyone walks, a surprising number of people think about walking, and its history is spread across many scholars' fields—so that nearly everyone I know contributed an anecdote, a ref-erence, or a perspective to my researches. The history of walking is everyone's history, but my version of it particularly benefited from the following friends, who have my heartfelt gratitude: Mike Davis and Michael Sprinker, who sup-plied fine ideas and much encouragement early on; my brother David, for luring me long ago into street marches and the pilgrimage-protests at the Nevada Test Site; my bicycle-activist brother Stephen; John and Tim O'Toole, Maya Gallus, Linda Connor, Jane Handel, Meridel Rubenstein, Jerry West, Greg Powell, Malin Wilson-Powell, David Hayes, Harmony Hammond, May Stevens, Edie Katz, Tom Joyce, and Thomas Evans; Jessica, Gavin, and Daisy in Dunkeld; Eck Finlay in Edinburgh and his father in Little Sparta; Valerie and Michael Cohen in June Lake; Scott Slovic in Reno; Carolyn from Reclaim the Streets in Brixton; Iain Boal; my agent Bonnie Nadell; my editor Paul Slovak at Viking Penguin, who took to the idea of a general history of walking immediately and made this one possible; and particularly Pat Dennis, who listened to me chapter by chapter, related much on mountaineering history and Asian mysticism to me, and walked alongside me for the duration of this book.

WANDERLUST

STILL WALKING

On January 1, 1999, at the age of 89, Doris Haddock, better known as Granny D, set out to walk across the United States to demand campaign finance reform; she arrived in the nation's capital fourteen months and 3,200 miles later. It was no coincidence that she chose an activity that required openness, engagement and few expenses to make her protest against the hidden corrosion of big money. Britons won a different battle with the right-to-roam legislation passed in 2000 but only now realized as the new ordnance-survey maps and other guides to the newly accessible rural areas appear. Battles against private-property owners continue, but much of the island is more accessible than before. Other victories, to pedestrianize cities and rethink urban design, to let children walk to school again, even to ban automobiles from city centers on Sundays or once a year or all the time, have been won. The new millenium arrived as a dialectic between secrecy and openness; between consolidation and dispersal of power; between privatization and public ownership, power, and life, and walking has as ever been on the side of the latter.

On February 15, 2003, police estimated three quarters of a million took to the streets of London, though organizers thought two million a more accurate figure. Fifty thousand or so walked in Glasgow, about a hundred thousand in Dublin, three times that many in Berlin, three million people in Rome, a hundred thousand in Paris, a million and a half in Barcelona and two million in Madrid.

South American demonstrations in Rio de Janeiro, Buenos Aires, Santiago and other cities took place that day; walkers gathered in Seoul, Tokyo, Tel Aviv, Baghdad, Karachi, Detroit, Cape Town, Calcutta, Istanbul, Montreal, Mexico City, New York, San Francisco, Sydney, Vancouver, Moscow, Tehran, Copenhagen—but to name only the large cities is to overlook the passion in Toulouse, in Malta, in smalltown New Mexico and Bolivia, in the Inuit homeland of northern Canada, in Montevideo, Mostar, in Sfax, Tunisia, where the marchers were beaten by police, in Chicoutimi, Quebec, where the wind chill brought the temperate down to −40 centrigrade, in Juneau, Alaska, and on Ross Island in Antarctica, where the scientists didn't walk far, but posed for antiwar photographs to testify that even the seventh continent was on board.

The global walk of more than thirty million people prompted the *New York Times* to call civil society "the world's other superpower." That day, February 15, 2003, didn't stop the war against Iraq, though it might have changed that war's parameters—Turkey, for example, under heavy citizen pressure declined to let its air bases be used for the assault. The twenty-first century has dawned as an era of people power and public protest. In Latin America in particular that power has been very tangible, toppling regimes, undoing coups, protecting resources from foreign profiteers, undermining the neoliberal agenda of the Free Trade Area of the Americas, but from students in Belgrade to farmers in Korea, collective public acts have mattered. Walking itself has not changed the world, but walking together has been a rite, tool and reinforcement of the civil society that can stand up to violence, to fear, and to repression. Indeed, it is hard to imagine a viable civil society without the free association and the knowledge of the terrain that comes with walking. A sequestered or passive population is not quite a citizenry.

The fifty-thousand-person march in Seattle that culminated in a shutdown of the 1999 World Trade Organization meeting on November 30, 1999, was one start of a new era in which a global movement stood up against the corporate version of globalization, with its threats to the local, the democratic, the unhomogenized and independent. September 11, 2001, and the collapse of the World Trade Towers is the other date usually selected as the stormy dawn of the new millenium, and perhaps the most profound response to that terrorism was the first: the tens of thousands of New Yorkers who walked away from danger together, on foot, as citizens familiar with their streets and as human beings willing to offer aid to strangers, filling avenues like a grim parade, turning the Brooklyn Bridge into a pedestrian route, eventually turning Union Square into an agora for public mourning and public debate. Those tens or hundreds of thousands living in public, unarmed, engaged and equal, were the opposite of the secrecy and violence that characterized both the attacks and Bush's revenge (and unrelated war in Iraq). That much of the antiwar movement has also consisted of massive groups of walkers is perhaps not coincidental.

The best evidence of the potency of unarmed people walking together in the streets is the aggressive measures taken in the US and the UK to control or altogether stop these crowds: at the Republican National Convention in New York in August 2004, in Gleneagles, Scotland during the G8 summit a year later, as well as at any corporate globalization conference since 1999, be it the WTO, IMF, World Bank, World Economic Forum or G8. These summits at which the power of the few is openly pitted against that of the many have routinely required that temporary police states be built around them, with millions of pounds, dollars, euros or yuan spent on security forces, armaments, surveillance, fences and barriers, a world brutalized in defense of brutal policy.

But more insidious forces are marshalled against the time, space and will to walk and against the version of humanity that act embodies. One force is the filling-up of what I think of as "the time inbetween," the time of walking to or from a place, of meandering, of running errands. That time has been deplored as a waste, reduced, and its remainder filled with earphones playing music and mobile phones relaying conversations. The very ability to appreciate this uncluttered time, the uses of the useless, often seems to be evaporating, as does appreciation of being outside—including outside the familiar; mobile-phone conversations seem to serve as a buffer against solitude, silence and encounters with the unknown. Technology as such is hard to finger as a culprit, since the global march of February 15, 2003, was coordinated on the Internet, but technology's commercial deployment is often against those things that are free in both senses, monetary and political. Other changes are easy to point to, factors that have mostly intensified in the years since I wrote *Wanderlust*.

Obesity and its related health crises seem to be becoming more and more of a transnational pandemic as people in more parts of the world become immobilized and overfed from childhood on, a downward spiral where the inactive body becomes less and less capable of action. That obesity is not just circumstantial—due to a world of digital amusements and parking lots, of sprawl and suburbs—

but conceptual in origin, as people forget that their bodies could be adequate to the challenges that face them and a pleasure to use. They perceive and imagine their bodies as essentially passive, a treasure or a burden but not a tool for work and travel. Promotional material for motorized Segway scooters, for example, asserts that traveling short distances in cities and even warehouses is a challenge that only machines can solve; the adequacy of feet alone to go the distance has been erased, along with the millennia we got around before machines. The fight against this collapse of imagination and engagement may be as important as the battles for political freedom, because only by recuperating a sense of inherent power can we begin to resist both oppressions and the erosion of the vital body in action.

And as the climate heats up and oil runs out, this recovery is going to be very important, more important perhaps than "alternative fuels" and the other modes of continuing down the motorized route rather than reclaiming the alternatives. I often find myself at odds with pedestrian and bicycle advocates who believe that infrastructure is everything; that if you build it they will come. I believe that most industrial-zone human beings need to rethink time, space and their own bodies before they will be equipped to be as urbane and as pedestrian (or at least nonmotorized) as their predecessors. Only in places like Manhattan and London do people—some people—seem to remember how to integrate public transit and their own legs into an effective, ethical and sometimes deeply pleasurable way of navigating the terrain of their daily lives.

I wrote *Wanderlust* at the end of the 1990s in a world that was already polarized, and readers and reviewers bemused me by taking so affectionately to it. Perhaps it was the pleasure of reading of pilgrimages and prostitutes' strolls that kept them from bristling at the ways this book was also a polemic against industrialization, privatization of open lands, the oppression and confinement of women, suburbia, the disembodiment of everyday life and a few other such things. The book opened up a huge territory for me that I continue to explore; in some ways, my 2003 book about Eadweard Muybridge continued my investigation of the industrialization of time and space and the acceleration of everyday life that began with *Wanderlust*; *Hope in the Dark* looked further at the power of citizens in the streets to change the world; and *A Field Guide to Getting Lost* expanded on the uses of wandering and uncertainty. I am still walking the terrain of *Wanderlust*, which was for me a map of the world, selective as all maps are, but extensive too.

One of the great pleasures of researching and writing this book was arriving at a set of conclusions and descriptions in which many familiar divisions were reunited. While walking, the body and the mind can work together, so that thinking becomes almost a physical, rhythmic act—so much for the Cartesian mind/body divide. Spirituality and sexuality both enter in; the great walkers often move through both urban and rural places in the same way; and even past and present are brought together when you walk as the ancients did or relive some event in history or your own life by retracing its route. And each walk moves through space like a thread through fabric, sewing it together into a continuous experience—so unlike the way air travel chops up time and space and even cars and trains do. This continuity is one of the things I think we lost in the industrial age—but we can choose to reclaim it, again and again, and some do. The fields and streets are waiting.

Part I

THE PACE OF

$\mathcal{T}$HOUGHTS

Chapter 1

TRACING A HEADLAND:

An Introduction

Where does it start? Muscles tense. One leg a pillar, holding the body upright between the earth and sky. The other a pendulum, swinging from behind. Heel touches down. The whole weight of the body rolls forward onto the ball of the foot. The big toe pushes off, and the delicately balanced weight of the body shifts again. The legs reverse position. It starts with a step and then another step and then another that add up like taps on a drum to a rhythm, the rhythm of walking. The most obvious and the most obscure thing in the world, this walking that wanders so readily into religion, philosophy, landscape, urban policy, anatomy, allegory, and heartbreak.

The history of walking is an unwritten, secret history whose fragments can be found in a thousand unemphatic passages in books, as well as in songs, streets, and almost everyone's adventures. The bodily history of walking is that of bipedal evolution and human anatomy. Most of the time walking is merely practical, the unconsidered locomotive means between two sites. To make walking into an investigation, a ritual, a meditation, is a special subset of walking, physiologically like and philosophically unlike the way the mail carrier brings the mail and the office worker reaches the train. Which is to say that the subject of walking is, in some sense, about how we invest universal acts with particular meanings. Like eating or breathing, it can be invested with wildly different cultural meanings, from the erotic to the spiritual, from the revolutionary to the artistic. Here this

---

Isn't it really quite extraordinary to see that, since man took his first step, no one has asked himself why he walks, history begins to become part of the history of the imagination and the culture, of what kind of pleasure, freedom, and meaning are pursued at different times by different kinds of walks and walkers. That imagination has both shaped and been shaped by the spaces it passes through on two feet. Walking has created paths, roads, trade routes; generated local and cross-continental senses of place; shaped cities, parks; generated maps, guidebooks, gear, and, further afield, a vast library of walking stories and poems, of pilgrimages, mountaineering expeditions, meanders, and summer picnics. The landscapes, urban and rural, gestate the stories, and the stories bring us back to the sites of this history.

This history of walking is an amateur history, just as walking is an amateur act. To use a walking metaphor, it trespasses through everybody else's field—through anatomy, anthropology, architecture, gardening, geography, political and cultural history, literature, sexuality, religious studies—and doesn't stop in any of them on its long route. For if a field of expertise can be imagined as a real field— a nice rectangular confine carefully tilled and yielding a specific crop—then the subject of walking resembles walking itself in its lack of confines. And though *the* history of walking is, as part of all these fields and everyone's experience, virtually infinite, *this* history of walking I am writing can only be partial, an idiosyncratic path traced through them by one walker, with much doubling back and looking around. In what follows, I have tried to trace the paths that brought most of us in my country, the United States, into the present moment, a history compounded largely of European sources, inflected and subverted by the vastly different scale of American space, the centuries of adaptation and mutation here, and by the other traditions that have recently met up with those paths, notably Asian traditions. The history of walking is everyone's history, and any written version can only hope to indicate some of the more well-trodden paths in the author's vicinity—which is to say, the paths I trace are not the only paths.

I sat down one spring day to write about walking and stood up again, because a desk is no place to think on the large scale. In a headland just north of the Golden Gate Bridge studded with abandoned military fortifications, I went out walking up a valley and along a ridgeline, then down to the Pacific. Spring had come after an unusually wet winter, and the hills had turned that riotous, exuberant green I forget and rediscover every year. Through the new growth poked grass from the

---

how he walks, if he has ever walked, if he could walk better, what he achieves in walking . . . questions that are tied year before, bleached from summer gold to an ashen gray by the rain, part of the subtler palette of the rest of the year. Henry David Thoreau, who walked more vigorously than me on the other side of the continent, wrote of the local, "An absolutely new prospect is a great happiness, and I can still get this any afternoon. Two or three hours' walking will carry me to as strange a country as I expect ever to see. A single farmhouse which I had not seen before is sometimes as good as the dominions of the King of Dahomey. There is in fact a sort of harmony discoverable between the capabilities of the landscape within a circle of ten miles' radius, or the limits of an afternoon walk, and the threescore years and ten of human life. It will never become quite familiar to you."

These linked paths and roads form a circuit of about six miles that I began hiking ten years ago to walk off my angst during a difficult year. I kept coming back to this route for respite from my work and for my work too, because thinking is generally thought of as doing nothing in a production-oriented culture, and doing nothing is hard to do. It's best done by disguising it as doing something, and the something closest to doing nothing is walking. Walking itself is the intentional act closest to the unwilled rhythms of the body, to breathing and the beating of the heart. It strikes a delicate balance between working and idling, being and doing. It is a bodily labor that produces nothing but thoughts, experiences, arrivals. After all those years of walking to work out other things, it made sense to come back to work close to home, in Thoreau's sense, and to think about walking.

Walking, ideally, is a state in which the mind, the body, and the world are aligned, as though they were three characters finally in conversation together, three notes suddenly making a chord. Walking allows us to be in our bodies and in the world without being made busy by them. It leaves us free to think without being wholly lost in our thoughts. I wasn't sure whether I was too soon or too late for the purple lupine that can be so spectacular in these headlands, but milkmaids were growing on the shady side of the road on the way to the trail, and they recalled the hillsides of my childhood that first bloomed every year with an extravagance of these white flowers. Black butterflies fluttered around me, tossed along by wind and wings, and they called up another era of my past. Moving on foot seems to make it easier to move in time; the mind wanders from plans to recollections to observations.

The rhythm of walking generates a kind of rhythm of thinking, and the pas-

---

to all the philosophical, psychological, and political systems which preoccupy the world.—HONORÉ DE BALZAC,

---

sage through a landscape echoes or stimulates the passage through a series of thoughts. This creates an odd consonance between internal and external passage, one that suggests that the mind is also a landscape of sorts and that walking is one way to traverse it. A new thought often seems like a feature of the landscape that was there all along, as though thinking were traveling rather than making. And so one aspect of the history of walking is the history of thinking made concrete—for the motions of the mind cannot be traced, but those of the feet can. Walking can also be imagined as a visual activity, every walk a tour leisurely enough both to see and to think over the sights, to assimilate the new into the known. Perhaps this is where walking's peculiar utility for thinkers comes from. The surprises, liberations, and clarifications of travel can sometimes be garnered by going around the block as well as going around the world, and walking travels both near and far. Or perhaps walking should be called movement, not travel, for one can walk in circles or travel around the world immobilized in a seat, and a certain kind of wanderlust can only be assuaged by the acts of the body itself in motion, not the motion of the car, boat, or plane. It is the movement as well as the sights going by that seems to make things happen in the mind, and this is what makes walking ambiguous and endlessly fertile: it is both means and end, travel and destination.

The old red dirt road built by the army had begun its winding, uphill course through the valley. Occasionally I focused on the act of walking, but mostly it was unconscious, the feet proceeding with their own knowledge of balance, of sidestepping rocks and crevices, of pacing, leaving me free to look at the roll of hills far away and the abundance of flowers close up: brodia; the pink papery blossoms whose name I never learned; an abundance of cloverlike sourgrass in yellow bloom; and then halfway along the last bend, a paperwhite narcissus. After twenty minutes' trudge uphill, I stopped to smell it. There used to be a dairy in this valley, and the foundations of a farmhouse and a few straggling old fruit trees still survive somewhere down below, on the other side of the wet, willow-crowded valley bottom. It was a working landscape far longer than a recreational one: first came the Miwok Indians, then the agriculturists, themselves rooted out after a century by the military base, which closed in the 1970s, when coasts became irrelevant to an increasingly abstract and aerial kind of war. Since the

---

THEORIE DE LA DEMARCHÉ   *An Eskimo custom offers an angry person release by walking the emotion out of his*

1970s, this place has been turned over to the National Park Service and to people like me who are heirs to the cultural tradition of walking in the landscape for pleasure. The massive concrete gun emplacements, bunkers, and tunnels will never disappear as the dairy buildings have, but it must have been the dairy families that left behind the live legacy of garden flowers that crop up among the native plants.

Walking is meandering, and I meandered from my cluster of narcissus in the curve of the red road first in thought and then by foot. The army road reached the crest and crossed the trail that would take me across the brow of the hill, cutting into the wind and downhill before its gradual ascent to the western side of the crest. On the ridgetop up above this footpath, facing into the next valley north, was an old radar station surrounded by an octagon of fencing. The odd collection of objects and cement bunkers on an asphalt pad were part of a Nike missile guidance system, a system for directing nuclear missiles from their base in the valley below to other continents, though none were ever launched from here in war. Think of the ruin as a souvenir from the canceled end of the world.

It was nuclear weapons that first led me to walking history, in a trajectory as surprising as any trail or train of thought. I became in the 1980s an antinuclear activist and participated in the spring demonstrations at the Nevada Test Site, a Department of Energy site the size of Rhode Island in southern Nevada where the United States has been detonating nuclear bombs—more than a thousand to date—since 1951. Sometimes nuclear weapons seemed like nothing more than intangible budget figures, waste disposal figures, potential casualty figures, to be resisted by campaigning, publishing, and lobbying. The bureaucratic abstractness of both the arms race and the resistance to it could make it hard to understand that the real subject was and is the devastation of real bodies and real places. At the test site, it was different. The weapons of mass destruction were being exploded in a beautifully stark landscape we camped near for the week or two of each demonstration (exploded underground after 1963, though they often leaked radiation into the atmosphere anyway and always shook the earth). We— that *we* made up of the scruffy American counterculture, but also of survivors of Hiroshima and Nagasaki, Buddhist monks and Franciscan priests and nuns, veterans turned pacifist, renegade physicists, Kazakh and German and Polynesian activists living in the shadow of the bomb, and the Western Shoshone, whose land it was—had broken through the abstractions. Beyond them were the actual-

---

or her system in a straight line across the landscape; the point at which the anger is conquered is marked with a ities of places, of sights, of actions, of sensations—of handcuffs, thorns, dust, heat, thirst, radiation risk, the testimony of radiation victims—but also of spectacular desert light, the freedom of open space, and the stirring sight of the thousands who shared our belief that nuclear bombs were the wrong instrument with which to write the history of the world. We bore a kind of bodily witness to our convictions, to the fierce beauty of the desert, and to the apocalypses being prepared nearby. The form our demonstrations took was walking: what was on the public-land side of the fence a ceremonious procession became, on the off-limits side, an act of trespass resulting in arrest. We were engaging, on an unprecedentedly grand scale, in civil disobedience or civil resistance, an American tradition first articulated by Thoreau.

Thoreau himself was both a poet of nature and a critic of society. His famous act of civil disobedience was passive—a refusal to pay taxes to support war and slavery and an acceptance of the night in jail that ensued—and it did not overlap directly with his involvement in exploring and interpreting the local landscape, though he did lead a huckleberrying party the day he got out of jail. In our actions at the test site the poetry of nature and criticism of society were united in this camping, walking, and trespassing, as though we had figured out how a berrying party could be a revolutionary cadre. It was a revelation to me, the way this act of walking through a desert and across a cattle guard into the forbidden zone could articulate political meaning. And in the course of traveling to this landscape, I began to discover other western landscapes beyond my coastal region and to explore those landscapes and the histories that had brought me to them—the history not only of the development of the West but of the Romantic taste for walking and landscape, the democratic tradition of resistance and revolution, the more ancient history of pilgrimage and walking to achieve spiritual goals. I found my voice as a writer in describing all the layers of history that shaped my experiences at the test site. And I began to think and to write about walking in the course of writing about places and their histories.

Of course walking, as any reader of Thoreau's essay "Walking" knows, inevitably leads into other subjects. Walking is a subject that is always straying. Into, for example, the shooting stars below the missile guidance station in the northern headlands of the Golden Gate. They are my favorite wildflower, these small magenta cones with their sharp black points that seem aerodynamically shaped for a flight that never comes, as though they had evolved forgetful of the

---

stick, bearing witness to the strength or length of the rage.—LUCY LIPPARD, OVERLAY   *We learn a place and how*

---

fact that flowers have stems and stems have roots. The chaparral on both sides of the trail, watered by the condensation of the ocean fog through the dry months and shaded by the slope's northern exposure, was lush. While the missile guidance station on the crest always makes me think of the desert and of war, these banks below always remind me of English hedgerows, those field borders with their abundance of plants, birds, and that idyllic English kind of countryside. There were ferns here, wild strawberries, and, tucked under a coyote bush, a cluster of white iris in bloom.

Although I came to think about walking, I couldn't stop thinking about everything else, about the letters I should have been writing, about the conversations I'd been having. At least when my mind strayed to the phone conversation with my friend Sono that morning, I was still on track. Sono's truck had been stolen from her West Oakland studio, and she told me that though everyone responded to it as a disaster, she wasn't all that sorry it was gone, or in a hurry to replace it. There was a joy, she said, to finding that her body was adequate to get her where she was going, and it was a gift to develop a more tangible, concrete relationship to her neighborhood and its residents. We talked about the more stately sense of time one has afoot and on public transit, where things must be planned and scheduled beforehand, rather than rushed through at the last minute, and about the sense of place that can only be gained on foot. Many people nowadays live in a series of interiors—home, car, gym, office, shops—disconnected from each other. On foot everything stays connected, for while walking one occupies the spaces between those interiors in the same way one occupies those interiors. One lives in the whole world rather than in interiors built up against it.

The narrow trail I had been following came to an end as it rose to meet the old gray asphalt road that runs up to the missile guidance station. Stepping from path to road means stepping up to see the whole expanse of the ocean, spreading uninterrupted to Japan. The same shock of pleasure comes every time I cross this boundary to discover the ocean again, an ocean shining like beaten silver on the brightest days, green on the overcast ones, brown with the muddy runoff of the streams and rivers washing far out to sea during winter floods, an opalescent mottling of blues on days of scattered clouds, only invisible on the foggiest days, when the salt smell alone announces the change. This day the sea was a solid blue running toward an indistinct horizon where white mist blurred the transition to cloudless sky. From here on, my route was downhill. I had told Sono about an ad

to visualize spatial relationships, as children, on foot and with imagination. Place and the scale of place must be

I found in the *Los Angeles Times* a few months ago that I'd been thinking about ever since. It was for a CD-ROM encyclopedia, and the text that occupied a whole page read, "You used to walk across town in the pouring rain to use our encyclopedias. We're pretty confident that we can get your kid to click and drag." I think it was the kid's walk in the rain that constituted the real education, at least of the senses and the imagination. Perhaps the child with the CD-ROM encyclopedia will stray from the task at hand, but wandering in a book or a computer takes place within more constricted and less sensual parameters. It's the unpredictable incidents between official events that add up to a life, the incalculable that gives it value. Both rural and urban walking have for two centuries been prime ways of exploring the unpredictable and the incalculable, but they are now under assault on many fronts.

The multiplication of technologies in the name of efficiency is actually eradicating free time by making it possible to maximize the time and place for production and minimize the unstructured travel time in between. New timesaving technologies make most workers more productive, not more free, in a world that seems to be accelerating around them. Too, the rhetoric of efficiency around these technologies suggests that what cannot be quantified cannot be valued— that that vast array of pleasures which fall into the category of doing nothing in particular, of woolgathering, cloud-gazing, wandering, window-shopping, are nothing but voids to be filled by something more definite, more productive, or faster paced. Even on this headland route going nowhere useful, this route that could only be walked for pleasure, people had trodden shortcuts between the switchbacks as though efficiency was a habit they couldn't shake. The indeterminacy of a ramble, on which much may be discovered, is being replaced by the determinate shortest distance to be traversed with all possible speed, as well as by the electronic transmissions that make real travel less necessary. As a member of the self-employed whose time saved by technology can be lavished on daydreams and meanders, I know these things have their uses, and use them—a truck, a computer, a modem—myself, but I fear their false urgency, their call to speed, their insistence that travel is less important than arrival. I like walking because it is slow, and I suspect that the mind, like the feet, works at about three miles an hour. If this is so, then modern life is moving faster than the speed of thought, or thoughtfulness.

Walking is about being outside, in public space, and public space is also being

---

measured against our bodies and their capabilities.—GARY SNYDER, "BLUE MOUNTAINS CONSTANTLY

---

abandoned and eroded in older cities, eclipsed by technologies and services that don't require leaving home, and shadowed by fear in many places (and strange places are always more frightening than known ones, so the less one wanders the city the more alarming it seems, while the fewer the wanderers the more lonely and dangerous it really becomes). Meanwhile, in many new places, public space isn't even in the design: what was once public space is designed to accommodate the privacy of automobiles; malls replace main streets; streets have no sidewalks; buildings are entered through their garages; city halls have no plazas; and everything has walls, bars, gates. Fear has created a whole style of architecture and urban design, notably in southern California, where to be a pedestrian is to be under suspicion in many of the subdivisions and gated "communities." At the same time, rural land and the once-inviting peripheries of towns are being swallowed up in car-commuter subdivisions and otherwise sequestered. In some places it is no longer possible to be out in public, a crisis both for the private epiphanies of the solitary stroller and for public space's democratic functions. It was this fragmentation of lives and landscapes that we were resisting long ago, in the expansive spaces of the desert that temporarily became as public as a plaza.

And when public space disappears, so does the body as, in Sono's fine term, adequate for getting around. Sono and I spoke of the discovery that our neighborhoods—which are some of the most feared places in the Bay Area—aren't all that hostile (though they aren't safe enough to let us forget about safety altogether). I have been threatened and mugged on the street, long ago, but I have a thousand times more often encountered friends passing by, a sought-for book in a store window, compliments and greetings from my loquacious neighbors, architectural delights, posters for music and ironic political commentary on walls and telephone poles, fortune-tellers, the moon coming up between buildings, glimpses of other lives and other homes, and street trees noisy with songbirds. The random, the unscreened, allows you to find what you don't know you are looking for, and you don't know a place until it surprises you. Walking is one way of maintaining a bulwark against this erosion of the mind, the body, the landscape, and the city, and every walker is a guard on patrol to protect the ineffable.

Perhaps a third of the way down the road that wandered to the beach, an orange net was spread. It looked like a tennis net, but when I reached it I saw that it fenced off a huge new gap in the road. This road has been crumbling since I began to walk on it a decade ago. It used to roll uninterruptedly from sea to

---

WALKING"   *Then one day walking round Tavistock Square I made up, as I sometimes make up my books,* To

---

ridgetop. Along the coastal reach of the road a little bite appeared in 1989 that one could edge around, then a little trail detoured around the growing gap. With every winter's rain, more and more red earth and road surface crumbled away, sliding into a heap at the ruinous bottom of the steep slope the road had once cut across. It was an astonishing sight at first, this road that dropped off into thin air, for one expects roads and paths to be continuous. Every year more of it has fallen. And I have walked this route so often that every part of it springs associations on me. I remember all the phases of the collapse and how different a person I was when the road was complete. I remember explaining to a friend on this route almost three years earlier why I liked walking the same way over and over. I joked, in a bad adaptation of Heraclitus's famous dictum about rivers, that you never step on the same trail twice; and soon afterward we came across the new staircase that cut down the steep hillside, built far enough inland that the erosion wouldn't reach it for many years to come. If there is a history of walking, then it too has come to a place where the road falls off, a place where there is no public space and the landscape is being paved over, where leisure is shrinking and being crushed under the anxiety to produce, where bodies are not in the world but only indoors in cars and buildings, and an apotheosis of speed makes those bodies seem anachronistic or feeble. In this context, walking is a subversive detour, the scenic route through a half-abandoned landscape of ideas and experiences.

I had to circumnavigate this new chunk bitten out of the actual landscape by going to a new detour on the right. There's always a moment on this circuit when the heat of climbing and the windblock the hills provide give way to the descent into ocean air, and this time it came at the staircase past the scree of a fresh cut into the green serpentine stone of the hill. From there it wasn't far to the switchback leading to the other half of the road, which winds closer and closer to the cliffs above the ocean, where waves shatter into white foam over the dark rocks with an audible roar. Soon I was at the beach, where surfers sleek as seals in their black wet suits were catching the point break at the northern edge of the cove, dogs chased sticks, people lolled on blankets, and the waves crashed, then sprawled into a shallow rush uphill to lap at the feet of those of us walking on the hard sand of high tide. Only a final stretch remained, up over a sandy crest and along the length of the murky lagoon full of water birds.

It was the snake that came as a surprise, a garter snake, so called because of the yellowish stripes running the length of its dark body, a snake tiny and en-

the Lighthouse, *in a great, apparently involuntary rush.*—VIRGINIA WOOLF, MOMENTS OF BEING   *In my* chanting as it writhed like waving water across the path and into the grasses on one side. It didn't alarm me so much as alert me. Suddenly I came out of my thoughts to notice everything around me again—the catkins on the willows, the lapping of the water, the leafy patterns of the shadows across the path. And then myself, walking with the alignment that only comes after miles, the loose diagonal rhythm of arms swinging in synchronization with legs in a body that felt long and stretched out, almost as sinuous as the snake. My circuit was almost finished, and at the end of it I knew what my subject was and how to address it in a way I had not six miles before. It had come to me not in a sudden epiphany but with a gradual sureness, a sense of meaning like a sense of place. When you give yourself to places, they give you yourself back; the more one comes to know them, the more one seeds them with the invisible crop of memories and associations that will be waiting for you when you come back, while new places offer up new thoughts, new possibilities. Exploring the world is one of the best ways of exploring the mind, and walking travels both terrains.

---

room, the world is beyond my understanding; / But when I walk I see that it consists of three or four hills and a

---

Chapter 2

THE MIND AT THREE MILES
AN HOUR

I. PEDESTRIAN ARCHITECTURE

Jean-Jacques Rousseau remarked in his *Confessions*, "I can only meditate when I am walking. When I stop, I cease to think; my mind only works with my legs." The history of walking goes back further than the history of human beings, but the history of walking as a conscious cultural act rather than a means to an end is only a few centuries old in Europe, and Rousseau stands at its beginning. That history began with the walks of various characters in the eighteenth century, but the more literary among them strove to consecrate walking by tracing it to Greece, whose practices were so happily revered and misrepresented then. The eccentric English revolutionary and writer John Thelwall wrote a massive, turgid book, *The Peripatetic*, uniting Rousseauian romanticism with this spurious classical tradition. "In one respect, at least, I may boast of a resemblance to the simplicity of the ancient sages: I pursue my meditations on foot," he remarked. And after Thelwall's book appeared in 1793, many more would make the claim until it became an established idea that the ancients walked to think, so much so that the very picture seems part of cultural history: austerely draped men speaking gravely as they pace through a dry Mediterranean landscape punctuated with the occasional marble column.

This belief arose from a coincidence of architecture and language. When Aristotle was ready to set up a school in Athens, the city assigned him a plot of

------

cloud.—WALLACE STEVENS, "OF THE SURFACE OF THINGS"   *As a result of walking tours in Scotland while he*

------

land. "In it," explains Felix Grayeff's history of this school, "stood shrines to Apollo and the Muses, and perhaps other smaller buildings. . . . A covered colonnade led to the temple of Apollo, or perhaps connected the temple with the shrine of the Muses; whether it had existed before or was only built now, is not known. This colonnade or walk (peripatos) gave the school its name; it seems that it was here, at least at the beginning, that the pupils assembled and the teachers gave their lectures. Here they wandered to and fro; for this reason it was later said that Aristotle himself lectured and taught while walking up and down." The philosophers who came from it were called the Peripatetic philosophers or the Peripatetic school, and in English the word *peripatetic* means "one who walks habitually and extensively." Thus their name links thinking with walking. There is something more to this than the coincidence that established a school of philosophy in a temple of Apollo with a long colonnade—slightly more.

The Sophists, the philosophers who dominated Athenian life before Socrates, Plato, and Aristotle, were famously wanderers who often taught in the grove where Aristotle's school would be located. Plato's assault on the Sophists was so furious that the words *sophist* and *sophistry* are still synonymous with deception and guile, though the root *sophia* has to do with wisdom. The Sophists, however, functioned something like the chautauquas and public lecturers in nineteenth-century America, who went from place to place delivering talks to audiences hungry for information and ideas. Though they taught rhetoric as a tool of political power, and the ability to persuade and argue was crucial to Greek democracy, the Sophists taught other things besides. Plato, whose half-fabricated character Socrates is one of the wiliest and most persuasive debaters of all times, is somewhat disingenuous when he attacks the Sophists.

Whether or not the Sophists were virtuous, they were often mobile, as are many of those whose first loyalty is to ideas. It may be that loyalty to something as immaterial as ideas sets thinkers apart from those whose loyalty is tied to people and locale, for the loyalty that ties down the latter will often drive the former from place to place. It is an attachment that requires detachment. Too, ideas are not as reliable or popular a crop as, say, corn, and those who cultivate them often must keep moving in pursuit of support as well as truth. Many professions in many cultures, from musicians to medics, have been nomadic, possessed of a kind of diplomatic immunity to the strife between communities that keeps others local. Aristotle himself had at first intended to become a doctor, as his father

was an undergraduate, he recalls in his autobiography, Pilgrim's Way (1940), *that "the works of Aristotle are* had been, and doctors in that time were members of a secretive guild of travelers who claimed descent from the god of healing. Had he become a philosopher in the era of the Sophists, he might have been mobile anyway, for settled philosophy schools were first established in Athens in his time.

It is now impossible to say whether or not Aristotle and his Peripatetics habitually walked while they talked philosophy, but the link between thinking and walking recurs in ancient Greece, and Greek architecture accommodated walking as a social and conversational activity. Just as the Peripatetics took their name from the *peripatos* of their school, so the Stoics were named after the stoa, or colonnade, in Athens, a most unstoically painted walkway where they walked and talked. Long afterward, the association between walking and philosophizing became so widespread that central Europe has places named after it: the celebrated Philosophenweg in Heidelberg where Hegel is said to have walked, the Philosophen-damm in Königsberg that Kant passed on his daily stroll (now replaced by a railway station), and the Philosopher's Way Kierkegaard mentions in Copenhagen.

And philosophers who walked—well, walking is a universal human activity. Jeremy Bentham, John Stuart Mill, and many others walked far, and Thomas Hobbes even had a walking stick with an inkhorn built into it so he could jot down ideas as he went. Frail Immanuel Kant took a daily walk around Königsberg after dinner—but it was merely for exercise, because he did his thinking sitting by the stove and staring at the church tower out the window. The young Friedrich Nietzsche declares with superb conventionality, "For recreation I turn to three things, and a wonderful recreation they provide!—my Schopenhauer, Schumann's music, and, finally, solitary walks." In the twentieth century, Bertrand Russell recounts of his friend Ludwig Wittgenstein, "He used to come to my rooms at midnight, and for hours he would walk backwards and forwards like a caged tiger. On arrival, he would announce that when he left my rooms he would commit suicide. So, in spite of getting sleepy, I did not like to turn him out. One such evening after an hour or two of dead silence, I said to him, 'Wittgenstein, are you thinking about logic or about your sins?' 'Both' he said, and then reverted to silence." Philosophers walked. But philosophers who thought about walking are rarer.

---

forever bound up with me with the smell of peat and certain stretches of granite and heather." —ON JOHN BUCHAN,

---

II. CONSECRATING WALKING

It is Rousseau who laid the groundwork for the ideological edifice within which walking itself would be enshrined—not the walking that took Wittgenstein back and forth in Russell's room, but the walking that took Nietzsche out into the landscape. In 1749 the writer and encylopedist Denis Diderot was thrown into jail for writing an essay questioning the goodness of God. Rousseau, a close friend of Diderot's at the time, took to visiting him in jail, walking the six miles from his home in Paris to the dungeon of the Château de Vincennes. Though that summer was extremely hot, says Rousseau in his not entirely reliable *Confessions* (1781–88), he walked because he was too poor to travel by other means. "In order to slacken my pace," writes Rousseau, "I thought of taking a book with me. One day I took the *Mercure de France* and, glancing through it as I walked, I came upon this question propounded by the Dijon Academy for the next year's prize: Has the progress of the sciences and arts done more to corrupt morals or improve them? The moment I read that I beheld another universe and became another man." In this other universe, this other man won the prize, and the published essay became famous for its furious condemnation of such progress.

Rousseau was less an original thinker than a daring one; he gave the boldest articulation to existing tensions and the most fervent praise to emerging sensibilities. The assertion that God, monarchical government, and nature were all harmoniously aligned was becoming untenable. Rousseau, with his lower-middle-class resentments, his Calvinist Swiss suspicion of kings and Catholicism, his desire to shock, and his unshakable self-confidence, was the person to make specific and political those distant rumblings of discord. In the *Discourse on the Arts and Letters*, he declared that learning and even printing corrupt and weaken both the individual and the culture. "Behold how luxury, licentiousness, and slavery have in all periods been punishment for the arrogant attempts we have made to emerge from the happy ignorance in which eternal wisdom had placed us." The arts and sciences, he asserted, lead not to happiness nor to self-knowledge, but to distraction and corruption.

Now the assumption that the natural, the good, and the simple are all aligned seems commonplace at best; then, it was incendiary. In Christian theology, nature and humanity had both fallen from grace after Eden; it was Christian civilization that redeemed them, so that goodness was a cultural rather than a natural state. This Rousseauian reversal that insists that men and nature are better in their original condition is, among other things, an attack on cities, aristocrats, technology, sophistication, and sometimes theology, and it is still going on today (though curiously the French, who were his primary audience and whose revolution he contributed to, have in the long run been less responsive to these ideas than the British, the Germans, and the Americans). Rousseau developed these ideas further in his *Discourse on the Origin and Foundation of Inequality* (1754) and in his novels *Julie* (1761) and *Emile* (1762). Both novels portray, in various ways, a simpler, more rural life—though none of them acknowledge the hard manual labor of most rural people. His fictional characters lived, as he himself did at his happiest, in unostentatious ease, supported by invisible toilers. The inconsistencies in Rousseau's work don't matter, for it is less a cogent analysis than the expression of a new sensibility and its new enthusiasms. That Rousseau wrote with great elegance is one of those inconsistencies and one of the reasons he was so widely read.

In the *Discourse on Inequality*, Rousseau portrays man in his natural condition "wandering in the forests, without industry, without speech, without domicile, without war and without liaisons, with no need of his fellow-men, likewise with no desire to harm them," even while he admits that we cannot know what this condition was. The treatise offhandedly ignores Christian narratives of human origins and reaches toward a prescient comparative anthropology of social evolution instead (and though it reiterates Christianity's theme of the fall from grace, it reverses the direction of this fall: it is no longer into nature but into culture). In this ideology, walking functions as an emblem of the simple man and as, when the walk is solitary and rural, a means of being in nature and outside society. The walker has the detachment of the traveler but travels unadorned and unaugmented, dependent on his or her own bodily strength rather than on conveniences that can be made and bought—horses, boats, carriages. Walking is, after all, an activity essentially unimproved since the dawn of time.

In portraying himself so often as a pedestrian, Rousseau claimed kin to this ideal walker before history, and he did walk extensively throughout his life. His wandering life began when he returned to Geneva from a Sunday stroll in the country, only to find that he had come back too late: the gates of the city were shut. Impulsively, the fifteen-year-old Rousseau decided to abandon his birth-

---

himself began to walk around at a lively pace in a "Keplerian ellipse," all the time explaining in a low voice his place, his apprenticeship, and eventually his religion; he turned from the gates and walked out of Switzerland. In Italy and France he found and left many jobs, patrons, and friends during a life that seemed aimless until the day he read the *Mercure de France* and found his vocation. Ever after, he seemed to be trying to recover the carefree wandering of his youth. He writes of one episode, "I do not remember ever having had in all my life a spell of time so completely free from care and anxiety as those seven or eight days spent on the road. . . . This memory has left me the strongest taste for everything associated with it, for mountains especially and for travelling on foot. I have never travelled so except in my prime, and it has always been a delight to me. . . . For a long while I searched Paris for any two men sharing my tastes, each willing to contribute fifty louis from his purse and a year of his time for a joint tour of Italy on foot, with no other attendant than a lad to come with us and carry a knapsack."

Rousseau never found serious candidates for this early version of a walking tour (and never explained why companions were necessary to its execution, unless they were to pay the bills). But he continued to walk at every opportunity. Elsewhere he claimed, "Never did I think so much, exist so vividly, and experience so much, never have I been so much myself—if I may use that expression—as in the journeys I have taken alone and on foot. There is something about walking which stimulates and enlivens my thoughts. When I stay in one place I can hardly think at all; my body has to be on the move to set my mind going. The sight of the countryside, the succession of pleasant views, the open air, a sound appetite, and the good health I gain by walking, the easy atmosphere of an inn, the absence of everything that makes me feel my dependence, of everything that recalls me to my situation—all these serve to free my spirit, to lend a greater boldness to my thinking, so that I can combine them, select them, and make them mine as I will, without fear or restraint." It was, of course, an ideal walking that he described—chosen freely by a healthy person amid pleasant and safe circumstances—and it is this kind of walking that would be taken up by his countless heirs as an expression of well-being, harmony with nature, freedom, and virtue.

Rousseau portrays walking as both an exercise of simplicity and a means of contemplation. During the time he wrote the *Discourses*, he would walk alone in the Bois de Boulogne after dinner, "thinking over subjects for works to be written and not returning till night." The *Confessions*, from which these passages come,

---

thoughts on "complementarity." He walked with bent head and knit brows: from time to time, he looked up at me

---

were not published until after Rousseau's death (in 1762 his books had been burned in Paris and Geneva, and his life as a wandering exile had begun). Even before the *Confessions* were finished, however, his readers already associated him with peripatetic excursions. When an adoring James Boswell came to visit Rousseau near Neuchâtel, Switzerland, in 1764, Boswell wrote, "To prepare myself for the great Interview, I walked out alone. I strolled pensive by the side of the River Ruse in a beautifull Wild Valley surrounded by immense Mountains, some covered with frowning rocks, others with glittering snow." Boswell, who was at twenty-four as self-conscious as Rousseau and more foppish about it, already knew that walking, solitude, and wilderness were Rousseauian and clad his mind in their effects as he might have adorned his body for a more conventional meeting.

Solitude is an ambiguous state throughout Rousseau's writings. In the *Discourse on the Origin and Foundations of Inequality*, he portrays human beings in their natural state as isolated dwellers in a hospitable forest. But in his more personal work, he often portrays solitude not as an ideal state but as a consolation and refuge for a man who has been betrayed and disappointed. In fact, much of his writing revolves around the question of whether and how one should relate to one's fellow humans. Hypersensitive almost to the point of paranoia and convinced of his own rightness under the most dubious circumstances, Rousseau overreacted to the judgments of others, yet never could or would subdue his unorthodox and often abrasive ideas and acts. It is now popularly proposed that his writing universalizes his experience, and that his picture of man's fall from simplicity and grace into corruption is little more than a portrait of Rousseau's fall from Swiss simplicity and security or merely from childhood naïveté into his uncertain life abroad among aristocrats and intellectuals. Whether this is so or not, his version has been so influential that few are entirely beyond its reach nowadays.

Finally, at the end of his life, he wrote *Reveries of a Solitary Walker* (*Les Rêveries du promeneur solitaire* in the original; 1782), a book that is and is not about walking. Each of its chapters is called a walk, and in the Second Walk, he states his premise: "Having therefore decided to describe my habitual state of mind in this, the strangest situation which any mortal will ever know, I could think of no simpler or surer way of carrying out my plan than to keep a faithful record of my solitary walks and the reveries that occupy them." Each of these short personal essays resembles the sequence of thoughts or preoccupations one might enter-

---

and underlined some important point by a sober gesture. As he spoke, the words and sentences which I had read tain on a walk, though there is no evidence they are the fruit of specific walks. Several are meditations on a phrase, some are recollections, some are little more than aired grievances. Together the ten essays (the eighth and ninth were still drafts and the tenth was left unfinished at the time of his death in 1778) portray a man who has taken refuge in the thoughts and botanical pursuits of his walks, and who through them seeks and recalls a safer haven.

A solitary walker is in the world, but apart from it, with the detachment of the traveler rather than the ties of the worker, the dweller, the member of a group. Walking seems to have become Rousseau's chosen mode of being because within a walk he is able to live in thought and reverie, to be self-sufficient, and thus to survive the world he feels has betrayed him. It provides him with a literal position from which to speak. As a literary structure, the recounted walk encourages digression and association, in contrast to the stricter form of a discourse or the chronological progression of a biographical or historical narrative. A century and a half later, James Joyce and Virginia Woolf would, in trying to describe the workings of the mind, develop the style called stream of consciousness. In their novels *Ulysses* and *Mrs. Dalloway*, the jumble of thoughts and recollections of their protagonists unfolds best during walks. This kind of unstructured, associative thinking is the kind most often connected to walking, and it suggests walking as not an analytical but an improvisational act. Rousseau's *Reveries* are one of the first portraits of this relationship between thinking and walking.

Rousseau walks alone, and the plants he gathers and strangers he encounters are the only beings toward whom he expresses tenderness. In the Ninth Walk, he reminisces about earlier walks, which seem to slide out from each other like sections of a telescope to focus on his distant past. He begins with a walk two days before to the Ecole Militaire, then moves to one outside Paris two years before, and then to a garden excursion with his wife four or five years before, and finally recounts an incident that pre-dated even this last recollection by many years, in which he bought all the apples a poor girl was selling and distributed them among hungry urchins loitering nearby. All these recollections were prompted by reading an obituary of an acquaintance that mentioned her love for children and triggered Rousseau's guilt about his own abandoned children (though modern scholars sometimes doubt he had any children to begin with, his *Confessions* say he had five by his common-law wife Thérèse and put all of them in orphanages). These recollections argue against a charge no one but he himself has lev-

---

before in his papers suddenly took life and became loaded with meaning. It was one of the few solemn moments that eled, and they do so by declaring his affection for children, as demonstrated in these casual encounters. The essay is a ruminative defense for an imagined trial. The conclusion shifts the subject to the tribulations his fame has brought him and his inability to walk unrecognized and in peace among people. The implication is that even in this most casual of social exchanges he has been thwarted, so that only the terrain of the reverie leaves him freedom to roam. Most of the book was written while he was living in Paris, isolated by his fame and his suspicion.

If the literature of philosophical walking begins with Rousseau, it is because he is one of the first who thought it worthwhile to record in detail the circumstances of his musing. If he was a radical, his most profoundly radical act was to revalue the personal and the private, for which walking, solitude, and wilderness provided favorable conditions. If he inspired revolutions, revolutions in imagination and culture as well as in political organization, they were for him only necessary to overthrow the impediments to such experience. The full force of his intellect and his most compelling arguments had been made in the cause of recovering and perpetuating such states of mind and life as he describes in *Reveries of a Solitary Walker.*

In two walks, he recollects the interludes of rural peace he most treasured. In the famous Fifth Walk, he describes the happiness he found on the island of Saint-Pierre on Lake of Bienne, to which he fled after being stoned and driven out of Motiers, near Neuchâtel, where Boswell had visited him. "Wherein lay this great contentment?" he asks rhetorically, and goes on to describe a life in which he owned little and did little, save botanize and boat. It is the Rousseauian peaceable kingdom, privileged enough that no manual labor is required, but without the sophistication and socializing of an aristocratic retreat. The Tenth Walk is a paean to the similar rural happiness he had with his patroness and lover, Louise de Warens, when he was a teenager. It was written when he had finally found a replacement for Saint-Pierre, the estate of Ermenonville. He died at the age of seventy-five, leaving the Tenth Walk unfinished. The marquis de Girardin, Ermenonville's owner, buried Rousseau on an isle of poplars there and established a pilgrimage for the sentimental devotees who came to pay tribute. It included an itinerary that instructed the visitor not only how to walk through the garden toward the tomb but how to feel. Rousseau's private revolt was becoming public culture.

---

count in an existence, the revelation of a world of dazzling thought.—LEON ROSENFELD, ON A 1929 ENCOUNTER

III. Walking and Thinking and Walking

Søren Kierkegaard is the other philosopher who has much to say about walking and thinking. He chose cities—or one city, Copenhagen—as his place to walk and study his human subjects, though he compared his urban tours to rural botanizing: human beings were the specimens he gathered. Born a hundred years later in another Protestant city, he had a life in some ways utterly unlike Rousseau's: the harsh ascetic standards he set for himself could not be less like Rousseau's self-indulgence, and he kept to his birthplace, to his family, and to his religion throughout his life, though he quarreled with them all. In other respects—in his social isolation, his prolific writing of works both literary and philosophical, his chafing self-consciousness—the resemblance is strong. The son of a wealthy and grimly devout merchant, Kierkegaard lived off his inheritance and under his father's thumb for most of his life. In a memory he ascribes to one of his pseudonyms but which is almost certainly his own, he tells of how his father, rather than let him leave the house, would walk back and forth in a room with him, describing the world so vividly that the boy seemed to see all the variety evoked. As the boy grew older, his father let him join in: "What had at first been an epic now became a drama; they conversed in turn. If they were walking along well-known paths they watched one another sharply to make sure that nothing was overlooked; if the way was strange to Johannes, he invented something, whereas the father's almighty imagination was capable of shaping everything, of using every childish whim as an ingredient of the drama. To Johannes it seemed as if the world were coming into existence during the conversation, as if the father were the Lord God and he was his favorite."

The triangle between Kierkegaard, his father, and his God would consume his life, and sometimes it seems that he made his God in his father's image. With these walks in the room, his father seems to be consciously shaping the strange character Kierkegaard would become. He described himself as already an old man in childhood, as a ghost, as a wanderer, and this pacing back and forth seems to have been instruction in living in a disembodied magical realm of the imagination that had only one real inhabitant, himself. Even the myriad pseudonyms under which he published many of his best-known works seem devices to lose himself while revealing himself and to make a crowd out of his solitude.

WITH NIELS BOHR   *Last Sunday I took a Walk toward highgate and in the lane that winds by the side of Lord*

Throughout his adult life, Kierkegaard almost never received guests at home, and indeed, throughout his life he almost never had anyone he could call a friend, though he had a vast acquaintance. One of his nieces says that the streets of Copenhagen were his "reception room," and Kierkegaard's great daily pleasure seems to have been walking the streets of his city. It was a way to be among people for a man who could not be with them, a way to bask in the faint human warmth of brief encounters, acquaintances' greetings, and overheard conversations. A lone walker is both present and detached from the world around, more than an audience but less than a participant. Walking assuages or legitimizes this alienation: one is mildly disconnected because one is walking, not because one is incapable of connecting. Walking provided Kierkegaard, like Rousseau, with a wealth of casual contacts with his fellow humans, and it facilitated contemplation.

In 1837, just as his literary work was beginning, Kierkegaard wrote, "Strangely enough, my imagination works best when I am sitting alone in a large assemblage, when the tumult and noise require a substratum of will if the imagination is to hold on to its object; without this environment it bleeds to death in the exhausting embrace of an indefinite idea." He found the same tumult on the street. More than a decade later, he declared in another journal, "In order to bear mental tension such as mine, I need diversion, the diversion of chance contacts on the streets and alleys, because association with a few exclusive individuals is actually no diversion." In these and other statements, he proposes that the mind works best when surrounded by distraction, that it focuses in the act of withdrawing from surrounding bustle rather than in being isolated from it. He reveled in the turbulent variety of city life, saying elsewhere, "This very moment there is an organ-grinder down in the street playing and singing—it is wonderful, it is the accidental and insignificant things in life which are significant."

In his journals, he insists that he composed all his works afoot. "Most of _Either / Or_ was written only twice (besides, of course, what I thought through while walking, but that is always the case); nowadays I like to write three times," says one passage, and there are many like it protesting that although his extensive walks were perceived as signs of idleness they were in fact the foundation of his prolific work. The recollections of others show him during his pedestrian encounters, but there must have been long solitary intervals in which he could compose his thoughts and rehearse the day's writing. Perhaps it was that the city

---

Mansfield's park I met Mr. Green our Demonstrator at Guy's in conversation with Coleridge—I joined them, after

---

strolls distracted him so that he could forget himself enough to think more productively, for his private thoughts are often convolutions of self-consciousness
and despair. In a journal passage from 1848, he described how on his way home,
"overwhelmed with ideas ready to be written down and in a sense so weak that I
could scarcely walk," he would often encounter a poor man, and if he refused to
speak with him, the ideas would flee "and I would sink into the most dreadful
spiritual tribulation at the idea that God could do to me what I had done to that
man. But if I took the time to talk with the poor man, things never went that way."

Being out in public gave him almost his only social role, and he fretted over
how his performance on the stage of Copenhagen would be interpreted. In a way,
his appearances on the street were like his appearances on the printed page: en-
deavors to be in touch, but not too closely and on his own terms. Like Rousseau,
he had an exacting relationship with the public. He chose to publish many of his
works under pseudonyms and then to complain that he was considered an idler,
since none knew he went home from his roaming to write. After he broke off his
engagement with Regine Olsen in what was to be the defining tragedy of his life,
he continued to see her on the street but nowhere else. Years later, they would
both appear repeatedly at the same time on a portside street, and he worried over
what this meant. The street, which is the most casual arena for people with full
private lives, was the most personal for him.

The other great crisis of his uneventful life came when he wrote a small attack
on Denmark's scurrilous satirical magazine the *Corsair*. Though its editor admired
him, the magazine began to publish mocking pictures and paragraphs about him,
and the Copenhagen public took up the joke. Most of the jokes were mild
enough—they depicted him as having trouser legs of uneven lengths, made fun
of his elaborate pseudonyms and compositional style, published pictures of him
as a spry figure in a frock coat that belled out around his spiky legs. But the par-
odies made him better known than he wished to be, achingly anxious about being mocked and seeing mockery everywhere. Kierkegaard seems to have
exaggerated the effect of the *Corsair*'s jabs and suffered horribly—not least because he no longer felt free to roam the city. "My atmosphere has been tainted for
me. Because of my melancholy and my enormous work I needed a situation of
solitude in the crowd in order to rest. So I despair. I can no longer find it.
Curiosity surrounds me everywhere." One of his biographers says that it was this
final crisis of his life, after those of his father and his fiancée, that pushed him into

---

enquiring by a look whether it would be agreeable—I walked with him at his alderman-after-dinner pace for nearly

---

his last phase as a theological rather than a philosophical and aesthetic writer. Nevertheless, he continued to walk the streets of Copenhagen, and it was on one of those walks that he collapsed and was taken to the hospital, where he died some weeks later.

Like Rousseau, Kierkegaard is a hybrid, a philosophical writer rather than a philosopher proper. Their work is often descriptive, evocative, personal, and poetically ambiguous, in sharp contrast to the closely reasoned argument central to the Western philosophical tradition. It has room for delight and personality and something as specific as the sound of an organ grinder in a street or rabbits on an island. Rousseau branched out into the novel, the autobiography, and the reverie, and play with forms was central to Kierkegaard's work: creating a massive postscript to a relatively short essay, layering pseudonymous authors like Chinese boxes within his texts. As a writer his heirs seem to be literary experimentalists like Italo Calvino and Jorge Luis Borges, who play with the way form, voice, reference, and other devices shape meaning.

Rousseau and Kierkegaard's walking is only accessible to us because they wrote about it in more personal, descriptive, and specific works—Rousseau's *Confessions* and *Reveries*, Kierkegaard's journals—rather than staying in the impersonal and universal realm of philosophy at its most pure. Perhaps it is because walking is itself a way of grounding one's thoughts in a personal and embodied experience of the world that it lends itself to this kind of writing. This is why the meaning of walking is mostly discussed elsewhere than in philosophy: in poetry, novels, letters, diaries, travelers' accounts, and first-person essays. Too, these eccentrics focus on walking as a means of modulating their alienation, and this kind of alienation was a new phenomenon in intellectual history. They were neither immersed in the society around them nor—save in Kierkegaard's later years, after the *Corsair* affair—withdrawn from it in the tradition of the religious contemplative. They were in the world but not of it. A solitary walker, however short his or her route, is unsettled, between places, drawn forth into action by desire and lack, having the detachment of the traveler rather than the ties of the worker, the dweller, the member of a group.

---

two miles I suppose. In those two Miles he broached a thousand things—let me see if I can give you a list—

IV. THE MISSING SUBJECT

In the early twentieth century, a philosopher actually addressed walking directly as something central to his intellectual project. Of course walking had been an example earlier. Kierkegaard liked to cite Diogenes: "When the Eleatics denied motion, Diogenes, as everyone knows, came forward as an opponent. He literally did come forward, because he did not say a word but merely paced back and forth a few times, thereby assuming he had sufficiently refuted them." The phenomenologist Edmund Husserl described walking as the experience by which we understand our body in relationship to the world, in his 1931 essay, "The World of the Living Present and the Constitution of the Surrounding World External to the Organism." The body, he said, is our experience of what is always here, and the body in motion experiences the unity of all its parts as the continuous "here" that moves toward and through the various "theres." That is to say, it is the body that moves but the world that changes, which is how one distinguishes the one from the other: travel can be a way to experience this continuity of self amid the flux of the world and thus to begin to understand each and their relationship to each other. Husserl's proposal differs from earlier speculations on how a person experiences the world in its emphasis on the act of walking rather than on the senses and the mind.

Still, this is slim pickings. One would expect that postmodern theory would have much to say about walking, given that mobility and corporeality have been among its major themes—and when corporeality gets mobile, it walks. Much contemporary theory was born out of feminism's protest at the way earlier theory universalized the very specific experience of being male, and sometimes of being white and privileged. Feminism and postmodernism both emphasize that the specifics of one's bodily experience and location shape one's intellectual perspective. The old idea of objectivity as speaking from nowhere—speaking while transcending the particulars of body and place—was laid to rest; everything came from a position, and every position was political (and as George Orwell remarked much earlier, "The opinion that art should not be political is itself a political opinion"). But while dismantling this false universal by emphasizing the role of the ethnic and gendered body in consciousness, these thinkers have apparently generalized what it means to be corporeal and human from their own specific ex-

----

Nightingales, poetry—on Poetical Sensation—Metaphysics—Different genera and species of Dreams—

----

perience—or inexperience—as bodies that, apparently, lead a largely passive existence in highly insulated circumstances.

The body described again and again in postmodern theory does not suffer under the elements, encounter other species, experience primal fear or much in the way of exhilaration, or strain its muscles to the utmost. In sum, it doesn't engage in physical endeavor or spend time out of doors. The very term "the body" so often used by postmodernists seems to speak of a passive object, and that body appears most often laid out upon the examining table or in bed. A medical and sexual phenomenon, it is a site of sensations, processes, and desires rather than a source of action and production. Having been liberated from manual labor and located in the sensory deprivation chambers of apartments and offices, this body has nothing left but the erotic as a residue of what it means to be embodied. Which is not to disparage sex and the erotic as fascinating and profound (and relevant to walking's history, as we shall see), only to propose that they are so emphasized because other aspects of being embodied have atrophied for many people. The body presented to us in these hundreds of volumes and essays, this passive body for which sexuality and biological function are the only signs of life, is in fact not the universal human body but the white-collar urban body, or rather a theoretical body that can't even be theirs, since even minor physical exertions never appear: this body described in theory never even aches from hauling the complete works of Kierkegaard across campus. "If the body is a metaphor for our locatedness in space and time and thus for the finitude of human perception and knowledge, then the postmodern body is no body at all," writes Susan Bordo, one feminist theorist at odds with this version of embodiment.

Travel, the other great theme of recent postmodern theory, is about being utterly mobile; the one has failed to modify the other, and we seem to be reading about the postmodern body shuttled around by airplanes and hurtling cars, or even moving around by no apparent means, muscular, mechanical, economic, or ecological. The body is nothing more than a parcel in transit, a chess piece dropped on another square; it does not move but is moved. In a sense, these are problems arising from the level of abstraction of contemporary theory. Much of the terminology of location and mobility—words like *nomad, decentered, marginalized, deterritorialized, border, migrant,* and *exile*—are not attached to specific places and people; they represent instead ideas of rootlessness and flux that seem as much the result of the ungrounded theory as its putative subject. Even in these endeav-

Nightmare—a dream accompanied by a sense of touch—single and double touch—A dream related—First and ors to come to terms with the tangible world of bodies and motion, abstraction dematerializes them again. The words themselves seem to move freely and creatively, unburdened by the responsibilities of specific description.

Only in maverick writings does the body become active. In Elaine Scarry's magisterial book *The Body in Pain: The Unmaking and Making of the World,* she considers first how torture destroys the conscious world of its subjects, then theorizes how creative efforts—making both stories and objects—construct that world. She describes tools and manufactured objects as extensions of the body into the world and thus ways of knowing it. Scarry documents how the tools become more and more detached from the body itself, until the digging stick that extends the arm becomes a backhoe that replaces the body. Though she never discusses walking directly, her work suggests philosophical approaches to the subject. Walking returns the body to its original limits again, to something supple, sensitive, and vulnerable, but walking itself extends into the world as do those tools that augment the body. The path is an extension of walking, the places set aside for walking are monuments to that pursuit, and walking is a mode of making the world as well as being in it. Thus the walking body can be traced in the places it has made; paths, parks, and sidewalks are traces of the acting out of imagination and desire; walking sticks, shoes, maps, canteens, and backpacks are further material results of that desire. Walking shares with making and working that crucial element of engagement of the body and the mind with the world, of knowing the world through the body and the body through the world.

---

second consciousness—the difference explained between will and Volition—so many metaphysicians from a

---

Chapter 3

RISING AND FALLING:

The Theorists of Bipedalism

It was a place as blank as a sheet of paper. It was the place I had always been look-ing for. Out train and car windows, in my imagination, and on my walks through more complicated terrain, flat expanses would call to me, promising walking as I imagined it. And now I had arrived at the pure plane of a dry lake bed where I could walk uninterrupted and utterly free. The desert holds many of these dry lake beds or playas, washed long ago or annually to a surface as flat and inviting as a dance floor when dry. These are the places where the desert is most itself: stark, open, free; an invitation to wander, a laboratory of perception, scale, light, a place where loneliness has a luxurious flavor, like in the blues. This one, near Joshua Tree National Park, in southeastern California's Mojave Desert, was occa-sionally a lake bed but mostly a pure plain of cracked dust in which nothing grew. To me these big spaces mean freedom, freedom for the unconscious activity of the body and the conscious activity of the mind, places where walking hits a steady beat that seems to be the pulse of time itself. Pat, my companion on this walk across the lake bed, prefers rock climbing, in which every move is an iso-lated act that absorbs the whole of his attention and seldom rises to a rhythm. It's a difference of style that cuts deep in our lives: he is something of a Buddhist and conceives of spirituality as being conscious in the moment; while I am a sucker for symbolisms, interpretations, histories, and a Western kind of spirituality that is located less in the here than in the there. But both of us share the same notion of being out in the land as an ideal way to exist.

Walking, I realized long ago in another desert, is how the body measures itself against the earth. On this lake bed, each step brought us minutely closer to one of the ranges of mountains, blue in the late afternoon light, that circled our horizon like the bleachers rising above a field. Picture the lake bed as a pure geometric plane that our steps measured like the legs of a protractor swinging back and forth. The measurements recorded that the earth was large and we were not, the same good and terrifying news most walks in the desert provide. On this afternoon even the cracks in the ground cast long sharp shadows, and a shadow like a skyscraper stretched from Pat's van. Our shadows moved alongside us on our right, growing longer and longer, longer than I had ever seen them. I asked him how long he thought they were, and he told me to stand still and he'd pace it off. I faced east into my shadow, toward the closest mountains that all the shadows stretched toward, and he began to walk.

I stood alone, my shadow like a long road Pat traveled. He seemed, in that pellucid air, not to grow distant but only to grow smaller. When I could frame him between my thumb and forefinger held close together and his own shadow stretched almost to the mountains, he had reached the shadow of my head—but as he arrived, the sun suddenly slipped below the horizon. With that, the world changed: the plain lost its gilding, the mountains became a deeper blue, and our sharp shadows grew blurry. I called for him to stop at the now-vague shadow of my head, and when I had myself covered the distance between us, he told me he'd gone a hundred paces—250 or 300 feet—but what constituted my shadow had become harder and harder to distinguish as he went. We walked back to the van as night approached, the experiment concluded. But where did it begin?

Rousseau thought that humanity's true nature could be found in its origins, and that to understand those origins was to understand who we were and who we should be. The subject of human origins has itself evolved immensely since he cobbled together a few sketchy descriptions of non-European customs with some groundless speculation on the "noble savage." But the argument that who we were originally—whether *originally* means 1940 or three million years ago—is

---

*Southey's belief too much diluted—A Ghost story—. . . . —*JOHN KEATS, IN A LETTER TO GEORGE AND who we are or ought to be has only become stronger with time. Popular books and scientific articles debate again and again whether we are a bloodthirsty, violent species or a communitarian one and what kind of differences between the genders are encoded in our genes. Both are often just-so stories about who we are, could be, or should be, told by everyone from conservatives arguing the adequacy of tradition to health seekers arguing that we ought to eat some just-discovered primordial diet. This, of course, makes who we were an intensely political subject. The scientists researching human origins have been contentious about these questions of human nature, and in recent years walking has become a central part of their conversation.

While philosophers have had little to say about what walking means, scientists have of late had a great deal to say. Paleontologists, anthropologists, and anatomists have launched a passionate and often partisan argument over when and why the ancestral ape got up on its hind legs and walked so long that its body became our upright, two-legged, striding body. They were the philosophers of walking I had been looking for, speculating endlessly about what each bodily shape says about function and about how those forms and functions eventually added up to our humanity—though what that humanity consists of is equally debatable. The only given is that upright walking is the first hallmark of what became humanity. Whatever its causes, it caused much more: it opened up vast new horizons of possibility, and among other things, it created the spare pair of limbs dangling from the upright body, seeking something to hold or make or destroy, the arms freed to evolve into ever more sophisticated manipulators of the material world. Some scholars see two-legged walking as the mechanism that set our brains expanding, others as the structure that established our sexuality. So, although the debate about the origins of bipedalism is full of detailed descriptions of hip joints and foot bones and geologic dating methods, it is ultimately about sex, landscape, and thinking.

Usually the uniqueness of human beings is portrayed as a matter of consciousness. Yet the human body is also unlike anything else on earth, and in some ways has shaped that consciousness. The animal kingdom has nothing else like this column of flesh and bone always in danger of toppling, this proud unsteady tower. The few other truly two-legged species—birds, kangaroos—have tails and other features for balance, and most of these bipeds hop rather than walk. The alternating long stride that propels us is unique, perhaps because it is such a pre-

---

GEORGIANA KEATS   *Sir, I have received your new book written against the human race, and I thank*

---

arious arrangement. Four-legged animals are are as stable as a table when all four eet are on the ground, but humans are already precariously balanced on two be-fore they begin to move. Even standing still is a feat of balance, as anyone who as watched or been a drunk knows.

Reading the accounts of human walking, it is easy to begin to think of the Fall in terms of the falls, the innumerable spills, possible for a suddenly upright crea-ture that must balance all its shifting weight on a single foot as it moves. John Napier, in an essay on the ancient origins of walking, wrote, "Human walking is a unique activity during which the body, step by step, teeters on the edge of ca-tastrophe. . . . Man's bipedal mode of walking seems potentially catastrophic be-cause only the rhythmic forward movement of first one leg and then the other keeps him from falling flat on his face." This is easiest to see in small children for whom the many aspects that will later unite seamlessly into walking are still dis-tinct and awkward. They learn to walk by flirting with falling—they lean forward with their body and then rush to keep their legs under that body. Their plump bowed legs always seem to be lagging behind or catching up, and they often tumble into frustration before they master the art. Children begin to walk to chase desires no one will fulfill for them: the desire for that which is out of reach, for freedom, for independence from the secure confines of the maternal Eden. And so walking begins as delayed falling, and the fall meets with the Fall.

Genesis may seem out of place in a discussion of science, but it is often the scientists who have dragged it in with them, unwittingly or otherwise. The sci-entific stories are as much an attempt to account for who we are as any creation myth, and some of them seem to hark back to the central creation myth of Western culture, that business of Adam and Eve in the Garden. Many of the hy-potheses have been wildly speculative, seemingly based less on the evidence than on modern desires or old social mores, particularly as they relate to the roles of the sexes. During the 1960s, the Man the Hunter story was widely accepted and made popular by such books as Robert Ardrey's *African Genesis*, with its famous opening line "Not in innocence, and not in Asia, was man born." It suggested that violence and aggression are ineradicable parts of human disposition, but re-deemed them by proposing that they were the means by which we evolved (or males evolved; most of the mainstream theories have tended to leave females do-ing little but passing along the genes of their evolving mates). Early challengers of the Man the Hunter scenario, writes the feminist anthropologist Adrienne

you. . . . Never was so much intelligence used to make us stupid. While reading it, one longs to go on all fours.

Zihlman, "point out parallels between the interpretation of hunting as propelling humankind into humanity, on the one hand, and the biblical myth of expulsion from Eden, after Eve's eating of the tree of knowledge, on the other. The authors argue that both fates—that of hunting and of the expulsion—were precipitated by an act of eating—meat in the first instance and forbidden fruit in the other." And they argue that the division of labor—men as hunters, women as gatherers—reflects the distinct division of roles given Adam and Eve in Genesis. Similarly, during the 1960s and 1970s, the theory went that human walking evolved during a time of radical climate change, when the species was transformed from an arboreal forest dweller to a creature of the savannah, another expulsion from Eden. Nowadays both the dominance of hunting and the residence on the savannah have fallen from favor as evolutionary explanations. But the language remains: scientists now pursuing human origins not in fossils but in genes describe our hypothetical common ancestor as "African Eve" or "Mitochondrial Eve."

These scientists have sometimes looked for what they wanted to find, or found what they were looking for. The Piltdown man hoax was believed from 1908 to its denouement in 1950 because British scientists were eager to believe the evidence of a large-brained creature with an animal jaw. The bones suggested that our intelligence was of great age and gratified them by showing up in England. Much was made of clever Piltdown man as an Englishman, until new technologies proved him a liar cobbled together from a modern ape's jaw and a human skull. When Raymond Dart found a child's skull in South Africa in 1924 that, unlike Piltdown man, turned out to be genuine, it was widely discredited as a human ancestor by the British masters so pleased by Piltdown. It was discredited because the scientists of the era preferred not to come from Africa and because the skull of the Taung child, as it was called, had a small cranium but evidently walked upright, suggesting that our intelligence had come late rather than early in our evolution. At the base of the skull is an opening called the foramen magnum through which the spinal cord connects to the brain. The foramen magnum of the Taung child was in the center of the skull, as it is in us, rather than at the back, as it is in apes, and so it was evident that this creature had walked upright, its head poised atop the spine rather than hanging down from it. Like most of the skulls of the australopithecine hominids who would evolve into humans, this one looks to the modern eye like a house with odd proportions: the porch of the brow and jutting jaw is enormous, the attic where the modern brain rises is

---

—VOLTAIRE TO ROUSSEAU, ON THE DISCOURSE ON THE ORIGIN OF INEQUALITY   *The diminution of the* nonexistent. Most early evolutionists proposed that our human characteristics—walking, thinking, making—originated together, perhaps because they found it hard or unpleasant to imagine a creature who shared only a part of our humanity. Dart's counter-hypothesis was advanced by Louis and Mary Leakey's spectacular Kenyan finds in the 1950s, 1960s, and 1970s and all but confirmed by Donald Johanson's celebrated discovery of the "Lucy" skeleton and related fossils in Ethiopia in the 1970s. Walking came first.

Nowadays walking upright is considered to be the Rubicon the evolving species crossed to become hominid, distinct from all other primates and ancestral to human beings. The list of what we eventually got from bipedalism is long and alluring, full of all the gothic arches and elongations of the body. Start with the straight row of toes and high arch of the foot. Go up the long straight walker's legs to the buttocks, round and protruberant thanks to the massively developed gluteus maximus of walkers, a minor muscle in apes but the largest muscle in the human body. Then go on to the flat stomach, the flexible waist, the straight spine, the low shoulders, the erect head set atop a long neck. The upright body's various sections are balanced on top of each other like the sections of a pillar, while the weight of quadrupeds' heads and torsos hangs from their spines like the roadway from a suspension bridge, with a pair of pierlike legs toward either end. The great apes are knuckle-walkers: creatures adapted to life in tropical forests who for the most part move only short distances on the ground between trees, on long forelimbs that give them a kind of diagonal posture. Apes have—when compared to humans—arched backs, no waists, short necks, chests shaped like inverted funnels, protruberant abdomens, scrawny hips and bottoms, bandy legs, and flat feet with opposable big toes.

When I think about this evolutionary history of walking, I see a small figure, like my companion on the lake bed, only this time it is dawn and the figure is moving toward me, an indecipherable dot in the distance that seems somehow unfamiliar as it becomes distinguishable as an upright figure and finally, when it draws close, is just another walker. But what was that casting a long shadow in the middle distance? Lucy—as they named the small 3.2-million-year-old *Australopithecus afarensis* skeleton found in Ethiopia in 1974, presuming from various details that it was female—was apelike in many respects; she had little in the way of a waist or neck, short legs, longish arms, and the funnel-like rib cage of an ape. Her pelvis, however, was wide and shallow, and so she had a stable gait with

---

olfactory stimuli seems itself to be a consequence of man's raising himself from the ground, of his assumption of an

---

hip joints far apart tapering to close-together knees like humans and unlike chimps (whose narrow hips and far-apart knees make them lurch from side to side when they walk upright). Some say she would have been a terrible runner and not much of a walker. But she walked. This much is certain, and then come the arguments.

Dozens of scientists have interpreted her bones, reconstructed her flesh, her gait, her sex life, in dozens of different ways and argued over whether she walked well or poorly. Discovery conveys a certain privilege of interpretation, and so Johanson, who worked at the Cleveland Museum, took the bones he found in Hadar, Ethiopia, to his friend Owen Lovejoy, an anatomist at Cleveland State University and an expert on human locomotion. Lovejoy issued the orthodox verdict. In his book *Lucy*, Johanson reports that Lovejoy said of the *afarensis* knee joint he had brought in the year before,

"This is like a modern knee joint. This little midget was fully bipedal."

"But could he walk upright?" I persisted.

"My friend, he could walk upright. Explain to him what a hamburger was and he'd beat you to the nearest McDonald's nine times out of ten."

Johanson's knee joint came along as the first material support for Lovejoy's bold theory that bipedalism had begun and been perfected far earlier than anyone else had assumed. The following year, the Lucy skeleton—or the 40 percent of it that was recovered—further confirmed his hypothesis about the antiquity of human walking, as did the 3.7-million-year-old footprints of a pair of walkers Mary Leakey's team found at Laetoli, Tanzania, in 1977. But why had these creatures become bipedal?

By 1981 Lovejoy had evolved a complicated explanation for why we got up and walked. His 1981 *Science* article "The Origin of Man" has become the focal point for the arguments in the field about the reasons why walking appeared 4 million or more years ago. Lovejoy evolved an elaborate thesis that decreasing the time between births would increase the survival rate of the species. "In most primate species," he wrote, "male fitness is largely determined by consort success of one sort or another"—that is, in the ability or opportunity to mate and thereby pass along their genes. He proposed that in the Miocene era, 5 million and more

---

upright gait; this made his genitals, which were previously concealed, visible and in need of protection, and so

---

years ago, the human ancestor changed its—or rather his—behavior. Males, he proposed, began to bring back provisions for the females; the females thus provided for were able to bear more children as the challenge of feeding themselves and their young was lessened, and the male-headed nuclear family was born. In other words, male fitness had expanded to include provisioning, which would allow them to pass along those genes more frequently and certainly. "Bipedalism," he wrote in a 1988 summary, "figured in this new reproductive scheme because by freeing the hands it made it possible for the male to carry food gathered far from his mate." But, he added, such daily separation of the sexes would only genetically favor males if they could come home and propagate their own genes and no one else's—thus the behavior must have selected for monogamous females as well as responsible males. Lovejoy explained, "The highly unusual sexual behavior of man may now be brought into focus. Human females are continually sexually receptive and . . . male approach may be considered equally stable." Since unlike the females of most species this one no longer signaled her fertile times, they had sex a lot to procreate and to bond. If we regard it as a creation myth, it is one in which the two-parent family is far older than the human species, hominid males are mobile and responsible partners and parents, and females are needy, faithful, stay-at-home mates who are *not* the instruments of bipedal evolution.

The 1960s myth of Man the Hunter had been succeeded by two theories in the 1970s. One dubbed Woman the Gatherer proposed that the primordial diet was probably mostly vegetarian and was mostly collected then, as in hunter-gatherer societies today, by females. The other emphasized food sharing as instrumental in ensuring survival and generating a home base to which food was brought and shared, resulting in more complex social consciousness. In this theory, a communitarian First Supper takes the place of Ardrey's blood sports as the event that propelled us into humanity. Lovejoy combined aspects of both these new theories to create his Man the Gatherer, who brought food home and shared it, though only with his mate and offspring. His theory suggested not only that walking had been a male business, and that the males in question had been full of family virtues, but that the virtues in question had made us walkers. In fact, he said, Lucy and her ilk could walk better than we do, and further, the species had lost its ability to climb.

---

provided feelings of shame in him.—FREUD, *CIVILIZATION AND ITS DISCONTENTS*   *Hand in hand with equal plod*

I was staying with Pat in his shack just outside Joshua Tree National Park while I wrote this chapter. Preoccupied and trying to sort out the sea of material before me, I kept recounting theories to him about why we became bipedal, about details of anatomy and function, and he laughed incredulously at the more outlandish ones. "People get grants and tenure for *that?*" he'd say. His favorite was R. D. Guthrie's 1974 proposal that when hominids became bipedal, the males used their now-exposed penises as a "threat display organ" to intimidate opponents, and we speculated on the origins of human laughter. The following day, after he came home from guiding clients up and down rock faces all day and was lounging with a drink, I read him anthropologist Dean Falk's attack on Lovejoy. Lovejoy's term "copulatory vigilance" caught his attention, and he laughed more at the strange stuff I was immersed in. Not that his world was exactly a bastion of seriousness: while he was climbing for pleasure the day before, I had lain in the shade idly flipping through his guidebook and been entertained by some of the names of the climbing routes up and down the park's myriad giant boulders: "Presbyterian Dental Floss" was right next to "Episcopalian Toothpick," while "Boogers on a Lampshade" mocked the climb genteelly called "Figures in a Landscape," and innumerable poodle, political, and anatomical jokes described other vertical routes up the rocks. That evening, as I read bipedal theory to him and the quail bobbed about the backyard and the setting sun pushed the shadows of the hills farther and farther across the valley, he swore he would get his friends who founded and named many of the park's climbing routes to name the next one "Copulatory Vigilance," an obscure monument to a theory that we had lost our ability to climb and to his opinion of the more far-flung theories of human origins. Lovejoy's theory has become famous, if only because no one can resist attacking it.

Among the earlier critics were the anatomists Jack Stern and Randall Sussman at the State University of New York at Stonybrook, who I visited. Two unathletic men with identical clipped gray mustaches, they looked something like the Walrus and the Carpenter, with Stern as the compact Carpenter and Sussman the expansive Walrus. They talked to me for hours in an office full of bones and books, and periodically one or the other would grab a chimp pelvis or a cast of a fossil femur to illustrate a point. Obviously enthusiastic about their work, they often went off on conversational tangents with each other that left me far behind, and they delighted too in dishing their colleagues in this contentious field. They

---

they go. In the free hands—no. Free empty hands. Backs turned both bowed with equal plod they go. The child

---

had argued that Johanson's Lucy-era *Australopithecus afarensis* fossils were those of apprentice walkers who, based on the evidence—big arms and smallish legs, curved fingers and toes—continued climbing trees well and frequently for a long time afterward. Another feature of the *afarensis* fossils they took up was gender size: if the large and small skeletons Johanson and company had found in Ethiopia were the same species (which Richard Leakey and others contest), then the sizes must represent small females and large males, which made it unlikely they practiced Lovejoy's monogamous arrangement. Living primate species where the males are far larger—baboons, gorillas—are usually polygamous; only those without size differences, such as gibbons, are monogamous. So their version of Lucy was that she was a lousy walker with big floppy feet, a pretty good climber with long, strong arms, and probably part of a polygamous group in which small females spent more time in the trees than large males.

Sussman said, "Back when we started this work, and I don't think it's unhumble to say it, the majority of the people in the field would say we evolved in the savannah, in the open country of the veldt of South Africa or the savannah of East Africa. I think that's a load of crap. I think that what happened was that *afarensis* was living in forest and open country mosaics like you see today in places like the French Congo or along rivers where there's a lot of trees. I mean, that probably went on for a million years when you had an animal that was climbing and an apprentice biped." He added that in the old pictures re-creating this phase of evolution, the creatures were strolling across the grassland; newer ones showed them in much more mixed habitat, and the most recent *National Geographic* articles had paintings that placed these creatures in forests with some of them in the trees. That the creatures were forest dwellers and tree climbers had become, Stern said, so obvious that no one bothered to credit Stern and Sussman for pushing the idea early on.

The argument before had been circular: that hominids had learned to walk in order to venture onto the savannah, and that if they survived on the savannah, they must have been competent walkers. And the savannah seemed to be an image of freedom, of unlimited space in which the possibilities were likewise unlimited, a nobler space than the primeval forest that was less like the open forest of Rousseau's solitary wanderers and more like the jungles from which Jane Goodall and Dian Fossey sent back their primate reports. Stern said a little later on, "I worry most about the manner of their bipedal walking. I wrote a paper say-

---

band raised to reach the holding hand. Hold the old holding hand. Hold and be held. Plod on and never recede.

---

ing they could not have walked as we do. It's not fast, it's not energetically efficient. . . . Are we wrong? Was their method of bipedalism actually pretty good?"
Sussman cut in, "Or did they combine very good tree-climbing with shitty
bipedalism and gradually the proportions reversed . . ." Stern continued, "The argument that I sometimes soothe myself with is that chimpanzees are really pretty
crappy quadrupeds themselves, as four-footed animals go. So if they can be
pretty crappy quadrupeds for seven million years, then we could've been pretty
crappy bipeds for a couple of million years."

At the 1991 Conference on the Origins of Bipedalism in Paris, three anthropologists had reviewed all the current theories on walking as a kind of academic
stand-up comedy routine. They described the "schlepp hypothesis," which explained walking as an adaptation for carrying food, babies, and various other
things; "the peek-a-boo hypothesis," which involved standing up to see over the
grass of the savannah; "the trench coat hypothesis," which, like Guthrie's theory
that so amused Pat, connected bipedalism to penile display, only this time to impress females rather than intimidate other males; "the all wet hypothesis," which
involved wading and swimming during a proposed aquatic phase of evolution;
"the tagalong hypothesis," which involved following migratory herds across that
ever-popular savannah; "the hot to trot hypothesis," which was one of the more
seriously reasoned theories, claiming that bipedalism limited solar exposure in
the tropical midday sun and thus freed the species up to move into hot, open
habitat; and the "two feet are better than four" hypothesis, which proposes that
bipedalism was more energy-efficient than quadrupedalism, at least for the primates who would become humans.

It was quite a collection of theories, though since talking to Stern and
Sussman I had grown accustomed to the fluctuating interpretations of what to a
lay person exposed to only one source sounds like established fact. The bones
unearthed in Africa in ever greater quantity remain enigmatic in crucial ways, and
the business of their interpretation recalls the ancient Greeks reading the entrails
of animals to divine the future, or the Chinese throwing I Ching sticks to understand the world. They are constantly being rearranged to correspond to a new
evolutionary family tree, a new set of measurements. Two Zurich anthropologists, for example, recently declared that the famous Lucy skeleton is actually
that of a male, while Falk argues that she is not a human ancestor. Paleontology
sometimes seems like a courtroom full of lawyers, each waving around evidence

---

Slowly with never a pause plod on and never recede. Backs turned. Both bowed. Joined by holding holding hands.

---

that confirms their hypotheses and ignoring the evidence that contradicts it (though Stern and Sussman impressed me as being exceptionally committed to evidence rather than ideology). Only one thing seemed agreed upon in all these competing stories of the bones, the thing that Mary Leakey had said when she wrote about the footprints her team had found in Laetoli: "One cannot overemphasize the role of bipedalism in hominid development. It stands as perhaps the salient point that differentiates the forebears of man from other primates. This unique ability freed the hands for myriad possibilities—carrying, tool-making, intricate manipulation. From this single development, in fact, stems all modern technology. Somewhat oversimplified, the formula holds that this new freedom of forelimbs posed a challenge. The brain expanded to meet it. And mankind was formed."

Falk wrote the most devastating reply to Lovejoy's hypothesis in a 1997 essay titled "Brain Evolution in Human Females: An Answer to Mr. Lovejoy." She declared, "According to this view, early hominid females were left not only fourfooted, pregnant, hungry and in fear of too much exercise in a central core area, they were also left 'waiting for their man.'" And she went on to say, after reviewing details such as the unlikelihood of monogamy between such differently scaled males and females, to comment, "The Lovejoy hypothesis may also be viewed at an entirely different level, i.e., as being preoccupied with questions/anxieties about male sexuality. At its most basic level, the hypothesis focuses on the evolution of how men got/get sex." She goes on to point out that the behavior of terrestrial female primates suggests that female ancestral hominids chose multiple partners for reproductive and recreational sex, and "much of the world appears to fear that this might still be the case as indicated by the universal close observation and control of sexual conduct in human communities, not to mention all those male insecurities simmering beneath the surface of Lovejoy's hypothesis."

Having dismissed the notion that a providing male brought home the bacon to a monogamous, immobilized mate, Falk took up the alternate and much simpler theory that walking upright minimized the amount of direct sun the earliest hominids received as they moved in the open spaces between patches of trees, thereby freeing them to move farther and farther out from the shade of the forest. Falk explains that Peter Wheeler, whose hypothesis it was, proposed that "these features led to 'whole-body cooling' that regulated temperature of blood

---

Plod on as one. One shade. Another shade.—SAMUEL BECKETT   *John and the Austrian walked one way along*

circulating to (among other regions) the brain, helped prevent heatstroke, and thereby released a physiological constraint on brain size in *Homo*." Thus the changes freed the species to grow larger and larger brains, as well as to wander farther and farther. She buttresses Wheeler's theory with information drawn from her own research into brain evolution and structure and concludes, as Mary Leakey did, though for a different reason, that becoming upright walkers didn't create but did make possible the rise of intelligence.

Intelligence may be located in the brain, but it affects other parts of the anatomy. Consider the pelvis as a secret theater where thinking and walking meet and, according to some anatomists, conflict. One of the most elegant and complicated parts of the skeleton, it is also one of the hardest to perceive, shrouded as it is in flesh, orifices, and preoccupations. The pelvis of all other primates is a long vertical structure that rises nearly to the rib cage and is flattish from back to front. The hip joints are close together, the birth canal opens backward, and the whole bony slab faces down when the ape is in its usual posture, as do the pelvises of most quadrupeds. The human pelvis has tilted up to cradle the viscera and support the weight of the upright body, becoming a shallow vase from which the stem of the waist rises. It is comparatively short and broad, with wide-set hip joints. This width and the abductor muscles that extend from the iliac crests—the bone on each side that sweeps around toward the front of the body just below the navel—steady the body as it walks. The birth canal points downward, and the whole pelvis is, from the obstetrical point of view, a kind of funnel through which babies fall—though this fall is one of the most difficult of human falls. If there is a part of anatomical evolution that recalls Genesis, it is the pelvis and the curse, "In sorrow thou shalt bring forth children."

Giving birth for apes, as for most mammals, is a relatively simple process, but for humans it is difficult and occasionally fatal for mother and child. As hominids evolved, their birth canals became smaller, but as humans have evolved, their brains have grown larger and larger. At birth the human infant's head, already containing a brain as big as that of an adult chimpanzee, strains the capacity of this bony theater. To exit, it must corkscrew down the birth canal, now facing forward, now sideways, now backward. The pregnant woman's body has already increased pelvic capacity by manufacturing hormones that soften the ligaments binding the pelvis together, and toward the end of pregnancy the cartilage of the pubic bone separates. Often these transformations make walking more difficult

---

the shore discussing the formation of sand banks and the theories of the tides, and Charlotte & I went in the opposite

---

during and after giving birth. It has been argued that the limitation on our intelligence is the capacity of the pelvis to accommodate the infant's head, or contrarily that the limitation on our mobility is the need for the pelvis to accommodate birth. Some go further to say that the adaptation of the female pelvis to large-headed babies makes women worse walkers than men, or makes all of us worse walkers than our small-brained ancestors. The belief that women walk worse is widespread throughout the literature of human evolution. It seems to be another hangover from Genesis, the idea that women brought a fatal curse to the species, or that they were mere helpmeets along the evolutionary route, or that if walking is related to both thinking and freedom, they have or deserve less of each. If learning to walk freed the species—to travel to new places, to take up new practices, to think—then the freedom of women has often been associated with sexuality, a sexuality that needs to be controlled and contained. But this is morality, not physiology.

I got so annoyed by the ambiguous record on gender and walking that early one fine morning in Joshua Tree, while the cottontails were hopping in the yard, I called up Owen Lovejoy. He pointed to some differences between male and female anatomy that, he said, *ought* to make women's pelvises less well adapted to walking. "Mechanically," he said, "women are less advantaged." Well, I pressed, do these differences actually make a practical difference? No, he conceded, "it has no effect on their walking ability at all," and I walked back out into the sunshine to admire a huge desert tortoise munching on the prickly pear in the driveway. Stern and Sussman had laughed when I asked them whether women were indeed worse walkers and said that as far as they knew, no one had ever done the scientific experiments that would back up this assertion. Great runners tend to converge in certain body types, whichever gender they are, they ruminated, but walking is not running, and the question of what constitutes greatness there is more ambiguous. What, they asked, does better mean? Faster? More efficient? Humans are slow animals, they said, and what we excel at is distance, sustaining a pace for hours or days.

Those in other disciplines who speculate about walking speculate about what meanings it can be invested with—how it can be made an instrument of contemplation, of prayer, of competition. What makes these scientists, for all their squabbles, significant is their attempt to discuss what meanings are intrinsic to walking—not what we make it but how it made us. Walking is an odd fulcrum in

---

direction for above two hours and lastly lay down among the long grass and gathered shells until our

---

human evolutionary theory. It is the anatomical transformation that propelled us out of the animal kingdom to eventually occupy our own solitary position of dominion over the earth. Now it remains as a limitation, no longer leading us into a fantastic future but linking us to an ancient past as the same gait of a hundred thousand or a million, or if you go with Lovejoy, three million years ago. It may have made possible the work of the hands and the expansion of the mind, but it remains as something not particularly powerful or fast. If it once separated us from the rest of the animals, it now—like sex and birth, like breathing and eating—connects us to the limits of the biological.

The morning before I left I went walking in the national park, starting out from the rocks where Pat was teaching climbing, pacing myself to stay cool and hydrated. His father had told him, and he had told me, that the landscape never looks the same coming and going, so turn around periodically and look at the view you'll see coming back. It's good advice for this confusing landscape. I started amid a big cluster of rocks, an archipelago or a neighborhood of rock piles each the size of a huge building; like buildings they cut off views, so you have to know the lay of the land and local landmarks rather than counting on distant sights to steer by as in other deserts. With the morning sun at my left, I went south along a path that crossed a road to become a fainter road itself, with tufts of grass in the center; it curved along to the southwest and ended in another, much-used road. Small lizards darted into the bushes as I went by, and a faint flush of tender green grass was everywhere in the shade, spears an inch or two high from the downpour a few weeks ago. Drifting across the vast space, silent except for wind and footsteps, I felt uncluttered and unhurried for the first time in a while, already on desert time. My road reached the dead end of a private property boundary, so I circled around, guessing I could find another path back to the rock cluster, flirting with being lost. Mountain ranges appeared and disappeared on the horizon as I rotated around the plain and returned to the rocks. Eventually I met the point where my trail crossed the disused road, found my own footprints going the other way, printed crisply atop the softer footprints of people who'd passed this way on previous days, and followed that trace of my own passing an hour or so ago back to where I started.

Handkerchiefs were quite full.—EFFIE GRAY RUSKIN   *You've got to walk / that lonesome valley / Walk it*

THE UPHILL ROAD TO GRACE:
Some Pilgrimages

Walking came from Africa, from evolution, and from necessity, and it went everywhere, usually looking for something. The pilgrimage is one of the basic modes of walking, walking in search of something intangible, and we were on pilgrimage. The red earth between the piñon and juniper trees was covered with a shining mix of quartz pebbles, chips of mica, and the cast-off skins of cicadas who had gone underground again for another seventeen years. It was a strange pavement to be walking on, both lavish and impoverished, like much of New Mexico. We were walking to Chimayó, and it was Good Friday. I was the youngest of the six people setting out cross country for Chimayó that day, and the only nonlocal. The group had coalesced a few days before, when various characters, myself included, asked Greg if he would mind company. Two of the others were members of Greg's cancer survivors' group, a surveyor and a nurse, and my friend Meridel had brought her neighbor David, a carpenter.

Although we were on our own route—or rather Greg's route—we had joined the great annual pilgrimage to the Santuario de Chimayó and thus were walking as pilgrims. Pilgrimage is one of the fundamental structures a journey can take—the quest in search of something, if only one's own transformation, the journey toward a goal—and for pilgrims, walking is work. Secular walking is often imagined as play, however competitive and rigorous that play, and uses gear and techniques to make the body more comfortable and more efficient. Pilgrims, on the other hand, often try to make their journey harder, recalling the origin of the word travel in *travail*, which also means work, suffering, and the pangs of childbirth. Since the Middle Ages, some pilgrims have traveled barefoot or with stones in their shoes, or fasting, or in special penitential garments. Irish pilgrims at Croagh Patrick still climb that stony mountain barefoot on the last Sunday of every July, and pilgrims in other places finish the journey on their knees. An early Everest mountaineer noted a still more arduous mode of pilgrimage in Tibet. "These devout and simple people travel sometimes two thousand miles, from China and Mongolia, and cover every inch of the way by measuring their length on the ground," wrote Captain John Noel. "They prostrate themselves on their faces, marking the soil with their fingers a little beyond their heads, arise and bring their toes to the mark they have made and fall again, stretched full length on the ground, their arms extended, muttering an already million-times-repeated prayer."

In Chimayó, a few pilgrims every year come carrying crosses, from lightweight and relatively portable models to huge ones that must be dragged step by weary step. Inside the chapel that is their destination one such cross is preserved to the right of the altar, and a small metal plaque by its carrier declares, "This cross is a symbol in thanking God for the safe return of my son Ronald E. Cabrera from combat duty in Viet-Nam. I Ralph A. Cabrera promised to make a pilgrimage, which consisted of walking 150 miles from Grants New Mexico to Chimayó. This pilgrimage was finished on the 28th day of November 1986." Cabrera's plaque and knobby wooden crucifix, about six feet high with a folkloric carved Christ attached to it, make it clear that a pilgrimage is work, or rather labor in a spiritual economy in which effort and privation are rewarded. Nobody has ever quite articulated whether this economy is one in which benefits are incurred for labor expended or the self is refined into something more worthy of such benefit—and nobody needs to; pilgrimage is almost universally embedded in human culture as a literal means of spiritual journey, and asceticism and physical exertion are almost universally understood as means of spiritual development.

Some pilgrimages, such as that to Santiago de Compostela in northwest Spain, are entirely on foot from beginning to end; the pilgrimage begins with the first step, and the journey itself is the most important part. Others, such as the Islamic hajj in Mecca or various denominations' visits to Jerusalem, nowadays are

---

there by yourself.—TRADITIONAL GOSPEL SONG   *But if a man walketh in the night, he stumbleth, because there*

---

as likely to begin with airplanes, and the walking only begins upon arrival (though West African Muslims may spend a lifetime or generations slowly walking toward Saudi Arabia, and a whole culture of nomads has grown up whose eventual goal is Mecca). Chimayó is still a walking pilgrimage, though most walkers have a driver who dropped them off and will pick them up. It's a pilgrimage in an intensely automotive culture, alongside the highway north from Santa Fe and then on the shoulder of the smaller road northeast to Chimayó. The roadside for the last several miles is studded with cars whose drivers are keeping track of family or friends, and in town the air can be noxious with carbon monoxide from the traffic jam; from Santa Fe onward, it's also studded with signs to drive slowly and watch for pilgrims.

Greg's route began about twelve miles north of Santa Fe and cut across country to join up with the rest of the pilgrims only a few miles from Chimayó. We had arrived at eight in the morning at the land Greg and his wife MaLin had bought long ago, and for him the walk tied their land to the holy land due north some sixteen or so miles. It made sense for the rest of us too; none of us were Catholics or even Christians, and walking cross-country let us be in that nonbeliever's paradise, nature, before we arrived at this most traditional of religious destinations. I kept having to remind myself it wasn't a hike and get over my desire to move at my own speed and make good time. As it turned out, it was slowness that would make this walk hard.

Like much of northern New Mexico, the town of Chimayó exudes a sense of ancientness that sets it apart from the rest of the forgetful United States. The Indians here embedded the landscape with stone buildings, potsherds, and petroglyphs, and Pueblo, Navajo, and Hopi people have remained a very visible portion of the population. The Hispanic population is also large and old, and their ancestors established Santa Fe as the first European-inhabited town in what would become the United States. Neither of these peoples has been forgotten or eradicated as they have in other parts of the country; nobody imagines that this landscape was uninhabited wilderness before the Yankees came. And in fact the Yankees who come tend to borrow and revel in the cultures, becoming connoisseurs of adobe architecture and Indian silver work, of Pueblo dances and Hispanic crafts and everyone's customs, including the pilgrimage.

---

is no light in him.—JOHN 11:10   *But as for me, I will walk in mine integrity: redeem me, and be merciful unto*

Before the Conquistadors came, Chimayó had been inhabited by ancestors of
the contemporary Tewa Pueblo people, and they named the hill above the
Santuario Tsi Mayo, "the place of good flaking stone." Records of Spanish settlement in the Chimayó valley date back to 1714, and the plaza at the north end of
this narrow, well-watered agricultural valley is said to be one of the best remaining examples of colonial architecture in the region. Like much of New Mexico,
it is insular; one of its children, Don Usner, says in his history of the place
that those of the plaza didn't intermarry with people at the Potrero in the southern end of the valley. In colonial times the Spanish settlers were forbidden to
travel without permission, and an extremely local, land-based identity evolved.
In another northern New Mexico village I had lived in the year before this
pilgrimage, someone once tartly remarked of a neighbor, "They're not from
here. We remember when their great-grandfather moved here." The Spanish
spoken here is old-fashioned, and it is often noted that the culture derives
from pre-Enlightenment Spain. In its strong agricultural and local ties and traditions, its widespread poverty, its conservative social views, and its devout,
magical Catholicism, this culture often seems like a last outpost of the Middle
Ages.

The Santuario is in the southern end of Chimayó, on its own little unpaved
plaza past a street of crumbling adobe houses and shops with hand-lettered signs
and chile _ristras_. Graves fill the courtyard of this small, sturdily built adobe
church. Inside it's covered in faded murals depicting the saints and Christ hung
on a green cross in a style reminiscent of both Byzantine and Pennsylvania Dutch
painting. The northern chapels are what make the church exceptional, though.
The first is full of pictures of Jesus, Mary, and the saints brought in by devotees,
and hand-painted images mingle with 3D and decoupage icons, a silver-glitter
Virgin of Guadalupe, and a printed, varnished, cracked Last Supper. The outer
wall of this chapel is covered with crucifixes, in front of which hang a solid row
of crutches, their silvery aluminum forming a surface as regular as prison bars
through which many Christs peer. Through a low doorway to the west is the
most important part of the church, a little chapel where the hole in the unpaved
floor yields up the dirt pilgrims take home. This year it had in it a small green
plastic scoop from a detergent carton with which to take up the moistly crumbling sandy earth. People used to drink this earth dissolved in water, and they
still collect it to apply to diseased and injured areas and write to the church of

me. My foot standeth in an even place.—PSALMS 26:1–12   _The farther pilgrims move from their common_ miraculous cures. The crutches here testify, as they do in many pilgrimage sites, to cures of lameness.

When I first came here several years before, I had heard of many holy wells of water, but I was astonished to find a holy well of dirt. The Catholic church doesn't generally consider dirt much of a medium for holiness, but the dirt well in Chimayó is exceptional. The anthropologists Victor and Edith Turner use the term "baptizing the customs" to describe how the Catholic church assimilated local practices as it spread across Europe and the Americas—which is why, for example, so many of Ireland's holy wells were holy before they were Christian. It is now thought that the Tewa considered the earth here sacred or at least of medicinal virtue before the Spanish came, and that in the smallpox plague of the 1780s the Spanish women acquired some of their customs. To consider earth holy is to connect the lowest and most material to the most high and ethereal, to close the breach between matter and spirit. It subversively suggests that the whole world might potentially be holy and that the sacred can be underfoot rather than above. On earlier visits, I was given to understand that the well was supposed to replenish itself magically, and such inexhaustibility has been the stuff of miracles since the bottomless drinking horns of Celtic literature and Jesus' own multiplying loaves and fishes. Certainly the hole in the dirt floor of the chapel is still only about the size of a bucket after nearly two centuries of devotees scooping out soil to take home. But the religious literature I bought next door made it clear that the priests add earth from elsewhere that has been blessed, and on Good Friday a large box of such earth rests on the altar.

The story goes that during Holy Week early in the nineteenth century a local landowner, Don Bernardo Abeyta, was performing the customary penances of his religious society in the hills. He saw a light shining from a hole in the ground and found in it a silver crucifix that, when brought to other churches, would be found again in the hole in Chimayó. After the crucifix returned to the hole three times, Don Bernardo understood that the miracle was tied to the site, and he built a private chapel there in 1814–16. The curative properties of the earth were already known in 1813—a pinch of it in the fire was said to abate storms. The miracle story fits the pattern for many pilgrimage sites, notably the medieval "cycle of the shepherds" in which a cowherd, shepherd, or farmer discovers a holy image in the earth or some other humble place amid miraculous light or music or homage by the beasts, an image that cannot be relocated, for the miracle and the place are

---

world, the closer they come to the realm of the divine. We might mention that in Japanese the word for "walk" is the

---

one. The Turners write of Christian pilgrimage, "All sites of pilgrimage have this in common: they are believed to be places where miracles once happened, still happen, and may happen again."

Pilgrimage is premised on the idea that the sacred is not entirely immaterial, but that there is a geography of spiritual power. Pilgrimage walks a delicate line between the spiritual and the material in its emphasis on the story and its setting: though the search is for spirituality, it is pursued in terms of the most material details—of where the Buddha was born or where Christ died, where the relics are or the holy water flows. Or perhaps it reconciles the spiritual and the material, for to go on pilgrimage is to make the body and its actions express the desires and beliefs of the soul. Pilgrimage unites belief with action, thinking with doing, and it makes sense that this harmony is achieved when the sacred has material presence and location. Protestants, as well as the occasional Buddhist and Jew, have objected to pilgrimages as a kind of icon worship and asserted that the spiritual should be sought within as something wholly immaterial, rather than out in the world.

There is a symbiosis between journey and arrival in Christian pilgrimage, as there is in mountaineering. To travel without arriving would be as incomplete as to arrive without having traveled. To walk there is to earn it, through laboriousness and through the transformation that comes during a journey. Pilgrimages make it possible to move physically, through the exertions of one's body, step by step, toward those intangible spiritual goals that are otherwise so hard to grasp. We are eternally perplexed by how to move toward forgiveness or healing or truth, but we know how to walk from here to there, however arduous the journey. Too, we tend to imagine life as a journey, and going on an actual expedition takes hold of that image and makes it concrete, acts it out with the body and the imagination in a world whose geography has become spiritualized. The walker toiling along a road toward some distant place is one of the most compelling and universal images of what it means to be human, depicting the individual as small and solitary in a large world, reliant on the strength of body and will. In pilgrimage, the journey is radiant with hope that arrival at the tangible destination will bring spiritual benefits with it. The pilgrim has achieved a story of his or her own and in this way too becomes part of the religion made up of stories of travel and transformation.

---

same word which is used to refer to Buddhist practice; the practitioner (gyōja) is then also the walker, one who does

---

Tolstoy captures this in a longing that comes to Princess Marya in *War and Peace* as she feeds the myriad Russian pilgrims that pass by her home: "Often as she listened to the pilgrims' tales she was so fired by their simple speech, natural to them but to her full of deep meaning, that several times she was on the point of abandoning everything and running away from home. In imagination she already pictured herself dressed in coarse rags and with her wallet and staff, walking along a dusty road." She has imagined her life of genteel seclusion become clear, sparse, and intense with a purpose she can move toward. Walking expresses both the simplicity and the purposefulness of the pilgrim. As Nancy Frey writes of the long-distance pilgrimage to Santiago de Compostela in Spain, "When pilgrims begin to walk several things usually begin to happen to their perceptions of the world which continue over the course of the journey: they develop a changing sense of time, a heightening of the senses, and a new awareness of their bodies and the landscape. . . . A young German man expressed it this way: 'In the experience of walking, each step is a thought. You can't escape yourself.'"

In going on pilgrimage, one has left behind the complications of one's place in the world—family, attachments, rank, duties—and become a walker among walkers, for there is no aristocracy among pilgrims save that of achievement and dedication. The Turners talk about pilgrimage as a liminal state—a state of being between one's past and future identities and thus outside the established order, in a state of possibility. Liminality comes from the Latin *limin*, a threshold, and a pilgrim has both symbolically and physically stepped over such a line: "Liminars are stripped of status and authority, removed from a social structure maintained and sanctioned by power and force, and leveled to a homogeneous social state through discipline and ordeal. Their secular powerlessness may be compensated for by a sacred power, however—the power of the weak, derived on the one hand from the resurgence of nature when structural power is removed, and on the other from the reception of sacred knowledge. Much of what has been bound by social structure is liberated, notably the sense of comradeship and communion, or communitas."

We started easily enough, on a flat wooden bridge across a stream that watered the banks around it into rare lushness, then up through Greg and MaLin's dogleg cornfield bordered by oaks. From there we went over an irrigation ditch and

---

not reside anywhere, who abides in emptiness. All of this is of course related to the notion of Buddhism as a path:

---

through the fence that divided their land from the Nambe reservation, the first of many fences we would crawl under, scramble over, or unlatch a wire-fastened gate and pass through. On the Nambe reservation, we passed Nambe Falls, which we could hear roaring in its gorge but not quite see. I liked its invisibility as a reminder that we were not on a scenic walk or the territory of people imbued with the mainstream European tradition of such walks. We could hear it as we approached and, by going to a promontory point and craning, could see part of it, but the only possible clear view on our route would be the quick one during the plummet from the cliff into the deep channel below. So we glimpsed the foaming white edges and lower streambed and went on. We all kept pace with each other for the first half of the expedition, and though the way utterly failed to resemble the route that had looked so coherent when Greg had shown it to us on the topographical maps, the roads and irrigation ditches and landmarks made it clear enough to him.

"Wherever you go, there you are," he said whenever someone asked him if we were lost yet. We had a cheerful morning of it. Sue said that she had expected us to proceed in somber silence, but everyone told stories and made observations. We ate a first snack under a roadside cottonwood tree past the San Juan Reservoir on the Nambe reservation, which adjoins Greg's land, then walked through the outskirts of the reservation town with its horses, fruit trees, sweat lodge, buffalo pasture, and many scattered houses. For the whole length of that road into Nambe, Meridel told us about her first New Age experience in Santa Fe, having her aura balanced in the 1970s, and we variously inquired and wisecracked about the notion. Sue taught us the acronym AFGO, "another fucking growth opportunity," for the plethora of spiritual opportunities (and opportunists) in Santa Fe. Three in our party had had Christian upbringings, and I had come out partly to help Meridel celebrate her fiftieth birthday with a revisionist Passover dinner the day after our walk (she was raised as a nonreligious Jew, and I was raised as nothing in particular by a lapsed Catholic and a nonpracticing Jew). Since the Last Supper was a Passover seder, even Good Friday and Easter are overlaid on the Jewish holiday celebrating the flight from Egypt, and this pilgrimage was built on top of all those layers of meeting, suffering, moving, dying.

We began to drift apart north of the Nambe settlement when we reached the rough sandstone expanse of the badlands, with wind-carved pillars of red stone studding a hot, airless expanse of sand and gravel and ruddy dirt stretching to the

practice is a concrete approach to Buddhahood.—ALLAN G. GRAPARD, "FLYING MOUNTAINS AND WALKERS OF red cliffs in the distance. The two other women began to trail, and the two men I didn't know went on ahead. We all met up at the windmill, which marked a turn in terrain and in direction, and lounged around the shade of its waterless tank. Afterward, Greg and Sue decided to go around a hill the rest of us were going to go straight over, because she was wearing out. The badlands had given way to more of that intricate terrain of hillocks so hard to navigate in, and rather than going over the single hill I had expected, we found ourselves surmounting and descending innumerable tree-studded red-soil rises. We shouted, but we couldn't find them, so we kept walking. One of the other men had gone on far ahead; the other was walking faster than Meridel could. She is an athletic woman, but she is small and had pulled something in her knee, and her steps had grown short.

This drifting apart was dispiriting. When I think about what we were doing, it seems as if it ought to have been an experience of paradise attained—dear friends and amiable new acquaintances moving across a varied landscape toward a remarkable goal under an azure sky. But, alas, we had various bodies and various styles. I had been frustrated for the last few hours by the pace. Someone would stop to pull out binoculars or to confer, and everyone would come to a halt that would grow protracted. Standing or wandering slowly makes my feet hurt; it's why museums and malls are more painful than mountains. And if the devil is in the details, mine was in the heavy-duty boots I thought I had broken in but which had begun to break my feet in all over again. So I oscillated between the man ahead and the woman behind until we finally reached the open grassland. Three of us arrived at the road on the far side of the grassland together. A steady stream of walkers and cars was going by—the former all uphill, the latter in both directions—and Meridel and I joined it. We were now part of the much larger community spread out for dozens of miles along the highway that is the main pilgrimage route. The trail of empty water bottles and orange peels bore evidence to the volunteers farther down the road, people who came every year and set up tables bearing slices of oranges, water, soft drinks, cookies, and occasionally Easter candy that everyone was welcome to take. This was one of the most moving parts of the pilgrimage to me, these people who were out not to earn their own salvation but to support others doing so.

On Good Friday of the year before, I had been struck by how little preparation most of the pilgrims seemed to have made for a long walk. Their everyday clothes had been something of a rebuke to me that this was not a hike, and many

---

stout people who looked as if they never walked much otherwise persevered. This year the day was much warmer, and everything seemed different: with our aching feet and our packs, *we* looked more serious, more dogged, than the jaunty young pilgrims in their colorful shorts and jeans and T-shirts (though Meridel's husband Jerry told us when he met us in Chimayó that he had seen a woman from a very small town walking in a fancy white dress—"the kind of dress you would get married in, or buried in"—and two days earlier and thirty miles west I had seen two men in fatigues walking eastward, one of them carrying a large cross). Both times I joined this pilgrimage I had the strange sense that I was walking alongside people in another world, the world of believers, people for whom the Santuario up ahead contained a definite power in a cosmos organized around the Trinity, the mother of God, the saints, and the geography of churches, shrines, altars, and sacraments. But I had suffered like a pilgrim; my feet were killing me.

Pilgrimages are not athletic events, not only because they often punish the body but because they are so often gone on by those who are seeking the restoration of their own or a loved one's health. They are for the least equipped rather than the most. Greg told me, when I called him up to ask if I could join in, that when he had leukemia he made a deal with the gods. Framed in the same easygoing humor he brought to other subjects, the deal's terms were flexible: that if he lived, he would try to go on the pilgrimage when he could. This was his third year of walking it, and it got easier every year. Four years before, when he was deathly ill, Jerry and Meridel walked for him and brought him back some dirt from the Santuario.

This Easter week in which we were walking to Chimayó, a similar pilgrimage from Paris to Chartres would be taking place again, and far larger crowds of Christians would be gathering in Rome and Jerusalem. In the last half century or so, a wide variety of secular and nontraditional pilgrimages have evolved that extend the notion of the pilgrimage into political and economic spheres. Not long before I had set out, a march in San Francisco commemorated the farmworker organizer César Chávez's birthday with a crosstown "Walk for Justice"; and in Memphis, Tennessee, civil rights activists commemorated the thirtieth anniversary of Martin Luther King's assassination there with another march. In the

---

count inhalations and exhalations as you walk slowly around the room. Begin walking with the left foot and walk

---

southwest in April, I could have instead joined the Franciscan-led Nevada Desert Experience on their annual peace walk from Las Vegas to the Nevada Test Site (akin to another pilgrimage route from Chimayó to Los Alamos, birthplace of the atomic bomb, thirty miles west). Then there was the Muscular Dystrophy Association's annual walkathon on the first week of April and the March of Dimes's WalkAmerica the last weekend of that month. I had come across a flyer in Gallup, New Mexico, for "Native Americans for Community Action, Inc. 15th Annual Sacred Mountain 10k Prayer Run and 2k Fun Run/Walk" to be held in Flagstaff in June, which sounded like the Spirit Runs held by the five tribes fighting the proposed Ward Valley nuclear waste dump in southeastern California, and I knew that the annual breast cancer and AIDS walks were coming up in San Francisco's Golden Gate Park and other locations around the country. And no doubt somewhere somebody was walking across the continent for some other good cause. All these were outgrowths of the pilgrimage, or adaptations of its terms.

Imagine all those revisionist versions of pilgrimage as a mighty river of walkers flowing from many sources. The first small trickle comes, like March ice melt from a high glacier, from a single woman almost half a century ago. On January 1, 1953, a woman known to the world only as Peace Pilgrim set out, vowing "to remain a wanderer until mankind has learned the way of peace." She had found her vocation years before when she walked all night through the woods and felt, in her words, "a complete willingness, without any reservations, to give my life to God and to service," and she prepared for her vocation by walking 2,000 miles on the Appalachian Trail. Raised on a farm and active in peace politics before she abandoned her name and began her pilgrimage, she was a peculiarly American figure, plainspoken and confident that the simplicity of life and thought that worked for her could work for everyone. Her cheery accounts of her long years of walking the roads and talking to the people she met are unburdened by complexity, dogma, or doubt and rife with exclamation marks.

She started her pilgrimage by joining the Rose Bowl Parade in Pasadena, and something about setting out on her long odyssey from this corny festivity recalls Dorothy in *The Wizard of Oz*, with her own farmgirl can-do determination, starting down the Yellow Brick Road amid dancing munchkins. Peace Pilgrim kept walking for twenty-eight years through all kinds of weather and every state and Canadian province as well as parts of Mexico. An older woman at the time she

---

in such a way that the foot sinks into the floor, first the heel and then the toes. Walk calmly and steadily, with poise

---

first set out, she wore navy blue pants and shirt, tennis shoes, and a navy blue tunic whose front was stenciled with the words "Peace Pilgrim" and whose back text changed over the years from "walking coast to coast for peace" to "walking 10,000 miles for world disarmament" to "25,000 miles on foot for peace." Something of her brisk, practical piety comes across in her explanation of the choice of dark blue—"it doesn't show dirt," she wrote, and "does represent peace and spirituality." Though she attributes her extraordinary health and stamina to her spirituality, it is hard not to wonder if it was the other way around. She continued her pilgrimage in her simple outfit through snowstorms, rain, a harsh dust storm, and heat, sleeping in cemeteries, in Grand Central Station, on floors, and on an endless succession of the couches of new acquaintances.

Though most of her writings are nonpartisan, she took a strong stand on national and global politics, arguing against the Korean War, the cold war, the arms race, and war in general. The war in Korea was still going on when she set out from Pasadena, as was Senator Joe McCarthy's anticommunist intimidation. It was one of the bleakest periods in American history, with fear of nuclear war and communism driving most Americans into the bunkers of conformity and repression. Even to argue for peace took heroic courage. To set out, as Peace Pilgrim did on the first day of 1953, with nothing more than her single outfit, whose pockets contained "a comb, a folding toothbrush, a ballpoint pen, copies of her message and her current correspondence," was astonishing. While the economy was booming and capitalism was becoming enshrined as a sacrament of freedom, she had dropped out of the money economy—she never carried or used money for the rest of her life. She says of her lack of material possessions, "Think of how free I am! If I want to travel, I just stand up and walk away. There is nothing to tie me down." Though her models were largely Christian, her pilgrimage seems to have arisen from the same 1950s crisis of culture and spirituality that pushed John Cage, Gary Snyder, and many other artists and poets into investigations of Zen Buddhism and other nonwestern traditions and sent Martin Luther King to India to study Gandhi's teachings on nonviolence and *satyagraha,* or soul-force.

Most people who diverge from the mainstream withdraw from its spaces, but Peace Pilgrim had withdrawn from the former to enter the latter, where she would be most required to mediate the gap between her beliefs and national ideology—she was as much an evangelist as a pilgrim. She had set out to walk 25,000 miles for peace, and it took her nine years to do so. Afterward, she con-

---

and dignity. The walking must not be done absentmindedly, and the mind must be taut as you concentrate on the

---

tinued walking for peace but stopped counting the miles. As she put it, "I walk until given shelter, fast until given food. I don't ask—it's given without asking. Aren't people good! . . . I usually average twenty-five miles a day walking, depending on how many people stop to talk to me along the way. I have gone up to fifty miles in one day to keep an appointment or because there was no shelter available. On very cold nights I walk through the night to keep warm. Like the birds, I migrate north in the summer and south in the winter." Later she became a widely recognized public speaker and occasionally accepted a ride to get her to her speaking engagements. She died, ironically, in a head-on car crash in July 1981.

Like a pilgrim, she had entered the liminal condition the Turners would later describe, leaving behind an ordinary identity and the goods and circumstances that bolster such identities to achieve that state of anonymous simplicity and clear purpose Tolstoy's Princess Marya longed for. Her walking became a testament to the strength of her convictions and suggests several things. One is that the world was in such trouble that she herself had to drop her ordinary name and ordinary life to try to heal it. Another is that if she could break with the ordinary and go forth unprotected by money, by buildings, and by a place in the world, then perhaps profound change and profound trust were possible on a larger scale. A third is that of the carrier: like Christ taking on the sins of all his followers or the Hebrew scapegoat driven out into the wilderness, burdened with the sins of the community, she had taken personal responsibility for the state of the world, and her life was testimony and expiation as well as example. But what makes her unorthodox is that she adapted a religious form, the pilgrimage, to carry political content. The pilgrimage traditionally dealt with disease and healing of self or loved ones, but she had taken on war, violence, and hate as plagues ravaging the world. The political content that motivated her and the way in which she endeavored to achieve change through influencing her fellow human beings rather than through divine intervention make her the first of a horde of modern political pilgrims.

She foreshadowed this shift in the nature of the pilgrimage, from appealing for divine intervention or holy miracle to demanding political change, making the audience no longer God or the gods, but the public. Perhaps the postwar era marked the end of belief that divine intervention alone was adequate; God had failed to prevent the Jewish Holocaust, and the Jews had seized their promised

---

counting.—INSTRUCTIONS ON WALKING MEDITATION IN *THREE PILLARS OF ZEN*   *Sigmund Freud believed, for*

---

land through political and military means. African Americans, who had long used metaphors of the Promised Land, stopped waiting too. At the height of the civil rights movement, Martin Luther King said that he was going to Birmingham to lead demonstrations until "Pharaoh lets God's people go." The collective walk brings together the iconography of the pilgrimage with that of the military march and the labor strike and demonstration: it is a show of strength as well as conviction, and an appeal to temporal rather than spiritual powers—or perhaps, in the case of the civil rights movement, both.

Because of the involvement of so many ministers, the practice of nonviolence, and the language of religious redemption and, occasionally, martyrdom, the civil rights movement was more saturated with the temperament and imagery of pilgrimage than most struggles. It was in large part about the rights of access of black people, and it was first fought on the contested sites: sitting down in and then boycotting buses, bringing children into schools, sitting in at lunch counters. But it found its momentum in events that united the protest or the strike with the pilgrimage: the march from Selma to Montgomery to petition for voting rights, the many marches in Birmingham and throughout the country, the culminating March on Washington. In fact, the first major event organized by the newly founded Southern Christian Leadership Conference (SCLC) was the "prayer pilgrimage" at the Lincoln Memorial in Washington, D.C., on May 17, 1957, the third anniversary of the Supreme Court ruling in favor of desegregating schools. It was so called to make it sound less threatening; a pilgrimage makes an appeal while a march makes a demand. King was profoundly influenced by the writings and actions of Mahatma Gandhi, and he adapted from Gandhi both the general principle of nonviolence and the specifics of marches and boycotts that had hastened India's liberation from British rule. Perhaps Gandhi was the founder of the political pilgrimage with his famous 200-mile-long Salt March in 1930, in which he and many people living inland walked to the sea to make their own salt in violation of British law and British taxes. Nonviolence means that activists are asking their oppressors for change rather than forcing it, and it can be an extraordinary tool for the less powerful to wring change out of the more powerful.

Six years after the founding of the SCLC, Martin Luther King decided that nonviolent resistance by itself was inadequate, and the violence the southern segregationists inflicted on blacks should be made as public as possible. The audience would no longer be merely the oppressors, but the world. This was the

----

example, that the psychical foundation of all travel was the first separation and the various other departures from

----

strategy of the Birmingham struggle, perhaps the central episode of the civil rights movement, which began on Good Friday of 1963 with the first of many marches, or processions. It is from these protests that the most famous images come, of people being blasted by high-pressure fire hoses and savaged by police dogs, images that provoked worldwide indignation. King and hundreds of others were arrested for marching in Birmingham, and after the supply of willing adults began to run out, high school students were recruited, and their younger siblings volunteered. They marched for freedom with bold jubilance, and on May 2 of that year 900 of these children were arrested. To go out onto the streets knowing they risked attack, injury, arrest, and death took an extraordinary resolve, and the religious ardor of Southern Baptists as well as the Christian iconography of martyrdom seems to have strengthened them. A month after the Birmingham campaign had begun, writes one of King's biographers, "Reverend Charles Billups and other Birmingham ministers led more than 3,000 young people on a prayer pilgrimage to Birmingham jail singing 'I Want Jesus to Walk with Me' as they moved."

A photograph of the 1965 Selma-to-Montgomery march has been on my refrigerator for months, and it speaks of this inspired walking. Taken by Matt Heron, it show a steady stream of marchers three or four wide moving from right to left across the photograph. He must have lain low to take it, for it raises its subjects up high against a pale, clouded sky. They seem to know they are walking toward transformation and into history, and their wide steps, upraised hands, the confidence of their posture, express the will with which they go to meet it. They have found in this walk a way to make their history rather than suffer it, to measure their strength and test their freedom, and their movement expresses the same sense of destiny and meaning that resonates in King's deep-voiced, indomitable oratory.

In 1970 the form of the pilgrimage was moved yet further from its origins when the first Walkathon was held by the March of Dimes. Tony Choppa, who has been working on these walks since 1975 and is their unofficial historian, says it was risky at the time, since walking the streets en masse was associated with more radical demonstrations. The first walkers were high school students in San Antonio, Texas, and Columbus, Ohio, and this first "walkathon" was modeled af-

---

one's mother, including the final journey into death. Journeying is therefore an activity related to a larger feminine ter a fund-raiser for a hospital in Canada. It rained on both walks, he says, and there was "no money but great potential. People did actually come out and walk." Over the years the route was trimmed from the initial twenty-five miles to ten kilometers, and participation mushroomed. The year we walked to Chimayó from Greg's land, nearly a million people were expected to join what the March of Dimes now calls WalkAmerica, and they would raise about $74 million for infant and prenatal health care and supporting research. The walk was cosponsored by K-Mart and Kellogg's, among others. This walkathon structure, with corporations sponsoring the event in return for promotional opportunities and walkers raising the money for the charity, has been adopted by hundreds of organizations, the great majority of them dealing with disease and health care.

The summer before I had accidentally run into the eleventh annual AIDS Walk San Francisco in Golden Gate Park. A huge throng of people in shorts and caps milled around the starting area that sunny day, holding various free beverages, advertisements, and product samples. The hundred-page booklet for the walk consisted almost entirely of advertisements for the dozens of corporate sponsors—clothing companies, brokerage houses—who also had tables set up around the lawn. It was a strange atmosphere, a cross between a gym and a convention, crawling with logos and ads. Yet it must have been profound for some of its participants. The next day the paper said 25,000 walkers had raised $3.5 million for local AIDS organizations and described a walker who wore a T-shirt printed with photographs of his two sons who had died of AIDS and said, "You never get over it. The walk is a way to cope with it."

These fund-raising walks have become the mainstream American version of the pilgrimage. In many ways they have traveled far from its original nature, notably in the evolution from devoutly appealing for divine intervention to pragmatically asking friends and family for money. And yet, however banal these walks are, they retain much of the content of the pilgrimage: the subject of health and healing, the community of pilgrims, and the earning through suffering or at least exertion. Walking is crucial to these events, or at least it has been. Bikeathons have come into being, and the last indignity dealt to this highly mutated form of pilgrimage came with the virtual walk, including the San Francisco Art Institute's "nonwalk," in which people were asked to give money and were given a T-shirt but weren't obliged to show up, and AIDS Action's "Until It's Over

realm, so that it is not surprising that Freud himself was ambivalent about it. Of the landscape he said, "All of these e-March," which proposed that participants electronically sign their names to a letter on the Internet as a substitute for marching or walking.

Fortunately, walkathons are not the end of the story. Though mutant forms of the pilgrimage keep springing up, the older ones thrive, from religious pilgrimages to long political walks. A month after 25,000 people walked ten kilometers to raise money for AIDS organizations in San Francisco, gang counselor Jim Hernandez and antiviolence organizer Heather Taekman finished a 500-mile walk from East Los Angeles to Richmond, California, carrying more than 150 photographs of young murder victims and meeting with teenagers along the way. In 1986 hundreds of people joined together to form the Great Peace March. They walked across the United States together to ask for disarmament in a mass pilgrimage that created its own culture and support structure and had a large impact in some of the small towns through which they trekked. The walk began as a sort of publicity event, but somewhere along the long way the walking itself took over, and the walkers became less concerned with media and message and more with what was happening within themselves. In 1992 two more cross-continental peace walks did much the same thing, and like the walkers of the Great Peace March they drew inspiration from Peace Pilgrim. Similar walks went across the Soviet Union and Europe during the early 1990s, and in 1993 strawberry pickers and other United Farm Workers (UFW) supporters reenacted the great three-hundred-mile Delano-to-Sacramento march César Chávez had organized in 1966 and called a pilgrimage.

Even the most sophisticated yield to the pilgrim's impulse, and even without the superstructure of religion, the ordeal of walking makes sense. The filmmaker Werner Herzog writes, "At the end of November, 1974, a friend from Paris called and told me that Lotte Eisner [a film historian] was seriously ill and would probably die. I said that this must not be, not at this time, German cinema could not do without her now, we would not permit her death. I took a jacket, a compass and a duffel bag with the necessities. My boots were so solid and new that I had confidence in them. I set off on the most direct route to Paris, in full faith, believing that she would stay alive if I came on foot. Besides, I wanted to be alone with myself." He walked the several hundred miles from Munich in winter weather, often wet, often smelly, often thirsty, and usually suffering from great pain in some part of his feet and legs.

---

dark woods, narrow defiles, high grounds and deep penetrations are unconscious sexual imagery, and we are

---

Herzog, as anyone who has seen his films knows, is fond of deep passions and extreme behavior, however obtuse, and in his journals of his long walk to Paris he took on the qualities of one of the obsessives in his films. He walked in all weather, though he occasionally accepted a lift, and he slept in barns and a display mobile home he broke into as well as in strangers' homes and inns. The sparse prose describes walking, suffering, minor encounters, and fragments of scenery. Elaborate fantasies that themselves sound like outlines for Herzog movies are woven into the description of his ordeal. On the fourth day, he writes, "While I was taking a shit, a hare came by at arm's length without noticing me. Pale brandy on my left thigh which hurts from my groin downwards with every step. Why is walking so full of woe?" On the twenty-first day, he put his feet up in Eisner's room, and she smiled at him. "For one splendid fleeting moment something mellow flowed through my deadly tired body. I said to her, open the window, from these last days onward I can fly."

We had arrived too, along the curving road into Chimayó. Sal and I sat down and waited for Meridel on a sidewalk. Cars, policemen, and children carrying Sno-Cones passed by in front of us; behind us bloomed a few stunted fruit trees in a knobby pasture. Afterward, Sal went to stand in the long line in front of the Santuario, and I went off to buy us some lemonade at a little mobile food-stand around the corner, near the Santo Niño Chapel, where people used to offer up children's shoes because the Santo Niño, a version of the Christ child, is said to have worn out his own running errands of mercy around the countryside at night. It was nice to be back on familiar ground. I knew what was inside the Santuario and thought of the thousands of crosses woven into the cyclone fence behind the outdoor chapel below, crosses made of grapevine and cottonwood twigs and larger sticks, and then of the irrigation ditch that flowed just the other side of the fence, of the swift shallow river that runs through the town, of the burrito stand that sold meatless alternatives for Lent, of the old adobe houses and the trailer homes that are beginning to look old, and of the many unwelcoming signs: "Notice: Please Don't Leave Your Belongings Unattended at Any Time," "Not Responsible for Theft," "Beware of Dog." Chimayó is a desperately poor town, known for drugs, violence, and crime as well as for sanctity. Jerry West was waiting for his wife, Meridel, in front of that chapel, and I made my last foot journey

exploring a woman's body."—PAUL SHEPARD, *NATURE AND MADNESS*   *The geographical pilgrimage is the* back with the lemonade, bade Sal farewell, and went off to my own culminating destination. About ten thousand pilgrims would come into town and stand in line to go into the chapel that day, and Jerry found Greg and Sue standing in line to go in too. When we left after the moon had risen, there were still more figures walking along the narrow shoulder of the road in the night, shadowy groups that no longer looked festive, but dedicated and fragile in the dark.

symbolic acting out of an inner journey. The inner journey is the interpolation of the meanings and signs of the

LABYRINTHS AND CADILLACS:
Walking into the Realm
of the Symbolic

I didn't mind not getting into the church at Chimayó along with all the long patient line of pilgrims, because I had another destination. The year before I'd
walked the last six or so miles of the pilgrimage, and later, trying to catch up with
my friend who'd driven in, I walked past the Cadillac with the stations of the
cross painted on it. I kept going after a cursory inspection, and then I did the
world's slowest double take. A Cadillac with the fourteen stations began, during
the interim between those two Good Fridays, to seem more and more extraordinary, a gorgeous compression of many symbolic languages and desires into one
divinely strange chariot. Jerry said, in front of the Santo Niño Chapel, that it was
just up the road a hundred yards, and so I limped off to see it again.

Long and pale blue and somehow soft-looking, as though the metal body
were dissolving into velvet or veils, this 1976 Cadillac was a contrary thing. The
stations of the cross were wrapped around its long lean body, below the chrome
line that bisected it horizontally. Jesus was condemned at the rear end of the driver's side and carried the cross, stumbled, and encountered his way around the car
to be crucified in the middle of the passenger's side, next to the door handle, and
he was buried at the back end of that side. All along those sides was painted a

---

outer pilgrimage. One can have one without the other. It is best to have both.—THOMAS MERTON   *I was the* dark gray sky full of lightning that made the place of his suffering into New Mexico, with its volatile thunderclouds. There was Jesus again on the trunk as a big soft-focus head with a crown of thorns, flanked by angels, thorny roses, and the same kind of undulating ribbons that bear inscriptions in medieval and old Mexican religious paintings. The thorns everywhere seemed like further reminders that Chimayó and Jerusalem were both arid landscapes, and the same thorny roses adorned the hood, where Mary, the Sacred Heart, an angel, and a centurion were.

This car was designed to be looked at standing still, but it retained the possibility of moving. It didn't matter if the car ever went far, just that it could, that these images could hurtle down the highway, whipped by wind and drops of rain running sideways. Imagine it doing seventy on the interstate, passing mesas and crumbling adobes and cattle and maybe some billboards for fake Indian trading posts, Dairy Queens, and cheap motels, an eight-cylinder Sistine Chapel turned inside out and speeding toward a stark horizon under changing skies. The artist, Arthur Medina, a slender, restless-looking man with wavy black hair, showed up while I was admiring it and leaned against the adjacent wooden shed to receive compliments and questions. Why a Cadillac? I asked, and he didn't seem to understand my premise that a luxury car is not the most natural and neutral thing on which to paint holy pictures. So I asked him why he painted the car with this subject matter, and he said, "To give the people something for Lent," and indeed he displayed it here every year.

He had, he said, painted other cars and had an Elvis car, and then he darkly intimated that other local artists were imitating him. It was true that another long 1970s car was parked nearer the Santuario, in front of a white-painted adobe shop, and that very shop was painted with perfect accuracy on the side of the car facing the street, while a radiant image of the Santuario itself covered the hood. This made it almost as dizzying a vehicle of meaning as Medina's car, a transformation of immobile place into speeding representations. But the tradition of customized low-rider cars goes back more than a quarter of a century in northern New Mexico, and this other car was painted much more professionally—which is not to say that Medina was a lesser artist, only that most such cars have an orthodox aesthetic that comes from a particular way of handling the airbrush, and Medina had made his figures simpler and flatter and created a much more lushly

---

first in six generations to leave the Valley, the only one in my family to ever leave home. But I didn't leave all the misty atmosphere. You could say that most low-rider cars are baroque, with a slightly cynical hyperreality of form, while Medina's had something of the flat devout force of medieval painting about it.

It was an extraordinarily quixotic object, a car about walking, a luxury item about suffering, sacrifice, and humiliation. And the car united two radically different walking traditions, one erotic and one religious. Customized cars exist both as art objects and as the vehicles for an updated version of an old Spanish and now Latin American custom, the paseo or *corso*. For hundreds of years, promenading the plaza in the center of town has been a social custom in these places, one that allows young people to meet, flirt, and stroll together and dictates that villages and cities from Antigua, Guatemala, to Sonoma, California, have a central plaza in which to do so (the more casual promenades of northern Europe take place in parks, quays, and boulevards). In some parts of Mexico and elsewhere the custom was once so formal that the men strolled in one direction and the women in the other, like the indefinitely extended steps of a line dance, but in most nowadays the plaza is the site of less structured promenading. The promenade is a special subset of walking with an emphasis on slow stately movement, socializing, and display. It is not a way of getting anywhere, but a way of being somewhere, and its movements are essentially circular, whether on foot or by car.

During the days I was writing this, I ran into my brother Steve's friend José in Dolores Park after San Francisco's May Day Parade and asked him about the custom. At first he said he knew nothing about it, but as we talked, more and more came back to him, and his eyes shone with the old memories flooding back in a new light. In his hometown in El Salvador, the custom was called "going around the park," though *park* meant the plaza at the center of town. Mostly teenagers used the park for this socializing, in part because the small houses and warm weather made it uncomfortable to socialize at home, at least at that age. Girls didn't go to the park alone, so he was much in request as a sort of midget chaperone by his older sister and his three beautiful cousins. Many Saturday and Sunday evenings of his childhood were spent licking an ice cream cone and ignoring their conversations with boys. The paseo, like less structured courtship walks in other places, allows people to remain visually in public but verbally in private, giving them enough room to talk and enough supervision to do little more. Nobody could afford to stay in the village, he said, and so the romances

---

parts of me: I kept the ground of my own being. On it I walked away, taking with me the land, the Valley, kindled during strolls in the parks rarely led to marriage. But when people came back home, they would go around the park again, not to meet people but in reminiscence of this part of their life. Every small town and village in El Salvador and, he ventured, Guatemala had some form of this custom, and "the smaller the town the more important it was for keeping people's sanity." Other versions of the pedestrian paseo exist in Spain, southern Italy, and much of Latin America; the custom turns the world into a kind of ballroom and walking into a slow waltz.

It is hard to say how the customized car and the cruise came together, but the cruise is very much the successor to the paseo or *corso*, with the cars moving at promenade speed and the young people within flirting with and challenging each other. Meridel, my companion on the Chimayó pilgrimage, had in 1980 made one of her earliest series of photographs about New Mexico, a documentary project on low riders. At that time the subculture was booming, and the cars would slowly cruise the old plaza at the center of Santa Fe. Like low riders in most places, these ones met with the hostility of the civic authorities, who turned the four streets around the plaza into a one-way roundabout and took other steps to ban the practice. But when Meridel's series was complete, she organized a show of her work in the plaza, to which the low riders were invited and at which many of their cars were on display. By resituating them within the context of high art, she had reopened the space to them and introduced their work and world to the others in the region. It was the biggest art opening in Santa Fe history, with all kinds of people milling around the plaza to look at the cars, the photographs, and each other, an art paseo.

Though cruising came from the paseo, the cars' imagery sometimes spoke of a very different tradition. In devout New Mexico they bore far more religious imagery than, for example, low-rider cars in California, and Meridel came to see many of them as chapels, reliquaries, and, because of the plush velvet upholstery, even caskets. They express the culture of young people who are both devout and hard-partying as an indivisible whole, not a set of contradictions. And they express something of the centrality of the car in New Mexico, where sidewalks and roadside trails are often hard to find and both rural and urban life are built around the car (even on the pilgrimage, low riders cruised the road and did the occasional doughnut for us pedestrians). Still I find it strange that the paseo should have ceased to be a pedestrian event and become a vehicular one. Cars function best as exclusionary devices, as mobile private space. Even driven as slowly as

---

Texas.—GLORIA ANZALDUA   *An active line on a walk moving freely, without goal. A walk for a walk's*

possible, they still don't allow for the directness of encounter and fluidity of contact that walking does. Medina's car, however, was no longer a vehicle but an object. He stood beside it to receive compliments, and we walked around it less as devotees would walk the stations of the cross than as connoisseurs would tour a gallery.

The stations of the cross are themselves one of those cultural things made up of many strata laid down upon each other. The first layer is the presumed course of events from Jesus's condemnation to the laying of his dead body in the tomb in the cave, a walk from Pilate's house to Golgotha, the walk that the pilgrims dragging crosses to Chimayó imitate. During the Crusades pilgrims in Jerusalem would tour the sites of these events, praying as they went, laying down a second layer, a layer of devout retracing that brought pilgrimage close to tourism. In the fourteenth and fifteenth centuries Franciscan friars created the third layer by formalizing the route as a series of fixed events—the fourteen stages—and abstracting them from their site. From this tradition come the stations of the cross artworks—usually fourteen small paintings or prints running up and down the nave of the church—that adorn nearly all Catholic churches, and it is an amazing abstraction. No longer is it necessary to be in Jerusalem to trace these events two millennia ago. The time is past, the place is elsewhere, but walking and imagining are adequate means to enter into the spirit of those events. (Most of the recommendations on praying the stations emphasize reliving the events of the crucifixion, so that it is an act not merely of prayer but of identification and imagination.) Christianity is a portable religion, and even this route once so specific to Jerusalem was exported around the world.

A path is a prior interpretation of the best way to traverse a landscape, and to follow a route is to accept an interpretation, or to stalk your predecessors on it as scholars and trackers and pilgrims do. To walk the same way is to reiterate something deep; to move through the same space the same way is a means of becoming the same person, thinking the same thoughts. It's a form of spatial theater, but also spiritual theater, since one is emulating saints and gods in the hope of coming closer to them oneself, not just impersonating them for others. It's this that makes pilgrimage, with its emphasis on repetition and imitation, distinct amid all the modes of walking. If in no other way one can resemble a god, one can at least walk like one. And indeed, in the stations of the cross, Jesus appears at his most

----

sake.—PAUL KLEE, ALLEGORIZING DRAWING   *Trebuchant sur les mots comme sur les paves (stumbling against*

----

human, stumbling, sweating, suffering, falling three times, and dying in the course of redeeming the Fall. But by the time the stations of the cross had become a sequence of pictures in any church, anywhere, devotees were tracing a path that was no longer through a place but through a story. The stations are set up all along the nave of churches so that worshipers can walk themselves into Jerusalem, into the central story of Christianity.

There are many other devices besides the stations of the cross that let people bodily enter a story. I found one last summer. I had a date to meet some friends for drinks at the famously kitschy old mock-Polynesian bar the Tonga Room in the Fairmont Hotel atop Nob Hill. After walking over Nob Hill, past a grocery store advertising caviar, past a Chinese boy skipping with joy, past the less joyful adults in this posh neighborhood, and around the back of Grace Cathedral, I walked through a courtyard where a fountain was playing and a young man was waving a Bible around and mumbling something. At the far side of the space I saw, to my delight, something new there, a labyrinth. In pale and dark cement it repeated the same pattern made of stone in Chartres Cathedral: eleven concentric circles divided into quadrants through which the path winds until it ends at the six-petaled flower of the center. I was early for my rendezvous, and so I stepped onto the path. The circuit was so absorbing I lost sight of the people nearby and hardly heard the sound of the traffic and the bells for six o'clock.

Inside the labyrinth the two-dimensional surface ceased to be open space one could move across anyhow. Keeping to the winding path became important, and with one's eyes fixed upon it, the space of the labyrinth became large and compelling. The very first length of path after the entrance almost reaches the center of the eleven rings, then turns away to snake round and round, nearer and farther, never so close as that initial promise until long afterward, when the walker has slowed down and become absorbed in the journey—which even on a maze forty feet in diameter like this can take a quarter hour or more. That circle became a world whose rules I lived by, and I understood the moral of mazes: sometimes you have to turn your back on your goal to get there, sometimes you're farthest away when you're closest, sometimes the only way is the long one. After that careful walking and looking down, the stillness of arrival was deeply moving. I

---

words as against cobblestones)—CHARLES BAUDELAIRE, "LE SOLEIL"   *At the other extreme is a group of* looked up at last to see that white clouds like talons and feathers were tumbling east in a blue sky. It was breathtaking to realize that in the labyrinth, metaphors and meanings could be conveyed spatially. That when you seem farthest from your destination is when you suddenly arrive is a very pat truth in words, but a profound one to find with your feet.

The poet Marianne Moore famously wrote of "real toads in imaginary gardens," and the labyrinth offers us the possibility of being real creatures in symbolic space. I had thought of a children's story as I walked, and the children's books that I loved best were full of characters falling into books and pictures that became real, wandering through gardens where the statues came to life and, most famously, crossing over to the other side of the mirror, where chess pieces, flowers, and animals all were alive and temperamental. These books suggested that the boundaries between the real and the represented were not particularly fixed, and magic happened when one crossed over. In such spaces as the labyrinth, we cross over; we are really traveling, even if the destination is only symbolic, and this is in an entirely different register than is thinking about traveling or looking at a picture of a place we might wish to travel to. For the real is in this context nothing more or less than what we inhabit bodily. A labyrinth is a symbolic journey or a map of the route to salvation, but it is a map we can really walk on, blurring the difference between map and world. If the body is the register of the real, then reading with one's feet is real in a way reading with one's eyes alone is not. And sometimes the map *is* the territory.

In medieval churches these labyrinths—once common, but now existing only in a few churches—were sometimes called *chemins à Jerusalem*, "roads to Jerusalem," and the center was Jerusalem or heaven itself. Though the historian of mazes and labyrinths W. H. Matthews cautions that there is no written evidence on their intended use, it is widely thought that they offered the possibility of compressing a pilgrimage into the compact space of a church floor, with the difficulties of spiritual progress represented by the twists and turns. At Grace Cathedral in San Francisco, the labyrinth was commissioned by cathedral canon Lauren Artress in 1991. "Labyrinths," she writes, "are usually in the form of a circle with a meandering but purposeful path, from the edge to the center and back out again. Each one has only one path, and once we make the choice to enter it, the path becomes a metaphor for our journey through life." Since then Artress has started something of a labyrinth cult, which has trained nearly 130 people to present

---

figurative monuments in Kelly Ingram Park in Birmingham, which try to draw the viewer back into the tumult of labyrinth workshops and programs called "the theater of enlightenment," even publishing a quarterly newsletter on the labyrinth project (including a few pages hawking labyrinth tote bags, jewelry, and other items). Labyrinths as spiritual devices are proliferating around the country, and garden mazes are also undergoing a revival. In the 1960s and 1970s a very different kind of labyrinth proliferation took place, in the work of artists such as Terry Fox, and in the late 1980s Adrian Fisher became a wildly successful maze designer in Britain, designing and building garden mazes at Blenheim Palace and dozens of other locations.

Labyrinths are not merely Christian devices, though they always represent some kind of journey, sometimes one of initiation, death and rebirth, or salvation, sometimes of courtship. Some seem merely to signify the complexity of any journey, the difficulty of finding or knowing one's way. They were much mentioned by the ancient Greeks, and although the legendary labyrinth of Crete in which the minotaur was imprisoned has never been found and probably never existed, the shape now called the Cretan labyrinth appeared on its coins. Other labyrinths have been found: carved in the rock in Sardinia; cleared in the stony desert surface in southern Arizona and California; made of mosaic by the Romans. In Scandinavia there are almost five hundred known labyrinths made of stones laid out upon the earth; until the twentieth century, fishermen would walk them before putting out to sea to ensure good catches or favorable winds. In England turf mazes—mazes cut into the earth—were used by young people for erotic games, often in which a boy ran toward a girl at the center, and the twists and turns of the maze seem to symbolize courtship's complexities. The much better known hedge mazes of that country are a later, more aristocratic innovation of the Renaissance garden. Many who've written about mazes and labyrinths distinguish between the two of them. Mazes, including most garden mazes, have many branchings and are made to perplex those who enter, whereas a labyrinth has only one route, and anyone who stays with it can find the paradise of the center and retrace the route to the exit. Another metaphorical moral seems built into these two structures, for the maze offers the confusions of free will without a clear destination, the labyrinth an inflexible route to salvation.

Like the stations of the cross, the labyrinth and maze offer up stories we can walk into to inhabit bodily, stories we trace with our feet as well as our eyes. There is

---

the past. Several works designed by James Drake along a path named Freedom Walk commemorate the brutal police a resemblance not only between these symbolically invested structures but between every path and every story. Part of what makes roads, trails, and paths so unique as built structures is that they cannot be perceived as a whole all at once by a sendentary onlooker. They unfold in time as one travels along them, just as a story does as one listens or reads, and a hairpin turn is like a plot twist, a steep ascent a building of suspense to the view at the summit, a fork in the road an introduction of a new storyline, arrival the end of the story. Just as writing allows one to read the words of someone who is absent, so roads make it possible to trace the route of the absent. Roads are a record of those who have gone before, and to follow them is to follow people who are no longer there—not saints and gods anymore, but shepherds, hunters, engineers, emigrants, peasants to market, or just commuters. Symbolic structures such as labyrinths call attention to the nature of all paths, all journeys.

This is what is behind the special relationship between tale and travel, and, perhaps, the reason why narrative writing is so closely bound up with walking. To write is to carve a new path through the terrain of the imagination, or to point out new features on a familiar route. To read is to travel through that terrain with the author as guide—a guide one may not always agree with or trust, but who can at least be counted upon to take one somewhere. I have often wished that my sentences could be written out as a single line running into the distance so that it would be clear that a sentence is likewise a road and reading is traveling (I did the math once and found the text of one of my books would be four miles long were it rolled out as a single line of words instead of being set in rows on pages, rolled up like thread on a spool). Perhaps those Chinese scrolls one unrolls as one reads preserve something of this sense. The songlines of Australia's aboriginal peoples are the most famous examples conflating landscape and narrative. The songlines are tools of navigation across the deep desert, while the landscape is a mnemonic device for remembering the stories: in other words, the story is a map, the landscape a narrative.

So stories are travels and travels are stories. It is because we imagine life itself as a journey that these symbolic walks and indeed all walks have such resonance. The workings of the mind and the spirit are hard to imagine, as is the nature of time—so we tend to metaphorize all these intangibles as physical objects located in space. Thus our relationship to them becomes physical and spatial: we move toward or away from them. And if time has become space, then the unfolding of

---

repression of the famous marches in the spring of 1963. In one work, the walkway passes between two vertical slabs,

---

time that constitutes a life becomes a journey too, however much or little one travels spatially. Walking and traveling have become central metaphors in thought and speech, so central we hardly notice them. Embedded in English are innumerable movement metaphors: steering straight, moving toward the goal, going for the distance, getting ahead. Things get in our way, set us back, help us find our way, give us a head start or the go-ahead as we approach milestones. We move up in the world, reach a fork in the road, hit our stride, take steps. A person in trouble is a lost soul, out of step, has lost her sense of direction, is facing an uphill struggle or going downhill, through a difficult phase, in circles, even nowhere. And there are the far more flowery phrases of sayings and songs—the primrose path, the road to ruin, the high road and the low road, easy street, lonely street, and the boulevard of broken dreams. Walking appears in many more common phrases: set the pace, make great strides, a great step forward, keep pace, hit one's stride, toe the line, follow in his footsteps. Psychic and political events are imagined as spatial ones: thus in his final speech Martin Luther King said, "I've been to the mountaintop," to describe a spiritual state, echoing the state Jesus attained after his literal mountain ascent. King's first book was called *Stride to Freedom*, a title echoed more than three decades later by Nelson Mandela's autobiography, *Long Walk to Freedom* (while his former countrywoman Doris Lessing called the second volume of her memoirs *Walking in the Shade*, and then there's Kierkegaard's *Steps on Life's Way* or the literary theorist Umberto Eco's *Six Walks in the Fictional Woods*, in which he describes reading a book as wandering in a forest).

If life itself, the passage of time allotted to us, is described as a journey, it's most often imagined as a journey on foot, a pilgrim's progress across the landscape of personal history. And often, when we imagine ourselves, we imagine ourselves walking; "when she walked the earth" is one way to describe someone's existence, her profession is her "walk of life," an expert is a "walking encyclopedia," and "he walked with God" is the Old Testament's way of describing a state of grace. The image of the walker, alone and active and passing through rather than settled in the world, is a powerful vision of what it means to be human, whether it's a hominid traversing grasslands or a Samuel Beckett character shuffling down a rural road. The metaphor of walking becomes literal again when we really walk. If life is a journey, then when we are actually journeying our lives have become tangible, with goals we can move toward, progress we can see,

---

from which bronze attack dogs emerge on either side and lunge into the pedestrian's space. In another the walkway

---

achievement we can understand, metaphors united with actions. Labyrinths, pilgrimages, mountain climbs, hikes with clear and desirable destinations, all allow us to take our allotted time as a literal journey with spiritual dimensions we can understand through the senses. If journeying and walking are central metaphors, then all journeys, all walks, let us enter the same symbolic space as mazes and rituals do, if not so compellingly.

There are many other arenas in which walking and reading are conflated. Just as the church labyrinth had its secular sibling in the garden maze, so the reading of the stations of the cross has its secular equivalent in the sculpture garden. Premodern Europeans were expected to recognize a large cast of characters in painting, sculpture, and stained glass, from the saints—Saint Peter with his key, Saint Lucy with her eyes on a plate—to the graces, cardinal virtues, and deadly sins. Most churches would have some portion of the Bible translated into art; a particularly elaborate cathedral like Chartres would include such features as the Seven Liberal Arts and the Wise and Foolish Virgins as well as scenes from the life of Christ arranged symbolically. Though book literacy was far lower, image literacy was incomparably higher, and the more educated would be able to recognize the gods and mortals from classical mythology as well as Christian iconography. Because the sources were usually literary, each figure represented a story, and these stories could be arranged in various sequences and often were—sequences that could be "read" by strolling past (embodiments such as Liberty or Spring were not narrative, but they might be arranged in a sequence that was, while gods and heroes often appeared in some climactic moment from a familiar tale, making the sculpture equivalent to a film still). Many gardens were sculpture gardens, not in our modern sense of greenery as a sort of picture frame for various individual objects, but as whole spaces that could be read, making the garden as much an intellectual space as the library. Sculptures and, sometimes, architectural elements were arranged in sequences that the viewer-stroller interpreted as she passed, and part of the charm of these gardens is that walking and reading, body and mind, were harmoniously united there.

The cloisters that were part of every monastery and convent sometimes bore elaborate Christian stories. Usually a square arcade around a garden with a central well, pool, or fountain, the cloister was where monks or nuns could walk without leaving the contemplative space of the order. Renaissance gardens had elaborately arranged mythological and historical statues. Because the walker al-

---

leads through an opening in a metal wall faced by two water cannons; just off the wall, by the walk, are two bronze

---

ready knew the story, no words need be said, but in the space and time of the walk and its encounter with the statuary, the story was in a sense retold just by being called to mind. This makes the garden a poetic, literary, mythological, and magical space. The great gardens of the Villa d'Este in Tivoli had a series of bas-reliefs that told the tales of Ovid's *Metamorphoses*. A more completely lost narrative was the labyrinth at Versailles, destroyed in 1775. In it were placed, along with a statue of Aesop, figure groupings from his fables, and "each of the speaking characters represented in the fable groups," writes W. H. Matthews, "emitted a jet of water, representing speech, and each group was accompanied by an engraved plate displaying more or less appropriate verses by the poet de Benserade." The labyrinth was thus a three-dimensional anthology in which walking, reading, and looking united into a journey into the fables' morals and meanings. Versailles, the largest of all Europe's formal gardens, had the most complex sculptural program, in which the Aesop maze was only a minor diversion. It organized nearly all its sculptures around the central image of Louis XIV as the Sun King (subsequent additions and subtractions make it hard to decipher now). Seventy sculptors labored that the sculptures, fountains, and very plants would speak to strollers of the power of the king, a power naturalized and endorsed by the imagery of the sun and the classical sun god Apollo, on a scale that made the symbolic not a scale model but a vast expanse of the world. A century later, the celebrated formal garden at Stowe in Buckingham, England, was transformed into a more naturalistic landscape, but its rolling hills and groves were studded with even more pointedly political architectural motifs. The Temple of Ancient Virtue was located near both the ruined Temple of Modern Virtue and, across a pool, the Temple of British Worthies, featuring the poets and statesmen most appealing to the garden's Whig owner. The conjunction deplored the state of the eighteenth-century world while setting up the Whigs as heirs to the noble ancients. Other elements at Stowe were more humorous for those who could read space and symbolism: the hermitage located near the Temple of Venus, for example, pitting asceticism against sensuality. If a narrative is a sequence of related events, then these sculpture gardens made the world into a book by situating these events in real space, far enough apart to be "read" by walking (and made Versailles and Stowe into books of political propaganda). Sometimes what is to be read in the garden is less literal. "A garden path," write the landscape architects Charles W. Moore, William J. Mitchell, and William Turnbull, "can become the thread of a

figures of African Americans, a man crumpled to the ground and a woman standing with her back against the plot, connecting moments and incidents into a narrative. The narrative structure might be a simple chain of events with a beginning, middle, and end. It might be embellished with diversions, digressions, and picaresque twists, be accompanied by parallel ways (subplots), or deceptively fork into blind alleys like the alternative scenarios explored in a detective novel." Los Angeles's contribution to this genre is the Walk of the Stars on Hollywood Boulevard, in which tourists read celebrity names as they tread them underfoot.

Sometimes walkers overlay their surroundings with their imaginings and tread truly invented terrain. The American minister and walking enthusiast John Finlay wrote a friend, "You may be interested to know that I have a little game that I play alone: namely, that of walking in some part of the world as many miles as I actually walk here day by day, with the result that I have walked nearly 20,000 miles here in the last six years, which means that I have covered the land part of the earth in a circuit of the globe. I finished last night 2,000 miles since the first of January 1934 and in doing so reached Vancouver from the north." The Nazi architect Albert Speer traversed the world in his imagination while pacing back and forth in his prison yard, like Kierkegaard and his father. The art critic Lucy Lippard found that after her return to Manhattan she could continue to take the daily walks that had been so important a part of her year's residence in rural England "in a kind of out-of-body form—step by step, weather, texture, views, seasons, wildlife encounters."

There is a very practical sense in which to trace even an imaginary route is to trace the spirit or thought of what passed there before. At its most casual, this retracing allows unsought memories of events to return as one encounters the sites of those events. At its most formal it is a means of memorizing. This is the technique of the memory palace, another inheritance from classical Greece widely used until the Renaissance. It was a means of committing quantities of information to memory, an important skill before paper and printing made the written word replace the memory for much storage of rote information. Frances Yates, whose magnificent *Art of Memory* recovered the history of this strange technique for our time, describes the workings of the system in detail. "It is not difficult to get hold of the general principles of the mnemonic," she writes. "The first step

---

imagined force of the water. Integrated into the pedestrian experience of the park, these monuments invite everyone—

---

was to imprint on the memory a series of loci or places. The commonest, though not the only, type of mnemonic place system used was the architectural type. The clearest description of the process is that given by Quintilian. In order to form a series of places in memory, he says, a building is to be remembered, as spacious and various a one as possible, the forecourt, the living room, bedrooms, and parlours, not omitting statues and other ornaments with which the rooms are decorated. The images by which the speech is to be remembered . . . are then placed in imagination in the places which have been memorized in the building. This done, as soon as the memory of the facts requires to be revived, all these places are visited in turn and the various deposits demanded of their custodians. We have to think of the ancient orator as moving in imagination through his memory building whilst he is making his speech, drawing from the memorized places the images that he has placed on them. The method ensures that the points are remembered in the right order, since the order is fixed by the sequence of places in the building."

Memory, like the mind and time, is unimaginable without physical dimensions; to imagine it as a physical place is to make it into a landscape in which its contents are located, and what has location can be approached. That is to say, if memory is imagined as a real space—a place, theater, library—then the act of remembering is imagined as a real act, that is, as a physical act: as walking. The scholarly emphasis is always on the device of the imaginary palace, in which the information was placed room by room, object by object, but the means of retrieving the stored information was walking through the rooms like a visitor in a museum, restoring the objects to consciousness. To walk the same route again can mean to think the same thoughts again, as though thoughts and ideas were indeed fixed objects in a landscape one need only know how to travel through. In this way, walking *is* reading, even when both the walking and reading are imaginary, and the landscape of the memory becomes a text as stable as that to be found in the garden, the labyrinth, or the stations.

But if the book has eclipsed the memory palace as a repository of information, it has retained some of its pattern. In other words, if there are walks that resemble books, there are also books that resemble walks and use the "reading" activity of walking to describe a world. The greatest example is Dante's *Divine Comedy*, in which the three realms of the soul after death are explored by Dante, guided by

---

black or white, young or old—to step for a moment into someone else's shoes. —KIRK SAVAGE   *I stride along*

Virgil. It is an unearthly travelogue of sorts, moving past sights and characters steadily, always keeping the pace of a tour. The book is so specific about its geography that many editions contain maps, and Yates suggests that in fact this masterpiece was a memory palace of sorts. Like a vast number of stories before and after, it is a travel story, one in which the movement of the narrative is echoed by the movement of the characters across an imaginary landscape.

---

with calm, with eyes, with shoes, / with fury, with forgetfulness—PABLO NERUDA

Part II

FROM THE
GARDEN TO THE
*W*ILD

Chapter 6

THE PATH OUT OF THE GARDEN

I. TWO WALKERS AND THREE WATERFALLS

Two weeks before the end of the century, a brother and sister went walking across the snow. Both were dark-complexioned, and their friends remarked that you could see their bad posture when they walked, but the resemblance ended there. He was tall, Roman-nosed, calm, while she was small and had fiery eyes that everyone noticed. The first day of their journey, December 17, they had gone twenty-two miles on horseback before they parted with their friend, the horses' owner, and walked another twelve miles to their lodgings, "having walked the last three miles in the dark and two of them over hardfrozen road to the great annoyance of our feet and ancles. Next morning the earth was thinly covered with snow, enough to make the road soft and prevent its being slippery." As they had the day before, the travelers turned aside to see a waterfall amid this mountainous landscape. "Twas a keen frosty morning," the brother went on in his Christmas Eve letter, "showers of snow threatening us but the sun bright and active; we had a task of twenty one miles to perform in a short winter's day. . . . On a nearer approach the water seemed to fall down a tall arch or rather nitch which had shaped itself by insensible moulderings in the wall of an old castle. We left this spot with reluctance but highly exhilarated."

In the afternoon they came upon another waterfall, whose water seemed to turn to snow as it fell amid the ice. He continued, "The stream shot from between the rows of icicles in irregular fits of strength and with a body of water that momently varied. Sometimes it threw itself into the basin in one continued curve, sometimes it was interrupted almost midway in its fall and, being blown towards

---

As some fond virgin, whom her mother's care / Drags from the town to wholesome country air . . . / She went from

---

us, part of the water fell at no great distance from our feet like the heaviest thunder shower. In such a situation you have at every moment a feeling of the presence of the sky. Above the highest point of the waterfall large fleecy clouds drove over our heads and the sky appeared of a blue more than usually brilliant." After the detour to the waterfall, they walked the next ten miles in two and a quarter hours "thanks to the wind that drove behind us and the good road," and he seemed to relish their prowess in walking almost as much as the scenery. Seven more miles took them to their next resting spot, and in the morning they walked into Kendal, the gateway to the Lake District, where they had come to live.

The century they were approaching as fast as their new home was the nineteenth century, and the home was a cottage on the outskirts of the small lakeside village of Grasmere; the two vigorous walkers themselves were, as many may have already guessed, William and Dorothy Wordsworth. What they did on those four days across the Pennine Mountains of northern England, what they had done and would do as walkers, was extraordinary. What exactly makes it so is hard to pin down. People had traveled by foot much farther and in far worse conditions before. People had begun, by the time of the poet's and his sister's birth nearly thirty years before, to admire some of the wildest features of the British countryside—mountains, cliffs, moors, storms, and the sea, as well as waterfalls. In France and Switzerland a few people had begun to climb mountains—the summit of Mont Blanc, Europe's highest peak, had first been reached fourteen years earlier. Wordsworth and his companions are said to have made walking into something else, something new, and thereby to have founded the whole lineage of those who walk for its own sake and for the pleasure of being in the landscape, from which so much has sprung. Most who have written about this first generation of Romantics propose that they themselves introduced walking as a cultural act, as a part of aesthetic experience.

Christopher Morley wrote in 1917, "I have always fancied that walking as a fine art was not much practiced before the Eighteenth Century. We know from Ambassador Jussurand's famous book how many wayfarers were abroad on the roads in the Fourteenth Century, but none of these were abroad for the pleasures of moving meditation and scenery. . . . Generally speaking, it is true that cross-country walks for the pure delight of rhythmically placing one foot before the other were rare before Wordsworth. I always think of him as one of the first to employ his legs as an instrument of philosophy." Morley is not far off the mark,

---

opera, park, assembly, play / To morning walks, and prayers three hours a day . . . —ALEXANDER POPE, "EPISTLE

---

in his first sentence, though much of the eighteenth century had passed before Wordsworth was born in 1770. But then he conflates walking as a fine art with cross-country walking, which is where the confusion slips in. Since Morley, the subject of walking and English culture has been taken up in three books, all of which go further in proposing that it was in the late eighteenth century, when Wordsworth and his peers set out afoot, that this walking began.

Morris Marples's delightful 1959 *Shanks's Pony: A Study of Walking*, Anne D. Wallace's 1993 *Walking, Literature, and English Culture*, and Robin Jarvis's 1998 *Romantic Poetry and Pedestrian Travel* all use as their demonstration case the German minister Carl Moritz. During his walk across England in 1782, Moritz often found himself scorned and ejected by innkeepers and their employees, while coachmen and carters continually asked him if he wanted a ride. He concluded that it was his mode of travel that made him seem out of place to those he encountered: "A traveller on foot in this country seems to be considered as a sort of wild man, or an out-of-the-way-being, who is stared at, pitied, suspected, and shunned by everybody that meets him." Reading his book, one is moved to speculate on whether his dress, manner, or accent disconcerted the people he encountered, rather than his walking. But his explanation is largely accepted by the three who cite him.

Travel itself was enormously difficult until the late eighteenth century in England. The roads were atrocious and plagued by highwaymen and their pedestrian equivalents, footpads. Those who could afford to went by horse or by coach, carriage, or at worst, wagon, sometimes with weapons; walking along the public roads often signified that one was either a pauper or a footpad, at least until the 1770s, when various intellectuals and eccentrics began to walk there for pleasure. By the late eighteenth century, the roads were improving in both quality and safety, and walking was becoming a more respectable mode of travel. On the cusp of the next century, the Wordsworths were having a splendid time walking not only roads but fells and byways; fear of crime and denigration seem to be the furthest things from their mind as they admired the view and enjoyed their own powers of walking in weather that would keep most people huddled indoors.

They had visited the Lake District six years before their midwinter walk. "I walked with my brother at my side, from Kendal to Grasmere, eighteen miles, and afterwards from Grasmere to Keswick, fifteen miles, through the most de-

TO MISS BLOUNT"   *To Hyde-park they repaired; sir Philip boasting all the way they walked, of the superior* lightful country that ever was seen," wrote Dorothy in the initial flush of pleasure after that excursion in 1794, and then she wrote defensively to her aunt, "I cannot pass unnoticed that part of your letter in which you speak of my 'rambling about the country on foot.' So far from considering this as a matter of condemnation, I rather thought it would have given my friends pleasure to hear that I had courage to make use of the strength with which nature has endowed me, when it not only procured me infinitely more pleasure than I should have received from sitting in a post chaise—but was also the means of saving me at least thirty shillings." If we take Dorothy Wordsworth in 1794 rather than Carl Moritz in 1782 as our witness, we find walking cross-country was nothing worse than unladylike and unconventional.

Though Wordsworth is in some sense the founding father (and therefore Dorothy the aunt) of a modern taste that has done much to shape the more pleasant parts of our world and the imaginations of those in it, he himself was heir to a long tradition, and so it is more accurate to see him as a transformer, a fulcrum, a catalyst for the history of walking in the landscape. His precursors, it is true, had not walked much on the public roads (and for the most part, neither do his modern descendants, since cars have made roads dangerous and miserable again). Though many traveled on foot out of necessity before him, few did so for pleasure, and these historians therefore conclude that walking for pleasure was a new phenomenon. In fact, walking had already become an important activity, though not as travel. Few of Wordsworth's pedestrian antecedents are to be found traveling along the public roads, but many of them were strolling in gardens and parks.

II. THE GARDEN PATH

Halfway through the nineteenth century, Thoreau wrote, "When we walk, we naturally go to the fields and woods: what would become of us, if we walked only in a garden or a mall?" For Thoreau, the desire to walk in the unaltered landscape no longer seemed to have a history, but to be natural—if nature means the timeless truth we have found, not the historic specific we have made. Though many nowadays go to the fields and woods to walk, the desire to do so is largely the result of three centuries of cultivating certain beliefs, tastes, and values. Before that,

----

strength of his head. Clarence protested that his own was stronger than any man's in England, and observed, that

----

the privileged seeking pleasure and aesthetic experience did indeed walk only in a garden or a mall. The taste for nature already entrenched in Thoreau's time and magnified in our own has a peculiar history, one that has made nature itself cultural. To understand why people chose to walk out in certain landscapes with certain agendas, one must first understand how that taste was formed in and launched from English gardens.

We tend to consider the foundations of our culture to be natural, but every foundation had builders and an origin—which is to say that it was a creative construction, not a biological inevitability. Just as a twelfth-century cultural revolution ushered in romantic love as first a literary subject and then a way of experiencing the world, so the eighteenth century created a taste for nature without which William and Dorothy Wordsworth would not have chosen to walk long distances in midwinter and to detour from their already arduous course to admire waterfalls. This is not to say that no one felt a tender passion or admired a body of water before these successive revolutions; it is instead to say that a cultural framework arose that would inculcate such tendencies in the wider public, give them certain conventional avenues of expression, attribute to them certain redemptive values, and alter the surrounding world to enhance those tendencies. It is impossible to overemphasize how profound is the effect of this revolution on the taste for nature and practice of walking. It reshaped both the intellectual world and the physical one, sending populations of travelers to hitherto obscure destinations, creating innumerable parks, preserves, trails, guides, clubs, and organizations and a vast body of art and literature with almost no precedent before the eighteenth century.

Some influences stand out like a landmark and leave a traceable legacy with evident heirs. But the most profound influences soak into the cultural landscape like rain and nourish everyday consciousness. Such an influence is likely to go undetected, for it comes to seem the way things have always been, the natural or even the only way to look at the world. This is the influence Shelley had in mind when he wrote, "Poets are the unacknowledged legislators of the world." Such an influence is the Romantic taste for landscape, for wild places, for simplicity, for nature as an ideal, for walking in the landscape as the consummation of a relationship with such places and an expression of the desire for simplicity, purity, solitude. Which is to say, walking is natural, or rather part of natural history, but choosing to walk in the landscape as a contemplative, spiritual, or aesthetic ex-

---

at this instant he walked better than any person in company, sir Philip Baddely not excepted. Now, sir Philip

---

perience has a specific cultural ancestry. This is the history that had already become naturalized for Thoreau and that took walkers farther and farther afield—for the changing history of walking is inseparable from the changing taste in places in which to walk.

The real reason Wordsworth and his peers seem to be the founders rather than the transformers of a tradition of walking for aesthetic reasons is because the walks that preceded theirs are so unremarkable. In fact these short walks in safe places are only incidental to the histories of architecture and gardens; they have no literature of their own, only mentions in novels, journals, and letters. The core of their history is concealed within another history, of making places to walk, places that became larger and more culturally significant as the eighteenth century wore on. It is also the history of a radical transformation of taste, from the formal and highly structured to the informal and naturalistic. It seems, in its origins, a trivial history of the idle aristocracy and their architecture, but in its results it created some of the most subversive and delightful places and practices in the contemporary world. The taste for walking and landscape became a kind of Trojan horse that would eventually democratize many arenas and in the twentieth century literally bring down the barriers around aristocratic estates.

The practice of walking can be traced through places. By the sixteenth century, as castles were beginning to turn into palaces and mansions, galleries—long narrow rooms like corridors, though often leading nowhere—often began to be part of the design. They were used for exercise indoors. "Sixteenth-century doctors stressed the importance of daily walking to preserve health, and galleries made exercise possible when the weather would otherwise have prevented it," writes Mark Girouard in his history of the country house. (The gallery eventually became a place for displaying paintings, and though museum galleries are still a place where people stroll, the strolling is no longer the point.) Queen Elizabeth added a raised terrace walk to Windsor Castle and walked there for an hour before dinner on every day that was not too windy. Walking was still more for health than for pleasure, though gardens were also being used for walking, and some kind of pleasure must have accrued there. But the taste for landscape was still fairly limited. On October 11, 1660, Samuel Pepys went walking in St. James's Park after dinner, but he only notes the water pumps at work there. Two years later, on May 21, 1662, he writes that he and his wife went walking in White Hall Garden, but he seemed most interested in the lingerie of the king's

---

Baddely was a noted pedestrian, and he immediately challenged our hero to walk with him for any money he

mistress in the privy garden, evidently hung there to dry. It was society that interested him, not nature, and landscape was not yet a significant subject for British painting and poetry, as it was to become. Until the surroundings became important, the walk was just movement, not experience.

A revolution was under way, however, in gardens. The medieval garden had been surrounded by high walls, in part for security in unstable times. In pictures of these gardens, the occupants most often sit or recline, listening to music or conversing (the enclosed garden had been, since the Song of Songs, a metaphor for the female body, and at least since the rise of the courtly love tradition, the site of much courtship and flirtation). Flowers, herbs, fruit-bearing trees, fountains, and musical instruments made them places that speak to all the senses, and the world outside this voluptuous sanctum seemed to provide more than enough exercise, since medieval nobles were still bodily involved in military and household matters. As the world became safer and the aristocratic residence became more a palace than a fortress, the gardens of Europe began to expand. Flowers and fruit were disappearing from the gardens; it was the eye to which these expanded realms appealed. The Renaissance garden was a place in which one could take a walk as well as sit, and the Baroque garden grew vast. Just as walking was exercise for those who need no longer work, so these vast gardens were cultivated landscapes that need no longer produce anything more than mental, physical, and social stimulation for walkers.

Were the Baroque garden not so ostentatious a display of wealth and power, its abstractness could be called austere. Trees and hedges were forced into squares and cones; paths, avenues, and walks were laid out as straight lines; water was pumped into fountains or poured into geometrical pools. A platonic order, a superimposition of the ideal on the messy material of the real, triumphed. Such gardens extended the geometry and symmetry of architecture into the organic world. But they still provided opportunities for informal and private behavior: throughout their history, one of the major functions of aristocratic gardens was to give people a place to retreat from the household into contemplation or private conversation. In England, William and Mary added new gardens to Hampton Court in 1699, gardens in which one could walk for a mile before reaching the wall. Walks, or paths, were becoming increasingly important parts of gardens, and they are indirect evidence of the increasing popularity of walking (in this context, "a walk" meant a path broad enough for two to walk abreast; it could

---

pleased.—MARIA EDGEWORTH, *BELINDA*   *In the evening walked alone down to the Lake by the side of Crow-*

---

be called a conversational route). English traveler and chronicler Celia Fiennes wrote of a garden she visited near the beginning of the eighteenth century, "There is gravel walks and grass and close walks, there is one walk all the length of the Garden called the Crooked Walke, of grass well cut and rowled, it is indented in and out in corners and so is the wall, which makes you thinke you are at the end of the walke several times before you are." But the walls of the garden were disappearing, and the distinction between it and the landscape beyond became harder and harder to find. Renaissance Italian gardens had been built by preference upon slopes that gave views of the countryside beyond, connecting the garden to the world, but French and English gardens seldom had such settings. The line of sight only extended to the garden wall, then eventually through a variety of openings in the garden wall.

When the ha-ha came into being in the early decades of the eighteenth century, the walls came down in Britain. A ditch relatively invisible from any distance, the ha-ha—so named because strollers were said to exclaim "Ha ha!" in surprise when they came upon it—provided an invisible barrier that allowed the garden's inhabitants to gaze into the distance uninterrupted. Where the eye went, the walker would soon follow. Most English estates consisted of a series of increasingly controlled spaces: the park, the garden, and the house. Originally hunting preserves, parks remained as a kind of buffer zone between the leisure classes and the agricultural land and workers around them and often provided timber and grazing space. The garden was typically a much smaller space surrounding the house. Susan Lasdun, in her history of these parks, writes of the straight avenues of trees planted in parks and gardens in the seventeenth century: "These avenues provided the shade and shelter for walks which, having been made fashionable by Charles II, were now becoming de rigueur in parks. . . . Certainly the liking for air and exercise was already considered an 'English' taste. Walks were now laid out by private owners in their country parks, and walking became as much a part of the pleasure of a park as hunting, driving and riding. The walks themselves were made increasingly interesting, with aesthetic considerations developing from the simple static vista from a window or terrace, to something that took account of a more mobile point of view. . . . The walker in fact made a circuit, and in the eighteenth century this was to become the standard manner for viewing gardens and parks. The days when it was only safe to walk on the castle terrace—the allure—had long since passed."

Park after sun-set and saw the solemn colouring of night draw on, the last gleam of sunshine fading away on the

The formal garden, with its patterns made of clipped hedges, geometric pools, and trees in orderly ranks, had suggested that nature was a chaos on which men imposed order (though starting in Italy in the Renaissance, paintings of unaltered landscapes, if not the unaltered land itself, were appreciated). In England the garden would become less and less formal as the eighteenth century progressed, and this idea of naturalistic landscaping that would be called the *jardin anglais*, the English garden, or the landscape garden is one of the great English contributions to Western culture. As the visual barrier that separated it from its surroundings vanished, the design of the garden became less distinctly separate too. In 1709 Anthony Ashley Cooper, earl of Shaftesbury, had effused, "O glorious Nature! Supremely Fair, and sovereignly Good! . . . I shall no longer resist the Passion growing in me for Things of a natural kind where neither Art nor the Conceit or Caprice of Man has spoiled their genuine Order, by breaking in upon that primitive State. Even the rude Rocks, the mossy Caverns, the irregular unwrought Grottos and broken Falls of waters, with all the horrid Graces of the Wilderness itself, as representing Nature more, will be the more engaging, and appear with a Magnificence beyond the formal Mockery of Princely Gardens." Rhetoric raced ahead of practice. It would be many more decades before princely gardens gave way to wilderness. But Shaftesbury's optimistic view of nature as inherently good joined with the optimism that men could appropriate, improve upon, or invent nature in their gardens.

"Poetry, Painting, and Gardening, or the science of Landscape, will forever by men of Taste be deemed Three Sisters, or the Three New Graces who dress and adorn nature," famously declared Horace Walpole, the wealthy aesthete who did much to inculcate romantic tastes in his peers. One of the premises of this declaration is that gardening is as much an art as the more traditionally respected practices of poets and painters, and the period was a sort of golden age for attention to gardens—or a kind of age of incubation, in which the taste for nature was hatched out of those gardens, poems, and paintings. Another premise is that nature needs to be dressed and adorned, at least in the garden, and paintings suggested some of the ways in which this could be done. Among the influences on the emerging English landscape garden were the seventeenth-century Italian landscapes of Claude Lorrain, Nicholas Poussin, and Salvator Rosa, with their rolling ground stretching toward far horizons, their clumps of feathery trees framing the distance, their serene bodies of water and their classical buildings

---

hilltops, the deep serene of the asters, and the long shadows of the mountains thrown across them, till they nearly

---

and ruins (and, in Rosa's case, the cliffs, torrents, and bandits that made him the most gothic of the three). Pillared temples and Palladian bridges were added to make English gardens resemble the Italian campagna of these paintings and to suggest that England was heir to Rome's virtues and beauties. "All gardening is landscape painting," said Alexander Pope, and people were learning to look at landscape in gardens as they had learned to look at landscape in paintings.

And though architectural items—ruins, temples, bridges, obelisks—continued to be sprinkled over gardens for many decades, the subject of gardens was becoming nature itself—but a very specific version of nature, nature as a visual spectacle of plants and water and space, a serene thing to be contemplated serenely. Unlike the formal garden and the painting, which had a single ideal point of view from which they could be regarded, the English landscape garden "asked to be explored, its surprises and unsuspected corners to be discovered on foot," writes garden historian John Dixon Hunt. Carolyn Bermingham adds, in her history of the relations between class and landscape, "Whereas the French formal garden was based on a single axial view from the house, the English garden was a series of multiple oblique views that were meant to be experienced while one walked through it." To use anachronistic terms, the garden was becoming more cinematic than pictorial; it was designed to be experienced in motion as a series of compositions dissolving into each other rather than as a static picture. It was now designed aesthetically as well as practically for walkers, and walking and looking were beginning to become linked pleasures.

There were other factors in the increasing naturalization of the garden. Perhaps the most important was the equation of the landscape garden with English liberty. The English aristocrats cultivating a taste for nature were, in a sense, politically positioning themselves and their social order as natural, in contrast to French artifice. Thus their pursuit of country pastimes, their penchant for portraits of themselves in the landscape, their creation of naturalistic gardens, their cultivation of a taste for landscape, all had a political subtext, as Bermingham has so brilliantly pointed out. Yet other influences include reports of Chinese gardens, in which the paths and waterways were sinuous and winding, the overall effect celebrating rather than subduing natural complexity. Neither the early chinoiseries nor the imitations of nature bore much resemblance to their originals, but the intent was there, and evolving. Finally, this changing taste manifests an extraordinary confidence. The formal, enclosed garden and the castle are

----

touched the hithermost shore. At distance heard the murmur of many waterfalls not audible in the day-time. Wished

----

corollaries to a dangerous world from which one needs to be protected literally and aesthetically. As the walls come down, the garden proposes that there is already an order in nature and that it is in harmony with the "natural" society enjoying such gardens. The growing taste for ruins, mountains, torrents, for situations provoking fear and melancholy, and for artwork about all these things suggests that life had become so placidly pleasant for England's privileged that they could bring back as entertainment the terrors people had once strived so hard to banish. Too, private experience and informal art were blooming elsewhere, notably in the rise of the novel.

The exemplary garden for this evolution is Stowe in Buckingham. Stowe itself went through most of the phases of the English garden in the eighteenth century and stands now as a kind of lexicon of eighteenth-century gardening, from its temples, grotto, hermitage, and bridges to its lake and landscaping. It had some of the earliest chinoiserie and Gothic-revival architecture in England. Its owner, Viscount Cobham, had replaced the formal "parlour garden" made in 1680 with a far larger formal garden that he slowly revised and erased as the new century advanced. First the Elysian Fields, with their Temples of British Worthies and of Ancient and Modern Virtue, mentioned in the preceding chapter, were transformed into something with softer, more undulating lines, and the rest of the garden eventually followed. Straight walks became serpentine, and their walkers no longer promenaded but wandered. Christopher Hussey describes Stowe, the political capital of the Whigs, as transforming politics into garden architecture, loosening the formal landscape design "into harmony with the age's humanism, its faith in disciplined freedom, its respect for natural qualities, its belief in the individual, whether man or tree, and its hatred of tyranny whether in politics or plantations." Most of the great landscape architects of the age worked for Cobham, and many of the great poets and writers were among his guests. And the gardens continually expanded, annexing dozens of acres at a time. "Within thirty years," summarizes one of the garden's historians, "his taste had moved from a preoccupation with regular arrangements of terraced lawns, statues and straight paths . . . to an essay in three-dimensional landscape painting, the creation of an ideal landscape."

Celebrated in many poems, pictures, and journals, Stowe was a central site in the cultural foment of the era, both as a subject and a retreat. "O lead me to the wide-extended walks / The fair majestic paradise of Stowe . . . While there with

---

for the moon, but she was dark to me and silent, hid in her vacant interlunar cave.—THOMAS GRAY, "JOURNAL IN

---

th' enchanted round I walk / The regulated wild," wrote James Thomson, a guest during most of 1734 and 1735, in the "Autumn" section of his poem *The Seasons*. This enormously successful poem with its blank verse describing the changing year and minor dramas in the landscape probably did more than any other literary work to inculcate a taste for scenery; in the nineteenth century J.M.W. Turner was still appending big chunks of the poem to his paintings. Pope wrote at length of Stowe's glories too, and in a letter described a typical day at Stowe in the 1730s: "Everyone takes a different way, and wanders about till we meet at noon." Walpole visited Cobham's heir at Stowe in 1770. After breakfast, the party spent the day walking in the gardens "or drove about it in cabriolets, till it was time to dress" for dinner. It had become enormous, a place it takes a whole day to explore on foot, and no clear boundary but a ha-ha separates it from the surrounding countryside.

That year, the Gothic architect Sanderson Miller walked there with various people, including Lancelot "Capability" Brown, the landscape architect who was to complete the revolution in garden design with his unadorned expanses of water, trees, and grass. Brown created the Grecian Valley in Stowe, the largest and plainest stretch of the garden (and though it looks wholly natural, the valley itself was dug by hand by many laborers, whose views of landscape gardening do not survive). The Brownian garden, having largely banished sculpture and architecture, no longer commemorated human history and politics. Nature was no longer a setting, but the subject. And the walkers in such a garden were no longer being steered toward ready-made reflections on virtue or Virgil; they were free to think their own thoughts as they followed the meandering paths (though those thoughts might well be about nature, or rather Nature, as taught by myriad texts). From being an authoritarian, public, and essentially architectural space, the garden was becoming a private and solitary wilderness.

Not everyone was ready to accept the landscape garden as realized by Brown. Sir Joshua Reynolds, president of the Royal Academy, wrote, "Gardening, as far as Gardening is an Art, or entitled to the appellation, is a deviation from nature; for if the true taste consists, as many hold, in banishing every appearance of Art, or any traces of the footsteps of man, it would then no longer be a garden." Reynolds was onto something. The garden, in the course of becoming more and more indistinguishable from the surrounding landscape, had become unneces-

---

THE LAKES"   *On the day after Mary Wollstonecraft first made love to William Godwin she retreated in concern* sary—Walpole had said of the landscape architect William Kent that he had "leapt the fence and saw all nature was a garden." If a garden was nothing more than a visually pleasing space in which to wander, then gardens could be found rather than made, and the tradition of the garden walk could expand to become the tourist's excursion. Rather than looking at the work of man, the scenic stroller could look at the works of nature, and to look at nature as a work of art completed a momentous revolution. In Shaftesbury's terms, princely gardens had finally given way to wilderness; the nonhuman world had become a fit subject for aesthetic contemplation.

The aristocratic garden had begun as part of the fortified castle, and slowly its boundaries had melted away; the melting of the garden into the world is a mark of how much safer England had become (and to a lesser degree, much of western Europe, where the fashion for the English garden soon caught on). Since about 1770, England had undergone a "transportation revolution" of improved roads, decreased roadside crime, and cheaper fares. The very nature of travel changed. Before the mid-eighteenth century, travel accounts have little to say about the land between religious or cultural landmarks. Afterward, an entirely new way of travel arose. In pilgrimage and practical travel, the space between home and destination had been an inconvenience or an ordeal. When this space became scenery, travel became an end in itself, an expansion of the garden stroll. That is to say, the experiences along the way could replace destinations as the purpose of travel. And if the whole landscape was the destination, one arrived as soon as one set out in this world that could be looked at as a garden or a painting. Walking had long been recreational, but travel had joined it, and it was only a matter of time before traveling on foot would itself become a widespread part of the pleasures of scenic travel, its slowness finally a virtue. The point at which a poor poet and his sister might travel across a snowy countryside for the pleasure of looking and walking was drawing near.

Afterward, Wordsworth himself was moved to write a guidebook to the Lake District, in which he summarized the history traced here. "Within the last sixty years," he wrote in 1810, "a practice, denominated Ornamental Gardening, was at that time becoming prevalent over England. In union with an admiration of this art, and in some instances in opposition to it, had been generated a relish for select parts of natural scenery: and Travellers, instead of confining their observa-

---

and self-doubt: "Consider what has passed as a fever of your imagination . . . and I will become again a Solitary

---

tions to Towns, Manufactories, or Mines, began (a thing till then unheard of) to wander over the island in search of sequestered spots, distinguished . . . for the sublimity or beauty of the forms of Nature there to be seen."

III. Inventing Scenic Tourism

The unhappy German traveler Carl Moritz, who felt rejected at many points on his pedestrian journey, in fact encountered a plethora of walkers, though neither he nor his modern readers made much of them. He takes little note of the many people he saw walking from Greenwich to London, but he does say of London's St. James's Park that what "greatly compensates for the mediocrity of this park, is the astonishing number of people who, towards evening, in fine weather, resort here; our finest walks are never so full even in the midst of summer. The exquisite pleasure of mixing freely with such a concourse of people, who are for the most part well dressed and handsome, I have experienced this evening for the first time." Moritz, in fact, is suggesting that walking is *more* genteel a pastime, or more public a genteel pastime, in England than in Germany, even if traveling on foot is not (he is also revealing that he is a snob, which may be why he resented road-walking's plebeian status). During his time in London, he also visited Ranelagh and Vauxhall Gardens. Cousins of the country fair and the modern amusement park, these popular sites offered music, spectacles, strolls, and refreshments in a garden atmosphere, and both the gentry and the middle class flocked there for evening amusements. Like modern strollers in Latin American plazas and parks or any carnival or mall now, they were there to look at each other as well as the scenery, and the scenery was often augmented with orchestras, pantomimes, refreshments, and other diversions. Social promenading was another aspect of a thriving culture of walking, whose more solitary moments developed in the private garden and park. "The People of London are as fond of walking as our friends at Pekin of riding," wrote Oliver Goldsmith in the guise of a Chinese visitor describing Vauxhall. "One of the principal entertainments of the citizens here in summer is to repair about nightfall to a garden not far from town, where they walk about, shew their best cloaths and best faces, and listen to a concert provided for the occasion."

Another significant aspect of Moritz's travels was his visit to the famous cav-

---

Walker."—E. P. THOMPSON   *I spent the following day roaming through the valley. I stood beside the sources* ern in the Peak District of Derbyshire in northern England, not far from the Lakes. Significantly, there was already a guide in place to collect a fee and show him its marvels. Scenic tourism was coming into existence in the Peak District, the Lake District, Wales, and Scotland. And just as the development of the English landscape garden had been surrounded by a flurry of descriptive poems and epistles, so the growth of tourism was encouraged and informed by guidebooks. Like modern guidebooks and travel narratives, these tell of what is to be seen and where to find it. Some of them—notably the work of the clergyman William Gilpin—also tell *how* to see. A taste for landscape was a sign of refinement, and those wishing to become refined took instruction in landscape connoisseurship. One suspects that the contemporaries who made Gilpin so influential a writer consulted him much the way later generations consulted guides on which fork to use or how to thank a hostess, for Gilpin wrote when the middle class was acquiring the hitherto aristocratic taste for landscape. A landscape garden was a luxury that only a few could create or use, but the unaltered landscape was available to virtually everyone, and more and more middle-class people could travel to enjoy it as the roads became safer and smoother and transportation became cheaper. A taste for landscape was something to be learned, and Gilpin was many people's guide.

"She would have every book that tells her how to admire an old twisted tree," remarks Edward of the romantic Marianne in Jane Austen's *Sense and Sensibility*. Critic John Barrell writes that "there is a sense in which, in late eighteenth-century England, one can say that the simple contemplation of landscape, quite apart from its expression in painting, writing or whatever, came to be regarded as an important pursuit for the cultivated and almost in itself the practice of an art. To display a correct taste in landscape was a valuable social accomplishment quite as much as to sing well, or to compose a polite letter. The heroines of a number of late eighteenth-century novels are made to display this taste with an almost ostentatious virtuosity, and not only the simple fact of having a taste for landscape or not, but also variations of taste within the general one, are regarded by some novelists as legitimate indications of differences in character." Marianne Dashwood is asserting her romanticism with her taste for old twisted trees, though she apologizes for the fashionability of the taste: "It is very true . . . that admiration of landscape scenery is become a mere jargon. Everybody pretends to feel and tries to describe with the taste and elegance of him who first defined

of the Arveiron, which take their rise in a glacier, that with slow pace is advancing down from the summit of the what picturesque beauty was." She too is speaking of Gilpin, who brought into common usage the word *picturesque,* which originally meant any landscape that resembled or could be perceived as a picture and eventually came to mean a wild, gnarled, rough, intricate kind of landscape.

For Gilpin was teaching people to look at landscape as pictures. Nowadays, his books give a sense of what a heady new pastime looking at landscape was and how much assistance was required. Gilpin tells his readers what to look for and how to frame it in the imagination. Of Scotland, for example, he declares, "Were it not for this general deficiency of objects, particularly of wood, in the Scotch views, I have no doubt but that they would rival those of Italy. The grand outlines are all laid in; a little finishing is all we want"—which is to say that the new subject of Scottish terrain can be understood through comparison to both art and the already hallowed landscapes of Italy. He wrote guidebooks to many parts of England, notably the Lake District, as well as to Wales and Scotland, enumerating the proper sites to visit. Others joined in; Richard Payne Knight wrote, in his abominable but influential 1794 *Landscape: A Didactic Poem in Three Books,* "Let us learn, in real scenes, to trace / The true ingredients of the painter's grace."

Like the taste for landscape, the emphasis on the pictorial and the existence of scenic tourism seem unremarkable things to present-day readers, and yet they were all invented in the eighteenth century. The poet Thomas Gray's celebrated Lake District tour of 1769 came two years after the first tourist came specifically to admire the scenery and write about it, and Gray wrote about it too. By the end of the century the Lakes were an established tourist destination, as they have remained since, thanks to Gilpin, Wordsworth—and Napoleon: English travelers who once might have gone abroad began to travel around their own island during the turmoil of the French Revolution and Napoleonic wars. Tourists traveled by coach, then train (and eventually car and plane). They read their guidebooks. They looked at their landscapes. They bought souvenirs. And when they arrived, they walked. Originally, the walking seems to have been incidental, part of the process of moving around to find the best view. But by the turn of the century walking was a central part of some touristic ventures, and walking tours and mountain climbing were coming into being.

---

hills to barricade the valley. . . . These sublime and magnificent scenes afforded me the greatest consolation that I

IV. MUD ON HER PETTICOAT

Though Jane Austen famously ignored the Napoleonic Wars in her novels, she pointedly addressed other topical subjects. In *Northanger Abbey* she mocked the current taste for the gothic novel, with its macabre and unlikely thrills, and in *Sense and Sensibility* she was almost as sarcastic about Marianne Dashwood's romantic views on love and landscape. Later in her life, she seems to have accepted the cult of landscape far more, and in her late novel, *Mansfield Park*, she more than once equates the heroine's sensitivity to natural beauty with her moral virtues. Her novels with their genteel young women in rural circumstances are also a wonderful index of the uses of the walk at the end of the eighteenth century and beginning of the nineteenth, and none so much as *Pride and Prejudice*. A tour of Elizabeth Bennet's walks will close our inspection of the circumstances in which William and Dorothy Wordsworth set out for Grasmere in December of 1799 (and here it should be noted that though *Pride and Prejudice* was published in 1813, the first version was composed in 1799). Austen was their peer, and she lets us glimpse the staid world they walked out on.

Walks are everywhere in *Pride and Prejudice*. The heroine walks on every possible occasion and in every location, and many of the crucial encounters and conversations in the book take place while two characters are walking together. The very incidental role of the walks indicates how much a part of the fabric of everyday life walking was for such people as Austen's genteel characters. Throughout the eighteenth century and into the nineteenth in England, walking was a particularly feminine pursuit—"They were country ladies, and of course fond of the country lady's amusement, walking," wrote Dorothy Wordsworth in a letter in 1792. It was something to do. In the writings of men we find much about designing and admiring gardens, but it is in the letters and novels of women that we most often find people actually walking in them, perhaps because they address more minute daily life, or perhaps because Englishwomen—or, rather, ladies—had so few other activities open to them. Between social functions Elizabeth Bennet, the heroine of *Pride and Prejudice*, reads copiously, writes letters, sews a little, plays the piano passably, and walks.

Not long after the novel opens, Jane Bennet catches a cold riding to Netherfields, the house of her suitor Mr. Bingley, and her sister Elizabeth walks over to nurse her. Going by foot is in part an act of necessity, since she is "no horsewoman," and only one horse, rather than a pair to pull the carriage, is available. But the bold verve that makes her so charming a heroine also makes her an avid walker—"I do not wish to avoid the walk. The distance is nothing when one has a motive; only three miles"—and the walk is the first major demonstration of her unconventionality. Though not going nearly as far as did Dorothy Wordsworth when reprimanded by her aunt, Elizabeth is likewise walking beyond the bounds of propriety for women of her class, and the characters at Mr. Bingley's house have much to say about it. The transgression seems to be both that she went out into the world alone, and that she turned the idyll of the genteel walk into something utilitarian. "That she should have walked three miles so early in the day, in such dirty weather, and by herself, was almost incredible to Mrs. Hurst and Miss Bingley; and Elizabeth was convinced that they held her in contempt for it." When she is out of earshot caring for her sister, who has become seriously ill, they expatiate on the mud on her petticoat and her "abominable sort of conceited independence, a most country town indifference to decorum." Mr. Bingley, on the other hand, remarks that the unorthodox excursion "shews an affection for her sister that is very pleasing," and Mr. Darcy notes that it has "brightened" her eyes.

Soon afterward, while Jane and Elizabeth are marooned at this worldly house, its inhabitants demonstrate the correct sort of walking—within the bounds of both garden shrubbery and society. Miss Bingley is still railing to Mr. Darcy about Elizabeth. "At that moment they were met from another walk, by Mrs. Hurst and Elizabeth herself." Mrs. Hurst takes Mr. Darcy's disengaged arm and leaves Elizabeth to walk alone. "Mr. Darcy felt their rudeness and immediately said,—

"'This walk is not wide enough for our party. We had better go into the avenue.'

"But Elizabeth, who had not the least inclination to remain with them, laughingly answered—

"'No, no; stay where you are.—You are charmingly group'd, and appear to uncommon advantage. The picturesque would be spoilt by admitting a fourth. Good bye.'"

They have castigated her cross-country walk across the boundaries of decorum; she is mocking their garden propriety by suggesting that they have become part of the garden's array of aesthetic objects, objects that she can contemplate as

---

they subdued and tranquilized it.—MARY SHELLEY, _FRANKENSTEIN_   _He who does not know these sensations has_

---

impersonally as trees and water. That evening Miss Bingley strolls about the narrower confines of the drawing room, where all the Netherfields characters but Jane are gathered. "Her figure was elegant, and she walked well," says Austen. The acuity of idle people about each other's conduct extended to critiques of movement and posture, and a person's walk was considered an important part of his or her appearance. When she invites Elizabeth to join her, Mr. Darcy remarks that they walk either to discuss things privately or because "you are conscious that your figures appear to the greatest advantage in walking." Walking can be for display, withdrawal, or both.

This novel and other novels of the time suggest that walking provided a shared seclusion for crucial conversations. Etiquette at the time required residents and guests of the country house to pass their day in the main rooms together, and the garden walk provided relief from the group, either in solitude or in tête-à-têtes (in a twist on this practice, modern political figures have often held crucial conversations on walks in order to avoid being bugged). Soon after Jane's recovery, she and Elizabeth gossip while walking in their own family's shrubbery. For *Pride and Prejudice* is also an incidental inventory of the types of landscape available to walk in. Toward the end of the book, further features of the Bennet gardens appear when Lady Catherine storms in to harangue Elizabeth about her intentions toward Mr. Darcy; "'Miss Bennet, there seemed to be a prettyish kind of a little wilderness on one side of your lawn. I should be glad to take a turn in it, if you will favour me with your company,'" she dissembles, seeking private conversation. "'Go, my dear,' cried her mother, 'and shew her ladyship about the different walks. I think she will be pleased with the hermitage.'" This lets us know that it is a mid-eighteenth-century garden of some size, with at least one architectural adornment in it.

What exactly Lady Catherine's park included we never learn, only that during her stay nearby Elizabeth's "favourite walk . . . was along the open grove which edged that side of the park, where there was a nice sheltered path, which no one seemed to value but herself, and where she felt beyond the reach of Lady Catherine's curiosity." Not Mr. Darcy's, however: "More than once did Elizabeth in her ramble within the Park, unexpectedly meet Mr. Darcy.—She felt all the perverseness of the mischance." She tells him it is her "favorite haunt," for she still wishes to avoid him. He, of course, is in love with her and repeatedly joins her in the park seeking private conversation: "it struck her in the course of their third

rencontre that he was asking some odd unconnected questions—about her pleasure in being at Hunsford, her love of solitary walks . . ."

For the author and her readers, as for Mr. Darcy, these solitary walks express
the independence that literally takes the heroine out of the social sphere of the
houses and their inhabitants, into a larger, lonelier world where she is free to
think: walking articulates both physical and mental freedom. Though Austen has
not nearly as much to say about scenery in this novel as in *Mansfield Park*, Elizabeth's sensitivity to landscape is another of the features that signifies her refined
intelligence. It is not Mr. Darcy but Pemberly, his estate, that begins to change
her mind about him, and walking in his park becomes a peculiarly intimate act.
She "had never seen a place for which nature had done more, or where natural
beauty had been so little counteracted by an awkward taste. . . . At that moment
she felt, that to be mistress of Pemberley might be something!" Evidently a student of Gilpin, she inspects the view from each window of the house, and after
they have left it to walk toward the river, the owner of both house and river appears. Her uncle "expressed a wish of going round the whole Park, but feared it
might be beyond a walk. With a triumphant smile, they were told, that it was ten
miles round." Like Elizabeth's fondness for solitary walks, Mr. Darcy's possession
of a magnificent naturalistic landscape evidently in the modern style of Capability Brown is a sign of character. When they unexpectedly meet in this landscape,
a more civil and conscious relationship begins, as they "pursued the accustomed
circuit; which brought them again, after some time, in a descent among hanging
woods, to the edge of the water, in one of its narrowest parts. They crossed it by
a simple bridge, in character with the general air of the scene . . . and the valley,
here contracted into a glen, allowed room only for the stream, and a narrow walk
amidst the rough coppice-wood which bordered it. Elizabeth longed to explore
its windings. . . ."

It is this shared taste for scenery that finally provides the literal common
ground on which they resolve their differences. Of course, the hero and heroine
of the novel have been brought together in the glories of Pemberley because her
aunt and uncle had offered to take her to the Lake District (to which Elizabeth
"rapturously cried, 'what delight! what felicity! You give me fresh life and vigour.
Adieu to disappointment and spleen. What are men to rocks and mountains?'").
Though Miss Bingley despises this aunt and uncle for being in trade and residing
in an unfashionable part of London, they have demonstrated *their* refinement by

---

no sympathy, and Charlotte does not allow me to enjoy the melancholy consolation of bathing her hand in my

---

taking up this moderately avant-garde form of scenic tourism. The trip has been cut short, bringing them to Derbyshire and Pemberley, not far south of the Lakes, and gathering together all the most admirably conscious characters in the book. Austen interrupts the high abstract plane of her narration, in which only the most necessary details of the material world briefly intrude, to offer us luscious descriptions of Pemberley. Of the country in which it is located, she remarks, however, "It is not the object of this work to give a description of Derbyshire." Still, she lists the magnificent estate of Chatsworth and the natural wonders of Dove Dale, Matlock, and the Peak as among the attractions these tourists have visited.

The multiplicity of walking's uses are notable in this novel. Elizabeth walks to escape society and to converse privately with her sister and, at the end of *Pride and Prejudice*, with her suitor. The landscapes she enjoys include old-fashioned and new gardens, wild landscapes of the north and Kentish countryside. She walks for exercise, as did Queen Elizabeth, for conversation, as did Samuel Pepys, and walks in gardens, as did Walpole and Pope. She walks in scenic spots as did Gray and Gilpin, and even walks for transportation, as did Moritz and the Wordsworths, and like them she meets with disapproval for it. Once or twice she promenades, as did they all. New purposes keep being added to the pedestrian repertoire, but none are dropped, so that the walk constantly increases in meanings and uses. It has become an expressive medium. It is also both socially and spatially the widest latitude available to the women contained within these social strictures, the activity in which they find a chance to exert body and imagination. On a walk where they manage to lose all their companions and "she went boldly on with him alone," Elizabeth and Darcy finally come to an understanding, and their communications and newfound happiness take up so much time that "'My dear Lizzy, where can you have been walking to?' was a question which Elizabeth received from Jane as soon as she entered the room, and from all the others when they sat down to table. She had only to say in reply, that they had wandered about, till she was beyond her own knowledge." Consciousness and landscape have merged, so that Elizabeth has literally gone "beyond her own knowledge" into new possibilities. It is the last service the walk performs for the restless heroine of this novel.

Notable too are the many times in which walking appears as a noun rather than a verb in this book and in this era: "Within a short walk of Longbourn lived

---

tears, I tear myself from her and roam through the country, climb some precipitous cliff, or make a path through a a family"; "a walk to Meryton was necessary to amuse their morning hours"; "they had a pleasant walk of about half a mile across the park"; "her favourite walk . . . was along the open grove" and so forth. These uses of the word express that the walk is a set piece with known qualities, like a song or a dinner, and that in going on such a walk one does not merely move one's legs alternately but does so for a certain duration neither too long nor too short, for purposes sufficiently unproductive of anything but health and pleasure, in pleasing surroundings. The language implies a conscious attention to the refinement of everyday acts. People had always walked, but they had not always invested it with these formal meanings, meanings about to expand further.

V. OUT OF THE GATE

The Romantic poets are popularly portrayed as revolutionaries breaking with everything that had come before. The young Wordsworth was radical in politics, as well as poetic style and subject matter, but he carried much polite eighteenth-century convention forward with him. Still in his mother's womb when Gray arrived in the Lake District, he helped further popularize the region's beauties, and though he was born on the edge of its steep, stony expanses, it was conventional aesthetics as well as personal associations that brought him back to live out the last fifty years of his life there. From Wales to Scotland to the Alps, Wordsworth chose already-celebrated landscapes to walk in and write about. He was, in some ways, the ideal tourist, a tourist with a unique gift for remembering and describing what he saw, and his relationship to the Lake District is an odd balancing act between the clear-eyed intimacy of the local and the enthusiasm of the tourist. He and his sister were consciously steeping themselves in the existing literature on landscape, educating themselves to see the same way Marianne Dashwood or Elizabeth Bennet might have, and bringing that sight into their everyday excursions. In 1794 Wordsworth asked his brother in London to send his books to him and singled out the volumes of Gilpin's Scottish and northern English tours as important to include. And in 1800, seven months after that long walk across the snow, Dorothy wrote in her journal, "In the morning, I read Mr Knight's *Landscape* [*The Landscape: A Didactic Poem*, quoted earlier]. After tea we rowed down to Loughrigg Fell, visited the white foxglove, gathered wild strawberries and

---

trackless wood, where I am wounded and torn by thorns and briars; and there I find some relief. . . . Ossian has

---

walked up to view Rydale. We lay a long time looking at the lake: the shores all embrowned with the scorching sun. The ferns were turning yellow, that is, here and there one was quite turned. We walked round by Benson's wood home. The lake was now most still, and reflected the beautiful yellow and blue and purple and grey colours of the sky." The passage reads as though she took instruction in landscape in the morning and carried it out in the afternoon. It also illustrates the Wordsworths' most common kind of walking—not as travel but as daily outings in the region around them, in some respects like the daily garden walks of the ladies and gentlemen whose traditions they were extending, and in some respects radically different.

-----

superseded Homer in my heart. What a world into which that magnificent poet carries me! To wander over the

Chapter 7

THE LEGS OF
WILLIAM WORDSWORTH

"His legs were pointedly condemned by all the female connoisseurs in legs that I ever heard lecture on that topic," wrote Thomas De Quincey of William Wordsworth, with the mixture of admiration and animosity most of the next generation of poets brought to that looming presence. "There was no absolute deformity about them; and undoubtedly they had been serviceable legs beyond the average standard of human requisition; for I calculate, upon good data, that with these identical legs Wordsworth must have traversed a distance of 175 to 180,000 English miles—a mode of exertion, which to him, stood in the stead of wine, spirits, and all other stimulants whatsoever to the animal spirits; to which he has been indebted for a life of unclouded happiness, and we for much of what is most excellent in his writings." While others walked before and after him, and many other Romantic poets went on walking tours, Wordsworth made walking central to his life and art to a degree almost unparalleled before or since. He seems to have gone walking nearly every day of his very long life, and walking was both how he encountered the world and how he composed his poetry.

To understand his walking, it is important to break away from the idea of "the walk" as meaning a brief stroll about a pleasant place and from that other definition of the recent writers on Romantic walking, of walking as long-distance travel. For Wordsworth walking was a mode not of traveling, but of being. At twenty-one, he set off on a two-thousand-mile journey on foot, but during the

---

heath, blown about by the winds, which conjure up by the feeble light of the moon the spirit of our ancestors. . . . At

---

last fifty years of his life, he paced back and forth on a small garden terrace to compose his poetry, and both kinds of walking were important to him, as was cruising about the streets of Paris and of London, climbing mountains, and walking with sister and friends. All this walking found a way into his poetry. I could have written about his walking earlier, with the philosophical writers who made walking part of their thinking process, or later, when I turn to the histories of walking in the city. But he himself linked walking with nature, poetry, poverty, and vagrancy in a wholly new and compelling way. And of course Wordsworth himself emphatically valued the rural over the urban:

> Happy in this, that I with nature walked
> Not having a too early intercourse
> With the deformities of crowded life. . . .

Too, he is the figure to which posterity looks in tracing the history of walking in the landscape: he has become a trailside god.

Born in 1770 in Cockermouth, just north of the more wild and steep scenery of the Lake District, Wordsworth liked in later years to portray himself as a simple man born amid a kind of pastoral republic of lakeland freeholders and shepherds. In fact, his father was the agent of Lord Lowther, an immensely wealthy despot who owned much of the region. The future poet was not yet eight when his mother died; Dorothy was sent away to be raised by relatives, and he himself was sent to school in Hawkshead, in the heart of the Lakes. The death of their father when Wordsworth was thirteen left the children dependent on the goodwill of unenthused relations, for Lord Lowther managed to deprive the five Wordsworth children of their legacy from this successful father for nearly twenty years. But the years at Hawkshead's excellent school were idyllic despite or perhaps because of all the family turmoil. There he set snares, ice-skated, climbed the cliffs for birds' eggs, boated, and walked incessantly, at night and often in the morning before school, when he and a friend would go the five miles around the nearby lake. Or so says *The Prelude*, his great autobiographical poem of several thousand lines, which even with its scrambled chronologies and deleted facts provides a spectacular portrait of the poet's early life. Called by his family "The Poem to Coleridge," to whom it is addressed, it is also subtitled "The Growth of a Poet's Mind," signifying exactly what kind of an autobiography it is, and it was

---

noon I went to walk by the river—I had no appetite. Everything around seemed gloomy.—GOETHE, THE SORROWS meant to be a prelude to a monumental philosophical poem *The Recluse*, of which only *The Prelude* and "The Excursion" were completed.

The Prelude reads almost as a single long walk that, though interrupted, never altogether stops, and this recurrent image of the walker gives it continuity amid all its digressions and detours. One pictures Wordsworth like Christian in *Pilgrim's Progress* or Dante in the *Divine Comedy*, a small figure touring the whole world on foot, only this time around it is a world of lakes, dances, dreams, books, friendships, and many many places. The poem is also a kind of atlas of the making of a poet, showing us the role of this city and that mountain, for places loom larger than people. In the same respectfully spiteful vein as De Quincey remarking on Wordsworth's legs, the essayist William Hazlitt once quipped, "He sees nothing but himself and the universe." In the history of English literature, the rise of the novel is often linked to the rise of awareness and interest about personal life— personal life as private thoughts, emotions and relations between people. Wordsworth went much further than the novels of his time in charting his own thoughts, emotions, memories, and relations to place, but his seems a curiously impersonal life, since he remains reticent on his personal relationships—thus Hazlitt's quip.

His passion for walking and for landscape seems to have originated in childhood, or been that curiosity so many children have, salvaged and refined into art in his later years, but the passion begins too early and goes too far to be merely the fashionable taste for admiring and describing landscapes. In the fourth of the *Prelude's* thirteen books, he describes walking home from an all-night dance somewhere in the Lakes, sometime in his late teens, to witness a dawn "more glorious than I had ever beheld." Early on this morning, while "The sea was laughing at a distance; all / The solid mountains were as bright as clouds" he committed to his vocation as poet—"I made no vows but vows / Were then made for me"—and he became a "dedicated spirit. On I walked / In blessedness, which even yet remains." In his early twenties, he seems to have set about to systematically fail at every alternative to being a poet and chosen wandering and musing as the preliminaries for realizing his vocation.

> Should the guide I choose
> Be nothing better than a wandering cloud,
> I cannot miss my way,

OF YOUNG WERTHER   *When his [Coleridge's] health was good, which it certainly was for long spells, he did the*

---

he asserts amid the opening lines of this massive poem first finished in 1805, revised repeatedly during his lifetime, and only published after his death in 1850.

The turning point in both his life and *The Prelude* is his amazing 1790 walk with his fellow student Robert Jones across France into the Alps, when they should have been studying for their Cambridge University exams. Wordsworth's most recent biographer, Kenneth Johnston, dramatically declares, "With this act of disobedience his career as a Romantic poet may be said to have begun." Travel has its rogue and rebel aspects—straying, going out of bounds, escaping—but this journey was as much a quest for an alternate identity as an escapade. The Grand Tour had been a standard feature of English gentlemen's educations, usually they went by coach to meet people of their own class and see the artworks and monuments of France and Italy. Those connoisseurs of gardens and landscapes Horace Walpole and Thomas Gray went on such a tour in 1739, where they each wrote excitedly of the Alps they crossed en route to Italy. To go on foot and to make Switzerland, rather than Italy, the destination of the trip expressed a radical shift in priorities, away from art and aristocracy toward nature and democracy. To go in 1790 meant joining the flood of radicals converging on Paris to breathe the heady atmosphere of the early days of the French Revolution, before the blood had begun to pour. The Alps themselves, already central objects in the cult of the landscape sublime, were part of the attraction, but so was Switzerland's republican government and its associations with Rousseau. Their final destination before they boated back down the Rhine was the island of Saint-Pierre, which Rousseau wrote about in the *Confessions* and the *Reveries of a Solitary Walker* as a version of the natural paradise. Rousseau is an obvious precursor for Wordsworth, who walked as both a means and an end—to compose and to be.

They had landed in Calais on July 13 and woke the next day to the joyous celebrations of the first anniversary of the storming of the Bastille, when France was "standing on top of golden hours / And human nature seeming born again." They walked through

> hamlets, towns,
> Gaudy with relics of that festival,
> Flowers left to wither on triumphal arcs, and window garlands. . . .
> Unhoused beneath the evening star we saw

---

most amazing walks and mountain climbs all round the Lakes single-handed. He was in effect the first of the modern

---

> Dances of liberty, and in late hours
> Of darkness, dances in the open air.

Wordsworth and Jones had charted their journey with care, however, and walked about thirty miles a day in order to carry out their ambitious plans:

> A march it was of military speed
> And earth did change her images and form
> Before us fast as clouds are changed in heaven.
> Day after day, up early and down late,
> From vale to vale, from hill to hill we went,
> From province on to province did we pass,
> Keen hunters in a chase of fourteen weeks.

So vigorous were they that they crossed the Alps without realizing it, much to their disappointment. Already over the final pass and still thinking they had far higher to go, they had cut off on an uphill trail when a peasant set them straight and sent them to finish their descent into Italy, where they made a quick loop past Lake Como before reentering Switzerland. Wordsworth breaks off this narrative at Lake Como, but *The Prelude* recounts his returns to France in 1791, where his politics continued to develop.

It is entirely Wordsworthian that he tried to understand the Revolution by walking the streets of Paris and visiting "each spot of old and recent fame" from the "dust of the Bastille" to the Champ de Mars and Montmartre. Among the Britons he may have met there are Colonel John Oswald and "Walking Stewart," two examples of a new kind of pedestrian. Johnston writes, "Oswald had traveled to India, become a vegetarian and nature mystic, walked back to Europe overland, thrown himself into the French Revolution with the direct intent of carrying it back to England." He would later appear under his own surname in Wordsworth's early verse drama *The Borderers*. Stewart was a similar character whose nickname commemorated his remarkable walks—he too had walked back from India, as well as all over Europe and North America—but whose books were diatribes on other subjects. De Quincey wrote of Walking Stewart, "No region, pervious to human feet except, I think, China and Japan, but had been visited by Mr. Stewart in this philsophical style; a style which compels a man to move

---

fell walkers, the first known outsider to set out to climb the mountain tops, just for the pleasure of doing so. His

---

slowly through a country, and to fall in continually with the natives of that country." A third eccentric, John Thelwall (mentioned in chapter 2), suggests something of a pattern: autodidacts who took the trinity of radical politics, love of nature, and pedestrianism to extremes. Thelwall became well acquainted with Wordsworth and Coleridge in the early 1790s, and later in that decade, after he narrowly escaped hanging for his politics, sought refuge with them. Wordsworth owned a copy of Thelwall's *Peripatetic,* which amid its digressions on philosophy takes stock of the living and working conditions of the laborers being drawn into the beginnings of the industrial revolution. These characters suggest that traveling any distance on foot was the act of a political radical in England, expressing an unconventionality and a willingness to identify and be identified with the poor. Wordsworth himself wrote in a letter of 1795, "I have some thoughts of exploring the country westward of us, in the course of next summer, but in an humble evangelical way; to wit *à pied,*" and in *The Prelude* he wrote, "So like a peasant I pursue my way."

To walk in this way summoned up Rousseau's complex equation of virtue with simplicity with childhood with nature. At the beginning of the eighteenth century, English aristocrats had linked nature with reason and the current social order, suggesting that things were as they should be. But nature was a dangerous goddess to enthrone. At the latter end of that century, Rousseau and romanticism equated nature, feeling, and democracy, portraying the social order as highly artificial and making revolt against class privilege "only natural." In his history of eighteenth-century ideas of nature, Basil Willey remarks, "Throughout that turbulent time 'Nature' remained the dominant concept," but its meaning was protean. "The Revolution was made in the name of Nature, Burke attacked it in the name of Nature, and in *eodem nomine* Tom Paine, Mary Wollstonecraft, and [radical philosopher William] Godwin replied to Burke." To walk in the gracious and expensive confines of the garden was to associate walking, nature, the leisure classes, and the established order that secured that leisure. To walk in the world was to link walking with a nature aligned instead with the poor and whatever radicalism would defend their rights and interests. Too, if society deformed nature, then children and the uneducated were, in a radical reversal, the purest and the best. Wordsworth, perfect sponge of his age, soaks up these values and pours them forth as his extraordinary poetry of childhood—his own, and those of his many fictional characters—and of the poor. He took up Rousseau's task and im-

---

ascent in 1802 of Scafell Pike, the highest Lakeland peak, is the first recorded climb of that magnificent mountain.

---

proved upon it, portraying rather than arguing a relationship between childhood, nature, and democracy. Though only the first two of this trinity are remembered by the worshipers of the trailside god, the third is central to at least the early work. "You know perhaps already that I am of that odious class of men called democrats," he wrote a friend in 1794, continuing with a confidence that proved unwarranted, "and of that class I shall for ever continue."

Somewhere on these roads, among these people and these questions, Wordsworth met up with his style. His earliest poetry is lofty, vague, and studded with conventional images, in the mode of Thomson's _Seasons_, but it seems to be his revolutionary ardor and sympathetic identification with the poor that saved him from being a minor landscape poet (during the same decade of the 1790s, Dorothy's writing undergoes a similar transformation, from the aphoristic abstruseness of a Dr. Johnson or Jane Austen to something vividly descriptive and down-to-earth). It changed both subject matter and style. In his retroactive preface to the _Lyrical Ballads_, the epochal book of poems by Wordsworth and Coleridge published in 1798, he wrote, "The principal object, then, proposed in these poems, was to choose incidents and situations from common life, and to relate or describe them throughout, as far as was possible, in a selection of language really used by men, and, at the same time, to throw over them a certain coloring of imagination. . . . Humble and rustic life was generally chosen, because in that condition the essential passions of the heart find a better soil . . . and speak a plainer and more emphatic language." He wrote about the poor as people rather than as figures in fables of virtue or pity, as he wrote about landscapes in their specific details rather than in high-flown generalizations and classical allusions. Choosing plainer language was a political act, with spectacular artistic results.

What is marvelous about Wordsworth's early poetry is its union of the radical walk for the sake of encounters with the scenic stroll of aesthetic connoisseurs. Looking back, it seems there should have been some tensions between scenery and poverty as subjects, but for the young Wordsworth in that exuberant moment there were none. The landscapes are the more incandescent for being populated by vagrants rather than nymphs, and that incandescence is the more necessary as the birthright and backdrop of the desperate. The recurrent structure of these early poems is a walk interrupted by an encounter with those displaced by the economic turbulence of the time into fellow wanderers. Earlier poets and artists had looked at the cottages and bodies of the poor and found

---

—HUNTER DAVIES, _WILLIAM WORDSWORTH: A BIOGRAPHY_   _I said he has just finished an exquisite ode to Pan_ them picturesque or pitiful, but no one with such a voice had found it worthwhile to talk to them before. "When we walk, we naturally go to the fields and woods," remarked Thoreau, but Wordsworth headed as eagerly to the public roads as to mountains and lakes. People walk streets for the sake of encounters and paths for solitude and scenery; on the road Wordsworth seems to have found an ideal intermediary, a space providing long quiet spells broken by the occasional meeting. He affirmed:

> I love a public road: few sights there are
> That please me more—such object has had power
> O'er my imagination since the dawn
> Of childhood, when its disappearing line
> Seen daily afar off, on one bare steep
> Beyond the limits which my feet had trod,
> Was like a guide into eternity,
> At least to things unknown and without bound.

Which is to say that the road had a kind of perspectival magic, an allure of the unknown. But it also had a populace:

> When I began to enquire,
> To watch and question those I met, and held
> Familiar talk with them, the lonely roads
> Were schools to me in which I daily read
> With most delight the passions of mankind,
> There saw into the depth of human souls
> Souls that appear to have no depth at all
> To vulgar eyes. . . .

This education had begun during his schooldays, when he boarded with a retired carpenter and his wife and met peddlers, shepherds, and similar characters. These early experiences seem to have set him at ease with people of another class and at least partially relieved him of that mental barrier that separates the English classes from each other. He once remarked, "Had I been born in a class which would have deprived me of what is called a liberal education, it is not unlikely

---

—and as he had not a copy I begged Keats to repeat it—which he did in his usual half chant, (most touchingly)

---

that, being strong in body, I should have taken to a way of life such as that in which my Pedlar passed the greater part of his days." The terrible uncertainty of his own early life, with parents dead and relatives shuttling the children around, seems to have generated a sympathy for the displaced, while his passion for traveling made these mobile characters, in a word, romantic to him. The times themselves were uncertain; the old order had been shaken by the revolutions and insurrections in France, America, and Ireland, and the poor were being displaced by the changing rural scene and dawning industrial revolution. The modern world of people cast adrift, unanchored by the securities of place, work, family, had dawned.

The mobile figure recurs in the work of Wordsworth's contemporaries too, and walking seems to have provided literal common ground between those traveling to seek adventure and pleasure and those on the road to seek survival. Even now English people tell me that walking plays so profound a role in English culture in part because it is one of the rare classless arenas in which everyone is roughly equal and welcome. The young Wordsworth wrote about discharged soldiers, tinkers, peddlers, shepherds, stray children, abandoned wives, "The Female Vagrant," "The Leech Gatherer," "The Old Cumberland Beggar," and others who tended to be nomadic or displaced; even the Wandering Jew made an appearance in his poetry and that of many other Romantics. Or as Hazlitt put it in describing the revolutionary transformation of English poetry at the hands of Coleridge, Wordsworth, and Robert Southey, "They were surrounded, in company with Muses, by a mixed rabble of idle apprentices and Botany Bay convicts, female vagrants, gipsies, meek daughters in the family of Christ, of ideot boys and mad mothers, and after them 'owls and night-ravens flew.'"

The peddler Wordsworth might have been is the principal narrator of his first long narrative poem, "The Ruined Cottage." It is typical of his early poetry in that in it a fortunate young man encounters, while walking, someone who tells him the tale that makes up the body of the poem, so that the young man and his saunters make a kind of frame around the sad picture, serving as frames do both to underscore the value and to isolate the work within. This time around, the Wordsworth figure arrives at a ruined cottage where the Pedlar tells him the pathos-drenched tale of the last residents of the place: a family torn apart into wanderers and lingerers by economic hardship. Everyone in the story is in some

---

walking up & down the room. . . . —BENJAMIN HAYDON   *Our walk before breakfast, and after the bath, is the* kind of pedestrian motion: the strolling narrator, the nomadic Pedlar, the husband enlisted and gone to a distant land, the heartbroken wife wearing a path into the grass by pacing back and forth, watching the road for his return.

The walkers in the garden had been anxious to distinguish their walking for pleasure from that of those who walked for necessity, which is why it was important to stay within the garden's bounds and not to walk as travel—but Wordsworth sought out meetings with those who represented this other kind of walking (or, frequently, borrowed those characters as met and vividly described by Dorothy in her journals, from which he gathered much). For all its meaty radical politics, *The Prelude* is a thirteen-book sandwich whose bread is landscape. The poem ends with a visionary experience atop Mount Snowdon in Wales that leads into another long soliloquy—but no further geographical details. A shepherd—shepherds were among the first mountain guides in Europe—leads him and an unnamed friend up during the night so they can see the sunrise from the peak. Because the young men are so fit, they arrive early at their destination. The narrative leaves Wordsworth atop the mountain in a sudden flood of moonlight, scenery, and revelation. Climbing a mountain has become a way to understand self, world, and art. It is no longer a sortie from but an act of culture.

But walking wasn't only a subject for Wordsworth. It was his means of composition. Most of his poems seem to have been composed while he walked and spoke aloud, to a companion or to himself. The results were often comic; the Grasmere locals found him spooky, and one remarked, "He won't a man as said a deal to common fwoak, but he talked a deal to hiseen. I oftenn seead his lips a ganin," while another recalled, "He would set his head a bit forrad, and put his hands behint his back. And then he would start a bumming, and it was bum, bum, bum, stop; then bum, bum bum, reet down till t'other end; and then he'd set down and git a bit o'paper and write a bit." In *The Prelude* he describes a dog he used to walk with who would, when a stranger drew near, cue him to shut up and avoid being taken for a lunatic. He possessed a remarkable memory that allowed him to recollect with visual detail and emotional vividness scenes long past, to quote long passages of the poets he admired, and to compose afoot and write the result down later. Most modern writers are deskbound, indoor creatures when they write, and nothing more than outline and ideas can be achieved elsewhere; Wordsworth's method seemed a throwback to oral traditions and explains why

best meal of the day. Anna and Elizabeth are beginning to taste and find out how good it is for mind and body. It the best of his work has the musicality of songs and the casualness of conversation. His steps seem to have beat out a steady rhythm for the poetry, like the metronome of a composer.

One of his best-known poems—"Lines Composed a Few Miles Above Tintern Abbey, on Revisiting the Banks of the Wye During a Tour," to give it its full title—was composed on foot during a walking tour in Wales with Dorothy in 1798. Upon arriving back in Bristol, he jotted the whole thing down and tacked it unrevised onto the *Lyrical Ballads*, where it appears as the last and one of the best poems in his book, his work, and perhaps the English language. Very much a walking poem, "Tintern Abbey" captures that state of musing, of shifting about in time from recollection to experience to hope while exploring a place. And like much of his blank verse, it is written in language so close to actual speech that it reads with conversational ease, but speaking it aloud revives the strong rhythms of those walks two hundred years ago.

In 1804 Dorothy wrote to a friend, "At present he is walking and has been out of doors these two hours though it has rained heavily all the morning. In wet weather he takes out an umbrella; chuses the most sheltered spot, and there walks backwards and forwards and though the length of his walk be sometimes a quarter or half a mile, he is as fast bound within the chosen limits as if by prison walls. He generally composes his verses out of doors and while he is so engaged he seldom knows how the time slips by or hardly whether it is rain or fair." There is a path at the top of the small garden at Dove Cottage, where he could see over the house to the lake and most of the ranges rising around it, and it was there he most often paced, composing. Many thousand of the "175 to 180,000 English miles" De Quincey estimated he had walked were walked here, on this terrace about twelve paces long, and on the similar terrace of the larger home he moved to in 1813. Seamus Heaney, writing about the "almost physiological relation of a poet composing and the music of the poem," says of Wordsworth's pacing back and forth that it "does not forward a journey but habituates the body to a kind of dreamy rhythm." It also makes composing poetry into physical labor, pacing back and forth like a ploughman turning his furrows up or wandering across the heights like a shepherd in search of a sheep. Perhaps because he was producing beauty out of arduous physical toil, he shamelessly identified himself with the working and walking poor. Though he was basically a rugged and athletic man, the stress of composing gave him headaches and a recurrent pain in the side, so

---

was meant that the whole season should be put into us, as it is into a flower.—AMOS BRONSON ALCOTT fiercely did he drive himself in this act of poetry as bodily labor. Heaney concludes, "Wordsworth at his best, no less than his worst, is a pedestrian poet."

Had Wordsworth been a perfect Romantic poet, he would have died in his late thirties, still pacing back and forth at humble Dove Cottage, leaving us the first, best version of *The Prelude*, all his early ballads and narratives about the poor, his odes and lyrics of childhood, and his image as a radical intact. Unfortunately for his reputation, though happily enough for self and family, he lingered in Grasmere and then in the large house in neighboring Rydal to the age of eighty, becoming increasingly conservative and decreasingly inspired. One might say that he went from being a great Romantic to a great Victorian, and the transition required much renouncement. Though he did not keep faith with his early politics, he kept faith with his walking. And oddly, it is his legacy not as a writer but as a walker that carries on the joyful insurrection of his early years.

One of his own last twinges of democracy came in 1836, when he was sixty-six. He had taken Coleridge's nephew walking on a private estate when, as one biographer recounts it, "the lord who owned the ground came up and told them they were trespassing. Much to his companion's embarrassment, William argued that the public had always walked this way and that it was wrong of the lord to close it off." The nephew recalled that "Wordsworth made his point with somewhat more warmth than I either liked or could well account for. He had evidently a pleasure in vindicating these rights, and seemed to think it a duty." Another version situates the confrontation at Lowther Castle, where Wordsworth, Coleridge's nephew, and the lord in question were dining. The latter declared that his wall had been broken down and he would have horsewhipped the man who did it. "The grave old bard at the end of the table heard the words, the fire flashed into his face and rising to his feet, he answered: 'I broke your wall down, Sir John, it was obstructing an ancient right of way, and I will do it again. I am a Tory, but scratch me on the back deep enough and you will find the Whig in me yet.'"

Of all the other Romantics, only De Quincey seems to have had a lifelong passion for walking comparable to Wordsworth's, and though it is impossible to measure pleasure, it is possible to say something about effects: walking was neither a subject nor a compositional method for the younger writer in the way it had been for the older. His innovations were elsewhere—Morris Marples credits

---

At length, as we plodded along the dusty roads, our thoughts became as dusty as they; all thought indeed stopped, him with being the first to go on a walking tour with a tent, which he slept in during an early sojourn in Wales to save money (the beginnings of the outdoor equipment industry show up here, in the special coats Wordsworth and Robert Jones had a tailor make them for their continental tour, in Coleridge's walking sticks, in De Quincey's tent, in Keats's odd travel outfit). De Quincey's best writing about walking was about prowling the streets of London as a destitute youth, a very different kind of walking—and writing. His fellow essayist William Hazlitt wrote the first essay on walking, but it began another genre of walking literature rather than extending the tradition Wordsworth took up, and it depicts walking as a pastime rather than an avocation. Shelley was too aristocratic an anarchist and Byron too lame an aristocrat to have much to do with walking; they sailed and rode instead.

Coleridge, on the other hand, had a decade of avid walking—1794–1804—which is reflected in his poetry from that time. Even before he met Wordsworth, he set out on a walking tour to Wales with a friend named Joseph Hucks and then another tour in Somerset in southern England with his fellow poet and future brother-in-law Robert Southey. In 1797 Coleridge and Wordsworth began their extraordinary collaborative years, with walks in the same parts of southern England; on one of these tours, when Dorothy joined them, Coleridge composed his most famous poem, the "Rime of the Ancient Mariner" (which is, like his friend's work of the time, a poem about wandering and exile). He and the Wordsworths walked together many more times: there was the epochal walking tour in the Lake District with William Wordsworth and his younger brother John, during which Wordsworth decided to return to this scene of his childhood, and there were many shorter walks after Coleridge and Southey moved to Keswick in the north of that district, as well as one final, blighted tour of Scotland with William, Dorothy, and a donkey cart. The two men got on each other's nerves, split up, and never quite resumed their great friendship. During the course of a solitary and athletic tour of the Lakes, Coleridge also became the first recorded person to reach the summit of Scafell Peak, though he lost some of the glory he might have achieved with this difficult climb by getting stuck on his descent and then tumbling down the mountain. After 1804, Coleridge went on no more long walks. Although the links between walking and writing are neither so explicit nor so profuse in his work as in his friend's, the critic Robin Jarvis does point out that Coleridge ceased to write blank verse when he ceased to walk.

----

thinking broke down, or proceeded only passively in a sort of rhythmical cadence of the confused material of

----

These walking tours on the part of poets who would not walk much later suggest that there was indeed an emerging fashion for traveling on foot. Certainly the very unpoetic literature of the guidebook began to address itself to walkers at this point, and the very notion of a walking tour suggests that the parameters of how to walk and what it meant were beginning to be established. Like the garden stroll, the long walk was acquiring conventions of both meaning and doing. This is easily seen in John Keats's one great experiment with walking. In 1818 the young Keats set out on a walking tour for the sake of poetry, suggesting that such an excursion was a familiar rite of passage as well as a refinement of sensibility. "I purpose within a month to put my knapsack at my back and make a pedestrian tour through the north of England, and part of Scotland—to make a sort of prologue to the life I intend to pursue—that is to write, to study and to see all Europe at the lowest expense. I will clamber through the clouds and exist," he wrote, and soon afterward wrote to another friend, "I should not have consented to myself these four Months tramping in the Highlands but that I thought it would give me more experience, rub off more Prejudice, use [me] to more hardship, identifying finer scenes, load me with grander Mountains, and strengthen more my reach in Poetry, than would stopping at home among Books even though I should read Homer." In other words, roughing it and growing acquainted with mountains was poetic training. Yet like the walkers who came after him, he wanted only so much hardship and experience. He turned back from Ireland appalled by the harsh poverty on that oppressed island, and in reading of this rejection of experience one thinks of a key moment in *The Prelude* and evidently in Wordsworth's life. He was walking in France with the revolutionary soldier Michel Beaupuy; they encountered a "hunger-bitten girl . . . who crept along" a lane, and Beaupuy explained that she was the reason they were fighting. Wordsworth had connected walking to both pleasure and suffering, to politics and scenery. He had taken the walk out of the garden, with its refined and restricted possibilities, but most of his successors wanted the world in which they walked to be nothing but a larger garden.

---

thought, and we found ourselves mechanically repeating some verse of the Robin Hood ballads.—THOREAU, "A

Chapter 8

A THOUSAND MILES OF
CONVENTIONAL SENTIMENT:
The Literature of Walking

I. THE PURE

Other kinds of walk survived, and early in Thomas Hardy's novel *Tess of the D'Urbervilles*, one of them collides with the traditions drawn from romanticism. Tess and her fellow peasant girls are celebrating May Day by going "club-walking," a pre-Christian spring ceremony in which they walk in procession across the countryside. Dressed all in white, the young women and a few older ones go in "a processional march of two and two round the parish" and in the designated meadow begin to dance. Looking on "were three young men of a superior class, carrying small knapsacks strapped to their shoulders and stout sticks in their hands. The three brethren told casual acquaintances that they were spending their Whitsun holidays in a walking tour through the Vale. . . ." Two of these three sons of a devout clergyman are themselves ministers; the third, who is less sure of the order of the world and his own place in it, chooses to leave the road and dance with the celebrants. The peasant women on their procession and the young gentlemen on their walking tour are both engaged in nature rituals, in very different ways. The men, with their costumes of knapsack and staff, are being artificially natural, for their version of how to connect to nature involves leisure, informality, and travel. The women, with their highly structured rite handed down from an unremembered past, are being naturally artificial. Their acts speak of the two things specifically excluded from the walking tour, work and sex, since it is a kind of crop fertility rite they are engaged in and since the local young men will come to dance with them when their day's work is done. Nature, after all, is not where they take their vacations but where they lead their lives, and work, sex, and the fertility of the land are part of that life. But pagan survivals and peasant rites are not the dominant cult of nature.

Nature, which had been an aesthetic cult in the eighteenth century and become a radical cult at the end of that century, was by the middle of the next century an established religion for the middle classes and, in England far more than the United States, for much of the working classes as well. Sadly, it had become as pious, sexless, and moral a religion as the Christianity it propped up or supplanted. Going out into "nature" was a devout act for those English, American, and Central European heirs of romanticism and transcendentalism. In a cheerfully malicious essay entitled "Wordsworth in the Tropics," Aldous Huxley asserted, "In the neighborhood of latitude fifty north, and for the last hundred years or thereabouts, it has been an axiom that Nature is divine and morally uplifting. For good Wordsworthians—and most serious-minded people are now Wordsworthians—either by direct inspiration or at second hand—a walk in the country is the equivalent of going to church, a tour through Westmoreland is as good as a pilgrimage to Jerusalem."

The first essay specifically on walking is William Hazlitt's 1821 "On Going a Journey," and it establishes the parameters for walking "in nature" and for the literature of walking that would follow. "One of the pleasantest things in the world is going a journey; but I like to go by myself," it opens. Hazlitt declares that solitude is better on a walk because "you cannot read the book of nature, without being perpetually put to the trouble of translating it for the benefit of others" and because "I want to see my vague notions float like the down of the thistle and not to have them entangled in the briars and thorns of controversy." Much of his essay is about the relationship between walking and thinking. But his solitude with the book of nature is very questionable, since in the course of the short piece he manages to quote from other books by Virgil, Shakespeare, Milton, Dryden,

asked if they could give me a bed. "Is your name Mr. Trevelyan?" they answered. "No," I said, "are you expecting

Gray, Cowper, Sterne, Coleridge, and Wordsworth, along with the Book of Revelation. He describes a day of walking through Wales launched by reading
Rousseau's *Nouvelle Heloise* the night before and quoting Coleridge's landscape poetry as he goes. Clearly, the books set forth the kind of experience of walking in
nature he should have—pleasant, mingling thoughts, quotations, and scenery—
and Hazlitt manages to have it. If nature is a religion and walking its principal
rite, then these are its scriptures being organized into a canon.

Hazlitt's essay became the foundation of a genre. It appears in each of the
three anthologies of walking essays—an English one from 1920 and two American ones from 1934 and 1967—that I own, and many of the later essayists cite it.
The walking essay and the kind of walking described in it have much in common:
however much they meander, they must come home at the end essentially un-
changed. Both walk and essay are meant to be pleasant, even charming, and so no
one ever gets lost and lives on grubs and rainwater in a trackless forest, has sex in
a graveyard with a stranger, stumbles into a battle, or sees visions of another
world. The walking tour was much associated with parsons and other Protestant
clergymen, and the walking essay has something of their primness. Most of the
classic essays cannot resist telling us how to walk. Individually, some of these are
very fine pieces of writing. Leslie Stephen, who in his "In Praise of Walking" takes
up Hazlitt's theme of the musings of the mind, writes, "The walks are the unobtrusive connecting thread of other memories, and yet each walk is a little drama
itself, with a definite plot with episodes and catastrophes, according to the requirements of Aristotle; and it is naturally interwoven with all the thoughts, the
friendships, and the interests that form the staple of ordinary life." Which is very
interesting in its way, and Stephen, who distinguished himself as a scholar, an
early Alpine climber, and an athletic walker, is himself interesting until he goes
on to tell us that Shakespeare walked and so did Ben Johnson and many others,
on up to, inevitably, Wordsworth. And then moralizing sneaks in; he says of Byron that his "lameness was too severe to admit of walking, and therefore all the
unwholesome humours which would have been walked off in a good cross-country
march accumulated in his brain and caused the defects, the morbid affectation
and perverse misanthropy, which half ruined the achievement of the most masculine intellect of his time." Stephen goes on to announce, after throwing in a few
dozen more English authors, "Walking is the best of panaceas for the morbid tendencies of authors." And then come the instructional shoulds, the shoulds that

---

him?" "Yes," they said, "and his wife is here already." This surprised me, as I knew it was his wedding day. I found

---

none of these essayists seems able to resist. He writes that monuments and land-marks "should not be the avowed goal but the accidental addition to the interest of a walk."

It doesn't take Robert Louis Stevenson nearly as long to get to that fateful word. Two or three pages after he has begun his celebrated 1876 essay "Walking Tours," he declares, "A walking tour should be gone on alone, because freedom is of the essence; because you should be able to stop and go on, and follow this way or that, as the freak takes you; and because you must have your own pace, and neither trot alongside a champion walker, nor mince in time with a girl." He goes on to praise and criticize Hazlitt: "Notice how learned he is in the theory of walking tours. . . . Yet there is one thing I object to in these words of his, one thing in the great master's practice that seems to me not wholly wise. I do not ap-prove of that leaping and running." On his own long walking tour in France's Cévennes mountain range, described in *Travels with a Donkey*, Stevenson carried a pistol but described only picturesque and lightly comic situations. Few of the canonical essayists can resist telling us that we should walk because it is good for us, nor from providing directions on how to walk. In 1913 the historian G. M. Trevelyan begins his "Walking" with "I have two doctors, my left leg and my right. When body and mind are out of gear (and those twin parts of me live at such close quarters that the one always catches the melancholy from the other) I know that I shall have only to call in my doctors and I shall be well again. . . . My thoughts start out with me like blood-stained mutineers debauching themselves on board the ship they have captured, but I bring them home at nightfall, larking and tumbling over each other like happy little boy scouts at play."

The possibility that some of us would prefer that happy little boy scouts keep their distance doesn't occur to him, but it must have to one writer, who blas-phemed against the cult in 1918. In his "Going Out on a Walk," the Anglo-German satirist Max Beerbohm exploded, "Whenever I was with friends in the country, I knew that at any moment, unless rain were actually falling, some man might suddenly say, 'Come out for a walk!' in that sharp imperative tone which he would not dream of using in any other connection. People seem to think there is something inherently noble and virtuous in the desire to go for a walk." Beer-bohm's heresy goes further; he claims that walking is not at all conducive to thinking because though "the body is going out because the mere fact of its do-ing so is a sure indication of nobility, probity, and rugged grandeur," the mind re-

---

her languishing alone, as he had left her at Truro, saying that he could not face the whole day without a little walk.

---

fuses to accompany it. He was, however, a voice crying out in a densely populated but otherwise convinced wilderness.

On the other side of the Atlantic, one essay on walking had lurched toward greatness, but even Henry David Thoreau could not resist preaching. "I wish to speak a word for Nature, for absolute freedom and wildness," he famously begins his 1851 essay "Walking," for like all the other essayists he connects walking in the organic world with freedom—but like all the others, he instructs us on how to be free. "I have met with but one or two persons in the course of my life who understood the art of Walking, that is, of taking walks—who had a genius, so to speak, for sauntering." A page later, "We should go forth on the shortest walk, perchance, in the spirit of undying adventure, never to return. . . . If you are ready to leave father and mother, and brother and sister, and wife and child and friends, and never see them again—if you have paid your debts, and made your will, and settled all your affairs, and are a free man, then you are ready for a walk." His are the most daring, wildest instructions, but they are still instructions. Soon afterward comes the other word, *must*: "You must be born into the family of Walkers." And then, "You must walk like a camel, which is said to be the only beast which ruminates when walking. When a traveler asked Wordsworth's servant to show him her master's study, she answered, 'Here is his library, but his study is out of doors.'"

Although the walking essay was officially a celebration of bodily and mental freedom, it was not actually opening up the world for that celebration—that revolution had already taken place. It was instead domesticating the revolution by describing the allowable scope of that freedom. And the sermonizing never let up. In 1970, a century and a half after Hazlitt, Bruce Chatwin wrote an essay that set out to be about nomads but detoured to include Stevenson's *Travels with a Donkey*. Chatwin wrote divinely, but he always declined to distinguish nomadism—a persistent travel by any means, seldom primarily by foot—from walking, which may or may not be travel. Blurring those distinctions by conflating nomadism and his own British walking-tour heritage made nomads Romantics, or at least romantic, and allowed him to fancy himself something of a nomad. Soon after Chatwin cites Stevenson, he falls into step with the tradition: "The best thing is to walk. We should follow the Chinese poet Li Po in 'the hardships of travel and the many branchings of the way.' For life is a journey through a wilderness. This concept, universal to the point of banality, could not have survived unless it were biologi-

---

He arrived about ten o'clock at night, completely exhausted, having accomplished the forty miles in record time, but cally true. None of our revolutionary heroes is worth a thing until he has been on a good walk. Che Guevera spoke of the 'nomadic phase' of the Cuban Revolution. Look what the Long March did for Mao Tse-Tung, or Exodus for Moses. Movement is the best cure for melancholy, as Robert Burton (the author of *The Anatomy of Melancholy*) understood."

A hundred and fifty years of moralizing! A century and a half of gentlemanly exhortation! Doctors have asserted many times over the centuries that walking is very good for you, but medical advice has never been one of the chief attractions of literature. Besides, only a walk that is guaranteed to exclude certain things— assailants, avalanches—is truly wholesome, and only such walking is advocated by these sermonizing gentlemen who seem not to see the boundaries they have put around the act (one of the delights of urban walking is how unwholesome it is). Gentlemen, I say, because all the writers on walking seem to be members of the same club—not one of the real walking clubs, but a kind of implicit club of shared background. They are generally privileged—most of the English ones write as though everyone else also went to Oxford or Cambridge, and even Thoreau went to Harvard—and of a vaguely clerical bent, and they are always male—neither dancing peasant lasses nor mincing girls, with wives rather than husbands to leave, as the above passages make clear. Thoreau considerately adds, "How womankind, who are confined to the house still more than men, stand it I do not know." Many women after Dorothy Wordsworth went on long solitary walks, and Sarah Hazlitt, Hazlitt's estranged wife, even went on a walking tour alone and kept a journal of it, which like most of these documents of female walking went unpublished in its time. Flora Thompson's account of her journeys on foot across rural Oxfordshire to deliver mail in all seasons and weather is one of the most enchanting descriptions of country walks, but it is not part of the canon because it is by a poor woman, about work (and sex, in that a gamekeeper whose grounds she regularly crosses courts her, unsuccessfully), and buried in a book about many other things. Like the great women travelers of the nineteenth century—Alexandra David-Neel in Tibet, Isabelle Eberhardt in North Africa, Isabella Bird in the Rockies—they are anomalies, these walking women (the reasons why will be dealt with at length later, in chapter 14).

By the late nineteenth century the word *tramp* as both noun and verb was popular among the walking writers, as was *vagabond* and *gypsy* and, far down the road in a different world, *nomad*, but to play at tramp or gypsy is one way of demon-

it seemed to me a somewhat curious beginning for a honeymoon.—BERTRAND RUSSELL   *"And that's to be life!"*

strating that you are not really one. You must be complex to want simplicity, settled to desire this kind of mobility. Bruce Chatwin to the contrary, Bedouins do
not go on walking tours. Stephen Graham, an Englishman who early in the twentieth century took remarkable long walks through eastern Europe, Asia, and the
Rocky Mountains, wrote, along with his books on specific travels, a hybrid volume called *The Gentle Art of Tramping*. It gives cheery anecdotal instructions on the
art for 271 pages, in chapters on boots, "marching songs," "drying after rain," and
"trespassers' walk." Thoreau alone seems to get lost in his own thinking and to
find himself in surprising places, advocating abandonment, manifest destiny, am-
nesia, and, for his work, a rare nationalism, but by the time he is advocating the
latter, ax-swinging frontiersmen rather than unarmed walkers are his protagonists. Perhaps the limits are implicit in the form of the essay, which is widely regarded as a kind of literary birdcage capable of containing only small chirping
subjects, as distinct from the lion's den of the novel and the open range of the
poem. Writing and walking were reduced to fit each other, at least in this major
tradition in the English-speaking world.

II. THE SIMPLE

This belief in walking—rural walking, anyway—as virtuous persists. Examples
are everywhere. Recently, I found one particularly annoying essay in a Buddhist
magazine asserting that all the world's problems would be solved if only the
world's leaders would walk. "Perhaps walking can be the way to peace in the
world. Let world leaders walk to the conference site instead of riding in a power-
contagious limousine. Take away the conference tables—whatever their size and
shape—and have a meeting of minds along the shores of Lake Geneva." Another
example by a world leader suggests how dubious this idea is. Ronald Reagan
wanted to start his memoirs with the most important moment of his presidency,
writes the editor Michael Korda, who tried to make them work as a book. The
moment was during his first meeting with Mikhail Gorbachev, near Geneva.
Geneva is Rousseau's birthplace, and it was a Rousseauian scene that Reagan described. "Reagan had realized . . . that the summit meeting was going nowhere.
The two leaders were surrounded by advisers and specialists as they discussed
disarmament, and were unable to make any human contact, so Reagan had

---

said Helen, with a catch in her throat. "How can you, with all the beautiful things to see and do—with music—

---

tapped Gorbachev on the shoulder and invited him to go for a walk. The two went outside, and Reagan took Gorbachev down toward the shore of Lake Geneva." Reagan went on to say that during "a long, heartfelt discussion" on that occasion they agreed toward mutual inspection and verification as well as the first steps toward nuclear disarmament. Korda objected to an aide that the anecdote as Reagan had told it, though deeply moving, was problematic. Gorbachev and Reagan didn't speak each other's language. If any such walk took place, a retinue of translators and security people must have gone with them to make the event more resemble a state procession than a friendly ramble.

To propose that the world's problems would be solved by two old men walking by a Swiss lakeside (in Rousseau's hometown, what's more) was to propose that the simple, the good, and the natural were still aligned, and that these world leaders who held the power to destroy the earth were themselves simple men (and to suggest that they were simple is to imply that they were good and thus that their regimes were just and their achievements honorable, a series of dominoes lined up behind the first Romantic assumption). The aesthetic of the simple virtues had continued to triumph over the aesthetic of the royal procession, with its signs of complexity, sophistication, its many people signifying society. Jimmy Carter actually walked down Pennsylvania Avenue for his inauguration as president, but Reagan brought a new level of pomp and ceremony to the White House and came as close as American presidents ever have to being a Sun King. He did so by telling us simple stories about our lost innocence, our corruption by education and the arts, our ability to fall back on log-cabin virtues and thereby to dispense with the complex interdependencies of society, economic and otherwise. Portraying himself as a Rousseauian walker was one of those stories. The history of rural walking is full of people who wish to portray themselves as wholesome, natural, a brother to all man and nature, and who in that wish often reveal themselves to be powerful and complicated—though other walkers are true radicals out to undermine the laws and authorities that stifle others as well as themselves.

---

with walking at night—" "Walking is well enough when a man's in work," he answered. "Oh I did talk a lot of

---

III. THE FAR

Just as the walking essay seems to have been the dominant form for writing about walking in the nineteenth century, so the lengthy tale of the very long walk is for the twentieth century. Perhaps the twenty-first will bring us something altogether new. In the eighteenth century, travel literature was commonplace, but the long-distance walkers left little written record of their feats. Wordsworth's walking tour across the Alps, as described in *The Prelude*, was not published until 1850, and *The Prelude* is not exactly travel writing. Thoreau wrote accounts of walks in which his own experience is charted with the same scientific acuity as is the natural world around him, but these are more nature essays than walking literature. The first significant account of a long-distance walk for the sake of walking I know is John Muir's *Thousand Mile Walk to the Gulf*, describing a journey from Indianapolis to the Florida Keys in 1867 (published after his death in 1914). The South he walked through was an open wound still festering from the Civil War, and Civil War historians must be frustrated by Muir's neglect of social observation for the sake of botanizing, though it is still the most populated of his many books. The wilderness writings make him a kind of John the Baptist come back from a suddenly appealing wilderness to preach its wonders to the rest of us (wilderness because its indigenous inhabitants had been forcibly removed and decimated before Muir arrived, but that's another story). For Muir is the United States's evangelist of nature, adapting the language of religion to describe the plants, mountains, light, and processes that he so loved. As close an observer as Thoreau, he is far more apt to read religion into what he sees. He was also one of the great mountaineers of the nineteenth century, achieving in his woolens and hobnailed boots feats that most with modern gear would be hard-pressed to follow. Lacking Wordsworth's poetic gifts and Thoreau's radical critique, Muir nevertheless walked as they only imagined walking, for weeks alone in the wilderness, coming to know a whole mountain range as a friend and turning his passion for the place into political engagement. But that came decades after his walk in the South.

A Thousand Mile Walk is episodic, as are most such walking books. In such travel literature there is no overarching plot, except for the obvious one of getting from point A to point B (and for the more introspective, the self-transformation along the way). In a sense these books on walks for their own sakes are the liter-

---

nonsense once, but there's nothing like a bailiff in the house to drive it out of you. When I saw him fingering my ature of paradise, the story of what can happen when nothing profound is wrong, and so the protagonist—healthy, solvent, uncommitted—can set out seeking minor adventure. In paradise, the only things of interest are our own thoughts, the character of our companions, and the incidents and appearance of the surroundings. Alas, many of these long-distance writers are not fascinating thinkers, and it's a dubious premise that someone who would be dull to walk round the corner with must be fascinating for a six-month trek. To hear about walking from people whose only claim on our attention is to have walked far is like getting one's advice on food from people whose only credentials come from winning pie-eating contests. Quantity is not everything. But Muir has far more to offer than quantity. An acute and often ecstatic observer of the natural world around him, he says nothing at all about why he is walking in *A Thousand Mile Walk to the Gulf*, though it seems clear enough that it is because he is hardy, poor, and possessed of botanical passions best fulfilled on foot. But though he is one of history's great walkers, walking itself is seldom his subject. There is no well-defined border between the literature of walking and nature writing, but nature writers tend to make the walking implicit at best, a means for the encounters with nature which they describe, but seldom a subject. Body and soul seem to disappear into the surrounding environment, but Muir's body reappears when his paradisiacal luck runs out and he starves waiting for money to arrive and later becomes mortally ill. Thoreau wrote accounts of walks in which his own experience is charted with the same scientific acuity as the natural world around him, but these are more nature essays than walking literature.

Seventeen years after Muir, another young man in his twenties set out to walk more than a thousand miles, from Cincinnati to Los Angeles. Charles F. Lummis says at the outset of his *Tramp Across the Continent*, "But why tramp? Are there not railroads and Pullmans enough, that you must walk? That is what a great many of my friends said when they learned of my determination to travel from Ohio to California on foot; and very likely it is the question that will first come to your mind in reading of the longest walk for pure pleasure that is on record." Which is to say, he starts out thinking of his friends, readers, and the record, as well as pleasure. But he goes on to say, "I was after neither time nor money, but life—not life in the pathetic meaning of the poor health-seeker, for I was perfectly well and a trained athlete; but life in the truer, broader, sweeter sense, the exhilarant joy of living outside the sorry fences of society, living with a perfect body and a wak-

----

Ruskins and Stevensons, I seemed to see life straight real, and it isn't a pretty sight."—E. M. FORSTER, *HOWARDS*

----

ened mind. . . . I am an American and felt ashamed to know so little of my country as I did, and as most Americans do." Seventy-nine pages later, he says of a brief companion, "He was the only live, real walker I met on the whole long journey, and there was a keen zest in reeling off the frosty miles with such a companion." Lummis is vain; there are anecdotes where he outshoots and outtoughs westerners, rattlesnakes, and snowstorms, and his solemn attempts at jokes, in the vein of Twain, often fall flat. But he redeems himself by his great (and for the time, unusual) affection for the people and land of the Southwest and occasional anecdotes at his own expense. It is a remarkable story, of toughness and navigatory ability and adaptability. Long-distance walking in North America never had the gentility of the walking tour. In England, you can walk from pub to pub or inn to inn (or, nowadays, hostel to hostel); in America a long-distance walk is usually a plunge into the wilderness or at least un-English scale and uninviting spaces such as highways and hostile towns.

There seem to be three motives for these long-distance trips: to comprehend a place's natural or social makeup; to comprehend oneself; and to set a record; and most are a combination of the three. An extremely long walk is often taken up as a sort of pilgrimage, a proof of some kind of faith or will, as well as a means of spiritual and practical discovery. Too, as travel became more common, travel writers often sought out more extreme experience and remote places. One of the implicit premises of the latter kind of writing is that the journey, rather than the traveler, must be exceptional to be worth reading about (though Virginia Woolf wrote a brilliant essay about going out into a London evening to buy a pencil, and James Joyce managed to write the greatest novel of the twentieth century about a pudgy ad salesman trudging Dublin's streets). For writers, the long-distance walk is an easy way to find narrative continuity. If a path is like a story, as I was proposing a few chapters ago, then a continuous walk must make a coherent story, and a very long walk makes a full-length book. Or so goes the logic of these recent books, and to some extent it is true; a walker does not skip over much, sees things close up, and makes herself vulnerable and accessible to local people and places. On the other hand, a walker may be so consumed by athletic endeavor as to be unable to participate in his surroundings, particularly when driven by a schedule or competition. Some of them are happy with these limits, as is Colin Fletcher, one of those inevitable Englishmen whose first long walk is a journey up the eastern side of California in 1958. The resultant book, entitled

---

END   *Rhythm is originally the rhythm of the feet. Every human being walks, and since he walks on two legs*

The Thousand-Mile Summer, is a sort of trail mix made up of bite-size epiphanies, moral lessons, blisters, social encounters, and recounted practical details. He took other walks later, and like Graham wrote a guidebook, *The Complete Walker*, still used by backpackers. Another Englishman, John Hillaby, walked the length of Britain—a thousand miles—in 1968 and wrote a best-seller about it, as well as several other books about other walks.

By the time Peter Jenkins set out to walk more than three thousand miles across the United States in 1973 (with *National Geographic* sponsorship), the cross-country expedition had become a kind of rite of passage of American manhood, though by that time the means were more often vehicular. Crossing the continent seemed to embrace or encompass it at least symbolically, the route wrapped around it like a ribbon around a package. The movie *Easy Rider*, which had recently been released, seemed to draw some of its sensibility from Jack Kerouac's road stories, which themselves often sprawled more like travel books than novels (Kerouac's *Dharma Bums* recounts how the poet and ecologist Gary Snyder got Kerouac out of the car and into the mountains). Jenkins set out to have social encounters; the America he was looking for was, unlike Muir's, made up of people rather than places. Like Wordsworth in his incessant encounters with characters eager to tell their tale, he takes the time to listen to everyone he meets and tells about them in his naively earnest *Walk Across America* and *Walk Across America II*. In part a reaction against the anti-Americanism of the young radicals of the time, Jenkins's journey brings him into close contact and, often, friendship with the white southerners so reviled by northern civil rights activists. In the course of his travels, he stays with an Appalachian living off the land, lives with a poor black family for several weeks, and in Louisiana falls in love with a Southern Baptist seminarian, undergoes a religious conversation, marries the woman, and after several months resumes his walk with her, arriving on the Oregon coast a far different person from the one who set out. This is truly a journey as life, for Jenkins goes as slowly as experience demands.

The literature of the long-distance walk is a sort of downhill slope. Toward the bottom come books by people who are athletic walkers but not necessarily writers, for the necessary combination of silver tongue and iron thighs seems to be a rare one. The most impressive of the contemporary long-distance walkers I have read—there are many now—is Robyn Davidson, who didn't exactly set out to write about walking at all, but did so brilliantly in the course of her *Tracks*, a

---

with which he strikes the ground in turn and since he only moves if he continues to do this, whether intentionally or book recounting her 1,700-mile trek across the Australian outback to the sea with three camels (sponsored, like Jenkins's odyssey, by the National Geographic Society). Midway in her journey, she explains its effect on her mind: "But strange things do happen when you trudge twenty miles a day, day after day, month after month. Things you only become totally conscious of in retrospect. For one thing I had remembered in minute and Technicolor detail everything that had ever happened in my past and all the people who belonged there. I had remembered every word of conversation I had had or overheard way, way back in my childhood and in this way I had been able to review these events with a kind of emotional detachment as if they had happened to somebody else. I was rediscovering and getting to know people who were long since dead and forgotten. . . . And I was happy, there is simply no other word for it." She brings us back to the territory of the philosophers and the walking essayists, to the relationship between walking and the mind, and she does it from a kind of extreme experience few have had.

The 1970s seem to have been a golden age of long-distance walks; Jenkins, Davidson, and Alan Booth all set out in the mid-1970s. Booth's delightful *Roads to Sata: A Two-Thousand-Mile Walk Through Japan* is a milestone in how far the literature of walking had come. An Englishman who had lived in Japan for seven years and come to know the language and culture well, he is unfailingly humorous and modest, a great evoker of place and recounter of comic conversations, respectful but not reverent about the culture. He describes his trip—dirty socks, hot springs, sake and more sake, comic and tragic figures, sultry weather, lechers of both sexes—with élan. He comments wryly, "In properly developed countries, the inhabitants regard walkers with grave suspicion and have taught their dogs to do the same," but enjoys himself all the same. Yet like most of these travel books, his is not really a book about walking. That is to say, it is not about the acts but about the encounters, just as *A Thousand Mile Walk to the Gulf* is really about botany and natural epiphanies—and *On the Road* and *Easy Rider* are only implicitly about the internal combustion engine and its implications. Walking is only a means to maximize those encounters and perhaps test body and soul.

The test is central to Ffyona Campbell's prolific walks, as recounted in her book *The Whole Story: A Walk Around the World*. The daughter of a harsh military man, she seems to be on a quest to prove herself to him and to herself, with her walking an obsessive activity not unlike her sister's anorexia (which crops up in

---

not, a rhythmic sound ensues. . . . Animals too have their familiar gait, their rhythms are often richer and more

---

her book). In 1983, at the age of sixteen, Campbell successfully walked the length of Britain—a thousand miles—sponsored by London's *Evening Standard* and seeking to raise money for a hospital. She then set out to walk around the world—not literally, for the continuous line that links up many walkers' narratives has nothing to do with her: "The Guinness Book of Records defines a walk around the world as beginning and finishing in the same place, crossing four continents, and covering a total of at least 16,000 miles," says the preface of her book. She set off across the United States two years later, Australia five years later, and the length of Africa eight years later, finishing up eleven years after the English walk with a trek northward from Spain to the English Channel. It is as discontinuous as could be—she flies back to Africa and the States to complete segments she left out earlier—and only a kind of accounting holds it all together as a single act.

Perhaps it is a mistake to include Campbell in the literature of walking, even though she has produced books, but she is certainly part of the culture of walking. There is another ancestry for her in the pedestrian athletes of the late eighteenth and early nineteenth century, who seemed indifferent whether they went their thousand miles around a track or down a road, and who were the subjects of heavy betting. After all, almost no landscape appears in her narratives of several continents; we cannot in it trace an inheritance from Wordsworth. Yet the notion that walking is somehow redemptive and walking farther is more so seems to have taken on a fearful life of its own, and surely this is something of a Victorian heritage, and those Victorians were themselves heirs of Wordsworth. Such is the winding road down which history comes, now with one set of desires in view, now with another. Like Davidson, Campbell seems driven, but Davidson represents a more intellectual, insightful version of the wounded self seeking redemption through an ordeal, and comes equipped with vastly more literary and landscape sensibility. The fierce alienation is much the same, the sense of a young woman clinging to her stubbornness and her arduous goal because that's all she has. Jenkins is softer, less locked up, maybe because it's easier for a man, maybe because he's more openly a seeker: he knows what kind of pilgrimage he is on.

To some extent Campbell resembles the Walkathon walkers, in that she is often walking to raise money for a cause (or more often looking for a cause to represent so she can also raise money for her expeditions, which with support staff, publicity, and so forth were often expensive). Still, to walk fifty miles in a day is

---

audible than those of men; hoofed animals flee in herds, like regiments of drummers. The knowledge of the animals

---

remarkable, to get up and do it again the next day is stunning, and to do it day after day across the Australian outback alongside a road in ugly weather is brutal. Campbell did it, walking 3,200 miles across that continent in ninety-five days, a world record. Her legs are indefatigably strong and relentless in their pursuit, but nothing is left in her walks but accomplishment—no scenery, no pleasure, few encounters. For 20,000 miles she is struggling to understand herself well enough to outwalk her suffering, but she is alarmingly unclear about her values, seeking corporate sponsorship and media attention at some points and condemning journalists and capitalists at others, insulting people who drive cars on her second walk in the United States, after having been trailed across the country by a motor home driven by her support staff the first time. Her book ends with an anecdote that undermines all her effort, one of many passages of fuzzy reverence for indigenous peoples. It is a tale of the military men who challenge some aboriginal Australians to a footrace across the desert, which the latter abandon to track down honeycomb. Telling it, she suggests she is on the side of the aborigines in disdaining rigid goals, quantifiable experience, competition, even record-keeping or -making, as deeply flawed ways of being in the world. The tragedy is that all along she has been on the side of the military men.

Perhaps Campbell shows us pure walking. It is impurity that makes it worthwhile, the views, the thoughts, the encounters—all those things that connect mind and world through the medium of the roving body, that leaven the self-absorption of the mind. These books suggest how slippery a subject is walking, how hard it is to keep one's mind on it. Walking is usually about something else—about the walker's character or encounters, about nature or about achievement, sometimes so much so it ceases to be about walking. Yet together all these things—the canons of walking essays and travel literature—constitute a coherent, if meandering, two-hundred-year history of reasons to walk across the land.

---

by which he was surrounded, which threatened him and which he hunted, was man's oldest knowledge. He learnt

---

Chapter 9

MOUNT OBSCURITY AND
MOUNT ARRIVAL

Ffyona Campbell's tale of the military men racing across the Australian outback toward the finish line and their aboriginal rivals straying from it to gather honeycomb suggests some of the various ways and reasons to walk and to live, or at least some of the questions. Can one weigh public glory against private pleasure, and are they mutually exclusive? What portions of an act can be measured and compared? What does it mean to arrive, and what to wander without destination? Is competition an ignoble motive? Can the soldiers be imagined as students of discipline and the aboriginal men as students of detachment? After all, there are pilgrims for whom arrival at their journey's end is spiritual consummation, but there are other pilgrims and mystics who wander without cease or destination, from the Chinese sages of antiquity to the anonymous nineteenth-century Russian peasant who wrote *The Way of a Pilgrim*. These questions about how one travels and why become most pressing, or at least most evident, with mountaineering.

Mountaineering is the art of getting up mountains by foot and occasionally by hand, and though the climbing is usually emphasized, most ascents are mostly a matter of walking (and since good climbers climb with their legs as much as possible, climbing could be called the art of taking a vertical walk). In the steepest places the steady semiconscious rhythm of walking slows down, every step can become a separate decision about direction and about safety, and the simple

to know animals by the rhythm of their movement. The earliest writing he learnt to read was that of their tracks, it act of walking is transformed into a specialized skill that often calls for elaborate equipment. Here I want to address mountaineering that includes climbing but leave aside the separate discipline of climbing without mountaineering, a somewhat artificial division, but one with reasons. The latter is a recently explored side canyon in the history of mountaineering in which technique has been vastly refined to ascend ever-more-challenging surfaces. A supremely hard climb can be less than a hundred feet long, and a single move can become a famous "problem" to be worked out by intense application and training. And while mountaineering is traditionally motivated by a taste for mountain scenery, technical climbing seems to involve other pleasures. Since the eighteenth century, nature has been imagined as scenery, and scenery is what is seen at a certain distance, but climbing puts one face-to-face with the rock, with a wholly different kind of engagement. Perhaps tactile encounters, sensations of gravity (and, sometimes, mortality), and the kinesthetic pleasures of one's body moving at its limit of ability are an equally valid if less culturally hallowed experience of nature. With climbing, sometimes scenery disappears altogether, at lest in the rapidly proliferating indoor climbing gyms. Too, walking fosters one kind of awareness in which the mind can stray away from and return to the immediate experience of traversing a particular place; rock climbing, on the other hand, is demanding enough that one guide told me, "Climbing is the only time my mind doesn't wander." Climbing is about climbing. Mountaineering, on the other hand, is still about mountains.

Most standard histories of mountaineering and of landscape aesthetics start with the poet Petrarch, "the first man to climb a mountain for its own sake, and to enjoy the view from the top," as the art historian Kenneth Clark put it. Long before Petrarch climbed Italy's Mount Ventoux in 1335, there were others ascending mountains in other parts of the world. Petrarch prefigures the Romantic-generated practice of traveling among mountains for aesthetic pleasure and getting to their summits for secular reasons. This history of mountaineering really begins in Europe in the late eighteenth century, when curiosity and changed sensibilities spurred a few bold individuals not just to travel through the Alps but to try to get to their summits. The practice was gradually consolidated into mountaineering, a set of skills and assumptions—for example, the assumption that getting to the top of a mountain is a uniquely meaningful act, distinct from walking among the passes or foothills. In Europe mountaineering developed largely as a gentleman's pastime and a guide's profession, since the former so of-

---

was a kind of rhythmic notation imprinted on the soft ground. . . . the large numbers of the herd which they hunted

---

ten relied upon the latter; in North America the first recorded ascents were made by explorers and surveyors in far remoter places (some ascents in the Alps could and can be watched through telescopes from the villages below; some in North America took weeks of wilderness trekking to reach). Of course, as the great geologist and mountaineer Clarence King recounts, when in 1871 he got to the top of one of the highest peaks in the Sierra Nevada, hoping to make a first ascent, he found that "a small mound of rock was piled on the peak, and solidly built into it an Indian arrow-shaft, pointing due west." Mountains attracted attention and walkers long before romanticism spawned mountaineering.

A lone peak or high point is a natural focal point in the landscape, something by which both travelers and locals orient themselves. In the continuum of landscape, mountains are discontinuity—culminating high points, natural barriers, unearthly earth. On mountains, latitude's imperceptible changes can become altitude's striking transformations. Ecology and climate change rapidly from balmy foothills to glacial heights: there's the timberline and, farther up, what could be called the lifeline, beyond which nothing lives or grows, and, above about 18,000 feet, what mountaineers call the death zone, the icy low-oxygen realm where the body starts to die, judgment is impaired, and even the most acclimated alpinists lose brain cells. Up high, biology vanishes to reveal a world shaped by the starker forces of geology and meteorology, the bare bones of the earth wrapped in sky. Mountains have been seen around the world as thresholds between this world and the next, as places where the spirit world comes close. In most parts of the world, sacred meanings are ascribed to mountains, and though the spirit world may be terrifying, it is seldom evil. Christian Europe seems to be alone in having seen mountains as ugly and almost hellish realms. In Switzerland, dragons, the souls of the unhappy dead, and the Wandering Jew were supposed to haunt the heights (sentenced in the legend to wander the earth until the Second Coming because he slighted Jesus, the Wandering Jew suggests that European Christians often took a dim view of wandering as well as of Jews). Many seventeenth-century English writers express their detestation of mountains as "high and hideous," "rubbish of the earth," "deformities," and even damage caused to a formerly smooth earth by the Deluge. So though Europeans led the world in the development of modern mountaineering, that mountaineering came out of romanticism's recovery of an appreciation for natural places that much of the rest of the world had never lost.

---

blended into their feelings with their own numbers which they wished to be large, and they expressed this in a specific

---

One of the first individuals whose ascent of a mountain is recorded is China's "First Emperor," who in the third century B.C. drove his chariot up T'ai Shan against the advice of his sages, who thought he should walk. Better known for starting the Great Wall and for burning all the books so that Chinese history would start with him, the First Emperor may have eradicated the record of those who ascended before him. Most people since have walked to T'ai Shan's summit—for many centuries on the 7,000-step staircase leading from the City of Peace at the foot of the mountain through three Heavenly Gates to the Temple of the Jade Emperor on top. American writer and Buddhist Gretel Ehrlich walked up T'ai Shan and other mountain pilgrimage sites in China and wrote, "The Chinese phrase for 'going on a pilgrimage,' ch'ao-shan chin-hsiang, actually means 'paying one's respects to the mountain,' as if the mountain was an empress or an ancestor before whom one must kneel." In the fourth century A.D. a very different kind of pilgrim climbed mountains on the other side of Eurasia: the Christian pilgrim Egeria. Almost no trace of her but her pilgrimage diary survives, though that manuscript suggests she was an abbess or other religious figure of some stature and that Mount Sinai deep in the Egyptian desert was among the sites of Christian pilgrimage then. She was guided by resident holy men through "the vast and very flat valley where the children of Israel tarried during those days when the holy man Moses climbed the mountain of God" on their flight from slavery in Egypt. She and her unnamed companions scaled the nearly 9,000-foot peak of Mount Sinai on foot—"straight up, as if scaling a wall." Egeria noted that "this seems to be a single mountain all around; however, once you enter the area you see there are many, but the whole range is called the Mountain of God." For Egeria, Sinai was the mountain on which God had descended and Moses had ascended to receive the Tablets of the Law: climbing it was a profession of faith in Scripture and a return to the site of its greatest moments. Since her time stairs have been built up Sinai too, and one fourteenth-century mystic ascended them every day as his religious expression.

Mountains, like labyrinths and other built structures, function as metaphorical and symbolic space. There is no more clear geographical equivalent to the idea of arrival and triumph than the topmost peak beyond which there is no farther to go (though in the Himalayas many pilgrims circumambulate mountains, believing it would be sacrilegious to stand on the summit). The athletically gifted and enormously ambitious Victorian mountaineer Edward Whymper said of

---

state of communal excitement which I shall call the rhythmic or throbbing crowd. The means of achieving this state

---

reaching the top of the Matterhorn, "There is nothing to look up to; all is below," in a telling mix of literal and figurative language. "The man who is there is somewhat in the position of one who has attained all that he desires—he has nothing to aspire to." The appeal of climbing to the top of mountains may also be drawn from language metaphors. English and many other languages associate altitude, ascent, and height with power, virtue, and status. Thus we speak of being on top of the world or at the top of one's field, at the height of one's ability, on the way up; of peak experiences and the peak of a career; of rising and moving up in the world; to say nothing of social climbers, upward mobility, high-minded saints and lowly rascals, and of course the upper and the lower classes. In Christian cosmology, heaven is above us and hell below, and Dante portrays Purgatory as a conical mountain he arduously ascends, conflating spiritual and geographical travel (starting with what modern climbers would call a chimney: "We climbed up through the narrow cleft, / rock pressed in on us from either side, / and that ground needed both feet and hands"). A walk uphill traverses these metaphysical territories; a goalless ramble across the same mountain moves through very different metaphysics.

In Japan mountains have been imagined as the centers of vast mandalas spreading across the landscape like, in one scholar's words, "overlapping flowers," and approaching the center of the mandala means approaching the source of spiritual power—but the approach may be indirect. In a labyrinth one can be farthest from the destination when one is closest; on a mountain, as Egeria found, the mountain itself changes shape again and again as one ascends. The famous Zen parable about the master for whom, before his studies, mountains were only mountains, but during his studies mountains were no longer mountains, and afterward mountains were again mountains could be interpreted as an allegory about this perceptual paradox. Thoreau noticed it and wrote, "To the traveller, a mountain outline varies with every step, and it has an infinite number of profiles, though absolutely but one form," and that form is best apprehended from a distance. In every print but one of the Japanese artist Hokusai's famous *Thirty-Six Views of Mount Fuji*, the perfect cone of Mount Fuji looms largely nearby or small far away, giving orientation and continuity to city, road, field, and sea. Only in the print of pilgrims actually ascending the mountain does the familiar shape that unites the other prints vanish. When we are attracted, we draw near; when we draw near, the sight that attracted us dissolves: the face of the beloved blurs or

---

was first of all the rhythm of their feet, repeating and multiplied.—ELIAS CANETTI, *CROWDS AND POWER*

---

fractures as one draws near for a kiss, the smooth cone of Mount Fuji becomes rough rock rising from underfoot to blot out the sky in Hokusai's print of the mountain pilgrims. The objective form of the mountain seems to dissolve into subjective experience, and the meaning of walking up a mountain fragments.

A walk, I have claimed, is like a life in miniature, and a mountain ascent is a more dramatic walk: there is more danger and more awareness of death, more uncertainty about the outcome, more triumph at what is more unequivocally arrival. "To climb up rocks is like all the rest of your life, only simpler and safer," wrote the British mountaineer Charles Montague in 1924. "Each time that you get up a hard pitch, you have succeeded in life." What fascinates me about mountaineering is how one activity can mean so many disparate things. Though the idea of pilgrimage almost always seems to be present, many ascents derive their meaning from sports and military action as well. Pilgrimage draws meaning from following hallowed routes to established destinations, while the most revered mountaineers are often those who are first on a route or summit, who like athletes make a record. Mountaineering has often been seen as a pure form of the imperial mission, calling into play all its skills and heroic virtues, with none of its material gains or oppositional violence (which is why the superb French alpinist Lionel Terray called his memoir *Conquistadors of the Useless*). On March 17, 1923, while on a speaking tour to raise money for an Everest expedition, the great mountaineer George Mallory apparently got exasperated with the continual questions about why he wanted to climb it, and uttered the most famous line in mountaineering history, the one sometimes cited as a Zen koan: "Because it's there." His usual reply was, "We hope to show that the spirit that built the British Empire is not yet dead." Mallory and his companion Andrew Irvine themselves died on that expedition, and mountaineering historians still debate whether they got to the summit before vanishing. (Mallory's battered, frozen body was discovered seventy-five years later, on May 1, 1999.)

The measurable part of an experience translates most easily, so the highest peaks and worst disasters are the best known aspects of mountaineering, along with all the records—first ascent, first ascent by the north face, first American, first Japanese, first woman, fastest, first without this or that piece of gear. Mount Everest has always been about these calculables for Westerners, to whose attention it first came through trigonometry. In 1852 a clerk in the office of the British Trigonometrical Survey in India calculated that what they called "Peak XV" and

---

Mountains, admired, arouse feeling of horror, attraction of, as background, barrenness admired, beauty of,

---

the Tibetans "Chomalungma" was taller than all the Himalayan peaks clustered around it. The man who had just measured it named it after a man who had never noticed it, former surveyor general of India Sir George Everest (thereby giving it a kind of sex change, since *chomalungma* means "goddess of the place"). The locals consider Chomalungma one of the less significant sacred mountains, but mountaineering writers sometimes call Everest (which is at the same latitude as southern Florida) the top or the roof of the world, as though our spherical planet were instead some kind of pyramid. The widely traveled mountaineer and religious scholar Edwin Bernbaum writes, wryly, "Whatever Western society regards as number one tends to take on an aura of ultimacy that makes it seem more real and worthwhile than anything else—in a word, sacred." And number one is generally determined by measurement. Triumph in mountaineering, as in sports, is measured in firsts, fastests, and mosts.

Like sports, mountaineering is exertion with only symbolic results, but the nature of that symbolism dictates everything—why, for example, French mountaineer Maurice Herzog could consider his 1950 expedition to Annapurna, the world's seventh-highest mountain, a great victory because they made it to the top and not a failure because he got so severely frostbitten he lost all his fingers and toes and had to be carried down by sherpas. Perhaps it was that Herzog trod the terrain of history as selflessly as Egeria did Scripture. In the mid-1960s, David Roberts led the second-ever ascent to the summit of Alaska's Mount Huntington. As he recounted it in his book *The Mountain of My Fear,* the expedition seems to have begun in Massachusetts with his study of photographs of the mountain, his surmise of a new route up it, and his desire to do something that hadn't been done before. That is, the expedition began with visual representation and desire to situate himself in the historical record, with months of planning, fund-raising, recruiting, collecting gear, and writing lists; it only became a bodily engagement with the mountain long afterward. This tension between history and experience, between aspiration, memory, and the moment, fascinates me, and though it exists throughout human activity, it seems to become, so to speak, more transparent at high altitudes. History, let me clarify, means an act imagined as being situated in the context of other such acts and as it will be perceived by others; it arises from a social imagination of how one's private acts fit into public life. History is carried in the mind to the remotest places to determine what one's acts mean even there, and who can say how much it weighs for those who carry it?

---

enjoyment of, "know thyself" philosophy, and men, mysticism, romantic feeling towards, scientific attitude,

---

Because mountain heights are usually so remote from inhabited earth, because mystics and outlaws have so often gone there to vanish from sight, because climbing is "the only time my mind doesn't wander," making history in the mountains seems a particularly paradoxical idea and mountaineering a particularly paradoxical sport—when it is regarded as a sport. Being first up a mountain means entering the unknown, but for the sake of putting the place into human history, of making it known. There are those who decline to record their ascents or name their climbs, who see their mountaineering as a retreat from history. Gwen Moffat, who became Britain's first certified woman climbing guide in 1953, wrote about the immediate satisfactions: "And before I started to move I felt the familiar feeling that came when I was about to do something hard. Mental and physical relaxation, a loosening of the muscles so complete that even the face relaxes and the eyes widen; one's body becomes light and supple—a pliable and coordinated entity to be shown a climb as a horse is shown a jump. In that exquisite moment before the hard move, when one looks and understands, may lie an answer to the question why one climbs. You are doing something hard, so hard that failure could mean death, but because of knowledge and experience you are doing it safely." She and a partner once decided to set the record for the slowest traverse ever of a ridge on the Isle of Skye and, with the help of a surprise blizzard, probably succeeded.

European mountaineering history had its beginnings in a competition of sorts. Decades before Mont Blanc was climbed, the glacier coming down from it to the Chamonix Valley and the valley itself had become tourist destinations (as they have remained ever since). The locals were, like those of north Wales and the Lake District, beneficiaries of travelers' growing taste for wild and rugged scenery. One outcome of this growing tourist economy was that a twenty-year-old gentleman scientist from Geneva, Horace Benedict de Saussure, arrived in 1760, became so fascinated by glaciers that he dedicated the rest of his life to studying them, and posted a handsome prize for the first person to reach the 15,782-foot summit of Mont Blanc. Mont Blanc, the highest point in Europe, was a magnet in the early years of the cult of mountains and a cultural icon for landscape romantics, the subject of a major poem by Shelley, the first measure of ambition of mountaineers. In 1786 a local doctor reached the summit with the aid of a local hunter. An attempt a few years before had so frightened the four guides who tried it that they declared it unclimbable, and no one in Europe was then certain whether human beings could survive at such high altitudes. Chamonix resident Dr. Michel Gabriel Paccard, writes a notable later mountaineer, Eric Shipton, "turned his keen intelligence and his already keen experience as a climber to the problems of mountain survival. . . . He did not seek notoriety, and he spoke little of his exploits, many of which showed great resolution and physical stamina. His wish to climb Mont Blanc was apparently inspired more by his desire to be first for France—and in the interests of science—than by any desire to win fame for himself. Among other things he was anxious to make barometric observations at the top. . . ."

After four unsuccessful attempts, the doctor hired Jacques Balmat, a strong climber who made a living as a hunter and collector of crystals. They set out on a night of the full moon in August, without the ropes and ice axes of modern mountaineering, crossing the deep ice crevasses with nothing more than a pair of long poles. When they reached the dread Valley of Snow, the deep recess surrounded by icy walls where the four guides had given up earlier, Balmat begged to turn back, but Paccard convinced him to continue, and they climbed up a snow ridge in a high wind. They reached the summit early in the evening, fourteen hours after they had set out; Paccard made his measurements, and they descended to spend the night under a boulder. In the morning both were badly windburned and frostbitten, and Paccard was snow-blind as well and had to be led downward. "Judged by sheer physical effort alone, the first ascent of Mont Blanc was a remarkable performance," Shipton concludes. But the story didn't end there. The scheming Balmat began to spread stories that it was he who had explored the route and led the expedition, and that Paccard was little more than baggage he dragged along. His stories grew until he was claiming that Paccard had collapsed several hundred feet below the summit and Balmat alone had completed the ascent. It wasn't until the twentieth century that the truth was uncovered and the brave doctor was restored to his place among the heroes of mountaineering. One of the mountaineers had betrayed his companion and the truth for the sake of history, publicity, and the reward (and a century later the explorer Frederick Cook lied and faked photographs to claim he had made the first ascent of Alaska's Mount Denali; for him history counted for everything, experience for nothing).

As soon as Mont Blanc was proved climbable, many others began to climb it. By the middle of the nineteenth century, forty-six parties, many of them English,

----

the days of Leslie Stephen, the intelligent justifications for a life of climbing have been few, far between, and (vide had reached the summit, and the focus turned to other Alpine peaks and routes. Though there are many greater mountaineers, I can't get over my affection for Henriette d'Angeville. It may be the effusiveness of her *My Ascent of Mont Blanc* that charms me, since it proves that great physical stamina need not be coupled with stoicism, or it may be that real mountaineering literature is for real mountaineers, who love passages full of hand-jams, mantelshelf moves, crampon or belaying technique, and so forth. D'Angeville was forty-four when she went up the mountain in 1838, though she had grown up among the Alps and walked in them before. She cleared up the inevitable question about why she climbed early in her book, writing, "The soul has needs, as does the body, peculiar to each individual. . . . I am among those who prefer the grandeur of natural landscapes to the sweetest or most charming views imaginable . . . and that is why I chose Mont Blanc." Later she earned popular scorn by quipping that she climbed it to become as famous as the novelist George Sand, but she continued to climb mountains into her sixties without receiving further attention and wrote, "It was not the puny fame of being the first woman to venture on such a journey that filled me with the exhilaration such projects always called forth; rather it was the awareness of the spiritual well-being that would follow." Her climb is a tender drama of arduous ascent bracketed by extravagant packing lists beforehand and a victory dinner with her ten guides afterward. Guiding was already becoming a profession, and technique and tools had evolved much since Paccard's time.

Golden ages usually end with a fall, and the golden age of mountaineering was no exception. Usually described as the period between 1854 and 1865 when many of the Alps were climbed for the first time, it was a largely British golden age in which climbing mountains became a recognized, but by no means popular, sport (far more people continued to walk in the Alps without striving for summits). About half the major first ascents of that age were made by well-heeled British amateurs with local guides. The Alpine Club, founded in 1857 as a sort of cross between a gentleman's club and a scientific society, has so long been an accepted part of the mountaineering world that its oddness—a British club focused on Continental mountains—has seldom been remarked. But in those years the Alps were almost the exclusive focus of this new sport, or pastime, or passion; mountains farther afield and smaller, more technically demanding climbs in places like the Peak District or the Lakes had yet to receive much attention, and climbing in North America took place in a radically different context. The British

---

Mallory) cryptic, at best. . . . Love of nature, by the way, seems to have little to do with it. Superclimbers are, on

audience for this activity was far larger than its practitioners, and in Europe mountaineers and climbers still sometimes become celebrities. Albert Smith's popular entertainment *Mont Blanc*, based on his 1851 ascent, ran in a London theater for years, and books like Alfred Wills's *Wanderings Among the Alps* and the Alpine Club's *Peaks, Passes and Glaciers* series were well received.

Lured by this literature, the twenty-year-old engraver Edward Whymper managed to get an assignment to make images of the Alps. He spent his spare time exploring the mountains and turned out to have a talent for getting up them. Though he made a number of first ascents elsewhere, it was the Matterhorn that captured his imagination. Between 1861 and 1865 he made seven unsuccessful attempts on the spectacular peak, racing against other climbers to be the first. He finally succeeded, and his success is said to have ended the golden age. Whether it ended because Whymper had brought a different or at least more overtly ambitious spirit to the enterprise, because the Matterhorn was the last major Alpine peak to be summitted, or because of the ensuing disaster is unclear. His eighth ascent had been made in collaboration with the greatest amateur climber of the time, the Reverend Charles Hudson, two other young Englishmen, and three local guides. On the descent Hudson, the two young men, and the outstanding guide Michel Croz, who were all roped together, fell to their deaths when one of them slipped. The Victorian equivalent of a media circus ensued, with much condemnation of mountaineering itself as unjustifiably dangerous and much muttering about whether Whymper and the guides had behaved professionally and ethically. Whymper's *Scrambles in the Alps* became a classic anyway, and perhaps it's why the Matterhorn has become a ride at Disneyland.

The history of mountaineering is about the firsts, mosts, and disasters, but behind the dozens of famous faces are countless mountaineers whose rewards have been entirely private and personal. What is recorded as history seldom represents the typical, and what is typical seldom becomes visible as history—though it often becomes visible as literature. Something of this dichotomy is present in the two major genres of mountaineering book, the epics that the general public generally reads and the memoirs that seem to have a far smaller audience. The epics are heroic accounts of an attempt on a major summit; they are books about History and, almost always, Tragedy (high-altitude mountaineering literature, with its emphasis on bodily suffering, survival through sheer will, and the grisly details of frostbite, hypothermia, high-altitude dementia, and fatal falls, often reminds

the whole, uncheerful about hiking, impatient with the weather, insensitive to the subtleties of landscape.—DAVID me of books about concentration camps and forced marches, except that mountaineering is voluntary and, for some, deeply satisfying). In contrast, the cheerful memoirs by even some of the greatest climbers—Joe Brown, Don Whillens, Gwen Moffat, Lionel Terray—often read as humorous idylls that deemphasize difficulty. The satisfactions in these narratives come from minor and major excursions, from friendships, freedoms, love of mountains, refinement of skill, low ambition, and high spirits, with only an occasional tragedy on the rocks. The best books' merit comes from the vividness rather than the historic importance of the events they recount.

If we look for private experience rather than public history, even getting to the top becomes an optional narrative rather than the main point, and those who only wander in high places become part of the story. That is to say, we can leave behind sports and records, and when we do, the discipline of the destination is once again balanced with the discipline of detachment. Smoke Blanchard, the guide who came of age climbing the Oregon peaks during the Great Depression, wrote in my favorite of all mountain memoirs, *Walking Up and Down in the World*, "For half a century I have tried to promote the idea that mountaineering is best approached as a combination of picnic and pilgrimage. Mountain picnic-pilgrimage is short on aggression and long on satisfaction. I hope that I can show that mild mountaineering can be happily pursued through a long lifetime without posting records. Can a love affair be catalogued?" The convivial, humorous Blanchard was as much a walker as a mountaineer, and among the pleasures he recounts are long hikes along the Oregon coast and across the width of California, from the White Mountains east of the Sierra Nevada to the sea, as well as many ascents in the Sierra Nevada and Pacific Northwest. Like a lot of other Pacific Coast mountaineers from John Muir to Gary Snyder, he approached the mountains in a way that reconciles wandering and arriving and recalls the older mountain traditions on the other side of the ocean, in China and Japan.

It wasn't ascending so much as being in the mountains that those poets, sages, and hermits celebrated, and the mountains so frequently portrayed in Chinese poetry and paintings were a contemplative retreat from politics and society. In China, wandering was celebrated—"To 'wander' is the Taoist code word for becoming ecstatic," writes a scholar—but arriving was sometimes regarded with ambiguity. One of the eighth-century poet Li Po's compositions is titled "On Visiting a Taoist Master in the Tai-T'ien Mountains and Not Finding Him," a common theme in Chinese poetry then. Mountains had both physical and symbolic geography, so that literal walking has metaphorical overtones:

> People ask the way to Cold Mountain
> Cold Mountain? There is no road that goes through. . . .
> How can you hope to get there by aping me?
> Your heart and mine are not alike.

writes Li Po's contemporary, the ragged, humorous Buddhist hermit Han-Shan.

In Japan mountains have had religious significance since prehistoric times, though Bernbaum writes, "Before the sixth century A.D. the Japanese did not climb their sacred mountains, which were regarded as a realm apart from the ordinary world, too holy for human presence. The people built shrines at their feet and worshipped them from a respectful distance. With the introduction of Buddhism from China in the sixth century came the practice of climbing the sacred peaks all the way to their summits, there to commune directly with the gods." Afterward, though monks and ascetics wandered, the indeterminate geography of wandering was overshadowed by a determinate one of pilgrimage to the mountains. Climbing mountains became a central part of religious practice, notably in Shugendō, which is more or less a Buddhist mountaineering sect. "Every aspect of Shugendō is conceptually or physically related to the power of sacred mountains and the benefit of reverential behavior within sacred mountains," writes the foremost Western scholar of this sect, H. Byron Earhart. Though festivals, temple ceremonies, and extended periods of mountain asceticism were also part of Shugendō, ascending mountains was central to it both for priests and for lay people, and a kind of priestly guide service emerged. Mountains themselves were perceived as Buddhist mandalas, and ascent paralleled the six stages of spiritual progress toward enlightenment (one stage involved dangling initiates over an abyss while they confessed their sins). The seventeenth-century Zen poet Bashō ascended some of Shugendō's most sacred mountains in the course of his meanders, as he recounts in his haiku-and-travel-narrative masterpiece *The Narrow Road to the Deep North:* "I . . . set off with my guide on a long march of eight miles to the top of the mountain. I walked through mists and clouds, breathing the thin air of high altitudes and stepping on slippery ice and snow, till at last through a gateway of clouds, as it seemed, to the very paths of the sun and moon, I reached the

----

simplicity, the escape from a normal petty existence, the finding of values, of beauty, of vision. These are worth

----

summit, completely out of breath and nearly frozen to death." After Shugendō was banned late in the nineteenth century, it ceased to be a major religion in Japan, but it still has shrines and practitioners, Mount Fuji remains a major pilgrimage site, and the Japanese remain among the most avid mountaineers in the world.

Gary Snyder, pretty good mountaineer and great poet, seems to unite the spiritual and secular traditions. After all, he studied Buddhism in Asia but learned how to climb mountains far earlier, with Oregon's Mazamas (a mountaineering club founded atop Mount Hood in Oregon in the 1890s). In an afterword to his book-length poem named after a Chinese scroll, *Mountains and Rivers Without End*, begun in 1956 and finished nearly forty years later, he writes, "I had been introduced to the high snow peaks of the Pacific Northwest when I was thirteen and had climbed a number of summits even before I was twenty. East Asian landscape paintings, seen at the Seattle Art Museum from the age of ten on, also presented such a space." During his years in Japan, he practiced walking meditation and made contact with surviving Shugendō practitioners, "and I was given a chance to see how walking the landscape can become both ritual and meditation. I did the five-day pilgrimage on the Omine ridge and established a tentative relationship with the archaic Buddhist mountain deity Fudo. This ancient exercise has one visualizing the hike from peak to valley floor as an inner linking of the womb and diamond mandala realms of Vajrayana Buddhism."

In 1956, just before he left for Japan, Snyder led Jack Kerouac on an overnight hike to the sea and back across Mount Tamalpais, a 2,571-foot peak on the other side of the Golden Gate from San Francisco. On that walk, Snyder told his footsore companion, "The closer you get to real matter, rock air fire wood, boy, the more spiritual the world is." The scholar David Robertson comments, "This sentence states what is perhaps not only the central idea of Gary Snyder's poetry and prose, but the fixed point around which rotate the thought and practice of many who take to trails. If one habit beats in the ritual heart of the lives and their literature, surely this is it: the practice of 'mattering,' of repeatedly accessing the thing that is at one and the same time both spirit and matter. . . . Hiking for Snyder is a way of furthering a political, social, and spiritual revolution. . . . The essential nature of things is not an Aristotelian plot nor a Hegelian dialectic, and does not lead to a goal. Therefore, it cannot be the object of a quest, as for the grail. Instead, it goes round and round and on and on, rather like the hike that

---

living for—and possibly dying for.—HAMISH BROWN, IN AN ACCOUNT OF HOW HE CLIMBED ALL 279

Kerouac and Snyder took and even more like the poem that Snyder projected writing and told Kerouac about as they walked."

That poem is *Mountains and Rivers Without End*, and one of the pieces in it, "The Circumambulation of Mount Tamalpais," describes the sites and recounts the chants of his daylong excursion there with Philip Whalen (now a Zen *roshi*) and Allen Ginsberg in 1965 "to show respect and to clarify the mind." The Himalayan-style circumambulation has been taken up by local Buddhists to become a several-times-a-year walk of some fifteen miles and ten stations, from near the foot to Tam's east peak and down again (which, when I went on it, preserved Snyder's humor by reading from his "Smoky the Bear Sutra" in the penultimate station, a roadside parking lot appropriately sprinkled with cigarette butts). The peak isn't a culmination, just one of the ten stations on this circuit, which wraps the mountain in a spiral of interpretations drawn from mostly Asian religious sources. Mountains have been a recurrent subject of Snyder's poetry. He once reset Muir's description of his ascent of Mount Ritter to make a poem of it, wrote his own *Cold Mountain Poems* after Han-Shan, and described not only climbing and walking in mountains but living in them and working in them as a fire lookout and a trail builder. In *Mountains and Rivers Without End*, says Snyder, "I translate space from its physical sense to the spiritual sense of space as emptiness—spiritual transparency—in Mahayana Buddhist philosophy." The book opens with what at first seems to be a long description of landscape but is in fact a description of a Chinese painting, and Snyder travels through all kinds of space—paintings, cities, wildernesses—in the same spirit. In "Walking the New York Bedrock / Alive in the Sea of Information," Snyder traverses Manhattan, thinking of the Indians' encounters early on with European settlers, seeing the skyscrapers as corporate deities—"Equitable god" and "Old Union Carbide god"—seeing trees, peregrines nesting "at the thirty-fifth floor," homeless people wandering amid the street-canyons whose buildings become "arêtes and buttresses rising above them." But real mountains delight him in ways Manhattan does not, as a short poem with a long title, "On Climbing the Sierra Matterhorn Again After Thirty-One Years," suggests:

> Range after range of mountains
> Year after year after year.
> I am still in love.

MUNROES—OR PEAKS OVER 3,000 METERS—IN SCOTLAND   *There's all sorts of walking—from heading out*

Chapter 10

OF WALKING CLUBS AND
LAND WARS

I. THE SIERRA NEVADA

"Another perfect Sierra Nevada day," said Michael Cohen, hovering over his coffee and managing to sound caustic about it, to me, hovering over my tea, as we looked at the morning light glittering on the lake. Valerie Cohen wasn't up yet, and I wasn't all that awake myself early that morning in the Cohens' June Lake cabin, on the eastern side of the Sierra Nevada, a little southeast of the highlands of Yosemite National Park. I don't remember what made him say all of a sudden, "The Sierra Club likes to say that John Muir founded the Sierra Club. But California culture founded it." We were products of that culture ourselves. The Cohens had both grown up in the Los Angeles area and spent a lot of time in the Sierra from an early age. I wasn't nearly so dedicated a wilderness explorer as they were, nor so athletic, even if my father's parents had met in immigrant hiking clubs in L.A. The high Sierra was definitely the Cohens' territory, in which they had skied, climbed, hiked, worked, and even gotten married thirty years before, and I let them pick the destination for our day's hike.

It was a gorgeous cloudless day in mid-August, and winter had been so late and so wet that the meadows were still green and wildflowers were everywhere.

---

across the desert in a straight line to a sinuous weaving through undergrowth. Descending rocky ridges and talus

---

So were other hikers. Valerie led off at a good clip down the trail that began southwest of Tuolumne Meadows, and for the first mile or so through the pines she reminisced for my benefit about when she was a law enforcement ranger, this trail was her beat, and she was responsible for dealing with the demented and drugged of the high country. In the meadow where the trail had been trodden into a narrow trench several inches deep she told me about the time the campers complained that there was a crazy guy in their campground who stayed up all night walking in circles muttering to himself, a guy who turned out to be an eminent but deranged mathematician. Somewhere in the course of these stories— maybe during the one about the babysitter and the amanita mushrooms— Michael commented that the consequence of the theory that nature is supposed to make you happy is that those most desperately in search of happiness tend to show up there. Certainly they do, along with a few million others every year, in Yosemite National Park, one of the most famous and heavily visited natural places in the world.

Yosemite is also a major historical site, not least for the history of walking, mountaineering, and the environmental movement. It was my good fortune that Michael had written the history of the Sierra Club and an intellectual biography of John Muir, so that in walking along the Mono Pass trail we were traversing the terrain of his scholarship. Dorothy and William Wordsworth walking together through the Pennines just before the nineteenth century began seem lonely figures, choosing an unpopular activity in an unpopulated countryside, and John Muir tramping across Yosemite and the Sierra Nevada in the decades after his arrival in California in 1868 seems part of that tradition of solitary wandering, pursuing the aesthetic while those all around pursued the utilitarian. But Muir, as Michael had been saying, was a founder—if not the founder—of the Sierra Club, and the club would further transform the social landscape in its efforts to keep the natural landscape untransformed (except by trails; trail building was an important activity of the early club). A little more than a hundred years after the Wordsworths set off on their lonely winter walk, almost a century before the Cohens and I set out from the roadside bustle, ninety-six Sierra Club members—including their president, Muir—spent two weeks walking, mountaineering, and camping in Tuolumne Meadows. That first Sierra Club High Trip in July 1901 is a milestone in the history of the taste for walking in the landscape. Not the only such milestone, for club secretary William Colby wrote, "An excursion of this

---

slopes is a specialty in itself. It is an irregular dancing—always shifting—step of walk on slabs and scree. The

---

sort, if properly conducted, will do an infinite amount of good toward awakening the proper kind of interest in the forests and other natural features of our mountains, and will also tend to create a spirit of good-fellowship among our members. The Mazamas and Appalachian Clubs have for many years shown how successful and interesting such trips may be made." Walking had become so entrenched a part of the culture that it could be, by means of walking clubs, a foundation for further change.

Since English mountaineers founded the Alpine Club in 1857, outdoor organizations had been proliferating across Europe and North America, many, like the Alpine and Appalachian Clubs, combining the pleasures of a social club with the publications and explorations of a scientific society. But the Sierra Club was different. "The proper kind of interest in the forests and other natural features" was, in the ideology of the club, a political interest. Mountaineering and hiking were ends in themselves for most of the clubs, but the Sierra Club had been founded as a dual-purpose organization. In 1890 Muir and such friends as the painter William Keith and the lawyer Warren Olney had started meeting to discuss defending Yosemite National Park from the developers who sought to raid its timber and mineral resources. They had merged with professors at the University of California, Berkeley, who were considering founding a mountaineering club, and the new organization's name came from the range they would explore, just as the Appalachian Club's name came from its members' local mountains. On June 4, 1892, the Sierra Club was formed.

To pretend that the world is a garden is an essentially apolitical act, a turning away from the woes that keep it from being one. But to try to make the world a garden is often a political endeavor, and it is this taste that the more activist walking clubs around the world have taken up. Walking in the landscape had long been considered a vaguely virtuous act, but Muir and the club had at last defined that virtue as defense of the land. This made it a self-perpetuating virtue, securing the grounds of its existence, and made the club an ideological organization. Walking—or hiking and mountaineering, as the club tended to call it—became its ideal way of being in the world: out of doors, relying on one's own feet, neither producing nor destroying. The club's mission statement said its purpose was "to explore, enjoy, and render accessible the mountain regions of the Pacific Coast; To publish authentic information concerning them; To enlist the support

---

breath and eye are always following this uneven rhythm. It is never paced or clocklike, but flexing—little jumps—

---

and cooperation of the people and the government in preserving the forests and other natural features of the Sierra Nevada Mountains."

From the beginning, the Sierra Club had a lot of built-in contradictions. It was founded as a combination mountaineering and preservation society, because Muir and some of the other founders believed that those who spent time in the mountains would come to love them, and that that love would be an active love, a love willing to go into political battle to save them. Though the premise proved to be good enough, there are plenty of mountaineers whose love has no political dimension and plenty of environmentalists who, for various reasons, don't travel in remote places. The other contradiction had to do with the fact that environmental devastation is usually done in the name of economic growth. The middle-class club found itself fighting innumerable battles in a war that dare not speak its name, a war against economic exploitation of the environment in the name of progress and free enterprise. John Muir took a stand against anthropocentrism, against the idea that trees, animals, minerals, soil, water, are there for humans to use, let alone to destroy, but by positioning wilderness as a place apart from society and the economy he avoided addressing the wider politics of land and money. For most of its history, the club would tender the milder, more anthropocentric argument that the exploitation of beautiful places destroyed them as recreational sites. Eventually it became clear that recreation was destroying Yosemite Valley almost as much as resource extraction had destroyed the neighboring Hetch-Hetchy Valley by damming it as a reservoir for San Francisco during World War I. The club would have to rescind the "render accessible" clause in its mission statement and begin advocating for survival of species, then ecosystems, then the planet, as nature began to be imagined as a necessity rather than a pleasure.

Most of the Sierra Club's troubles and transformations were far ahead, however, when the first High Trip set out in July 1901. The world was far larger and less paved then than now, and they spent three days walking from relatively accessible Yosemite Valley to Tuolumne Meadows, accompanied by a vast caravan of mules and horses carrying stoves, blankets, camp beds, and quantities of food (nowadays, the Meadows are a few hours by car from the valley). Once arrived, they settled into their large camp, from which smaller parties made forays into the surrounding mountains and canyons. It was a strange halcyon era between

---

sidesteps—going for the well-seen place to put a foot on a rock, hit flat, move on—zigzagging along and all the violent settlement of California by avaricious Yankees and the overdevelopment of the state later. Wrote Ella M. Sexton of that first High Trip, "There were solemn hours, too, when the mountaineers looked disdainfully at us feeble 'tenderfeet' as we set off with trusty alpenstocks, a light lunch, and much courage to conquer the jagged peaks, loose talus, and snow-fields of Mt. Dana. . . . The climbers were so delayed by ten long miles to the foot of the mountain, the hard ascent and a weary ten miles back to camp, that relief parties had to go out to kindle fires at stream-crossings, and it was nine o'clock before the last straggler was ferried over on the shaky raft." With unbridged rivers and unmapped routes, it was a far wilder place than it is today. Few besides club members, fishermen, and the surviving Indians ventured into these regions then, and during those early years the club included many leading mountaineers among its members and sponsored many first ascents.

But it is the ordinary experiences that give something of the flavor of these mass expeditions into the mountains. Nelson Hackett was a high-school student when two of his female teachers recruited him, and the experience did exactly what it was supposed to: incorporate him into a community of activist nature lovers. He later became editor of the *Sierra Club Bulletin* and a member of the board. While on the 1908 High Trip to the Kings Canyon region of the Sierra, he wrote to his parents about the club leaders, "Mr. Colby goes like lightning and Mr. Parsons is very fat and very slow so there is no need of not finding someone to suit your pace. Of course when half a dozen are ahead you can't miss the trail for the tracks they make. I sort of imagined that the 120 people would all walk along in a row but they are so scattered that you are hardly ever in sight of more than a half dozen or so." Several days later: "Next morning we turned out in the cold star-light at 3:30 and started at 4:30 for Mt. Whitney. The climb is easy but tedious and the rocks are hard on the feet. I arrived at the top at nine o'clock. We ate lunch and made some chocolate sherbet, enjoyed the view for a couple of hours and then returned. We could see the desert, and Owen's Lake, eleven thousand feet below us." And in a second letter written that day, July 18, 1908, "I had a long talk with Mr. Muir this aft—or rather he did all the talking—about a thousand mile walk he took thro the South, the year after the Rebellion. Also, how he first became interested in Botany. Camp-fire ready. Good-bye. . . ."

Light on tradition and heavy on new juxtapositions, California has long been a wellspring of fresh cultural possibilities. At the turn of the century, a regional

---

deliberate. The alert eye looking ahead, picking the footholds to come, while never missing the step of the moment.

---

culture including painters, bad poets, and good architects was responding to the state's distinctive influences and environment, and the early Sierra Club was part of this response. Unlike organizations such as the Alpine Club, which excluded women, the Sierra Club made them welcome and seems to have provided many with opportunities for mountaineering they might have found in few other places. At a time when a woman could hardly go unchaperoned around London, it says something for the freedom of the West Coast or the club that women seem to have gone wherever they liked, with whomever they liked, in the mountains. Populated by professionals of both sexes, the Sierra Club had some intellectual force behind it in its early days, and evenings around the campfire were lively with discussion, music, and performances. Muir was the most influential member then, but the club would later become a home for the men who invented American nature photography—Ansel Adams and Eliot Porter—and for many who redefined American wilderness in both law and imagination, such as George Marshall and David Brower. But California culture didn't come out of nowhere. The campers on those early trips were making their own culture, but much of the material came from points east. It's not hard to trace the lineage. After all the dean of New England transcendentalism, Ralph Waldo Emerson, had visited with both Wordsworth and John Muir, seeming to transmit—and transmute—the legacy from the peripatetic poet who had walked through the French Revolution to the evangelical mountaineer who died at the beginning of World War I. The members of the Sierra Club had imported their taste for nature, but it may have been the nature itself—the colossal wilderness of the West—that transformed that taste into something new.

That first High Trip in 1901 suggested how far the culture of walking had come from the aristocratic stroll in the garden and the solitary ramble in the woods when it arrived in the mountains of California. It had become not only mainstream culture but politics, and if landscape could shape its walkers, these California walkers were returning the favor by shaping that landscape through both legislation and cultural representation. In recent decades the Sierra Club has been excoriated by younger environmental organizations for its compromises and missteps and for having been of its time rather than ours on such issues as dams and nuclear power. But environmental awareness and the Sierra Club grew up together. In the postwar years the club began to expand its scope and eventually its membership. It went from being a regional club whose several

The body-mind is so at one with this rough world that it makes these moves effortlessly once it has had a bit of

thousand members were mostly participants in outdoor activities to being a national organization whose half-million members include many who have never participated in a club excursion. It was the first major force for environmental protection in the United States and remains one of the most influential, achieving major victories on forests, air, water, species, parks, toxics. And it still sponsors thousands of local hikes and wilderness outings every year.

Our own walk came out of the woods and proceeded across some beautiful meadows with streams running through them. Michael and Valerie had led some of the last High Trips the club held, in 1968, when "the old man of the mountains," the legendary climber and curmudgeon Norman Clyde, still came by, but the impact of large-scale camps and expeditions was beginning to dismay the club, and soon afterward the tradition came to an end. As we approached Mono Pass, we came across the same wildflowers blooming here that I had seen in the Marin Headlands in March, not three hundred miles away. And then we reached the saddleback that the signpost announced as Mono Pass, 10,600 feet high, and sat down in the gravel and tufts of lupine. The crest of the Sierra Nevada is one of the few real borders in the world, besides the ebbing and flowing borders dividing land from water. These mountains scrape off the stormclouds sailing in from the west, and the clouds' bounty becomes snowmelt running westward again to water some of the greatest temperate forests of the world, the sequoia, ponderosa, and fir groves of the Sierra, and thence to the valleys and salmon-run rivers to the ocean—and farms and cities—below. Though a little of the mountain runoff flows down the east side of the Sierra, everything east of the peaks is desert. At Mono Pass, we were sitting facing a bright green meadow full of tender wildflowers, and a few miles behind us began a thousand miles of aridity. We were also sitting within view of the results of two great battles over land. Yosemite National Park's boundaries had been set in the 1890s, and John Muir had drawn them up. Mono Lake, the blue oval in the dusty east, had been saved in the 1990s when environmentalists, after many years of fighting, finally prevented Los Angeles from diverting some of the lake's tributaries into the vast hydraulic system that waters the city.

We fell to talking about the Sierra Club again. Although I admire the club's staunch work over the decades, I worry that equating the love of nature with certain kinds of leisure activity and visual pleasure leaves out those with other tastes and tasks. Walking in the landscape can be a demonstration of a specific heritage,

---

practice. The mountain keeps up with the mountain.—GARY SNYDER, "BLUE MOUNTAINS CONSTANTLY and when it is mistaken for a universal experience, those who don't participate can be seen as less sensitive to nature, rather than less acculturated to the northern European romantic tradition. Michael told me about a Sierra Club outing he led and Valerie cooked for in which some well-meaning members brought along two inner-city African-American boys who were totally bewildered. The wilderness alarmed them, and the point of exerting oneself in it escaped them. Only the man who took them fishing and the hamburgers Valerie made them every day redeemed the experience. Michael wrote about it in *The Pathless Way*, his book on Muir: "We were shocked to discover firsthand that the taste for wilderness was culturally determined, a privilege enjoyed only by the sons and daughters of a certain comfortable class of Americans. One could cultivate a sense of utopian community on the outings only by beginning with a group of people who already agreed closely about certain basic values." (Since then, the Sierra Club and other organizations have sponsored "inner-city outings" better equipped to mediate the experience.) Afterward we left the trail and went cross-country, straying near a small lake tucked under a dark cliff face that seemed to increase its depths and then venturing through marshy green expanses of wild onion splashed with the scarlet of Indian paintbrush to a windswept slope above Bloody Canyon.

II. The Alps

One of the monuments to John Muir—along with the John Muir Trail from Mount Whitney to Yosemite Valley and dozens of California public schools—is the expanse of redwoods called Muir Woods, on the foothills of Mount Tamalpais, a dozen miles north of the Golden Gate Bridge. Mount Tamalpais is the small peak where Gary Snyder and friends instituted the Buddhist practice of ritual circumambulation, but there are other ways to interpret mountains and walking, and this one has had many interpreters. Above Muir Woods, there's an inconspicuous trail that runs for half a mile or so, then comes around a bend to a very different and disorienting monument on the steep slope above the woods. It looks like a perfect Alpine chalet, with its outdoor dance floor, pitched roof, and tiers of balconies made of pine planks cut out in folkloric designs, and it is one of the few surviving American outposts of the Austria-based organization Die

WALKING"   *And the meaning of Earth completely changes: with the legal model, one is constantly*

Naturfreunde. The Naturfreunde, or Nature Friends, was founded in Vienna in 1895 by teacher Georg Schmiedl, blacksmith Alois Rohrauer, and student Karl Renner, at a time when the Hapsburg monarchy and other elites still controlled access to most of the Austrian mountains. "Berg frei"—free mountains—was their slogan. They were socialists and antimonarchists, and they were immensely successful. Sixty people attended the organization's first meeting, and within a few decades there were 200,000 members, mostly in Austria, Germany, and Switzerland. Each local chapter bought land and built a clubhouse, which was open to all members of the Naturfreunde. They sponsored hikes, environmental consciousness, and folk festivals, and advocated access to the mountains for working people.

The late nineteenth to early twentieth century was a golden age of organizations. Some provided social cohesion for the displaced of a rapidly changing world; others offered resistance to industrialization's inhuman appetite for the time, health, energy, and rights of workers. Many were organized around utopian ideals or pragmatic social change, and all of them created communities—of Zionists, feminists, labor activists, athletes, charities, and intellectuals. Walking clubs were part of this larger movement, and each of the major political walking clubs was founded in some kind of opposition to the mainstream of its society. For the Sierra Club, this mainstream was the rampant destruction of a pristine ecosystem by a rapidly developing country. In most of Europe, the remaining open space was in more stable but less accessible condition. For the Austrian Naturfreunde as well as many British groups, the aristocratic monopoly on open space was the problem. Manfred Pils, the current Naturfreunde secretary general, wrote me, "The Friends of Nature were founded because leisure time and tourism was a privilege for upper class people at that time. They wanted to open up such opportunities also for common people . . . it was the Friends of Nature who campaigned against the efforts to exclude people from private meadows and forests in the Alps. The campaign was called 'Der verbotene Weg' (the forbidden path). So the Friends of Nature achieved finally a legalistic regulation which guaranteed access by walking to forests and alpine meadows for everyone." As a result, "the Alps are not a national territory, they stayed in private property but we (and all tourists) have access to all footpaths and generally to forests and alpine meadows."

When German and Austrian radicals arrived in the United States, they

---

reterritorializing around a point of view, on a domain, according to a set of constant relations, but with the brought their organization with them. In San Francisco, immigrants who met at the German workers' hall on Valencia Street went forth in big groups to hike on Mount Tam. After the 1906 earthquake, local Naturfreunde historian Erich Fink told me, many more craftsmen arrived in the region, the number of weekend hikers mushroomed, and they decided to buy property to start their own branch of the Naturfreunde. Five young people bought a whole steep hillside on Mount Tam for two hundred dollars, and the members built themselves a rural outpost. Fink's wife told me that until the 1930s you had to show a union card to join. This Bavarian lodge perched above the redwoods provided a workers' alternative to the Sierra Club, a local place for people who had only the weekend in which to escape the city.

The Naturfreunde paid for its success. Its socialism provoked the Nazi regime to repress it in Austria and Germany, while the Germanness of the organization made it suspect in the United States during that era. After the end of World War II, socialism became an issue in the United States too. McCarthyism in the United States so traumatized the organization that one local leader was still reluctant to talk to me about the club's history. "They are very political today in Europe," he said in a heavy Teutonic accent, "which we cannot be. We stay away from any politics because they almost took away what we built up through all the years." During the years when being or having been a socialist or Communist was a dangerous offense, all the branches of the Naturfreunde in the eastern United States collapsed, and the clubhouses bought, built, and owned by the members fell into private hands. Only three California outposts survived by being adamantly apolitical, and a fourth one recently opened up in northern Oregon. Of the 600,000 Naturfreunde members in twenty-one countries, less than a thousand remain in the United States, and they are anomalies for their apolitical stance.

The German youth movement, the Wandervogel, did not survive World War II, but its history demonstrates that no ideology had a monopoly on walking. A reaction against the authoritarianism of the German family and government, it began inauspiciously enough in a suburb of Berlin in 1896, where a group of shorthand students began to go on expeditions together to the woods nearby and then farther away. By 1899 they were setting off for weeks at a time to wander in the mountains. The most charismatic member of that circle, Karl Fischer, trans-

---

ambulant model, the process of deterritorialization constitutes and extends the territory itself.—DELEUZE &

formed the organization, formalizing its behavior and spreading its ideas. When the Wandervogel Ausschuss für Schulerfahrten (Wandervogel Committee for Schoolboys' Rambles) was founded on November 4, 1901, it was a Romantic rambling society. *Wandervogel* means a magical bird; a word taken from a poem, it suggests the free and weightless identity the members would seek. Medieval wandering scholars were the first role models for the thousands of boys who joined up, and rambling on long excursions together was their principal activity. There were other cultural activities—the lasting legacy of the Wandervogel, and, according to historians, its only first-rate cultural contribution, was the revival of folk songs. Most of its members were in the throes of adolescence's heady idealism, and heated philosophical debates as well as music filled their evenings. The movement seemed to be forever splintering over some minor point or other. "On the main thing—rambling—we are in complete agreement," concluded a Wandervogel statement.

Theirs was an odd antiauthoritarianism, since the Wandervogel was exclusive, hierarchical, organized into small groups giving unquestioning obedience to a leader, with semiformal uniforms (usually shorts, dark shirts, and neckerchiefs) and initiation rituals of various degrees of difficulty and danger. Though the Wandervogel was detached from practical politics, most members subscribed to an ethnic nationalism, and so the folk culture that meant working-class culture for the Naturfreunde meant ethnic identity for the Wandervogel. The members were almost exclusively middle-class; girls were admitted to some groups after 1911 or encouraged to form their own groups. "The Jewish problem" meant that Jews—and often, Catholics—were generally unwelcome (though certainly one prominent Jew, Walter Benjamin, was involved in a radical splinter group of the youth movement in his own youth). At its height, the Wandervogel had about sixty thousand members. The Wandervogel seems to have started out as a real rebellion against German authoritarianism, and to this extent it was a political club, but it had neither the strength nor the insight to truly oppose its country's slide toward fascism.

There were other organizations for young people to join, church groups and the Protestant Youth Movement and, after 1909, a German version of the Boy Scouts, while working-class youths had Communist and socialist youth clubs. The Boy Scouts, like the Wandervogel, like so many situations in the history of walking, raise the question of when walking becomes marching. Most walking

GUATTARI, TREATISE ON *NOMADOLOGY*   . . . *malformations of the spine are very frequent among mill-hands;*

clubs were groups come together to celebrate and protect individual and private experience, but some embraced authoritarianism. Marching subordinates the very rhythms of individual bodies to group and to authority, and any group that marches is marching toward militarism if it is not already there. The scouting movement was adapted by the Boer War veteran Sir Baden-Powell from ideas of his own and ideas plagiarized from the Anglo-Canadian Ernest Thompson Seton. Seton's goal had been to introduce boys to outdoor life with a strong focus on Native American skills and values, and he is sometimes credited with starting the pagan revival among adults instead. Baden-Powell brought a more militaristic, conservative sensibility to the idea of living in the woods. Even now, each scouting group seems to have its own style; some teach outdoor skills, some train the boys as little soldiers. After World War I, the Wandervogel collapsed, but the German Boy Scouts—the Pathfinders, they were called—rebelled against their adult leaders and largely replaced the original movement.

Werner Heisenberg, the physicist most famous for his uncertainty principle, became the leader of one of these New Pathfinder troops. Playing at adventure must have been a relief to him after the war, during which he and his brother had undergone real risks smuggling food into besieged Munich. Like many other Germans, he had a tradition of hiking and love of mountains to draw on: his paternal grandfather had gone on the "wander year" that was a rite of passage for young artisans, and his maternal grandfather was an avid hiker who went on long walking tours. But the Pathfinder movement, with its idealism and its camaraderie, had other attractions. The movement instilled in him a love of his country and close ties to his peers that made him deeply ambivalent and deeply troubled during World War II, when he was in charge of the Nazi program to develop an atomic bomb. "After 1919, the militant dictatorships in Russia, Italy, and Germany built up youth organizations of their own," writes one historian of the era. "The Hitler Youth took over many of the symbols and rituals of the original Youth Movement, but it was no more than a caricature."

III. The Peak District and Beyond

Everywhere but Britain, organized walking seems to become hiking, then camping, and eventually something as nebulous as, in contemporary terminology, out-

some of them consequent upon mere overwork, others the effect of long work upon constitutions originally feeble, or door recreation or wilderness adventure. The clubs are "walking and" organizations: walking and climbing and environment activism, walking and socialism and folk songs, walking and adolescent dreaming and nationalism. Only in Britain has walking remained the focus all along, even if the word *rambling* is often used to describe it. Walking has a resonance, a cultural weight, there that it does nowhere else. On summer Sundays, more than eighteen million Britons head for the country, and ten million say they walk for recreation. In most British bookstores walking guides occupy a lot of shelf space, and the genre is so well established that there are classics and subversive texts—among the former, Alfred Wainwright's handwritten, illustrated guides to the wilder parts of the country, and among the latter the Sheffield land-rights activist Terry Howard's itinerary of walks that are all trespasses. The American magazine *Walking* is nothing but a health and fitness publication aimed at women—walking appears there as just another exercise program—but Britain has half a dozen outdoor magazines in which walking is about the beauty of landscape rather than the body. "Almost a spiritual thing," the outdoor writer Roly Smith told me, "a religion almost. A lot of people walk for the social aspects—there are no barriers on the moors and you say hello to everyone—overcome our damn British reserve. Walking is classless, one of the few sports that is classless."

But accessing the land has been something of a class war. For a thousand years, landowners have been sequestering more and more of the island for themselves, and for the past hundred and fifty, landless people have been fighting back. When the Normans conquered England in 1066, they set aside huge deer parks for hunting, and ever since, the penalties for poaching and interfering with hunting land have been fierce—castration, deportation, and execution were some of the punishments meted out over the centuries (after 1723, for example, taking rabbits or fish, let alone deer, was an offense punishable by death). The commons were usually privately owned land to which locals retained rights to gather wood and graze animals, while the traditional rights-of-way—footpaths across the fields and woods that the public had the right to walk no matter whose property they traversed—were necessary for work and travel. In Scotland, common land was abolished by an act of Parliament in 1695, and in England enclosure acts and unauthorized but fiercely enforced seizures of hitherto common land accelerated in the eighteenth century.

Corollaries of the glorious open gardens of the era, the lucrative enclosures

----

weakened by bad food. Deformities seem even more frequent than these diseases; the knees were bent inward, the

----

were vast areas fenced off and filled with sheep or farmed by a single large landowner, and they were often created by shutting landworkers out from agricultural and common land. In the nineteenth century, an upper-class mania for hunting inspired many more landowners to sequester public land that formerly supported many people. The Highland Clearances of 1780–1855 in Scotland were particularly brutal, displacing quantities of people, many of whom emigrated to North America, while some were driven to the coast, where they eked out a bare survival on small farms. Hunting grouse, pheasant, and deer for a few weeks annually has become the excuse for denying access to thousands of miles of Britain's wildest countryside year-round, and while hunting in the United States is sometimes a source of food for poor, rural, and indigenous people, hunting in Britain is an elite sport. Armies of gamekeepers patrolled and patrol such land, and some have used extreme measures to keep people out: spring guns and mantraps, dogs, brandished guns and shots fired overhead, assault with sticks or fists, threats, and usually, the support of local law enforcement.

When Britain was still a rural economy of landworkers, the struggle over access was about economics. But by the middle of the nineteenth century, half the nation's population lived in cities and towns, and nowadays more than 90 percent does. The cities they moved to, particularly the new industrial cities, were often bleak. Densely built, without adequate fresh water, sewers, or garbage collection systems and with a constant pall of soot in the air from the coal-burning mills and homes, the English cities of the nineteenth century were foul places, and the poor lived in the foulest. It's a chicken-and-egg question as to whether the taste for the rural or the awfulness of the cities came first, but the British have always sworn allegiance to footpaths, not boulevards. People wanted to get out of the cities whenever they could, and many of these cities were still compact enough that one could walk out of them into the country. During this period, the conflict over the commons and the rights-of-way stopped being about economic survival and became about psychic survival—about a reprieve from the city.

As more and more people chose to spend their spare time walking, more and more of the traditional rights-of-way were closed to them. In 1815 Parliament passed an act allowing magistrates to close any path they considered unnecessary (and throughout these land wars, the administration of rural Britain has been largely in the hand of landowners and their associates). In 1824 the Association for the Protection of Ancient Footpaths was formed near York, and in 1826 a

ligaments very often relaxed and enfeebled, and the long bones of the legs bent. The thick ends of these long bones

Manchester association of the same name was formed. The Scottish Rights of Way Society, formed in 1845, is the oldest surviving such society, but the Commons, Open Spaces, and Footpath Preservation Society, founded in 1865, is still active as the Open Space Society. It fought and won the war of Epping Forest near London. In 1793 the forest was a 9,000-acre expanse used by the public; by 1848 it had been reduced to 7,000 acres, and a decade later it was fenced off. Three laborers who cut wood there were given harsh sentences, and in protest of the sentences and the fences—which had been ordered removed by a court order—five to six thousand people came out to exercise their right to be there. In 1884 the Forest Ramblers' Club was formed by London businessmen to "walk through Epping Forest and report obstructions we have seen." Countless other walking clubs were formed in these years.

The conflict is over two ways of imagining the landscape. Imagine the countryside as a vast body. Ownership pictures it divided into economic units like internal organs, or like a cow divided into cuts of meat, and certainly such division is one way to organize a food-producing landscape, but it doesn't explain why moors, mountains, and forests should be similarly fenced and divided. Walking focuses not on the boundary lines of ownership that break the land into pieces but on the paths that function as a kind of circulatory system connecting the whole organism. Walking is, in this way, the antithesis of owning. It postulates a mobile, empty-handed, shareable experience of the land. Nomads have often been disturbing to nationalism because their roving blurs and perforates the boundaries that define nations; walking does the same thing on the smaller scale of private property.

Certainly one of the pleasures of walking in England is this sense of cohabitation right-of-way paths create—of crossing stiles into sheep fields and skirting the edges of crops on land that is both utilitarian and aesthetic. American land, without such rights-of-way, is rigidly divided into production and pleasure zones, which may be one of the reasons why there is little appreciation for or awareness of the immense agricultural expanses of the country. British rights-of-way are not impressive compared to those of other European countries—Denmark, Holland, Sweden, Spain—where citizens retain much wider rights of access to open space. But rights-of-way do preserve an alternate vision of the land in which ownership doesn't necessarily convey absolute rights and paths are as significant a principle as boundaries. Nearly 90 percent of Britain is privately

----

were especially apt to be bent and disproportionately developed, and these patients came from the factories in which

----

owned, so gaining access to the countryside means gaining access to private land, while in the United States a lot of land remains public—if not always conveniently located for Sunday strolls. Thus the Sierra Club fought for boundaries, while British walking activists fight against them, but the boundaries laid down in America are to keep the land public, wild, and indivisible, to keep private enterprise out, while in Britain they kept the public out.

When I went to see the great garden of Stowe, I ran into a docent who told me that the gardens were built by destroying the village around the church and relocating "the dirty little people" a mile or so away. She added that these people were not allowed back in unless they wore smocks that made them picturesque. Three hours later I ran into this subversive, charming docent near that church, now hidden behind trees and shrubs, and we fell to talking again. About right of access, she said that as a little girl she lived near a farmer whose signs said, "Trespassers Will Be Prosecuted." She believed this meant they would be executed and used to wonder how a man who would chop people's heads off had the temerity to show himself in church. Later in life, she lived in Russia with her diplomat husband, and there and many other places, she said, trespassing was hardly a concept. Most of the British people I spoke with had a sense that the landscape was their heritage and they had a right to be there. Private property is a lot more absolute in the United States, and the existence of vast tracts of public land serves to justify this, as does an ideology in which the rights of the individual are more often upheld than the good of the community.

So I was thrilled when I got to England and discovered a culture in which trespassing is a mass movement and the extent of property rights is open to question. If walking sews together the land that ownership tears apart, then trespassing does so as a political statement. The Liberal member of Parliament James Bryce, who introduced an unsuccessful bill to allow access to privately held moors and mountains in 1884, declared a few years later, "Land is not property for our unlimited and unqualified use. Land is necessary so that we may live upon it and from it, and that people may enjoy it in a variety of ways; and I deny therefore, that there exists or is recognized by our law or in natural justice, such a thing as an unlimited power of exclusion." This position is widely held by British moderates as well as radicals. The author of a pleasant guidebook to Derbyshire remarks of the Peak District, "It is the one thing that is unpleasant, this watchful herding of holiday-makers, where in a space so wide all must keep to a path a few

long work-hours were of frequent occurrence."—FRIEDRICH ENGELS, THE CONDITION OF THE WORKING CLASS IN paces across. I have thought: what an incitement to any who believe in the public ownership of all land." Unfortunately even the rights-of-way "a few paces across" are limited, and though it is legal to travel on them, sitting, picnicking, and straying may be illegal. Most footpaths were established for practical purposes and don't go through some of the wildest and most spectacular parts of Britain.

Thus came the great trespasses and walks that changed the face of the English countryside. They took place in the Peak District, where the laborers of the industrial north converged by foot, bicycle, and train during their time off. In the south of England, Leslie Stephen got by with "a little judicious trespassing," and his gentlemanly Sunday Tramps could and did intimidate the gamekeepers they met, while for serious expeditions there were always the Alps. "By the last quarter of the nineteenth century, in all parts of urban Britain, especially the industrial towns, the people's rambling movement was emerging, and gradually they began to take over the leadership of the struggle for access," writes Howard Hill. "The major reason for this was the growing popularity of the Swiss mountains which, being completely free to walk and climb on, drew the gentlemen ramblers and climbers away from Britain." The YMCA was one early sponsor of walking clubs, and in the 1880s members of the Manchester YMCA Rambling Club would walk seventy miles between Saturday afternoon, when work ended, and Sunday evening. In 1888 the Polytechnic Club of London was founded as a walking club; in 1892 the West of Scotland Ramblers' Alliance was organized; in 1894 women teachers formed the Midlands Institute of Ramblers; in 1900 the Sheffield Clarion Ramblers—a socialist organization—was founded by G. B. H. Ward; in 1905 a London Federation of Rambling Clubs was formed; in 1907 came the Manchester Rambling Club; in 1928 the nationwide British Workers Sports Federation—the BWSF; and in 1930 the Youth Hostels Association began to provide, like the Naturfreunde, lodging for young and poor travelers (the YHA had its beginnings in Germany in 1907; among the rules in Britain in early years was one that no one could arrive in an automobile). So many went out walking in the first three or four decades of the twentieth century that some speak of it as a movement. As historian Raphael Samuels put it, "Hiking was a major, if unofficial, component of the socialist lifestyle." Laborers had developed—or retained from their peasant parents and grandparents—a passion for the land, and a whole culture of working-class botanists and naturalists emerged, as did a legion of walk-

---

ENGLAND   *"The fellow, by his agent, or secretary, or somebody, writes to me, 'Sir Leicester Dedlock, Baronet,* ers. Walking in groups was partly a matter of safety—there were the gamekeepers, and one Sheffield rambler reported "a genuine hatred of ramblers by countryfolk who sometimes 'beat up' those they found walking alone."

Before the industrial revolution, the Peak District was a major tourist destination: the Wordsworths went there, and so did Carl Moritz, and Jane Austen sent the heroine of *Pride and Prejudice* to scenic spots there. Afterward it became an anomaly, a forty-mile-wide open space wedged between the great manufacturing cities of Manchester and Sheffield, much loved by its locals. The Peak District encompasses every variety of terrain, from the luxurious grounds of Chatsworth, landscaped by Capability Brown, to gentle Dove Dale, to the rough moors with their superb gritstone rock-climbing areas (in which two Manchester plumbers, Joe Brown and Don Whillans, carried out "the working class revolution in climbing" in the 1950s, taking the art to new levels of difficulty). In between Chatsworth's gardens and the gritstone climbs is Kinder Scout, focus of the most famous battle for access. The highest and wildest point in the Peak District, it was "king's land"—that is, public land—until 1836, when an enclosure act divided the land up among the adjacent landowners, giving the lion's share to the duke of Devonshire, owner of Chatsworth. The fifteen square miles of Kinder Scout became completely inaccessible to the public, for no footpath went near its summit. Walkers called it "the forbidden mountain." An old Roman road across the base had been the main way of traversing the region, but in 1821 this right-of-way—Doctor's Gate, it was called—was illegally closed by the land's owner, Lord Howard. At the end of the nineteenth century, negotiations to open it began, and the rambling clubs of Manchester and Sheffield began to take direct action. In 1909 the Sheffield Clarion Ramblers walked the length of Doctor's Gate, and the Manchester Ramblers "defiantly" walked it for five years. The lord continued posting No Road signs, wiring up the gate at one end, padlocking the way, but he finally lost. Today Doctor's Gate is, with a few minor changes of route, the public route it had been for nearly two millennia before.

The crest of Kinder Scout posed a bigger problem. Benny Rothman, the secretary of the Manchester branch of the British Workers Sports Federation, writes of the grim cities during the industrial depression of the 1930s, "Town dwellers lived for weekends when they could go camping in the country, while unemployed young people would return home just to 'sign on' at the Labor Exchanges and collect their dole money. Rambling, cycling and camping clubs grew in

---

presents his compliments to Mr. Lawrence Boythorn, and has to call his attention to the fact that the green

---

membership. . . . The feeling of being close to nature receded as the crowds grew, and ramblers looked longingly at the acres of empty peat bogs, moorlands and the tops, which were forbidden territory. They were not just forbidden, they were guarded by gamekeepers armed with sticks, which some were not afraid to use against solitary walkers." In 1932 the BWSF decided to organize a mass trespass to publicize the situation, and Rothman gave interviews to newspapers. Though opposed by other ramblers' clubs, the young radicals drew four hundred ramblers to the nearby town of Hayfield anyway, along with a third of the Derbyshire Police Force. Partway up, Rothman gave a stirring speech about the history of the access-to-mountains movement, to much applause. Farther up the steep approach to Kinder Scout's plateau, about twenty to thirty gamekeepers appeared, shouting, threatening the walkers with their sticks, and getting the worst of the scuffles they initiated. At the crest, the trespassers were joined by members of the Sheffield clubs and latecomers from Manchester.

For this temporary victory and scenic view, Rothman and five others were arrested. One case was dismissed. The others received jail sentences from two to six months for "incitement to riotous assembly." Outrage over the sentences galvanized other ramblers and members of the public and sent both the curious and the committed to Kinder Scout. Annual rallies protesting lack of access had been held at Winants Pass in the Peak before, but the one that year brought in ten thousand ramblers, and further mass trespasses and demonstrations were held in the wake of this verdict. The politics of walking heated up. In 1935 the national federation of rambling associations became the Ramblers' Association, which stepped up activism on behalf of access, and in 1939 a bill for access was put before Parliament, unsuccessfully. In 1949 a stronger bill succeeded. The National Parks and Access to the Countryside Act changed the rules. The national parks didn't amount to much, but the access did. Every county council in England and Wales was required to map all the rights-of-way in its jurisdiction, and once the paths had been mapped, they were considered definitive. The burden had shifted to the landowner to prove that a right-of-way didn't exist, rather than to the walker to prove that one did. And these rights-of-way have ever since appeared on the Ordnance Survey maps, making the routes accessible to everyone. Local councils were also required to create a "review map" of appropriate open-space areas and then to negotiate for them to become accessible to walkers—not as strong as an absolute right of access, but a great improvement. More recently a

---

pathway by the old parsonage-house, now the property of Mr. Lawrence Boythorn, is Sir Leicester's right number of long-distance trails have been created, making it possible for people to walk or backpack across Britain for days or weeks. In recent years, walkers have grown restless. On the fiftieth anniversary of its creation, the Ramblers' Association began holding "Forbidden Britain" mass trespasses of its own, and in 1997 the Labour party campaigned on a promise to support "right to roam" legislation that would, more than a century since Bryce's 1884 bill, at last open the countryside to the citizens. Recently, more radical new groups such as This Land Is Ours and Reclaim the Streets have taken direct action to enlarge the public sphere, and though walking is less central to their democratic and ecological agenda, the same populist issues of access and preservation prevail.

And this is the great irony—or poetic justice—of the history of rural walking; that a taste that began in aristocratic gardens should end up as an assault on private property as an absolute right and privilege. The gardens and parks in which the culture of walking had begun were closed spaces, often walled or secured by ditches, accessible to a privileged few, and sometimes created on land seized by enclosure. Yet a democratic principle had been implicit in the development of the English garden, in the way trees, water, and land were allowed their natural contours rather than being pushed into geometric forms, in the dissolution of the walls around the garden, in the increasingly mobile experience of walking through these increasingly informal spaces. The spread of the taste for walking in the landscape obliged some of the descendants of these aristocrats to live up to the principles implicit in their gardens. It may yet open the whole of Britain to walkers.

Walking for pleasure had joined the repertoire of human possibilities, and some of those enjoying the expansion returned the favor and changed the world, making it into a version of the garden—this time a public garden without walls. The terrain shaped by walkers' clubs is spread differently across different countries. In the United States it's a patchwork of wild places and a broad political movement bent on saving the organic world. Radiating from Austria are several hundred lodges scattered across twenty-one countries and more than half a million outdoor types with their own environmentalist bent. In Britain it's 140,000 miles of paths and a truculent attitude about the landed gentry. Walking has become one of the forces that has made the modern world—often by serving as a counter-principle to economics.

---

of way, being in fact a portion of the park of Chesney Wold, and that Sir Leicester finds it convenient to

---

The impulse to organize around walking is at first an odd one. After all, those who value walking often speak of independence, solitude, and the freedom that comes from lack of structure and regimentation. But there are three prerequisites to going out into the world to walk for pleasure. One must have free time, a place to go, and a body unhindered by illness or social restraints. These basic freedoms have been the subjects of countless struggles, and it makes perfect sense that the laborers' organizations campaigning first for eight- or ten-hour workdays and then for five-day work weeks—struggling for free time—should also concern themselves with securing space in which to enjoy this hard-won time. Others too have campaigned for space, and though I have focused on wilderness and rural space, another rich history concerns the development of urban parks such as Central Park, a democratic and Romantic project to bring the rural virtues to city dwellers without resources to leave the city. The unhindered body is a more subtle subject. The early Sierra Club, with unchaperoned women sleeping on pinebough beds and climbing mountains in bloomers, suggests that in California, liberation—or some genteel degree of it—was a by-product: for Victorian clothing imprisoned women in the proprieties of shallow breaths, short steps, precarious balance. The nudism of early German and Austrian outdoor clubs suggests that for some, heading for the hills was part of a wider project of embracing the natural, a natural defined to include the erotic, and even for those who remained clothed, the clothes were the informal shorts that displayed the body. As for British workers—one only has to read Friedrich Engels's *Condition of the Working Class in England*, about living and working conditions so dire they deformed and diseased factory workers' bodies, to understand why striding across open space under clean skies was a liberation many were willing to fight for. Walking in the landscape was a reaction against the transformations that were making the middle-class body an anachronism locked away in homes and offices and laborers' bodies part of the industrial machinery.

The writers at the beginning of this history of walking in the landscape, Rousseau and Wordsworth, linked social liberation with a passion for nature (though, fortunately, neither of them could have envisioned the Boy Scouts, the outdoor equipment industry, and other far-flung effects of the culture of walking). The walking clubs brought many ordinary people closer to their notion of the ideal walker, moving without impediments across the landscape.

----

close up the same.' "—CHARLES DICKENS, *BLEAK HOUSE*

Part III

LIVES OF THE
STREETS

Chapter 11

THE SOLITARY STROLLER
AND THE CITY

I lived in rural New Mexico long enough that when I came back home to San Francisco, I saw it for the first time as a stranger might. The exuberance of spring was urban for me that year, and I finally understood all those country songs about the lure of the bright lights of town. I walked everywhere in the balmy days and nights of May, amazed at how many possibilities could be crammed within the radius of those walks and thrilled by the idea I could just wander out the front door to find them. Every building, every storefront, seemed to open onto a different world, compressing all the variety of human life into a jumble of possibilities made all the richer by the conjunctions. Just as a bookshelf can jam together Japanese poetry, Mexican history, and Russian novels, so the buildings of my city contained Zen centers, Pentecostal churches, tattoo parlors, produce stores, burrito places, movie palaces, dim sum shops. Even the most ordinary things struck me with wonder, and the people on the street offered a thousand glimpses of lives like and utterly unlike mine.

Cities have always offered anonymity, variety, and conjunction, qualities best basked in by walking: one does not have to go into the bakery or the fortune-teller's, only to know that one might. A city always contains more than any inhabitant can know, and a great city always makes the unknown and the possible spurs to the imagination. San Francisco has long been called the most European of American cities, a comment more often made than explained. What I think its

---

There are few greater delights than to walk up and down them in the evening alone with thousands of other people,

---

speakers mean is that San Francisco, in its scale and its street life, keeps alive the idea of a city as a place of unmediated encounters, while most American cities are becoming more and more like enlarged suburbs, scrupulously controlled and segregated, designed for the noninteractions of motorists shuttling between private places rather than the interactions of pedestrians in public ones. San Francisco has water on three sides and a ridge on the fourth to keep it from sprawling, and several neighborhoods of lively streets. Truly urban density, beautiful buildings, views of the bay and the ocean from the crests of its hills, cafés and bars everywhere, suggest different priorities for space and time than in most American cities, as does the (gentrification-threatened) tradition of artists, poets, and social and political radicals making lives about other things than getting and spending.

My first Saturday back, I sauntered over to nearby Golden Gate Park, which lacks the splendor of a wilderness but has given me many compensatory pleasures: musicians practicing in the reverberant pedestrian underpasses, old Chinese women doing martial arts in formation, strolling Russian émigrés murmuring to each other in the velvet slurp of their mother tongue, dog walkers being yanked into the primeval world of canine joys, and access by foot to the shores of the Pacific. That morning, at the park's bandshell, the local radio variety show had joined forces with the "Watershed Poetry Festival," and I watched for a while. Former poet laureate of the United States Robert Hass was coaching children to read their poetry into the microphone onstage, and some poets I knew were standing in the wings. I went up to say hello to them, and they showed me their brand-new wedding rings and introduced me to more poets, and then I ran into the great California historian Malcolm Margolin, who told me stories that made me laugh. This was the daytime marvel of cities for me: coincidences, the mingling of many kinds of people, poetry given away to strangers under the open sky.

Margolin's publishing house, Heydey Press, was displaying its wares along with those of some other small presses and literary projects, and he handed me a book off his table titled *920 O'Farrell Street*. A memoir by Harriet Lane Levy, it recounted her own marvelous experiences growing up in San Francisco in the 1870s and 1880s. In her day, walking the streets of the city was as organized an entertainment as a modern excursion to the movies. "On Saturday night," she wrote, "the city joined in the promenade on Market Street, the broad thoroughfare that begins at the waterfront and cuts its straight path of miles to Twin Peaks.

---

up and down, relishing the lights coming through the trees or shining from the facades, listening to the sounds of

---

The sidewalks were wide and the crowd walking toward the bay met the crowd walking toward the ocean. The outpouring of the population was spontaneous as if in response to an urge for instant celebration. Every quarter of the city discharged its residents into the broad procession. Ladies and gentlemen of imposing social repute; their German and Irish servant girls, arms held fast in the arms of their sweethearts; French, Spaniards, gaunt, hard-working Portuguese; Mexicans, the Indian showing in reddened skin and high cheekbone—everybody, anybody, left home and shop, hotel, restaurant, and beer garden to empty into Market Street in a river of color. Sailors of every nation deserted their ships at the water front and, hurrying up Market Street in groups, joined the vibrating mass excited by the lights and stir and the gaiety of the throng. 'This is San Francisco,' their faces said. It was carnival; no confetti, but the air a criss-cross of a thousand messages; no masks, but eyes frankly charged with challenge. Down Market from Powell to Kearny, three long blocks, up Kearny to Bush, three short ones, then back again, over and over for hours, until a glance of curiosity deepened to one of interest; interest expanded into a smile, and a smile into anything. Father and I went downtown every Saturday night. We walked through avenues of light in a world hardly solid. Something was happening everywhere, every minute, something to be happy about. . . . We walked and walked and still something kept happening afresh." Market Street, which was once a great promenade, is still the city's central traffic artery, but decades of tearing it up and redeveloping it have deprived it of its social glory. Jack Kerouac managed to have two visions on it late in the 1940s or early in the 1950s, and he would probably embrace its freeway-shadowed midtown population of panhandlers and people running sidewalk sales out of shopping carts. Levy's downtown stretch is now trod by office workers and shoppers and by tourists swarming around the Powell Street cable car turnaround; more than a mile farther uptown, Market Street finally bursts into vigorous pedestrian life again for a few blocks before it crosses Castro Street and begins its steep ascent of Twin Peaks.

The history of both urban and rural walking is a history of freedom and of the definition of pleasure. But rural walking has found a moral imperative in the love of nature that has allowed it to defend and open up the countryside. Urban walking has always been a shadier business, easily turning into soliciting, cruising,

---

music and foreign voices and traffic, enjoying the smell of flowers and good food and the air from the nearby sea.

---

promenading, shopping, rioting, protesting, skulking, loitering, and other activities that, however enjoyable, hardly have the high moral tone of nature appreciation. Thus no similar defense has been mounted for the preservation of urban space, save by a few civil libertarians and urban theorists (who seldom note that public space is used and inhabited largely by walking it). Yet urban walking seems in many ways more like primordial hunting and gathering than walking in the country. For most of us the country or the wilderness is a place we walk through and look at, but seldom make things in or take things from (remember the famous Sierra Club dictum, "Take only photographs, leave only footprints"). In the city, the biological spectrum has been nearly reduced to the human and a few scavenger species, but the range of activities remains wide. Just as a gatherer may pause to note a tree whose acorns will be bountiful in six months or inspect a potential supply of basket canes, so an urban walker may note a grocery open late or a place to get shoes resoled, or detour by the post office. Too, the average rural walker looks at the general—the view, the beauty—and the landscape moves by as a gently modulated continuity: a crest long in view is reached, a forest thins out to become a meadow. The urbanite is on the lookout for particulars, for opportunities, individuals, and supplies, and the changes are abrupt. Of course the city resembles primordial life more than the country in a less charming way too; while nonhuman predators have been radically reduced in North America and eliminated in Europe, the possibility of human predators keeps city dwellers in a state of heightened alertness, at least in some times and places.

Those first months at home were so enchanting that I kept a walking journal and later that glorious summer wrote, "I suddenly realized I'd spent seven hours at the desk without a real interruption and was getting nervous and hunchbacked, walked to the Clay Theater on upper Fillmore via a passage on Broderick I'd never seen before—handsome squat old Victorians near the housing projects— and was pleased as ever when the familiar yielded up the unknown. The film was *When the Cat's Away*, about a solitary young Parisienne forced to meet her Place de Bastille neighbors when her cat vanishes, full of uneventful events and people with seesaw strides and rooftops and mumbling slang, and when it got out I was exhilarated and the night was dark with a pearly mist of fog on it. I walked back fast, first along California, past a couple—her unexceptional, him in a well-tailored brown suit with the knock knees of someone who'd spent time in leg braces—and ignored the bus, and did the same on Divisadero with that bus.

The sidewalks are lined with small shops, bars, stalls, dance halls, movies, booths lighted by acetylene lamps, and

---

Slowed down at an antique store window to look at a big creamy vase with blue Chinese sages painted on it, then a few doors down saw a balding Chinese man holding a toddler boy up to the glass of a store, where a woman on the inside was playing with him through the glass. To their confusion, I beamed. There's a way the artificial lights and natural darkness of nightwalks turn the day's continuum into a theater of tableaux, vignettes, set pieces, and there's always the unsettling pleasure of your shadow growing and shrinking as you move from streetlight to streetlight. Dodging a car as a traffic light changed, I broke into a canter and it felt so good I loped along a few more blocks without getting winded, though I got warm.

"All along Divisadero keeping an eye on the other people and on the open venues—liquor stores and smoke shops—and then turned up my own street. At a cross street a young black guy in a watch cap and dark clothes was running downhill at me at a great clip, and I looked around to suss up my options just in case—I mean if Queen Victoria was moving toward you that fast you'd take note. He saw my hesitation and assured me in the sweetest young man's voice, 'I'm not after you; I'm just *late*' and dashed past me, so I said, 'Good luck' and then, when he was into the street and I had time to collect my thoughts, 'Sorry to look suspicious, but you were kind of speedy.' He laughed, and then I did, and in a minute I recalled all the other encounters I'd had around the 'hood lately that might have had the earmarks of trouble but unfolded as pure civility and was pleased that I'd been prepared without being alarmed. At that moment, I looked up and saw in a top-floor window the same poster of Man Ray's *A l'heure de l'observatoire*—his painting of the sunset sky with the long red lips floating across it—that I'd seen in another window somewhere else in town a night or two before. This poster was bigger, and this night was more exuberant; seeing *A l'heure* twice seemed magic. Home in about twenty minutes at most."

Streets are the space left over between buildings. A house alone is an island surrounded by a sea of open space, and the villages that preceded cities were no more than archipelagos in that same sea. But as more and more buildings arose, they became a continent, the remaining open space no longer like the sea but like rivers, canals, and streams running between the land masses. People no longer moved anyhow in the open sea of rural space but traveled up and down the

---

everywhere are strange faces, strange costumes, strange and delightful impressions. To walk up such a street into the

---

streets, and just as narrowing a waterway increases flow and speed, so turning open space into the spillways of streets directs and intensifies the flood of walkers. In great cities, spaces as well as places are designed and built: walking, witnessing, being in public, are as much part of the design and purpose as is being inside to eat, sleep, make shoes or love or music. The word *citizen* has to do with cities, and the ideal city is organized around citizenship—around participation in public life.

Most American cities and towns, however, are organized around consumption and production, as were the dire industrial cities of England, and public space is merely the void between workplaces, shops, and dwellings. Walking is only the beginning of citizenship, but through it the citizen knows his or her city and fellow citizens and truly inhabits the city rather than a small privatized part thereof. Walking the streets is what links up reading the map with living one's life, the personal microcosm with the public macrocosm; it makes sense of the maze all around. In her celebrated *Death and Life of Great American Cities*, Jane Jacobs describes how a popular, well-used street is kept safe from crime merely by the many people going by. Walking maintains the publicness and viability of public space. "What distinguishes the city," writes Franco Moretti, "is that its spatial structure (basically its concentration) is functional to the intensification of mobility: spatial mobility, naturally enough, but mainly social mobility."

The very word *street* has a rough, dirty magic to it, summoning up the low, the common, the erotic, the dangerous, the revolutionary. A man of the streets is only a populist, but a woman of the streets is, like a streetwalker, a seller of her sexuality. Street kids are urchins, beggars, and runaways, and the new term *street person* describes those who have no other home. *Street-smart* means someone wise in the ways of the city and well able to survive in it, while "to the streets" is the classic cry of urban revolution, for the streets are where people become the public and where their power resides. *The street* means life in the heady currents of the urban river in which everyone and everything can mingle. It is exactly this social mobility, this lack of compartments and distinctions, that gives the street its danger and its magic, the danger and magic of water in which everything runs together.

In feudal Europe only city dwellers were free of the hierarchical bonds that structured the rest of society—in England, for example, a serf could become free by living for a year and a day in a free town. The quality of freedom within cities

---

quieter, more formal part of town, is to be part of a procession, part of a ceaseless ceremony of being initiated into

---

then was limited, however, for their streets were usually dirty, dangerous, and dark. Cities often imposed a curfew and closed their gates at sunset. Only in the Renaissance did the cities of Europe begin to improve their paving, their sanitation, and their safety. In eighteenth-century London and Paris, going out anywhere at night was as dangerous as the worst slums are supposed to be nowadays, and if you wanted to see where you were going, you hired a torchbearer (and the young London torch carriers—link boys, they were called—often doubled as procurers). Even in daylight, carriages terrorized pedestrians. Before the eighteenth century, few seem to have walked these streets for pleasure, and only in the nineteenth century did places as clean, safe, and illuminated as modern cities begin to emerge. All the furniture and codes that give modern streets their orderliness—raised sidewalks, streetlights, street names, building numbers, drains, traffic rules, and traffic signals—are relatively recent innovations.

Idyllic spaces had been created for the urban rich—tree-lined promenades, semipublic gardens and parks. But these places that preceded the public park were anti-streets, segregated by class and disconnected from everyday life (unlike the pedestrian *corsos* and paseos of the plazas and squares of Mediterranean and Latin countries and Levy's Market Street promenade—or London's anomalous Hyde Park, which accommodated both carriage promenades for the rich and open-air oratory for the radical). Though politics, flirtations, and commerce might be conducted in them, they were little more than outdoor salons and ballrooms. And from the mile-long Cours de la Reine built in Paris in 1616 to Mexico City's Alameda to New York's Central Park built during the 1850s, such places tended to attract people whose desire to display their wealth was better served by promenading in carriages than walking. On the Cours de la Reine, the carriages would gather so thickly a traffic jam would result, which may be why in 1700 a fashion for getting out and dancing by torchlight on the central round developed.

Though Central Park was shaped by more-or-less democratic impulses, English landscape garden aesthetics, and the example of Liverpool's public park, poor New Yorkers often paid to go to private parks akin to Vauxhall Gardens instead, where they might drink beer, dance the polka, or otherwise engage in plebeian versions of pleasure. Even those who wished only to have an uplifting stroll, as the park's codesigner Frederick Law Olmsted had intended them to, found obstacles. Central Park became a great promenade for the rich, and once

the city and rededicating the city itself.—J. B. JACKSON, "THE STRANGER'S PATH"   . . . *after scrambling under* again carriages segregated the society. In their history of the park and its city, Ray Rosenzweig and Elizabeth Blackmar write, "Earlier in the [nineteenth] century the late afternoon, early evening, and Sunday promenades of affluent New Yorkers had evolved into parades of high fashion; the wide thoroughfares of Broadway, the Battery, and Fifth Avenue had become a public setting in which to see and be seen. By midcentury, however, the fashionable Broadway and Battery promenades had declined as 'respectable' citizens lost control over these public spaces. . . . Both men and women wanted grander public space for a new form of public promenading—by carriage. In the mid-nineteenth century, carriage ownership was becoming a defining feature of urban upper-class status." The rich went to Central Park, and a populist journalist said, "I hear that pedestrians have acquired a bad habit of being accidentally run over in that neighborhood."

Just as poorer people continued to promenade in New York's Battery, so their Parisian counterparts strolled along the peripheries of the city, often under avenues of trees planted to shade just such excursions. After the Revolution, Paris's Tuileries could be entered by anyone the guards deemed properly dressed. Private pleasure gardens modeled after London's famous Vauxhall Gardens, including Ranelagh and Cremorne Gardens in London itself; Vienna's Augarten; New York's Elysian Fields, Castle Gardens, and Harlem Gardens; and Copenhagen's Tivoli Gardens (sole survivor of them all) sorted out people by the simpler criterion of ability to pay. Elsewhere in these cities, markets, fairs, and processions brought festivity to the sites of everyday life, and the stroll was not so segregated. To me, the magic of the street is the mingling of the errand and the epiphany, and no such gardens seem to have flourished in Italy, perhaps because they were unneeded.

Italian cities have long been held up as ideals, not least by New Yorkers and Londoners enthralled by the ways their architecture gives beauty and meaning to everyday acts. Since at least the seventeenth century, foreigners have been moving there to bask in the light and the life. Bernard Rudofsky, nominally a New Yorker, spent a good deal of time in Italy and sang its praises in his 1969 *Streets for People: A Primer for Americans.* For those who consider New York the exemplary American pedestrian city, Rudofsky's conviction that it is abysmal is startling. His book uses primarily Italian examples to demonstrate the ways plazas and streets can function to tie a city together socially and architecturally. "It simply never occurs to us to make streets into oases rather than deserts," he says at the begin-

----

bellies of horses, through wheels, and over posts and rails, we reached the gardens, where were already many ning. "In countries where their function has not yet deteriorated into highways and parking lots, a number of arrangements make streets fit for humans. . . . The most refined street coverings, a tangible expression of civic solidarity—or, should one say, of philanthropy, are arcades. Apart from lending unity to the streetscape, they often take the place of the ancient forums." Descendants of the Greek stoa and *peripatos*, arcaded streets blur the boundaries between inside and out and pay architectural tribute to the pedestrian life that takes place beneath them. Rudofsky singles out Bologna's famous *portici*, a four-mile-long covered walkway running from the central square to the countryside; Milan's Galleria, less strictly commercial in its functions than the upscale shopping malls modeled and named after it; the winding streets of Perugia; the car-free streets of Siena; and Brisinghella's second-story public arcades. He writes with passionate enthusiasm about the Italian predinner stroll—the *passaggiata*—for which many towns close down their main streets to wheeled traffic, contrasting it with the American cocktail hour. For Italians, he says, the street is the pivotal social space, for meeting, debating, courting, buying, and selling.

The New York dance critic Edwin Denby wrote, about the same time as Rudofsky, of his own appreciation of Italian walkers. "In ancient Italian towns the narrow main street at dusk becomes a kind of theatre. The community strolls affably and looks itself over. The girls and the young men, from fifteen to twenty-two, display their charm to one another with a lively sociability. The more grace they show the better the community likes them. In Florence or in Naples, in the ancient city slums the young people are virtuoso performers, and they do a bit of promenading any time they are not busy." Of young Romans, he wrote, "Their stroll is as responsive as if it were a physical conversation." Elsewhere, he instructs dance students to watch the walk of various types: "Americans occupy a much larger space than their actual bodies do. This annoys many Europeans; it annoys their instinct of modesty. But it has a beauty of its own, that a few of them appreciate. . . . For myself I think the walk of New Yorkers is amazingly beautiful, so large and clear." In Italy walking in the city is a universal cultural activity rather than the subject of individual forays and accounts. From Dante pacing out his exile in Verona and Ravenna to Primo Levi walking home from Auschwitz, Italy has not lacked great walkers—but urban walking itself seems to be more part of a universal culture than the focus of particular experience (save that by foreigners, copiously recorded, and the cinematic strolls of such characters as the

---

thousand persons. . . . We walked twice round and were rejoiced to come away, though with the same difficulties

---

streetwalker in Federico Fellini's *Nights of Cabiria* and the protagonists in Vittorio De Sica's *Bicycle Thief* and in many of Michelangelo Antonioni's films). However, the cities that are neither so accommodating as Naples nor so forbidding as Los Angeles—London, New York—have produced their own fugitive culture of walking. In London, from the eighteenth century on, the great accounts of walking have to do not with the cheerful and open display of ordinary life and desires but with nocturnal scenes, crimes, sufferings, outcasts, and the darker side of the imagination, and it is this tradition that New York assumes.

In 1711 the essayist Joseph Addison wrote, "When I am in a serious Humour, I very often walk by my self in Westminster Abbey; where the Gloominess of the Place, and the Use to which it is applied . . . are apt to fill the Mind with a kind of Melancholy, or rather Thoughtfulness, that is not disagreeable." At the time he wrote, walking the city streets was perilous, as John Gay pointed out in his 1716 poem *Trivia; or, The Art of Walking the Streets of London.* Travel through the city was as dangerous as cross-country travel: the streets were full of sewage and garbage, many of the trades were filthy, the air was already bad, cheap gin had ravaged the city's poor the way crack did American inner cities in the 1980s, and an underclass of criminals and desperate souls thronged the streets. Carriages jostled and mangled pedestrians without fear of reprisal, beggars solicited passersby, and street sellers called out their wares. The accounts of the time are full of the fears of the wealthy to go out at all and of young women lured or forced into sexual labor: prostitutes were everywhere. This is why Gay focuses on urban walking as an *art*—an art of protecting oneself from splashes, assaults, and indignities:

> Though you through cleanlier allies wind by day,
> To shun the hurries of the publick way,
> Yet ne'er to those dark paths by night retire;
> Mind only safety, and contemn the mire.

Like Dr. Johnson's 1738 poem "London," Gay's *Trivia* uses a classical model to mock the present. Divided into three books—the first on the implements and techniques of walking the streets, the second on walking by day, the third on walking by night—the poem makes it clear that the minutia of everyday life can

as at our entrance.—HORACE WALPOLE, IN A LETTER TO GEORGE MONTAGU ON A "RIDOTTO" AT VAUXHALL only be observed scornfully. The high-flown style cannot but contrast abrasively with such small subjects, with something of the same mockery he brought to his *Beggars' Opera*. Gay tries—

> Here I remark each walker's diff'rent face,
> And in their look their various bus'ness trace.

—but he ends by despising everyone, assuming he can read their tawdry lives in their faces. At the end of Gay's century Wordsworth "goes forward with the crowd," seeing a mystery in the face of each stranger; while William Blake wanders "each charter'd street / And mark in every face I meet / Marks of weakness, marks of woe:"—the cry of a chimney sweep, the curse of a young harlot. Earlier eighteenth-century literary language was not supple enough or personal enough to connect the life of the imagination to that of the street. Johnson had been one of those desperate London walkers in his early years there—in the late 1730s, when he and his friend, the poet and rogue Richard Savage, were too poor to pay for lodgings, they used to walk the streets and squares all night talking insurrection and glory—but he didn't write about it. Boswell did in his *Life of Johnson*, but for Boswell, the darkness of night and anonymity of the streets were a less reflective opportunity, as his London diary records: "I should have been at Lady Northumberland's rout tonight, but my barber fell sick [meaning his hair was not properly powdered]; so I sallied to the streets, and just at the bottom of our own, I picked up a fresh, agreeable young girl called Alice Gibbs. We went down a lane to a snug place. . . ." Of Alice Gibbs's impression of the streets and the night, we have no record.

That few women other than prostitutes were free to wander the streets and that wandering the street was often enough to cause a woman to be considered a prostitute are matters troubling enough to be taken up elsewhere. Here I merely want to comment on their presence in the street and in the night, habitats in which they more than almost any other kind of walker became natives. Until the twentieth century women seldom walked the city for their own pleasure, and prostitutes have left us almost no records of their experience. The eighteenth century was immodest enough to have a few famous novels about prostitutes, but Fanny Hill's courtesan life was all indoors, Moll Flanders's was entirely practical, and both of them were creations of male authors whose work was at least partly

GARDENS, 1769   *Walking the streets so constantly as he did . . . gave him an opportunity of examining into* speculative. Then as now, however, a complex culture of working the streets must have existed, each city mapped according to safety and the economics of male desire. There have been many attempts to confine such activity; Byzantine-era Constantinople had its "street of harlots," Tokyo from the seventeenth to the twentieth century had a gated pleasure district, nineteenth-century San Francisco had its notorious Barbary Coast, and many turn-of-the-century American cities had red-light districts, the most famous of which was New Orleans's Storyville, where jazz is reputed to have been born. But prostitution wandered outside these bounds, and the population of such women was enormous: 50,000 in 1793, when London had a total population of one million, estimated one expert. By the mid-nineteenth century they were to be found in the most fashionable parts of London too: social reformer Henry Mayhew's report refers to "the circulating harlotry of the Haymarket and Regent Street," as well as to the women working in the city's parks and promenades.

Twenty-odd years ago a researcher on prostitution reported, "Prostitution streetscapes are composed of *strolls*, loosely defined areas where the women solicit. . . . On the stroll the prostitute moves around to entice or enjoin customers, reduce boredom, keep warm and reduce visibility [to the police]. Part of most streetscapes resemble common greens, areas to which all have unimpeded access. Here women assemble in groups of two to four, laughing, talking and joking among themselves. . . . Working the same stroll infuses much needed predictability into an illegal, sometimes dangerous environment." And Dolores French, an advocate for prostitutes' rights, worked the streets herself and reports that her fellow streetwalkers "think that women who work in whorehouses have too many restrictions and rules" while the street "welcomed everyone democratically. . . . They felt they were like cowboys out on the range, or spies on a dangerous mission. They bragged about how free they were. . . . They had no one to answer to but themselves." The same refrains—freedom, democracy, danger—come up in this as in the other ways of occupying the streets.

In the eighteenth-century city, a new image of what it means to be human had arisen, an image of one possessed of the freedom and isolation of the traveler, and travelers, however wide or narrow their scope, became emblematic figures. Richard Savage proposed this early with a 1729 poem called *The Wanderer;* and the aptly named George Walker inaugurated the new century with his novel *The Vagabond,* followed in 1814 by Fanny Burney's *Wanderer.* Wordsworth had his

---

the condition of every poor person that he met. Which he did, with so well practiced a sagacity, as could seldom be

Excursion (whose first two sections were titled "The Wanderer" and "The Solitary"); Coleridge's Ancient Mariner was condemned like the Wandering Jew to roam; and the Wandering Jew himself was a popular subject for Romantics in Britain and on the continent.

The literary historian Raymond Williams remarks, "Perception of the new qualities of the modern city had been associated, from the beginning, with a man walking, as if alone, in its streets." He cites Blake and Wordsworth as founders of this tradition, but it was De Quincey who wrote of it most poignantly. In the beginning of *Confessions of an English Opium Eater*, De Quincey tells of how at the age of seventeen he had run away from a dull school and his unsympathetic guardians and landed in London. There he was afraid to contact the few people he knew and unable to seek work without connections. So for sixteen weeks in the summer and fall of 1802 he starved, having found no other support in London but a home in an all-but-abandoned mansion whose other resident was a forlorn female child. He fell into a spectral existence shared with a few other children, and he wandered the streets restlessly. Streets were already a place for those who had no place, a site to measure sorrow and loneliness in the length of walks. "Being myself at that time, of necessity, a peripatetic, or walker of the streets, I naturally fell in more frequently with those female peripatetics who are technically called street-walkers. Many of these women had occasionally taken my part against watchmen who wished to drive me off the steps of houses where I was sitting." He was befriended by one, a girl named Ann—"timid and dejected to a degree which showed how deeply sorrow had taken hold of her young heart"— who was younger than he and who had turned to the streets after being cheated of a minor inheritance. Once when they were "pacing slowly along Oxford Street, and after a day when I had felt unusually ill and faint, I requested her to turn off with me into Soho Square," and he fainted. She spent what little she had on hot spiced wine to revive him. That he was never able to find her again after his fortune changed was, he declares, one of the great tragedies of his life. For De Quincey, his sojourn in London was one of the most deeply felt passages in his long life, though it had no sequel: the rest of his book is given over to its putative subject, the effects of opium, and the rest of his life to rural places.

Charles Dickens was different, in that he chose such urban walking and his writing explored it thoroughly over the years. He is the great poet of London life, and some of his novels seem as much dramas of place as of people. Think of

imposed upon. And every man that follows his example, will soon find, that this practice will lead him into the

Our Mutual Friend, where the great euphemistic piles of dust, the dim taxidermy and skeleton shop, the expensively icy interiors of the wealthy, are portraits of those associated with them. People and places become one another—a character may only be identified as an atmosphere or a principle, a place may take on a full-fledged personality. "And this kind of realism can only be gained by walking dreamily in a place; it cannot be gained by walking observantly," wrote one of his best interpreters, G. K. Chesterton. He attributed Dickens's acute sense of place to the well-known episode in his boyhood when his father was locked up in a debtor's prison and Dickens himself was put to work in a blacking factory and lodged in a nearby roominghouse, a desolate child abandoned to the city and its strangers. "Few of us understand the street," Chesterton writes. "Even when we step into it, we step into it doubtfully, as into a house or room of strangers. Few of us see through the shining riddle of the street, the strange folk that belong to the street only—the street-walker or the street arab, the nomads who, generation after generation have kept their ancient secrets in the full blaze of the sun. Of the street at night many of us know less. The street at night is a great house locked up. But Dickens had, if ever man had, the key of the street. . . . He could open the inmost door of his house—the door that leads onto the secret passage which is lined with houses and roofed with stars." Dickens is among the first to indicate all the other things urban walking can be: his novels are full of detectives and police inspectors, of criminals who stalk, lovers who seek and damned souls who flee. The city becomes a tangle through which all the characters wander in a colossal game of hide and seek, and only a vast city could allow his intricate plots so full of crossed paths and overlapping lives. But when he wrote about his own experiences of London, it was often an abandoned city.

"If I couldn't walk fast and far, I should explode and perish," he once told a friend, and he walked so fast and far that few ever managed to accompany him. He was a solitary walker, and his walks served innumerable purposes. "I am both a town traveller and a country traveller, and am always on the road," he introduces himself in his essay collection *The Uncommercial Traveller.* "Figuratively speaking, I travel for the great house of Human Interest Brothers, and have rather a large connection in the fancy goods way. Literally speaking, I am always wandering here and there from my rooms in Covent-garden, London." This metaphysical version of the commercial traveler is an inadequate description of his role, and he tried on many others. He was an athlete: "So much of my travelling

---

exercise of more charity, than is possible to be practiced in carriages of any kind.—PATRICK DELANY, OBSERVATIONS is done on foot, that if I cherished better propensities, I should probably be found registered in sporting newspapers under some such title as the Elastic Novice, challenging all eleven stone mankind to competition in walking. My last special feat was turning out of bed at two, after a hard day, pedestrian and otherwise, and walking thirty miles into the country to breakfast. The road was so lonely in the night that I fell asleep to the monotonous sound of my own feet, doing their regular four miles an hour." And a few essays later, he was a tramp, or a tramp's son: "My walking is of two kinds: one straight on end to a definite goal at a round pace; one, objectless, loitering, and purely vagabond. In the latter state, no gypsy on earth is a greater vagabond than myself; it is so natural to me, and strong with me, that I think I must be the descendant, at no great distance, of some irreclaimable tramp." And he was a cop on the beat, too ethereal to arrest anyone but in his mind: "It is one of my fancies, that even my idlest walk must always have its appointed destination. . . . On such an occasion, it is my habit to regard my walks as my beat, and myself as a higher sort of police-constable doing duty on the same."

And yet despite all these utilitarian occupations and the throngs who populate his books, his own London was often a deserted city, and his walking in it a melancholy pleasure. In an essay on visiting abandoned cemeteries, he wrote, "Whenever I think I deserve particularly well of myself, and have earned the right to enjoy a little treat, I stroll from Covent-garden into the City of London, after business-hours there, on a Saturday, or—better yet—on a Sunday, and roam about its deserted nooks and corners." But the most memorable of them all is "Night Walks," the essay that begins, "Some years ago, a temporary inability to sleep, referable to a distressing impression, caused me to walk about the streets all night, for a series of several nights." He described these walks from midnight till dawn as curative of his distress, and during them "I finished my education in a fair amateur experience of houselessness"—or what is now called homelessness. The city was no longer as dangerous as it had been in Gay's and Johnson's time, but it was lonelier. Eighteenth-century London was crowded, lively, full of predators, spectacles, and badinage between strangers. By the time Dickens was writing about houselessness in 1860, London was many times as large, but the mob so feared in the eighteenth century had in the nineteenth been largely domesticated as the crowd, a quiet, drab mass going about its private business in public: "Walking the streets under the pattering rain, Houselessness would walk and

---

UPON LORD ORRERY'S "REMARKS ON THE LIFE AND WRITINGS OF JONATHAN SWIFT," 1754   *They don't want*

---

walk and walk, seeing nothing but the interminable tangle of streets, save at a corner, here and there, two policemen in conversation, or the sergeant or inspector looking after his men. Now and then in the night—but rarely—Houselessness would become aware of a furtive head peering out of a doorway a few yards before him, and, coming up with the head, would find a man standing bolt upright to keep within the doorway's shadow, and evidently intent upon no particular service to society. . . . The wild moon and clouds were as restless as an evil conscience in a tumbled bed, and the very shadow of the immensity of London seemed to lie oppressively upon the river." And yet he relishes the lonely nocturnal streets, as he does the graveyards and "shy neighborhoods" and what he quixotically called "Arcadian London"—London out of season, when society had gone en masse to the country, leaving the city in sepulchural peace.

There is a subtle state most dedicated urban walkers know, a sort of basking in solitude—a dark solitude punctuated with encounters as the night sky is punctuated with stars. In the country one's solitude is geographical—one is altogether outside society, so solitude has a sensible geographical explanation, and then there is a kind of communion with the nonhuman. In the city, one is alone because the world is made up of strangers, and to be a stranger surrounded by strangers, to walk along silently bearing one's secrets and imagining those of the people one passes, is among the starkest of luxuries. This uncharted identity with its illimitable possibilities is one of the distinctive qualities of urban living, a liberatory state for those who come to emancipate themselves from family and community expectation, to experiment with subculture and identity. It is an observer's state, cool, withdrawn, with senses sharpened, a good state for anybody who needs to reflect or create. In small doses melancholy, alienation, and introspection are among life's most refined pleasures.

Not long ago I heard the singer and poet Patti Smith answer a radio interviewer's question about what she did to prepare for her performances onstage with "I would roam the streets for a few hours." With that brief comment she summoned up her own outlaw romanticism and the way such walking might toughen and sharpen the sensibility, wrap one in an isolation out of which might come songs fierce enough, words sharp enough, to break that musing silence. Probably her roaming the streets didn't work so well in a lot of American cities,

anything to do with a roof and four walls. How can that be compared to the street? The vice of the children is the where the hotel was moated by a parking lot surrounded by six-lane roads without sidewalks, but she spoke as a New Yorker. Speaking as a Londoner, Virginia Woolf described anonymity as a fine and desirable thing, in her 1930 essay "Street Haunting." Daughter of the great alpinist Leslie Stephen, she had once declared to a friend, "How could I think mountains and climbing romantic? Wasn't I brought up with alpenstocks in my nursery, and a raised map of the Alps, showing every peak my father had climbed? Of course, London and the marshes are the places I like best." London had more than doubled in size since Dickens's night walks, and the streets had changed again to become a refuge. Woolf wrote of the confining oppression of one's own identity, of the way the objects in one's home "enforce the memories of our own experience." And so she set out to buy a pencil in a city where safety and propriety were no longer considerations for a no-longer-young woman on a winter evening, and in recounting—or inventing—her journey, wrote one of the great essays on urban walking.

"As we step out of the house on a fine evening between four and six," she wrote, "we shed the self our friends know us by and become part of that vast republican army of anonymous trampers, whose society is so agreeable after the solitude of one's room." Of the people she observes she says, "Into each of these lives one could penetrate a little way, far enough to give one the illusion that one is not tethered to a single mind, but can put on briefly for a few minutes the bodies and minds of others. One could become a washerwoman, a publican, a street singer." In this anonymous state, "the shell-like covering which our souls have excreted for themselves, to make for themselves a shape distinct from others, is broken, and there is left of all these wrinkles and roughnesses a central oyster of perceptiveness, an enormous eye. How beautiful a street is in winter! It is at once revealed and obscured." She walked down the same Oxford Street De Quincey and Ann had, now lined with windows full of luxuries with which she furnished an imaginary house and life and then banished both to return to her walk. The language of introspection that Wordsworth helped develop and De Quincey and Dickens refined was her language, and the smallest incidents—birds rustling in the shrubbery, a dwarf woman trying on shoes—let her imagination roam farther than her feet, into digressions from which she reluctantly returns to the actualities of her excursion. Walking the streets had come into its own, and the solitude and introspection that had been harrowing for her predecessors was a joy

---

street itself. The street is an addiction even stronger than the thinner they buy in the hardware store. . . . Only the for her. That it was a joy because her identity had become a burden makes it modern.

Like London, New York has seldom prompted unalloyed praise. It is too big, too harsh. As one who knows only smaller cities intimately, I continually underestimate its expanse and wear myself out on distances, just as I do by car in Los Angeles. But I admire Manhattan: the synchronized beehive dance of Grand Central Station, the fast pace people set on the long grids of streets, the jaywalkers, the slower strollers in the squares, the dark-skinned nannies pushing pallid babies before them through the gracious paths of Central Park. Wandering without a clear purpose or sense of direction, I have often disrupted the fast flow of passersby intent on some clear errand or commute, as though I were a butterfly strayed into the beehive, a snag in the stream. Two-thirds of all journeys around downtown and midtown Manhattan are still made on foot, and New York, like London, remains a city of people walking for practical purposes, pouring up and down subway stairs, across intersections—but musers and the nocturnal strollers move to a different tempo. Cities make walking into true travel: danger, exile, discovery, transformation, wrap all around one's home and come right up to the doorstep.

The Italophile Rudofsky uses London to scorn New York: "On the whole North America's Anglo-Saxomania has had a withering effect on its formative years. Surely, the English are not a desirable model for an urban society. No other nation developed such a fierce devotion to country life as they did. And with good reason; their cities have been traditionally among Europe's least wholesome. Englishmen may be intensely loyal to their towns, but the street—the very gauge of urbanity—does not figure large in their affections." New York's streets do figure large in the work of some of its writers. "Paris, c'est une blonde," goes the French song, and Parisian poets have often made their city a woman. New York, with its gridded layout, its dark buildings and looming skyscrapers, its famous toughness, is a masculine city, and if cities are muses, it is no wonder this one's praises have been sung best by its gay poets—Walt Whitman, Frank O'Hara, Allen Ginsberg, and the prose-poet David Wojnarowicz (though everyone from Edith Wharton to Patti Smith has paid homage to this city and its streets).

----

street is theirs. It consoles them for their loneliness and lack of love. It has a dizzying appeal. It gives them the money

----

In Whitman's poems, though he often speaks of himself as happy in the arms of a lover, the passages in which he appears as a solitary walking the streets in quest of that lover—a precursor of the gay cruiser—ring more true. In "Recorders Ages Hence," the immodest Whitman states for the record that he was one "Who often walk'd lonesome walks thinking of his dear friends, his lovers." A few poems later in the final version of *Leaves of Grass*, he begins another poem with the oratorical address "City of orgies, walks and joys." After listing all the possible criteria for a city's illustriousness—houses, ships, parades—he chooses "not these, but as I pass O Manhattan, your frequent and swift flash of eyes offering me love": the walks rather than the orgies, the promises rather than the delivery, are the joys. Whitman was a great maker of inventories and lists to describe variety and quantity and one of the first to love the crowd. It promised new liaisons; it expressed his democratic ideals and oceanic enthusiasms. A few poems past "City of Orgies" comes "To a Stranger": "Passing stranger! You do not know how longingly I look upon you. . . ." For Whitman the momentary glimpse and the intimacy of love were complementary, as were his own emphatic ego and the anonymous mass of crowds. Thus he sang the praises of the swelling metropolis of Manhattan and the new possibilities of urban scale.

Whitman died in 1892, just as everyone else was beginning to celebrate the city. For the first half of the new century, the city seemed emblematic—the capital of the twentieth century, as Paris had been of the nineteenth century. Destiny and hope were urban for both radicals and plutocrats in those days, and New York with its luxury steamers docking and immigrants pouring off Ellis Island, with its skyscrapers even Georgia O'Keeffe couldn't resist painting during her time as a New Yorker, was the definitive modern city. In the 1920s a magazine was devoted to it, the *New Yorker*, whose Talk of the Town section compiled minor street incidents made incandescent by its writers in the tradition of eighteenth-century London's *Spectator* and *Rambler* essays, and it had jazz and the Harlem Renaissance uptown and radical Bohemia down in the Village (and in Central Park was the Ramble, an area so well known for gay cruising it was nicknamed "the fruited plain"). Before World War II, Berenice Abbott roamed New York's streets photographing buildings, and after it, Helen Levitt photographed children playing in the streets while Weegee photographed the underworld of fresh corpses on sidewalks and prostitutes in paddy wagons. One imagines them wandering purposefully like hunter-gatherers with the camera a sort of basket

they never got at home. It gives them rhythm, a tempo, and immediate compensation.—ELENA PONIATOWSKA, "IN laden with the day's spectacles, the photographers leaving us not their walks, as poets do, but the fruits of those walks. Whitman, however, had no successor until after the war, when Allen Ginsberg stepped into his shoes, or at least his loose long lines of celebratory ranting.

Ginsberg is sometimes claimed as a San Franciscan, and he found his poetic voice during his time there and in Berkeley in the 1950s, but he is a New York poet, and the cities of his poems are big, harsh cities. He and his peers were passionate urbanists at a time when the white middle class was abandoning city life for the suburbs (and though many of the so-called Beats gathered in San Francisco, most wrote poetry about things more personal or more general than the streets they thronged, or used the city as a gateway to Asia and the western landscape). He did write about suburbs, notably in his "Supermarket in California," in which he summoned up a supermarket where the abundance of produce and shopping families makes wry comedy of the dead gay poets—Whitman and Federico García Lorca (a New Yorker from 1929 to 1930)—cruising the aisles. But otherwise his early poems burst with snow, tenements, and the Brooklyn Bridge. Ginsberg walked considerably in San Francisco and in New York, but in his poems walking is always turning into something else, since the sidewalk is always turning into a bed or a Buddhist paradise or some other apparition. The best minds of his generation were "dragging themselves through the negro streets at dawn looking for an angry fix," but they immediately commenced to see angels staggering on tenement roofs, eat fire, hallucinate Arkansas and Blake-light tragedy, and so on, even if they did afterward stumble to unemployment offices and walk "all night with their shoes full of blood on the snowbank docks waiting for a door in the East River to open. . . ."

For the Beats, motion or travel was enormously important, but its exact nature was not (save for Snyder, the true peripatetic of the bunch). They caught the tail end of the 1930s romance of freighthoppers, hobos, and railroad yards, they led the way to the new car culture in which restlessness was assuaged by hundreds of miles at 70 m.p.h. rather than dozens at 3 or 4 on foot, and they blended such physical travel with chemically induced ramblings of the imagination and a whole new kind of rampaging language. San Francisco and New York seem pedestrian anchors on either side of the long rope of the open road they traveled. In the same mode, one can see the shift in country ballads: sometime in the 1950s

---

THE STREET"   *In a charming sally, Mme de Girardin one day said that for the Parisian, walking is not taking* disappointed lovers stopped walking away or catching the midnight train and began driving, and by the 1970s the apotheosis of eighteen-wheeler songs had arrived. Had he lived that long, Kerouac would've loved them. Only in the first section of *Kaddish*, when Ginsberg gives over singing of his generation and his pals to mourn his mother, do the act and the place remain particular. The streets are repositories of history, walking a way to read that history. "Strange now to think of you, gone without corsets & eyes, while I walk on the sunny pavement of Greenwich Village," it opens, and as he walks Seventh Avenue he thinks of Naomi Ginsberg in the Lower East Side, "where you walked 50 years ago, little girl—from Russia / . . . then struggling in the crowds of Orchard Street toward what? / —toward Newark—" in an antiphony of her city and his, joined in later sections by their shared experiences during his childhood.

Handsome as a marble statue, Frank O'Hara was as unlike Ginsberg as a gay poet born the same year could be, and he wrote about far more delicate diurnal adventures. Ginsberg's poetry was oratorical—jeremiads and hymns to be shouted from the rooftops; O'Hara's poetry is as casual as conversation and sequenced by strolls in the street (among his book titles are *Lunch Poems*—not about eating but about lunchtime excursions from his job at the Museum of Modern Art—*Second Avenue*, and the essay collection *Standing Still and Walking in New York*). While Ginsberg tended to speak to America, O'Hara's remarks often addressed a "you" who seemed to be an absent lover in a silent soliloquy or a companion on a stroll. The painter Larry Rivers recalls, "It was the most extraordinary thing, a simple walk" with O'Hara, and O'Hara wrote a poem titled "Walking with Larry Rivers." Walking seems to have been a major part of his daily repertoire, as well as a kind of syntax organizing thought, emotion, and encounter, and the city was the only conceivable site for his tender, street-smart, and sometimes campy voice celebrating the incidental and the inconsequential. In the prose-poem "Meditations in an Emergency" he affirmed, "I can't even enjoy a blade of grass unless I know there's a subway handy, or a record store or some other sign that people do not totally *regret* life. It is more important to affirm the least sincere; the clouds get enough attention as it is. . . . " The poem "Walking to Work" ends

> I'm becoming
> the street.

---

exercise—it is searching. . . . The Parisian truly seems an explorer, always ready to set off again, or, better like

---

> Who are you in love with?
>
> me?
>
> Straight against the light I cross.

Yet another walking poem begins:

> I'm getting tired of not wearing underwear
> And then again I like it
>   strolling along
> feeling the wind blow softly on my genitals

and goes on to speculate on "who dropped that empty carton / of cracker jacks," before turning to the clouds, the bus, his destination, the "you" to whom he speaks, Central Park. The texture is that of everyday life and of a connoisseur's eye settling on small things, small epiphanies, but the same kind of inventory that studs Whitman's and Ginsberg's poems recurs in O'Hara's. Cities are forever spawning lists.

David Wojnarowicz's *Close to the Knives: A Memoir of Disintegration* reads like a summary of all the urban experience that came before him. Like De Quincey he was a runaway, but like De Quincey's friend Ann he supported himself as a child prostitute, and like Dickens and Ginsberg he brought an incandescant, hallucinatory clarity to the moods and scenes of his city. Most who took up the Beat subject of the urban underworld of the erotic, the intoxicated, and the illegal took it up in William Burroughs's amoral vein, more interested in its coolness than its consequences or its politics, but Wojnarowicz raged at the system that created such suffering, that created his suffering as a runaway child, a gay man, a person with AIDS (of which he died in 1991). He writes in a collage of memories, encounters, dreams, fantasies, and outbursts studded with startling metaphors and painful images, and in his writings walking appears like a refrain, a beat: he always returns to the image of himself walking alone down a New York street or a corridor. "Some nights we'd walk seven or eight hundred blocks, practically the whole island of Manhattan," he wrote of his hustling years, for walking remained the recourse for those with nowhere to sleep, as it had been for Johnson and Savage.

Wojnarowicz's 1980s New York had come full circle to resemble Gay's early

---

some marvelous alchemist of life.—F. BLOCH, *TYPES DU BOULEVARD*   *To rove about, musing, that is to say* eighteenth-century London. It had the scourges of AIDS, of the vast new population of homeless people, and of the drug-damaged staggering around like something out of William Hogarth's Gin Lane, and it was notoriously violent, so that the well-to-do feared its streets as they once had London's. Wojnarowicz writes of seeing "long legs and spiky boots and elegant high heels and three prostitutes suddenly surround a business man from the waldorf and they're saying: 'Come on honey' and rubbing his dick . . . and his wallet appears behind his back in the hands of one of them and they all drop away as he continues to giggle" and we're back to Moll Flanders stripping a passed-out trick of his silver gloves, snuffbox, and even his periwig. He writes of the years when he was suffering from malnutrition and exposure, living on the streets until he was eighteen, "I had almost died three times at the hands of people I'd sold my body to in those days and after coming off the street. . . . I could barely speak when in the company of other people. . . . That weight of image and sensation wouldn't come out until I picked up a pencil and started putting it down on paper." "Coming off the street": the phrase describes all streets as one street and that street as a whole world, with its own citizenry, laws, language. "The street" is a world where people in flight from the traumas that happen inside houses become natives of the outside.

One of the book's sections, "Being Queer in America: A Journal of Disintegration," is as tidy a chronicle of the uses of walking for a queer man of the streets in 1980s urban America as *Pride and Prejudice* is of the uses of walking for a country lady almost two centuries before. "I'm walking through these hallways where the windows break apart a slow dying sky and a quiet wind follows the heels of the kid as he suddenly steps through a door frame ten rooms down," it opens. He follows the kid into the room, which resembles the long wharves and warehouses he used to cruise, sucks him off, and a few sections later his walking becomes mourning for his friend, the photographer Peter Hujar, dead of AIDS. "I walked for hours through the streets after he died, through the gathering darkness and traffic, down into the dying section of town where bodies litter the curbsides and dogs tear apart the stinking garbage by the doorways. There was a green swell to the clouds above the buildings. . . . I turned and left, walking back into the gray haze of traffic and exhaust, past a skinny prostitute doing the junkie walk bent over at the waist with knuckles dragging the sidewalk." He meets a friend—"man on second avenue at 2:00 am"—who tells him about a third man being jumped on West Street by a carload of kids from Jersey and brutally beaten

loitering, is, for a philosopher, a good way of spending time; especially in that kind of mock rurality, ugly but odd, for being gay. And then comes his refrain, "I walk this hallway twenty-seven times and all I can see are the cool white walls. A hand rubbing slowly across a face, but my hands are empty. Walking back and forth from room to room trailing bluish shadows I feel weak. . . ." His city is not hell but limbo, the place in which restless souls swirl forever, and only passion, friendship, and visionary capacity redeem it for him.

I began walking my own city's streets as a teenager and walked them so long that both they and I changed, the desperate pacing of adolescence when the present seemed an eternal ordeal giving way to the musing walks and innumerable errands of someone no longer wound up so tight, so isolated, so poor, and my walks have now often become reviews of my own and the city's history together. Vacant lots become new buildings, old geezer bars are taken over by young hipsters, the Castro's discos become vitamin stores, whole streets and neighborhoods change their complexion. Even my own neighborhood has changed so much it sometimes seems as though I have moved two or three times from the raucous corner I started out on just before I turned twenty. The urban walkers I have surveyed suggest a kind of scale of walking, and on it, I have moved from near the Ginsberg-Wojnarowicz end of the spectrum to that of a low-rent Virginia Woolf.

Two days before the end of the year, I went to one of the local liquor stores for milk early one Sunday morning. Around the corner a guy was sitting in a doorway drinking and singing falsetto, with that knack some local drunks have for sounding like fallen angels. The word *Alooooone* trilled out of nowhere, echoing beautifully in the stairwell. On my way back I saw him weaving so intently down the street he didn't notice me pass a few feet away. Merely walking seemed to take all the singer's concentration, as though he were forcing himself through an atmosphere that had become thick around him. When I started watering the tree in front of my building, he was still winding around the corner. The old lady who always wears a dress and always speaks so politely in word-salad non sequiturs was walking in the other direction. I said hello to her as she passed me, but she didn't notice me any more than he did. All of a sudden, when she had reached the same point on her side of the street that he had on his, she broke into a sort of soft-shoe shuffle that carried on until she turned out of sight down the

and partaking of two natures, which surrounds certain large cities, particularly Paris.—VICTOR HUGO, LES facing corner. The two of them seemed to be listening to some inaudible music that carried them along and made them joyous as well as haunted.

Later on the churchgoers would appear. When I first moved here, there were no cafés, and all the churchgoers walked—on Sunday mornings the streets were busy and sociable with black women in resplendent hats, walking in all directions to their churches, not with the dogged steps of pilgrims but with the festive stride of celebrants. That was long ago; gentrification has dispersed the Baptist congregations to other neighborhoods, from which many now drive to church. Young African-American men still saunter by, their legs nonchalant while their arms and shoulders jump around as though staking a bodily territory, but most of the churchgoers have been replaced on the sidewalks these weekend mornings by joggers and dog walkers pumping towards that great secular temple of the middle class, the garden as represented by Golden Gate Park, while the hung-over drift towards the cafés. But this early the street belonged to us three walkers, or to the two of them, for they made me feel like a ghost drifting through their private lives out in public on that cold, sunny Sunday morning, in the communal solitude of urban walkers.

MISÉRABLES   *Bored, we stroll aimlessly about and look at things, and by way of curing our state we buy two*

Chapter 12

PARIS, OR BOTANIZING
ON THE ASPHALT

Parisians inhabit their public gardens and streets as though they were salons and corridors, and their cafés face the street and overflow into it as though the theater of passersby were too interesting to neglect even for the duration of a drink. Nude bronze and marble women are everywhere out of doors, standing on pedestals and springing from walls as though the city were both museum and boudoir, while victory arches and pillars punctuate the avenues like the yonis and lingams of a militant sexuality. Streets turn into courtyards, the largest buildings wrap around other courtyards that are actually parks, the national buildings are as long as avenues, and avenues are lined with trees and chairs just like the parks. Everything—houses, churches, bridges, walls—is the same sandy gray so that the city seems like a single construction of inconceivable complexity, a sort of coral reef of high culture. All this makes Paris seem porous, as though private thought and public acts were not so separate here as elsewhere, with walkers flowing in and out of reveries and revolutions. More than any other city, it has entered the paintings and novels of those under its sway, so that representation and reality reflect each other like a pair of facing mirrors, and walking Paris is often described as reading, as though the city itself were a huge anthology of tales. It exerts a magnetic attraction over its citizens and its visitors, for it has always been the capital of refugees and exiles as well as of France.

"Now a landscape, now a room," Walter Benjamin wrote of the walker's expe-

old Saint-Cloud teapots, embossed with silver gilt in a box with a fleur-de-lys lock.—THE GONCOURT JOURNALS, rience of Paris. Benjamin is one of the great scholars of cities and the art of walking them, and Paris drew him into its recesses as it had drawn so many before, coming to overshadow all the other subjects of his writing during the last decade before his death in 1940. He first visited Paris in 1913 and returned for longer and longer visits until he finally settled there at the end of the 1920s. Even in writing of his birthplace, Berlin, Benjamin's words wandered toward Paris. "Not to find one's way in a city may well be uninteresting and banal. It requires ignorance—nothing more. But to lose oneself in a city—as one loses oneself in a forest—that calls for quite a different schooling. Then signboards and street names, passers-by, roofs, kiosks, or bars must speak to the wanderer like a crackling twig under his feet, like the startling call of a bittern in the distance, like the sudden stillness of a clearing with a lily standing erect at its center. Paris taught me this art of straying," he said in his essay on his Berlin childhood. "It fulfilled a dream that had shown its first traces in the labyrinths on the blotting pages of my school exercise books." He had been brought up as a good turn-of-the-century German to revere mountains and forests—a photograph of him as a child shows him holding an alpenstock before some painted Alps, and his wealthy family often took long vacations in the Black Forest and Switzerland—but his enthusiasm for cities was both a rejection of that musty romanticism and an immersion in modernism's urbanism.

Cities fascinated him as a kind of organization that could only be perceived by wandering or by browsing, a spatial order in contrast to the tidily linear temporal order of narratives and chronologies. In that Berlin essay, he speaks of a revelation he had in a Paris café—"it had to be in Paris, where the walls and quays, the places to pause, the collections and the rubbish, the railings and the squares, the arcades and the kiosks, teach a language so singular"—that his whole life could be diagrammed as a map or a labyrinth, as though space rather than time were its primary organizing structure. His *Moscow Diary* mixed his own life into an account of that city, and he wrote a book whose form seems to mimic a city, *One-Way Street*, a subversive confection of short passages titled as though they were city sites and signs—Gas Station, Construction Site, Mexican Embassy, Manorially Furnished Ten-Room Apartment, Chinese Curios. If a narrative is like a single continuous path, this book's many short narratives are like a warren of streets and alleys.

He was himself a great wanderer of streets. I picture Benjamin walking the

1856   *The end of her life was terrible. She who had been the most beautiful and most desired woman of her time* streets of Paris—"I don't think I ever saw him walk with his head erect. His gait had something unmistakable about it, something pensive and tentative, which was probably due to his shortsightedness," said one friend—passing without noticing another exile with worse eyesight, James Joyce, who lived there from 1920 to 1940. There is a sort of symmetry between the exiled Catholic who had written a novel studded and layered with obscure information about a Jew wandering the streets of Dublin and the exiled Berlin Jew strolling the Paris streets while writing lyrical histories about a Catholic—Charles Baudelaire—walking and writing the streets of Paris. The kind of homage Joyce received in his lifetime has come far later to Benjamin, with the rediscovery of his works first in Germany in the 1960s and 1970s and later in English. He has become the patron saint of cultural studies, and his writing has spawned hundreds more essays and books. It may be the hybrid nature of this writing—more or less scholarly in subject, but full of beautiful aphorisms and leaps of imagination, a scholarship of evocation rather than definition—that has made him so rich a source for further interpreters. His Parisian studies have been of particular interest—he left a huge collection of quotes and notes for an unwritten book, the *Arcades Project*, which would have expanded further on the linked subjects of Baudelaire, Paris, the Parisian arcades, and the figure of the flâneur. It was he who named Paris "the capital of the nineteenth century" and he who made the flâneur a topic for academics at the end of the twentieth.

What exactly a flâneur is has never been satisfactorily defined, but among all the versions of the flâneur as everything from a primeval slacker to a silent poet, one thing remains constant: the image of an observant and solitary man strolling about Paris. It says something about the fascination public life exerted over Parisians that they developed a term to describe one of its types, and something about French culture that it theorized even strolling. The word only became common usage in the early nineteenth century, and its origins are shrouded. Priscilla Parkhurst Ferguson says it comes from "old Scandinavian (*flana, courir etourdiment ca et la* [to run giddily here and there])," while Elizabeth Wilson writes, "The nineteenth-century *Encylopedie Larousse* suggests that the term may be derived from an Irish word for 'libertine.' The writers of this edition of Larousse devoted a long article to the flâneur, whom they defined as a loiterer, a fritterer away of time. They associated him with the new urban pastimes of shopping and crowd watching. The flâneur, Larousse pointed out, could exist only in the great

---

became a half-mad woman driven by a mania for walking. She was living at 26 bis, Place Vendôme, and every

---

city, the metropolis, since provincial towns would afford too restricted a stage for his strolling."

Benjamin himself never clearly defined the flâneur, only associated him with certain things: with leisure, with crowds, with alienation or detachment, with observation, with walking, particularly with strolling in the arcades—from which it can be concluded that the flâneur was male, of some means, of a refined sensibility, with little or no domestic life. The flâneur arose, Benjamin argues, at a period early in the nineteenth century when the city had become so large and complex that it was for the first time strange to its inhabitants. Flâneurs were a recurrent subject of the feuilletons—the serialized novels in the newly popularized newspapers—and the *physiologies*, those popular publications that purported to make strangers familiar but instead underscored their strangeness by classifying them as species one could identify on sight, like birds or flowers. In the nineteenth century, the idea of the city so intrigued and overwhelmed its inhabitants that they eagerly devoured guidebooks to their own cities as modern tourists peruse those of other cities.

The crowd itself seemed to be something new in human experience—a mass of strangers who would remain strange—and the flâneur represented a new type, one who was, so to speak, at home in this alienation: "The crowd is his domain, just as the air is the bird's, and water that of the fish," wrote Baudelaire in a famous passage often used to define flâneurs. "His passion and his profession is to merge with the crowd. For the perfect idler, for the passionate observer it becomes an immense source of enjoyment to establish his dwelling in the throng, in the ebb and flow, the bustle, the fleeting and infinite. To be away from home and yet to feel at home anywhere . . ." The flâneur, Benjamin wrote in his most famous passage on the subject, "goes botanizing on the asphalt. But even in those days it was not possible to stroll about everywhere in the city. Before Haussmann [remodeled the city] wide pavements were rare, and the narrow ones afforded little protection from vehicles. Strolling could hardly have assumed the importance it did without the arcades." "Arcades," he wrote elsewhere, "where the flâneur would not be exposed to the sight of carriages that did not recognize pedestrians as rivals were enjoying undiminished popularity. There was the pedestrian who wedged himself into the crowd, but there was also the flâneur who demanded elbow room and was unwilling to forego the life of a gentleman of leisure." One demonstration of this leisureliness, Benjamin goes on to say, was the fashion,

evening, dressed in black, her face hidden by veils, dragging along two miserable, fat, asthmatic dogs, she would around 1840, for taking turtles for walks in the arcades. "The flâneurs liked to have the turtles set the pace for them. If they had their way, progress would have been obliged to accommodate itself to this pace."

His final, unfinished work, the *Arcades Project*, was devoted to teasing out the meanings of these shopping arcades that had arisen during the first decades of that century. The arcades intensified the blurring of interior and exterior: they were pedestrian streets paved with marble and mosaic and flanked by shops, they had roofs made of the new building materials of steel and glass, and they were the first places in Paris to be lit by the new gaslight. Precursors of Paris's great department stores (and later America's shopping malls), they were elegant environments for selling luxury goods and accommodating idle strollers. The arcades allowed Benjamin to link his fascination with the stroller to other, more Marxist themes. The flâneur, visually consuming goods and women while resisting the speed of industrialization and the pressure to produce, is an ambiguous figure, both resistant to and seduced by the new commercial culture. The solitary walker in New York or London experiences cities as atmosphere, architecture, and stray encounters; the promenader in Italy or El Salvador encounters friends or flirts; the flâneur, the descriptions suggest, hovers on the fringes, neither solitary nor social, experiencing Paris as an intoxicating abundance of crowds and goods.

The only problem with the flâneur is that he did not exist, except as a type, an ideal, and a character in literature. The flâneur is often described as detective-like in his aloof observation of others, and feminist scholars have debated whether there were or could be female flâneurs—but no literary detective has found and named an actual individual who qualifies or was known as a flâneur (Kierkegaard, were he less prolific and less Danish, might be the best candidate). No one has named an individual who took a tortoise on a walk, and all who refer to this practice use Benjamin as their source (though during the flâneurs' supposed heyday, the writer Gérard de Nerval famously took a lobster on walks, with a silk ribbon for a leash, but he did so in parks rather than arcades, and for metaphysical rather than foppish reasons). No one quite fulfilled the idea of the flâneur, but everyone engaged in some version of flâneury. Benjamin to the contrary, it was not only "possible to stroll about everywhere in the city" but widely done. The solitary walker in other cities has often been a marginal figure, shut out of the private life that takes place between intimates and inside buildings—

---

leave her house, taking care not to be recognized, go to the arcades of the street whose name she was once so proud

---

but in nineteenth-century Paris, real life was in public, on the street and among society.

Paris before Baron Georges-Eugène Haussmann's massive remodeling of the city from 1853 to 1870 was still a medieval city. "Narrow crevices," Victor Hugo calls "those obscure, contracted, angular lanes, bordered by ruins eight stories high. . . . The street was narrow and the gutter wide, the passerby walked along a pavement which was always wet, beside shops that were like cellars, great stone blocks encircled with iron, immense garbage heaps. . . ." It was a remarkably unsegregated city: the very courtyard of the Louvre had a kind of slum built into it, and the outdoor arcade-courtyard of the Palais Royale offered sex, luxury goods, books, and drinks for sale, while social spectacles and political discourse were free. In 1835 the writer Frances Trollope went out to shop in a fashionable boutique "which I reached without any other adventure than being splashed twice and nearly run over thrice"; on her way back with her parcels she stopped to look at "the monuments raised over some half-dozen or half-score of revolutionary heroes, who fell and were buried on a spot at no great distance from the fountain" and eavesdropped, along with a gathering crowd, on an artisan telling his daughter why he and those heroes fought in 1830. On other days she reported on an uprising and on the fashionable promenaders of the boulevard des Italiens. Shopping and revolution, ladies and artisans, mingled on these dirty, enchanted streets.

A Moroccan who had visited Paris in 1845–46 was impressed by the pedestrian life there: "In Paris there are places where people take walks, which is one of their forms of entertainment. A fellow takes the arm of his friend, man or woman, and together they go to one of the spots known for it. They stroll along, chatting and taking in the sights. Their idea of an outing is not eating or drinking, and certainly not sitting. One of their favorite promenades is a place called the Champs-Élysées." The popular places for strolling were the Champs-Élysées, the Tuileries gardens, the avenue de la Reine, the Palais Royale, and the boulevard des Italiens, all on the right bank, and the Jardin des Plantes and Luxembourg Gardens on the left, where Baudelaire had grown up. Writing to his mother in 1861, Baudelaire recollected their "long walks and constant affection! I recall the quais, so sad in the evenings," and a friend remembered that when the poet was young they had "strolled about all evening on the boulevards and in the Tuileries" together.

People went to the boulevards for society. They went to the streets and alleys

----

to bear, in the direction of the Rue de Rivoli. For hours and hours she would walk, coming back to her house only

----

for adventure, proud that they could navigate the vast network that had yet to be adequately mapped. Even before the French Revolution, some writers and walkers had cherished this idea of the city as a kind of wilderness, mysterious, dark, dangerous, and endlessly interesting. Restif de la Bretonne's _Les Nuits de Paris, ou le Spectateur Nocturne_ is the classic book of prerevolutionary walks (and after the revolution it was expanded to include _Les Nuits de la Révolution_; the book was first published in 1788 and expanded in the 1790s). A peasant who became a printer, then a Parisian, then a writer, Bretonne is one of French literature's great eccentrics, little remembered now. He wrote book after book, emulating Rousseau's _Confessions_ with a sixteen-volume autobiography, imitating while claiming to revile the marquis de Sade's _Justine_ in his own _Anti-Justine_ (sold, like Sade's works, in a pornographic bookshop in the Palais Royale's arcades), and producing dozens of novels, as well as some journalism about Paris that foreshadows the _physiologies_ of the nineteenth century. The _Nuits_ is unique, a collection of hundreds of anecdotes about his adventures on hundreds of nights on the streets of Paris. Each brief chapter covers a night, and the pretext of the book is that he was working as a missionary to rescue distressed maidens and bring them to his patroness, the marquise de M————, though he has many other kinds of adventure as well. The episodic quality of the book makes it recall the innumerable adventures of the Native American trickster Coyote or of the comic-strip Spiderman.

In his late-night wanderings, Bretonne meets with shop girls, blacksmiths, drunkards, servants, and of course prostitutes, spies on politicians in debate and aristocrats in adultery (notably in the Tuileries), sees crimes, fires, mobs, crossdressers, a freshly murdered corpse. He writes of Paris in the way many others would later: as a book, a wilderness, and a sort of erogenous zone, or bedroom. The Île Saint-Louis was his favorite haunt, and from 1779 to 1789 he chiseled onto its stone walls dates of great personal significance, along with a few evocative words. Thus Paris became both the source of his adventures and a book recording them, a tale to be both written and read by walking. As Proust's famous madeleine served to recall his past, so did these inscriptions for Bretonne: "Whenever I had stopped along the the parapet [of the Île Saint-Louis] to ponder some sorrowful thought, my hand would trace the date and the thought that had just stirred me. I would walk on then, wrapped in the darkness of the night whose silence and loneliness were touched with a horror I found pleasing." He reads the

---

when the dawn was beginning to disperse the darkness she now cherished.—ANDRE CASTELOT ON LOUIS-PHILIPPE'S

---

first date he had carved: "I cannot describe the emotion I felt as I thought back to the year before. . . . A rush of memories came to me; I stood motionless, preoccupied with linking the present moment to the preceding year's, to make them one." He relived love affairs, nights of desperation, and ruptured friendships. His Paris is a bedroom full of liaisons in the gardens and lechery on the streets (fittingly enough, Bretonne was a foot fetishist and sometimes followed women with small feet and high heels). In his Paris, the privacy of erotic life is constantly spilling forth in public, and the city is a wilderness, because its public and private spaces and experiences are so intermingled and because it is lawless, dark, and full of dangers.

In the nineteenth century, the theme of the city as wilderness would come up again and again in novels, poems, and popular literature. The city was called a "virgin forest," its explorers were sometimes, in Benjamin's famous phrase, naturalists "botanizing on the asphalt," but its indigenous inhabitants were often "savages." "What are the dangers of the forest and the prairie compared with the daily shocks and conflicts of civilization?" wrote Baudelaire in a passage Benjamin cites. "Whether a man grasps his victim on a boulevard or stabs his quarry in unknown woods—does he not remain both here and there the most perfect of all beasts of prey?" In admiration of James Fenimore Cooper's novels of the American wilderness, Alexandre Dumas titled a novel *Mohicans du Paris;* it features the adventures of a flâneur-detective who lets a blowing scrap of paper lead him to adventures that always involve crimes; a minor novelist, Paul Feval, installed an unlikely Native American character in Paris, where he scalps four enemies in a cab; Balzac, says Benjamin, refers to "Mohicans in spencer jackets" and "Hurons in frock coats"; later in the century, loiterers and petty criminals were nicknamed "Apaches." These terms invested the city with the allure of the exotic, turning its types into tribes, its individuals into explorers, and its streets into a wilderness. One of its explorers was George Sand, who found that "on the Paris pavement I was like a boat on ice. My delicate shoes cracked open in two days, my pattens sent me spilling, and I always forgot to lift my dress. I was muddy, tired and runny-nosed, and I watched my shoes and my clothes . . . go to rack and ruin with alarming rapidity." She put on men's clothes, and though that act is frequently described as a subversive social one, she described it as a practical one. Her new costume gave her a freedom of movement she reveled in: "I can't convey how much my boots delighted me. . . . With those steel-tipped heels I was solid on the sidewalk at last. I dashed back and forth across Paris and felt I was going around the world. My clothes were weatherproof too. I was out and about in all weathers, came home at all hours, was in the pits of all the theaters."

But it was not the same medieval wilderness Bretonne had ventured into. In Baudelaire some of the same figures recur—the prostitute, the beggar, the criminal, the beautiful stranger—but he does not speak to them, and the content of their lives remains speculative to him. Window-shopping and people-watching have become indistinguishable activities; one may attempt to buy but not to know them. "Multitude, solitude: identical terms, and interchangeable by the active and fertile poet," wrote Baudelaire. "The man who is unable to people his solitude is equally unable to be alone in a bustling crowd. The poet enjoys the incomparable privilege of being able to be himself or someone else. . . . Like those wandering souls who go looking for a body, he enters as he likes into each man's personality. For him alone everything is vacant." Baudelaire's city is like a wilderness in another way: it is lonely.

The old Paris was cut down like a forest by Baron Haussmann, who carried out Napoleon III's vision of a splendid—and manageable—modern city. Since the 1860s it has been popular to say that Haussmann's destruction of the medieval warrens of streets and his creation of the grand boulevards was a counterrevolutionary tactic, an attempt to make the city penetrable by armies, indefensible by citizens. After all, citizens had revolted in 1789, 1830, and 1848, in part by building barricades across the narrow streets. But this does not explain the rest of Haussmann's project. The wide new avenues accommodated the flow of a vastly increased population, commerce, and on occasion troops, but below them were new sewers and waterways, eliminating some of the stench and disease of the old city—and the Bois de Boulogne was landscaped as a great public park in the English style. As a political project, it seems an attempt not to subdue but to seduce Parisians; as a development project, it displaced the poor from the center of the city to its edges and suburbs, where they remain today (the opposite of most postwar American cities—Manhattan and San Francisco are exceptions—abandoned to the poor when the middle class flocked to the suburbs). Other efforts were made to civilize the "wilderness" of the city in the nineteenth century: streetlights, house numbers, sidewalks, regularly posted street names, maps, guidebooks, increased policing, and the registration, prosecution, or both of prostitutes.

---

window displays were like pastry erotica. I discovered I particularly liked a vanilla custard pastry cut into

---

The real complaint against Haussmann seems to be twofold. The first is that in tearing down so much of the old city, he obliterated the delicate interlace of mind and architecture, the mental map walkers carried with them and the geographical correlatives to their memories and associations. In a poem about walking through one of Haussmann's construction sites near the Louvre, Baudelaire complained

> Paris is changing! but nothing within my melancholy
> has shifted! New palaces, scaffoldings, piles of stone
> Old neighborhoods—everything has become allegory for me
> and my dear memories are heavier than stones.

Baudelaire being Baudelaire, the poem ends "in the forest of my exiled soul." And the brothers Edmond and Jules Goncourt wrote in their journal on November 18, 1860, "My Paris, the Paris in which I was born, the Paris of the manners of 1830 to 1848, is vanishing, both materially and morally. . . . I feel like a man merely passing through Paris, a traveller. I am foreign to that which is to come, to that which is, and a stranger to these new boulevards that go straight on, without meandering, without the adventures of perspective. . . ."

The second complaint is that with his broad, straight avenues, Haussmann turned the wilderness into a formal garden. The new boulevards continued a project begun two centuries before by André Le Nôtre, who went on to design the vast gardens of Versailles for Louis XIV. It was Le Nôtre who had designed the gardens of the Tuileries and the garden-boulevard of the Champs-Élysées extending west from the Tuileries to the Étoile, where Napoleon later placed his Arc de Triomphe. Most of these designs of Le Nôtre were outside the city walls and thus outside the economic life of the city, but the city expanded to absorb them. Thus the boulevards that Le Nôtre built for pleasure alone in the 1660s were developed for pleasure and industry by Haussmann in the 1860s (and these long axes had been widely emulated long before; Washington, D.C., is one of the cities that derives from this imperial geometry). Haussmann was as much an aesthete as Le Nôtre; he annoyed his emperor by leveling hills and taking other pains to make his streets utterly straight, opening up the long vistas that now seem so characteristic of Paris. It is a great irony that though the English garden had triumphed and gardens had become "natural"—irregular, asymmetrical, full

---

segments like a wheel of Brie. Walking along the street, Eiffel Tower in sight ahead, eating the pastry out of my of serpentine rather than straight lines—a formal French garden had been hacked out of the wilds of Paris.

The damp, intimate, claustrophobic, secretive, narrow, curving streets with their cobblestones sinuous like the scales of a snake had given way to ceremonial public space, space full of light, air, business, and reason. And if the old city had so often been compared to a forest, it may have been because it was an organic accretion of independent gestures by many creatures, rather than the implementation of a master plan made by one; it had not been designed but grown. No map had dictated that meandering organic form. And many hated the change: "For the promenaders, what necessity was there to walk from the Madeleine to the Étoile by the shortest route? On the contrary, the promenaders like to prolong their walk, which is why they walk the same alley three or four times in succession," wrote Adolphe Thiers. Walking in the wilderness is one kind of pleasure, demanding daring, knowledge, strength—for savages, detectives, women in men's clothes; walking in a garden is a far milder one. Haussmann's boulevards made far more of the city a promenade and far more of its citizens promenaders. The arcades began their long decay as the streets bloomed with boutiques and the grand department stores were born—and during the Commune of 1871 the barricades of street revolutionaries were built across the great boulevards.

It wasn't Baudelaire who had first drawn Benjamin's attention to the arcades and to the possibility of configuring walking as a cultural act, but Benjamin's contemporaries—fellow Berliner and friend Franz Hessel and the surrealist writer Louis Aragon. He found Aragon's 1926 book _Paysan de Paris (Paris Peasant)_ so exhilarating that "evenings in bed I could not read more than a few words of it before my heartbeat got so strong I had to put the book down. . . . And in fact the first notes of the _Passagenwerk_ [or Arcades Project] come from this time. Then came the Berlin years, in which the best part of my friendship with Hessel was nourished by the Passagen-project in frequent conversations." In his Berlin essay, Benjamin describes Hessel as one of those guides who had introduced him to the city, and Hessel himself had written about walking Berlin (and, with Benjamin, worked on a translation of Marcel Proust's _Remembrance of Things Past_, a novel that with its themes of memory, walks, chance encounters, and Parisian salons fits neatly be-

---

band, was not unlike sex.—E-MAIL TO THE AUTHOR FROM DAVID HAYES, TORONTO, 1998   _He began to take_

---

tween the two bodies of French literature Benjamin took on). It is these twentieth-century writers and artists who best fit the descriptions of the nineteenth-century flâneur.

Aragon's *Paysan de Paris* is one of a trio of surrealist books published in the late 1920s; the other two are André Breton's *Nadja* and Philippe Soupault's *Last Nights of Paris*. All three are first-person narratives about a man wandering in Paris, give very specific place names and descriptions of places, and make prostitutes one of their main destinations. Surrealism prized dreams, the free associations of an unconscious or unself-conscious mind, startling juxtapositions, chance and coincidence, and the poetic possibilities of everyday life. Wandering around a city was an ideal way to engage with all these qualities. Breton wrote, "I still recall the extraordinary role that Aragon played in our daily strolls through Paris. The localities that we passed through in his company, even the most colourless ones, were positively transformed by a spellbinding romantic inventiveness that never faltered and that needed only a street-turning or a shop-window to inspire a fresh outpouring."

Paris, which had been stripped of its mystery by Haussmann, had recovered it to serve once again as a kind of muse to its poets. Both *Nadja* and *Last Nights* are organized around the pursuit of an enigmatic young woman met through a chance encounter, and it is this pursuit that gives the books their narratives. Such encounters are a staple of city-walking literature: Bretonne follows women with beautiful feet; Whitman eyeballs men in Manhattan; both Nerval and Baudelaire wrote poems about a passing glimpse of a woman who could have been their great love. Breton "spoke to this unknown woman, though I must admit that I expected the worst." Soupault's nameless narrator stalked his subject like a detective and came to know the underworld she and her associates inhabited, though this sordid realm of the ambitious, the demented, and the murderous neither explains nor fully dispels her fascination. Aragon's book, the least conventional of the three, has no narrative and is organized, like Benjamin's *One-Way Street*, around geography: it explores a few Parisian places—the first of which is the passage de l'Opéra, a shopping arcade already slated for destruction when Aragon wrote about it. (It was, tidily enough, torn down to make way for the expansion of the boulevard Haussmann.) *Paysan de Paris* demonstrated how rich a subject the city itself was for wandering, on foot and in the imagination.

Aragon made the city itself his subject, but Breton and Soupault pursued

---

long walks along the Champs-Élysées to the Étoile, and exercise became a kind of punishment. As he wrote Miss women who were embodiments of the city: Nadja and Georgette. Soupault writes of his protagonist spying on Georgette as she takes a customer to a hotel near the Pont Neuf and returns to the streets. Afterward, "Georgette resumed her stroll about Paris, through the mazes of the night. She went on, dispelling sorrow, solitude or tribulation. Then more than ever did she display her strange power: that of transfiguring the night. Thanks to her, who was no more than one of the hundred thousands, the Parisian night became a mysterious domain, a great and marvelous country, full of flowers, of birds, of glances and of stars, a hope launched into space. . . . That night, as we were pursuing, or more exactly, tracking Georgette, I saw Paris for the first time. It was surely not the same city. It lifted itself above the mists, rotating like the earth on its axis, more feminine than usual. And Georgette herself became a city." Once again and yet more deliriously, Paris is a wilderness, bedroom, and book to be read by walking. The protagonist—nameless, without a profession, the perfect flâneur at last—has taken up Bretonne's task of exploring the night, but by pursuing a single woman entangled with a single crime, a murder whose aftermath they both witnessed. The protagonist is a detective on the trail of crime and aesthetic experience, and Georgette embodies both.

Later Georgette tells him she took up her profession because she and her brother needed to live, and "Everything is so simple when one knows all the streets as I do, and all the people who move in them. They are all seeking something without seeming to do so." Like Nadja, she is a flâneuse, one who has made of the street a sort of residence. While *Last Nights of Paris* is a novel, *Nadja* is based on Breton's encounters with a real woman, and to underscore his book's nonfictionality, he reproduces photographs of people (though not of pseudonymous Nadja), places, drawings, and letters in the pages of his narrative. On one of their dates, Nadja leads him to the place Dauphine at the west end of the Île de la Cité, and he writes, "Whenever I happen to be there, I feel the desire to go somewhere else gradually ebbing out of me, I have to struggle against myself to get free from a gentle, over-insistent, and finally, crushing embrace."

Thirty years later, in his *Pont Neuf*, Breton, in the words of one critic, "famously proposes a detailed 'interpretation' of the topography of central Paris according to which the geographical and architectural layout of the Île de la Cité, and the bend of the Seine where it is situated, are seen to make up the body of a recumbent woman whose vagina is located in the place Dauphine, 'with its triangular,

---

Weaver on August 30, 1921, "I have been training for a Marathon race by walking 12 or 14 kilometers every day

slightly curvilinear form bisected by a slit separating two wooded spaces.'" Breton spends the night in a hotel with Nadja, and Soupault's narrator hires Georgette for sex, but in these tales eroticism is not focused on bodily intimacy in bed but diffused throughout the city, and noctural walking rather than copulating is the means by which they bask in this charged atmosphere. The women they pursue are most themselves, most enchanting, and most at home on the streets, as though the profession of streetwalker was at last truly to walk the streets (no longer victims of or refugees from the streets, as so many earlier heroines had been). Nadja and Georgette are, like most surrealist representations of women, too burdened with being incarnations of Woman—degraded and exalted, muse and whore, city incarnate—to be individual women, and this is most evident in their magical strolls through the city, strolls that lure the narrators to follow these sirens on a chase that is also an homage to and tour of Paris. The love of a citizen for his city and the lust of a man for a passerby has become one passion. And the consummation of this passion is on the streets and on foot. Walking has become sex. Benjamin concurred in this transformation of city into female body, walking into copulating, when he concluded his passage about Paris as labyrinth, "Nor is it to be denied that I penetrated to its innermost place, the Minotaur's chamber, with the only difference being that this mythological monster had three heads: those of the occupants of the small brothel on rue de la Harpe, in which, summoning my last reserves of strength . . . I set my foot." Paris is a labyrinth whose center is a brothel, and in this labyrinth it is the arrival, not the consummation, that seems to count, and the foot that seems to be the crucial anatomical detail.

Djuna Barnes wrote a sort of coda to these books in her 1936 *Nightwood*, where once again the erotic love of an enchanted madwoman mingles with the fascinations of Paris and the night. The heroine of Barnes's great lesbian novel, Robin Vote, walks the streets "rapt and confused," abandoning her lover Nora Flood and directing "her steps toward that night life that was a known measure between Nora and the cafés. Her meditations, during this walk, were a part of the pleasure she expected to find when the walk came to an end. . . . Her thoughts were in themselves a form of locomotion." A cross-dressing Irish doctor who frequents the pissoirs of the boulevards explains the night in a long soliloquy to Nora, and Barnes must have known what she was doing when she housed this Dr. O'Connor on the rue Servandoni by the place Saint-Sulpice, the same small street in which Dumas had housed one of his Three Musketeers and Hugo had settled *Les*

---

and looking carefully in the seine to see if there is any place where I could throw Bloom in with a 50 lb. weight

---

Misérables' hero Jean Valjean. Such a density of literature had accumulated in Paris by the time of *Nightwood* that one pictures characters from centuries of literature crossing paths constantly, crowding each other, a Metro car full of heroines, a promenade populated by the protagonists of novels, a rioting mob of minor characters. Parisian writers always gave the street address of their characters, as though all readers knew Paris so well that only a real location in the streets would breathe life into a character, as though histories and stories themselves had taken up residence throughout the city.

Walter Benjamin described himself as "a man who has, with great difficulty, pried open the jaws of a crocodile and set up housekeeping there." He managed to live most of his life drifting about like a minor character in the literature he preferred. Perhaps it was French literature that led him to his death, for he delayed leaving Paris until it was too late. Boys' adventure books and the chronicles of the explorers would have better prepared him for his last years in the shadow of the Third Reich. When war broke out in September of 1939, he was rounded up with other German men in France and marched to a camp in Nevers, more than a hundred miles to the south. Now plump and afflicted with heart trouble that even on the streets of Paris had made him stop every few minutes, he collapsed several times on the march, but revived enough during his nearly three months of internment in the camp to teach courses in philosophy for a fee of a few cigarettes. His release secured by the P.E.N. club, he returned to Paris, where he continued to work on the *Arcades Project*, tried to secure a visa, and wrote the piercingly lyrical "Theses on the Philosophy of History." After the Nazi occupation of France, he fled south and with several others walked the steep route over the Pyrenees into Port Bou, Spain. He carried a heavy briefcase with him containing, he said, a manuscript more precious than his life, and in a steep vineyard he was so overcome that his companions had to support him on the walk. "No one knew the path," wrote a Frau Gurland who went with him. "We had to climb part of the way on all fours." In Spain the authorities demanded an exit visa from France and refused to honor the entrance visa for the United States Benjamin's friends had finally secured. In despair at his circumstances and the prospect of having to walk back over the mountains, he took an overdose of morphine in Spain and died on September 26, 1940—"whereupon the border officials, upon whom this suicide

---

fixed to his feet."—RICHARD ELLMANN, *JAMES JOYCE*   *Fantine, in those labyrinths of the hill of the Pantheon,*

---

had made an impression," writes Hannah Arendt, "allowed his companions to proceed to Portugal." His briefcase vanished.

In the same essay, Arendt, who had lived in Paris herself in the 1960s, wrote, "In Paris a stranger feels at home because he can inhabit the city the way he lives in his own four walls. And just as one inhabits an apartment, and makes it comfortable, by living in it instead of just using it for sleeping, eating, and working, so one inhabits a city by strolling through it without aim or purpose, with one's stay secured by the countless cafés which line the streets and past which the life of the city, the flow of pedestrians moves along. To this day Paris is the only one among the large cities which can be comfortably covered on foot, and more than any other city it is dependent for its liveliness on people who pass by in the streets, so that the modern automobile traffic endangers its very existence not only for technical reasons." When I ran away to Paris at the end of the 1970s, the city was still more or less a walker's paradise, if you discounted the petty lecheries and rudeness of some of its men, and I was so poor and so young that I walked everywhere, for hours, and in and out of the museums (which are free to people under eighteen). Now I know that even I was living in a Paris that was disappearing. The vast void on the Right Bank was the site where the great Les Halles markets had recently been eradicated, but I didn't know that the spiral-walled pissoirs like little labyrinths for the mystery of male privilege were vanishing too, that traffic lights would come to the crooked old streets of the Latin Quarter and illuminated plastic signs for fast food would mar the old walls, that the old hulk on the quai d'Orsay was to become a flashy new museum, that the Tuileries' and Luxembourg's metal chairs with their spiral arms and perforated circular seats (in much the same aesthetic vein as the pissoirs) would be replaced by more rectilinear and less beautiful chairs painted the same green. It was nothing like the transformations Parisians experienced during the Revolution, or during Haussmannization or at many other times, but this small register of changes has made me too the possessor of a lost city, and perhaps Paris is always a lost city, a city full of things that only live in imagination. Most dismaying of all when I returned recently was the change Arendt had foreseen: the dominance of the streets by cars. Cars had returned Paris's streets to the dirty and dangerous state in which they once had been, in the days when Rousseau was run over by a coach and walking the streets was a feat. To compensate for the automotive apotheosis, cars are banished on Sundays from certain streets and quays so that people might

---

where so many ties are knotted and unloosed, long fled from Tholomyès, but in such a way as always to meet him

---

once again promenade there, as they always have in the gardens and on the wide sidewalks of the boulevards (and as I write, efforts are being made to take back more space—notably the great expanse of the place de la Concorde, which has in recent decades become a congested traffic circle).

One glory remains to Paris, that of possessing the chief theorists of walking, among them Guy DeBord in the 1950s, Michel de Certeau in the 1970s, and Jean Christophe Bailly in the 1990s. DeBord addressed the political and cultural meanings of cities' architecture and spatial arrangements; deciphering and reworking those meanings was one of the tasks of the Situationist Internationale he cofounded and whose principal documents he wrote. "Psychogeography," he declared in 1955, was a discipline that "could set for itself the study of the precise laws and specific effects of the geographical environment, consciously organized or not, on the emotions and behaviors of individuals." He decried the apotheosis of the automobile in that essay and elsewhere, for psychogeographies were best perceived afoot: "The sudden change of ambience in a street within the space of a few meters; the evident division of the city into zones of distinct psychic atmospheres; the path of least resistance which is automatically followed in aimless strolls (and which has no relation to the contour of the ground)" were among the subtleties he charted, proposing "the introduction of psychogeographic maps, or even the introduction of alterations" to "clarify certain wanderings that express not subordination to randomness but complete insubordination to habitual influences (influences generally categorized as tourism, that popular drug as repugnant as sports or buying on credit)." Another of DeBord's pugnacious treatises was the "Theory of the Dérive" (*dérive* is French for *drifting*), "a technique of transient passage through varied ambiances. . . . In a dérive one or more persons during a certain period drop their usual motives for movement and action, their relations, their work and leisure activities, and let themselves be drawn by the attractions of the terrain and the encounters they find there." That flâneury seemed to DeBord a radical new idea all his own is somewhat comic, as are his authoritarian prescriptions for subversion—but his ideas for making urban walking yet more conscious an experiment are serious. "The point," writes Greil Marcus, who has studied Situationism, "was to encounter the unknown as a facet of the known, astonishment on the terrain of boredom, innocence in the face of experience. So you can walk up the street without thinking, letting your mind drift, letting your legs, with their internal memory, carry you up and down and around turns, at-

---

again. There is a way of avoiding a person which resembles a search.—VICTOR HUGO, *LES MISÉRABLES*   On

---

tending to a map of your own thoughts, the physical town replaced by an imaginary city." The Situationists' combination of cultural means and revolutionary ends has been influential, nowhere more so than in Paris's 1968 student uprising, when Situationist slogans were painted on the walls.

De Certeau and Bailly are far more mild, though they see futures as dark as DeBord's. The former devotes a chapter of his *Practice of Everyday Life* to urban walking. Walkers are "practitioners of the city," for the city is made to be walked, he wrote. A city is a language, a repository of possibilities, and walking is the act of speaking that language, of selecting from those possibilities. Just as language limits what can be said, architecture limits where one can walk, but the walker invents other ways to go, "since the crossing, drifting away, or improvisation of walking privilege, transform or abandon spatial elements." Further, he adds, "the walking of passers-by offers a series of turns (tours) and detours that can be compared to 'turns of phrase' or 'stylistic figures.'" De Certeau's metaphor suggests a frightening possibility: that if the city is a language spoken by walkers, then a postpedestrian city not only has fallen silent but risks becoming a dead language, one whose colloquial phrases, jokes, and curses will vanish, even if its formal grammar survives. Bailly lives in this car-choked Paris and documents this decline. In the words of an interpreter, he states that the social and imaginative function of cities "is under threat from the tyranny of bad architecture, soulless planning and indifference to the basic unit of urban language, the street, and the 'ruissellement de paroles' (stream of words), the endless stories, which animate it. Keeping the street and the city alive depends on understanding their grammar and generating the new utterances on which they thrive. And for Bailly, the principal agency of this process is walking, what he calls the 'grammaire generative de jambes' (generative grammar of the legs)." Bailly speaks of Paris as a collection of stories, a memory of itself made by the walkers of the streets. Should walking erode, the collection may become unread or unreadable.

---

his walks along the coast, this subject took shape for him, thanks to one of the enormous antitheses that were

---

CITIZENS OF THE STREETS:
Parties, Processions, and
Revolutions

I turned all the way around to see that it was his wings that had made the angel just behind me look so odd out of the corner of my eye. At least, he was dressed as an angel, and various space aliens, tarts, disco kings, and two-legged beasts were all streaming down the street in the same direction, toward Castro Street, as they do every Halloween. The night before I had taken my bike down to the foot of Market Street to ride in Critical Mass, the group ride that is both a protest of the lack of safe space for bicyclists and a festive seizure of that space. Several hundred bicyclists riding together filled the streets, as they have the last Friday of every month since the event began here in 1992. (Cyclists stage Critical Masses around the world, from Geneva to Sydney to Jerusalem to Philadelphia.) Some of the more righteous bicyclists had taken to wearing T-shirts that say "One Less Car," so a trio of runners accompanied us wearing "One Less Bike" shirts, and in honor of the impending holiday some of the cyclists had donned masks or costumes.

Halloween in the Castro is a similarly hybrid event, both celebration and, at least in its origins, political statement—for asserting a queer identity is a bold po-litical statement in itself. Asserting such an identity festively subverts the long tradition of sexuality being secret and homosexuality being shameful—and in

indispensable to his inspiration. In Hugo the crowd enters literature as an object of contemplation. The surging dreary times joy itself is insurrectionary, as community is in times of isolation. Nowadays, the Castro's Halloween street party is a magnet for a lot of straight people as well, but everyone seems to operate under the aegis of tolerance, campiness, and shameless staring in this event that is nothing more than a few thousand people milling along several blocks of shut-down streets. Nothing is sold, no one is in charge, and everyone is both spectacle and spectator. Earlier Halloween night, several hundred people had marched from Castro Street to the Hall of Justice to protest and mourn the murder of a young gay man in Wyoming, a pretty routine demonstration for San Francisco and for the Castro, which is both a temple of consumerism and home base for a politically active community.

November 2, Día de los Muertos, the Day of the Dead, was celebrated on Twenty-fourth Street in the Mission District. As always, the Aztec dancers—barefoot, spinning and stamping, clad in loincloths, leg rattles, and four-foot-long feather plumes—led the parade. They were followed by participants who bore altars on long poles—a Virgin of Guadalupe atop one and an Aztec god on the other. Behind the altars walked people carrying huge crosses draped in tissue paper, people with faces painted as skulls, people carrying candles, perhaps a thousand participants in all. Unlike bigger parades, this one was made up almost entirely of participants, with only a few onlookers from the windows of their homes. Perhaps it is better described as a procession, for a procession is a participants' journey, while a parade is a performance with audience. Walking together through the streets felt very different than did milling around on Halloween; there was a more tender, melancholic mood about this festival of death and a delicate but satisfying sense of camaraderie in the air that might have come from nothing more than sharing the same space and same purpose while moving together in the same direction. It was as though in aligning our bodies we had somehow aligned our hearts. At Twenty-fifth and Mission another procession invaded ours, a louder one chanting against the impending execution of a death-row inmate, and though it was annoying to be demonstrated at as though we were the executioners, it was useful to be reminded of the reality of death. The bakeries stayed open late selling *pan de muerto*—sweet bread baked into human figures—and the holiday was a fine hybrid of Christian and indigenous Mexican tradition, revised and metamorphosed at the hands of San Francisco's many cultures. Like Halloween, the Day of the Dead is a liminal festival, celebrating the threshholds between life and death, the time in which everything is possible and

ocean is its model, and the thinker who reflects on this eternal spectacle is the true explorer of the crowd in which he identity itself is in flux, and these two holidays have become thresholds across which different factions of the city meet and the boundaries between strangers drop.

The great German artist Joseph Beuys used to recite, as a maxim and manifesto, the phrase "Everyone an artist." I used to think it meant that he thought everyone should make art, but now I wonder if he wasn't speaking to a more basic possibility: that everyone could become a participant rather than a member of the audience, that everyone could become a producer rather than a consumer of meaning (the same idea lies behind punk culture's DIY—do it yourself—credo). This is the highest ideal of democracy—that everyone can participate in making their own life and the life of the community—and the street is democracy's greatest arena, the place where ordinary people can speak, unsegregated by walls, unmediated by those with more power. It's not a coincidence that *media* and *mediate* have the same root; direct political action in real public space may be the only way to engage in unmediated communication with strangers, as well as a way to reach media audiences by literally making news. Processions and street parties are among the pleasant manifestations of democracy, and even the most solipsistic and hedonistic expressions keep the populace bold and the avenues open for more overtly political uses. Parades, demonstrations, protests, uprisings, and urban revolutions are all about members of the public moving through public space for expressive and political rather than merely practical reasons. In this, they are part of the cultural history of walking.

Public marches mingle the language of the pilgrimage, in which one walks to demonstrate one's commitment, with the strike's picket line, in which one demonstrates the strength of one's group and one's persistence by pacing back and forth, and the festival, in which the boundaries between strangers recede. Walking becomes testifying. Many marches arrive at rally points, but the rallies generally turn participants back into audiences for a few select speakers; I myself have often been deeply moved by walking through the streets en masse and deeply bored by the events after arrival. Most parades and processions are commemorative, and this moving through the space of the city to commemorate other times knits together time and place, memory and possibility, city and citizen, into a vital whole, a ceremonial space in which history can be made. The past becomes the foundation on which the future will be built, and those who

---

loses himself as he loses himself in the roaring of the sea.—WALTER BENJAMIN, *CHARLES BAUDELAIRE*   *Then we*

---

honor no past may never make a future. Even the most innocuous parades have an agenda: Saint Patrick's Day parades go back more than two hundred years in New York, and they demonstrate the religious convictions, ethnic pride, and strength of a once-marginal community, as do the much more glittering Chinese New Year's Day parade in San Francisco and colossal Gay Pride parades around the continent. Military parades have always been shows of strength and incitements to tribal pride or citizen intimidation. In Northern Ireland, Orangemen have used their marches celebrating past Protestant victories to symbolically invade Catholic neighborhoods, while Catholics have made the funerals of the slain into massive political processions.

On ordinary days we each walk alone or with a companion or two on the sidewalks, and the streets are used for transit and for commerce. On extraordinary days—on the holidays that are anniversaries of historic and religious events and on the days we make history ourselves—we walk together, and the whole street is for stamping out the meaning of the day. Walking, which can be prayer, sex, communion with the land, or musing, becomes speech in these demonstrations and uprisings, and a lot of history has been written with the feet of citizens walking through their cities. Such walking is a bodily demonstration of political or cultural conviction and one of the most universally available forms of public expression. It could be called marching, in that it is common movement toward a common goal, but the participants have not surrendered their individuality as have those soldiers whose lockstep signifies that they have become interchangeable units under an absolute authority. Instead they signify the possibility of common ground between people who have not ceased to be different from each other, people who have at last become the public. When bodily movement becomes a form of speech, then the distinctions between words and deeds, between representations and actions, begin to blur, and so marches can themselves be liminal, another form of walking into the realm of the representational and symbolic—and sometimes, into history.

Only citizens familiar with their city as both symbolic and practical territory, able to come together on foot and accustomed to walking about their city, can revolt. Few remember that "the right of the people peaceably to assemble" is listed in the First Amendment of the U.S. Constitution, along with freedom of the press, of speech, and of religion, as critical to a democracy. While the other

---

sallied forth into the streets, arm in arm, continuing the topics of the day, or roaming far and wide until a late hour,

---

rights are easily recognized, the elimination of the possibility of such assemblies through urban design, automotive dependence, and other factors is hard to trace and seldom framed as a civil rights issue. But when public spaces are eliminated, so ultimately is the public; the individual has ceased to be a citizen capable of experiencing and acting in common with fellow citizens. Citizenship is predicated on the sense of having something in common with strangers, just as democracy is built upon trust in strangers. And public space is the space we share with strangers, the unsegregated zone. In these communal events, that abstraction the public becomes real and tangible. Los Angeles has had tremendous riots—Watts in 1965 and the Rodney King uprising in 1992—but little effective history of protest. It is so diffuse, so centerless, that it possesses neither symbolic space in which to act, nor a pedestrian scale in which to participate as the public (save for a few relict and re-created pedestrian shopping streets). San Francisco, on the other hand, has functioned like the "Paris of the West" it was once called, breeding a regular menu of parades, processions, protests, demonstrations, marches, and other public activities in its central spaces. San Francisco, however, is not a capital, as Paris is, so it is not situated to shake the nation and the national government.

Paris is the great city of walkers. And it is the great city of revolution. Those two facts are often written about as though they are unrelated, but they are vitally linked. Historian Eric Hobsbawm once speculated on "the ideal city for riot and insurrection." It should, he concluded, "be densely populated and not too large in area. Essentially it should still be possible to traverse it on foot. . . . In the ideal insurrectionary city the authorities—the rich, the aristocracy, the government or local administration—will therefore be as intermingled with the central concentration of the poor as possible." All the cities of revolution are old-fashioned cities: their stone and cement are soaked with meanings, with histories, with memories that make the city a theater in which every act echoes the past and makes a future, and power is still visible at the center of things. They are pedestrian cities whose inhabitants are confident in their movements, familiar with the crucial geography. Paris is all these things, and it has had major revolutions and insurrections in 1789, 1830, 1848, 1871, and 1968, and in recent times, myriad protests and strikes.

---

seeking amid the wild lights and shadows of the populous city, that infinity of mental excitement which quiet

---

Hobsbawm addresses Haussmann's reshaping of Paris when he writes, "Urban reconstruction, however, had another and probably unintended effect on potential rebellions, for the new and wide avenues provided an ideal location for what became an increasingly important aspect of popular movements, the mass demonstration or rather procession. The more systematic these rings and cartwheels of boulevards, the more effectively isolated those were from the surrounding inhabited area, the easier it became to turn such assemblies into ritual marches rather than preliminaries to riot." In Paris itself, it seems that the saturation of ceremonial, symbolic, and public space makes the people there peculiarly susceptible to revolution. That is to say, the French are a people for whom a parade is an army if it marches like one, for whom the government falls if they believe it has, and this seems to be because they have a capital where the representational and the real are so interfused and because their imaginations too dwell in public, engaged with public issues, public dreams. "I take my desires for reality, because I believe in the reality of my desires," said graffiti on the Sorbonne in the student-led uprising of May 1968. That uprising captured its most crucial territory, the national imagination, and it was on this territory as well as the Latin Quarter and the strike sites around France that they came within a hairsbreadth of toppling Europe's strongest government. "The difference between rebellion at Columbia and rebellion at the Sorbonne is that life in Manhattan went on as before, while in Paris every section of society was set on fire, in the space of a few days," wrote Mavis Gallant, who was there in the streets of the Latin Quarter. "The collective hallucination was that life can change, quite suddenly and for the better. It still strikes me as a noble desire."

Everyone knows how the French Revolution began. On July 11, 1789, Louis XVI dismissed the popular minister Jacques Necker, further stirring up his already turbulent capital. Parisians must have been imagining an armed revolt, for 6,000 of them spontaneously assembled to storm the Invalides and seize the rifles stored there, then went on to conquer the Bastille across the river for more military supplies, with results still celebrated in parades and festivals throughout France every July 14, Bastille Day. Life did change, suddenly and, in the long run, for the better. The liberation of that medieval fortress-prison symbolically ended centuries of despotism but the revolution didn't really begin until the march of the market women three months later. The revolution's intellectual origins lay in the ideals of liberty and justice prompted in part by Enlightenment philosophers

---

observation can afford.——EDGAR ALLAN POE, "THE MURDERS IN THE RUE MORGUE"   *In cities men cannot be* such as Thomas Paine, Rousseau, and Voltaire, but it also had bodily origins. In the summer of 1788 a devastating hailstorm had wiped out much of the harvest across France, and in 1789 the people felt the effects. Bread rose in price and became scarce, ordinary people often began standing in line at the bakeries at 4 A.M. in the hope of buying a loaf that day, and the poor began to become the hungry. Bodily causes had bodily effects; it was to be a revolution not merely of ideas but of bodies liberated, starving, marching, dancing, rioting, decapitated, on the stage of Parisian streets and squares. Revolutions are always politics made bodily, politics when actions become the usual form of speech. Britain and France had had food and tax riots before, but nothing quite like this combination of hunger for food and for ideals.

In the heady days after the fall of the Bastille, the market women and *poissardes*, or fishwives, had grown accustomed to marching together, and they must have first felt their common desires and collective strength during the religious processions they went on that season. At least one local was alarmed "at the discipline, pageantry, and magnitude of the almost daily processions of market women, laundresses, tradesmen, and workers of different districts that, during August and September, wound up the rue Saint-Jacques to the newly built church of Sainte-Genevieve [patroness of Paris] for thanksgiving services." Simon Schama points out that on the feast-day of Saint Louis, August 25, the market women of Paris traditionally went to Versailles to present the queen with bouquets. It is as though having learned the form of the procession, they could give it new content: having marched to pay homage to church and state, they were ready to march to demand terms.

On the morning of October 5, 1789, a girl took a drum to the central markets of Les Halles, while in the insurrectionary faubourg Saint-Antoine a woman compelled a local cleric to ring the church bells in his church. Drum and bells gathered a crowd. The women—now numbering in the thousands—chose a hero of the Bastille to lead them, Stanislas-Marie Maillard, who found himself constantly preaching moderation to his followers. Though made up mostly of poor working women—fishwives, market women, laundresses, portresses—the crowd included some women of means and a few noted revolutionaries, such as Theroigne de Mericourt, known as Theroigne the Amazon. (Prostitutes and men dressed as women loomed large in contemporary accounts of the march, but this seems to

---

prevented from concerting together, and awakening a mutual excitement which prompts sudden and passionate

---

have been because many believed "respectable" women were incapable of such insurrection.) The women insisted on moving straight through the Tuileries, still the gardens of the king, and when a guard pulled his sword on one of the women in the lead, Maillard came to her defense—but "she delivered such a blow with her broom to the crossed swords of the men that they were both disarmed." They continued on chanting "Bread and to Versailles!" Later that day the marquis de Lafayette, hero of the American Revolution, led an army of about 20,000 national guards after them in equivocal support.

By early evening they were at the National Assembly in Versailles, demanding that this new governing body deal with the food shortage, and a few women were taken before the king to make their case. Before midnight the crowd was at the palace gates; and early in the morning the crowd came inside. It was a gory arrival—after a guardsman shot a young woman, the crowd decapitated two guards and rushed the royal apartments looking for the hated queen, Marie Antoinette. That day, the terrified royal family was forced to return to Paris with the jubilant, exhausted, victorious crowd. At the head of the long procession— Lafayette estimated it at 60,000—came the royal family in a carriage surrounded by women carrying branches of laurel, followed by the National Guard, escorting wagonloads of wheat and flour. At the rear, writes one historian, marched more women, "their decorated branches amidst the gleaming iron of pikes and musket barrels giving the impression, as one observer thought, of 'a walking forest.' It was still raining, and the roads were ankle deep in mud, yet they all seemed content, even cheerful." They shouted to passersby, "Here come the Baker, the Baker's Wife, and the Baker's Little Boy." The king in Paris was a very different entity than the king in Versailles. There the once absolute power of the French monarchy ebbed away, and he became a constitutional monarch, then a prisoner, and within a few years a victim of the guillotine as the revolution spiraled down into factions and bloodbaths.

History is often described as though it were made up entirely of negotiations in closed spaces and wars in open ones—of talking and fighting, of politicians and warriors. Earlier events of that revolution—the birth of the National Assembly and the storming of the Bastille—correspond to these versions. Yet the market women had managed to make history as ordinary citizens engaged in ordinary gestures. During the walk of the thousands of women to Versailles, they

---

assemblies. Cities may be looked upon as large assemblies, of which all the inhabitants are members; their populace

---

had overcome the weight of the past in which they had been deferential to all the usual authorities, while the traumas of the future were yet unforeseen. They had one day in which the world was with them, they feared nothing, armies followed in their wake, and they were not grist for history's mill but the grinders. Like mass marchers everywhere, they displayed a collective power—the power at the very least to withdraw their support and at the most to revolt violently—but they managed to start the revolution largely as marchers. They carried branches as well as muskets—for muskets operate in the realm of the real, but branches in that of the symbolic.

This intertwining of religious festivity, huge gatherings in public squares, and mass marches would appear again on the two hundredth anniversary of the beginning of the French Revolution. The revolutionary year began inauspiciously with government tanks literally crushing the student democracy movement in Beijing's Tiananmen Square, but across Europe Communist governments had lost their appetite for or their confidence in violent repression. Violence itself had become a far less casual tool than it had been before Gandhi spread his doctrine of nonviolence, human rights had become far more established, and media had made events around the world more visible. The American civil rights movement had demonstrated its effectiveness in the West, and peace movements and nonviolent direct-action tactics had become a global language of citizen resistance. As Hobsbawm points out, marching down the boulevard had largely replaced rioting in the quarter. Throughout Eastern Europe the insurrectionaries made it clear that nonviolence was part of their ideology. The revolution in Poland worked the way nonviolent changes are supposed to—slowly, with lots of outside political pressure and inside political negotiation, culminating in the free election of June 4, 1989—and all the revolutions benefited from Mikhail Gorbachev's shrewd dismantling of the Soviet Union. But in Hungary, East Germany, and Czechoslovakia, history was made in the streets, and their old cities accommodated public gatherings beautifully.

It was, reported Timothy Garton Ash, a funeral held thirty-one years late for Imre Nagy, executed for his part in the unsuccessful 1956 revolt, that started the revolution in Hungary. On June 16, two hundred thousand people marched in a gathering that would have been violently crushed in previous years. In the exhil-

---

exercise a prodigious influence upon the magistrates, and frequently execute their own wishes without the

---

aration of having recovered their history and their voice, dissidents stepped up their efforts, and on October 23, the new Hungarian Republic was born. East Germany was next. Repressive measures were at first stepped up—students on their way home from school and employees returning for work were arrested just for being in the vicinity of disturbances in East Berlin: even the everyday freedom to walk about had become criminalized (as, with curfews and bans on assembly, it often is in turbulent times or under repressive regimes). But Leipzig's Nikolaikirche had long held Monday-evening "prayers for peace" followed by demonstrations on adjacent Karl-Marx-Platz, and there the numbers began to grow. On October 2, fifteen to twenty thousand gathered at that square by the church in the largest spontaneous demonstration in East Germany since 1953, and by October 30, nearly half a million people marched. "From that time forward," writes Ash, "the people acted and the Party reacted." On November 4 a million people gathered in East Berlin's Alexanderplatz, carrying flags, banners, and posters, and on November 9 the Berlin Wall fell. A friend who was there told me it fell because so many people showed up when a false report circulated that the wall was down that they made it into a real event—the guards lost their nerve and let them through. It became true because enough people were there to make it true. Once again people were writing history with their feet.

Czechoslovakia's "Velvet Revolution" was the most marvelous of them all, and the last (Romania's Christmastime violence was something else altogether). In January of that magic year, playwright Václav Havel had been imprisoned for participating in a twentieth-anniversary commemoration of a student who had burned himself to death in Prague's heart, Wenceslas Square, in protest of the crushed "Prague Spring" revolution of 1968. November 17, 1989, was the anniversary of another Czech student martyr, killed by Nazis during the occupation, and this commemorative procession was far larger and far bolder than that of January. The crowd marched from Charles University, and when the official itinerary was over at dusk, they lit candles, produced flowers, and continued on through the streets, singing and chanting antigovernment slogans—the past once again becoming an occasion to address the present. At Wenceslas Square, policemen surrounded them and began clubbing anyone within reach. Marchers stampeded down side streets, where some slipped away or were taken into nearby homes, but many were injured. False accounts that one student had joined the ranks of student martyrs infuriated the nation. Afterward came spontaneous

---

intervention of public officers.—ALEXIS DE TOQUEVILLE, DEMOCRACY IN AMERICA   *We are nothing if we walk*

---

marches, strikes, and gatherings in Wenceslas Square—really a kilometer-long, immensely wide boulevard in the heart of the city—with hundreds of thousands of participants. Behind the scenes, in the Magic Lantern Theater, the recently released Havel brought together all the opposition groups into a political force to make something pragmatic of the power being taken in the streets (the Czech opposition was called the Civic Forum; the Slovak equivalent was called the Public Against Violence).

Czechoslovakians had begun to live in public, gathering every day in Wenceslas Square and proceeding down adjoining Národní Avenue, getting their news from other participants, making and reading posters and signs, creating altars of flowers and candles—reclaiming the street as public space whose meaning would be determined by the public. "Prague," reported one journalist, "seemed hypnotized, caught in a magical trance. It had never ceased to be one of Europe's most beautiful cities, but for two long decades a cloud of repressive sadness had enveloped the Gothic and baroque towers. Now it vanished. The crowds were calm, confident and civilized. Each day, people assembled after work at 4pm, filing politely, patiently and purposefully into Wenceslas Square. . . . The city burst with color: posters were plastered on walls, on shop windows, on any inch of free space. After each mass rally, the crowd sang the National Anthem." Four days later the country's two most famous dissidents—Havel and the hero of 1968, Alexander Dubček—appeared on a balcony above the square, the latter in his first public appearance after twenty-one years of enforced silence. Dubček said at this time, "The government is telling us that the street is not the place for things to be solved, but I say the street was and is the place. The voice of the street must be heard."

The revolution that began by remembering a student peaked by celebrating a saint. Saint Agnes of Bohemia, great-granddaughter of the saintly Wenceslas, had been canonized a few weeks earlier. Prague's archbishop, a supporter of the opposition, held an outdoor mass for hundreds of thousands in the snow a few days after Dubček reappeared. Like the Hungarians, the Czechoslovakians had wrested their future free by remembering the heroes and martyrs of the past, for by December 10 there was a new government. Michael Kukral, a young American geographer who was there throughout the Velvet Revolution, wrote, "The time of massive and daily street demonstrations was over after November 27th, and thus, the entire character of the revolution metamorphosed. I did not

alone; we are everything when we walk together in step with other dignified feet.—SUBCOMMANDANTE MARCOS, awaken the next morning to find myself transformed into a giant bug, but I did feel a sense of sadness knowing that I will probably never again experience the momentum, spontaneity, and exhilaration of these past ten days."

Nineteen-eighty-nine was the year of the squares—of Tiananmen Square, of the Alexanderplatz, of Karl-Marx-Platz, of Wenceslas Square—and of the people who rediscovered the power of the public in such places. Tiananmen Square serves as a reminder that marches, protests, and seizures of public space don't always produce the desired results. But many other struggles lie somewhere in between the Velvet Revolution and the bloodbaths of repression, and the 1980s were a decade of great political activism: in the colossal antinuclear movements in Kazakhstan, Britain, Germany, and the United States, in the myriad marches against U.S. intervention in Central America, in the students around the world who urged their universities to divest from South Africa and helped topple the apartheid regime there, in the queer parades increasing through the decade and the radical AIDS activists at the end of the decade, in the populist movements that took to the streets of the Philippines and many other countries.

A few years earlier another insurrection found a square for its stage. The saga of the Mothers of the Plaza de Mayo began when these women started to notice each other at the police stations and government offices, making the same fruitless inquiries after children who had been "disappeared" by agents of the brutal military junta that seized power in 1976. "Secrecy," writes Marguerite Guzman Bouvard, "was a hallmark of the junta's Dirty War. . . . In Argentina the abductions were carried out beneath a veneer of normalcy so that there would be no outcry, so that the terrible reality would remain submerged and elusive even to the families of the abducted." Mostly homemakers with little education and no political experience, these women came to realize that they had to make the secret public, and they pursued their cause with a stunning lack of regard for their own safety. On April 30, 1977, fourteen mothers went to the Plaza de Mayo in the center of Buenos Aires. It was the place where Argentinean independence had been proclaimed in 1810 and where Juan Perón had given his populist speeches, a plaza at the heart of the country. Sitting there was, a policeman shouted, tantamount to holding an illegal meeting, and so they began walking around the obelisk in the center of the plaza.

1995   *She's gravely ill now from a hunger strike, and she's told the generals that she'll gladly leave. But she*

There and then, wrote a Frenchman, the generals lost their first battle and the Mothers found their identity. It was the plaza that gave them their name, and their walks there every Friday that made them famous. "Much later," writes Bouvard, "they described their walks as marches, not as walking, because they felt that they were marching toward a goal and not just circling aimlessly. As the Fridays succeeded one another and the numbers of Mothers marching around the plaza increased, the police began to take notice. Vanloads of policemen would arrive, take names, and force the Mothers to leave." Attacked with dogs and clubs, arrested and interrogated, they kept returning to perform this simple act of remembrance for so many years that it became ritual and history and made the name of the plaza known around the world. They marched carrying photographs of those children mounted like political placards on sticks or hung around their neck, and wearing white kerchiefs embroidered with the names of their disappeared children and the dates of their disappearances (later they were embroidered instead, "Bring Them Back Alive").

"They tell me that, while they are marching they feel very close to their children," wrote the poet Marjorie Agosin, who walked with them. "And the truth is, in the plaza where forgetting is not allowed, memory recovers its meaning." For years these women taking the national trauma on a walk were the most public opposition to the regime. By 1980 they had created a network of mothers around the country, and in 1981 they began the first of their annual twenty-four-hour marches to celebrate Human Rights Day (they also joined religious processions around the country). "By this time the Mothers were no longer alone during their marches; the Plaza was swarming with journalists from abroad who had come to cover the strange phenomenon of middle-aged woman marching in defiance of a state of siege." When the military junta fell in 1983, the Mothers were honored guests at the inauguration of the newly elected president, but they kept up their weekly walks counterclockwise around the obelisk in the Plaza de Mayo, and the thousands who had been afraid before joined them. They still walk counterclockwise around the tall obelisk every Thursday.

There are many ways to measure the effectiveness of protest. There's its impact on the wider public, directly and through the media, and there's its impact on the

---

said, "I want all political prisoners released, and I want to walk to the airport." It's twenty miles from her house to

---

government—on its audiences. But what's often forgotten is its impact on the protesters, who themselves suddenly become the public in literal public space, no longer an audience but a force. I had a taste, once, of this public life during the first weeks of the Gulf War, of living there more intensely than in San Francisco's many annual marches and parades before and since. Not much was written then or has been since about the huge protests all over the country in January 1991— surrounding Philadelphia's Independence Hall, gathering in Lafayette Park across from the White House, occupying the Washington State and Texas legislatures, shutting down the Brooklyn Bridge, covering Seattle in posters and demonstrations, holding "gas-pump protests" across the South. But there was, amid the fear and more deferential versions of patriotism, a huge outcry that continued for weeks in San Francisco. I don't mean to suggest that we had the courage of the Mothers of the Plaza de Mayo or the impact of the people of Prague, only that we too lived for a while in public. The whole strategy of that war—its speed, its colossal censorship, its reliance on high-tech weaponry, its very limited ground combat—was organized to defeat opposition at home by limiting information and U.S. casualties, which suggests that protest and popular opinion were so strong a force that the war (and the little wars like it since) was a preemptive strike against them.

We went out into the streets anyway, and the very space of the city was transformed. Before the first bombs dropped, people began to gather spontaneously, to march together, to make bonfires out of the old Christmas trees put out on the streets, to organize rituals and gatherings, to plaster the city with posters that seemed to make the very walls break their silence with calls for specific actions and caustic commentaries on the meaning of the war. Many of the demonstrations here, as elsewhere, instinctively headed for the traffic arteries—bridges, highways—or for the power points—the federal building, the stock exchange— and shut them down. There were protests almost daily into February. The city was being remade as a place whose center did not belong to business or to cars, but to pedestrians moving down the street in this most bodily form of free speech. The streets were no longer antechambers to the interiors of homes, schools, offices, shops, but a colossal amphitheater. I wonder now if anyone has ever protested or paraded simply because such occasions provide the only time when American city streets are a perfect place to be a pedestrian, safe from as-

---

the airport. And she has so rallied the spirit of her people that the generals rightly fear that the whole country sault by cars and strangers if not, occasionally, police. From the middle of the street, the sky is wider and the shop windows are opaque.

The Saturday evening before the war began, I ditched my car and walked in the boisterous march that coalesced spontaneously, drawing people out of bars and cafés and homes. I marched in the well-organized protest the day before the war broke out with a few thousand others. I joined more thousands the afternoon the war broke out to march again through the dark and our own horror to the Federal Building. The next morning I blockaded Highway 101 with the group of activists I spent much of the war with, until the highway patrol began clubbing away and broke one man's leg, and later that morning I walked with twenty or thirty others again down the city streets into the financial and commercial district. On the weekend after the war broke out, I walked with 200,000 others who gathered to protest the war with banners and placards, puppets and chants. For those weeks my life seemed to be one continuous procession through the transformed city. Private concerns and personal fears faded away in the incendiary spirit of the time. The streets were our streets, and all our fear was for others. There were mutterings about using nuclear weapons and suggestions that Israel might be drawn into a conflict that seemed as though it could spread like wildfire into a worldwide conflagration. The horror about what was happening far away and the strength of the incendiary resistance inside us and around us generated extraordinary feeling. I have never felt anything as intensely as I did that war except for the most passionate love and the most mourned deaths (and it was a war with plenty of deaths, though few were of Americans until the effects of the war's toxic materials began to materialize).

The afternoon of the first day of the war, I got caught up in a police sweep and spent a few hours sitting down for a change, handcuffed in a bus near the center of activity, looking out the window, and in an odd truce, listening with the policemen to an arrested journalist's shortwave radio broadcasting the war. Missiles were being fired on Israel, and the radio said the inhabitants of Tel Aviv were all in sealed rooms wearing gas masks. That image stuck with me, of a war in which civilians lost sight of the world and of each others' faces and, from behind their hideous masks, lost even the ability to speak. Most Americans weren't much better off, voiceless in front of televisions running the same uninformative footage of the censored war over and over again. In living on the streets we were refusing

would turn out to cheer her if she took that twenty-mile walk.—PAUL MONETTE, ON AUNG SAN SUU KYI IN to consume the meaning of that war and instead producing our own meaning, on our streets and in our hearts if not in our government and media.

In those moments of moving through the streets with people who share one's beliefs comes the rare and magical possibility of a kind of populist communion—perhaps some find it in churches, armies, and sports teams, but churches are not so urgent, and armies and teams are driven by less noble dreams. At such times it is as though the still small pool of one's own identity has been overrun by a great flood, bringing its own grand collective desires and resentments, scouring out that pool so thoroughly that one no longer feels fear or sees the reflections of oneself but is carried along on that insurrectionary surge. These moments when individuals find others who share their dreams, when fear is overwhelmed by idealism or by outrage, when people feel a strength that surprises them, are moments in which they become heroes—for what are heroes but those so motivated by ideals that fear cannot sway them, those who speak for us, those who have power for good? A person who feels this all the time may become a fanatic or at least an annoyance, but a person who never feels it is condemned to cynicism and isolation. In those moments everyone becomes a visionary, everyone becomes a hero.

Histories of revolutions and uprisings are full of stories of generosity and trust between strangers, of incidents of extraordinary courage, of transcendence of the petty concerns of everyday life. In *1793*, Victor Hugo's novel of revolution, he wrote, "People lived in public: they ate at tables spread outside the doors; women seated on the steps of the churches made lint as they sang the 'Marseillaise.' Park Monceaux and the Luxembourg Gardens were parade-grounds. . . . Everything was terrible and no one was frightened. . . . Nobody seemed to have leisure: all the world was in a hurry." At the beginning of the Spanish Civil War, George Orwell wrote of Barcelona's transformation, "The revolutionary posters were everywhere, flaming from the walls in clean reds and blues that made the few remaining advertisements look like daubs of mud. Down the Ramblas, the wide central artery of the town where crowds of people streamed constantly to and fro, the loud-speakers were bellowing revolutionary songs all day and far into the night. . . . Above all there was a belief in the revolution and the future, a feeling

---

BURMA   *The Orthodox forbid women to pray together in groups, to pray out loud, and to hold a Torah.*

---

of having suddenly emerged into an era of equality and freedom." To use a Situationist word, there seems to be a psychogeography of insurrection in which life is lived in public and is about public issues, as manifested by the central ritual of the march, the volubility of strangers and of walls, the throngs in streets and plazas, and the intoxicating atmosphere of potential freedom that means the imagination has already been liberated. "Revolutionary moments are carnivals in which the individual life celebrates its unification with a regenerated society," writes Situationist Raoul Vaneigem.

But nobody remains heroic forever. It is the nature of revolutions to subside, which is not the same thing as to fail. A revolution is a lightning bolt showing us new possibilities and illuminating the darkness of our old arrangements so that we will never see them quite the same way again. People rise up for an absolute freedom, a freedom they will only find in their hopes and their acts at the height of that revolution. Sometimes they may have overthrown a dictator, but other dictators will arise and bring with them other ways of intimidating or enslaving the populace. Sometimes everyone will have a vote at last, food and justice will be adequate if not ideal, but ordinary traffic will return to the streets, the posters will fade, revolutionaries will go back to being housewives or students or garbage collectors, and the heart will become private again. On the first anniversary of the storming of the Bastille came the Fête de la Federation, a national festival of dances, visits, parades, and overflowing joy, and it was the spontaneous participation of all classes of Parisians in readying the Champ de Mars for their fête, rather than the fete itself, that was most exhilarating. A year later, on July 12, 1791, there was a military parade commemorating Voltaire, and the people who had participated in history ferociously and then joyously had become spectators again.

"Resistance is the secret of joy," proclaimed the pamphlet someone from Reclaim the Streets handed me in the middle of a Birmingham street, in the midst of one of their street parties. Reclaim the Streets was founded in London in May 1995 with the understanding that if the twin forces of privatized space and globalized economies are alienating us from each other and from local culture, the reclaiming of public space for public life and public festival is one way to resist both. The very act of revolting—happily and communally and in the middle of the street—

These women gathered to pray at the Western Wall in Jerusalem, and were assaulted by the Orthodox men, their was no longer a means to an end but victory itself. Imagined thus, the difference between revolutions and festivals becomes even less distinct, for in a world of dreary isolation festivals are inherently revolutionary. The RTS party in Birmingham three years later was intended as a counterpoint to the Group of Eight meeting that weekend, in which leaders from the world's top economic powers would make the world's future without consulting citizens or the poorer nations. Hundreds of thousands gathered by the group Christian Aid formed a human chain around the central city to demand that third-world debt be forgiven. Reclaim the Streets wasn't asking, but taking what they wanted.

There was a glorious moment when trumpeters blew a sort of pedestrian charge, and the thousands who'd come for this Global Street Party surged out of the bus station into Birmingham's main street. People quickly shimmied up light poles and hung banners: "Beneath the Tarmac the Grass," said one about sixty feet long, copping a line from May '68 in Paris, and "Stop the Car/Free the City" said another. Once people settled in, the great spirit of the move forward subsided into a fairly standard party of mostly young and scruffy people, dancing, mingling, stripping down in the steamy heat, not notably different from, say, Halloween in the Castro, except that it was illegal and obstructionist. Walking and marching are communal in spirit in ways that mingling after arrival is not. It wasn't, an RTS activist told me later, one of their great street parties, nothing compared to their three-day street party with the striking Liverpool dockworkers, or the rave-style protest of an intrusive new highway near London that included giant puppets wearing hoop skirts beneath which hid jackhammer operators putting holes in the overpass that were then planted with trees, or RTS spinoff the Revolutionary Pedestrian Front's pranks at an Alfa Romeo promotional event, or the taking over of Trafalgar Square. Perhaps some of the other places where sister street parties were held that day—Ankara, Berlin, Bogotá, Dublin, Istanbul, Madrid, Prague, Seattle, Turin, Vancouver, Zagreb—lived up to the glorious rhetoric of Reclaim the Streets' publications. Though Reclaim the Streets may not have fulfilled its goal, it has set a new one for every street action—now every parade, every march, every festival, can be regarded as a triumph over alienation, a reclaiming of the space of the city, of public space and public life, an opportunity to walk together in what is no longer a journey but already an arrival.

---

case is still pending in the Israeli Supreme Court.—MARTHA SHELLEY, *HAGGADAH: A CELEBRATION OF FREEDOM*

WALKING AFTER MIDNIGHT:
Women, Sex, and Public Space

Caroline Wyburgh, age nineteen, went "walking out" with a sailor in Chatham, England, in 1870. Walking had long been an established part of courtship. It was free. It gave the lovers a semiprivate space in which to court, whether in a park, a plaza, a boulevard, or a byway (and such rustic landscape features as lovers' lanes gave them private space in which to do more). Perhaps, in the same way that marching together affirms and generates solidarity between a group, this delicate act of marching the rhythms of their strides aligns two people emotionally and bodily; perhaps they first feel themselves a pair by moving together through the evening, the street, the world. As a way of doing that something closest to doing nothing, strolling together allows them to bask in each other's presence, obliged neither to converse continually nor to do something so engaging as to prevent them from conversing. And in Britain the term "walking out together" sometimes meant something explicitly sexual, but more often expressed that an ongoing connection had been established, akin to the modern American phrase "going steady." In James Joyce's novella *The Dead*, the husband who has just discovered that his wife had a suitor in her youth asks if she loved that now-dead boy, and she replies, devastatingly, "I used to go out walking with him."

Caroline Wyburgh, age nineteen, was seen walking with her soldier, and because of it she was dragged from her bed late one night by a police inspector. The Contagious Diseases Acts in effect at that time gave police in barracks towns the

---

A female ophthalmologist, who is herself veiled, discounted the problem. "There is no proof it affects the vision at

---

power to arrest anyone they suspected of being a prostitute. Merely walking about in the wrong time or place could put a woman under suspicion, and the law allowed any woman so accused or suspected to be arrested. If the arrested woman refused to undergo a medical examination, she could be sentenced to months in jail; but the painful and humiliating medical examination constituted punishment too; and if she was found to be infected, she was confined to a medical prison. Guilty till proven innocent, she could not escape unscathed. Wyburgh supported herself and her mother by washing doorsteps and basements, and her mother, fearing the loss of their income for so long, tried to persuade her to submit to the examination rather than to serve the three-month prison sentence. She refused, and so the officers of the law strapped her to a bed for four days. On the fifth day she agreed to be examined, but her willingness failed her after she was taken to the surgery, straitjacketed, thrust onto an examining couch with her feet strapped apart, and held down by an assistant who planted an elbow on her chest. She struggled, rolled off the couch with her ankles still strapped in, and severely injured herself. But the surgeon laughed, for his instruments of inspection had deflowered her, and blood poured between her legs. "You have been telling the truth," he said. "You are not a bad girl."

The soldier was never named, arrested, inspected, or otherwise drawn into the legal system, and men have usually had an easier time walking down the street than have women. Women have routinely been punished and intimidated for attempting that most simple of freedoms, talking a walk, because their walking and indeed their very beings have been construed as inevitably, continually sexual in those societies concerned with controlling women's sexuality. Throughout the history of walking I have been tracing, the principal figures—whether of peripatetic philosophers, flâneurs, or mountaineers—have been men, and it is time to look at why women were not out walking too.

"Being born a woman is my awful tragedy," wrote Sylvia Plath in her journal when she too was nineteen. "Yes, my consuming desire to mingle with road crews, sailors and soldiers, barroom regulars—to be part of a scene, anonymous, listening, recording—all is spoiled by the fact that I am a girl, a female always in danger of assault and battery. My consuming interest in men and their lives is often misconstrued as a desire to seduce them, or as an invitation to intimacy. Yes, God, I want to talk to everybody I can as deeply as I can. I want to be able to sleep in an open field, to travel west, to walk freely at night." Plath seems to have

---

all," she said. "And if women see less well at night, well, no good Muslim woman should be out at night been interested in men for the very reason she was unable to investigate them—because their greater freedom made their lives more interesting to a young woman just setting out on her own. There are three prerequisites to taking a walk—that is, to going out into the world to walk for pleasure. One must have free time, a place to go, and a body unhindered by illness or social restraints. Free time has many variables, but most public places at most times have not been as welcoming and as safe for women. Legal measures, social mores subscribed to by both men and women, the threat implicit in sexual harassment, and rape itself have all limited women's ability to walk where and when they wished. (Women's clothes and bodily confinements—high heels, tight or fragile shoes, corsets and girdles, very full or narrow skirts, easily damaged fabrics, veils that obscure vision—are part of the social mores that have handicapped women as effectively as laws and fears.)

Women's presence in public becomes with startling frequency an invasion of their private parts, sometimes literally, sometimes verbally. Even the English language is rife with words and phrases that sexualize women's walking. Among the terms for prostitutes are streetwalkers, women of the streets, women on the town, and public women (and of course phrases such as a public man, man about town, or man of the streets mean very different things than do their equivalents attached to women). A woman who has violated sexual convention can be said to be strolling, roaming, wandering, straying—all terms that imply that women's travel is inevitably sexual or that their sexuality is transgressive when it travels. Had a group of women called themselves the Sunday Tramps, as did a group of Leslie Stephen's male friends, the moniker would have implied not that they went walking but that they engaged in something salacious on Sundays. Of course women's walking is often construed as performance rather than transport, with the implication that women walk not to see but to be seen, not for their own experience but for that of a male audience, which means that they are asking for whatever attention they receive. Much has been written about how women walk, as erotic assessment—from the seventeenth-century miss whose "feet beneath her petticoat / like little mice, stole in and out" to Marilyn Monroe's wiggle—and as instruction on the right way to walk. Less has been written about where we walk.

Other categories of people have had their freedom of movement limited, but limitations based on race, class, religion, ethnicity, and sexual orientation are local and variable compared to those placed on women, which have profoundly

---

unaccompanied."—JAN GOODWIN, *PRICE OF HONOR: MUSLIM WOMEN LIFT THE VEIL OF SILENCE ON THE ISLAMIC*

---

shaped the identities of both genders over the millennia in most parts of the world. There are biological and psychological explanations for these states of affairs, but the social and political circumstances seem most relevant. How far back can one go? In Middle Assyria (circa the seventeenth to eleventh centuries B.C.), women were divided into two categories. Wives and widows "who go out onto the street" may not have their heads uncovered, said the law; prostitutes and slave girls, contrarily, must not have their heads covered. Those who illicitly wore a veil could be given fifty lashes or have pitch poured over their heads. The historian Gerda Lerner comments, "Domestic women, sexually serving one man and under his protection, are here designated as 'respectable' by being veiled; women not under one man's protection and sexual control are designated as 'public women,' hence unveiled. . . . This pattern of enforced visible discrimination recurs throughout historical time in the myriad regulations which place 'disreputable women' in certain districts or certain houses marked with clearly identifiable signs or which force them to register with the authorities and carry identification cards." Of course "respectable" women have been equally regulated, but more by social constraints than legal ones. Many things are remarkable about the appearance of this law, whose ordering of the world seems to have prevailed ever since. It makes women's sexuality a public rather than a private matter. It equates visibility with sexual accessibility, and it requires a material barrier rather than a woman's morality or will to make her inaccessible to passersby. It separates women into two publicly recognized castes based on sexual conduct but allows men, whose sexuality remains private, access to both castes. Membership in the respectable caste comes at the cost of consignment to private life; membership in the caste with spatial and sexual freedom comes at the cost of social respect. Either way, the law makes it virtually impossible to be a respected public female figure, and ever since, women's sexuality has been public business.

Homer's Odysseus travels the world and sleeps around. Odysseus's wife Penelope stays dutifully at home, rebuffing the suitors she lacks the authority to reject outright. Travel, whether local or global, has remained a largely masculine prerogative ever since, with women often the destination, the prize, or keepers of the hearth. By the fifth century B.C. in Greece, these radically different roles were defined as those of the interior and exterior, the private and the public spheres. Athenian women, writes Richard Sennett, "were confined to houses because of their supposed physiological defects." He quotes Pericles concluding his funeral

---

WORLD   *I could not walk out alone, without giving suspicion to the whole family; should I be watched, and seen* oration with advice to the women of Athens—"The greatest glory of a woman is to be least talked about by men, whether they are praising you or criticizing you"—and Xenophon telling wives, "Your business will be to stay indoors." Women in ancient Greece lived far from the celebrated public spaces and public life of the cities. Throughout much of the Western world into the present, women have remained relatively housebound, not only by law in some countries even now, but by custom and fear in others. The usual theory for this control of women is that in cultures where patrilineal descent is important for inheritance and identity, controlling women's sexuality has been the means of ensuring paternity. (Anyone who thinks such matters are archaic or irrelevant need merely remember the anatomist-evolutionist Owen Lovejoy, discussed in chapter 3, attempting to naturalize this social order by theorizing that female monogamy and immobility were important for our species long before we became human.) But there are many other factors pertaining to the creation of a dominant gender whose privileges include controlling and defining the female sexuality often viewed as chaotic, threatening, and subversive—a sort of wild nature to be subdued by masculine culture.

Architectural historian Mark Wiggins writes, "In Greek thought women lack the internal self-control credited to men as the very mark of their masculinity. This self-control is no more than the maintenance of secure boundaries. These internal boundaries . . . cannot be maintained by a woman because her fluid sexuality endlessly overflows and disrupts them. And more than this she endlessly disrupts the boundaries of others, that is, men. . . . In these terms the role of architecture is explicitly the control of sexuality, or more precisely, women's sexuality, the chastity of the girl, the fidelity of the wife. . . . While the house protects the children from the elements, its primary role is to protect the father's genealogical claims by isolating women from other men." Thus, women's sexuality is controlled via the regulation of public and private space. In order to keep women "private," or sexually accessible to one man and inaccessible to all others, her whole life would be consigned to the private space of the home that served as a sort of masonry veil.

Prostitutes have been more regulated than any other women, as though the social constraints they had escaped pursued them as laws. (Prostitutes' customers,

---

to meet a man—judge of the consequence!—MARY WORTLEY MONTAGU, 1712   *How beautiful are thy feet in*

---

of course, have almost never been regulated in any way, either by law or by social condemnation: think of Walter Benjamin and André Breton a few chapters ago, who managed to write about their relations with prostitutes without fear of losing their status as public intellectuals or marriageable men.) Throughout the nineteenth century, many European governments attempted to regulate prostitution by limiting the circumstances in which it could be carried out, and this often became a limitation of the circumstances in which any woman could walk. Nineteenth-century women were often portrayed as too frail and pure for the mire of urban life and compromised for being out at all if they didn't have a specific purpose. Thus women legitimized their presence by shopping—proving they were not for purchase by purchasing—and stores have long provided safe semipublic havens in which to roam. One of the arguments about why women could not be flâneurs was that they were, as either commodities or consumers, incapable of being sufficiently detached from the commerce of city life. Once the stores closed, so did much of their opportunity to wander (which was hardest on working women, for whom the evening was their only free time). In Germany the vice squad persecuted women who were out alone in the evening, and a Berlin doctor commented, "The young men strolling on the streets think only that a woman of good reputation does not allow herself to be seen in the evening." Public visibility and independence were still equated, as they had been three thousand years earlier, with sexual disreputability; women's sexuality could still be defined by geographical as well as temporal locale. Think of Dorothy Wordsworth and her fictional sister Elizabeth Bennet upbraided for going out walking in the country, or Edith Wharton's New York heroine in *The House of Mirth* risking her social status at the beginning of the novel to walk into a man's house unchaperoned for a cup of tea and ruining that status for good by being seen to leave another man's house in the evening (while the law controls "disreputable women," "respectable women" often patrol each other).

By the 1870s in France, Belgium, Germany, and Italy, prostitutes were only allowed to solicit at certain times. France was particularly cynical in its regulation of prostitution; the practice was licensed, and both the licensing and the banning of unlicensed sexual commerce allowed the police to control women. Any woman could be arrested for soliciting merely because she appeared in the times and places associated with the sex industry, while known prostitutes could be arrested for appearing in any other time or place—women had been divided into

---

shoes, O prince's daughter! the joints of thy thighs are like jewels.—SONG OF SOLOMON 7:1   *"You're wearing*

---

diurnal and nocturnal species. One prostitute was arrested for "shopping in Les Halles at nine o'clock in the morning and was charged with speaking to a man (the stall holder), and with being off the beat stipulated on her registration license." By that time, the Police des Moeurs, or Morals Police, could arrest working-class women for anything or nothing, and they would sometimes round up groups of female passersby on the boulevards to meet their quotas. At first watching the women get arrested was a masculine pastime, but by 1876 the abuses became so extreme that boulevardiers sometimes tried to interfere and got arrested themselves. The mostly young, mostly poor, unmarried women and girl children arrested were seldom found innocent; many were incarcerated behind the high walls of Saint Lazare prison, where they lived in dire circumstances, cold, malnourished, unwashed, overworked, and forbidden to speak. They were released when they agreed to register as prostitutes, while women who ran away from licensed brothels were given the choice of either returning to the brothel or being sent to Saint Lazare—thus women were forced into rather than out of prostitution. Many committed suicide rather than face arrest. The great champion of human rights for prostitutes Josephine Butler visited Saint Lazare in the 1870s: "I asked what the crime was for which the greater number were in prison and was told it was for walking in streets which are forbidden, and at hours which are forbidden!"

Butler, a well-educated, upper-class woman who grew up amid progressives, was the most effective opponent of Britain's Contagious Diseases Acts passed in the 1860s. A devout Christian, she opposed the laws both because they put the state in the business of regulating prostitution and thus, implicitly, of condoning it and because they enforced a double standard. Women could be punished by incarceration or by the inspections dubbed "surgical rape" for the slightest suspicion of being a prostitute, and a woman found to carry a venereal disease was confined and treated, while men were left free to continue spreading it (similar measures have been considered and sometimes carried out in regards to prostitutes and AIDS in recent years). The law had been passed to protect the health of the army, whose soldiers had a much higher incidence of such diseases than the general public; it seems to have been based on a cynical recognition that the health, freedom, and civil rights of men were of greater value to the state than those of women. Many more extreme abuses than that of Caroline Wyburgh were carried out, and at least one woman—a widowed mother of three—was

---

flat 'eels. Are you a Lesbian?"—LONDON PASSERBY TO A STREETWALKER   *Her body is perfectly balanced, she*

---

hounded into suicide. Going out walking had become evidence of sexual activity, and sexual activity on the part of women had been criminalized. Though the laws in the United States were never quite so bad, similar circumstances sometimes prevailed. In 1895 a young working-class New Yorker named Lizzie Schauer was arrested as a prostitute because she was out alone after dark and had stopped to ask directions of two men. Though she was in fact on her way to her aunt's house on the Lower East Side, the act and the time were interpreted as signs that she was soliciting. Only after a medical examination proved she was a "good girl" was she released. Had she not been a virgin, she might well have been found guilty of a crime compounded of the twin acts of having been sexual and of walking alone in the evening.

Though protecting respectable women from vice had long been one rationale for state regulation and prosecution of prostitution, the eminently respectable Butler took on the formidable task of protecting women from the state, for which she was vilified and chased by mobs (often hired by brothel owners). On one occasion the mob caught her and she was badly beaten and smeared with dirt and excrement, her hair and clothes torn; on another, a prostitute she came across as she fled a mob led her through a labyrinth of back streets and empty warehouses to safety. Of course she herself had transgressed by moving into the public sphere of political discourse and challenging the sexual conduct of men, and she was decried by one member of Parliament as "worse than prostitutes." As she lay dying in 1906, far more women were moving into that sphere and meeting with similar treatment. The women's suffrage movement in the United States and Britain, after decades of quiet and ineffectual effort to gain the vote for women, became militant in the first decade of the twentieth century, with an extraordinary campaign of marches, demonstrations, and public meetings—the now-usual forms of outdoor politicking available to those denied entrée to the system. These demonstrations were met with an unusual degree of violence—by the police in Britain, and by crowds of soldiers and other men in the United States. Union activists, religious nonconformists, and others had been met by violence before, but some of the things that happened to the suffragettes were unique. In Britain archaic laws were invoked to criminalize the women's public gatherings, and current laws that gave all citizens the right to petition the government were violated. In both the United States and Britain these women arrested for exercising their right to be and to speak in public went on hunger strike, demanding

holds herself straight, and yet nothing suggests a ramrod. She takes steps of medium length, and like all people who they be recognized as political prisoners. Both governments responded by force-feeding the prisoners, and the agonizing procedure—which involved restraining the woman, forcing a tube down her nostrils to her stomach, and pumping in food—became a new form of institutional rape. Once again women who had attempted to participate in public life by walking down the street were locked up and found the privacy of their bodily interiors violated by the state.

But women won the vote, and in recent decades most of this strange duet between public space and private parts has been not between women and the government but between women and men. Feminism has largely addressed and achieved reforms of interactions indoors—in the home, the workplace, the schools, and the political system. Yet access to public space, urban and rural, for social, political, practical, and cultural purposes is an important part of everyday life, one limited for women by their fear of violence and harassment. The routine harassment women experience ensures, in the words of one scholar of the subject, "that women will not feel at ease, that we will remember our role as sexual beings, available to, accessible to men. It is a reminder that we are not to consider ourselves equals, participating in public life with our own right to go where we like when we like, to pursue our own projects with a sense of security." Both men and women may be assaulted for economic reasons, and both have been incited by crime stories in the news to fear cities, strangers, the young, the poor, and uncontrolled spaces. But women are the primary targets of sexualized violence, which they encounter in suburban and rural as well as urban spaces, from men of all ages and income levels, and the possibility of such violence is implicit in the more insulting and aggressive propositions, comments, leers, and intimidations that are part of ordinary life for women in public places. Fear of rape puts many women in their place—indoors, intimidated, dependent yet again on material barriers and protectors rather than their own will to safeguard their sexuality. Two-thirds of American women are afraid to walk alone in their own neighborhoods at night, according to one poll, and another reported that half of British women were afraid to go out after dark alone and 40 percent were "very worried" about being raped.

Like Caroline Wyburgh and Sylvia Plath, I was nineteen when I first felt the full force of this lack of freedom. I had grown up on the suburban edge of the country in the days before children were closely supervised and I went to town or to the hills at will, and at seventeen I ran away to Paris, where the men who

---

move and dance well, walks from the hip, not the knee. On no account does she swing her arms, nor does she rest a

often propositioned and occasionally grabbed me in the streets seemed more annoying than terrifying. At nineteen, I moved to a poor San Francisco neighborhood with less street life than the gay neighborhood I had moved from and
discovered that at night the day's constant threats were more likely to be carried
out. Of course it wasn't only poor neighborhoods and nighttime in which I was
threatened. I was, for example, followed near Fisherman's Wharf one afternoon
by a well-dressed man who murmured a long stream of vile sexual proposals to
me; when I turned around and told him off, he recoiled in genuine shock at my
profanity, told me I had no right to speak to him like that, and threatened to kill
me. Only the earnestness of his death threat made the incident stand out from
hundreds of others more or less like it. It was the most devastating discovery of
my life that I had no real right to life, liberty, and pursuit of happiness out-of-
doors, that the world was full of strangers who seemed to hate me and wish to
harm me for no reason other than my gender, that sex so readily became violence, and that hardly anyone else considered it a public issue rather than a private problem. I was advised to stay indoors at night, to wear baggy clothes, to
cover or cut my hair, to try to look like a man, to move to someplace more expensive, to take taxis, to buy a car, to move in groups, to get a man to escort me—
all modern versions of Greek walls and Assyrian veils, all asserting it was my
responsibility to control my own and men's behavior rather than society's to ensure my freedom. I realized that many women had been so successfully socialized
to know their place that they had chosen more conservative, gregarious lives
without realizing why. The very desire to walk alone had been extinguished in
them—but it had not in me.

The constant threats and the few incidents of real terror transformed me. Still,
I stayed where I was, became more adept at navigating the dangers of the street,
and became less of a target as I grew older. Almost all my interactions nowadays
with passersby are civil, and some are delightful. Young women receive the brunt
of such harassment, I think, not because they are more beautiful but because they
are less sure of their rights and boundaries (though such unsureness manifested as
naïveté and timidity are often part of what is considered beauty). The years of
harassment received in youth constitute an education in the limits of one's life,
even long after the daily lessons stop. Sociologist June Larkin got a group of
Canadian teenagers to keep track of their sexual harassment in public and found
they were leaving the less dramatic incidents out because, as one said, "If I wrote

---

hand on her hip! Nor, when walking, does she wave her hands about in gesticulation.—EMILY POST, down every little thing that happened on the street, it would take up too much time." Having met so many predators, I learned to think like prey, as have most women, though fear is far more minor an element of my everyday awareness than it was when I was in my twenties.

The movements for women's rights often came out of the movements for racial justice. The first great women's convention at Seneca Falls, New York, was organized by abolitionists Elizabeth Cady Stanton and Lucretia Mott out of anger over the discrimination they faced even while trying to fight against slavery—they had attended the World's Anti-Slavery Convention in London, only to find that the male-dominated organization would not seat any female delegates. "Stanton and Mott," writes one historian, "began to see similarities between their own circumscribed status and that of slaves." Josephine Butler and the English suffrage leader Emmeline Pankhurst also came from abolitionist families, and in recent years some of the most original and important feminists have been black women—bell hooks, Michelle Wallace, June Jordan—who address both race and gender.

When I wrote of the gay poets of New York, I left out the Harlem-born James Baldwin, because for him Manhattan was not a deliciously liberatory place where he could lose himself, as it was for Whitman and Ginsberg. It threatened instead never to let him forget himself, whether it was the policemen near the Public Library telling him to stay uptown, the pimps on uptown Fifth Avenue trying to recruit him, when he was a boy, to become one of the dangers, or the people in his own neighborhood keeping track of him as do people in small towns. He wrote about walking the city as a black man rather than a gay one, though he was both; his race limited his roaming until he moved to Paris. Black men nowadays are seen as working-class women were a century ago: as a criminal category when in public, so that the law often actively interferes with their freedom of movement. In 1983 an African-American man, Edward Lawson, won a Supreme Court case challenging a California statute that "required persons who loiter or wander on the streets to provide a credible and reliable identification and to account for their presence when requested by a peace officer." Lawson, who, the *New York Times* reported, "liked to walk and was often stopped late at night in residential areas," had been arrested fifteen times for refusing to identify himself under this

------

ETIQUETTE   *"I call them limousine shoes," she says of the pointy toes that will make the rounds this fall. "One*

------

statute criminalizing walking. An athletic man with tidy dreadlocks, he used to dance at the same nightclub I did then.

But in public space, racism has often been easier to recognize than sexism and far more likely to become an issue. Late in the 1980s two young black men died for being in "the wrong place at the wrong time." Michael Griffith was chased by a gang of hostile white men in Howard Beach, ran out into traffic to escape their persecution, and was killed by a car. Yusef Hawkins was bludgeoned to death for being a black man in another white Queens neighborhood, Bensonhurst. An enormous outcry arose over these two cases; people rightly understood that these young men's civil rights had been stripped from them when they were attacked for walking down the street. Not long after Griffith and Hawkins died in Queens, a large group of teenage boys from uptown Manhattan went into Central Park at night and found a white female jogger. She was gang-raped, cut with knives, beaten with rocks and pipes, her skull was crushed, and she lost most of her blood. Expected to die, she survived with brain damage and physical disabilities.

"The Central Park Jogger Case" was discussed in startlingly different terms. Considerable public outrage had been expressed that the two murdered men had been denied the basic liberty to roam the city, and the crimes were universally recognized as racially motivated. But in a careful study of the Central Park case, Helen Benedict wrote, "Throughout the case, even up to the start of the trial, the white and black press kept running articles trying to analyze why the youths had committed this heinous crime. . . . They looked for answers in race, drugs, class, and in the ghetto's 'culture of violence.'" The reasons preferred, she concludes, "were woefully inadequate as an explanation . . . because the press never looked at the most glaring reason of all for rape: society's attitude toward women." Portraying it as a case about race—the assailants were Latino and black—rather than gender failed to make an issue at all of violence against women. And almost no one at all discussed the Central Park case as a civil rights issue—as part of a pattern of infringements on women's right to roam the city (women of color rarely show up in crime reportage at all, apparently since they lack men's status as citizens and white women's titillating appeal as victims). A decade after Bensonhurst and Central Park, the gruesome lynching of a black man in Texas has been greeted with outrage as a hate crime and an infringement on the civil rights of people of color, as has the brutal death of a young gay man in

woman wrote to me, 'My boyfriend wants me to wear high heels, but they hurt my feet.' I said, 'Tell him you'll wear

Wyoming—for gays and lesbians are also frequent targets of violence that "teaches them their place" or punishes them for their nonconformity. But similar murders motivated by gender, though they fill the newspapers and take the lives of thousands of women every year, are not contextualized as anything but isolated incidents that don't require social reform or national soul-searching.

The geography of race and gender are different, for a racial group may monopolize a whole region, while gender compartmentalizes in local ways. Many people of color find the whiter parts of rural America unwelcoming, to say the least, even in the places where a white woman might feel safe (white supremacists seem to arise from or flock to some of the most scenic parts of the country). Evelyn C. White writes that when she first tried to explore rural Oregon, memories of southern lynchings "could leave me speechless and paralyzed with the heart-stopping fear that swept over me as when I crossed paths with loggers near the McKenzie River or whenever I visited the outdoors." In Britain the photographer Ingrid Pollard made a series of wry portraits of herself in the Lake District, where she apparently went to try to feel like Wordsworth and felt nervous instead. Nature romanticism, she seemed to be saying, is not available to people of her color. But many white women too feel nervous in any isolated situation, and some have personal experience to draw upon. When she was young, the great climber and mountaineer Gwen Moffat went to the beautiful Isle of Skye off Scotland's west coast to climb by herself. After a drunken neighbor broke into her bedroom in the middle of the night, she cabled for a man to join her and recounts, "Had I been older and more mature, I could have coped with life on my own, but living as I did I laid myself open to all kinds of advances and speculations. Ordinary, conventional men thought this way of life an open invitation and I couldn't face the resentment which I knew they felt when they were rebuffed."

Women have been enthusiastic participants in pilgrimages, walking clubs, parades, processions, and revolutions, in part because in an already defined activity their presence is less likely to be read as sexual invitation, in part because companions have been women's best guarantee of public safety. In revolutions the importance of public issues seems to set aside private matters temporarily, and women have found great freedom during them (and some revolutionaries, such as

the shoes if he provides curb-to-curb service.'"—HARPER'S BAZAAR, 1997   *After the [Korean] city gates were*

Emma Goldman, have made sexuality one of the fronts on which they sought freedom). But walking alone also has enormous spiritual, cultural, and political resonance. It has been a major part of meditation, prayer, and religious exploration. It has been a mode of contemplation and composition, from Aristotle's peripatetics to the roaming poets of New York and Paris. It has supplied writers, artists, political theorists, and others with the encounters and experiences that inspired their work, as well as the space in which to imagine it, and it is impossible to know what would have become of many of the great male minds had they been unable to move at will through the world. Picture Aristotle confined to the house, Muir in full skirts. Even in times when women could walk by day, the night—the melancholic, poetic, intoxicating carnival of city nights—was likely to be off limits to them, unless they had become "women of the night." If walking is a primary cultural act and a crucial way of being in the world, those who have been unable to walk out as far as their feet would take them have been denied not merely exercise or recreation but a vast portion of their humanity.

Women from Jane Austen to Sylvia Plath have found other, narrower subjects for their art. Some have broken out into the larger world—Peace Pilgrim (in middle age), George Sand (in men's clothes), Emma Goldman, Josephine Butler, Gwen Moffat, come to mind—but many more must have been silenced altogether. Virginia Woolf's famous *Room of One's Own* is often recalled as though it were literally a plea for women to have home offices, but it in fact deals with economics, education, and access to public space as equally necessary to making art. To prove her point, she invents the blighted life of Shakespeare's equally talented sister, and asks of this Judith Shakespeare, "Could she even get her dinner in a tavern or roam the streets at midnight?"

Sarah Schulman wrote a novel that is, like Woolf's essay, a commentary on the circumscription of women's freedom. Titled *Girls, Visions and Everything* after a phrase from Jack Kerouac's *On the Road*, it is among other things an investigation into how useful Kerouac's credo is for a young lesbian writer, Lila Futuransky. "The trick," thinks Futuransky, "was to identify with Jack Kerouac instead of with the women he fucks along the way," for like Odysseus, Kerouac was a traveling man in a landscape of immobile women. She explores the charms of Lower East Side Manhattan in the mid-1980s as he did America in the 1950s, and among "the things she loved best" was to "walk the streets for hours with nowhere to go but where she ended up." But as the novel progresses, her world becomes more

closed . . . the city was turned over to women, who were then free to walk abroad. They strolled and chatted in intimate rather than more open: she falls in love and the possibility of a free life in public space recedes.

Near the end of the novel, she and her lover go out for an evening walk in Washington Square Park and come back to eat ice cream together in front of her apartment building when they overhear a man in a group of men: "That's gay liberation. They think they can do whatever they want whenever they want it." They have been, like lovers since time immemorial, walking out together. Like Lizzie Schauer, arrested in the Lower East Side ninety years earlier for walking alone, their venture into public space threatens to become an invasion of their private lives and their bodies:

"Lila didn't want to go upstairs, because she didn't want them to see where she lived. They started walking slowly away, but the men followed.

"'Come on you cunt. I bet you've got a nice pussy, you suck each other's pussy, right? I'll show you a cock that you'll never forget. . . .'

"For Lila, this was a completely normal though unnecessary part of daily life. As a result she had learned docility, to keep quiet and do a shuffle, to avoid having her ass kicked in. . . . Lila walked in the streets like someone who had always walked in the streets and for whom it was natural and rich. She walked with the illusion that she was safe and that the illusion would somehow keep her that way. Yet, that particular night as she went out for cigarettes, Lila walked uneasily, her mind wandering until it stopped of its own accord on the simple fact that she was not safe. She could be physically hurt at any time and felt, for a fleeting moment that she would be. She sat on the trunk of a '74 Chevy and accepted that this world was not hers. Even on her own block."

---

groups with their friends carrying paper lanterns. —ELIZABETH WILSON, *THE SPHINX IN THE CITY*

Part IV

PAST THE END
OF THE ℛOAD

AEROBIC SISYPHUS AND THE
SUBURBANIZED PSYCHE

Freedom to walk is not of much use without someplace to go. There is a sort of golden age of walking that began late in the eighteenth century and, I fear, expired some decades ago, a flawed age more golden for some than others, but still impressive for its creation of places in which to walk and its valuation of recreational walking. This age peaked around the turn of the twentieth century, when North Americans and Europeans were as likely to make a date for a walk as for a drink or meal, walking was often a sort of sacrament and a routine recreation, and walking clubs were flourishing. At that time, nineteenth-century urban innovations such as sidewalks and sewers were improving cities not yet menaced by twentieth-century speedups, and rural developments such as national parks and mountaineering were in first bloom. Thus far this book has surveyed pedestrian life in rural and urban spaces, and the history of walking is a history of cities and countryside, with a few towns and mountains thrown in for good measure. Perhaps 1970, when the U.S. Census showed that the majority of Americans were—for the first time in the history of any nation—suburban, is a good date for this golden age's tombstone. Suburbs are bereft of the natural glories and civic pleasures of those older spaces, and suburbanization has radically changed the scale and texture of everyday life, usually in ways inimical to getting about on foot. This transformation has happened in the mind as well as on the ground. Ordinary Americans now perceive, value, and use time, space, and their own

---

Walking as a form of transport in modern middle-class Euro-American life is essentially obsolete. It is the rare

---

bodies in radically different ways than they did before. Walking still covers the ground between cars and buildings and the short distances within the latter, but walking as a cultural activity, as a pleasure, as travel, as a way of getting around, is fading, and with it goes an ancient and profound relationship between body, world, and imagination. Perhaps walking is best imagined as an "indicator species," to use an ecologist's term. An indicator species signifies the health of an ecosystem, and its endangerment or diminishment can be an early warning sign of systemic trouble. Walking is an indicator species for various kinds of freedoms and pleasures: free time, free and alluring space, and unhindered bodies.

I. SUBURBIA

In *Crabgrass Frontier: The Suburbanization of the United States*, Kenneth Jackson outlines what he calls "the walking city" that preceded the development of middle-class suburbs: it was densely populated; it had "a clear distinction between city and country," often by means of walls or some other abrupt periphery; its economic and social functions were intermingled (and "factories were almost non-existent" because "production took place in the small shops of artisans"); people rarely lived far from work; and the wealthy tended to live in the center of the city. His walking city and my golden age find their end in the suburbs, and the history of suburbia is the history of fragmentation.

Middle-class suburban homes were first built outside London in the late eighteenth century, writes Robert Fishman in another history of suburbs, *Bourgeois Utopias*, so that pious merchants could separate family life from work. Cities themselves were looked upon askance by these upper-middle-class evangelical Christians: cards, balls, theaters, street fairs, pleasure gardens, taverns were all condemned as immoral. At the same time the modern cult of the home as a consecrated space apart from the world began, with the wife-mother as a priestess who was, incidentally, confined to her temple. This first suburban community of wealthy merchant families who shared each other's values sounds, in Fishman's account, paradisiacal and, like most paradises, dull: a place of spacious freestanding houses, with little for their residents to do outside the home and garden. These villas were miniaturized English country estates, and like such estates they aspired to a kind of social self-sufficiency. However, a whole community of farm-

individual who commutes to work on foot. Walking is usually linked with leisure. . . . One Irishwoman made a workers, gamekeepers, servants, guests, and extended families had inhabited the estate, which usually encompassed working farms and had thus been a place of production, while the suburban home housed little more than the nuclear family and was to become more and more a site only of consumption. Too, the estate was on a scale that permitted walking without leaving the grounds; the suburban home was not, but suburbia would eat up the countryside and diffuse the urban anyway.

It was in Manchester, during the industrial revolution, that the suburb came into its own. The suburb is a product of that revolution, radiating outward from Manchester and the north Midlands, which has so thoroughly fragmented modern life. Work and home had never been very separate until the factory system came of age and the poor became wage-earning employees. Those jobs, of course, fragmented work itself as craftsmanship was broken down into unskilled repetitive gestures in attendance on machines. Early commentators deplored how factory work destroyed family life, taking individuals out of the home and making family members strangers to each other during their prodigiously long workdays. Home for factory workers was little more than a place to recuperate for the next day's work, and the industrial system made them far poorer and unhealthier than they had been as independent artisans. In the 1830s Manchester's manufacturers began to build the first large-scale suburbs to escape the city they had created and to enhance family life for their class. Unlike the London evangelicals, they were fleeing not temptation but ugliness and danger—industrial pollution, the bad air and sanitation of a poorly designed city, and the sight and threat of their miserable workforce.

"The decision to suburbanize had two great consequences," says Fishman. "First the core emptied of residents as the middle class left and workers were pushed out by the conversion of their rooms in the back streets to offices. . . . Visitors were surprised to find an urban core that was totally quiet and empty after business hours. The central business district was born. Meanwhile, the once peripheral factories were now enclosed by a suburban belt, which separated them from the now-distant rural fields. The grounds of the suburban villas were enclosed by walls, and even the tree-lined streets on which they stood were often forbidden except to the residents and their guests. One group of workers attempted to keep open a once-rural footpath that now ran through the grounds of a factory owner's suburban villa. . . . Mr. Jones responded with iron gates and

---

similar observation: "Just think, the two most important forms of transport early this century are now highly

---

ditches." Fishman's picture shows a world where the fertile mix of urban life in the "walking city" has been separated out into its sterile constituent elements.

The workers responded by fleeing to the fields on Sundays and, eventually, fighting for access to the remaining rural landscape in which to walk, climb, cycle, and breathe (as chapter 10 chronicles). The middle class responded by continuing to develop and dwell in suburbs. Men commuted to work and women to shop by private carriages, then horse-drawn omnibuses (which, in Manchester, were priced too high to accommodate the poor), and eventually trains. In fleeing the poor and the city, they had left behind pedestrian scale. One could walk in the suburbs, but there was seldom anyplace to go on foot in these homogenous expanses of quiet residential streets behind whose walls dwelt families more or less like each other. The twentieth-century American suburb reached a kind of apotheosis of fragmentation when proliferating cars made it possible to place people farther than ever from work, stores, public transit, schools, and social life. The modern suburb as described by Philip Langdon is antithetical to the walking city: "Offices are kept separate from retailing. The housing is frequently divided into mutually exclusive tracts . . . with further subdivision by economic status. Manufacturing, no matter how clean and quiet—today's industries are rarely the noisy, smoke-belching mills of urban memory—is kept away from residential areas or excluded from the community entirely. Street layouts in new developments enforce apartness. To unlock the rigid geographic segregation, an individual needs to obtain a key—which is a motor vehicle. For obvious reasons those keys are not issued to those under sixteen, the very population for whom the suburbs are supposedly most intended. These keys are also denied to some of the elderly who can no longer drive."

Getting a license and a car is a profound rite of passage for modern suburban teenagers; before the car, the child is either stranded at home or dependent upon chauffeuring parents. Jane Holtz Kay, in her book on the impact of cars, *Asphalt Nation*, writes of a study that compared the lives of ten-year-olds in a walkable Vermont small town and an unwalkable southern California suburb. The California children watched four times as much television, because the outdoor world offered them few adventures and destinations. And a recent study of the effects of television on Baltimore adults concluded that the more local news television, with its massive emphasis on sensational crime stories, locals watched, the more fearful they were. Staying home to watch TV discouraged them from going out.

---

specialized hobbies!"—NANCY LOUISE FREY, *PILGRIM STORIES: ON AND OFF THE ROAD TO SANTIAGO*   *"People don't*

That *Los Angeles Times* advertisement for an electronic encyclopedia I cited at the beginning of this book—"You used to walk across town in the pouring rain to use our encyclopedias. We're pretty confident we can get your kid to click and drag"—may describe the options open to a child who no longer has a library within walking distance and may not be allowed to walk far alone anyway (walking to school, which was for generations the great formative first foray alone into the world, is likewise becoming a less common experience). Television, telephones, home computers, and the Internet complete the privatization of everyday life that suburbs began and cars enhanced. They make it less necessary to go out into the world and thus accommodate retreat from rather than resistance to the deterioration of public space and social conditions.

These American suburbs are built car-scale, with a diffuseness the unenhanced human body is inadequate to cope with, and just as gardens, sidewalks, arcades, and wilderness trails are a kind of infrastructure for walking, so modern suburbs, highways, and parking lots are an infrastructure for driving. Cars made possible the development of the great Los Angelean sprawls of the American West, those places not exactly suburbs because there is no urbanity to which they are subsidiary. Cities like Albuquerque, Phoenix, Houston, and Denver may or may not have a dense urban core floating somewhere in their bellies like a half-digested snack, but most of their space is too diffuse to be well served by public transit (if it exists) or to be traversed on foot. In these sprawls, people are no longer expected to walk, and they seldom do. There are many reasons why. Suburban sprawls generally make dull places to walk, and a large subdivision can become numbingly repetitious at three miles an hour instead of thirty or sixty. Many suburbs were designed with curving streets and cul-de-sacs that vastly expand distances: Langdon gives an example of an Irvine, California, subdivision where in order to reach a destination a quarter mile away as the crow flies the traveler must walk or drive more than a mile. Too, when walking is not an ordinary activity, a lone walker may feel ill at ease about doing something unexpected and isolated.

Walking can become a sign of powerlessness or low status, and new urban and suburban design disdains walkers. Many places have replaced downtown with shopping malls inaccessible by any means but cars, or by building cities that never had downtowns, buildings meant to be entered through parking garages

---

walk in Texas. Only Mexicans."—CHARACTER IN EDNA FERBER'S *GIANT*   *A black performance artist, Keith* rather than front doors. In Yucca Valley, the town near Joshua Tree National Park, all the businesses are strung out along several miles of highway, and crosswalks and traffic lights are rare: though, for example, my bank and food store are only a few blocks apart, they are on opposite sides of the highway, and a car is the only safe, direct way to travel between them. Throughout California more than 1,000 crosswalks have been removed in recent years, more than 150 of them in traffic-clogged Silicon Valley, apparently in the spirit of the L.A. planners who proclaimed in the early 1960s, "The pedestrian remains the largest single obstacle to free traffic movement." Many parts of these western sprawl-cities were built without sidewalks altogether, in both rich and poor neighborhoods, further signaling that walking has come to an end by design. Lars Eigner, who during a homeless and largely penniless phase of his life in the 1980s hitchhiked with his dog Lizbeth between Texas and southern California, wrote eloquently about his experiences, and one of the worst came about when a driver dropped him off in the wrong part of town: "South Tucson simply has no sidewalks. I thought at first this was merely in keeping with the general wretchedness of the place, but eventually it seemed to me that the public policy in Tucson is to impede pedestrians as much as possible. In particular, I could find no way to walk to the main part of town in the north except in the traffic lanes of narrow highway ramps. I could not believe this at first, and Lizbeth and I spent several hours wandering on the south bank of the dry gash that divides Tucson as I looked for a walkway."

Even in the best places, pedestrian space is continually eroding: in the winter of 1997–98, New York mayor Rudolph Giuliani decided that pedestrians were interfering with traffic (one could just as well have said, in this city where so many still travel and take care of their business on foot, that cars interfere with traffic). The mayor ordered the police to start citing jaywalkers and fenced in the sidewalks of some of the busiest corners of the city. New Yorkers, to their eternal glory, rebelled by staging demonstrations at the barriers and jaywalking more. In San Francisco, faster and denser traffic, shorter walk lights, and more belligerent drivers intimidate and occasionally mangle pedestrians. Here 41 percent of all traffic fatalities are pedestrians killed by cars, and more than a thousand walkers are injured every year. In Atlanta, the figures are 80 pedestrians killed per year and more than 1,300 injured. In Giuliani's New York, almost twice as many people are killed by cars as are murdered by strangers—285 versus 150 in 1997. Walking the city is not now an attractive prospect for those unequipped to dodge and dash.

Antar Mason, told me recently that he is now working increasingly in the only public spaces for African-

Geographer Richard Walker defines urbanity as "that elusive combination of density, public life, cosmopolitan mixing, and free expression." Urbanity and automobiles are antithetical in many ways, for a city of drivers is only a dysfunctional suburb of people shuttling from private interior to private interior. Cars have encouraged the diffusion and privatization of space, as shopping malls replace shopping streets, public buildings become islands in a sea of asphalt, civic design lapses into traffic engineering, and people mingle far less freely and frequently. The street is public space in which First Amendment rights of speech and assembly apply, while the mall is not. The democratic and liberatory possibilities of people gathered together in public don't exist in places where they don't have space in which to gather. Perhaps it was meant that way. As Fishman argues, the suburbs were a refuge—first from the sin and then from the ugliness and anger of the city and its poor. In postwar America "white flight" sent middle-class whites to the suburbs from multiracial cities, and in the new sprawl-cities of the West and suburbs around the country a fear of crime that often seems to be a broader fear of difference is further eliminating public space and pedestrian possibilities. Political engagement may be one of the things suburbs have zoned out.

Early on in the development of the American suburbs, the porch, an important feature for small-town social life, was replaced at the front of the home by the blind maw of the garage (and the sociologist Dean McCannell tells me some new homes have pseudo-porches that make them look sweetly old-fashioned but are actually too shallow to sit on). More recent developments have been more radical in their retreat from communal space: we are in a new era of walls, guards, and security systems, and of architecture, design, and technology intended to eliminate or nullify public space. This withdrawal from shared space seems, like that of the Manchester merchants a century and a half ago, intended to buffer the affluent from the consequences of economic inequity and resentment outside the gates; it is the alternative to social justice. The new architecture and urban design of segregation could be called Calvinist: they reflect a desire to live in a world of predestination rather than chance, to strip the world of its wide-open possibilities and replace them with freedom of choice in the marketplace. "Anyone who has tried to take a stroll at dusk through a neighborhood patrolled by armed security guards and signposted with death threats quickly realizes how merely notional, if not utterly obsolete, is the old idea of 'freedom of the city,'" writes Mike Davis of the nicer suburbs of Los Angeles. And Kierkegaard long ago exclaimed,

---

Americans that are supported actively by government—the prisons.—NORMAN KLEIN, THE HISTORY OF

"It is extremely regrettable and demoralizing that robbers and the elite agree on just one thing—living in hiding."

If there was a golden age of walking, it arose from a desire to travel through the open spaces of the world unarmored by vehicles, unafraid to mingle with different kinds of people. It emerged in a time when cities and countryside grew safer and desire to experience that world was high. Suburbia abandoned the space of the city without returning to the country, and in recent years a second wave of that impulse has beefed up this segregation with neighborhoods of high-priced bunkers. But even more importantly, the disappearance of pedestrian space has transformed perception of the relationship between bodies and spaces. Something very odd has happened to the very state of embodiment, of being corporeal, in recent decades.

II. THE DISEMBODIMENT OF EVERYDAY LIFE

The spaces in which people live have changed dramatically, but so have the ways they imagine and experience that space. I found a strange passage in a 1998 *Life* magazine celebrating momentous events over the past thousand years. Accompanying a picture of a train was this text: "For most of human history, all land transport depended on a single mode of propulsion—feet. Whether the traveller relied on his own extremities or those of another creature, the drawbacks were the same, low cruising speed, vulnerability to weather, the need to stop for food and rest. But on September 15, 1830, foot power began its long slide toward obsolescence. As brass bands played, a million Britons gathered between Liverpool and Manchester to witness the inauguration of the world's first fully steam-driven railway. . . . Despite the death of a member of Parliament who was run down by the train at the opening ceremony, the Liverpool and Manchester inspired a rash of track-laying round the world." The train was, like the factory and the suburb, part of the apparatus of the industrial revolution; just as factories mechanically sped up production, so trains sped up distribution of goods, and then of travelers.

Life magazine's assumptions are interesting; nature as biological and meteorological factors is a drawback rather than an occasional inconvenience; progress consists of the transcendence of time, space, and nature by the train and later the car, airplane, and electronic communications. Eating, resting, moving, experi-

---

FORGETTING   *The stationary cycle and the treadmill both have slot machines attached, allowing casino*

---

encing the weather, are primary experiences of being embodied; to view them as negative is to condemn biology and the life of the senses, and the passage does exactly that in its most lurid statement, that "foot power began its long slide toward obsolescence." Perhaps this is why neither *Life* nor the crowd apparently mourned the squashed Parliamentarian. In a way, the train mangled not just that one man's body, but all bodies in the places it transformed, by severing human perception, expectation, and action from the organic world in which our bodies exist. Alienation from nature is usually depicted as estrangement from natural spaces. But the sensing, breathing, living, moving body can be a primary experience of nature too: new technologies and spaces can bring about alienation from both body and space.

In his brilliant *The Railway Journey: The Industrialization of Time and Space in the Nineteenth Century*, Wolfgang Schivelbusch explores the ways trains changed their passengers' perceptions. Early railroad travelers, he writes, characterized this new technology's effects as the elimination of time and space, and to transcend time and space is to begin to transcend the material world altogether—to become disembodied. Disembodiment, however convenient, has side effects. "The speed and mathematical directness with which the railroad proceeds through the terrain destroy the close relationship between the traveller and the travelled space," Schivelbusch writes. "The train was experienced as a projectile, and travelling on it as being shot through the landscape—thus losing control of one's senses. . . . The traveller who sat inside that projectile ceased to be a traveller and became, as noted in a popular metaphor of the century, a parcel." Our own perceptions have sped up since, but trains were then dizzyingly fast. Earlier forms of land travel had intimately engaged travelers with their surroundings, but the railroad moved too fast for nineteenth-century minds to relate visually to the trees, hills, and buildings whipping by. The spatial and sensual engagement with the terrain between here and there began to evaporate. Instead, the two places were separated only by an ever-shortening amount of time. Speed did not make travel more interesting, Schivelbusch writes, but duller; like the suburb, it put its inhabitants in a kind of spatial limbo. People began to read on the train, to sleep, to knit, to complain of boredom. Cars and airplanes have vastly augmented this transformation, and watching a movie on a jetliner 35,000 feet above the earth may be the ultimate disconnection of space, time, and experience. "From the elimination of the physical effort of walking to the sensorimotor loss induced by

---

customers to sweat and bet at the same time. . . . "People are going crazy about this," said Kathy Harris, president

---

the first fast transport, we have finally achieved states bordering on sensory deprivation," writes Paul Virilio. "The loss of the thrills of the old voyage is now compensated for by the showing of a film on a central screen."

The *Life* writers may be right. Bodies are not obsolete by any objective standard, but they increasingly are perceived as too slow, frail, and unreliable for our expectations and desires—as parcels to be transported by mechanical means (though of course many steep, rough, or narrow spaces can only be traversed on foot, and many remote parts of the world can't be reached by any other means; it takes a built environment, with tracks, graded roads, landing strips, and energy sources, to accommodate motor transport). A body regarded as adequate to cross continents, like John Muir's or William Wordsworth's or Peace Pilgrim's, is experienced very differently than a body inadequate to go out for the evening under its own power. In a sense the car has become a prosthetic, and though prosthetics are usually for injured or missing limbs, the auto-prosthetic is for a conceptually impaired body or a body impaired by the creation of a world that is no longer human in scale. In one of the *Alien* movies the actress Sigourney Weaver lurches along in a sort of mechanized body armor that wraps around her limbs and magnifies her movements. It makes her bigger, fiercer, stronger, able to battle with monsters, and it seems strange and futuristic. But this is only because the relationship between the body and the prosthetic machine is so explicit here, the latter so obviously an extension of the former. In fact, from the first clasped stick and improvised carrier, tools have extended the body's strength, skill, and reach to a remarkable degree. We live in a world where our hands and feet can direct a ton of metal to go faster than the fastest land animal, where we can speak across thousands of miles, blow holes in things with no muscular exertion but the squeeze of a forefinger.

It is the unaugmented body that is rare now, and that body has begun to atrophy as both a muscular and a sensory organism. In the century and a half since the railroad seemed to go too fast to be interesting, perceptions and expectations have sped up, so that many now identify with the speed of the machine and look with frustration or alienation at the speed and ability of the body. The world is no longer on the scale of our bodies, but on that of our machines, and many need—or think they need—the machines to navigate that space quickly enough. Of course, like most "time-saving" technologies, mechanized transit more often produces changed expectations than free time; and modern Americans have sig-

of the Fitness Gaming Corporation in Fairfax, Va. . . . Ms. Harris pointed out that the machines were wired so nificantly less time than they did three decades ago. To put it another way, just as the increased speed of factory production did not decrease working hours, so the increased speed of transportation binds people to more diffuse locales rather than liberating them from travel time (many Californians, for example, now spend three or four hours driving to and from work each day). The decline of walking is about the lack of space in which to walk, but it is also about the lack of time—the disappearance of that musing, unstructured space in which so much thinking, courting, daydreaming, and seeing has transpired. Machines have sped up, and lives have kept pace with them.

The suburbs made walking ineffective transportation within their expanses, but the suburbanization of the American mind has made walking increasingly rare even when it is effective. Walking is no longer, so to speak, how many people think. Even in San Francisco, very much a "walking city" by Jackson's criteria, people have brought this suburbanized consciousness to their local travel, or so my observations seem to indicate. I routinely see people drive and take the bus remarkably short distances, often distances that could be covered more quickly by foot. During one of my city's public transit crises, a commuter declared he could *walk* downtown in the time it took the streetcar, as though walking was some kind of damning comparison—but he had apparently been traveling from a destination so near downtown he could've walked every day in less than half an hour, and walking was one transit option the newspaper coverage never proposed (obvious things could be said about bicycling here, were this not a book about walking). Once I made my friend Maria—a surfer, biker, and world traveler—walk the half mile from her house to the bars on Sixteenth Street, and she was startlingly pleased to realize how close they were, for it had never occurred to her before that they were accessible by foot. Last Christmas season, the parking lot of the hip outdoor equipment store in Berkeley was full of drivers idling their engines and waiting for a parking space, while the streets around were full of such spaces. Shoppers weren't apparently willing to walk two blocks to buy their out-door gear (and since then I have noticed that nowadays drivers often wait for a close parking spot rather than walk in from the farther reaches of the lot). People have a kind of mental radius of how far they are willing to go on foot that seems to be shrinking; in defining neighborhoods and shopping districts, planners say

----

"you can't gamble unless you're pedaling and you can't pedal unless you're gambling." The company's motto: "Put

----

it is about a quarter mile, the distance that can be walked in five minutes, but sometimes it hardly seems to be fifty yards from car to building.

Of course the people idling their engines at the outdoor equipment store may have been there to buy hiking boots, workout clothes, climbing ropes—equipment for the special circumstances in which people will walk. The body has ceased to be a utilitarian entity for many Americans, but it is still a recreational one, and this means that people have abandoned the everyday spaces—the distance from home to work, stores, friends—but created new recreational sites that are most often reached by car: malls, parks, gyms. Parks, from pleasure gardens to wilderness preserves, have long accommodated bodily recreation, but the gyms that have proliferated wildly in the past couple of decades represent something radically new. If walking is an indicator species, the gym is a kind of wildlife preserve for bodily exertion. A preserve protects species whose habitat is vanishing elsewhere, and the gym (and home gym) accommodates the survival of bodies after the abandonment of the original sites of bodily exertion.

III. THE TREADMILL

The suburb rationalized and isolated family life as the factory did manufacturing work, and the gym rationalizes and isolates not merely exercise but nowadays even each muscle group, the heart rate, the "burn zone" of most inefficient calorie use. Somehow all this history comes back to the era of the industrial revolution in England. "The Tread-Mill," writes James Hardie in his little book of 1823 on the subject, "was, in the year 1818, invented by Mr. William Cubitt, of Ipswich, and erected in the House of Correction at Brixton, near London." The original treadmill was a large wheel with sprockets that served as steps that several prisoners trod for set periods. It was meant to rationalize prisoners' psyches, but it was already an exercise machine. Their bodily exertion was sometimes used to power grain mills or other machinery, but it was the exertion, not the production, that was the point of the treadmill. "It is its monotonous steadiness and not its severity, which constitutes its terror, and frequently breaks down the obstinate spirit," Hardie wrote of the treadmill's effect in the American prison he oversaw. He added, however, that "the opinions of the medical officers in attendance at the various prisons, concur in declaring that the general health of the prisoners has,

your heart into gambling."—NEW YORK TIMES   _We've all heard of that future, and it sounds pretty lonely. In the_ in no degree suffered injury, but that, on the contrary, the labor has, in this re-spect, been productive of considerable benefit." His own prison of Bellevue on New York's East River included 81 male and 101 female vagrants, as well as 109 male and 37 female convicts, and 14 female "maniacs." Vagrancy—wandering without apparent resources or purpose—was and sometimes still is a crime, and doing time on the treadmill was perfect punishment for it.

Repetitive labor has been punitive since the gods of Greek myth sentenced Sisyphus—who had, Robert Graves tells us, "always lived by robbery and often murdered unsuspecting travellers"—to his famous fate of pushing a boulder up-hill. "As soon as he has almost reached the summit, he is forced back by the weight of the shameless stone, which bounces to the very bottom once more; where he wearily retrieves it and must begin all over again, though sweat bathes his limbs." It is hard to say if Sisyphus is the first weight lifter or the first tread-miller, but easy to recognize the ancient attitude to repetitive bodily exertion without practical results. Throughout most of human history and outside the first world nowadays, food has been relatively scarce and physical exertion abundant; only when the status of these two things is reversed does "exercise" make sense. Though physical training was part of ancient Greek citizens' education, it had so-cial and cultural dimensions missing from modern workouts and Sisyphean pun-ishments, and while walking as exercise had long been an aristocratic activity, industrial workers' enthusiasm for hiking, particularly in Britain, Austria, and Ger-many, suggests that it was far more than a way to make the blood circulate or calories burn. Under the heading "Alienation," Eduardo Galeano wrote a brief essay about fishermen in a remote village of the Dominican Republic puzzling over an advertisement for a rowing machine not very long ago. "Indoors? They use it indoors? Without water? They row without water? And without fish? And without the sun? And without the sky?" they exclaimed, telling the resident alien who has shown them the picture that they like everything about their work *but* the rowing. When he explained that the machine was for exercise, they said "Ah. And exercise—what's that?" Suntans famously became status symbols when most of the poor had moved indoors from the farm to the factory, so that browned skin indicated leisure time rather than work time. That muscles have become status symbols signifies that most jobs no longer call upon bodily strength: like tans, they are an aesthetic of the obsolete.

The gym is the interior space that compensates for the disappearance of out-

---

next century, the line of thinking goes, everyone will work at home, shop at home, watch movies at home and

---

side and a stopgap measure in the erosion of bodies. The gym is a factory for the production of muscles or of fitness, and most of them look like factories: the stark industrial space, the gleam of metal machines, the isolated figures each absorbed in his or her own repetitive task (and like muscles, factory aesthetics may evoke nostalgia). The industrial revolution institutionalized and fragmented labor; the gym is now doing the same thing, often in the same place, for leisure. Some gyms actually are born-again industrial sites. The Chelsea Piers in Manhattan were built in the first decade of this century for ocean liners—for the work of long-shoremen, stevedores, and clerks, and for the travel of emigrants and elites. They now house a sports center with indoor track, weight machines, pool, climbing gym, and most peculiarly, a four-story golf driving range, destinations in them-selves rather than points of arrival and departure. An elevator takes golfers to their stalls, where all the gestures of golf—walking, carrying, gazing, situating, removing, communicating, retrieving or following the ball—have vanished with the landscape of the golf course. Nothing remains but the single arc of a drive: four tiers of solitary stationary figures making the same gesture, the sharp sound of balls being hit, the dull thud of their landing, and the miniaturized armored-car vehicles that go through the green artificial-grass war zone to scoop up the balls and feed them into the mechanism that automatically pops up another ball as each one is hit. Britain has specialized in the conversion of industrial sites into climbing gyms. Among them are a former electrical substation in London, the Warehouse on Gloucester's Severn River waterfront, the Forge in Sheffield on one side of the Peak District, an early factory in downtown Birmingham, and, ac-cording to a surveyor friend, a "six-story former cotton mill near Leeds" I couldn't locate (not to mention a desanctified church in Bristol). It was in some of these buildings that the industrial revolution was born, with the Manchester and Leeds textile mills, Sheffield's iron- and steelworks, the innumerable manufactories of "the workshop of the world" that Birmingham once was. Climbing gyms are like-wise established in converted industrial buildings in the United States, or at least in those cities old enough to have once had industrial-revolution architecture. In those buildings abandoned because goods are now made elsewhere and First World work grows ever more cerebral, people now go for recreation, reversing the inclinations of their factory-worker predecessors to go out—to the outskirts of town or at least out-of-doors—in their free time. (In defense of climbing gyms, it should be said they allow people to polish skills and, during foul weather, to

communicate with all their friends through videophones and e-mail. It's as if science and culture have progressed for stay fit; for some the gym has only augmented the opportunities, not replaced the mountain, though for others the unpredictabilities and splendors of real rock have become dispensible, annoying—or unknown.)

And whereas the industrial revolution's bodies had to adapt to the machines, with terrible consequences of pain, injury, and deformity, exercise machines are adapted to the body. Marx said history happens the first time as tragedy, the second as farce; bodily labor here happens the first time around as productive labor and the second as leisuretime consumption. The deepest sign of transformation is not merely that this activity is no longer productive, that the straining of the arms no longer moves wood or pumps water. It is that the straining of the muscles can require a gym membership, workout gear, special equipment, trainers and instructors, a whole panoply of accompanying expenditures, in this industry of consumption, and the resulting muscles may not be useful or used for any practical purpose. "Efficiency" in exercise means that consumption of calories takes place at the maximum rate, exactly the opposite of what workers aim for, and while exertion for work is about how the body shapes the world, exertion for exercise is about how the body shapes the body. I do not mean to denigrate the users of gyms—I have sometimes been one myself—only to remark on their strangeness. In a world where manual labor has disappeared, the gym is among the most available and efficient compensations. Yet there is something perplexing about this semipublic performance. I used to try to imagine, as I worked out on one or another weight machine, that this motion was rowing, this one pumping water, this one lifting bales or sacks. The everyday acts of the farm had been reprised as empty gestures, for there was no water to pump, no buckets to lift. I am not nostalgic for peasant or farmworker life, but I cannot avoid being struck by how odd it is that we reprise those gestures for other reasons. What exactly is the nature of the transformation in which machines now pump our water but we go to other machines to engage in the act of pumping, not for the sake of water but for the sake of our bodies, bodies theoretically liberated by machine technology? Has something been lost when the relationship between our muscles and our world vanishes, when the water is managed by one machine and the muscles by another in two unconnected processes?

The body that used to have the status of a work animal now has the status of a pet: it does not provide real transport, as a horse might have; instead, the body is exercised as one might walk a dog. Thus the body, a recreational rather than

---

one purpose only: to keep us from ever having to get out of our pajamas. —SAN FRANCISCO CHRONICLE   *Some*

---

utilitarian entity, doesn't work, but works out. The barbell is only abstracted and quantified materiality to shift around—what used to be a sack of onions or a barrel of beer is now a metal ingot—and the weight machine makes simpler the act of resisting gravity in various directions for the sake of health, beauty, and relaxation. The most perverse of all the devices in the gym is the treadmill (and its steeper cousin, the Stairmaster). Perverse, because I can understand simulating farm labor, since the activities of rural life are not often available—but simulating walking suggests that space itself has disappeared. That is, the weights simulate the objects of work, but the treadmill and Stairmaster simulate the surfaces on which walking takes place. That bodily labor, real or simulated, should be dull and repetitive is one thing; that the multifaceted experience of moving through the world should be made so is another. I remember evenings strolling by Manhattan's many glass-walled second-floor gyms full of rows of treadmillers looking as though they were trying to leap through the glass to their destruction, saved only by the Sisyphean contraption that keeps them from going anywhere at all—though probably they didn't see the plummet before them, only their own reflection in the glass.

I went out the other day, a gloriously sunny winter afternoon, to visit a home-exercise equipment store and en route walked by the University of San Francisco gym, where treadmillers were likewise at work in the plate-glass windows, most of them reading the newspaper (three blocks from Golden Gate Park, where other people were running and cycling, while tourists and Eastern European emigrés were walking). The muscular young man in the store told me that people buy home treadmills because they allow them to exercise after work when it might be too dark for them to go out safely, to exercise in private where the neighbors will not see them sweating, to keep an eye on the kids, and to use their scarce time most efficiently, and because it is a low-impact activity good for people with running injuries. I have a friend who uses a treadmill when it's painfully cold outside in Chicago, and another who uses a no-impact machine whose footpads rise and fall with her steps because she has an injured hamstring (injured by driving cars designed for larger people, not by running). But a third friend's father lives two miles from a very attractive Florida beach, she tells me, full of low-impact sand, but he will not walk there and uses a home treadmill instead.

The treadmill is a corollary to the suburb and the autotropolis: a device with which to go nowhere in places where there is now nowhere to go. Or no desire

people walk with both eyes focused on their goal: the highest mountain peak in the range, the fifty-mile marker, the to go: the treadmill also accommodates the automobilized and suburbanized mind more comfortable in climate-controlled indoor space than outdoors, more comfortable with quantifiable and clearly defined activity than with the seamless engagement of mind, body, and terrain to be found walking out-of-doors. The treadmill seems to be one of many devices that accommodate a retreat from the world, and I fear that such accommodation disinclines people to participate in making that world habitable or to participate in it at all. It too could be called Calvinist technology, in that it provides accurate numerical assessments of the speed, "distance" covered, and even heart rate, and it eliminates the unpredictable and unforeseeable from the routine—no encounters with acquaintances or strangers, no sudden revelatory sights around a bend. On the treadmill, walking is no longer contemplating, courting, or exploring. Walking is the alternate movement of the lower limbs.

Unlike the prison treadmills, of the 1820s, the modern treadmill does not produce mechanical power but consumes it. The new treadmills have two-horsepower engines. Once, a person might have hitched two horses to a carriage to go out into the world without walking; now she might plug in a two-horsepower motor to walk without going out into the world. Somewhere unseen but wired to the home is a whole electrical infrastructure of power generation and distribution transforming the landscape and ecology of the world—a network of electrical cables, meters, workers, of coal mines or oil wells feeding power plants or of hydropower dams on rivers. Somewhere else is a factory making treadmills, though factory work is a minority experience in the United States nowadays. So the treadmill requires far more economic and ecological interconnection than does taking a walk, but it makes far fewer experiential connections. Most treadmillers read or otherwise distract themselves. *Prevention* magazine recommends watching TV while treadmilling and gives instructions on how treadmill users can adapt their routines to walking about outside when spring comes (with the implication that the treadmill, not the walk, is the primary experience). The *New York Times* reports that people have begun taking treadmill classes, like the stationary bicycling classes that have become so popular, to mitigate the loneliness of the long-distance treadmiller. For like factory labor, treadmill time is dull—it was the monotony that was supposed to reform prisoners. Among the features of the Precor Cardiologic Treadmill, says its glossy brochure, are "5 programmed courses" that "vary in distance, time and incline. . . . The Interactive

---

finish line. They stay motivated by anticipating the end of the journey. Since I tend to be easily distracted, I travel

Weight Loss course maintains your heart rate within your optimum weight loss zone by adjusting workload," while "custom courses allow you to easily create and store personalized programs of up to 8 miles, with variations as small as 1/10th mile increments." It's the custom courses that most amaze me; users can create an itinerary like a walking tour over varied terrain, only the terrain is a revolving rubber belt on a platform about six feet long. Long ago when railroads began to erode the experience of space, journeys began to be spoken of in terms of time rather than distance (and a modern Angeleno will say that Beverly Hills is twenty minutes from Hollywood rather than so many miles). The treadmill completes this transformation by allowing travel to be measured entirely by time, bodily exertion, and mechanical motion. Space—as landscape, terrain, spectacle, experience—has vanished.

somewhat differently—one step at a time, with many pauses in between. Occasionally the pauses become full stops

THE SHAPE OF A WALK

The disembodiment of everyday life I have been tracing is a majority experience, part of automobilization and suburbanization. But walking has sometimes been, at least since the late eighteenth century, an act of resistance to the mainstream. It stood out when its pace was out of keeping with the time—which is why so much of this history of walking is a First World, after-the-industrial-revolution history, about when walking ceased to be part of the continuum of experience and instead became something consciously chosen. In many ways, walking culture was a reaction against the speed and alienation of the industrial revolution. It may be countercultures and subcultures that will continue to walk in resistance to the postindustrial, postmodern loss of space, time, and embodiment. Most of these cultures draw from ancient practices—of peripatetic philosophers, of poets composing afoot, of pilgrims and practitioners of Buddhist walking meditation—or old ones, such as hiking and flâneury. But one new realm of walking opened up in the 1960s, walking as art.

Artists, of course, have walked. In the nineteenth century the development of photography and spread of plein-air painting made walking an important means for image makers—but once they found their view, they stopped traipsing around, and more importantly, their images stopped the view forever. There are countless wonderful paintings of walkers, from Chinese prints in which tiny hermits stray amid the heights to, for example, Thomas Gainsborough's *Morning Walk* or Gustave Caillebotte's *Paris Street, Rainy Day*, with its umbrella-carrying citizens going wherever they please on the Parisian cobblestones. But the aristocratic

that can last anywhere from two minutes to ten hours. More often they're less definite. . . . Trapped by our concepts young couple in *The Morning Walk* are forever frozen with their best foot forward. Among all the works that come to mind, only the nineteenth-century Japanese printmaker Hiroshige's *Fifty-three Views on the Tokuida Road* seem to suggest walking rather than stopping; they are, like stations of the cross, sequenced to reprise a journey, this time a 312-mile journey from Edo (now Tokyo) to Kyoto, which most then made on foot, as they do in the prints. It is a road movie from when roads were for walkers and movies were woodblock prints.

Language is like a road; it cannot be perceived all at once because it unfolds in time, whether heard or read. This narrative or temporal element has made writing and walking resemble each other in ways art and walking do not—until the 1960s, when everything changed and anything became possible under the wide umbrella of visual art. Every revolution has many parents. One godfather for this one is the abstract expressionist painter Jackson Pollock, at least as one of his offspring portrayed him. Allan Kaprow, himself an important performance and interdisciplinary artist, wrote in 1958 that Pollock shifted the emphasis from the painting as an aesthetic object to a "diaristic gesture." The gesture was primary, the painting secondary, a mere souvenir of that gesture which was now its subject. Kaprow's analysis becomes an exuberant, prophetic manifesto as he weighs the consequences of what the older artist had done: "Pollock's near destruction of this tradition may well be a return to the point where art was more actively involved in ritual, magic, and life than we have known it in our recent past. . . . Pollock, as I see him, left us at the point where we must become preoccupied with and even dazzled by the space and object of our everyday life, either our bodies, clothes, rooms, or, if need be, the vastness of Forty-second Street. Not satisfied with the suggestion through paint of our other senses, we shall utilize the specific substances of sight, sound, movements, people, odors, touch."

For the artists who took up the invitation Kaprow outlined, art ceased to be a craft-based discipline of making objects and become a kind of unbounded investigation into the relationship between ideas, acts, and the material world. At a time when the institutions of galleries and museums and the objects made for them seemed moribund, this new conceptual and dematerialized art sought a new arena and a new immediacy for artmaking. Art objects might be only the evidence of such an investigation or props and prompts for the viewers' own investigations, while artists could model themselves after scientists, shamans, detectives, or philosophers as they expanded the possible repertoire of gestures far beyond

---

and languages and the utter predictability of our five senses, we often forget to wonder what we're missing as we that of the painter at his canvas. Artists' bodies themselves became a medium for performances, and as art historian Kristine Stiles writes, "Emphasizing the body as art, these artists amplified the role of process over product and shifted from representational objects to presentational modes of action." In retrospect, it seems as though these artists were remaking the world, act by act, object by object, starting with the simplest substances, shapes, gestures. One such gesture—an ordinary one from which the extraordinary can be derived—is walking.

Lucy Lippard, who has been writing subversive histories of art for more than thirty years, traces the parentage for walking as a fine art to sculpture, not performance. She focuses on Carl Andre's 1966 sculpture *Lever* and his 1968 *Joint*, the former made of bricks lined up to extend from one room to another so that the viewer has to travel, the other a similar line but this time of hay bales in a meadow traversing a far greater distance. "My idea of a piece of sculpture is a road," Andre wrote then. "That is, a road doesn't reveal itself at any particular point or from any particular point. Roads appear and disappear. . . . We don't have a single point of view for a road at all, except a moving one, moving along it." Andre's minimal sculptures, like Chinese scrolls, reveal themselves over time in response to the movement of the looker; they incorporate travel into their form. "By incorporating an oriental notion of multiple viewpoints and both implied movement and direct intervention in the landscape, Andre set the scene for a subgenre of dematerialized sculpture which is simply, and not so simply, *walking*," concludes Lippard.

Other artists had already built roads of sorts: Carolee Schneemann built a labyrinth for friends to walk through out of a fallen tree of heaven and other tornado debris in her Illinois backyard in the summer of 1960, before she moved to New York and became one of the most radical artists in the burgeoning field of performance art. Kaprow himself was building environments for audiences and performers to move through and participate in by the early 1960s. The same year Andre built *Joint*, Patricia Johanson built *Stephen Long*. As Lippard describes it, "A 1,600-foot wooden trail painted in gradated pastels and laid out along an abandoned railroad track in Buskirk, New York, it was intended to take color and light beyond traditional impressionism by adding the elements of distance and time taken to perceive it." In the American West, even longer lines were being drawn, though they were no longer necessarily related to walking: Michael Heizer made his "motorcycle drawings" by using said vehicle to draw in the desert; Walter de

----

hurry along toward goals we may not even have chosen. I became a tracker by default, not design, when my

----

Maria commissioned a bulldozer to make similarly grandiose earth art on Nevada's arid surface, with lines that could be seen whole from a airplane or perceived over time and partially from the ground; but perhaps Robert Smithson's 1,500-foot-long *Spiral Jetty*, a rough but walkable path of rock and earth curling into the Great Salt Lake, was human in scale. Though its first inhabitants walked for millennia, the American West is often perceived as inimical to pedestrian scale; the earth art, as it came to be called, made there often seemed to echo the massive development projects of the conquest of the West, the railroads, dams, canals, mines.

England, on the other hand, has never ceased to be pedestrian in scale, and its landscape is not available for much further conquest, so artists there must use a lighter touch. The contemporary artist most dedicated to exploring walking as an artistic medium is the Englishman Richard Long. Much of what he has done since was already present in his early *Line Made by Walking* of 1967. The black-and-white photograph shows a path in grass running straight up the center to the trees at the far end of the meadow. As the title makes clear, Long had drawn the line with his feet. It was both more ambitious and more modest than conventional art: ambitious in scale, in making his mark upon the world itself; modest in that the gesture was such an ordinary one, and the resultant work was literally down to earth, underfoot. Like that of many other artists who emerged at the time, Long's work was ambiguous: was *A Line Made by Walking* a performance of which the line was a residual trace, or a sculpture—the line—of which the photograph was documentation, or was the photograph the work of art, or all of these?

Walking became Long's medium. His exhibited art since has consisted of works on paper documenting his walks, photographs of further marks in the landscape made in the course of those walks, and other sculptures made indoors that reference his outdoor activities. Sometimes the walk is represented by a photograph with text, or a map, or by text alone. On the maps the route of the walk is drawn in to suggest that walking is drawing on a grand scale, that his walking is to the land itself as his pen is to the map, and he often walks straight lines, circles, squares, spirals. Similarly, his sculptures in the landscape are usually made by rearranging (without relocating) rocks and sticks into lines and circles, a reductive geometry that evokes everything—cyclical and linear time, the finite and the infinite, roads and routines—and says nothing. Yet other works lay out those lines, circles, and labyrinths of sticks, stones, or mud on the gallery floor. But

---

tendency to be distracted by life's smallest signs grew into an unrelenting passion to trace those obscure, often walking in the landscape is always primary to the work. One magnificent early sculpture uniting these approaches was titled *A Line the Length of a Straight Walk from the Bottom to the Top of Silbury Hill.* With boots dipped in mud he had walked the distance not as a straight line but as a spiral on the gallery floor, so that the muddy path both represented the route he had taken elsewhere and became a new route indoors, evidence of and an invitation to walk. It plays with the concreteness of experience—the walk and its location (Silbury Hill is an ancient earthwork of unknown religious significance in southern England)—and with the abstractions of language and measurement in which that walk is described. The experience cannot be reduced to a place name and a length, but even this scant information is enough to start the imagination going. "A walk expresses space and freedom and the knowledge of it can live in the imagination of anyone, and that is another space too," Long wrote years later.

In some ways Long's works resemble travel writing, but rather than tell us how he felt, what he ate, and other such details, his brief texts and uninhabited images leave most of the journey up to the viewer's imagination, and this is one of the things that distinguishes such contemporary art, that it asks the viewer to do a great deal of work, to interpret the ambiguous, imagine the unseen. It gives us not a walk nor even a representation of a walk, only the idea of a walk and an evocation of its location (the map) or one of its views (the photograph). Formal and quantifiable aspects are emphasized: geometry, measurement, number, duration. There is, for example, Long's piece—a drawing of a squared-off spiral—captioned "A Thousand Miles A Thousand Hours A Clockwise Walk in England Summer 1974." It plays with correlations between time and space without showing or telling us anything further of the walk but the nation and the year, plays with what can be measured and what cannot. Yet it is enough to know that in 1974, as life seemed to get more complicated, crowded, and cynical, someone found the time and space to engage in such an arduous and apparently satisfying encounter with the land in quest of alignments between geography, body, and time. Then there was the map with inset text, " A Six Day Walk Over All Roads, Lanes and Double Tracks Inside a Six-Mile Wide Circle Centred on the Giant of Cerne Abbas," with the routes he had walked radiating like arteries out from the figure Long had placed at the heart of his walk. Another inset portrayed that figure—a 2,000-year-old chalk outline of a 180-foot-tall figure with a club and an erect penis on a Dorset hillside.

---

puzzling patterns somewhere, anywhere—to their source or end or simply to some midpoint in between. But when I

Long likes places where nothing seems to have broken the connection to the ancient past, so buildings, people, and other traces of the present or recent past rarely appear. His work revises the British tradition of country walks while representing its most enchanting and problematic faces. He has gone to Australia, the Himalayas, and the Bolivian Andes to make his work, and the idea that all these places can be assimilated into a thoroughly English experience smacks of colonialism or at least high-handed tourism. It raises once again the perils of forgetting that the rural walk is a culturally specific practice, and though it may be a civil, gentle thing in itself, imposing its values elsewhere is not. But while the literary art of the rural walk bogged down in convention, sentimentality, and autobiographical chatter, Long's art is austere, almost silent, and entirely new in its emphasis on the walk itself as having shape, and this is less a cultural legacy than a creative reassessment. His work is breathtakingly beautiful at times, and its insistence that the simple gesture of walking can tie the walker to the surface of the earth, can measure the route as the route measures the walker, can draw on a grand scale almost without leaving a trace, can be art, is profound and elegant. Long's friend and contemporary Hamish Fulton has also made walking his art, and his photographs-with-text pieces are almost indistinguishable from the other peripatetic Englishman's. But Fulton emphasizes a more spiritual-emotional side to his walking, more often choosing sacred sites and pilgrimage routes, and he makes no sculptures in the gallery or marks in the land.

There have been other kinds of walking artists. Probably the first artist to have made walking into performance art is a little-known emigré from Dutch Surinam, Stanley Brouwn. In 1960 he asked strangers on the street to draw him directions to locations around town and exhibited the results as a vernacular art of encounters or a collection of drawings; later he held a conceptual exhibition of "all the shoe-shops in Amsterdam" which would've called for viewers to take a walking tour; installed in a gallery signposts pointing out cities around the world and inviting viewers to take the first few steps toward Khartoum or Ottawa; spent a whole day in 1972 counting his steps; and otherwise explored the everyday world of urban walking. The magisterial German performance artist and sculptor Joseph Beuys, who often imbued simple acts with profound meaning, did one performance where he simply swept up after a political parade and another where he walked through one of the bogs he loved. This 1971 *Bog Action* was docu-

began tracking lost people, what had begun as an eccentric habit—following footprints on the ground—quickly mented in photographs that show him walking, sometimes with only his head and trademark fedora visible above water.

The New York performance artist Vito Acconci did his *Following Piece* over twenty-three days in 1969; like much conceptual art of the time, it played with the intersection between arbitrary rules and random phenomena by choosing a stranger and following him or her until he or she entered a building. Sophie Calle, a French photographer whose works arise from interactions and encounters, later revised Acconci's performance with two of her own, documented in photographs and text. *Suite Venitienne* recounts how she met a man at a party in Paris and surreptitiously followed him to Venice, where she tailed him like a detective until he confronted her; years later she had her mother hire an actual detective to do the same to her in Paris, and incorporated the detective's photographs of her into her own artwork as a kind of commissioned portraiture. These pieces explored the city's potential for suspicion, curiosity, and surveillance arising from the connections and disconnections between strangers on the street. In 1985 and 1986, the Palestinian-British artist Mona Hatoum used the street as a performance space, stenciling footprints containing the word *unemployed* down streets in Sheffield, as if to make visible the sad secrets of passersby in that economically devastated city, and performing two different walking acts in Brixton, a working-class outpost of London.

Of all the performances involving walking, the most dramatic, ambitious, and extreme was Marina Abramović and Ulay's 1988 *Great Wall Walk*. Radical performance artists from the Communist east—she from Yugoslavia, he from East Germany—they began to collaborate in 1976 on a series of what they called "relation works." They were interested in testing both their own and the audiences' physical and psychic boundaries with performances that threatened danger, pain, transgression, boredom; they were also interested in symbolically uniting the genders into an ideal whole; and they were increasingly influenced by shamanistic, alchemical, Tibetan Buddhist, and other esoteric traditions. Their work calls to mind what Gary Snyder described as the Chinese tradition of the "'four dignities'—Standing, Lying, Sitting, and Walking. They are 'dignities' in that they are ways of being fully ourselves, at home in our bodies, in their fundamental modes," or Vipassana Buddhism's similar emphasis on meditating in these four postures. In their first piece, *Relation in Space*, they walked rapidly from opposite

---

matured into an avocation. . . . I now commonly walk toward a single goal: to meet the person at the other end of

---

walls of a room toward each other until they collided, again and again. In 1977's *Imponderabilia* they stood nude and motionless in the doorway of a museum so that visitors had to decide who to face as they slipped sideways between them. In 1980's *Rest Energy*, they stood together while she held a bow and he held the arrow notched on the taut bowstring, pointing at her heart; their balanced tension and stillness prolonged this moment and stabilized its danger. That same year, they went to the Australian outback hoping to communicate with aboriginal people, who ignored them. They stayed and spent months of a scorching desert summer practicing sitting without moving, learning "immobility, silence and watchfulness" from the desert. Afterward, they found the locals more communicative. From this experience came their *Nightsea Crossing* performance in Sydney, Toronto, Berlin, and other cities: while remaining silent and fasting twenty-four hours a day, they spent several hours each day on successive days in a museum or public space sitting motionless, facing each other across a table, living sculptures displaying a kind of ferocious commitment.

"When I went to Tibet and the Aborigines I was also introduced to some Sufi rituals. I saw that all these cultures pushed the body to the physical extreme in order to make a mental jump, to eliminate the fear of death, the fear of pain, and of all the bodily limitations we live with," Abramović later said. "Performance was the form enabling me to jump to that other space and dimension." The *Great Wall Walk* was planned at the height of her collaboration with Ulay. They intended to walk toward each other from opposite ends of the 4,000-kilometer wall, meet, and marry. Years afterward, when they had finally cleared the bureaucratic hurdles set up by the Chinese government, their relationship had so changed that the walk became instead the end of their collaboration and relationship. In 1988 they spent three months walking toward each other from 2,400 miles away, embraced at the center, and went their separate ways.

The Great Wall, built to keep marauding nomads out of China, is one of the world's great emblems of the desire to define and secure self or nation by sealing its boundaries. For these two raised behind the Iron Curtain, this transformation of a wall separating north from south into a road linking east to west is full of political ironies and symbolic meanings. After all, walls divide and roads connect. Their performance could be read as a symbolic meeting of East and West, male and female, the architecture of sequestration and of connection. Too, the artists believed the wall had been, in the words of Thomas McEvilley, the critic who has

---

the tracks.—HANNAH NYALA, *POINT LAST SEEN*   *In the beginning of the 1940s, Paris was a six-day walk from* most closely followed their work, "mapped out over the millennia by feng shui experts, so if you followed the wall exactly you would be touching the serpent-power lines that bind together the surface of the earth." The book on the project records, "On March 30, 1988 Marina Abramović and Ulay began their walk over the Great Wall from opposite ends. Marina embarked from the east, by the sea. Ulay started far to the west, in the Gobi desert. On June 27, to the blare of horns, they met up in a mountain pass near Shenmu in Shaanxi Province, in the midst of Buddhist, Confucian and Taoist temples." McEvilley points out that this last performance also expanded upon their first, in which they strode toward each other until they collided.

Both artists have a section in this book in which sparse words and evocative photographs give a sense of their experience, functioning like Richard Long's photograph-and-text pieces to evoke carefully chosen fragments of a complex experience. In between the two texts McEvilley's essay revealed another face of the walk: its entanglement with endless layers of bureaucracy throughout the journey. Like Tolstoy's Princess Marya wishing to be a pilgrim on the road, Abramović and Ulay seem to have set out with an image of themselves walking alone in a clear, uncluttered space and state of mind, but McEvilley describes the minivans that took them to lodgings every night, the handlers, translators, and officials that bustled around them, ensuring they met the government's requirements and attempting to slow them down so they would spend more time and thus money in each province, the quarrel Ulay got into at a dance hall, the way schedules, rules, and geography had fragmented Ulay's walk (while Abramović made sure she started each morning where she stopped the night before, declaring, "I walk every fucking centimeter of the wall."). The wall was crumbling in many sections, calling for climbing as much as walking, and atop it the wind was often overwhelming. The walk had, in McEvilley's version, become another kind of performance, like a record-seeking one, in which the official goal is realized only at the cost of countless unofficial distractions and annoyances. But perhaps the two artists who had worked so long on their powers of concentration were able to shut out the surrounding clutter from their time on the wall. Their texts and images speak of the essence of walking, of the basic simplicity of the act amplified by the ancient emptiness of the desert around them. Like Long's pieces, theirs seem a gift to viewers of the assurance that a primeval purity of bodily encounter with the earth is still possible and that the human presence so crowded and dominating

---

the border, a three-hours' drive, and one hour by plane. Today the capital is only several minutes away from

---

elsewhere is still small when measured against the immensity of lonely places. "It took a great number of days before, for the first time, I felt the right pace," Ulay wrote. "When mind and body harmonized in the rhythmical sway of walking."

Afterward, Abramović began to make sculptures that invited viewers to participate in the basic acts her performances had explored. She set geodes, chunks of crystal, and polished stones into wooden chairs or on pedestals and mounts where they could be sat with or stood under—furniture for contemplation and for encounters with the elemental forces she believes the stones hold. The most spectacular of the sculptures were several pairs of amethyst shoes included in a big survey of her work at the Irish Museum of Modern Art in 1995. I had arrived there at the end of a long walk from downtown Dublin to find that the museum was housed in an elegant old military hospital, and the walk and the building's history seemed preparation for the shoes—great rough chunks of translucent mottled purple that had been hollowed out and polished inside, like a fairy-tale version of the wooden shoes European peasants once wore. Viewers were invited to put them on and close their eyes, and with them on I realized my feet were, in a sense, inside the earth itself, and though it was possible to walk, it was difficult to do so. I closed my eyes and saw strange colors, and the shoes seemed like fixed points around which the hospital, Dublin, Ireland, Europe, revolved; shoes not to travel in but to realize you might already be there. Later I read that they were made for walking meditation, to heighten awareness of every step. They were titled *Shoes for Departure*.

Kaprow's 1958 prophesy is fulfilled by all these walking artists: "They will discover out of ordinary things the meaning of ordinariness. They will not try to make them extraordinary but will only state their real meaning. But out of this they will devise the extraordinary." Walking as art calls attention to the simplest aspects of the act: the way rural walking measures the body and the earth against each other, the way urban walking elicits unpredictable social encounters. And to the most complex: the rich potential relations between thinking and the body; the way one person's act can be an invitation to another's imagination; the way every gesture can be imagined as a brief and invisible sculpture; the way walking reshapes the world by mapping it, treading paths into it, encountering it; the way each act reflects and reinvents the culture in which it takes place.

----

anywhere else . . . —PAUL VIRILIO, *SPEED AND POLITICS*   *An automobile which cuts out the use value from your*

Chapter 17

LAS VEGAS, OR THE LONGEST
DISTANCE BETWEEN TWO POINTS

I would have preferred to step out into the Peak District. I had been looking for a last tour of the sites of walking's history, and that locale seemed to have everything. I had envisioned starting in the hedge maze at the magnificent estate of Chatsworth, then wandering through the surrounding formal gardens into the Capability Brown–landscaped later gardens. From there I could go into the wilder reaches of the Peak, toward Kinder Scout, where the great right-of-way battles were fought, and past the famous gritstone climbs where "the working-class revolution in climbing" took place, then head for bordering Manchester with its formative suburbs or Sheffield with its industrial ruins and climbing gym in a former forge. Or I could begin with the industrial cities and work my way into the country and then to the garden and the maze. But all these picturesque schemes came to an end with the sneaking suspicion that proving that it was still possible to walk in Britain didn't count for much at all. Even Britain's industrial wastelands signify the pale northern European past, and it wasn't pedestrianism's past but its prognosis that I wanted to inspect. So one December morning I stepped out of Pat's van onto Fremont Street in downtown Las Vegas, and he set off to spend the day climbing the boulders and cliffs at Red Rocks.

Down most of Vegas's east-west avenues straight as latitude lines you can see the thirteen-mile-long escarpment of Red Rocks and, behind its ruddy sandstone domes and pillars, the ten-thousand-foot-high gray peaks of the Spring Range.

---

feet . . . I was recently told, "You're a liar!" when I said to somebody I walked down the spine of the Andes. The

---

One of the least celebrated aspects of this arid, amnesiac boomtown is its spectacular setting, with mountain ranges on three sides and glorious desert light, but Las Vegas has never been about nature appreciation. *Las vegas* means "the meadows" and makes it clear the Spanish got to this Southern Paiute oasis before the Anglos did, but the oasis didn't become a town until the twentieth century—until 1905, when the railroad from Los Angeles to Salt Lake City decided to put in a station here. Las Vegas remained a town for drifters and tourists long after the oasis was sucked dry. It lacked the mineral resources of much of the state and only began to flourish when gambling became legal in Nevada in 1931, while Hoover Dam was being built on the Colorado River, thirty miles to the southeast. In 1951 the Nevada Test Site was established sixty miles to the northwest, and in the decades since more than a thousand nuclear weapons have been detonated on its premises (until 1963, most of the tests were above ground, and there are some startling photographs of mushroom clouds rising up above the casinos' towering signs). Las Vegas is bracketed by these colossal monuments to the ambition to dominate rivers, atoms, wars, and to some extent, the world. It may be, however, a much smaller but more pervasive invention that most shaped this city in the Mojave Desert: air conditioning, which has much to do with the recent American mass migration south and west to places where many will spend all summer in climate-controlled interiors. Often portrayed as exceptional, Las Vegas is instead emblematic, an extreme version of new kinds of places being built around the United States and the world.

Las Vegas's downtown was built around the railroad station: visitors were expected to get off the train and walk to the casinos and hotels of downtown's compact Glitter Gulch area around Fremont Street. As cars came to supersede trains for American travelers, the focus shifted: in 1941 the first casino-hotel complex went in along what was then the highway to Los Angeles, Highway 91, and is now the Las Vegas Strip. Long ago, after falling asleep in a car headed for the annual antinuclear gathering at the Nevada Test Site, I woke up when we came to a halt at a traffic light on the Strip to see a jungle of neon vines and flowers and words dancing, bubbling, exploding. I still remember the shock of that spectacle after the blackness of the desert, heavenly and hellish in equal measure. In the 1950s, cultural geographer J. B. Jackson described the then-new phenomenon of roadside strips as another world, a world built for strangers and motorists. "The effectiveness of this architecture is finally a matter of what that other world is:

---

idea that somebody could just walk! He can jog perhaps in the morning, but be can't walk anywhere! The world

---

whether it is one that you have been dreaming about or not. And it is here that you begin to discover the real vitality of this new other-directed architecture along our highways: it is creating a dream environment for our leisure that is totally unlike the dream environment of a generation ago. It is creating and at the same time reflecting a new public taste." That taste, he said, was for something wholly new, something that dismissed earlier Eurocentric aping-one's-betters notions of recreation and taste, something adapted to cars and to the new futuristic and tropical fantasies of those cars' inhabitants: "those streamlined facades, flamboyant entrances and deliberately bizarre color effects, those cheerfully self-assertive masses of color and light and movement that clash so roughly with the old and traditional." This vernacular architecture invented for automotive America was celebrated in the famous 1972 architectural manifesto *Learning from Las Vegas*.

In recent years, however, something wholly unexpected has happened on the Strip. Like those islands where an introduced species reproduces so successfully that its teeming hordes devastate their surroundings and starve en masse, the Strip has attracted so many cars that its eight lanes of traffic are in continual gridlock. Its fabulous neon signs were made to be seen while driving past at a good clip, as are big signs fronting mediocre buildings on every commercial strip, but this Strip of Strips has instead in the last several years become a brand-new outpost of pedestrian life. The once-scattered casinos on the Strip have grown together into a boulevard of fantasies and lures, and tourists can now stow their car in one casino's behemoth parking lot and wander the Strip on foot for days, and they do, by the millions—more than 30 million a year, upward of 200,000 at once on the busiest weekends. Even in August, when it was about 100 degrees Fahrenheit after dark, I have seen the throngs stream back and forth on the Strip, slowly—though not much more slowly than the cars. Casino architecture itself has undergone radical changes since the prescient 1966 Caesars Palace played up fantasy architecture over neon signage and the 1989 Mirage presented the first facade specifically designed as a pedestrian spectacle. It seemed to me that if walking could suddenly revive in this most inhospitable and unlikely place, it had some kind of a future, and that by walking the Strip myself I might find out what that future was.

Fremont Street's old-fashioned glitter has suffered by comparison with the Strip's new fantasy environments, so it has been redesigned as a sort of cyber-

---

has become inaccessible because we drive there.—IVAN ILLICH, *WHOLE EARTH REVIEW*   *"After several hours, I* arcade. Its central blocks have been closed to cars so that pedestrians can mill around freely, and up above the resurfaced street is set a high, arched roof on which laser shows are beamed by night, so that what was once sky is now a kind of giant television screen. It's still a sad half-abandoned place in daylight, and it didn't take me long to tour it and wander south on Las Vegas Boulevard, which would eventually become the Strip. Before it becomes the Strip, the boulevard is a skid row of motels, shabby apartments, and sad souvenir, pornography, and pawn shops, the ugly backside of the gambling, tourism, and entertainment industries. A homeless black man huddled in a brown blanket at a bus stop looked at me walking by, and I looked at an Asian couple across the street coming out of one of the tiny wedding chapels, him in a dark suit, her in a chalk-white dress, so impersonally perfect they could have fallen off a colossal wedding cake. Here each enterprise seemed to stand on its own; the wedding chapel unintimidated by the sex shops, the fanciest casinos by the ruins and vacant lots around them. There weren't many people on the sidewalk with me in this sagging section between the two official versions of Vegas.

Farther on I came to the old El Rancho hotel, burned out and boarded up. The desert and the West had been romanticized by many of the earlier casinos: the Dunes, the Sands, the Sahara, and the Desert Inn on the Strip and the Pioneer Club, the Golden Nugget, the Frontier Club, and the Hotel Apache on Fremont Street, but more recent casinos have thrown regional pride to the winds and summoned up anyplace else, the less like the Mojave the better. The Sands is being replaced by the Venetian, complete with canals. I realized later that my walk was an attempt to find a continuity of experience here, the spatial continuity walking usually provides, but the place would defeat me with its discontinuities of light and fantasy. It defeated me another way too. Las Vegas, which had a population of 5 at the beginning of the twentieth century, 8,500 in 1940, and about half a million in the 1980s, when the casinos seemed to stand alone in the sweep of creosote bushes and yuccas, now has about 1.25 million residents and is the fastest growing city in the country. The glamorous Strip is surrounded by a colossal sprawl of trailer parks, golf courses, gated communities, and generic subdivisions—one of Vegas's abundant ironies is that it has a pedestrian oasis in the heart of the ultimate car suburb. I had wanted to walk from the Strip to the desert to connect the two, and I called the local cartographic company for recommendations about routes, since all my maps were long out of date. They told me that

---

begin to feel something new, something never before experienced. I strongly sense, with my whole self, that I am

---

the city was growing so fast they put out a new map every month and recommended some of the shortest routes between the southern Strip and the city edge, but Pat and I drove along them and saw they were alarming places for a solitary walker—a mix of warehouses, light industrial sites, dusty lots, and walled homes from which an aura of abandonment emanated, only occasionally interrupted by a car or grimy hobo. So I stuck to the pedestrian oasis and found that I could mentally move the great casinos like chess pieces from the flat board of the desert: ten years back the fantasy casinos were gone; twenty years back the casinos were scattered and there were almost no pedestrians; fifty years back there were only a few isolated outposts; and a century ago only a tiny whiskey-saloon hamlet disturbed the pale earth spreading in every direction.

Under the tired pavilion in front of the Stardust, an old French couple asked me for directions to the Mirage. I watched them walk slowly away from the old vehicular American fantasyland of glittering futures and toward the new nostalgic fantasyland at the Strip's heart and followed them south myself. The scattered walkers began to become crowds as I traveled south. The bride and groom I had seen come out of the wedding chapel showed up again walking down the boulevard near me, she with a delicate quilted jacket over her wedding dress and spike heels. Tourists come here from around the affluent world (and employees from some of the less affluent ones, notably Central America). Another of Vegas's ironies is that it is one of the world's most visited cities, but few will notice the actual city. In, for example, Barcelona or Katmandu, tourists come to see the locals in their natural habitat, but in Vegas the locals appear largely as employees and entertainers in the anywhere-but-here habitat built for tourists. Tourism itself is one of the last major outposts of walking. It has always been an amateur activity, one not requiring special skills or equipment, one eating up free time and feeding visual curiosity. To satisfy curiosity you must be willing to seem naive, to engage, to explore, to stare and be stared at, and people nowadays seem more willing or able to enter that state elsewhere than at home. What is often taken as the pleasure of another place may be simply that of the different sense of time, space, and sensory stimulation available anywhere one goes slowly.

The Frontier was the first casino I went inside. For six and a half years visitors could watch an outdoor floor show there, a round-the-clock picket of workers—maids, cocktail waitresses, busboys—fighting the union-busting new owners, testifying with their feet and their signs day and night, in summer's withering heat

---

moving from one place to another. . . . I am not passing through space, as one does in a car or airplane. I feel I am and winter's storms. During those years 101 babies were born and 17 people died among the Frontier strikers, and none of them crossed the picket line. It became the great union battle of the decade, a national inspiration to labor activists. In 1992 the AFL-CIO organized a related event, the Desert Solidarity March. Union activists and strikers walked three hundred miles from the Frontier across the desert to the courthouse in Los Angeles in a show of their willingness to suffer and prove their commitment. Vegas filmmaker Amie Williams commented, while showing me rushes from her documentary on the Frontier strike, that the union is like an American religion of family and solidarity: it has a credo, "An injury to one is an injury to all"—and in the Desert Solidarity March it got its pilgrimage. In Amie's footage, people who looked like they didn't walk much at all straggled in a line alongside old Route 66, bared their feet for bandaging in the evenings, and got up and did it again the next day. A carpenter and union representative named Homer, a bearded man who looked like a biker, testified to the pilgrimage's miracle: in the middle of a rainstorm, a sunspot followed them, and they stayed dry, and he sounded as enthused as one of the children of Israel for whom the Red Sea parted. Finally the union-busting family that had bought the Frontier was forced to sell, and on January 31, 1997, the new owners invited the union back in. Those who had spent six exhilarating years walking the line went back to mixing drinks and making beds. There was nothing of that struggle to see inside the Frontier, just the usual supernova of dizzily patterned carpet, jingling slots, flashing lights, mirrors, staff moving briskly and visitors milling slowly in the twilight that suffuses every casino. They are modern mazes, made to get lost in, with their windowless expanses full of odd angles, view-obscuring banks of slot machines, and other distractions designed, like those in malls and department stores, to prolong visitors' encounters with the temptations that might make them open their wallets before they find the well-concealed exits. Many casinos have "people movers"—moving ramps like those in airports—but here they are all inward-bound. Finding the way out is up to you.

Wandering and gambling have some things in common; they are both activities in which anticipation can be more delicious than arrival, desire more reliable than satisfaction. To put one foot in front of one another or one's cards on the table is to entertain chance, but gambling has become a highly predictable science for the casinos, and they and the law enforcement of Las Vegas are trying to control the odds on walking down the Strip too. The Strip is a true boulevard. It is

in a place, actually, in an infinite number of places. I am not in an undifferentiated space—what one feels in many exposed to the weather, open to its surroundings, a public space in which those glorious freedoms granted by the First Amendment can be exercised, but a mighty effort is being made to take them away, so that the Strip will instead be a sort of amusement park or mall, a space in which we can be consumers but not citizens. Next to the Frontier is the Fashion Show Shopping Center, where leafletters hang out together, forming one of the Strip's many subcultures. Many are undocumented Central Americans, Amie Williams said, and the leaflets most often pertain to sex (though Vegas has a huge sex industry, customers are sought largely by advertisements, not by street hustling; the dozens of clusters of news-stands along the Strip contain very few newspapers and a veritable library of brochures, cards, and leaflets with color photographs advertising an army of "pri-vate dancers" and "escort services"). Since the women themselves are largely in-visible, the visibility of the ads has come under assault. The county passed an ordinance making "off-premises canvassing" in the "resort district" a misdemeanor. The director of the Nevada outpost of the American Civil Liberties Union, Gary Peck, spoke to me of "the almost transparent paradox that Vegas markets itself as anything goes—sex, alcohol, gambling—and on the other hand has this almost obsessive attempt at thorough control of public space, advertising on billboards, in the airport, panhandling, free speech." The ACLU's fight over the handbill or-dinance had reached the Federal Court of Appeals, and other issues kept crop-ping up. Earlier that year, petition-gathers were harassed and a pastor and four companions were arrested for proselytizing in the Fremont Street Experience on charges of "blocking a sidewalk," though the now-pedestrian arcade is one vast sidewalk it would take dozens to obstruct.

The casinos and the county, Peck told me, are trying to privatize the very sidewalks, to give themselves more muscle for prosecuting or removing anyone engaging in First Amendment activities—speaking about religion, sex, politics, economics—or otherwise ruffling the smooth experience visitors are supposed to have (similarly, Tucson has recently looked into privatizing sidewalks by leasing them for one dollar to businesses, to allow them to drive out the homeless). Peck worries that if they succeed in taking away the ancient "freedom of the city" at the sidewalk level, it will set a precedent for the rest of the country, malling what were once genuine public spaces, making cities into theme parks. "The theme park," writes Michael Sorkin, "presents its happy regulated version of pleasure—all those artfully hoodwinking forms—as a substitute for the democratic urban

---

modern places that, really are non-places; they are simply repetitions of concepts—the concept of hospital space,

---

realm, and it does so appealingly by stripping troubled urbanity of its sting, of the presence of the poor, of crime, of dirt, of work." The Mirage has already posted a little sign on one of its lawns: "This sidewalk is the private property of the Mirage Casino Hotel upon which an easement has been granted to facilitate pedestrian movement. Anyone found loitering or otherwise impeding pedestrian movement is subject to arrest for trespass," and signs up and down the strip say, "Resort District: No Obstructive Uses Permitted on Public Sidewalks." The signs are there not to protect the freedom of movement of pedestrians, but to restrict what those pedestrians can do or see.

I was hot and weary from the four miles or so I'd gone from Fremont Street, for it was a warm day and the air was stale with exhaust. Distance is deceptive on the Strip: the major intersections are about a mile apart, but the new casinos with their twenty-or-thirty-story hotel towers tend to look closer because their scale doesn't register. Treasure Island is the first of the new theme-park casinos one reaches from the north, and one of the most fantastic—named not after a place or period like the rest, but after a boys' book about pirate life in the South Seas. With a facade of fake rock and picturesque building fronts behind its lagoon of palm trees and pirate ships, it resembles a hotel-resort version of Disneyland's Pirates of the Caribbean ride. But it was the adjoining Mirage that invented the pedestrian spectacle in 1989, with its volcano that erupts every fifteen minutes after dark, to the delight of gathered crowds. When Treasure Island opened in 1993, it upstaged the volcano with a full-fledged pirate battle climaxing with the sinking of a ship—but the battle only takes place a few times a day.

The authors of *Learning from Las Vegas* long ago groused that "the Beautification Committee would continue to recommend turning the Strip into a western Champs-Elysées, obscuring the signs with trees and raising the humidity with giant fountains." The fountains have arrived, and the vast sheets of water fronting the Mirage and Treasure Island are dwarfed by the eight-acre lake at Bellagio, down where the Dunes used to be, across Flamingo Road from Caesars Palace. Together these four casinos make something altogether new and surprisingly old-fashioned, a wild hybrid of the formal garden and the pleasure garden spread out along a public thoroughfare. The Mirage's volcano buried the old Vegas as decisively as Vesuvius did Pompeii, changing architecture and audiences together. The fountains are everywhere, and it *is* a kind of western Champs-Élysées, in that walking to look at the architecture and the other walkers has become a pastime. The Strip is replacing its neon-go-go Americana futurama vision with Europe, a fun pop-culture version of Europe, a Europe of architectural greatest hits and boulevardiers in shorts and T-shirts. Is there anything less peculiar about setting miniature Italian and Roman temples and bridges in English gardens than in putting up gargantuan ones in the desert, in building volcanoes in eighteenth-century gardens such as Wörlitz in Germany than on boulevards in Nevada? Caesars Palace, with its dark green cypresses, fountains, and classical statuary out front, calls up many of the elements of the formal garden, which was itself an Italian extension of Roman practices adapted by the French, Dutch, and English. Bellagio, with its frontage of fountains, recalls Versailles, whose scale was a demonstration of wealth, power, and triumph over nature. These places are mutant reprises of the landscapes in which walking as scenic pleasure was developed. Vegas has become the successor to Vauxhall, Ranelagh, Tivoli, and all the other pleasure gardens of the past, a place where the unstructured pleasures of walking and looking mingle with highly organized shows (stages for music, theater, and pantomimes were an important part of pleasure gardens, as were areas to dance, eat, drink, and sit). As a Vegas promoter might say, the garden is making a comeback, crossbred with the boulevard, and with them comes pedestrian life.

All the efforts to control who strolls and how suggest that walking may in some way still be subversive. At least it subverts the ideals of entirely privatized space and controlled crowds, and it provides entertainment in which nothing is spent or consumed. Though walking may be an inadvertent side effect of gambling—after all, the casino facades weren't built out of public-spiritedness—the Strip is now a place to walk. And after all, Paris's Champs-Élysées also belongs to tourists and foreigners nowadays, strolling, shopping, eating, drinking, and enjoying the sights. New pedestrian overpasses eliminate the intersection of people and cars where Flamingo Road crosses the Strip, and they are handsome bridges giving some of the best views around. But these bridges are entered and exited from within the casinos, so there may come a time when only the well-dressed can cross the street safely here, and the rabble will have to take their chances with the cars or make a long detour. The Strip is not the Champs-Élysées reborn for other reasons too; it lacks the perfect straightness Le Nôtre gave the older

---

unreproducible, as is every poem. Even if you walk exactly the same route every day—as with a sonnet—the road, the straightness that lets you see far into the distance. It bends and bulges, though there are always the cross-streets—and the bridge over Flamingo Road between Bellagio and Caesars provided the best view yet of the desert to the west and Red Rocks. From the other bridge, the one over the Strip from Bellagio to Bally's, I could see—Paris! I had forgotten that a Paris casino was under construction, but there rising out of the dusty soil of the Mojave like an urban mirage, a flâneur's apparition, was the Eiffel Tower, only half finished and half scale but already aggressively straddling what looked like a stumpy Louvre with the Arc de Triomphe jostling it in an antigeographic jumble of architectural greatest hits.

Of course Vegas is reinventing not only the garden, but the city: New York, New York is just down the road from Bellagio, the Tokyo-homage Imperial Palace is up the street, and a much older version of San Francisco—the Barbary Coast—faces Caesars. The 1996 New York, New York is, like the Paris casino, a cluster of famous features; inside is a funny little maze of streets made to look like various Manhattan neighborhoods, complete with street signs, shops (of which only the souvenir and food shops are real, as I found when I foolishly lunged for a bookstore), air conditioners jutting out third-floor windows, and even a graffiti corner—but, of course, without the variety, productive life, dangers, and possibilities of real urban life. Fronted by a Statue of Liberty welcoming gamblers rather than huddled masses yearning to be free, New York, New York is a walk-through souvenir of the city. No longer pocket-size and portable but a destination in itself, it performs a souvenir's function: recalling a few pleasant and reassuringly familiar aspects of a complicated place. I ate a late lunch in New York, New York and drank three pints of water to replenish what had evaporated from me in the desert aridity of my all-day walk.

Back on the boulevard, a young woman from Hong Kong asked me to take a picture of her with the Statue of Liberty behind her and then with the huge golden MGM lion across the street, and she looked ecstatic in both shots. Fat people and thin people, people in baggy shorts and in sleek dresses, a few children and a lot of old people streamed around us, and I handed the camera back and continued south with the crowd, to the last station on these stations of the odds, the Luxor, whose pyramid shape and sphinx say ancient Egypt, but whose shiny glass on which lasers play at night says technology. The newlyweds I had seen before were there in the entryway: she had laid aside her coat and purse to pose for his camera in front of one of the mock-Egyptian statues. I wondered

---

events along the route cannot be imagined to be the same from day to day. . . . If a poem is each time new, then it

---

about them, about why they had chosen to spend the first hours of their honeymoon strolling the Strip, about what past they brought to this encounter with global fantasy filtered through the Nevada desert's climate and gambling's economy. Who am I to say that because these people who streamed by to my right and my left were Las Vegas tourists they did not have other lives: that this English couple might not take their next vacation in the Lake District, that the old French couple might not live in Paris or near Plum Village where the Vietnamese Buddhist Thich Nhat Hanh teaches walking meditation, that the African-Americans might not have marched in Selma as children, that the beggar in a wheelchair could not have been hit by a car in New Orleans, that the bride and groom might not be Japanese climbers of Mount Fuji, Chinese descendants of mountain hermits, southern Californian executives with treadmills at home, that this Guatemalan handing out helicopter-ride coupons might not walk the stations of the cross in her church or once have promenaded the plaza in her hometown, that bartender going to work might not have gone on the AFL-CIO march across the desert? The history of walking is as expansive as human history, and the most attractive thing about this pedestrian oasis in the middle of suburban blight in the middle of a great desert expanse is that it hints at that history's breadth—not in its fake Rome and Tokyo, but in its Italian and Japanese tourists.

Las Vegas suggests that the thirst for places, for cities and gardens and wilderness, is unslaked, that people will still seek out the experience of wandering about in the open air to examine the architecture, the spectacles, and the stuff for sale, will still hanker after surprises and strangers. That the city as a whole is one of the most pedestrian-unfriendly places in the world suggests something of the problems to be faced, but that its attraction is a pedestrian oasis suggests the possibility of recovering the spaces in which walking is viable. That the space may be privatized to make the liberties of walking, speaking, and demonstrating illegal suggests that the United States is facing as serious a battle over rights-of-way as did English ramblers half a century ago, though this time the struggle is over urban, not rural, space. Equally scary is the widespread willingness to accept simulations of real places, for just as these simulations usually forbid the full exercise of civil liberties, so they banish the full spectrum of sights, encounters, experiences, that might provoke a poet, a cultural critic, a social reformer, a street photographer.

But the world gets better at the same time it gets worse. Vegas is not an anom-

is necessarily an act of discovery, a chance taken, a chance that may lead to fulfillment or disaster.—A. R.

aly but an intensification of mainstream culture, and walking will survive outside that mainstream and sometimes reenter it. When the automotive strip and suburb were being developed in the decades after World War II, Martin Luther King was studying Gandhi and reinventing Christian pilgrimage as something politically powerful at one edge of this continent, while at the other Gary Snyder was studying Taoist sages and walking meditation and rethinking the relationship between spirituality and environmentalism. At present, space in which to walk is being defended and sometimes enlarged by pedestrian activist groups springing up in cities across the United States, from Feet First in Seattle and Atlanta's PEDS to Philly Walks and Walk Austin, by the incendiary British-based Reclaim the Streets, by older organizations like the Ramblers' Association and other British insurrections for walking and access, and by pedestrian-favoring urban redesign from Amsterdam to Cambridge, Massachusetts. Walking traditions are maintained by the resurgence of the foot pilgrimage to Santiago de Compostela in Spain and the thriving one in Chimayó, New Mexico, the growing popularity of climbing and mountaineering, the artists working with walking as a medium and the writers with it as a means, the spread of Buddhism with its practices of walking meditation and circumambulating mountains, the newfound secular and religious enthusiasm for labyrinths and mazes. . . .

"This place is a *maze*," grumbled Pat when he found me in Caesars Forum, the arcade attached to the casino. The Forum is the capstone of the arch, the crowning jewel of Vegas's recreation of the past. It is an arcade in exactly the sense Walter Benjamin described Parisian arcades—he quoted an 1852 guidebook that said, "Both sides of these passageways, which are lighted from above, are lined with the most elegant shops, so that such an arcade is a city, even a world, in miniature," and added, "The arcades were a cross between a street and an *interieur*." With its arched roof painted to look like the sky and recessed lighting that changes from day to twilight and back every twenty minutes or so, this one is more so than Benjamin could have imagined. Its curving "streets" are disorienting and full of distractions: the stores full of clothes, perfumes, toys, knickknacks, a fountain whose backside is a huge tropical fish tank, the famous fountain of nubile gods and goddesses who periodically "come to life" during a simulated thunderstorm with laser lightning snaking across the skylike dome. I had visited the arcades of

AMMONS, "A POEM IS A WALK"   *Draw an imaginary map. / Put a goal mark where you want to go. / Go*

Paris only six months before, and they were beautiful dead places, like streambeds through which water no longer runs, with half their shops closed and few wanderers along their mosaic'd corridors, but Caesars Forum is constantly thronged (as are the arcades of Bellagio, modeled after Milan's famous Galleria). It is one of the most financially successful malls in the world, says the *Wall Street Journal,* adding that a new addition is planned, a re-creation of a Roman hill town with occasional appearances by horse-drawn chariots. An arcade was never much more than a mall, and though a flâneur was supposed to be more contemplative than the average mall rat, shallow gentlemen are as common as soulful shoppers. "Let's get out of here," I said to Pat, and we finished our drinks and headed for Red Rocks.

Red Rocks is as open, as public, as Las Vegas Boulevard, but nobody is promoting it, just as no one (unless they're selling gear) is promoting the free activity of walking in preference to the lucrative industry of cars. While tens of thousands of people wander the Strip, perhaps a hundred or so at most roam the larger terrain of Red Rocks, whose spires and buttresses are far taller and more spectacular than any casino. Many people only drive through or step out long enough to take a photograph, unwilling to surrender to the slower pace here, a twilight that comes only once a day, wildlife that does as it pleases, a place with no human trace to structure one's thoughts but a few trails, climbing bolts on the rocks, litter, and signs (and an entrenched tradition of nature-worship). Nothing happens here most of the time, except seasons, weather, light, and the workings of one's body and mind.

Musing takes place in a kind of meadowlands of the imagination, a part of the imagination that has not yet been plowed, developed, or put to any immediately practical use. Environmentalists are always arguing that those butterflies, those grasslands, those watershed woodlands, have an utterly necessary function in the grand scheme of things, even if they don't produce a market crop. The same is true of the meadowlands of imagination; time spent there is not work time, yet without that time the mind becomes sterile, dull, domesticated. The fight for free space—for wilderness and for public space—must be accompanied by a fight for free time to spend wandering in that space. Otherwise the individual imagination will be bulldozed over for the chain-store outlets of consumer appetite, true-crime titillations, and celebrity crises. Vegas has not yet decided whether to pave over or encourage that space.

---

walking on an actual street according to your map. / If there is no street where it should be according to

---

That night we would sleep out near Red Rocks, in an unofficial campground with figures silhouetted against the small fires burning here and there under the starry sky and the glow of Vegas visible over the hill. In the morning we would rendezvous with Paul, a young guide who often drove out from Utah to climb here and who had invited Pat to climb with him. He would lead us along a trail snaking up and down across small arroyos and a dry streambed, past the gorgeous foliage I remembered from earlier trips, junipers with desert mistletoe, tiny-leafed desert oaks, yuccas, manzanitas, and an occasional barrel cactus, all stunted and spread sparsely by the rocky soil, aridity, and scattered boulders in a way that re-calls Japanese gardens. Still limping from a fall six months earlier, Pat brought up the rear, while Paul and I talked as we went along about music, climbing, con-centration, bicycles, anatomy, apes. When I turned back to look at Las Vegas as I had so often looked toward Red Rocks the day before, he would say, "Don't look back," but I would stare, amazed how thick the city's smog was. The place ap-peared to be a brown dome with a only few spires murkily visible within it. This state of things whereby the desert could be seen clearly from the city but not the other way round seemed as neat an allegory as I'd ever met. It was as though one could look back from the future to the past but not forward from this ancient place to the future shrouded in trouble, mystery, and fumes.

Paul would lead us off the trail into the brush that led up steep, narrow Juniper Canyon, and I would manage to heave myself up the various shelves where the rock grew more and more gorgeous, sometimes striped red and beige in thin lay-ers, sometimes spotted with pink spots the size of coins, until we were at the foot of the climb. "Olive Oil: This route ascends obvious crack systems for 700 feet up the south side of the Rose Tower," I would read in Pat's battered *American Alpine Club Climber's Guide* for the region. I lounged and watched them climb with ease up the first few hundred feet and studied the mice, who were less glamorous than the white tigers and dolphins of the Mirage, but livelier. Afterward I would turn around and spend the afternoon wandering in flatter terrain, ambling along the few trails alongside the clear rushing water of Pine Creek, exploring another canyon, turning back to watch the shadows over the hills grow longer and the light thicker and more golden, as though air could turn to honey, honey that would dissolve into the returning night.

Walking has been one of the constellations in the starry sky of human culture, a constellation whose three stars are the body, the imagination, and the wide-

---

the map, make one by putting obstacles aside. / When you reach the goal, ask the name of the city and give open world, and though all three exist independently, it is the lines drawn between them—drawn by the act of walking for cultural purposes—that makes them a constellation. Constellations are not natural phenomena but cultural impositions; the lines drawn between stars are like paths worn by the imagination of those who have gone before. This constellation called walking has a history, the history trod out by all those poets and philosophers and insurrectionaries, by jaywalkers, streetwalkers, pilgrims, tourists, hikers, mountaineers, but whether it has a future depends on whether those connecting paths are traveled still.

---

flowers to the first person you meet.—YOKO ONO, "MAP PIECE," 1962

Notes

----

1. TRACING A HEADLAND: An Introduction

5   "An absolutely new prospect is a great happiness": Henry David Thoreau, "Walking," in *The Natural History Essays* (Salt Lake City: Peregrine Smith Books, 1980), 99.

7   It was nuclear weapons that first led: My early writing on walking and on nuclear politics appears in my 1994 book *Savage Dreams: A Journey into the Landscape Wars of the American West* (San Francisco: Sierra Club Books, 1994; Berkeley: University of California Press, 1999).

2. THE MIND AT THREE MILES AN HOUR

14   "I can only meditate when I am walking": Jean-Jacques Rousseau, *The Confessions* (Harmondsworth, England: Penguin Books, 1953), 382.

14   "In one respect, at least": John Thelwall, *The Peripatetic: or, Sketches of the Heart of Nature and Society* (1793; facsimile reprint, New York: Garland Publishing, 1978), 1, 8–9.

15   Felix Grayeff's history: *Aristotle and His School: An Inquiry into the History of the Peripatos* (London: Gerald Duckworth, 1974), 38–39.

16   The Stoics were named: Christopher Thacker, *The History of Gardens* (Berkeley: University of California Press, 1985), 21, is my source for the information on the stoa and the Stoics. Bernard Rudofsky's *Streets for People: A Primer for Americans* (New York: Van Nostrand Reinhold, 1982), also gives a précis of this information.

16   "For recreation I turn": *Selected Letters of Friedrich Nietzsche*, ed. Oscar Levy, trans. Anthony M. Ludovici (New York: Doubleday, 1921), 23.

16   "He used to come": Bertrand Russell, *Portraits from Memory*, quoted in A. J. Ayer, *Wittgenstein* (New York: Random House, 1985), 16.

17   "In order to slacken my pace": Rousseau, *Confessions*, 327.

17   "Behold how luxury": Jean-Jacques Rousseau, "First Discourse" ("Discourse on the Arts and Letters"), in *The First and Second Discourses* (New York: St. Martin's Press, 1964), 46.

18   "wandering in the forests": Rousseau, "Second Discourse," ibid., 137.

19   "I do not remember ever having had": Rousseau, *Confessions*, 64.

19   "Never did I think so much": Ibid., 158.

19   "thinking over subjects": Ibid., 363.

20   Boswell: "Dialogue with Rousseau," *The Portable Johnson and Boswell*, ed. Louis Kronenberger (New York: Viking, 1947), 417.

20   "Having therefore decided to describe": Jean-Jacques Rousseau, "Second Walk," in *Reveries of the Solitary Walker*, trans. Peter France (Harmondsworth, England: Penguin Books, 1979), 35.

22   "Wherein lay this great contentment?": "Fifth Walk," ibid., 83.

23   "What had at first been": Walter Lowrie, *A Short Life of Kierkegaard* (Princeton, N.J.: Princeton University Press, 1942), 45–46.

24   "Strangely enough, my imagination works best": *Søren Kierkegaard's Journals and Papers*, ed. and trans. Howard V. Hong and Edna H. Hong (Bloomington: Indiana University Press, 1978), 6:113.

24   "In order to bear mental tension": Ibid., 5:271 (1849–1851).

24   "This very moment there is an organ-grinder": Ibid., 5:177 (1841).

24   "Most of *Either/Or* was written only twice": Ibid., 5:341 (1846).

25   "overwhelmed with ideas": Ibid., 6:62–63 (1848).

25   "My atmosphere has been tainted": Ibid., 5:386 (1847).

27   Husserl described walking: "The World of the Living Present and the Constitution of the Surrounding World External to the Organism," in *Edmund Husserl: Shorter Works*, ed. Peter McCormick and Frederick A. Elliston (Notre Dame, Ind.: University of Notre Dame Press, Harvester Press, 1981). I benefited from Edward S. Casey's interpretation of this dense essay in his *The Fate of Place: A Philosophical History* (Berkeley: University of California Press, 1997), 238–50.

28   "If the body is a metaphor": Susan Bordo, "Feminism, Postmodernism, and Gender-Scepticism," in *Feminism/Postmodernism*, ed. Linda J. Nicholson (New York: Routledge, 1990), 145.

3. RISING AND FALLING: The Theorists of Bipedalism

33   "Human walking is a unique activity": John Napier, "The Antiquity of Human Walking," *Scientific American*, April 1967. Napier is one of the earliest to push the history of walking back further into prehuman history and insist on its formative importance there.

34   "point out parallels": Adrienne Zihlman, in "The Paleolithic Glass Ceiling," in *Women in Human Evolution*, ed. Lori D. Hager (London and New York: Routledge, 1997), 99. Zihlman and Dean Falk's readings of Lovejoy and the broader gender politics of human evolution in this book and in Falk's book *Braindance* (New York: Henry Holt, 1992) have been immensely helpful to my own reading.

36   "This is like a modern knee joint" and following: Donald Johanson and Maitland Edey, *Lucy: The Beginnings of Humankind* (New York: Simon and Schuster, 1981), 163. See also C. Owen Lovejoy with Kingsbury G. Heiple and Albert H. Burstein, "The Gait of Australopithicus," *American Journal of Physical Anthropology* 38 (1973): 757–80.

36   "In most primate species": C. Owen Lovejoy, "The Origin of Man," *Science* 211 (1981): 341–50.

37   "Bipedalism . . . figured": "Evolution of Human Walking," *Scientific American*, November 1988.

38   Dean Falk's attack on Lovejoy: "Brain Evolution in Females: An Answer to Mr. Lovejoy," in Hager, *Women in Human Evolution*, 115.

38   Jack Stern and Randall Sussman: Interview with the author, Stonybrook, New York, February 4, 1998. See also their comments in *Origine(s) de la Bipédie chez les Hominidés* (Paris: Editions du CNRS/Cahiers de Paléoanthropologie, 1991) and articles such as "The Locomotor Anatomy of *Australopithicus afarensis*," *American Journal of Physical Anthropology* 60 (1983). Representations of hominids in deep forest appeared in *National Geographic* in 1997.

40   1991 Conference on the Origins of Bipedalism: The three anthropologists at the Paris conference were Nicole I. Tuttle, Russell H. Tuttle, and David M. Webb; their paper "Laetoli Footprint Trails and the Evolution of Hominid Bipedalism" appears in *Origine(s) de la Bipédie;* the quoted passages appear on 189–90.

41   "One cannot overemphasize": Mary Leakey, *National Geographic*, April 1979, 453.

41   "According to this view": Falk, "Brain Evolution," 115.

41   "these features led to 'whole-body cooling' ": Falk, "Brain Evolution," 128, and at length in Falk, *Braindance*. See also E. Wheeler, "The Influence of Bipedalism on the Energy and Water Budgets of Early Hominids," *Journal of Human Evolution* 21 (1991): 117–36.

43   I called up Owen Lovejoy: C. Owen Lovejoy, interview by author, June 23, 1998.

4. THE UPHILL ROAD TO GRACE: Some Pilgrimages

46   "These devout and simple people": John Noel, *The Story of Everest* (New York: Blue Ribbon Books, 1927), 108.

46   Much of the information on Chimayó comes from Elizabeth Kay, *Chimayó Valley Traditions* (Santa Fe: Ancient City Press, 1987), and Don J. Usner, *Sabino's Map: Life in Chimayó's Old Plaza* (Santa Fe: Museum of New Mexico Press, 1995).

50   "All sites of pilgrimage": Victor Turner and Edith Turner, *Image and Pilgrimage in Christian Culture: Anthropological Perspectives* (New York: Columbia University Press, 1978), 41.

51   "Often as she listened to the pilgrims' tales": Leo Tolstoy, *War and Peace*, trans. Ann Dunnigan (New York: Signet Classics, 1965), bk. 2, pt. 3, ch. 26, 589.

51   "When pilgrims begin to walk": Nancy Louise Frey, *Pilgrim Stories: On and Off the Road to Santiago* (Berkeley: University of California Press, 1998), 72.

51   "Liminars are stripped of status and authority": Turner and Turner, *Image and Pilgrimage*, 37.

52   "Wherever you go, there you are": First said by Carl Franz, in his *People's Guide to Mexico*, Greg says.

55   "To remain a wanderer": Introduction, *Peace Pilgrim: Her Life and Work in Her Own Words* (Santa Fe: Ocean Tree Books, 1991), xiii.

55   "a complete willingness": Ibid., 7.

56   "it doesn't show dirt": Ibid., 56.

56   "a comb, a folding toothbrush": Ibid., xiii.

57   "I walk until given shelter": Ibid., 25.

59   "Reverend Charles Billups and other Birmingham ministers": Stephen B. Oates, *Let the Trumpet Sound: A Life of Martin Luther King, Jr.* (New York: Harper and Row, 1982), 236.

59   March of Dimes: Information from telephone conversation with Tony Choppa, April 1998.

61   "At the end of November, 1974": Werner Herzog, *On Walking in Ice* (New York: Tanam Press, 1980), 3.

62   "While I was taking a shit": Ibid., 27.

62   "For one splendid fleeting moment": Ibid., 57.

5. LABYRINTHS AND CADILLACS: Walking into the Realm of the Symbolic

70   W. H. Matthews cautions: W. H. Matthews, *Mazes and Labyrinths: Their History and Development* (1922; reprint, New York: Dover, 1970), 66, 69.

70   "Labyrinths . . . are usually in the form of a circle": Lauren Artress, handout at Grace Cathedral, n.d.

75   "each of the speaking characters": Matthews, *Mazes and Labyrinths*, 117.

75   "A garden path": Charles W. Moore, William J. Matchell, and William Turnbull, *The Poetics of Gardens* (Cambridge, Mass.: MIT Press, 1988), 35.

76   "I have a little game": John Finlay, ed., *The Pleasures of Walking* (1934; reprint, New York: Vanguard Press, 1976), 8.

76   "in a kind of out-of-body form": Lucy Lippard, *The Lure of the Local: Senses of Place in a Multicentered Society* (New York: New Press, 1996), 4.

76   "general principles of the mnemonic": Frances Yates, *The Art of Memory* (London: Pimlico, 1992), 18.

6. THE PATH OUT OF THE GARDEN

81   These descriptions of Dorothy Wordsworth occur on pages 132 and 188 of Thomas De Quincey, *Recollections of the Lakes and the Lake Poets* (Harmondsworth, England: Penguin Books, 1970).

81   "Twas a keen frosty morning": William Wordsworth, letter to Samuel Taylor Coleridge, December 24, 1799, in *Letters of William and Dorothy Wordsworth: The Early Years, 1787–1805*, ed. Ernest de Selincourt (Oxford: Clarendon Press, 1967), 273–80. It's worth noting that in this letter Wordsworth refers both to "Taylor's tour," a written account that described the first waterfall they visited, and to the waterfall itself as "a performance as you might expect from some giant gardiner employed by one of Queen Elizabeth's courtiers, if this same giant gardiner had consulted with Spenser," which is to say that his vision was framed in the literary and gardening traditions of England.

82   Wordsworth and his companions are said to have made walking into something new: See, for example, Marion Shoard, *This Land Is Our Land: The Struggle for Britain's Countryside*, 2d. ed. (London: Gaia Books, 1997), 79: "It is to Wordsworth as much as anyone that we also owe the idea that the proper way of communing with nature is by walking through the countryside."

82   "I have always fancied": Christopher Morley, "The Art of Walking" (1917), in Aaron Sussman and Ruth Goode, *The Magic of Walking* (New York: Simon and Schuster, 1967), a cheery evangelistic volume advocating walking for health, providing practical tips, and including an anthology of essays on the subject.

83   use as their demonstration case Carl Moritz: "Yet within less than ten years from the date of Moritz's tour a striking change had taken place, and the fashion of the walking-tour (or pedestrian-tour, as it was then called) had come in. It was the beginning of a movement . . ." (Morris Marples, *Shanks's Pony: A Study of Walking* [London: J. M. Dent and Sons, 1959], 31); "to the new phenomenon of the pedestrian tour, and to other less ambitious forms of walking for pleasure . . . established, in the last ten to fifteen years of the eighteenth century" (Robin Jarvis, *Romantic Writing and Pedestrian Travel* [Houndmills, Basingstoke, Hampshire: Macmillan Press, 1997], 4); "removing walking's long-standing implication of necessity and so of poverty and vagrancy" (Anne Wallace, *Walking, Literature and English Culture* [Oxford: Oxford University Press, 1993], 10); "changes in the practice of and attitudes toward travel in general, and walking in particular, which accompany the transport revolution beginning in the mid-eighteenth century" (ibid., 18). They all assert walking is travel; that it is not necessarily so is my argument.

83   "A traveller on foot": Carl Moritz, *Travels of Carl Philipp Moritz in England in 1782: A Reprint of the English Translation of 1795*, with an introduction by E. Matheson (1795; reprint, London: Humphrey Milford, 1924), 37.

83   "I walked with my brother at my side": Dorothy Wordsworth, quoted in Hunter Davies, *William Wordsworth: A Biography* (New York: Antheneum, 1980), 70.

84   "I cannot pass unnoticed": Dorothy Wordsworth to her proud aunt Crackanthorp, April 21, 1794, cited in de Selincourt, *Letters*, 117.

84   "When we walk, we naturally go to the fields and woods": Thoreau, "Walking," 98–99.

85   The eighteenth century created a taste for nature: See Christopher Thacker, *The Wildness Pleases: The Origins of Romanticism* (New York: St. Martin's Press, 1983), 1–2. He writes, "Aristotle claimed that all poetry was 'the imitation of men in action.' By poetry, he implied all forms of art, from sculpture to drama, from epic poetry to history, to painting and even to music. . . . Aristotle's definition of the scope of poetry cuts out many matters which we might consider wholly proper, indeed desirable, as the subject of a work of art. Above all, the depiction of 'nature' is a subject which we, living two centuries after the romantic explosion at the end of the eighteenth century, have come to accept almost without thinking." Naming many landscape paintings, Thacker goes on to say that such subject matter would have seemed incomprehensible, or at least inconsequential, to Aristotle and indeed to any educated onlooker before the transformation of perception that "took place in western Europe in the eighteenth century."

86   "Sixteenth-century doctors stressed": Mark Girouard, *Life in the English Country House: A Social and Architectural History* (New Haven: Yale University Press, 1978), 100.

86   Queen Elizabeth added a raised terrace: Susan Lasdun, *The English Park: Royal, Private & Public* (New York: Vendome Press, 1992), 35.

88   "There is gravel walks and grass and close walks": Celia Fiennes on the gardens at Agnes Burton, *The Journeys of Celia Fiennes*, ed. Christopher Morris (London: Cresset Press, 1949), 90–91.

88   "These avenues provided the shade and shelter for walks": Lasdun, *English Park*, 66.

89   "O glorious Nature!": Shaftesbury in John Dixon Hunt and Peter Willis, *The Genius of the Place: The English Landscape Garden, 1620–1840* (New York: Harper, 1975), 122; also a key text in Thacker, *The Wildness Pleases*, whose title comes from this effusion.

89   "Poetry, Painting, and Gardening": Walpole, quoted in Hunt and Willis, *Genius of the Place*, 11.

90   "asked to be explored": John Dixon Hunt, *The Figure in the Landscape: Poetry, Painting and Gardening during the Eighteenth Century* (Baltimore: Johns Hopkins University Press, 1976), 143.

90   "Whereas the French formal garden was based on a single axial view": Carolyn Bermingham, *Landscape and Ideology: The English Rustic Tradition, 1740–1860* (Berkeley: University of California Press, 1986), 12.

91   "into harmony with the age's humanism": Christopher Hussey, *English Gardens and Landscapes, 1700–1750* (London: Country Life, 1967), 101.

91   "Within thirty years": *Stowe Landscape Gardens* (Great Britain: National Trust, 1997), 45.

91   "O lead me to the wide-extended walks": James Thomson, *The Seasons* (Edinburgh and New York: T. Nelson and Sons, 1860), 139. Kenneth Johnston, in *The Hidden Wordsworth: Poet, Lover, Rebel, Spy* (New York: Norton, 1998), calls *The Seasons* the most successful poem of the century, and Andrew Wilton in *Turner and the Sublime* (Chicago: University of Chicago Press, 1981) documents its impact.

92   "Everyone takes a different way": Pope, letter of 1739, cited in *Stowe Landscape Gardens*, 66.

92   "or drove about it in cabriolets": Walpole, letter to George Montagu, July 7, 1770, in *Selected Letters of Horace Walpole* (London: J. M. Dent and Sons, 1926), 93.

92   "Gardening, as far as Gardening is an Art": Sir Joshua Reynolds, quoted in Hunt and Willis, *Genius of the Place*, 32.

93   "leapt the fence": Walpole, quoted in Hunt and Willis, *Genius of the Place*, 13.

93   "Within the last sixty years": Wordsworth, *Guide to the Lakes*, ed. Ernest de Selincourt (Oxford: Oxford University Press, 1977), 69.

94   "greatly compensates for the mediocrity of this park": *Travels of Carl Philipp Moritz*, 44.

94   "The People of London are as fond of walking": Oliver Goldsmith, *The Citizen of the World*, vol. 2 of the *Collected Works*, ed. Arthur Friedman (Oxford: Clarendon Press, 1966), 293.

95   "how to admire an old twisted tree": Jane Austen, *Sense and Sensibility* (New York: Washington Square Press, 1961), 80.

95   "there is a sense in which": John Barrell, *The Idea of Landscape and the Sense of Place* (New York: Cambridge University Press, 1972), 4–5.

95   "It is very true": Austen, *Sense and Sensibility*, 83–84.

96   "Were it not for this general deficiency of objects": William Gilpin, *Observations on Several Parts of Great Britain, particularly the Highlands of Scotland, relative chiefly to picturesque beauty, made in the year 1776* (London: T. Cadell and W. Davies, 1808), 2:119.

96   "Let us learn, in real scenes, to trace": Richard Payne Knight, "The Landscape: A Didactic Poem," in *The Genius of the Place*, 344.

96   "Thomas Gray's celebrated Lake District tour": Gray wrote about it in his "Journal in the Lakes," in *The Works of Thomas Gray in Prose and Verse*, vol. 1, ed. Edmund Gosse (New York: Macmillan, 1902).

97   "They were country ladies": Dorothy Wordsworth, Oct. 16, 1792, in de Selincourt, *Letters*, 84.

98–   "That she should have walked three miles": Jane Austen, *Pride and Prejudice* (Oxford:
101   Oxford University Press/Avenal Books, 1985), 30; "At that moment they were met," 49; "Her figure was elegant," 52; "Miss Bennet, there seemed to be a prettyish kind of a little wilderness," 340; "favourite walk," 164; "More than once did Elizabeth in her ramble," 176; "had never seen a place for which nature had done more," 234;

"rapturously cried, 'what delight! what felicity!," 150; "it is not the object of this work," 232; " 'My dear Lizzy, where can you have been walking to?,'" 360.

102 "In the morning, I read Mr Knight's *Landscape*": July 27, 1800, reprinted in *Home at Grasmere: Extracts from the Journal of Dorothy Wordsworth and from the Poems of William Wordsworth*, ed. Colette Clark (Harmondsworth, England: Penguin Books, 1978), 53–54.

7. THE LEGS OF WILLIAM WORDSWORTH

104 "His legs were pointedly condemned": Thomas De Quincey, *Recollections of the Lakes and the Lake Poets*, ed. David Wright (Harmondsworth, England: Penguin Books, 1970), 53–54.

105 "Happy in this, that I with nature walked": William Wordsworth, *The Prelude: The Four Texts (1798, 1799, 1805, 1850)*, ed. Jonathan Wordsworth (Harmondsworth, England: Penguin Books, 1995), 322. All quotes are from the 1805 version.

106 "He sees nothing but himself and the universe": Hazlitt, "The Lake School," in *William Hazlitt: Selected Writings* (Harmondsworth, England: Penguin Books, 1970), 218.

106 "more glorious than I had ever beheld": Wordsworth, *Prelude*, 158.

106 "Should the guide I choose": Ibid., 36.

107 "With this act of disobedience": Johnston, *Hidden Wordsworth*, 188.

107 "standing on top of golden hours": Wordsworth, *Prelude*, 226.

108 "each spot of old and recent fame": Ibid., 348.

108 "Oswald had traveled to India": Johnston, *Hidden Wordsworth*, 286.

108 "no region, pervious to human feet": Thomas De Quincey, "Walking Stewart— Edward Irving—William Wordsworth," in *Literary Reminiscences*, vol. 3 of *The Collected Works of Thomas De Quincey* (Boston: Houghton, Osgood and Co., 1880), 597.

109 "I have some thoughts:" in de Selincourt, *Letters*, 153; and "So like a peasant," Wordsworth, *Prelude*, 42.

109 "Throughout that turbulent time": Basil Willey, *The Eighteenth-Century Background* (Boston: Beacon Press, 1961), 205.

110 "that odious class of men called democrats": Wordsworth, letter to a friend, May 23, 1794, in de Selincourt, *Letters*, 119.

110 "The principal object, then, proposed in these poems": Wordsworth, preface to the second edition of *Lyrical Ballads*, in *Anthology of Romanticism*, ed. Ernest Bernbaum (New York: Ronald Press, 1948), 300–301.

111 "I love a public road": Wordsworth, *Prelude*, 496.

111 "Had I been born in a class": Johnston, *Hidden Wordsworth*, 57.

112 "They were surrounded": Hazlitt, "The Lake School," 217.

113 "He won't a man as said a deal to common fwoak": Local quoted in *Wordsworth Among the Peasantry of Westmorland*, cited in Davies, *Wordsworth*, 322.

113 "He would set his head a bit forrad": Andrew J. Bennett, "'Devious Feet': Words-
     worth and the Scandal of Narrative Form," *LELH* 59 (1992): 147.
114 "At present he is walking": Dorothy, in a letter to Lady Beaumont, May 1804, in
     Davies, *Wordsworth,* 166.
114 "almost physiological relation" and following: Seamus Heaney, "The Makings of a
     Music," in *Preoccupations* (New York: Farrar, Straus and Giroux, 1980), 66, 68.
115 "the lord who owned the ground": Davies, *Wordsworth,* 324. See also Wallace,
     Walking, Literature and English Culture, 117.
115 "The grave old bard": Letter published in the *Manchester Guardian,* October 7, 1887,
     cited in Howard Hill, *Freedom to Roam: The Struggle for Access to Britain's Moors and
     Mountains* (Ashbourne, England: Moorland Publishing, 1980), 40. The presence of a
     deferential "Mr. Justice Coleridge" on the walk and Sir John Wallace at the con-
     frontation make it appear that this is another version of the same event. Late in life
     Wordsworth, alas, also opposed the building of a railroad that would take tourists to
     Windermere, crustily remarking that workers could take their holidays closer to
     home. Though an unkind remark, it is not altogether wrong about the impact of
     tourism—a century later the Sierra Club would take the phrase "render accessible"
     out of its mission statement, realizing that people could love the landscape to death
     with tourism infrastructures and general trampling.
117 "I purpose within a month": Earle Vonard Weller, ed., *Autobiography of John Keats,
     Compiled from his Letters and Essays* (Stanford: Stanford University Press, 1933), 105.
117 "I should not have consented": Keats, in Marples, *Shanks's Pony,* 68.
117 "hunger-bitten girl": Wordsworth, *Prelude,* 374.

8. A THOUSAND MILES OF CONVENTIONAL SENTIMENT: The Literature of Walking

118 "a processional march": Thomas Hardy, *Tess of the d'Urbervilles* (New York: Bantam
     Books, 1971), 10.
119 "In the neighborhood of latitude": Aldous Huxley, "Wordsworth in the Tropics," in
     Collected Essays (New York: Bantam Books, 1960), 1.
119 "One of the pleasantest things in the world": William Hazlitt, "On Going a Journey,"
     in *The Lore of the Wanderer,* ed. Geoffrey Goodchild (New York: E. P. Dutton, 1920), 65.
120 "The walks are the unobtrusive connecting thread": Leslie Stephen, "In Praise of
     Walking," in Finlay, *Pleasures of Walking,* 20.
120 "lameness was too severe": Stephen, "In Praise," 24.
121 "A walking tour should be gone on alone": Robert Louis Stevenson, "Walking Tours,"
     in Goodchild, *Lore of the Wanderer,* 10–11.
121 "I have two doctors": G. M. Trevelyan, "Walking," in Finlay, *Pleasures of Walking,* 57.
121 "Whenever I was with friends": Max Beerbohm, "Going Out on a Walk," in Finlay,
     Pleasures of Walking, 39.

122   "I wish to speak a word for Nature" and following: Thoreau, "Walking," 93–98.

122   "The best thing is to walk": Bruce Chatwin, "It's a Nomad Nomad World," in *Anatomy of Restlessness: Selected Writings, 1969–1989* (New York: Viking, 1996), 103.

123   "How womankind, who are confined": Thoreau, "Walking," 97.

124   "Perhaps walking can be the way to peace": Mort Malkin, "Walk for Peace," *Fellowship* (magazine of the Buddhist Peace Fellowship), July/August 1997, 12. Malkin is the author of *Walk—The Pleasure Exercise* and *Walking—The Weight Loss Exercise*.

124   "Reagan had realized, he told us": Michael Korda, "Prompting the President," *New Yorker*, October 6, 1997, 92.

127   "But why tramp?" Charles F. Lummis, *A Tramp Across the Continent* (Omaha: University of Nebraska Press, 1982), 3.

130   "But strange things do happen": Robyn Davidson, *Tracks* (New York: Pantheon Books, 1980), 191–92.

130   "In properly developed countries, the inhabitants": Alan Booth, *The Roads to Sata: A Two-Thousand-Mile Walk Through Japan* (New York: Viking, 1986), 27.

131   "The Guinness Book of Records defines a walk": Ffyona Campbell, *The Whole Story: A Walk Around the World* (London: Orion Books, 1996), unpaginated preface.

9. MOUNT OBSCURITY AND MOUNT ARRIVAL

134   "the first man to climb a mountain": Kenneth Clark, *Landscape into Art* (Boston: Beacon Press, 1961), 7.

135   "a small mound of rock": Clarence King, *Mountaineering in the Sierra Nevada* (New York: W. W. Norton, 1935), 287.

135   Christian Europe seems to be alone: Both Francis Farquhar's brief bibliography of mountaineering literature and Edwin Bernbaum's *Sacred Mountains of the World* (Berkeley: University of California Press, 1997) agree on the peculiar European attitude toward mountains before the eighteenth century. Edward Whymper also speaks of the legend of the Wandering Jew, in Ronald W. Clark, *Six Great Mountaineers* (London: Hamish Hamilton, 1956), 14. The terms in which English writers described mountains come from Keith Thomas, *Man and the Natural World: Changing Attitudes in England* (Harmondsworth, England: Penguin Books, 1984), 258–59.

136   drove his chariot up T'ai Shan: The First Emperor's ascent is described in Bernbaum, *Sacred Mountains*, 31.

136   "The Chinese phrase for 'going on a pilgrimage'": Gretel Ehrlich, *Questions of Heaven: The Chinese Journeys of an American Buddhist* (Boston: Beacon Press, 1997), 15.

136   "the vast and very flat valley" and following: *Egeria: Diary of a Pilgrimage*, trans. George E. Gingras (New York: Newman Press, 1970), 49–51.

137   "There is nothing to look up to": Cited by Dervla Murphy in her introduction to Henriette d'Angeville's *My Ascent of Mont Blanc*, trans. Jennifer Barnes (London:

HarperCollins, 1991), xv. The first American woman atop Everest (the first woman was Japanese), Stacy Allison, similarly declared, "There was nowhere else to climb. I was standing on top of the world" (from www.everest.mountainzone.com).

137   "We climbed up through the narrow cleft": Dante, *The Divine Comedy, Purgatorio,* canto 4.

137   "To the traveller": Henry David Thoreau, *Walden* (Princeton: Princeton University Press, 1973), 290.

138   "To climb up rocks": Charles Edward Montague, "In Hanging Garden Gully" (from his book *Fiery Particles,* 1924), excerpted in *Challenge: An Anthology of the Literature of Mountaineering,* ed. William Robert Irwin (New York: Columbia University Press, 1950), 333.

138   "Because it's there," "We hope to show": Murray Sayle, "The Vulgarity of Success," *London Review of Books,* May 7, 1998, 8.

139   Chomalungma: See Bernbaum, *Sacred Mountains,* 7.

139   "Whatever Western society regards": Ibid., 236.

140   "And before I started to move": Gwen Moffat, *The Space Below My Feet* (Cambridge: Riverside Press, 1961), 66.

140   slowest traverse: "We made an epic traverse of the Cuillin Ridge at the end of June. The main ridge is seven or eight miles long with about sixteen peaks of over three thousand feet strong along the chain. The average time taken for the traverse was ten to thirteen hours; some parties took twenty-four, others were bringing the record down to fantastic times, as on the fourteen-peak walk in Snowdonia. We hated records; we decided to be different. We would take our time, sunbathe, enjoy the views, carry food for two days, sleep out on top of the ridge; we would set up the record for the longest time spent on the Cuillen traverse" (ibid., 101).

141   "turned his keen intelligence": Eric Shipton, *Mountain Conquest* (New York: American Heritage, 1965), 17.

141   forty-six parties . . . had reached the summit: Ronald W. Clark, *A Picture History of Mountaineering* (London: Hulton Press, 1956), 31.

142   "The soul has needs," "It was not the puny fame": D'Angeville, *My Ascent,* xx–xxi.

144   "For half a century": Smoke Blanchard, *Walking Up and Down in the World: Memories of a Mountain Rambler* (San Francisco: Sierra Club Books, 1985), xv.

144   "On Visiting a Taoist Master": Arthur Cooper, trans., *Li Po and Tu Fu* (Harmondsworth, England: Penguin Books, 1973), 105.

145   "People ask the way": *Cold Mountain: 100 Poems by the T'ang Poet Han-Shan,* trans. Burton Watson (New York: Columbia University Press, 1972), poem 82, 100.

145   "Before the sixth century A.D.": Bernbaum, *Sacred Mountains,* 58.

145   "Every aspect of Shugendō": H. Byron Earhart, *A Religious Study of the Mount Haguro Sect of Shugendō: An Example of Japanese Mountain Religion* (Tokyo: Sophia University, 1970), 31. Also see Allan G. Grapard, "Flying Mountains and Walkers of Emptiness:

Toward a Definition of Sacred Space in Japanese Religions," *History of Religion* 21, no. 3 (1982).

145 "I . . . set off": Bashō, *The Narrow Road to the Deep North and Other Travel Sketches,* trans. and ed. Nobuyuki Yuasa (Harmondsworth, England: Penguin Books, 1966), 125. Bashō was climbing Mount Gassan in the north, immediately after climbing better-known, adjacent Mount Haguro, a major focal point of Shugendō.

146 "I had been introduced to the high snow peaks": Gary Snyder, *Mountains and Rivers without End* (Washington, D.C.: Counterpoint Press, 1996), 153. Snyder also speaks about mountains, spirituality, and his mountaineering in the essay "Blue Mountains Constantly Walking," in *The Practice of the Wild* (San Francisco: North Point Press, 1990); in *Earth House Hold* (New York: New Directions, 1969); and most recently in an interview with John O'Grady, in *Western American Literature,* fall 1998, among many other places.

146 "I was given a chance to see": Snyder, *Mountains and Rivers,* 156.

146 "The closer you get to real matter": David Robertson quoting Kerouac in *Dharma Bums,* in *Real Matter* (Salt Lake City: University of Utah Press, 1997), 100.

146 "This sentence states what is perhaps": Ibid., 100, 108.

147 "I translate space from its physical sense": Snyder, interview with O'Grady, 289.

147 "On Climbing the Sierra Matterhorn Again": Gary Snyder, *No Nature: New and Selected Poems* (New York: Pantheon Books, 1992), 362.

10. OF WALKING CLUBS AND LAND WARS

149 "An excursion of this sort": William Colby, *Sierra Club Bulletin,* 1990.

150 outdoor organizations had been proliferating: "The formation of the [British] Alpine Club in 1857 had been followed by the foundation of the Swiss Alpine Club—and of the Societe de Touristes Savoyardes—in 1863. The Italian Alpine Club came later during the same year, while in 1865 there was founded for the further exploration of the Pyrenees the Societe Ramond. The Austrian and the German clubs came in 1869 and the French in 1874, while across the Atlantic the Williamstown Alpine Club had been founded as early as 1863 and was followed in 1873 and 1776 respectively by the White Mountain Club and the Appalachian Mountain Club" (Clark, *Picture History of Mountaineering,* 12). A Ladies' Alpine Club was founded in 1907.

152 "There were solemn hours": Ella M. Sexton, *Sierra Club Bulletin* 4 (1901): 17.

152 "Mr. Colby goes like lightning": Nelson Hackett in oral history transcripts, Sierra Club files, in Bancroft Library, letters of July 5 and July 18, 1908, transcribed at end of Hackett's interview.

155 "We were shocked to discover firsthand": Michael Cohen, *The Pathless Way: John Muir and the American Wilderness* (Madison: University of Wisconsin, 1984), 331.

156   "The Friends of Nature were founded": E-mail from Manfred Pils to the author, October 1998.

158   "On the main thing—rambling": Walter Laqueur, *Young Germany: A History of the German Youth Movement* (New Brunswick and London: Transaction Books, 1984), 33. This and Gerald Masur, *Prophets of Yesterday: Studies in European Culture, 1890–1914* (New York: Macmillan, 1961); Werner Heisenberg, *Physics and Beyond: Encounters and Conversations* (New York: Harper and Row, 1971); and David C. Cassidy, *Uncertainty: The Life and Science of Werner Heisenberg* (New York: W. H. Freeman, 1992), were my principal sources.

159   "After 1919, the militant dictatorships": Masur, *Prophets of Yesterday,* 368

160   eighteen million Britons head for the country: Shoard, *This Land Is Our Land,* 264; ten million walkers from *Country Walking* magazine editor in chief Lynn Maxwell, in conversation with the author, May 1998.

160   "Almost a spiritual thing": Roly Smith, conversation with the author, May 1998.

160   accessing the land has been something of a class war: Information on trespassing, poaching, and gamekeepers in various parts of Shoard, *This Land Is Our Land.*

161   Association for the Protection of Ancient Footpaths: Tom Stephenson, *Forbidden Land: The Struggle for Access to Mountain and Moorland,* ed. Ann Holt (Manchester and New York: Manchester University Press, 19), 59.

162   Forest Ramblers' Club: Hill, *Freedom to Roam,* 21.

162   not impressive compared to those of other European countries: Steve Platt, "Land Wars," *New Statesman and Society* 23 (May 10, 1991); Shoard, *This Land Is Our Land,* 451.

163   "Land is not property": James Bryce, quoted in Ann Holt, "Hindsight on Kinder," *Rambling Today,* spring 1995, 17. See also Raphael Samuel, *Theatres of Memory* (London: Verso, 1994), 294: "The Commons, Open Spaces and Footpath Society, founded in 1865—the remote ancestor of the National Trust—was a kind of Liberal front, championing the claims of villagers and commoners against the encroachments of landlords and property developers. . . . "

163   "It is the one thing that is unpleasant": Crichton Porteous, *Derbyshire* (London: Robert Hale Limited, 1950), 33.

164   "a little judicious trespassing": Leslie Stephen, "In Praise," 32.

164   "By the last quarter of the nineteenth century": Hill, *Freedom to Roam,* 24.

164   "Hiking was a major, if unofficial, component": Raphael Samuel, *Theatres of Memory,* 297. The passage continues, "and 'freedom to roam' was a left-wing campaigning issue. It had been given a mass basis, in Edwardian times, by the Clarion League, the 40,000 strong organization of the young who combined Sunday cycle meets with preaching the socialist message on the village green. In the inter-war years it was forwarded by the Woodcraft Folk—a kind of anti-militarist, co-educational version of the Boy Scouts and Girl Guides who combined pacifist advocacy and nature mys-

ticism; by the Youth Hostels Association, formed in 1930; and by that great army of hikers who on high days and holidays went rambling on the mountains and moors. Hiking had a particular appeal to working-class Bohemians, as a mainly intellectual alternative to the dance hall, and one that cost no money."

165 "a genuine hatred of ramblers": Ann Holt, *The Origins and Early Days of the Ramblers' Association*, booklet published by the Ramblers' Association from a speech given April 1995.

165 "Town dwellers lived for weekends": Benny Rothman, *The 1932 Kinder Scout Trespass: A Personal View of the Kinder Scout Mass Trespass* (Altrincham, England: Willow Publishing, 1982), 12.

11. THE SOLITARY STROLLER AND THE CITY

Philip Lopate's essay "The Pen on Foot: The Literature of Walking Around," Parnassus, vol. 18, no. 2 and 19, no 1, 1993, pointed me to Edwin Denby's writings and to specific poems of Walt Whitman's.

172 "On Saturday night . . . the city joined in the promenade": Harriet Lane Levy, *920 O'Farrell Street* (Berkeley: Heyday Books, 1997), 185–86.

173 Kerouac managed to have two visions on [Market Street]: see *Atlantic Monthly*, reprinting a May 1961 letter, November 1998, 68: "It [*On the Road*] was really a story about two Catholic buddies in search of God. And we found him. I found him in the sky, in Market Street San Francisco (those 2 visions)."

176 how a popular, well-used street is kept safe: Jane Jacobs, *The Death and Life of Great American Cities* (New York: Vintage Books, 1961), throughout the chapter "The Uses of Sidewalks: Safety."

176 "What distinguishes the city": Moretti, quoted in Peter Jukes, *A Shout in the Street: An Excursion into the Modern City* (Berkeley: University of California Press, 1991), 184.

177 little more than outdoor salons and ballrooms: *Cities and People* (New Haven and London: Yale University Press, 1985), 166–68, 237–38.

178 "Earlier in the [nineteenth] century," "I hear that pedestrians": Ray Rosenzweig and Elizabeth Blackmar, *The Park and the People: A History of Central Park* (Ithica: Cornell University Press, 1992), 27, 223.

178 "It simply never occurs to us": Bernard Rudofsky, *Streets for People: A Primer for Americans* (New York: Van Nostrand Reinhold, 1982), epigraph quoting his own *Architecture without Architects*.

179 "In ancient Italian towns the narrow main street": Edwin Denby, *Dancers, Buildings and People in the Streets*, introduction by Frank O'Hara (New York: Horizon Press, 1965), 183.

180 "When I am in a serious Humour": Addison in Joseph Addison and Richard Steele, *The Spectator, Vol. 1* (London: J. M. Dent and Sons, 1907), 96, from *Spectator*, no. 26 (March 30, 1711).

180 "Though you through cleaner allies": John Gay, "Trivia; or, the Art of Walking the Streets of London," book 3, line 126, in *The Abbey Classics: Poems by John Gay* (London: Chapman and Dodd, n.d.), 88.

181 "Here I remark": Ibid., ll. 275–82, 78.

181 "goes forward with the crowd": Wordsworth, *Prelude*, 286.

181 "each charter'd street": The famous opening of William Blake's "London," in *William Blake*, ed. J. Bronowski (Harmondsworth, England: Penguin Books, 1958), 52.

181 one of those desperate London walkers: See Richard Holmes, *Dr. Johnson and Mr. Savage* (New York: Vintage Books, 1993), 44, quoting Sir John Hawkins in the chapter on these walks: "Johnson has told me, that whole nights have been spent by him and Savage in conversations of this kind, not under the hospitable roof of a tavern, where warmth might have invigorated their spirits, and wine dispelled their care; but in a perambulation round the squares of Westminster, St. James's in particular, when all the money they could both raise was less than sufficient to purchase for them the shelter and sordid comforts of a night cellar."

181 "I should have been": James Boswell, *Boswell's London Journal*, ed. Frederick A. Pottle (New York: Signet, 1956), 235.

182 50,000 [prostitutes in London] in 1793: Henry Mayhew, *London Labour and the London Poor*, vol. 4 (1861–62; reprint, New York: Dover Books, 1968), 211, citing Mr. Colquhoun, a police magistrate, and his "tedious investigations."

182 "the circulating harlotry of the Haymarket and Regent Street": Ibid., 213. On 217, "They [the streetwalkers] are to be seen between three and five o'clock in the Burlington Arcade, which is a well known resort of cyprians of the better sort. They are well acquainted with its Paphian intricacies, and will, if their signals are responded to, glide into a friendly bonnet shop, the stairs of which leading to the coenacula or upper chambers are not innocent of their well formed 'bien chaussee' feet. The park is also, as we have said, a favorite promenade, where assignations may be made or acquaintances formed."

182 "Prostitution streetscapes are composed of *strolls*": Richard Symanski, *The Immoral Landscape: Female Prostitution in Western Societies* (Toronto: Butterworths, 1981), 175–76.

182 "think that women who work in whorehouses": Dolores French with Linda Lee, *Working: My Life as a Prostitute* (New York: E. P. Dutton, 1988), 43.

183 "Perception of the new qualities of the modern city": Raymond Williams, *The Country and the City* (New York: Oxford University Press, 1973), 233.

183 "Being myself at that time, of necessity, a peripatetic" and following: De Quincey, *Confessions of an English Opium Eater* (New York: Signet Books, 1966), 42–43.

184 "And this kind of realism," "Few of us understand the street": G. K. Chesterton, *Charles Dickens, a Critical Study* (New York: Dodd, Mead, 1906), 47, 44.

184 "If I couldn't walk fast and far": Dickens to John Forster, cited in Ned Lukacher, *Primal Scenes: Literature, Philosophy, Psychoanalysis* (Ithaca: Cornell University Press, 1986), 288.

184 "I am both a town traveller": Charles Dickens, *The Uncommercial Traveller and Reprinted Pieces Etc.* (Oxford and New York: Oxford University Press, 1958), 1.

184 "So much of my travelling is done on foot," "My walking is of two kinds": Dickens, "Shy Neighborhoods," ibid., 94, 95.

185 "It is one of my fancies": Dickens, "On an Amateur Beat," ibid., 345.

185 "Whenever I think I deserve particularly well of myself": Dickens, "The City of the Absent," ibid., 233.

185 "Some years ago, a temporary inability to sleep": Dickens, "Night Walks," ibid., 127.

186 "I would roam the streets": Patti Smith, when asked what she did to prepare to go onstage, *Fresh Air*, National Public Radio, Oct. 3, 1997.

187 "How could I think mountains and climbing romantic?": *The Letters of Virginia Woolf*, vol. 3, *A Change of Perspective*, ed. Nigel Nicholson (London: Hogarth Press, 1975–80), letter to V. Sackville-West, Aug. 19, 1924, 126.

187 "enforce the memories of our own experience": Virginia Woolf, "Street Haunting: A London Adventure," in *The Death of the Moth and Other Essays* (Harmondsworth, England: Penguin Books, 1961), 23.

187 "As we step out of the house," "the shell-like covering": Ibid., 23–24.

188 Two-thirds of all journeys . . . still made on foot: Tony Hiss, editorial, *New York Times*, January 30, 1998.

188 "On the whole North America's Anglo-Saxomania has had a withering effect": Rudofsky, *Streets for People*, 19.

189 "Who often walk'd lonesome walks": Walt Whitman, "Recorders Ages Hence," *Leaves of Grass* (New York: Bantam Books, 1983), 99.

189 "City of orgies, walks and joys": Ibid., 102.

189 "Passing stranger!": Ibid., 103.

189 "the fruited plain": Ken Gonzales-Day, "The Fruited Plain: A History of Queer Space," *Art Issues*, September/October 1997, 17.

190 "dragging themselves through the negro streets," "shoes full of blood": Allen Ginsberg, "Howl," in *The New American Poetry*, ed. Donald M. Allen (New York: Grove Press, 1960), 182, 186.

191 "Strange now to think of you, gone": Allen Ginsberg, *Kaddish and Other Poems, 1958–1960* (San Francisco: City Lights Books, 1961), 7.

191 "where you walked 50 years ago": Ibid., 8.

191 "It was the most extraordinary thing": Brad Gooch, *City Poet: The Life and Times of Frank O'Hara* (New York: Alfred A. Knopf, 1993), 217.

191 "I can't even enjoy a blade of grass": Frank O'Hara, "Meditations in an Emergency," in *The Selected Poems* (New York: Vintage Books, 1974), 87.

191 "I'm becoming": O'Hara, "Walking to Work," ibid., 57.

192 "I'm getting tired of not wearing": O'Hara, "F. (Missive and Walk) I. #53," ibid., 194.

192– "Some nights we'd walk seven or eight hundred blocks": David Wojnarowicz, *Close*
 94   *to the Knives: A Memoir of Disintegration* (New York: Vintage Books, 1991), 5; "long legs

and spiky boots," 182; "I had almost died three times," 228; "I'm walking through these hallways," 64; "I walked for hours," 67; "man on second avenue," 70; "I walk this hallway twenty-seven times," 79.

12. PARIS, OR BOTANIZING ON THE ASPHALT

196   "Now a landscape, now a room": Walter Benjamin, "On Some Motifs in Baudelaire," in *Reflections: Essays, Aphorisms, Autobiographical Writings* (New York: Schocken Books, 1978), 156.

197   "Not to find one's way in a city," "it had to be in Paris": Walter Benjamin, "A Berlin Chronicle," in *Reflections*, 8, 9.

197   holding an alpenstock before some painted Alps: On mountains, alpenstocks and Benjamin, see his letters of September 13, 1913; July 6–7, 1914; November 8, 1918; and July 20, 1921; and Monme Brodersen, *Walter Benjamin: A Biography* (London: Verso, 1996): "finally a crudely daubed backdrop of the Alps was brought for me. I stand there, bareheaded, with a tortuous smile on my lips, my right hand clasping a walking stick" (12), and "Another taken-for-granted feature of the boy's day-to-day life were the frequent lengthy journeys with the whole family: to the North Sea and the Baltic, to the high peaks of the Risengebirge between Bohemia and Silesia, to Freudenstadt in the Black Forest, and to Switzerland" (13).

198   "I don't think I ever saw him walk": Gershom Sholem, cited in Frederic V. Grunfeld, *Prophets without Honor: A Background to Freud, Kafka, Einstein and Their World* (New York: McGraw Hill, 1979), 233.

198   "old Scandinavian": Priscilla Park Ferguson, "The Flâneur: Urbanization and Its Discontents," in *From Exile to Vagrancy: Home and Its Dislocations in 19th Century France,* ed. Suzanne Nash (Albany: State University of New York, 1993), 60, n. 1. See also her *Paris as Revolution* (Berkeley: University of California Press, 1994).

198   "Irish word for 'libertine'": Elizabeth Wilson, "The Invisible Flâneur," *New Left Review* 191 (1992): 93–94.

199   "The crowd is his domain": Charles Baudelaire, "The Painter of Modern Life," *Selected Writings on Art and Artists* (Cambridge: University of Cambridge Press, 1972), 399.

199   "goes botanizing on the asphalt": Walter Benjamin, *Charles Baudelaire: A Lyric Poet in the Era of High Capitalism*, trans. Harry Zohn (London: Verso, 1973), 36.

199   "Arcades," "The flâneurs liked to have the turtles": Ibid., 53–54.

200   he did not exist: On the nonexistence of the flâneur, see Rob Shields, who, in "Fancy Footwork: Walter Benjamin's Notes on the Flâneur," in *The Flâneur*, ed. Keith Tester (London: Routledge, 1994), remarks, "In truth, it must be acknowledged that nineteenth-century visitors and travelogues do not appear to reference flânerie other than as an urban myth. The principal habitat of the flâneur is the novels of Honore de Balzac, Eugene Sue, and Alexandre Dumas."

200   Gerard de Nerval famously took a lobster on walks: Richard Holmes, *Footsteps: Adventures of a Romantic Biographer* (New York: Vintage Books, 1985), 213.

201   "Narrow crevices": Victor Hugo, *Les Misérables*, trans. Charles E. Wilbour (New York: Modern Library, 1992), bk. 12, *Corinth*, chap. 1, 939–40. See also Girouard, *Cities and People*, 200–201: "All visitors commented on these streets, which had no sidewalks, so that pedestrians were constantly in danger of being run down or spattered with mud by fast-moving traffic. 'Walking,' wrote Arthur Young in 1787, 'which in London is so pleasant and so clean, that ladies do it every day, is here a toil and a fatigue to a man, and an impossibility to a well-dress woman.' 'The renowned Tournefort,' according to the Russian traveller Karamzin writing in 1790, 'who had travelled almost the entire world, was crushed to death by a fiacre on his return to Paris because on his travels he had forgotten how to leap in the streets, like a chamois.' In this ambience, browsing in shop windows was not likely to flourish."

201   "which I reached without any other adventure" and following: Frances Trollope, *Paris and the Parisians in 1835* (New York: Harper and Brothers, 1836), 370.

201   "In Paris there are places where people take walks": Muhammed Saffar, *Disorienting Encounters: Travels of a Moroccan Scholar in France, 1845–46*, trans. and ed. Susan Gilson Miller (Berkeley: University of California Press, 1991), 136–37.

201   "long walks and constant affection!": Baudelaire to his mother, May 6, 1861, in Claude Pichois, *Baudelaire* (New York: Viking, 1989), 21.

202   "Whenever I had stopped": Nicholas-Edme Restif de la Bretonne, *Les Nuits de Paris or the Nocturnal Spectator (A Selection)*, trans. Linda Asher and Ellen Fertig, introduction by Jacques Barzun (New York: Random House, 1964), 176.

203   "virgin forest": Susan Buck-Morss, "The Flâneur, the Sandwichman and the Whore: The Politics of Loitering," *New German Critique* 39 (1986): 119: "The popular literature of flanerie may have referred to Paris as a 'virgin forest' (V, 551), but no woman found roaming there alone was expected to be one."

203   "What are the dangers": Benjamin, *Baudelaire*, 39.

203   "Mohicans in spencer jackets": Ibid., 42.

203   "on the Paris pavement": George Sand, *My Life*, trans. Dan Hofstadter (New York: Harper Colophon, 1979), 203–4.

204   "Multitude, solitude": Baudelaire, "Crowds," in *Paris Spleen*, trans. Louis Varese (New York: New Directions, 1947), 20.

204   Haussmann's project: On Haussmann I have been guided by David Pinkney, *Napoleon III and the Rebuilding of Paris* (Princeton: Princeton University Press, 1958), and to a lesser extent by Wolfgang Schivelbusch, *The Railway Journey: The Industrialization of Time and Space in the Nineteenth Century* (Berkeley: University of California Press, 1986). Schivelbusch insists that Haussmann—"the Attila of the straight line"—was entirely utilitarian in his street designs: "It is obvious that the avenues and boulevards were designed to be efficacious army routes, but that function

was merely a Bonapartist addendum to the otherwise commercially oriented new system" (181).

205 "Paris is changing!": Charles Baudelaire, "Le Cygne," *The Flowers of Evil*, trans. David M. Dodge for the author.

205 "My Paris, the Paris in which I was born": Jules and Edmond Goncourt, *The Goncourt Journals*, ed. and trans. Lewis Galantiere (New York: Doubleday, Doran, 1937), 93.

206 "For the promenaders, what necessity was there": Schivelbusch, *Railway Journey*, 185 n.

206 "evenings in bed I could not read more": Benjamin, quoted in Susan Buck Morss, *The Dialectics of Seeing: Walter Benjamin and the Arcades Project* (Cambridge, Mass.: MIT Press, 1991), 33.

207 "I still recall the extraordinary role": Andre Breton quoted in the introduction to Louis Aragon, *Paris Peasant*, trans. Simon Watson Taylor (Cambridge, Mass.: Exact Change, 1994), viii.

207 "spoke to this unknown woman": Andre Breton, *Nadja*, trans. Richard Howard (New York: Grove Press, 1960), 64.

208 "Georgette resumed her stroll": Philippe Soupault, *Last Nights of Paris*, trans. William Carlos Williams (Cambridge, Mass.: Exact Change, 1992), 45–46.

208 "Everything is so simple when one knows all the streets": Ibid., 64.

208 "Whenever I happen to be there": Ibid., 80.

208 "famously proposes a detailed 'interpretation' ": Michael Sheringham, "City Space, Mental Space, Poetic Space: Paris in Breton, Benjamin and Réda," in *Parisian Fields*, ed. Michael Sheringham (London: Reaktion Books, 1996), 89. Older metaphors of the city as a body existed, but not as a sexual body: in the nineteenth century, parks were often called the "lungs" of the city, and Richard Sennett, in *Flesh and Stone: The Body and the City in Western Civilization* (London and Boston: Faber and Faber, 1994), writes of the bodily metaphors that metaphorized Haussmann's sewers, waterways, and streets as various organs of bodily circulation, necessary for health.

209 "rapt and confused": Djuna Barnes, *Nightwood* (New York: New Directions, 1946), 59–60.

210 "a man who has, with great difficulty": Benjamin, quoted in Grunwald, *Prophets without Honor*, 245.

210 "No one knew the path": Ibid., 248.

210 "whereupon the border officials": Hannah Arendt, introduction, in *Illuminations: Essays and Reflections* (New York: Schocken Books, 1969), 18.

211 "In Paris a stranger feels at home": Ibid., 21.

212 "could set for itself the study": Guy DeBord, "Introduction to a Critique of Urban Geography," in *Situationist International Anthology*, ed. and trans. Ken Knabb (Berkeley: Bureau of Public Secrets, 1981), 5.

212 "The point . . . was to encounter the unknown": Greil Marcus, "Heading for the

Hills," *East Bay Express,* February 19, 1999. Marcus writes about situationism far more extensively in his *Lipstick Traces* (Cambridge, Mass.: Harvard University Press, 1990).

213 "practitioners of the city," "the walking of passers-by": Michel de Certeau, *The Practice of Everyday Life* (Berkeley: University of California Press, 1984), 93, 100.

213 "under threat from the tyranny of bad architecture": Jean-Christophe Bailly in Sheringham, "City Space, Mental Space, Poetic Space," *Parisian Fields,* 111.

13. CITIZENS OF THE STREETS: Parties, Processions, and Revolutions

Some of the material here comes from my essays "The Right of the People Peaceably to Assemble in Unusual Clothing: Notes on the Streets of San Francisco" published in *Harvard Design Magazine* in 1998, and "Voices of the Streets," *Camerawork Quarterly,* summer 1995; and my essay on Gulf War activism in *War After War* (San Francisco: City Lights Books, 1991).

218 "the ideal city for riot": Eric Hobsbawm, "Cities and Insurrections," in *Revolutionaries* (New York: Pantheon, 1973), 222. Elizabeth Wilson in *The Sphinx in the City* and Priscilla Parker Ferguson in *Paris as Revolution* also make astute links between the social space and revolutionary potential of a city.

219 "Urban reconstruction, however": Hobsbawm, "Cities and Insurrections," 224.

219 "I take my desires for reality": Angelo Quattrocchi and Tom Nairn, *The Beginning of the End* (London: Verso, 1998), 26.

219 "The difference between rebellion at Columbia and rebellion at the Sorbonne": Mavis Gallant, *Paris Notebooks: Essays and Reviews* (New York: Random House, 1988), 3.

220 the market women . . . had grown accustomed to marching: There are many conflicting versions of the market women's march. I relied on Shirley Elson Roessler's *Out of the Shadows: Women and Politics in the French Revolution, 1789–95* (New York: Peter Land, 1996) for the sequence and details of events, though I also used Michelet's history of the French Revolution (Wynnewood, Pa.: Livingston, 1972), Georges Rude's indispensable *Crowd in the French Revolution* (Oxford: Oxford University Press, 1972), Simon Schama's *Citizens* (New York: Knopf, 1989), and Christopher Hibbert's *The Days of the French Revolution* (New York: Morrow Quill Paperbacks, 1981).

220 "at the discipline, pageantry, and magnitude of the almost daily processions": Rude, *Crowd in the French Revolution,* 66.

221 "she delivered such a blow with her broom": Roessler, *Out of the Shadows,* 18.

221 "their decorated branches amidst the gleaming iron of pikes": Hibbert, *Days,* 104.

223 East Germany was next: On Germany I relied on Timothy Garton Ash, *The Magic Lantern: The Revolutions of 1989 Witnessed in Warsaw, Budapest, Berlin and Prague* (New York: Random House, 1990), and John Borneman, *After the Wall: East Meets West in the New Berlin* (New York: Basic Books, 1991).

223   arrested just for being in the vicinity of disturbances: Borneman, *After the Wall*, 23–24:
"In one example . . . a demonstrator was sentenced to six months imprisonment for
calling 'No Violence' about fifteen times."

223   "the people acted and the Party reacted": Ash, *Magic Lantern*, 83.

224   "Prague . . ˙. seemed hypnotized, caught in a magical trance": Michael Kukral, *Prague
1989: A Study in Humanistic Geography* (Boulder, Colo.: Eastern European Monographs,
1997), 110.

224   "The government is telling us": Alexander Dubček, quoted in *Time*, December 4,
1989, 21.

224   "The time of massive and daily street demonstrations": Kukral, *Prague 1989*, 95.

225   "Secrecy . . . was a hallmark": Marguerite Guzman Bouvard, *Revolutionizing Motherhood: The Mothers of the Plaza de Mayo* (Wilmington, Del.: Scholarly Resources, 1994),
30.

226   "Much later . . . they described their walks": Bouvard, *Revolutionizing Motherhood*, 70.

226   "They tell me that, while they are marching": Marjorie Agosin, *Circles of Madness:
Mothers of the Plaza de Mayo* (Freedonia: White Pine Press, 1992), 43.

229   "People lived in public": Victor Hugo, *1793*, trans. Frank Lee Benedict (New York:
Carroll and Graf, 1988), 116.

229   "The revolutionary posters were everywhere": George Orwell, *Homage to Catalonia*
(Boston: Beacon Press, 1952), 5.

230   "Revolutionary moments are carnivals in which the individual life celebrates its unification with a regenerated society": Situationist Raoul Vaneigem, quoted in *Do or
Die* (Earth First! Britain's newsletter), no. 6 (1997), 4.

14. WALKING AFTER MIDNIGHT: Women, Sex, and Public Space

232   "I used to go out walking": James Joyce, "The Dead," *Dubliners* (New York: Dover,
1991), 149. Anne Wallace, in her *Walking, Literature and English Culture*, pointed me to
this use of the term in this text; the Oxford English Dictionary also has a nice section on the phrase.

233   "You have been telling the truth": Glen Petrie, *A Singular Iniquity: The Campaigns of
Josephine Butler* (New York: Viking, 1971), 105, where the other details of the Caroline
Wyburgh story also appear.

233   "being born a woman": Sylvia Plath, quoted in Carol Brooks Gardner, *Passing By:
Gender and Public Harassment* (Berkeley: University of California Press, 1995), 26. Re
gender and travel, see Eric J. Leed, *The Mind of the Traveler: From Gilgamesh to Global
Tourism* (New York: Basic Books, 1991), 115–16: "The 'double standard' constructs
the spatial domains of interiority (female) and exteriority (male) as domains of, respectively, sexual constraint and sexual freedom. The chastity of women is a technique of inclusion and exclusion, which decrees memberships, rights, and relations

between males as well as sanctifying the male line of descent. Women's identification with place in conditions of settlement has been regarded as 'natural,' a result of reproductive necessities that require stability and protection by men; thus the genderization of space. . . . The antithesis between the exteriorizations of men and the interiorizations of women, the superfluity of the sperm and the parsimony of the ovum, has been mapped upon human mobility and come to be considered an element of human nature. But the immobilization of women is a historical achievement. . . . It is this territorialization that makes travel a gendering activity."

235   "who go out onto the street," "Domestic women": Gerda Lerner, *The Creation of Patriarchy* (Oxford: Oxford University Press, 1986), 134, 135–39.

235   "were confined to houses": Sennett, *Flesh and Stone*, 34. Pericles and Xenophon quotes are on pages 68 and 73.

236   "In Greek thought women lack": Mark Wiggins, "Untitled: The Housing of Gender," in *Sexuality and Space*, ed. Beatriz Colomina (Princeton: Princeton University Press, 1992), 335.

237   "The young men strolling on the streets": Joachim Schlor, *Nights in the Big City* (London: Reaktion Books, 1998), 139.

238   "shopping in Les Halles": Petrie, *A Singular Iniquity*, 160.

238   "I asked what the crime was": Ibid., 182.

239   hounded into suicide: The woman was a Mrs. Percy of Aldershot: see the preface and pages 149–54 of Petrie, *A Singular Iniquity*, and Paul McHugh, *Prostitution and Victorian Social Reform* (New York: St. Martin's Press, 1980), 149–51.

239   Lizzie Schauer in Glenna Matthews, *The Rise of Public Woman: Woman's Power and Woman's Place in the United States, 1630–1970* (New York, Oxford: Oxford University Press, 1992), 3.

240   force-feeding the prisoners: My sources were Midge Mackenzie, *Shoulder to Shoulder* (New York: Knopf, 1975), on British suffragists, and Doris Stevens, *Jailed for Freedom: American Women Win the Vote* (1920; new edition, edited by Carol O'Hare, Troutdale, Oregon: New Sage Press, 1995). Djuna Barnes volunteered to be force-fed so she could report on the process.

240   "that women will not feel at ease": B. Houston, "What's Wrong with Sexual Harassment," quoted in June Larkin, "Sexual Terrorism on the Street," in *Sexual Harassment: Contemporary Feminist Perspectives*, ed. Alison M. Thomas and Celia Kitzinger (Buckingham: Open University Press, 1997), 117.

240   Two-thirds of American women are afraid: Jalna Hanmer and Mary Maynard, eds., *Women, Violence and Social Control* (Houndmills, England: MacMillan, 1987), 77.

240   "very worried": Eileen Green, Sandra Hebron, and Diane Woodward, *Women's Leisure, What Leisure* (Houndmills, England: MacMillan, 1990): "One of the most severe restrictions on women's leisure time activities is their fear of being out alone after dark. Many women are afraid to use public transport after dark or late at night whilst for others it's having to walk to bus stops and wait there after dark which deters them.

The findings of the second British Crime Survey state that half the women interviewed only went out after dark if accompanied, and 40 percent were 'very worried' about being raped" (89).

241   "If I wrote down every little thing": Larkin, "Sexual Terrorism," 120.

242   "Stanton and Mott . . . began to see similarities": Stevens, *Jailed for Freedom*, 13.

242   Edward Lawson case: Abstract of *Kolender, Chief of Police of San Diego, et al., v. Lawson*, 461 U.S. 352, 103 S. Ct. 1855, 75 L. Ed. 2nd 903 (1983).

243   "Throughout the case," and following: Helen Benedict, *Virgin or Vamp: How the Press Covers Sex Crimes* (New York and London: Oxford University Press, 1992), 208.

244   "could leave me speechless": Evelyn C. White, "Black Women and the Wilderness," in *Literature and the Environment: A Reader on Nature and Culture,* ed. Lorraine Anderson, Scott Slovic, John O'Grady (New York: Addison Wesley, 1999), 319.

244   "Had I been older and more mature": Moffat, *Space Below My Feet*, 92.

245   "Could she even get her dinner": Virginia Woolf, *A Room of One's Own* (New York: Harcourt Brace Jovanovich, 1929), 50.

245   "The trick . . . was to identify with Jack Kerouac": Sarah Schulman, *Girls, Visions and Everything* (Seattle: Seal Press, 1986), 17, 97.

246   "That's gay liberation," "Lila walked in the streets": Ibid., 157, 159.

15. AEROBIC SISYPHUS AND THE SUBURBANIZED PSYCHE

250   "the walking city": Kenneth Jackson, *Crabgrass Frontier: The Suburbanization of the United States* (New York: Oxford University Press, 1985), 14–15.

250   Middle-class suburban homes: The source of much of the narrative here is Robert Fishman, *Bourgeois Utopias: The Rise and Fall of Suburbia* (New York: Basic Books, 1987), especially chap. 1, on London's evangelical merchants, and chapter 3, on Manchester's suburbia.

251   "The decision to suburbanize": Ibid., 81–82.

252   "Offices are kept separate": Philip Langdon, *A Better Place to Live: Reshaping the American Suburb* (Amherst: University of Massachusetts Press, 1994), xi.

252   study that compared the lives of ten-year-olds: Jane Holtz Kay, *Asphalt Nation: How the Automobile Took Over America and How We Can Take It Back* (New York: Crown Publishers, 1997), 25.

254   more than 1,000 crosswalks have been removed: Gary Richards, "Crossings Disappear in Drive for Safety: Traffic Engineers Say Pedestrians Are in Danger Between the Lines," *San Jose Mercury News,* November 27, 1998. Traffic engineers in the article blamed pedestrians for their own deaths by automobile in about half the cases and proposed restricting pedestrian access as the solution.

254   "The pedestrian remains the largest single obstacle": Rudofsky, *Streets for People,* 106.

254   "South Tucson simply has no sidewalks": Lars Eigner, *Travels with Lizbeth: Three Years on the Road and on the Streets* (New York: Fawcett Columbine, 1993), 18.

254   41 percent of all traffic fatalities: Betsy Thaggard, "Making the Streets a Safer Place," *Tube Times*, newsletter of the San Francisco Bicycle Coalition, December 1998–January 1999, 5.

254   Giuliani's New York: *San Francisco Chronicle*; also in *Tube Times*, 3, citing the Right of Way campaign organized by Time's Up! that is painting memorial stencils on the sites where NYC pedestrians and cyclists have been killed.

255   "that elusive combination": Richard Walker, "Landscape and City Life: Four Ecologies of Residence in the San Francisco Bay Area," *Ecumene* 2 (1995): 35.

255   "Anyone who has tried to take a stroll at dusk": Mike Davis, "Fortress Los Angeles," in *Variations on a Theme Park*, ed. Michael Sorkin (New York: Hill and Wang, 1992), 174.

256   "It is extremely regrettable": *Søren Kierkegaard's Journals and Papers*, ed. and trans. Howard V. Hong and Edna H. Hong (Bloomington: Indiana University Press, 1978), 5:415 (1847).

256   "For most of human history": *Life* magazine, special millennium issue (1998).

257   "The speed and mathematical directness": Schivelbusch, *Railway Journey*, 53.

257   "From the elimination of the physical effort of walking": Paul Virilio, *The Art of the Motor*, trans. Julie Rose (Minneapolis: University of Minnesota Press, 1995), 85.

260   "The Tread-Mill," "It is its monotonous steadiness": James Hardie, *The History of the Tread-Mill, containing an account of its origin, construction, operation, effects as it respects the health and morals of the convicts, with their treatment and diet . . .* (New York: Samuel Marks, 1824), 16, 18.

261   "always lived by robbery": Robert Graves, *The Greek Myths*, vol. 1 (Harmondsworth, England: Penguin Books, 1957), 168.

261   "Indoors?": Eduardo Galeano, *The Book of Embraces*, trans. Cedric Belfrage (New York, London: W. W. Norton, 1989), 162–63.

16. THE SHAPE OF A WALK

268   "Pollock's near destruction of this tradition": Allan Kaprow, "The Legacy of Jackson Pollock," in *Essays on the Blurring of Art and Life*, ed. Jeff Kelley (Berkeley: University of California Press, 1993), 7.

269   "Emphasizing the body as art": Peter Selz and Kristine Stiles, *Theories and Documents of Contemporary Art: A Sourcebook* (Berkeley: University of California Press, 1996), 679 (introduction to Performance section).

269   "My idea of a piece of sculpture": Lucy R. Lippard, *Overlay: Contemporary Art and the Art of Prehistory* (New York: Pantheon, 1993), 125.

269   "A 1,600-foot wooden trail": Lippard, *Overlay*, 132.

271   "A walk expresses space and freedom": Richard Long, "Five Six Pick Up Sticks, Seven Eight Lay Them Straight," in R. H. Fuchs, *Richard Long* (New York: Solomon

R. Guggenheim Museum/Thames and Hudson, 1986), 236. All works described are reproduced in this book.

272   Stanley Brouwn: Brouwn's work is mentioned in Lippard's *Six Years: The Dematerialization of the Art Object* (New York: Praeger Publishers, 1973) and described at length in the essay by Antje Von Graevenitz, "'We Walk on the Planet Earth': The Artist as a Pedestrian: The Work of Stanley Brouwn," *Dutch Art and Architecture,* June 1977. Acconci's *Following Piece* is also described in *Six Years.*

273   Marina Abramović and Ulay: On the performance work of Abramović and Ulay, and on Abramović's sculpture, see Thomas McEvilley, "Abramović/Ulay/Abramović," *Artforum International,* September 1983; McEvilley's essay in *The Lovers,* catalog/book on the Great Wall Walk (Amsterdam: Stedelijk Museum, 1989); and *Marina Abramović: objects performance video sound* (Oxford: Museum of Modern Art, 1995).

273   "'four dignities'": Gary Snyder, "Blue Mountains Constantly Walking," in *The Practice of the Wild* (San Francisco: North Point Press, 1990), 99.

274   "immobility, silence and watchfulness": McEvilley, "Abramović/Ulay/Abramović," 54.

274   "When I went to Tibet and the Aborigines": *Marina Abramović,* 63.

275   "mapped out over the millennia": Ibid., 50.

275   "On March 30, 1988": *The Lovers,* 175.

275   "I walk every fucking centimeter," "It took a great number of days": Ibid., 103, 31.

276   "They will discover out of ordinary things": Kaprow, *Essays on the Blurring of Art and Life,* 9.

17.   LAS VEGAS, OR THE LONGEST DISTANCE BETWEEN TWO POINTS

278   "The effectiveness of this architecture": J. B. Jackson, "Other-directed Houses," in *Landscapes: Selected Writings of J. B. Jackson,* ed. Ervin H. Jube (University of Massachusetts Press, 1970), 63.

279   "Those streamlined facades": Ibid., 62.

279   more than 30 million a year: A researcher at the Las Vegas Convention Center told me by phone, December 29, 1998.

281   round-the-clock picket: See Sara Mosle, "How the Maids Fought Back," *New Yorker,* February 26 and March 4, 1996, 148–56.

283   county passed an ordinance: See the *Las Vegas Review-Journal,* "Petitioners Claim Rights Violated," May 27, 1998; "Clark County Charts Its Strategy to Resurrect Handbill Ordinance," August 18, 1998; "Lawyers to Appeal Handbill Law Ruling," August 26, 1998; "Police Told to Mind Bill of Rights," October 20, 1998.

283   "The theme park": Introduction to Sorkin, *Variations on a Theme Park,* xv.

284   "the Beautification Committee would continue to recommend": Robert Venturi, Denise

Scott Brown, and Stephen Izenour, *Learning from Las Vegas: The Forgotten Symbolism of Architectural Form*, rev. ed. (Boston: MIT, 1977), xii.

288 "Both sides of these passageways, which are lighted from above": Benjamin, *Baudelaire*, 37.

290 "Olive Oil": Joanne Urioste, *The American Alpine Club Climber's Guide: The Red Rocks of Southern Nevada* (New York: American Alpine Club, 1984), 131.

Index

$\mathcal{S}ources\ for\ Foot\ Quotations$

I. THE PACE OF THOUGHTS

Honoré de Balzac, quoted in note 15 in Andrew J. Bennett, "Devious Feet: Wordsworth and the Scandal of Narrative Form," *ELH*, spring 1992.

Lucy R. Lippard, *Overlay: Contemporary Art and the Art of Prehistory* (New York: Pantheon, 1993).

Gary Snyder, "Blue Mountains Constantly Walking," *The Practice of the Wild*, (San Francisco: North Point Press, 1990), 98–99.

Virginia Woolf, *Moments of Being* (New York: Harcourt, Brace, Jovanovich, 1976), 82.

Wallace Stevens, "Of the Surface of Things," *The Collected Poems* (New York: Vintage Books, 1982), 57.

John Buchan, in William Robert Irwin, ed., *Challenge: An Anthology of the Literature of Mountaineering* (New York: Columbia University Press, 1950), 354.

Leon Rosenfeld, from his papers, in Niels Bladel, *Harmony and Unity: The Life of Niels Bohr* (Berlin, New York: Science Tech, Springer-Verlag, 1998), 195.

John Keats, letter, in Aaron Sussman and Ruth Goode, *The Magic of Walking* (New York: Simon and Schuster, 1967), 355.

Voltaire, letter to Rousseau, August 30, 1755, in Gavin de Beer, *Jean-Jacques Rousseau and His World* (New York: Putnam, 1972), 42.

Sigmund Freud, *Civilization and Its Discontents*, cited in Ivan Illich, *H2O and the Waters of Forgetfulness* (Dallas: Dallas Institute of Humanities and Culture, 1985), 34.

Samuel Beckett, cited in *The Nation*, July 28–August 4, 1997, 30.

Effie Gray Ruskin, in John Dixon Hunt, *The Wider Sea: A Life of John Ruskin* (London: Dent, 1982), 201

John 11:10 and Psalms 26:1–12, King James Bible.

Allan G. Grapard, "Flying Mountians and Walkers of Emptiness: Toward a Definition of Sacred Space in Japanese Religions," *History of Religion* 21, no. 3 (1982), 206.

The Three Pillars of Zen, ed. Philip Kapleau (Garden City, N.Y.: Anchor Press, 1980), 33–34.

Paul Shepard, *Nature and Madness* (San Francisco: Sierra Club Books, 1982), 161.

Thomas Merton, in Nancy Louise Frey, *Pilgrim Stories: On and Off the Road to Santiago* (Berkeley: University of California Press, 1998), 79.

Gloria Anzaldua, *Borderlands/La Frontera* (San Francisco: Aunt Lute Books, 1987), 3, 16.

Paul Klee, *Pedagogical Sketchbook*, 1925, cited in *The Oxford Dictionary of Quotations*, (Oxford: Oxford University Press, 1979), 305.

Charles Baudelaire, "Le Soleil," *Baudelaire*, selected and translated by Francis Scarfe (Harmondsworth, England: Penguin Books, 1964), 13.

Kirk Savage, "The Past in the Present," *Harvard Design Magazine*, fall 1999, 19.

Pablo Neruda, "Walking Around," *The Vintage Anthology of Contemporary World Poetry* (New York: Vintage Books, 1966), 527.

I. FROM THE GARDEN TO THE WILD

Alexander Pope, "Epistle to Miss Blount," *The Norton Anthology of English Literature*, vol. 1, 3rd ed. (New York: W. W. Norton, 1974), 2174.

Maria Edgeworth, *Belinda* (Oxford: Oxford University Editions, 1994), 90.

Thomas Gray, writing in 1769, "Journal in the Lakes," *Collected Works of Gray in Prose and Verse*, vol. 1, ed. Edmund Gosse (London: MacMillan and Co., 1902), 252.

E. P. Thompson, *Making History: Writings on History and Culture* (New York: New Press, 1995), 3.

Mary Shelley, *Frankenstein*, in *Three Gothic Novels* (Harmondsworth, England: Penguin Books, 1968), 360.

Johann Wolfgang von Goethe, *The Sorrow of Young Werther*, ed. and trans. Victor Lange (New York: Holt, Rinehart and Winston, 1949). "He who does not know," 4; "If in such moments I find," 52; "Ossian has superseded Homer," 83; "At noon I went to walk," 91.

Hunter Davies, *William Wordsworth: A Biography* (New York: Atheneum, 1980), 213.

Benjamin Haydon, cited in James Fenton, "A Lesson from Michelangelo," *New York Review of Books*, 1996.

Amos Bronson Alcott, cited in Carlos Baker, *Emerson Among the Eccentrics* (New York: Viking, 1996), 305–6.

Henry David Thoreau, "A Walk to Wachusett," *The Natural History Essays* (Salt Lake City: Peregrine Smith Books, 1980), 48.

Bertrand Russell, *The Autobiography of Bertrand Russell* (New York: Bantam Books, 1978), 78–79

E. M. Forster, *Howards End* (Harmondsworth, England: Penguin Books, 1992), 181.

Elias Canetti, *Crowds and Power* (New York: Viking, 1963), 31.

Morris Marples, *Shanks's Pony: A Study of Walking* (London: J. M. Dent and Sons, 1959), 190.

David Roberts, *Moments of Doubt: and Other Mountaineering Writings* (Seattle: Mountaineers, 1986), 186.

Hamish Brown, *Hamish's Mountain Walk: The First Traverse of All the Scottish Monroes in One Journey* (London: Victor Gollancz, 1978), 356–57. (A monroe is a Scottish peak over 3,000 feet.)

Gary Snyder, "Blue Mountains Constantly Walking," *The Practice of the Wild*, 113.

Gilles Deleuze and Felix Guattari, *Nomadalogy*, transl. Brian Massumi (New York: Semiotexte, 1986), 36–37.

Friedrich Engels, *The Condition of the Working Class in England* (Harmondsworth, England: Penguin Books, 1987), 173.

Charles Dickens, *Bleak House* (New York: New American Library, 1964), 517.

III. LIVES OF THE STREETS

J. B. Jackson, "The Stranger's Path," in *Landscapes: Selected Essays of J B Jackson* (Boston: University of Massachusetts Press, 1970), 102.

Horace Walpole, letter to George Montagu on a "ridotto" at Vauxhall Gardens, May 11, 1769, in *Letters of Horace Walpole* (London: J. M. Dent, 1926), 92.

Patrick Delany, in Carole Fabricant, *Swift's Landscape* (Baltimore: Johns Hopkins University Press, 1992).

Elena Poniatowska, "In the Street" (on the homeless children of Mexico City), *Doubletake*, winter 1998, 118–19.

F. Bloch, *Types du Boulevard*, cited in Margaret Cohen, *Profane Illumination: Walter Benjamin and the Paris of Surrealist Revolution* (Berkeley: University of California Press, 1995), 84

Victor Hugo, *Les Misérables*, trans. Charles E. Wilbour (New York: Modern Library, 1992), 506.

Jules and Edmond Goncourt, October 26, 1856, *The Goncourt Journals*, ed. and transl. Lewis Galantiere (Doubleday Doran, 1937), 38.

Andre Castelot, *The Turbulent City: Paris 1783–1871* (New York: Harper & Row, 1962), 186.

Richard Ellmann, *James Joyce* (New York: Oxford University Press, 1982), 518.

Victor Hugo, *Les Misérables*, 106–7.

Walter Benjamin, *Charles Baudelaire: A Lyric Poet in the Era of High Capitalism*, trans. Harry Zohn (London: Verso, 1973), 69.

Edgar Allan Poe, "The Murders in the Rue Morgue," in *The Fall of the House of Usher and Other Tales* (New York: New American Library, 1966), 53.

Alexis de Tocqueville, *Democracy in America* (New York: HarperPerennial, 1969), 108.

Subcommandante Marcos, cited in *Utne Reader*, May–June 1998, 55.

Paul Monette, "The Politics of Silence," in *The Writing Life* (New York: Random House, 1995), 210.

Martha Shelley, *Haggadah: A Celebration of Freedom* (San Francisco: Aunt Lute Books, 1997), 19.

Jan Goodwin, *Price of Honor: Muslim Women Lift the Veil of Silence on the Islamic World* (Boston: Little, Brown, 1994), 16

Mary Wortley Montagu, August 1712, letter to her future husband, *Letters of Mary Wortley Montagu* (London: J M Dent, n.d.), 32.

Song of Solomon 7:1, King James Bible.

London passerby to a streetwalker, in Richard Symanski, *The Immoral Landscape: Female Prostitution in Western Societies* (Toronto: Butterworths, 1984), 164.

Emily Post, *Etiquette* (1922 ed.), quoted by Edmund Wilson in "Books of Etiquette & Emily Post," *Classics and Commercials* (New York: Vintage, 1962), 378.

Harper's Bazaar, July 1997, 18.

Elizabeth Wilson, *The Sphinx in the City* (Berkeley: University of California Press, 1992), 16.

IV. PAST THE END OF THE ROAD

Nancy Louise Frey, *Pilgrim Stories*, 132.

Luz Benedict, in Edna Ferber, *Giant* (Garden City, N.Y.: Doubleday, 1952), 153.

Norman Klein, *History of Forgetting* (London: Verso, 1997), 118.

Brett Pulley, *New York Times*, Sunday, November 8, 1998, 3.

Mick LaSalle, *San Francisco Chronicle*, January 5, 1999, E1.

Hannah Nyala, *Point Last Seen* (Boston: Beacon Press, 1997), 1–3.

Paul Virilio, *Speed and Politics*, trans. Mark Polizzotti (New York: Semiotexte, 1986), 144.

Ivan Illich, *Whole Earth Review*, summer 1997.

Lee, "a Catholic American" pilgrim, in Nancy Louise Frey, *Pilgrim Stories*, 74–75.

A. R. Ammons, "A Poem Is a Walk," *Epoch* 18, no. 1 (1968), 116.

Yoko Ono, "Map Piece," summer 1962. © 1962 Yoko Ono. From the exhibition *Searchlight: Consciousness at Millennium*, CCAC Institute, San Francisco, 1999.